Personal Investing

The Irwin Series in Finance

Editors

Personal Investing

WILBUR W. WIDICUS
Associate Professor of Finance
and Associate Dean
School of Business
Oregon State University

THOMAS E. STITZEL
Professor of Finance
Boise State University

Revised Edition 1976

RICHARD D. IRWIN, INC. Homewood, Illinois 60430

Irwin-Dorsey Limited Georgetown, Ontario L7G 4B3

Revised Edition

First Printing, March 1976
Second Printing, November 1976
Third Printing, February 1977

ISBN 0-256-01832-4
Library of Congress Catalog Card No. 75–35092
Printed in the United States of America

To:

Jeffrey
Jennifer
Lisa
Matthew
Maura
Nancy
Peter
Shona

Preface

Much has happened in the world of investments since *Personal Investing* was first published in 1971. Security regulations have changed, new forms of investment have been created to better meet the needs of investors, and security markets themselves have been greatly altered. These developments and many others have been incorporated into this revised edition, but without altering the nature of the book. It remains a basic introductory text in investments which may be read by persons having no previous courses in accounting, finance, or economics.

The authors' approach to investing assumes that investors must first learn about the environment in which they will be operating. That is, they should know about the risks associated with different types of investments and the returns to be expected from them. They should be knowledgeable about the participants in the investment process—a group including organizations issuing and selling investment securities, firms which sell investment advice and information, and the regulators of the securities industry. After mastering these "basics" the investor may plan an investment program designed to use his or her financial resources to attain specific financial goals. This book provides information which allows investors to follow this approach to personal investing.

The world of investments is complex. To understand its operation one must speak its language fluently. To this end, detailed definitions of investment terms are written as they occur during the logical presentation of the material. In addition, an expanded glossary provides brief definitions of most investment terms. For the mathematically inclined, three end-of-chapter appendices show how to compute compound interest, present value, and bond values, and how to use a common stock valuation model. Numerous references and end-of-chapter reading lists enable students to pursue, at greater length, topics of special interest to them. Illustrations of security certificates, tax forms, and other investment-oriented documents are presented to provide more realism to the textual material. Of particular interest and uniqueness are chapters dealing with the tax aspects of investing, speculative investments, and planning and managing an investment program. At the suggestion of our readers a new chapter entitled "Analysis of Individual Securities, Industries, and Security Markets" has been added. The thrust of several other chapters has been altered to include more material about analysis of individual securities.

The world of investing is dynamic. New laws and regulations are passed and old ones are constantly being revised. Social conditions and national goals shift—witness the recent emphasis upon increasing our sources of energy, low cost housing, and ecological planning. These and countless other changes affect investors' decisions. The investor's successful quest for wealth and security requires a continuous effort to up-date and reappraise information of all types. Change is not necessarily bad or harmful because it often provides the alert investor with opportunity for profit. This book points out ways by which investors may identify changing conditions and describes ways to use this knowledge to best advantage.

Personal Investing has benefitted greatly from the many valuable criticisms and suggestions of colleagues and friends. We are particularly grateful to the stock exchanges, regulatory agencies, investment information services, brokers, financial advisors, and reviewers for the time and effort they have expended on our behalf. Any errors or omissions which remain are our joint responsibility, of course, and in no way reflect upon the efforts of the persons who have helped and advised us. We particularly welcome criticism of this book and suggestions for improving it. Chapters 1 through 4 and the last half of Chapters 6 and 12 were written by Professor Stitzel. The remaining chapters were written by Professor Widicus.

February 1976

Wilbur W. Widicus
Thomas E. Stitzel

Contents

part one

The What and Why of Investing

1
Investment Perspectives

INTRODUCTION

Anyone Can Still Make a Million[1] is the title of a recently written book. Dozens of other authors have dangled similar thoughts of wealth in front of a hungry public. Indeed, from the beginning of recorded history, people have struggled to increase their well-being through accumulation of money and/or its equivalent. This appetite for riches is insatiable for most people. At a time when the standard of living in the United States is beyond comprehension to much of the rest of the world, books, movies, and plays on the subject of wealth are produced at an unprecedented rate. The recurring theme of wealth accumulation is central to this book. This is not to say that anyone who reads further is an avaricious, gluttonous, ravenous person. Far from it. Just as the "Love of Money" is condemned in the Bible, this manuscript contains no get-rich-quick schemes or guarantees of huge financial rewards. A major purpose of this book is to provide the reader with a clear understanding of the investment environment. Opportunities and difficulties are discussed in a practical manner. Long established types of investments as well as the latest innovations are presented so that an individual can design a personalized investment plan. The reader will become a trained observer, aware of risks and returns, of the terminology of securities and procedures—or in other words the reader will become educated about the world of investments. A remark attributed to Frank Leahy, the outstanding Notre

[1] Morton Shulman, *Anyone Can Still Make a Million* (New York: McGraw-Hill, 1972).

Dame football coach, expresses this sentiment in another way, "Luck seems to always go to the side having the heaviest tackles." Knowing the ins and outs of investing does not guarantee success, but very few people have been consistently successful without a thorough comprehension of the field of investments.

Many investors get carried away with the feeling of the times. They see no change in sight and continue buying stocks well beyond levels where more prudent investors have ceased to buy. At times when everything seems bad, stock prices are down, and the outlook is for more of the same, they sell. Some people never get off the bandwagon of optimism or pessimism until it is too late. They end up buying high and selling low. The purpose of this discussion is to emphasize the following points: (1) change will occur, (2) securities will fluctuate in price, and (3) recognition of this pattern as an investment principle is the first step toward wisdom and profits. It is highly appropriate then, at the outset, to understand that the objective of this book is to provide a framework within which an individual can set investment goals and steer a course to achieve these desired results.

SUCCESSES AND FAILURES

Countless instances of dramatic investment results have been recorded. Typical of the prosperous examples is the overnight wealth that befell many investors in oil and various mineral ventures. Florida land booms have been well publicized. Polaroid, Xerox, and IBM are companies that have rewarded their original investors with phenomenal gains in short time spans. This list could go on and on. However, there is another side to the coin, and a different group of experiences remains all too vivid in the minds of many.

Thousands of people have made financial commitments to enterprises which subsequently declined in value and often went bankrupt. Many of these cases involved fraudulent schemes, but vast numbers were honest ventures that for one reason or another just did not work. In a delightfully written book entitled *Wiped Out* the author relates how a fortune was lost by investing in the stock market during a period in which stock prices in general were rising to unprecedented levels.[2] This experience is not uncommon!

The purpose of this discussion has not been to dampen the spirits of

[2] Anonymous investor, *Wiped Out: How I Lost a Fortune in the Stock Market While the Averages Were Making New Highs* (New York: Simon & Schuster, 1966).

the potential investor, but rather to emphasize the point that wealth is subject to both expansion and contraction. In other words, assets can grow or be depleted, and over a long period of time, both results will probably occur.

INVESTING DEFINED

Much confusion stems from lack of clear understanding of what is meant by various investment terms. Definitions will be stressed in each chapter to minimize this problem. The reader is advised to begin building an investment vocabulary immediately. Preparation of a glossary of terms similar to that appearing in the back of this book should prove to be most helpful.

At the end of a long day, a farmer announced to his wife that he ". . . was going to invest in the stock market because I would like to earn a dollar without having to sweat for it." An actor was sitting in an overstuffed chair in a thickly carpeted, air-conditioned Beverly Hills brokerage office. In these plush surroundings he remarked as he watched the stock prices flash on the screen before him, "This investing sure beats going down to the race track." A secretary described her resources for investing as "mad money" and as funds with which she could "gamble." Between classes one college student told another ". . . this investment is just a hunch on my part—pure speculation. . . ." A husband and wife asked how "they could accumulate funds for the purpose of their children's education." Each of these quotes illustrates a different concept of what is loosely called *investing*.

It is highly desirable that reader and authors have similar thoughts triggered by this the most important term used in this book. A framework for describing *investing* is presented in Table 1–1.

Each of these terms can be used appropriately to describe efforts designed to acquire and maintain wealth. Gambling is not limited to the Nevada casinos. It is a term that can be applied to actions based on tips, whims, or unexplained impulses. For example, a secretary repeats that her boss mentioned his golfing partner said that a rival company was about to unveil an amazing new product. The purchase of that company's stock based solely on that information would indeed be a "gamble." The decision would be made without any attempt to accumulate and analyze other facts. Short-term or even overnight profits would be expected. Furthermore, the gains en-

TABLE 1–1
Investing Distinguished

Term	*Research*	*Time Span*	*Expected Loss or Gain*
Gambling.	None	Short	Substantial
Speculating	Substantial	Short	Substantial
Investing	Substantial	Long	Moderate

visioned would occur rapidly so the annual return would be very high, even with a relatively small price rise.[3] Usually the gambler is aware that price declines could result. This is recognition of a potential risk, but no attempt is made to compare it with the anticipated gain.

Speculators also seek fast action, but they are careful to appraise the situation. A rumor may create interest in a security, but a thorough study will be undertaken before a commitment is made. In his first rule of investing, Bernard Baruch cautioned against speculation unless it is made a full-time job.[4] As in gambling the potential risks and rewards are high and the time horizon is short.

The distinguishing characteristics of investing are the time span and risk and reward considerations. While an investor would not be upset by a quick profit, neither would such a person be disheartened by an immediate drop in stock price. Patience is a virtue of the investor. True investing is a balancing of potential risks and rewards at a moderate level. In other words, investors are not trying to achieve wealth overnight by putting all their money on one horse.

It should be made perfectly clear that this presentation makes no value judgments regarding the activities of gambling, speculating, and investing. Such a decision is left entirely for each individual. It is interesting to observe, however, that any one person might undertake all of these activities at some time or other during a wealth-building career. This book focuses primarily on investment processes, with occasional discussions of speculative techniques.

The preceding paragraphs provide a framework for distinguishing between investing and other types of activities. There remains, however, additional discussion necessary to present a refined definition.

[3] Suppose the price rises from $10 to $11 per share in one week. This is a 10 percent gain. However, returns are usually expressed on an annual basis. In this instance the conversion is made by multiplying the percentage increase by the number of weeks in a year, for example $10\% \times 52 = 520\%$, a healthy rise!

[4] Bernard Baruch, *My Own Story* (New York: Henry Holt & Co., 1957), p. 254.

In the first place, what kinds of commitments are meant? While money is the most common form of a pledge, several other interpretations are used. For example, Mary is investing in her future by getting a college education, but in this book *investing* means the commitment of money.

Another point needing clarification involves the use for which money is to be committed. Collectors' items, real estate, and animals are but a few of literally thousands of different assets which people in general consider to be investment media, but this book is written primarily for those interested in acquiring securities, such as stocks or bonds. A later section in this chapter briefly describes investment opportunities outside the area of securities.

Investing then means *the committing of money for the purchase of securities based on a careful analysis of risks and rewards anticipated over a period of one year or more.*[5]

INVESTING PURPOSES

On the surface it might seem that all persons who invest desire to accumulate wealth. While this is perhaps the most common goal, it is certainly not the only purpose. One motivation has been superbly described in a best selling book, *The Money Game.*[6] In a most convincing manner the author tells how various individuals invest for the sheer excitement of being involved in the stock market. The playing of the game is the real stimulus for these people. The actual dollar gains and losses are secondary matters—a way of keeping score.

This gaming desire is evidenced in another manner. A host of parlor games based on the stock market has appeared in the last few years. "Transaction," "Buy or Sell," "Broker," "Stock Market," "Walstrete," "Acquire," and "Stocks and Bonds" are representatives. One game, "Corner," resembles an analog computer and costs in excess of $100.

Even those investors who are primarily concerned about wealth accumulation have differences in their investment purposes. One group desires cash returns on a regular basis for current needs. These people are also concerned about the safety of their investment. This need to preserve capital coupled with current income requirements dictates

[5] The terms *investing* and *speculating* will be used where it is important that they be distinguished. However, in the interest of writing brevity, investing may be understood to include speculative activity.

[6] Adam Smith, *The Money Game,* 2d ed. (New York: Random House, 1968).

the types of securities that will be held. Typical of this group of investors would be a retired couple that needs income for living expenses. They cannot afford to risk loss of principal, and they would be hesitant to consume any of the wealth they have previously accumulated.

Investors receive returns in two ways. *Income* is provided in the form of interest or dividends. The other source is known as a *capital gain*. This is achieved whenever a security is sold above its purchase price.[7] Gains occur sporadically and only when the price has advanced and when the investor *actually sells*. Income is normally received regularly. This difference in the time pattern of returns provides one way of studying an investor's objectives. If this person relies on a definite amount of return from security holdings the returns are probably needed for current uses. Thus, income often provides for present consumption; capital gains are the normal means of acquiring wealth for future consumption. This describes what is essentially a "tradeoff" situation. Emphasis on capital gains usually dictates holding securities that do not provide much income. Investments that offer substantial income payments normally have relatively stable prices. A young couple might represent the group hopeful of capital gain. Their salary provides for their living expenses, but they wish to build an estate for future needs, such as their children's educations and their own retirement.

The income versus capital gain is not strictly an either-or situation. It is a matter of emphasis. Many securities offer a combination of moderate income and some potential for price appreciation. So, there is really a broad spectrum of purposes for investors seeking monetary returns.

TYPES OF INVESTMENTS

The purpose of this section is to call attention to the myriad of potential investment media. A detailed examination of the "world of investments" would fill a library. The discussion that follows is meant to be suggestive and to make the reader aware of the hosts of possibilities.

---

[7] The opposite can and, of course, does occur, and is a capital loss. For income tax purposes a capital gain refers to net profits realized when the securities have been owned for at least six months. A discussion of tax aspects of investing is presented in Chapter 13.

Securities

Securities are certificates evidencing debt or ownership.[8] They are available in an abundant variety of types but are usually grouped into two broad classes—stocks and bonds. Common stocks are the most popular versions of ownership, with a lesser role being played by preferred stocks. Each of these categories has numerous sets of subclassifications. For example, sophisticated investors are aware of Class B, nonvoting, common stock and of Series D, 7 percent, cumulative, participating convertible preference shares. A detailed discussion of preferred and common stock may be found in Chapters 9 and 10, respectively.

Evidences of debt include bonds. They are classified according to the type of entity that has borrowed money and issued bond certificates. Knowledgeable persons have learned about *corporates,* including convertibles, and *governments* which embrace Treasury, agency, and municipal obligations. These issues are covered in Chapters 8 and 9.

Another category of securities may be broadly termed partnership interests. This group consists of many innovations and deserves investor attention. Many city dwellers have become absentee farmers through this vehicle. Several companies offer programs in which they will buy, feed, and breed animals in return for the investor's dollar. The value of this investment grows as offspring are sold. Beavers and beef cattle are available in this type of animal management contract. Interest in land, to be planted in citrus trees, for example, is offered under a similar plan. This, incidentally, has been advertised for people near retirement. The commitment is made, the land purchased, trees planted, watered, sprayed, and so on and in a few years when the investor retires and his or her salary income drops, the harvest begins and profits hopefully materialize!

Housing condominiums enjoyed popularity in the late 1960s. They, too, resemble the lease-a-cow plans. In this instance the buyer often acquires a vacation home and part interest in common facilities, such as a swimming pool and a restaurant. In nonvacation periods the management company will rent the property for the investor. Real Estate Investment Trusts are the forerunners of the condominium concept.

[8] Several types of savings plans use a certificate. These and passbook savings accounts are discussed in Chapter 7.

They stress investment in income-producing property, such as office buildings, apartments, and shopping centers.

Several billion dollars have been committed by investors in the past few years in oil drilling participations. Many of these are organized as limited partnerships and are designed mainly for wealthy individuals. Special tax laws that apply to the search for oil and gas make such investments especially attractive to persons having high incomes. The basic plan is again the same. For this and the other programs described, a syndication of investors is formed. Then a group of professionals, for example geologists, animal husbandmen, horticulturists, or real estate property managers, is employed to manage the assets for the interest of the investor.

Popularity of types of security investments waxes and wanes. Some of the alternatives mentioned above had fallen into disfavor with investors by the mid-1970s. At the same time other types have caught on. For example, the most rapidly growing security investment, in terms of investor interest, in 1975 was the *call option*. One should not be surprised to learn that at a later time, these options to buy common stock have faded from the forefront of investor appeal.

Land

"Land is not nearly so exciting as the stock market. You'll miss those big surprises every morning." These statements were used in an advertisement by a firm seeking to dramatize a difference between securities and land investments. These media can be differentiated by price patterns. Security prices, in general, and common stocks, in particular, tend to move up and down with some rapidity. Land values also change, but in many areas this pattern is seen as an almost uninterrupted price rise. Furthermore, securities are priced almost continuously and have instantaneous marketability. Land values, on the other hand, are not known unless someone provides the time and expense required for appraisals. Even then accurate results are not guaranteed and will not be revealed until an actual sale is completed. In spite of uncertain valuation and a lack of ready marketability, thousands of investors are attracted to ventures in land. This interest is especially keen when people experience anxieties over inflation and/or declining stock prices, such as during 1974. In the long run, investors realize the supply of land is fixed while the demand continues to grow. Expressed somewhat differently, "Land, air, and water will never go out of style. Combine this fact with the tremendous population rise and the great demand for investment capital to develop our natural resources to meet the needs of this population. . . ."[9]

There are several methods of classifying land investments, but perhaps the simplest division is between raw and developed land.[10] Placed in the former grouping would be areas close to population centers—out-of-town, but in a path of probable development. Recreational property such as river frontage is another example. Farms would be a third. In general, undeveloped land offers the greatest appreciation potential, *but* it is also accompanied by the highest risk.

Developed property is most often sought by persons seeking current income. These ventures are somewhat less risky. They might involve shopping centers, residential additions, and office buildings. These and other land investment opportunities are the subjects of many books.[11]

Notwithstanding the attractiveness of land investing, there are many people who choose to exclude this vehicle from their commitments. These individuals might say:

> Stocks have the advantage that they don't have to be mowed, picked clear of empty beer cans, and are not subject to curb, paving, and sewer assessments. If they don't produce current income, they aren't taxed. Higher and higher real estate taxes are becoming one of the best recommendations for stock ownership. Also if you don't like the weather in Mandan, North Dakota (35° below recently), you can put your stocks in your hat and move to Florida or Arizona. Try doing that with 160 acres, or six city lots.[12]

Commodities

A Chicagoan doubled his money in a recent three-week period. Arthur W. Cutten, a Canadian bookkeeper, parlayed $90 into $300 million over a 30-year time span at the turn of the century. J. Ogden

---

[9] Walter Youngquist, *Our Natural Resources: How to Invest in Them* (New York: Frederick Fell, 1966), p. 13. This book has been updated and extensively revised in Walter Youngquist, *Investing in Natural Resources: Today's Guide to Tomorrow's Needs* (Homewood, Ill.: Dow Jones-Irwin, 1975).

[10] This is somewhat analogous to separating securities into income and capital gain categories.

[11] James R. Cooper, *Real Estate Investment Analysis* (Lexington, Mass.: Lexington Books, 1974); J. Kirk, *How to Build a Fortune Investing in Land* (Englewood Cliffs, N.J.: Prentice-Hall, 1973); Douglas M. Temple, *Investing in Residential Income Property* (Chicago: Henry Regnery, 1974).

[12] Walter Youngquist, "Fortnight Notes," a bimonthly publication of Craig-Hallum, Inc., February 9, 1970, p. 2.

Armour, who headed his namesake meat packing firm familiar to most people, lost almost $150 million.[13] These fortunes were made and lost in the same activity, and in a manner that is unknown to thousands and not understood by millions of investors. The efforts involved *trading commodity futures*. This term refers to the buying and selling of mainly foodstuffs and metals. Beginning with apples and ending with zinc, the list includes mercury and molasses, platinum and plywood, potatoes and pork bellies, oats and orange juice—about three dozen types in total. A special section of Chapter 12 is devoted to a basic discussion of this type of investment.

Collectors' Items

Thousands of items are not particularly useful themselves, but they nevertheless have value because they offer pleasure to some people. These individuals are willing to pay for this. They are collectors. The goods they covet also provide a medium for investors. There is a limited supply of these items, whether there is only one, as an original painting, or only a limited number, as multiple copies of stamps. As more people become interested, the demand rises, forcing price increases. This situation provides the investor with the essential ingredient—an opportunity to buy low and sell high. So the connoisseurs are joined by others who want to profit by trading.

Paintings have long been a source of interest to both groups. Recent innovations have facilitated investor involvement. Several newly formed companies buy and sell art for profit.[14] Shares in these firms can be bought to give the individual an indirect interest. This allows participation in lesser amounts than would be required to deal directly. The stimulus for investing in art is shown in Table 1–2.

Thousands of people are numismatists and philatelists. These coin and stamp collectors also include investors in their groups.[15] "I saw the market conditions and realized my money was dwindling . . . I was fighting a losing cause in trying to set aside money for my children's educations. Stamps seemed the one way to assure me that the

[13] These experiences were discussed by Jonathan R. Laing in "A Risky Business," *The Wall Street Journal*, December 15, 1969, p. 1.

[14] See Lee Berton, "Art Funds: The Good, the Bad and the Beautiful," *Financial World*, May 22, 1974, pp. 20 ff.

[15] An unusual twist to coin collecting takes place every time a rise in subway fares occurs. Rather than reissue new tokens, the transit authorities often just begin selling the same tokens for a higher price. People can profit by buying tokens before the fares go up.

TABLE 1–2
Why Investors Like Art

	Number of Times by Which the Price Index Increased, 1950–69	*Percentage Increase 1970–73*
Dow Jones Industrial Index	3	18
Old master prints	37	50
Modern pictures.	29	60
Chinese porcelain	24½	40
Old books	13	30
Old master drawings	22	50
Impressionist pictures	18	50
Old master pictures.	7	40

Source: Adapted from data presented in Lee Berton, "Art as Investment Outpaces Stocks," *Financial World,* May 23, 1973, p. 22.

dollars wouldn't remain static or go downward."[16] This man and nine others put up $500,000 to establish a fund for stamp investing.

As the list of investment possibilities grows, it becomes more unusual. Collectors pay substantial sums for rare books, old bottles, and three-foot lengths of aged barbed wire. Wherever the collector's interest appears, the investor will not be far behind!

It is hoped that this discussion has helped the reader become aware of a wide variety of potential investment media because this is a book about *personal* investing. Aroused interest can be pursued in the references cited.

OUTLINE FOR THE BOOK

This book is written in four parts. In the first part the "what" and "why" of investing are discussed. Basic concepts are presented for application. The perspectives just discussed, and the investment returns and risks attending them, are considered. This provides a framework for analyzing any type of investment.

Part Two examines the organization of security markets, sources of investment information, financial statement interpretation, and investment analysis. The impact of regulation on the people who participate in the investment process is discussed. These chapters provide a background which is essential to a full understanding of the investment world.

16 Melodie Bowsher, "As Other Investments Sour, More Americans Turn to Rare Stamps," *The Wall Street Journal,* February 4, 1970, p. 1.

Part Three describes the many types of investments available to individuals. Characteristics of savings accounts at different financial institutions are discussed. A study of the major types of bonds follows. Preferred and common stock are examined, and a framework of analysis is given. Investment companies are treated in some detail. The last chapter in this part describes some special types of investments and techniques that are gaining in popularity.

Investing must be "personalized." That is to say, the individual is the key to any investment situation. Part Four, Managing Your Investments, emphasizes this belief. Tax considerations are presented so the reader can appreciate this aspect of the environment. The concluding chapters bring together the many factors that must be evaluated in establishing a personal investment program. The matters of personal objectives, resources to meet them, and individual constraints are emphasized. Special effort has been made to offer the reader information that will be of lasting value in this quest for wealth accumulation.

SUMMARY

The objective of this book is to provide a framework within which an individual can set personal investment goals and steer a course to achieve the desired results. The path of wealth accumulation is not free from difficulties and disappointments.

Security buying and selling activities can be identified as *gambling* when a person tries for large gains in short periods of time without making an effort to analyze each situation before acting. *Speculators* also look for quick, large profits, but they act only after carefully analyzing the relevant information about each opportunity. *Investing* also involves extensive research but is more directed toward long-term situations.

Some investors seek capital gains while others desire income on a regular basis. Still others invest for the psychological benefit derived from "playing the game." In many cases, two or more of these motives are combined in varying degrees.

Investors have a wide variety of opportunities to commit funds. Various types of savings plans are available, and bonds, preferred stocks, and common stocks are the most prevalent forms of securities. Partnership interests are offered in animal, housing, drilling, and land ventures. Commodities, consisting mainly of foodstuffs and metals, present another medium for investment. Collectors' items, such as stamps, coins, art objects, and even barbed wire are open to investor participation. The different opportunities are almost unlimited.

This is a basic book designed to cover the "what, why, where, how, and when" of personal investing.

PROBLEMS

1. Interview some people who are collectors. Ask them why they collect what they do. Do you think they are investors?
2. Look for the label or some identification of the manufacturer on an item of clothing which you are wearing. Go to a library and find out the following information about this company:
   a. Location of its headquarters.
   b. Sales and earnings for the latest year.
   c. Recent price of its stock.
3. Next time you go shopping make a list of each of the businesses which you have visited. Then look up the stock price of each of these firms. Why do you suppose this information is not available for some of the companies you listed?
4. Interview two or more persons who consider themselves to be investors. Determine what types of investments they make—stocks, bonds, real estate, commodities, and so on. Learn why they do or do not own some of the alternative investment types mentioned in this chapter.

QUESTIONS

1. Define *investing.*
2. Distinguish between investing, speculating, and gambling. Give an example of each activity in the area of securities.
3. What is the purpose of investing?
4. Briefly discuss opportunities to invest in securities, land, commodities, and collectors' items.
5. Cite advantages and disadvantages of each of the potential investment media listed in Question 4.
6. Discuss what makes an asset valuable.
7. Many books of the type you are now reading are titled "Investments." Why do you suppose the authors choose *Personal Investing* for the title of this book?

SELECTED READINGS

Anonymous investor. *Wiped Out: How I Lost a Fortune in the Stock Market While the Averages Were Making New Highs.* New York: Simon & Schuster, 1966.

Baruch, Bernard M. *My Own Story.* New York: Henry Holt & Co., 1957.

Cooper, James R. *Real Estate Investment Analysis.* Lexington, Mass.: Lexington Books, 1974.

Fisher, Philip A. *Conservative Investors Sleep Well.* New York: Harper & Row, 1975.

The Language of Investing, a Glossary. New York: The New York Stock Exchange, 1973.

Lindner, Edgar T., and Isaacs, Richard S. *A Layman's Guide to Investment Alternatives.* San Francisco: Chronicle Books, 1974.

Mader, Chris. *The Dow Jones-Irwin Guide to Real Estate Investing.* Homewood, Ill.: Dow Jones-Irwin, 1975.

Rush, Richard H. *Investments You Can Live with and Enjoy.* New York: Simon and Schuster, 1974.

Sarnoff, Paul. *The Wall Street Thesaurus.* New York: I. Obolinsky, 1963.

Seldin, Maury. *Land Investment.* Homewood, Ill.: Dow Jones-Irwin, 1975.

Shulman, Morton. *Anyone Can Still Make a Million.* New York: Bantam Books, 1973.

Smith, Adam. *The Money Game.* New York: Random House, 1968.

Stillman, Richard J. *Guide to Personal Finance.* Englewood Cliffs, N.J.: Prentice-Hall, 1975.

Temple, Douglas M. *Investing in Residential Income Property.* Chicago: Henry Regnery, 1974.

Wyckoff, Peter. *The Language of Wall Street.* New York: Hopkinson & Blake, 1973.

Youngquist, Walter. *Investing in Natural Resources: Today's Guide to Tomorrow's Needs.* Homewood, Ill.: Dow Jones-Irwin, 1975.

2
Risk and Return

INTRODUCTION

The concern that dominates the minds of most investors involves deciding what is a good stock to buy. This is an extremely difficult problem. Part of this difficulty is simply because no one really knows which particular shares will increase in price. A further complication concerns the individual seeking an investment, for it is this person's unique circumstances that will largely determine the answer. An analogy may help to illustrate this thought. The question "Where is a good place to go fishing?" will bring a wide range of replies, most of which will be a series of questions prefaced by the phrase, "It all depends on. . . ." How good a fisherman are you? What kind of tackle do you have? Are you patient? How far are you willing to drive? What kind of fish do you like to eat? The point is that whether one is trying to "gather" fish or dollars, the circumstances surrounding each individual situation must be carefully considered. A *suitable investment for one person may not be appropriate for another.* Does this mean that all investors do not share a common desire to buy securities which will increase in price? Not at all, because the main reason for investing is wealth accumulation. The various ways of properly matching investors and investments are the result of a complex of how two factors relate to the individual. These factors are known in broad terms as *risk* and *return.* They are the most important characteristics of any security. Investment risks must be recognized and understood before they can be avoided or at least minimized. Returns offered to investors should be appraised in the light of the risks that are incurred.

The surface relationship between risk and return is really quite straightforward. A moment's reflection should illustrate the connection. A test pilot earns more than an airline pilot. A college football coach is paid more than a professor of business administration. Many people earn more by working for themselves than they would if they were employed by someone else. The reader can probably think of numerous additional examples of past wealth accumulation that involved substantial risks of health, job security, or business failure. As a general statement, then, risk and return *tend* to move in the same direction. This is illustrated in Figure 2–1. The graph shows that

FIGURE 2–1
Relationship of Risk and Return in Investing

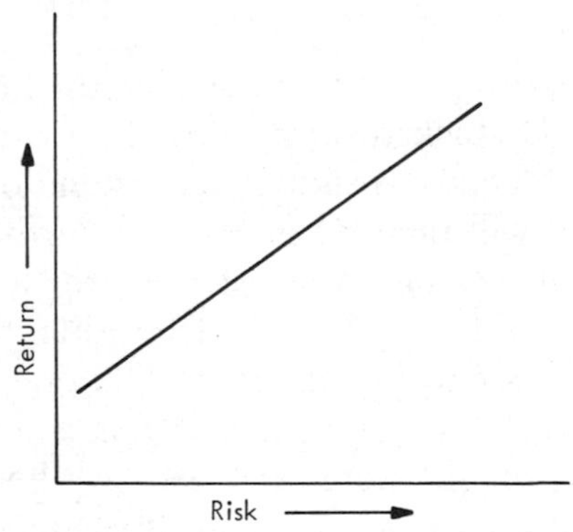

higher returns are achieved by accepting greater risks.[1] It should be emphasized that this is a general relationship and there are many exceptions. An individual does not acquire wealth simply by taking large risks. This is a tendency averaged over many cases and for long periods of time. In the short run and in particular instances, increasing risk may only lead to financial ruin.

The units of measurement are not given in Figure 2–1. This is because there are many ways to evaluate risk and return. Precise calculations and empirical evidence are best postponed until there is a clearer understanding of what is meant by the two factors. At the moment,

[1] For brevity the terms *return* and *risk* are used alone in this discussion. However, the reader should remember that the modifiers "expected" or "anticipated" are implied since it is the *future* that is of concern.

then, we must rely on an intuitive logic that risk and return, in general, are commensurate.

Risk is commonly defined as the chance or possibility of injury, damage, or loss. This exclusive emphasis on negative aspects is not necessary. The potential for gain is the attraction for most investments. Risk is involved here, too. This may sound odd, but it is really quite logical to consider change in either direction.[2] Note also that risk focuses on returns in the *future*. The words "chance," "possibility," and "potential" all refer to some event that is yet to happen. A determination of the degree of risk is based mainly on past records, but the purpose of the appraisal is definitely for application in the future.

The term *risk* shall be used in this book to mean the degree of the possibility of gain or loss occurring in investments.[3] A major objective of this book is to identify risks encountered in the investment process and to use this knowledge to maximize profits or minimize losses.

TYPES OF RISK

The previous definition presents a broad concept of risk. There is a need to be more precise because the term has many dimensions. The gain or loss from investments is the result of a number of different factors. Securities can be graded with respect to these factors or happenings. Grading is done by looking back and examining investment performance when certain events occur. The causative factors are identified with risk and referred to as *types of risk*.[4]

Financial Risk

The most obvious kind of risk is known as financial risk. This refers to *the uncertainty of future returns from a security because of changes*

---

[2] The concept of risk that includes both upward and downward movements is presented in Harry Sauvain, *Investment Management*, 4th ed. (Englewood Cliffs, N.J.: Prentice-Hall, 1973), p. 13. Some of the following discussion is also based on Sauvain's presentation in his Chapters 4–7.

[3] Some writers distinguish between risk and uncertainty, using the former term to describe situations in which future events can be described in probability terms. For example, the probability of a "head" appearing with the toss of a coin is 0.5. Uncertainty is used where probabilities cannot readily be assigned to the occurrence of future events.

[4] In a somewhat similar manner, students are evaluated by several criteria. To define a good student, one might examine such accomplishments as grade point average, leadership experience, communication skills, extracurricular activities, and so on.

in the financial capacity of the organization that issued the security. There is a wide range of possible variation in financial ability. To facilitate analysis of this risk, securities are grouped into the broad categories of bonds, preferred stocks, and common stocks.

Bonds and Preferred Stock. Almost all bonds promise to pay interest and principal according to a preset plan. The financial capacity of the bond issuer determines whether or not these pledges will be honored. Bonds are evaluated by appraising past records, current financial health, and future prospects. The organization least likely to undergo drastic change in financial ability is the U.S. government. So long as it has the power to levy taxes, it is hard to imagine that it could go "bankrupt." This means, then, that U.S. Treasury bonds are the safest form of security investment with respect to financial risk. By convention we say that these bonds are the highest grade.

Other governmental bodies also issue bonds—both foreign countries and domestic units such as state and local governments. These securities usually are considered to be slightly higher in financial risk. That is, they are assigned lower grades. The recent financial condition of New York City illustrates this point. Corporate bonds are also rated on the ability to keep the promises of payments. Many companies that issue bonds have unquestioned credit. Others are not financially strong. Some have had wide variations in their profits. These particular securities may represent situations in which the future returns are causes of concern. However, financial risk is a matter of degree. The bonds of some firms are superbly secure and are thus high grade while other corporate bonds might be of questionable value and be low grade.

Future returns from preferred stocks in general are less certain than those expected from corporate bonds. This is because failure to meet the bond obligations results in a default, whereas inability to pay preferred dividends has much less severe consequences. Firms are more hesitant to forego bond interest payments than they are to reduce preferred stock dividends.[5] Again, there is a wide range of grades of preferred stocks with each one being dependent upon the issuer's characteristics.

Common Stock. Common stockholders are residual owners. This means they are entitled to payments *only* after the other security

[5] An additional margin of safety is present for a firm's bondholders that is missing for the preferred stockholder. This is because the claims of the former group come first. If a company were liquidated, nothing would be paid to the owners of preferred stock until the claims of creditors, including bondholders, had been met. A further discussion of these priorities may be found in Chapter 8.

holders have had their claims satisfied. Future dividends may be quite uncertain in a company which has a large amount of bonds and/or preferred stock outstanding. This is especially true if the firm itself is not expected to enjoy uninterrupted prosperity. Being the last in line to receive company payments also means the owner of common stock will be the first to suffer when the firm experiences bad times. This event may be rather remote for some businesses, while in others a downturn must be considered a distinct possibility. In this group, too, there is a wide range of financial risks with grades being assigned accordingly.

Grading Securities. The preceding discussion can be summarized by the illustration in Figure 2–2. This chart shows a general pattern of increasing grade of security with regard to financial risk of common stock, preferred stock and corporate bonds, and government bonds, respectively. This is a general trend, and many exceptions exist. Hence, the graph has been drawn to show overlap between the different security categories. Some common stocks are of higher grade than some types of government bonds. Conversely, there are some bonds which carry a higher risk of future payments compared to common stock issues of other firms. This ranking is in spite of the priorities which add a protective factor to the bondholder claims.

So far, no mention has been made about what is specifically meant by financial ability. This term refers to income generating power and to a lesser extent to the composition of assets and liabilities. The financial risk of securities is appraised by a careful analysis of these figures for each issuing government or firm. In the former organization, the most crucial measure is the source of revenues. For the business group, the key information is the earning power of the firm. But these figures are only a beginning. A thorough analysis requires much additional data, the evaluation of which is a complicated task. Fortunately, there are professional security rating agencies. Their methods and other techniques are discussed in Chapters 8, 9, and 10.

Financial risk can also be called *business risk*. This term is used because it draws attention to the operation or *business* of an organization. The concern is that although a company's present financial condition may be sound, there is a possibility that its products might become outmoded. Few people doubt that the communications industry, in general, and American Telephone and Telegraph Company, in particular, are in any serious danger of survival in the near or even distant future. However, there is concern about the "staying power" of some firms, especially new firms or those producing certain

FIGURE 2–2
Security Grading and Financial Risk

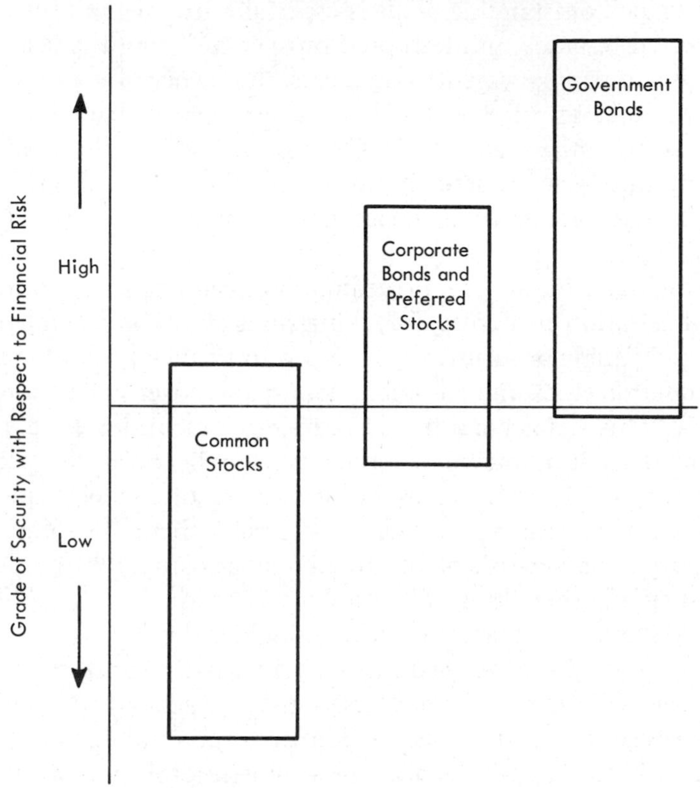

types of goods or a single product. Most people can readily recall several automobile makers who have gone out of business. Railroads and movie producers are other examples of companies having shaky pasts and rather uncertain futures. The term financial risk is used here in preference to business risk because the concept is applicable to governmental bodies as well as corporate forms of organization.

Market Risk

Market risk is the uncertainty of future prices because of changes in investor attitudes. This dimension of risk can be identified by observing the price movements of securities while they are being traded. One may ask why these prices change. Literally millions of people have pondered this question. Many answers have been given but most of them express, in one way or another, the notion that it is investor expectations which cause prices to move. These expectations are directly related to feelings about financial ability. However, waves of optimism and pessimism sweep investor minds. These shifts in attitudes sometimes occur without changes in financial capacity.[6] They may be termed broadly as *market psychology*.

It is usually very difficult to tell whether a price change has been caused by a change in financial ability or by a shift in investor attitudes or something else. Nonetheless, there can be no doubt that market psychology is a factor of influence on stock prices. Credence to this statement can be derived from a brief study of the severe decline on the New York Stock Exchange in 1974. Based on daily figures during the September 3–17 period, there were 4,108 instances of stock issues trading at new low prices for the year. This is a marked contrast to the ten cases during the same period in which issues reached record highs.[7] The extremely large number of record lows in proportion to new highs was not due just to changes in financial ability but was caused mainly by a widespread pessimistic feeling. Companies whose outlooks were not at all bleak were dragged down by the general fears that were then prevailing.

There are other times when the influence of market psychology can be identified rather easily. These situations arise when a crisis is created by the occurrence of some unforeseen event having widespread effects. Table 2–1 lists surprise announcements which had marked effects on stock prices.

Grading Securities. The concept of grading securities with respect to financial risk also applies to the analysis of market risk. In this case, the highest grade securities are those least susceptible to wide swings in investor favor. As a general rule, bonds, both government and corporate, are less affected by this factor than preferred stocks. In turn, these groups are less vulnerable than common stocks. In this latter category, the lowest grade securities are the *glamor* companies. These are firms which at times are especially appealing to investors. Past examples of favorites are conglomerates and firms in the electronic, publishing, franchising, and health care industries.

---

[6] One of the most widely adopted ways to measure investor attitudes toward a company is to examine the ratio of its stock market price to its earnings. A discussion of price-earnings ratios is presented in Chapters 6 and 10.

[7] Data taken from the Market Diary section of *The Wall Street Journal*. This period was selected because it covered the last weeks of the market downturn.

TABLE 2–1
Unpredictable News and Stock Market Behavior

	Days of Decline	*Percent Loss**
Battleship *Maine* sunk (1898)	32	16½
San Francisco earthquake (1906)	14	11
Lusitania sunk (1915)	32	11
Austrian crisis (1938)	31	25
Munich crisis (1938)	53	14
Czechoslovakian crisis (1939)	24	22
Poland invaded (1939)	17	7
Fall of France (1940)	26	25
Pearl Harbor (1941)	14	9
Berlin crisis (1948)	72	9
Korean crisis (1950)	13	12½
President Eisenhower's illness (1955)	12	10
Cuban crisis (1962)	6	5½
Kennedy assassination (1963)	1	6
Southeast Asia crisis (1964)	3	2
Czechoslovakian crisis (1968)	14	6

* Based on the Dow-Jones Industrial Average (DJIA)—a measure of average stock price movements on the New York Stock Exchange.

Source: "Rotnem Crisis Study," from *Market Interpretations* by Harris, Upham & Co., Inc., May 15, 1972.

Purchasing Power Risk

Once upon a time, a descendant of Rip Van Winkle became an investor by purchasing 100 shares of IBM and 200 shares of General Motors. Then, like the famous ancestor, this investor fell asleep for 20 years. Upon awakening, he called a stockbroker to ask how much his investments were worth. After some figuring, the broker reported his holdings now had a market value of $3 million. The man was thrilled, but before he could inquire as to why his stock had risen so much, the telephone operator interrupted to say, "Your time is up, please deposit $1 million dollars for your call!" The discovery of being a millionaire left this investor with very little to cheer about. He had become a victim of inflation.

One of the most widely recognized economic facts is the rising level of prices. School children know their lunches, gum, movies, and so on, all cost more as time passes. Adult see these and countless other examples. The 1 cent postcard, the 1 cent parking meter, the 5 cent daily paper, and the 75 cent haircut are all memories of a not-too-distant past. Similar rises in other costs are ample reasons for concern.

People invest mainly to accumulate wealth. Their records are usually kept in dollar terms. Mr. Van Winkle's experience illustrates a shortcoming of this measure. A more precise statement of investor aims would be a desire to build up *purchasing power.* Just having dollars is not enough. They must have the capability of being traded for goods and services which the consumer wants. Anyone in the past who "stuffed a mattress" with money to purchase items in the future was in for a big disappointment upon discovering the things wanted now cost two "mattresses of money."

Investors, then, are really concerned about purchasing power as opposed to dollars. The ability to buy goods and services is the critical factor. *Purchasing power risk is defined as the uncertainty of the purchasing power of future returns due to changes in the price level.*

Changes in the cost of living are usually measured by the *Consumer Price Index.*[8] Figure 2–3 traces the CPI for the post-World War II period. The Index shows a continual upward trend with the most rapid increases coming in 1973 and 1974. The long-run rise in the cost of living is a well-accepted fact which many people have adjusted to.[9] The problem is one of degree. Moderate increases can be accepted with relatively little inconvenience. But when the CPI rises at more than, say 3 percent per year, large groups of persons are affected. For example, an increase of 2 percent per year means the cost of living will double about every 36 years, which is a relatively long time. But if prices rise at an average rate of 12 percent per year, they will double in only six years![10] This rapid deterioration of purchasing power would be felt by virtually everyone but would pose an extreme hardship on those people having fixed incomes, mainly the elderly. Any person planning for needs ten or more years hence will be considerably affected by any moderate, but persistent, price rise.

The graph shows the United States has been fairly successful in preventing rampant inflation until recent times. In fact, the United

[8] This is a relatively elaborate measure of average retail prices of a broad range of consumer goods and services bought by moderate income groups within the U.S. urban population. It is compiled by the Bureau of Labor Statistics and is reported monthly.

[9] Although the long-run trend is definitely upward, price levels have declined in the past. This section has been written about inflation because it is widely held as being the most likely direction of future price level movements. Readers should be aware that *deflation* is possible and that fixed return securities are most desirable in those periods.

[10] An especially helpful "rule of thumb" to remember is called the *Rule of* 72. It states that the product of the growth rate and the time required to double will be approximately equal to 72. Thus, in the example above it was stated that a 2 percent growth rate would double the cost of living in 36 years ($2 \times 36 = 72$). Often this relationship is used to approximate growth rates. If the earnings per share for a company doubled in nine years, the rule would indicate that the profits had grown at an 8 percent compound annual rate ($72 \div 9 = 8$).

FIGURE 2-3
U.S. Cost of Living (1967 = 100)

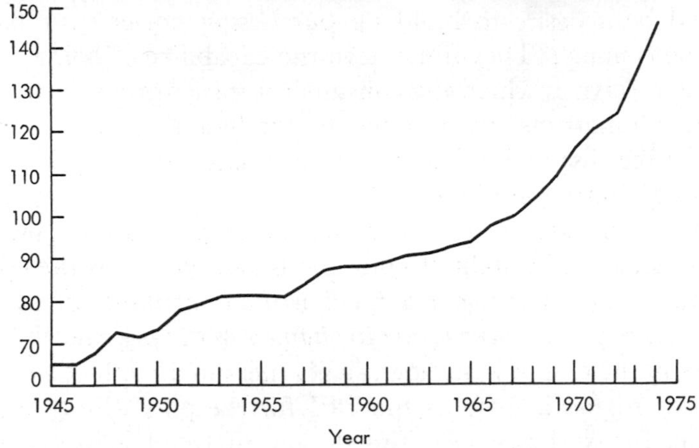

Source: Various issues of the *Handbook of Labor Statistics.*

States ranks high compared to the rest of the world.[11] It is the recent inflationary experience that is of utmost concern. In 1974 the cost of living rose 12 percent. These prices were reflecting rising raw material costs and wage increases. If high rates of inflation persist, the purchasing power risk may become the most critical type of risk for investors to recognize and react to.

Grading Securities. Grading of securities with respect to purchasing power risk is a very complex matter although it might seem relatively easy at first glance. The idea is simply to assign higher grades to the issues which offer returns that compensate best for the erosion of purchasing power. Traditionally, common stocks have been graded higher than bonds in this respect. This is mainly due to the flexibility in the pattern of stock returns compared to the fixed nature of bond yields. In the former instance, the arrangement that gives common stockholders the opportunity of sharing in the firm's earnings has been translated into a belief that this would provide for increasing returns. This has certainly been the experience over long periods of time, as

[11] For example, in the 1970–74 period, consumer prices rose 27 percent in the United States. Increases during the same period in several other countries were as follows: Germany, 27 percent; Canada, 29 percent; Netherlands, 37 percent; United Kingdom, 48 percent; Japan, 53 percent; Israel, 212 percent; and Chile, 8602 percent (through October 1974). See *International Financial Statistics,* International Monetary Fund, March 1975, p. 36.

shown in Figure 2–4. This graph indicates that during most of the 20th century common stocks have increased in price and paid dividends in sufficient amounts so as to more than offset the rises in the cost of living. However, when the time period is shortened a very different picture emerges. In 1974 when the consumer price index rose 12 percent, prices on the New York Stock Exchange declined 30 percent! So instead of offsetting a rise in the cost of living, common stock investment compounded the problem. Many persons who were attracted to equity issues for their protection against inflation learned, in a very painful way, that a considerable time period might have to pass before their investments provided them with the results they desired. A similar frustrating experience has resulted to shareholders in several other inflationary periods.[12]

Returns to stockholders are expected to grow because of two main reasons. First, companies expand their business by selling more of improved and/or new products. This often leads to increased profits, higher dividends, and stock price rises. The same results may occur when increases in the costs of doing business are passed on to the consumer in the form of higher prices. Thus, growth in sales, earnings, dividends, and stock prices may be the result of inflation as well as efforts on the part of a firm to expand operations. The effect of inflation on returns to stockholders varies for each industry and for companies within an industry. Firms having large reserves of natural resources such as oil, minerals, and timber are often thought to provide investors with protection against declines of purchasing power. Other firms may be good investments in inflationary periods because they are able to expand sales and profits. The electronics and the food industries are examples. On balance however, common stocks have *not* benefited from inflation and investors are cautioned against relying on them as being a good hedge. Remember that this is especially true for the short run.

Another concept will prove helpful in relating returns from bonds to the loss of purchasing power. Most financial data are expressed in dollars along with a particular time period. For example, Gross National Product (GNP) for the United States in 1973 and 1974 was reported as $1,295 and $1,397 billion, respectively. These numbers are known as current dollars. They indicate GNP rose almost 8 per-

[12] See F. K. Reilly, et al., "Inflation Hedges and Common Stocks," *Financial Analysts Journal*, January–February 1970, pp. 104–10, and Sauvain, *Investment Management*, pp. 124–31.

FIGURE 2–4
Common Stocks as Inflation Hedges

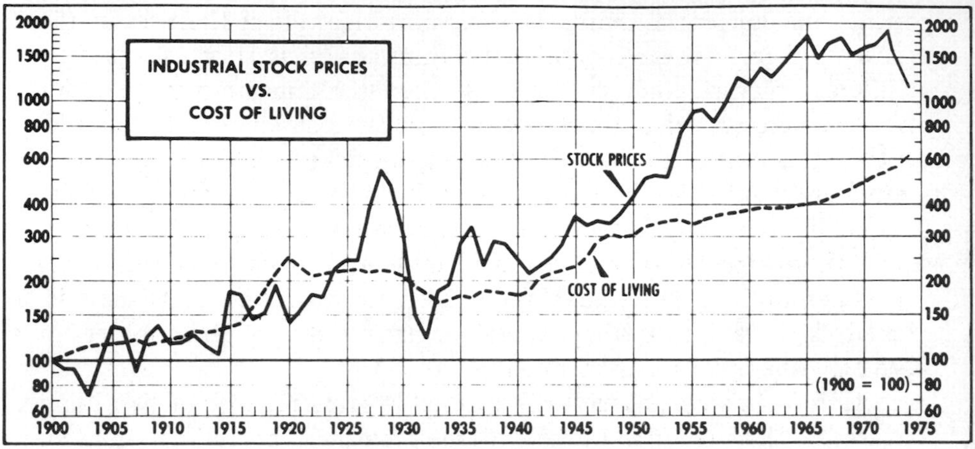

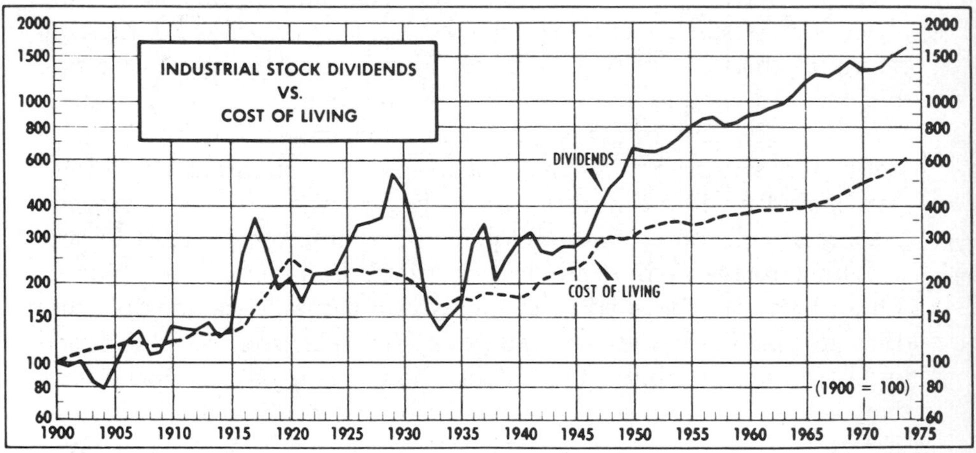

Source: Arthur Wiesenberger Financial Services, New York, 1975.

cent. However, it would not be proper to say that the economy expanded by that amount. The increase could have been caused in whole or in part by a *rise in the prices* which are used in valuing output. In order to determine what happened to the production of goods and services, the current dollar figures must be adjusted to account for a change in price levels. For GNP the base year is 1958. The reported figures, *after allowing for price increases,* were $839 and $821 billion in 1973 and 1974, respectively. This presents quite a

FIGURE 2–5
Aaa Corporate Bond Yields: Current versus Adjusted for Purchasing Power

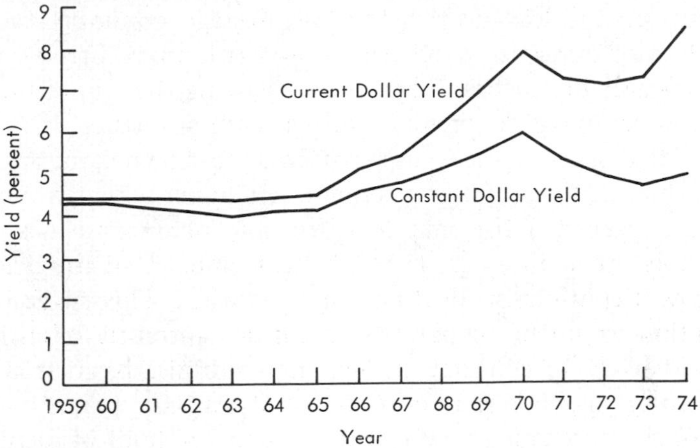

Source: Federal Reserve Bulletins.

different picture. It means that instead of expanding, the country actually experienced a *contraction!*

The adjusted figures are called *constant dollars.* In a similar manner adjustments can be made to returns from securities to show whether or not investors have gained purchasing power on balance. Data for returns from the bonds of the most credit-worthy corporations are plotted in Figure 2–5. The graph clearly shows that bonds have provided a long-run return sufficient to more than offset inflation. However, care must be exercised in interpreting this observation. In any one year bondholders may not have been protected against inflation. In 1974 for example, the bond yield of 8.6 percent was reduced by the 12 percent rise in the cost of living index to leave the investor with not a gain but instead a net loss of over 3 percent in terms of purchasing power! While this is the only year in recent history where the price rise has exceeded the yield, there have been numerous periods in which the purchasing power of returns from bonds has been quite low. People who own bonds paying low rates of interest are quite unhappy to see their returns wiped out by cost of living increases. Furthermore, when bonds are redeemed the principal is repaid in current dollars. These amounts will buy considerably less in comparison to the purchasing power of those dollars when the bonds were originally issued.[13] This, of course, is the reason why fixed income securities have been avoided at times when investors are worried about inflation.

Where does this leave us then? On the average, common stocks are low grade with respect to purchasing power risk. Fixed income securities are only slightly better. There is no denying that rapid increases in the cost of living do present problems for investors. If "double digit" inflation becomes a regular pattern, most owners of securities will face difficult times. The keypoint to remember is that while there has been a persistent rise in prices, the rate of increase has *varied* considerably. Economists are in general agreement that the degree of inflation will continue to fluctuate in the future. This suggests that one solution would be to purchase securities currently offering and considered likely to continue paying high returns. Regular receipts of these funds enable one to offset all or at least the majority of the erosion of the purchasing power of the dollar. Methods of identifying these opportunities will be treated in later chapters.

Interest Rate Risk

Interest rate risk is defined as the uncertainty of future returns due to changes in market rates of interest.

In 1946, American Telephone and Telegraph Company sold bonds to investors with the promise of paying a "coupon" or interest of 2⅝ percent each year until they mature in 1986 when the original amount borrowed would be repaid to the bondholder. In May 1975, these bonds could be purchased for as low as 59 percent of their original price. What happened? Why had the price of these bonds fallen so drastically? There had not been any developments that spelled doom to the company. They had never missed any interest payments. No technological breakthrough had been announced that would make the telephone obsolete. AT&T was not facing bankruptcy. Their continued existence was in no way in jeopardy. In fact, these bonds were superbly secure. There was virtually no question that the firm would not be able to make payments as promised. These aforementioned troubles have fallen on numerous other corporations in the past and, in some cases, caused their bond prices to decline. AT&T

[13] One method of attacking this problem is to adjust the payments each year so as to compensate for inflation and also offer some real rate of return. Such an arrangement is known as *indexing*. Brazil is the only country to have tried this technique. Lack of a clearcut success and many other complications have prevented other nations from putting the idea into practice.

had not suffered any traumatic setbacks, yet these bonds were being bought and sold at 59 percent of their original value. The reason for this decline is the subject of this section—*interest rate risk*.

Previous discussions have outlined other causes of variation in security prices. These were identified as changes in financial capacity, in investor psychology, and in price levels. Attention is now drawn to a fourth reason—changes in interest rates.

Security prices reflect changes in anticipated benefits. Bond interest is fixed. That is, it does not change over the life of the bond. In the example previously mentioned, AT&T promised to pay *no more or no less* than 2⅝ percent each year for the entire 40 years that particular bond was to be outstanding. This is constant, but the market rate of interest, which is essentially rent paid for the use of money, will change over time. The current price for money will be reflected in the new bonds that are sold. This is illustrated by AT&T, which has a large appetite for money. It sells more and more bonds as time passes. Whenever it does, it enters into a new agreement with investors and it pays the going rate for money. A partial listing of AT&T bonds outstanding as of April 1975, is presented in Table 2–2. The interest rates varied from 2⅝ percent in 1946 to 8⅘ percent in 1974. They were set each time based on what investors required when the offering was made.

After bonds have been originally purchased, they may be resold many times in the open market. Other investors buy them, but the

TABLE 2–2
American Telephone and Telegraph Company (bonds outstanding as of April 1975)

Year Issued	*Percent Interest*	*Year Issued*	*Percent Interest*
1945	2 3/4	1966	5 5/8
1946	2 5/8	1966	5 1/8
1947	2 3/4	1967	5 1/2
1947	2 7/8	1967	6
1948	3 3/8	1970	8 3/4
1950	2 3/4	1970	8 7/10
1954	3 1/4	1970	7 3/4
1956	3 7/8	1971	7
1957	4 3/8	1972	7 1/8
1960	4 3/4	1972	6 1/2
1961	4 3/4	1974	8 4/5
1962	4 3/8	1975	8 5/8
1962	4 5/8	1975	7 3/4
1963	4 3/8		

Source: Standard & Poor's *Bond Guide*, April 1975, p. 16.

price they pay is determined by the going interest rate at that moment. People buying bonds have the alternative of buying either new bonds or those which had been issued some time ago. If the current interest rate is higher than that paid on outstanding bonds, investors will not buy the older bonds unless their price drops enough so that the return is made equivalent to that currently being offered. In other words, people will pay less for AT&T's 2⅝ percent issue than they will for the 8⅘ percent one. Remember that the interest rate is quoted on the basis of par value, which is the same as or very close to the original purchase price. In the example just used, investors in 1975 would have the choice of receiving either $88.00 or $26.25 yearly interest for each $1,000 bond. Naturally they prefer the larger amount; so, if the 2⅝ percent bonds are going to find any buyers, their price must be lowered. In this case, the equilibrium point was about $590, which meant for this amount an investor could purchase a bond that would pay $26.25 per year until 1986, when AT&T would redeem the bond for $1,000.[14] Conversely, if the current level of interest rates happened to be below rates offered on outstanding bonds, investors would choose the old bonds. In so doing, they would bid up those prices above par to a point where the return was equivalent to the present rate.

This discussion identifies a very important relationship between prices of outstanding bonds and market rates of interest. This is shown in Figure 2–6. This graph indicates that bond prices vary inversely with interest rates. When interest rates increase, bond prices decrease, and vice versa. Note the dotted lines which show that when the market rate of interest is the same as the interest rate paid on the bond, the price will be $1,000.

Grading Securities. Securities having the highest grade in financial risk tend to be the lowest grade in interest rate risk because prices of these issues are determined almost entirely by the prevailing market rates of interest. This means that these bond prices will be very responsive to changes in the cost of money and therefore be low grade with respect to interest rate risk. On the other hand, bonds sold by organizations having questionable financial capacity will be purchased by investors seeking returns based primarily on the prospects of improvement in financial ability of the issuer. These people are not so concerned with interest rates, and those particular bond prices will not be so sensitive to changing money rates. This means the lower

[14] The mathematics of determining the relationship of interest rates and bond prices is presented in Chapter 8.

FIGURE 2–6
Relationship of Bond Prices and Interest Rates

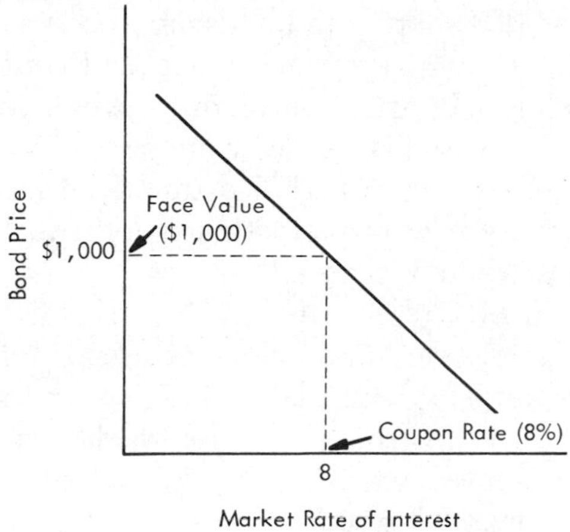

the grade of bonds in financial risk, the higher the grade will be in interest rate risk.

Another refinement has to do with the length of maturity of the bonds. As a general rule, the longer a bond has before it cxpires, the greater the change in price will be due to a change in interest rates.[15] Stated somewhat differently, a small price change in short-term bonds has a large cffect on returns. This means that interest rate risk grade is inversely proportional to length of maturity, or the longer a bond has before redemption, the lower the grade.

Attention has been focused exclusively on bond price changes. There are also returns in the form of interest to consider. Uncertainty of future income from this source can be reduced by purchasing long-term bonds. This is so because the interest rate on any particular bond is fixed over its lifetime. If a 9 percent, 25-year bond is bought, the owner will receive 9 percent for the quarter of a century that the bond is outstanding, regardless of any later changes in interest rates. If, on the other hand, a 9 percent five-year bond were selected, the owner would have to reinvest at the going money rate five years hence when the bond has matured. Interest rates could be higher or lower then. The uncertainty of the long-term bond is less simply because the investor is guaranteed a known amount for a longer period. The short-

[15] Proof of this relationship is given in Chapter 8.

term bondholder might possibly reinvest in four other five-year bonds, and at the end of 25 years have earned more interest than the investor that held the long-term bond. But the returns are *uncertain,* which by definition means that short-term bonds are lower grade when interest income is concerned. This grading arrangement contradicts that used for price. It is resolved by again considering the individual investor's circumstances. If this person is primarily interested in receiving a known and regular amount, then the choice would be long-term issues. If the dominant concern were protection of principal from loss, then short-term bonds would be chosen.[16]

The discussion of interest rate risk has thus far been limited to bonds. The basic relationship developed can also be applied to some preferred and common stocks. These would consist of those known as *income stocks.* They are issues which are sought mainly for dividends and not so much for the growth of price potential. Typical of this type would be some utility company stocks that traditionally have paid large dividends. If the general level of interest rates rises, income stocks will fall just like bonds until the yields they offer are equivalent to prevailing rates. Of course, most stocks have unlimited lives, which means that the factor of maturity as a refinement is not a consideration.

Political and Social Risks

There are at least two other identifiable causes of change in returns to holders of securities. One of these has to do with political developments. When a country devalues its currency, both good and bad effects will result to the financial capabilities of different organizations. A more serious development is the nationalization of facilities, which is usually quite damaging to companies whose assets were seized.

Social change is another factor to be recognized. This involves shifts in public attitudes. Examples may be found in the increasing concern about the quality of man's environment. Pollution and population control movements will have substantial impacts on some lines of business. An increasing social awareness may cause shifts in consumption patterns. That is, people may use less and less of some types of goods. The horsepower mania of Detroit appears to be yielding to smaller and less polluting autos. For the most part, social

---

[16] Losses due to price declines can be avoided by holding bonds until they mature. However, investors usually are not certain that they can do this. They might need to sell before the bonds are due.

changes are slow to evolve. This provides investors with sufficient time to react. Political change often takes place literally overnight. This latter risk can be taken into account by investors, but both of these types affect a rather limited segment of investment alternatives.

RETURNS FROM INVESTMENTS

The initial section of this chapter described the hypothesis that risk and return are commensurate. The following pages expanded the concept of risk, breaking it down into four major categories. Documentation was provided to establish the risk-return relationship for (1) market, (2) purchasing power and (3) interest rate risk types. The evidence of the risk-return connection for the fourth category, financial risk, has been withheld for special treatment at this point because it is usually considered the most dominant type. Whenever the term risk is used alone without any modifying adjective, it most often means financial risk. This usage will be adopted here.

Bonds

Bonds, it will be recalled, are issued with promises to pay interest and principal. They are graded on the likelihood that these pledges will be met. These grades are a measure of risk. Returns from bonds are known as yields and are expressed in percentages. The risk-return relationship for several classes of bonds over the past 25 years is shown in Figure 2–7. U.S. government bonds are the most creditworthy type issued. Aaa is the rating assigned to the safest corporate debt securities.[17] Baa bonds are considered lower medium-grade obligations. Note from the graph that while interest rates have varied considerably over the past quarter century, at all times the yields were lowest for U.S. government bonds and highest for the Baa category. This substantiates the claim that risk and return are commensurate.

The reason why this is so consistent with bonds is that there is widespread acceptance of the rating system. Investors, in general, do not like to take higher risks unless they are compensated for doing so. Lower grade bonds must provide higher yields. It is somewhat like the structure of life insurance premiums. Individuals pay more as they grow older because the risk of dying increases. In addition, some jobs are hazardous, and insurance rates for those workers reflect it. Like-

[17] These symbols are used by Moody's Investors Service in their bond rating system. An explanation of this procedure is presented in Chapter 8.

FIGURE 2–7
Yields on Different Risk Classes of Bonds

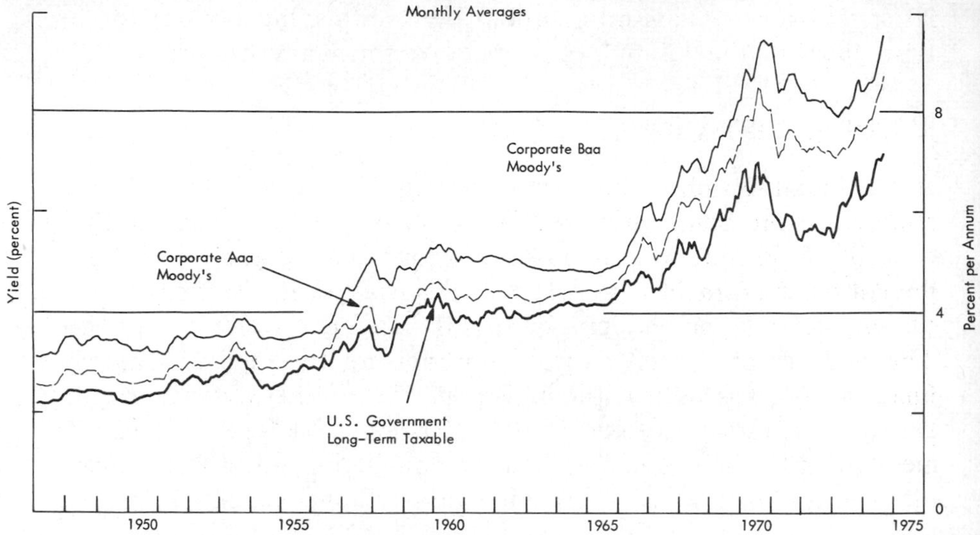

Source: Board of Governors of the Federal Reserve System, *Historical Chart Book,* 1974, p. 31.

wise, securities in different risk categories require different rates of return. Figure 2–7 provides clear support to the risk-return hypothesis applied to bonds.

Common Stocks

Equity issues, in general, are more risky than bonds because the claims of the former securities are junior to those of debtholders. According to the rule, then, returns from stock should be higher. Post-World War II stock and bond yields are plotted in Figure 2–8. Everything went according to form until 1958, when the curves crossed and bond yields rose above stock yields and remained higher. Something happened. Perhaps the risk-return hypothesis was no longer valid?[18] A moment's reflection will show no need to discard this relationship.

First of all, the graph shows that the change in yield position was developing over a number of years. This means that investors were gradually turning their attention to common stocks because they

[18] Actually, several other "inversions" have occurred in the past century. For example, in the late 1920s bond yields exceeded dividend yields.

FIGURE 2–8
Yields on High-Grade Debt Securities, Preferred and Common Stock

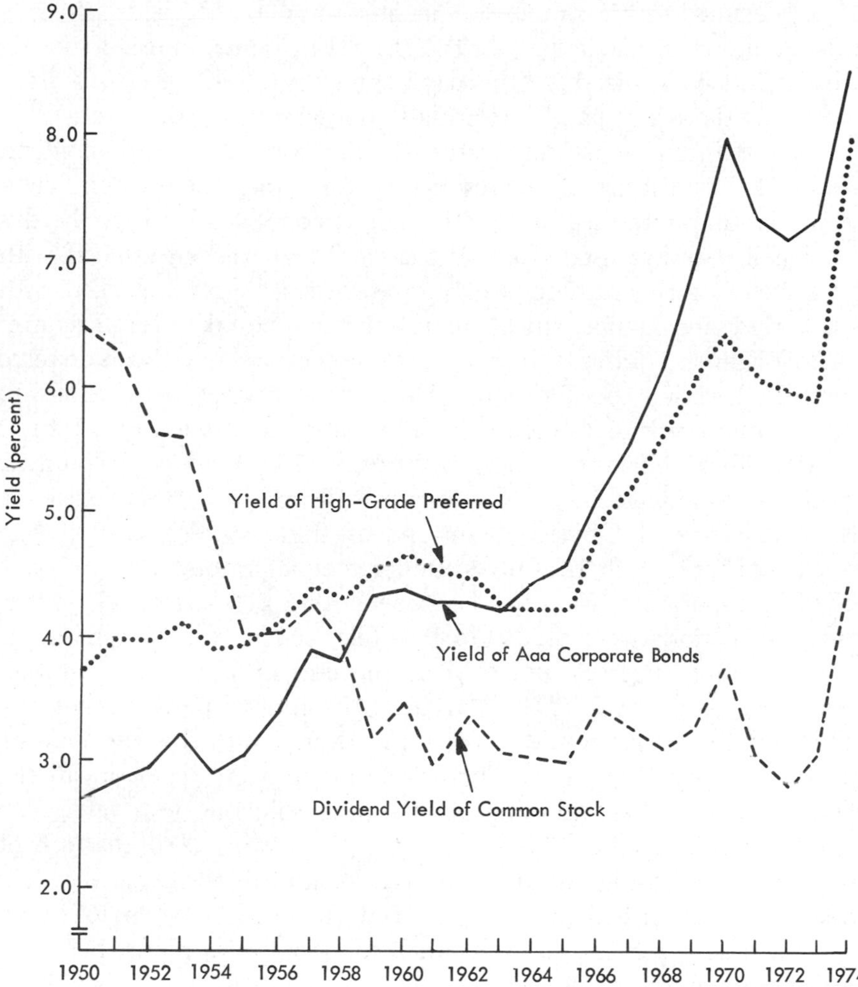

Source: Aaa Corporate Bond Interest series taken from *Federal Reserve Bulletins;* Dividend yield of Preferred from *Moody's Industrial Manual;* Common stock yields from Standard & Poor's 500 stock index.

offered returns not only from dividends but also through the opportunity for capital gain as stock prices rose. Remember that the interest rate paid on any particular bond will not change. As more investors became aware of the general rising trend in stock prices in the past, they anticipated a continuation of this trend. Thus, they were willing to pay higher prices in the present. The dividends on stock, while growing steadily, did not keep pace. Since the stock yields on the graph were calculated by dividing dividends by price, the ratio, or yield, declined. The comparison of stock and bond yields, then, is misleading. It only tells part of the story. For bonds, most of the return is indeed realized by the payment of interest.[19] Returns from stock, on the other hand, are usually dominated by the changes in price, and in the long run by the trend toward increased dividend payments by most firms. The result is that for stock the dividend yield is an inappropriate measure for this comparison. Notice that the discussion has always used risk and *return*. Yield was introduced with bonds because there it does measure return reasonably well. But with stock, the price change part of the return must be taken into account.

Risk-Return Studies. Numerous research efforts have been directed toward answering the question "What is the risk-return relationship in *common* stock investments?"[20] The most comprehensive attempt to determine what returns have been realized by holders of common stock was conducted by the Center for Research in Security Prices at the University of Chicago.[21] In one of these studies results were calculated for hypothetical investments of equal amounts in the stock of each corporation listed on the New York Stock Exchange. Different time periods were used. For example, stocks were purchased at the beginning of 1926 and sold at the end of that year. Another "purchase" was made at the start of 1926 and sold two years later. This procedure was repeated over and over, increasing the holding period one year each time. Then investments were made in all the listed stocks at the beginning of 1927 and sold one year later, two years later, and so on. This represented all possible combinations of buying in and selling out after one year or multiples of one year had passed. A total of 820 time periods were involved between 1926 and 1965. While the entire study is much too lengthy to report here, the major findings are as follows:

---

[19] Evidence of this can be found in an extensive study of investor experience with bonds by W. Braddock Hickman, *Statistical Measures of Corporate Bond Financing Since 1900* (Princeton, N.J.: National Bureau of Economic Research, 1960).

[20] One article lists 342 studies on this question. See Shannon P. Pratt, "Bibliography on Risks and Rates of Return for Common Stocks," *Financial Analysts Journal*, May–June 1968, pp. 155–66.

[21] Most significant results have been published in these three articles: Lawrence Fisher and James H. Lorie, "Rates of Return on Investments in Common Stock, the Year-by-Year Record, 1926–1965," *Journal of Business*, July 1968, pp. 291–316; Lawrence Fisher, "Outcomes for 'Random' Investments in Common Stocks Listed on the New York Stock Exchange," *Journal of Business*, April 1965, pp. 149–61; Lawrence Fisher and James H. Lorie, "Some Studies of Variability of Returns on Investments in Common Stocks," *Journal of Business*, April 1970, pp. 99–134.

1. The return over the longest time span covered was 9.3 percent. These returns are compound annual rates figured before taxes and with reinvestment of dividends. They can then be compared with interest rates paid by banks and published yields on most other investment media.

2. There is considerable variation of return, depending, of course, on dates of purchase and sale. During 1931 the return was a negative 48 percent. In 1933 a gain of 108 percent would have resulted. If someone had bought at the end of 1927, it would have been 14 years later before the securities could be sold out without having a loss. During the last 20 years covered by the study, the returns were consistently high with positive results in 95 percent of the 220 possible time periods. There was no ten-year time span in which the return was less than 11 percent.

These results present rather convincing evidence that common stocks have provided investors with substantial returns over the long run. But one might counter this remark by saying, "I'm an individual who can neither buy all listed stocks nor necessarily hold them for long periods." Is there any practical result supporting the case for common stock? Fisher and Lorie tackled this question with a gigantic computer program. They calculated results for every possible combination of month-end buy and sell dates for every stock during the 1926–60 period. This involved 87,900 different monthly buy-sell combinations for any one company. For all stocks listed, it meant tabulating results on 45,557,538 such possible transactions! Adjustments were made to allow for dividends and brokerage commissions. The returns were then expressed in a frequency distribution, which in turn showed the probability of gains and losses. For example, if someone randomly selected a company, purchased shares at the end of a randomly chosen month, and then sold that stock at the end of a later randomly selected month, the investor would have made money about three out of every four times. The tables also indicated a 50 percent chance that the return would have been at least 10 percent per annum. Furthermore, of every 100 transactions, 19 provided at least a 20 percent annual increase compared to only 6 that would have yielded losses at the annual rate of 20 percent or more. Other tests indicated that the chance of loss would have been considerably reduced and the amount of gain substantially increased if the investor had randomly chosen several stocks instead of just one and if the minimum holding period had been one year or more instead of one month.

FIGURE 2–9
Comparison of Dow-Jones Industrial Average and National Quotation Bureau Industrial Average

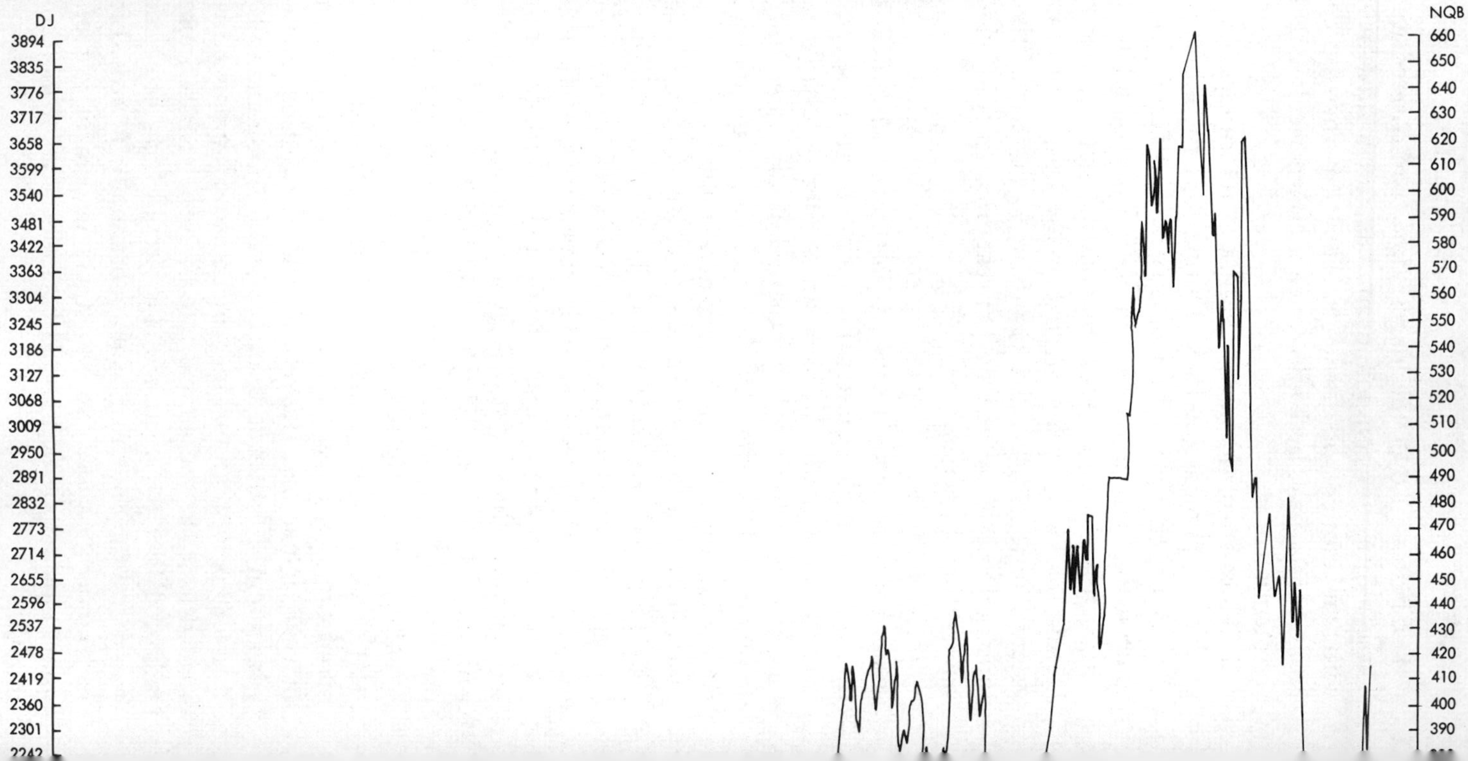

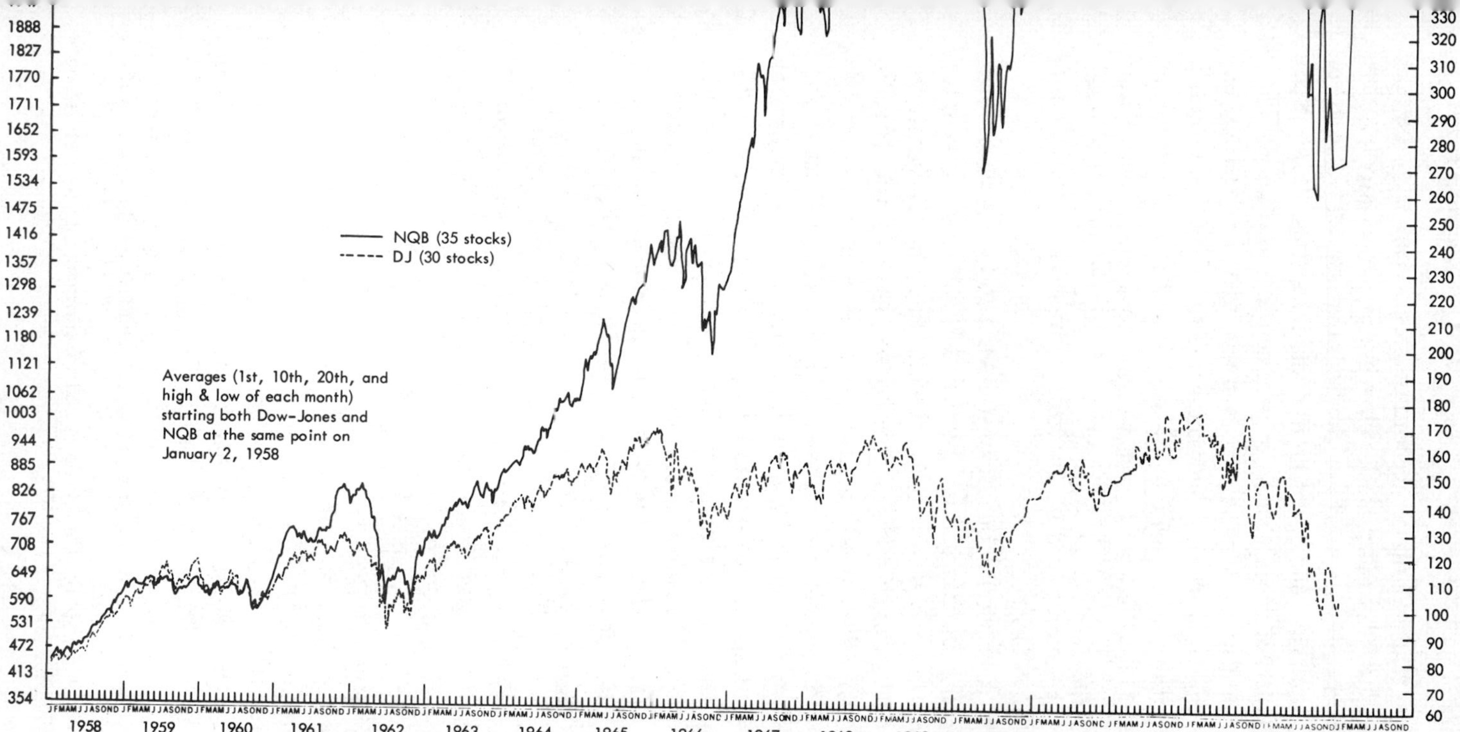

Source: Data supplied by National Quotation Bureau.

The risk-return relationship in common stocks can also be examined with the aid of Figure 2–9. This graph shows stock price performance in two different markets. The companies whose stock is traded in these markets have different characteristics. The New York Stock Exchange (NYSE) tends to list the older and larger firms with national reputations. Any securities not traded on a stock exchange are by definition in the over-the-counter (OTC) market.[22] The firms issuing these securities cover a very broad range from some that are old, well-established, and with worldwide operations to some that have been newly formed. The majority of this category are lesser known and have a smaller trading interest compared to those companies listed on the NYSE.

In general, the risks would be greatest in the OTC category and relatively less in the NYSE group. Figure 2–9 shows returns have been proportional to this classification of risk. The graph also shows wider price swings in the OTC compared to those in the NYSE. Variation in price, it will be recalled, is another measure of risk.

A word of caution must be given before leaving the risk-return discussion. All the empirical results shown are averages. These can cover up important information.[23] Many individual experiences will be different from what the averages would indicate. For example, it would be folly to feel assurance of large profits by buying stock in a company that had a very shaky past and an even more precarious future. The risk-return hypothesis does not say this at all. Instead, the preceding discussion has shown that for large numbers of stocks and over long periods of time, there is a greater return for the more risky situations. Remember then that this is a *tendency* which would become more uncertain as the time period is shortened and if only a very few investments are made. In order to reap the benefits of a plan following this hypothesis, the investor must be able to diversify holdings and be prepared to experience some losses, especially in the short run. The limitation as to how large returns are sought is determined by each individual's ability to sustain temporary setbacks. History has shown that the odds favor the risk-taker in the long run. To the extent that investors are able to expose themselves to greater risks, their wealth will tend to grow more rapidly.

---

[22] A detailed discussion of the organization of security markets can be found in the next chapter.

[23] One is reminded of the statistician who drowned while attempting to wade across a river which had an average depth of two feet.

SUMMARY

Risk is defined as the uncertainty of future returns from a security due to the occurrence of some causal event. These events can be grouped into four major categories. If the cause is the change in financial ability of the issuer, it is referred to as *financial risk.* Attitudes toward the value of securities vary over time. These are shifts in investor psychology and give rise to *market risk.* Inflation deteriorates the value of returns from securities. The uncertainty of what future dollars will buy due to this cause is known as *purchasing power risk.* Returns may also change as the result of a shift in market rates of interest and this particular cause is identified with the *interest rate* type of *risk.*

Securities can be rated according to their response to each of the different causes of change in returns. High grades are assigned to those issues which are relatively immune to the specific types of change, and low grades are given to securities that are quite sensitive to certain events. Table 2–3 shows how the major concepts of risk and security grading can be tabulated.

TABLE 2–3
Risks and Security Grades

Type of Risk	*Uncertainty of Future Returns Due to Changes in*	*High Grade*	*Low Grade*
1. Financial	Financial capacity	Bonds	Stock
2. Market	Investor psychology	Bonds	Stock
3. Purchasing power	Price level	Stock*	Bonds
4. Interest rate	Interest rates	Stock	Bonds

* This grading applies to the long run. In shorter periods common stock is lower grade.

The grading system is established by appraising the history of what happened to returns when each type of change occurred. Numerous studies have indicated risk and return are commensurate. These results are tendencies averaged for groups of securities and over long periods of time. Individual investments can and sometimes do lead to financial ruin. However, the odds in the long run have favored the risk-taker.

PROBLEMS

1. Make a list of occupations which have varying degrees of risk, either of being injured, losing money, or losing the job. Determine about how much a person in each of the categories would make. See if the highest risk jobs tend to offer the highest returns.
2. The following data are for three companies listed on the New York Stock Exchange:

	Stock Price Range (rounded)			*Earnings per Share*		
Year	*AT&T*	*Natomas*	*Northrop*	*AT&T*	*Natomas*	*Northrop*
1	71-60	12-08	35-20	3.41	1.62	2.10
2	64-50	16-10	32-20	3.69	2.18	2.51
3	63-50	24-11	46-27	3.79	1.60	2.86
4	58-48	40-16	54-31	3.75	0.58	3.28
5	58-49	131-34	54-33	4.00	(0.04)	3.80

   Based on the above data, rank the companies according to risk. What measures do you feel are most appropriate?
3. Look through the headings in the yellow pages of a telephone book and develop a list of industries which you feel offer investments which will be good hedges against inflation in the future.

QUESTIONS

1. What is the general relationship between risk and return?
2. Does investing in the more risky situations assure high returns? Explain.
3. What is *financial risk?*
4. Are bonds higher grade with respect to financial risk compared to common stocks? Why?
5. Define *market risk.*
6. Explain how investor psychology affects security prices.
7. Give a definition of *purchasing power risk.*
8. Would bonds issued by the U.S. government be high or low grade with respect to purchasing power risk? Support your answer.
9. What is *interest rate risk?*
10. What is the relationship between interest rates and bond prices?

11. Which is the more important consideration to investors in the U.S. companies, *political* or *social risk?* Explain.
12. Cite studies which support the risk-return hypothesis.
13. Suppose someone told you they had invested in common stocks to "hedge against inflation" and that the stocks had fallen while the cost of living had risen. What would you say to this person?
14. "Securities which are high grade with respect to one type of risk may be low grade with respect to another type of risk." Explain, using examples.

SELECTED READINGS

Campanella, Frank B. *The Measurement of Portfolio Risk Exposure.* Lexington, Mass.: Lexington Books, 1972.

Fisher, Lawrence. "Outcomes for 'Random' Investments in Common Stocks Listed on the New York Stock Exchange," *Journal of Business,* April 1965, pp. 149–61.

Fisher, Lawrence, and Lorie, James H. "Rates of Return on Investments in Common Stock, the Year-by-Year Record, 1926–1965," *Journal of Business,* July 1968, pp. 291–316.

———. "Some Studies of Variability of Returns on Investments in Common Stocks," *Journal of Business,* April 1970, pp. 90–134.

Hagin, Robert, and Mader, Chris. *The New Science of Investing.* Homewood, Ill.: Dow Jones-Irwin, 1973.

Sauvain, Harry. *Investment Management,* 4th ed. Englewood Cliffs, N.J.: Prentice-Hall, 1973.

part two

How and Where to Invest

3
Security Markets

INTRODUCTION

The first two chapters discussed the "what and why" of investing. They established a perspective for personal investing. Much of the material was conceptual. Attention is now turned to the considerations of "how and where" to invest. This chapter and the next are devoted to a description of the environment of the investing process—a complex arrangement of people, customs, and regulations.

FUNCTIONS OF SECURITIES MARKETS

Very few persons in Amcrica today are not aware of stock exchanges. Extensive publicity campaigns by professional investment people have caused widespread awareness, and many more people now own securities than ever before. While many individuals see the securities markets only as places to purchase and sell stocks and bonds, these institutions provide other basic functions for our free enterprise system.

The Economic Function

In the U.S. economy consumers are "kings"; efforts to satisfy their wishes keep the system going. The production of goods and services requires a combination of land, labor, and *capital*. Funds are needed to develop new ideas and to replace and expand facilities which are producing goods that are in demand. An important role of securities markets is to provide a channel through which money that is not presently needed by some can be used by others so that they can produce something to satisfy consumer wishes. *Facilitating flows of funds from sources to uses is the economic function of securities markets.* The more efficiently this can be done, the higher will be the living standard of the population. This not only means more cars, houses, and toys, but also more schools, roads, and water systems. Securities markets are not required in a system where the state owns the production facilities. In a free enterprise economy it is necessary that the savings of individuals, both large and small, be made available to those organizations that will build and produce.

Providing a Continuous Market with Fair Prices

One of the major attributes of most securities is that they can readily be sold for cash. This feature attracts many individuals who might otherwise invest in other assets, for example, land or rental property. The ability to buy or sell quickly without driving the price up or down is provided by securities markets, and is known as *marketability*. The transaction speed is one dimension of this term. A house, for example, is not very marketable because to achieve a quick sale the price might first have to be lowered considerably. Most securities can be bought or sold quickly. The other dimension of marketability involves the impact of an order on the price. Heavy demand for some new products causes their price to rise, and high production, such as in record agriculture crops, often results in price declines. Security prices are also determined by supply and demand, but most securities markets are capable of filling individual orders without the occurrence of wide price movements. The price of any security will increase or decrease if the orders are predominantly either to buy or to sell, but the movement caused by each order will be very small if the particular security is highly marketable.

Liquidity goes one step further in that it refers to the ability to convert assets into cash with little money loss in relation to the original purchase price. It is important to distinguish between these concepts. Securities can be marketable without being liquid, but they cannot be liquid unless they are marketable. Markets provide marketability but not necessarily liquidity because the latter depends on price movements of the security. Short-term U.S. government obligations—for example, Treasury Bills—are the most liquid type investments since their market values fluctuate very little. Common stocks, which typically have greater price volatility, are less liquid. A major function of the marketplace is to make known prices that both buyers or sellers can rely on in having their orders filled. The fact that these price quotes are always available is of great help to investors. They can continuously calculate the precise value of their holdings. They can also borrow money easier because reliable and continuous valuation makes securities highly acceptable collateral for loans.

In addition to continuous pricing the market system provides quotes that are "fair." This means that prices should deviate as little as possible from "true" investment value.[1] The worth of any security is determined by the future returns that are *expected* to accrue to the owner.[2] Note the emphasis on expected returns. These will, of course, vary depending on who is making the estimates. In fact, this is largely why so much security trading occurs. Investors who have a lower appraisal of the amount of future return than that indicated by the present price sell. Other persons figuring the future returns will be higher buy. A "good" market will produce quotes that represent the consensus of investor opinion regarding value. If the price is too high, people wanting to sell will be unable to find buyers. If too low a price is established, orders for purchase will go unfilled. A proper price level will result in maximum satisfaction to both buying and selling groups. At this point, trading activity will be the greatest.

An example will help illustrate the concept of a fair price. Imagine a group of investors interested in the stock of XYZ Company. Each person independently estimates the value of this security, and the tabulation of their appraisals is presented in Table 3–1. The highest

TABLE 3–1
Trading Interest in XYZ Stock*

Buy Orders	*Sell Orders*
100 shares @ 19¾	100 shares @ 20
200 shares @ 19½	300 shares @ 19¾
300 shares @ 19¼	600 shares @ 19½
600 shares @ 19	800 shares @ 19¼
200 shares @ 18¾	400 shares @ 19
300 shares @ 18½	300 shares @ 18¾
200 shares @ 18¼	300 shares @ 18½
100 shares @ 18	200 shares @ 18¼

* This illustration is based on one in Eiteman, Dice, and Eiteman, *The Stock Market*, p. 10.

[1] This particular section has benefited from W. J. Eiteman, C. A. Dice, and D. K. Eiteman, *The Stock Market*, 4th ed. (New York: McGraw-Hill, 1966), pp. 8–11.

[2] Returns, it will be recalled, are interest from bonds, dividends from stock, and the price at which the security may be sold in the future. Appropriate calculations may be found in the appendices at the end of Chapters 7, 8, and 10.

price anyone is willing to pay is $19¾ and the lowest is $18. On the sell side someone is willing to part with shares for $18¼, while another stockholder wants *at least* $20 per share. Notice the phrase "at least."

It means that the shares offered at $20 would also be available at any higher price. The person willing to pay $19¾ would be happier if the shares could be bought at a lower price. The investor appraisal information then can be retabulated on a basis that reflects this willingness to sell for "at least" or buy for "at most." This is done in Table 3–2.

TABLE 3–2
Cumulative Trading Interest in XYZ Common Stock

Shares Wanted	*Possible Prices*	*Shares Offered*
0	20	3,000
100	19¾	2,900
300	19½	2,600
600	19¼	2,000
1,200	19	1,200
1,400	18¾	800
1,700	18½	500
1,900	18¼	200
2,000	18	0

The question arises, "What is a fair price?" If $19¾ per share were established as the fair price, 100 shares would be purchased from the 2,900 shares offered. If the price were set at $18, no shares would exchange hands, leaving unfilled buy orders for 2,000 shares. At a price of $19, 1,200 shares would be traded. This is the maximum activity that could occur given the wishes of investors as set forth in Table 3–1. The function of a securities market is to facilitate trading at fair prices. This means disclosing the price which maximizes turnover, which in this example is $19 per share. The information is depicted graphically in Figure 3–1. The two curves show supply and demand for XYZ shares. At prices above and below $19 there is excess supply or demand. The greatest number of shares trades hands at $19. This presumably means more people are happy with that price than any other. Much of the remaining chapter will be devoted to a study of just how markets are organized so that fair prices can be disclosed.

FIGURE 3–1
Supply and Demand for XYZ Stock

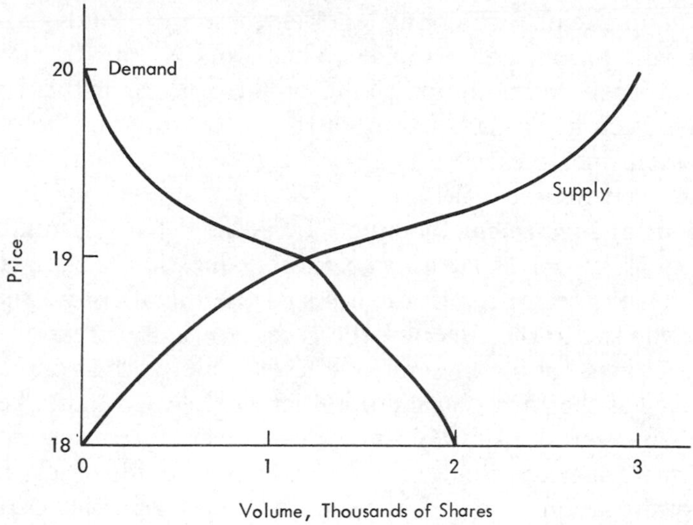

PRIMARY MARKETS

Recall that a major function of securities markets is economic and involves channeling savings into investments. This is accomplished in many ways. Banks accept deposits and make loans. Savings and loan associations, credit unions, and insurance companies are other financial institutions or intermediaries that help turn savings into investments. Individuals sometimes bypass the institutional intermediaries and invest directly. Whenever funds are made available to a user, regardless of whether they come directly or indirectly from the individual savers, new investment is said to be taking place. Securities of many types are sold by issuers to investors. This is different from the trading of securities *between* investors where no new investment takes place. The initial step of offering securities in exchange for cash involves what is known as *primary markets*. After securities are outstanding, they can be resold time and again in secondary markets.

Investment Banking

Investment banking is the business of assisting organizations in raising money. This aid is provided to both corporations and governmental units. It consists mainly of help in marketing new securities which are sold for the cash desired by the issuer. Investment bankers are middlemen who bring together those with funds to invest and those who have need for money. Their work is done in financial centers and small communities. Some of these firms in the United States have been in business for more than a century and help raise several billion dollars each year. Others are being formed every day and act on a very limited scale.

Functions of Investment Banking. Investment bankers fulfill two major roles. They act as *advisors* to the organization seeking funds and they sell the securities, if any are sold. In the advisory capacity they offer counsel to the issuer on the *type, terms,* and *timing* of the fund raising. Types of offerings include several categories of bonds and stocks as well as the particular method that will be used to market the security. Numerous decisions must be made on such terms as interest rates and maturities for bonds and the price of common stock. In addition, consideration should be given to a host of other features known as "sweeteners" that can be used to make the offering more attractive to potential investors. Finally, the decision must be made on *when* to sell the issue. Some offerings are postponed in hopes that investors will be more receptive later.

Literally thousands of combinations of terms can be used. However, there are relatively few alternatives that can be put together in an offering that will be both advantageous to the issuer and still be attractive to the investor. This is true because many characteristics that are desired most by investors, such as high interest rates, are least desirable to the issuer. Investors are a fickle group, and their requirements are constantly changing. Because investment bankers are in constant contact with the sources of funds, which are the investors, they develop a sense of what characteristics are currently held as being important.

After most of the details of the offering have been set, the investment bankers help assemble the relevant information required by various regulatory bodies. This activity will be discussed in the next chapter.

Advisory services are also provided by investment bankers to firms seeking to merge with or acquire other companies. Sometimes the investment banker actually initiates merger and acquisition activity.

The second major type of investment banking function is known as *underwriting*. This involves actually purchasing the securities to be sold from the issuer and then reselling them to the public. Underwriting means to assume liability in the event of loss or damage. The investment banker buys the securities at a stated price and then resells them immediately to the public at a higher price. At least this is the hope. But securities markets are constantly changing, and what appears attractive to investors one day will sometimes find no interest the next day. Underwriters assume the risk of being unable to sell the securities at a profit, but the issuers receive their money no matter what happens. The issuers are thus insured against loss due to a change in investor attitudes, and they are guaranteed the receipt of a certain amount of money at a certain date.

When small or new companies need capital, the investment banker may not wish to underwrite the offering because of the high degree of risk involved in marketing the securities. In these cases, a *best efforts* offering may be used. The investment banker attempts to sell the issue but does not *guarantee* that the offering will be successful. Any securities remaining unsold after employing "best efforts" will be returned to the issuer. This arrangement is like selling goods on consignment.

In practice, most offerings are usually sold to investors. The underwriter makes a profit by paying a certain price to the issuer and then reselling at a higher price to investors. The markup, or commission, as it is called, depends on (1) the type of security, (2) the issuer, and (3) the amount being sold. Commissions are lower on bonds than on stock because bonds are sold mainly to institutions and wealthy people. They buy in large amounts so the selling costs are lower. Common stock, on the other hand, is often sold to thousands of investors in small amounts. This requires more effort and results in higher costs.

Commissions are lower for the better known, financially sound issuers. Organizations having well-established reputations often have a following of investors who are willing to buy more of their securities.

The third major determinant of underwriting costs is the dollar amount of securities being sold. In general, the larger the offering, the smaller the percentage commission will be. This is because some parts of the fees charged are for items that require about the same expense whether half a million or half a billion dollars is being raised.

Documentation for the type of security and the effects of the size

TABLE 3–3
Costs of Selling Securities to the General Public (expressed as a percent of gross proceeds)

Size of Issue (millions of dollars)	*Debt*	*Preferred Stock*	*Common Stock*
Under 1.0	12.0	N.A.	22.2
1.0– 1.9	17.0	11.7	16.5
2.0– 4.9	6.2	N.A.	11.9
5.0– 9.9	3.1	2.5	8.7
10.0–19.9	1.9	1.8	6.6
20.0–49.9	1.4	1.7	5.0
50.0–99.9	1.2	1.6	4.2
100 and over	1.0	2.4	3.2
Average	1.6	1.9	12.4

Source: Securities and Exchange Commission, *Cost of Flotation of Corporate Securities, 1971–72* (Washington, D.C.: U.S. Government Printing Office, December 1974).

of the offering on the cost of selling securities is presented in Table 3–3.[3] In almost every instance the data confirm the relationships just described.

Negotiated Sale or Competitive Bid. Most new security offerings are made after the investment banker and the issuer decide on the type, terms, and timing of the issue. This procedure is known as a *negotiated sale* because the underwriter is directly involved in "putting together" the offering that will be sold. Certain types of organizations use a different process for raising funds. They invite investment bankers to *bid* for their securities. This system is known as *competitive bidding* and is required by regulation for many issuers. These are the federal, state, and local governments, railroads, and some public utilities. Investment bankers may, in some instances, furnish advice to these issuers, but they must then bid along with others for the opportunity of selling the issue. The reason for requiring competitive bidding is to prevent collusion between officials of the issuer and the investment banker.

Public Offering versus Private Placements. In many cases, funds are raised by selling an entire issue of securities to a small group of large investors such as insurance companies, mutual funds, pension funds, banks, and wealthy individuals. Sales of this type are known as *private placements* as opposed to the *public offerings* which occur when large numbers of investors are solicited. Private placements offer

[3] Evidence showing the influence of size of the issuing corporation on selling costs may be found in SEC, *Cost of Flotation of Corporate Securities, 1971–72*.

several advantages to the issuer. In the first place, the cost of selling is usually less. This is simply because the transaction often can be accomplished by a few telephone calls. Secondly, this procedure avoids legal requirements that are necessary for public offerings. Compliance with the regulations is a time-consuming and costly process. Finally, specific terms of the issue may be renegotiated with the small group of investors involved in a private placement. This provides flexibility that can be very helpful later if any difficulties arise.

The main disadvantage of private placements is that most investors are denied access to the issues. This may prevent the issuer from gaining an additional loyal group of customers, both for its products and for any of its subsequent security offerings. Also, since the issue really never meets the "test of the market," it is impossible to tell whether the lowest financing costs have been obtained.

Data showing the historical importance of private placements are presented in Table 3–4. These figures reveal the popularity of this method. Note the consistently greater reliance on private placements for debt securities as opposed to common stock.

TABLE 3–4
Relative Importance of Privately Placed Corporate Issues (private placements as a percent of the dollar value of issues offered both publicly and privately)

Year	*Debt Issues*	*Equity Issues*	*Total Issues*
1935	17.3	2.0	16.6
1940	31.7	2.4	28.6
1945	20.7	1.5	17.0
1950	52.0	8.2	42.1
1955	44.5	6.2	34.0
1960	40.5	10.7	34.4
1961	50.1	8.1	38.1
1962	50.5	6.4	43.3
1963	56.6	18.7	52.4
1964	66.7	8.4	53.8
1965	59.4	17.6	53.5
1966	48.5	6.3	42.6
1967	31.7	7.0	28.9
1968	38.3	6.8	31.7
1969	30.6	4.9	22.5
1970	16.1	2.8	13.2
1971	22.3	2.4	16.1
1972	33.8	10.3	26.2
1973	38.8	9.1	28.9

Source: *Annual Reports and Statistical Bulletins* of the Securities and Exchange Commission.

FIGURE 3–2
Example of a Private Placement Announcement

This announcement appears as a matter of record.

$25,000,000

Maryland Cup Corporation

Senior Notes due May 1995

The undersigned assisted in the direct placement of these Notes with institutional investors.

LEHMAN BROTHERS
INCORPORATED

NEW YORK • ATLANTA • BOSTON • CHICAGO • DALLAS • HOUSTON
LOS ANGELES • SAN FRANCISCO • WILMINGTON • LONDON • TOKYO

May 21, 1975

Source: *The Wall Street Journal*, April 24, 1975, p. 18.

An announcement of a private placement appears in Figure 3–2. The advertisement tells that Lehman Brothers, acting as an investment banker, arranged for a group of institutions such as life insurance firms and pension funds to purchase the notes issued by Maryland Cup Corporation.

Marketing of New Issues. In a typical public offering, the investment banker is faced with the task of selling an issue to raise many millions of dollars. This not only requires a large and effective group of sales personnel, but it exposes the underwriter to a very high risk. To better accomplish the marketing job and spread the risk, one firm will usually combine with others to form an *underwriting syndicate*. This is a temporary association organized for the sole purpose of selling a specific security issue. It may involve 100 or more investment bankers who each buy a portion of the offering. If the issue is very large, an additional set of securities firms will be organized as a *selling* *group*. Each member of the set receives an allotment from the underwriting syndicate or purchasing group, which they in turn sell for a commission. Both groups retail the issue to their customers.

After sales begin, some investors immediately sell what they just bought. If substantial numbers did this, the security price might decline considerably. Then any unsold securities could not be sold at the original price. To help minimize risks due to immediate price declines, the underwriters may *stabilize* the security price by buying back securities offered. This is perfectly legal for a period up to 30 days. Hopefully, the entire issue will have been sold by then. If not, the investment bankers may lose considerable sums of money. If, on the other hand, trading in the new issue is accompanied by a price rise, the underwriters cannot raise their price above the original offering price. This means that their profits are limited to underwriting fees, but their losses have no such restriction. In practice, most securities are sold at the intended price.

SECONDARY MARKETS

Once securities have been sold for the first time, they may be traded again and again. Buying and selling activities after the birth of the new issue comprise *secondary markets*. They are divided into two categories—*organized exchanges* and the *over-the-counter* (OTC) market. The first type consists of a number of organizations located in a few major cities. OTC markets literally exist all around the world, wherever securities are traded without the use of stock exchanges.

Stock Exchanges

The practice of trading securities at a specific place and with regulations governing activities is centuries old. The first exchange in America had its beginnings in New York City 16 years after the Declaration of Independence was signed. Today, there are 13 organized stock exchanges in the United States. A listing of the larger exchanges, together with sales volumes, appears in Table 3–5. Note that the New York and American exchanges account for almost 90 percent of the trading activity. Because of the dominant position of the New York Stock Exchange (NYSE), it will be discussed in detail.[4]

[4] The history and operation of stock exchanges throughout the world is described in Eiteman, Dice, and Eiteman, *The Stock Market*.

TABLE 3–5
Total Market Value of Listed Securities Sold on Major Stock Exchanges in the United States (1974 year-end data)

Exchange	*Millions of Dollars*
American Stock Exchange	$ 5,416.5
Boston Stock Exchange	1,470.0
Cincinnati Stock Exchange	79.7
Detroit Stock Exchange	268.9
Midwest Stock Exchange	5,642.8
New York Stock Exchange	105,563.8
Pacific Coast Stock Exchange	4,228.2
Phila.-Balt.-Wash. Stock Exchange	2,411.0
Spokane Stock Exchange	11.9
Total of all registered exchanges	125,099.3

Source: Securities and Exchange Commission, *Statistical Bulletin*, February 1975, p. 137.

The New York Stock Exchange

To most people, the stock market and the NYSE are synonymous. This is because it is the oldest and largest organized securities market in the United States. It began in 1792 with a gathering of those interested in selling stocks and bonds under a buttonwood tree on Wall Street. As the economy and business activity grew, security trading increased and the procedures became more formalized. Today, the NYSE is an association of members organized for the purpose of buying and selling securities for investors. The exchange itself only provides the facilities. The members, in effect, have a franchise to trade among themselves. There is a board of governors which establishes policies and regulations covering the activities of the membership. Since 1953, there have been only 1,366 members, or "seats" as they are often called. Entry is gained by buying a seat from an existing member or from the estate of a deceased member. Costs of a seat are determined largely by trading volume and stock price levels on the exchange. A record membership price set in 1929 at $495,000 held until 1968, when $515,000 was paid. The lowest price in this century was $42,000, paid in 1942. On May 5, 1975 a seat sold for $100,000.

Commission and Floor Brokers. The major types of memberships on the NYSE are shown in Table 3–6. The largest class is composed of *commission brokers*. These people execute orders for customers of their firms. Some brokerage houses have several seats to handle orders

TABLE 3–6
Classification of New York Stock Exchange Membership as of May 1973

Commission brokers	740
Specialists	383
Floor brokers	132
Registered traders	53
Odd-lot dealers and brokers	10
Others	48
Total membership	1,366

Source: Personal correspondence from the NYSE.

relayed to them by registered representatives in various cities throughout the world. Commission brokers act as agents for investors. When one of them has more orders than can be effectively handled, some of them may be given to a *floor broker* for execution. This type of member operates mainly on overflow business in heavy trading periods. Sometimes they assist commission brokers by handling large orders that require considerable time to be filled.

Specialists. One of the most important and yet least understood types of exchange members are the specialists. Their function is to maintain a fair and orderly market in one or more securities that have been assigned to them. They stay at a particular location or "post" on the floor of the exchange. Brokers come to them with their orders. Sometimes trades are effected immediately. In other cases the broker leaves the order with the specialist, who tabulates the information for later execution. They are constantly receiving orders and quoting prices based on them. They are able to match some of the buy and sell orders. They also maintain an inventory of shares which are used to fill other requests. Their inventory is used to dampen wide price fluctuations that might result if they relied solely on bringing buyers and sellers together. Strict regulations and close surveillance are employed to help assure that specialists do not use their positions for personal gain at the expense of the public.

Other Classes of Members. The remaining categories of membership are less important in the sense that they perform minor roles. At the end of 1974, there were 2,380 bond issues that were traded on the NYSE.[5] Orders for these securities were handled by *bond brokers*. *Registered traders* act exclusively for their own accounts. They buy and sell, seeking quick profits.

[5] New York Stock Exchange, *1975 Fact Book*, p. 77. Bond trading during 1974 accounted for less than 4 percent of the dollar volume of stocks on the NYSE.

Another group of members is on the wane. These are the *odd-lot dealers* who handle trades of less than 100 shares. They fill orders by selling from their inventory or by buying for it. When their holding is too high, they sell to the specialist. When they need more shares, they buy from the specialist. All of these trades and any others that do not involve odd lots are in *round lots* of 100 shares or multiples thereof, for example 300, 4,200, and so on.[6] In effect, then, the odd-lot dealer breaks up or accumulates round lots for people who wish to trade in fractions of 100. There is no trading in fractions of one share. Prices in odd-lot trading are determined by the next round-lot trade that occurs after the odd-lot order reaches the floor. Odd-lot transactions account for about 5 percent of the total share volume.[7]

Listing. Before securities can be traded on the NYSE, they must meet certain requirements for *listing*. These tests are designed to provide a group of stocks and bonds issued by larger, profitable firms in which there is a national interest.[8] From time to time, securities may be delisted due to a decline in trading interest, number of shareholders, profitability, and so on.

Types of Orders. Investors use several methods to instruct their brokers to buy or sell securities.[9] The most common order used on the exchange is the *market order*. This requests the broker to buy or sell at the best price obtainable at the moment. Sometimes investors wish to buy or sell at a particular price, so they use a *limit order*. In this case, a price is specified that is different from the prevailing market. For example, if XYZ shares were selling at $20, a limit order might be placed to buy at $19. If the quote fell to that level or below, the order would be executed. A seller might give a limit order at $22, which would be filled if and when the price rose to at least this level. A special type of limit order is known as the *stop* or *stop-loss order*. This is used in several ways, the most common being when an investor wants to "protect a profit." For example, suppose a stock, previously purchased at $10, is now quoted at $20. A stop order placed at some point below $20, say $18, assures the investor of a minimum profit of $18 minus $10 or $8 per share. If the stock does not drop but instead rises, the stop-order price can be increased.

---

[6] A few inactive common and preferred stocks use ten shares as the round lot. There is no odd-lot versus round-lot distinction made with bonds.

[7] NYSE *1975 Fact Book*, p. 17.

[8] Specific requirements are given in the NYSE *1975 Fact Book*, p. 26.

[9] The most common orders are described in this section. For a detailed description of 13 other types see Keith V. Smith and David K. Eiteman, *Essentials of Investing* (Homewood, Ill.; Richard D. Irwin, 1974), pp. 438–41.

In addition to specifying a price in all types of limit orders, a time period must be given to spell out how long the order is to be in effect. Usually the periods are for one day, one week, one month, or they may be "good 'til canceled" (GTC). If the stated price is not reached during the time period allowed, the order expires unfilled.

The difficulty with limit orders is that they may cause action or inaction which is not really best for the investor. When plain limit orders are used, execution may never take place. In the first example, an order was placed to buy at $19 when the market was $20. The price might only fall to $19⅛ and then rise to $30 or higher. The investor would have "missed the market." The same thing would happen with a sell order at $21 if the price rose to $20⅞ and then fell. Again profits would have been lost. In the case of stop orders, the price may drop just a little too far. In the example used, a decline from $20 to $18 would cause the shareholder to be sold out. If the price then reversed and started rising, an opportunity for profits would have been missed. The opponents of using limit orders as a technique are quick to point out the hazards of just barely missing the market. They argue that if someone wants to sell or buy, the stock should be closely watched. When a feeling develops that the time is right, action should be taken using a market order. Critics also say that use of limit orders which try to maximize profits just does not achieve that result very often, and in the long run the investor suffers losses because of them. Considerable care should be exercised in the use of limit orders.

Short Selling and Margin Trading. Two techniques can be used in conjunction with security orders. *Short selling* involves selling borrowed securities in the anticipation that the same issue can be bought back later at a lower price. Details of this procedure are discussed in Chapter 12. The other technique is known as *margin trading.* Margin is the amount of down payment required to purchase securities. The balance due is usually borrowed from the investor's broker or banker. Margin buying permits leverage, allowing more to be accomplished with a given amount of money. For example, if an investor purchased stock costing $10,000 and it increased 20 percent in value, the gain would be $2,000. With a 65 percent margin, $10,000 could be used in conjunction with a loan to purchase up to $15,400 in stock. If these shares rose the same 20 percent, the gross profit would be $15,400 × 1.2 − $10,000, or $8,480. The interest due on the $5,400 borrowed and commissions on the transaction would reduce this figure; however, the benefit of the margin technique in this example is obvious. Of course, if the stock price had fallen instead of rising, leverage would have increased the loss just as it increased the gain.

Furthermore, a decline in the price may result in a *margin call.* A NYSE regulation requires maintenance of a certain value in margin accounts in relation to the market value of the margined securities. If prices drop far enough, the investor will be called to put up more cash. Details of this procedure can be obtained at any brokerage office.

The painful reality of margin calls was dramatically illustrated in the speculative market boom of the late 1920s. Many investors had purchased stock on 10 percent margin. As stock prices declined, thousands were unable to put up the required cash. The stocks were sold, causing further price declines, more margin calls and so on.

After this debacle, margin activity has been more closely regulated. Since 1934 the Federal Reserve Board of Governors has set the margin requirement which has varied between 40 and 90 percent. On January 2, 1976, the margin requirement was 50 percent. The NYSE requires a minimum downpayment of $2,000 for securities bought on margin. The Securities and Exchange Commission (SEC) can require temporary 100 percent margins (no credit) on individual securities in situations where unusual speculative activity has occurred. As with limit orders, margin trading should be used with considerable care.

Commissions. Buying and selling securities is the business of investment firms or brokerage houses, as they are often called. They act as an agent for the investor much like the realtor does in real estate transactions. They charge a commission for this service. Minimum fees were fixed by the NYSE during the first 183 years of the Exchange's operation. Then, as of May 1, 1975, member firms were permitted to charge whatever rates they chose. The action of unfixing of commissions meant that for the first time investors might find different charges at each brokerage house. A survey by the authors a short time after "Mayday" revealed some differences among firms in the fee structure.[10] However, it is possible to illustrate a typical commission schedule; an abbreviated group of charges are shown in Table 3–7. The total commission appears in the top part of the table. Fees are expressed in dollars per share in the middle section and at the bottom part costs are figured as a percentage of the total value involved in the transaction. For example, an investor wishing to buy or sell 100 shares of a stock at $30 per share would pay this particular

[10] Also see "If You're Looking for Cheapest Way to Buy Stocks," *U.S. News and World Report,* May 12, 1975, pp. 85–87.

TABLE 3–7
Schedule of Commission Fees*

		Total Dollar Cost	
Price per Share	*50 Shares*	*100 Shares*	*500 Shares*
$10	$19.50	$30.00	$116.00
20	30.00	45.00	175.50
30	37.50	59.00	230.50
40	45.00	70.00	285.50
50	52.50	80.00	325.00
		Cost per Share	
Price per Share	*50 Shares*	*100 Shares*	*500 Shares*
$10	$0.39	$0.30	$0.23
20	0.60	0.45	0.35
30	0.75	0.59	0.46
40	0.90	0.70	0.57
50	1.05	0.80	0.65
		Cost as a Percentage of Transaction Amount	
Price per Share	*50 Shares*	*100 Shares*	*500 Shares*
$10	3.90%	3.00%	2.32%
20	3.00	2.25	1.75
30	2.50	1.97	1.54
40	2.25	1.77	1.43
50	2.10	1.60	1.30

* These figures do not include payments by the seller of (1) the New York state transfer tax of up to five cents per share and (2) the SEC fee of one cent for each $500 of transaction value.

Source: Survey of brokerage firms by the authors on May 8, 1975.

broker a commission of $59. This amounts to 59 cents per share or 1.97 percent of the $3,000 (100 shares times $30 per share) order.

Notice the cost per share declines as the number of shares in the order increases. Also, higher priced shares carry lower proportionate commissions. The two main variables in any transaction, the number of shares and the price per share, can be combined into a total value figure. The general observation then is *commission costs expressed as a percentage of the transaction will decrease as the order sizes become larger*. This is true at all brokerage firms. The main reason for this pattern is because the efforts involved do not increase proportionately to the value of the transaction.

FIGURE 3–3
Special Plans Offered by Brokers for Investors

It is not much harder to fill a 500-share order compared to a 100-share request. This experience is reflected in the cost schedule. Indeed, if one studies the different commission charges in effect over the years, a long-term trend to set fees more in line with costs is revealed. This has resulted in charges on smaller orders being increased proportionately more than the fees on the larger deals. Pressure by the SEC and large investors such as insurance companies and mutual funds hastened this shift to a cost-oriented commission schedule.

The unfixing of commissions stimulated brokerage firms to introduce a number of different plans designed to better meet needs of individual investors. Figure 3–3, showing parts of advertisements, illustrates this development. The old, uniform pricing system meant many investors were not using all the services that in effect were being paid for. Now, investors can better match their needs with a system of paying for these services. Details of these services and alternative plans are discussed in the next chapter.

The elimination of what was essentially price fixing of commissions means that investors can, in theory, negotiate fees with their brokers. However, it is unlikely that brokers will bargain with very many investors. Negotiating commissions is typically limited to the larger trades involving amounts of say $50,000 or more. This does not mean that fees for smaller orders will be approximately the same at all brokers. A typical schedule was presented in Table 3–7. Most firms are fairly close to this schedule unless the investor chooses some special plan that offers discounts on commissions.

Substantial discounts may be available on small trades but only because (1) few, if any other services are offered in addition to order executions, and (2) the price of the trade may not be the best available for the investor. This latter point needs special emphasis. The purpose of placing an order with a broker is to buy at the lowest price asked or to sell at the highest price bid. Executing an order to assure the best price is realized is the main concern; commission charges are really of secondary importance. Take the example of an investor wanting to buy 100 shares of a stock currently offered on an exchange for $30 per share. The price in the third market could be higher or lower but suppose it is $30.50. The commission charged by the broker for a third market transaction is typically lower than that quoted by a member of the NYSE, in this case say a 40 percent discount. From Table 3–7 the commission would then be .6 × $59 or $35.40, resulting in a net cost to the investor of $3,085.40 ($3,050 + $35.40). This order on the NYSE would cost a total of $3,059. Thus, the commission savings are more than offset by the higher price paid for the stock. In addition, the discount broker offers fewer, if any, complementary services. Sometimes the price comparisons may work the other way. In all cases, investors should be concerned with the *net* cost per share, a figure which includes price as well as commissions. Otherwise, they may "stumble over dollars to pick up pennies."

There are two additional considerations in examining transaction costs. One involves stock trades in the OTC market. This will be discussed in a later section. The other concerns bond trading. These orders tend to have commission charges of $5 per bond with some minimum fee per transaction of about $25. Variations in these costs are less than in the case of common stocks.

It is important to remember that the era of flexible commissions has just begun. Considerable experimentation in this area will likely take place. Investors are cautioned against devoting an undue amount of time and energy in shopping for the best net price on each order.

However, they are advised to be aware of transaction costs and to make an effort to be sure that they are "paying for only what they need."

Illustration of an Order. The operation of the New York Stock Exchange can perhaps be better understood by describing what happens when an order is placed. Suppose Mary Doe, an investor in Walla Walla, Washington, decides to invest in General Motors. She calls her broker or registered representative with instructions to buy 100 shares of GM common stock *at the market*. The broker, who is employed by a member firm of the NYSE, has this market order teletyped to the "floor" of the NYSE. This is a high-ceilinged, open room about half the size of a football field, located in a building near the southern tip of Manhattan Island. A photograph of the trading floor is shown in Figure 3–4. Around the edge of this room are message centers where trading information is received and transmitted by each of the member firms. A clerk, employed by the same firm as the Walla Walla broker, takes the order from the teletype and gives it to the firm's *commission broker*. If trading is especially active it might be given to a *floor broker* instead.

In either event, the clerk hands the order to a broker who then proceeds to the particular spot where GM is traded. This would be at one of 18 horseshoe-shaped counters called *trading posts*. A quote board above the post indicates that the last trade in GM was at $65; the broker knows the price will be close to this figure. In the hope of buying for less the broker asks the *specialist*, "How's GM?" The reply might be "three-quarters, one-quarter," meaning, I will pay $64¾ for GM, and I will sell it to you for $65¼. These are *bid* and *asked* prices; the bid is always given first. The difference between the two figures is the markup or spread on which the specialist makes a profit. The broker now knows that a market order can be executed by paying $65¼. However, he might say "65 for 100," which means he is offering to buy 100 shares at $65 per share. Somewhere between $65 and $65¼ a price will be agreed upon. Since this is a market order, the broker will not wait long before buying the shares. A *limit order* would have been left with the specialist to be filled when the price specified by Mary Doe was reached.

Perhaps some other brokers who also want to buy and sell GM arrive before the first broker leaves. They might also enter into the bidding. In any case the broker with a market order to fill will quickly purchase 100 shares of GM. Notes are made indicating who bought, who sold, the price, and the number of shares. The broker hurries

FIGURE 3–4
Trading Floor of New York Stock Exchange

Courtesy of New York Stock Exchange.

back to the clerk, who transmits details of the transaction back to the registered representative in Walla Walla. Mary Doe is then informed of prices and commissions directly. The whole process usually takes only five minutes or less. In two or three days she will receive a written confirmation of the transaction. Investors have five business days after the order was filled in which to pay for the stock. The stock certificate will be sent to them in about a month if desired, or sent to their broker for safekeeping.

In busy periods, trading on the NYSE is a fascinating display of "orderly pandemonium." A glass-enclosed visitors gallery enables people to view the proceedings below.[11] Everything is at a rapid pace with people scurrying all over much like ants in a broken bag of sugar. "How's GM? GMthreequartersonequarter Igohundredsixty-five Takeit" rolls into an unintelligible mumble. In a typical day, 20 million shares, representing values of $600 million will change hands, all in a symphonic, orderly, six-hour period of seeming chaos.

[11] Glass partitions were added after several hippies threw dollar bills down onto the trading floor.

Other Stock Exchanges

The other national exchange in the United States is the American Stock Exchange (AMEX). Though it is dwarfed by the NYSE, it represents a very active trading arena for investors.

The AMEX has had a colorful history since its birth during the California gold rush in 1849. Prior to 1953, it was called the New York Curb Exchange because trading activities over the first 72 years were carried out on the sidewalks of lower Manhattan under open skies. Brokers wore brightly colored hats and jackets so they could be identified in the street crowds by their message clerks who were perched on upper story windowsills in surrounding buildings. Finally, after succumbing to violent heat, extreme cold, driving rain, snow, and sleet, the exchange moved indoors in 1921.

Today there are many similarities between the two major exchanges. Trading procedures are the same in principle, though some details are different. Other characteristics are alike but on a reduced scale. For example, it costs less to become a member of the AMEX. In general, the companies listed are smaller and lesser known firms compared to their NYSE counterparts. Some investors have a special interest in the AMEX because stock prices there have tended to fluctuate widely. In 1974, the AMEX introduced trading in call options. This type of investment, which is described in Chapter 12, has proven very popular and has helped stimulate interest in the AMEX.

Regional stock exchanges are located in various metropolitan centers throughout the country. Major emphasis of these markets is to serve the population in the particular area. Around 90 percent of the stocks traded on most of these exchanges are also bought and sold on either the New York *or* the American Stock Exchange. This practice is known as *dual listing.* It provides a marketplace for issues with national interest to brokerage firms with a regional clientele. Different trading hours and slight variations in commission schedules are among the additional reasons why some stocks are traded on more than one exchange. Prices of any dually listed stock are always closely in line with the New York quotes.

The Midwest Stock Exchange, located in Chicago, is the largest regional exchange. Perhaps the most unique is the *Pacific Coast Stock Exchange,* with its two trading floors 400 miles apart in San Francisco and in Los Angeles. The system is organized so that transactions can be carried out in either city.

Over-the-Counter Markets

Securities traded without the use of stock exchange facilities are by definition traded in the OTC market.

It has been called an amorphous market because of the wide array of locations, participants, and securities involved. The majority of issues traded are government bonds—both federal and municipal—and corporate bonds and stocks in which there is too little investor interest for them to be listed on an exchange. By tradition, most banks and insurance companies, together with many nonfinancial corporations have chosen not to list their securities, even though many of these firms might well qualify for exchange trading. Because of the marketing techniques used to sell their shares, none of the mutual funds is listed. OTC trades are made in hundreds of cities and in thousands of different issues. It is easy to see why the market is usually defined in terms of what it is not.

The OTC Dealer. The central figures in the OTC trading are the dealers.[12] They perform a function similar to that carried out by the specialist on the NYSE. To do this dealers maintain inventories of securities. When someone wants to buy or sell, they come to the dealer. On the stock exchange there is usually only one "dealer" for each security, but in the OTC market there is no limit to how many people may set themselves up as dealers in any particular issue. They compete for business in a stock primarily on the basis of the price which they will pay and the price at which they offer to sell. Bid and asked prices are continually being quoted to brokerage firms around the country on a vast automated network known as NASDAQ (pronounced NAZDAK). This computerized system (acronym for National Association of Securities Dealers Automated Quotations) was introduced in 1971. It replaced a cumbersome communications procedure over telephone and teletype lines. As a result the OTC market was transformed into a nationwide, visible marketplace with a trading "floor" over 3,000 miles long. NASDAQ offers instantaneous quotations from OTC dealers. This is accomplished by the marketmakers, around the country, entering their names and bid and asked prices for stocks into a computer terminal. The information is transmitted to a central computer where it becomes available to any other broker/dealer who is tied into the system. When an investor places

[12] Most securities firms are broker-dealer businesses. They act as agents or ***brokers*** in handling buy and sell orders for investors. They assume the role of principal or *dealer* when they make a market in securities, buying and selling for their own account.

an order, the broker pushes a few buttons on a keyboard to access all this data. In an instant a display appears showing the quotations from around the nation. The broker will then place the order with the dealer offering the highest bid price if the investor is selling; a buy order will be executed with the dealer quoting the lowest asked price. The powerful system enables brokers to become very efficient shoppers for their clients. It is much like having someone give you up-to-the-second information on the price of XYZ canned beans in every grocery store.

NASDAQ has greatly stimulated OTC trading activity. During 1974, the volume of shares traded over this system was almost one third of the NYSE volume and 16 percent more than the share volume on all other exchanges combined.

OTC Commissions. OTC orders are filled in two different ways—on an *agency* or on a *principal* basis. In the former case, commissions are added to the price quoted for buy orders and subtracted from the price on sell orders. Most firms charge the same commissions on OTC trades as on listed security transactions. However, no odd-lot differential charges are levied in the OTC market.

In the other case the broker, acting as principal or dealer, fills the order from the firm's own account. The prices quoted to investors are on a net basis and no commissions per se are charged. Dealers hope to make money by buying at prices which are lower than their selling prices—just like any merchant.

The Third Market. This involves OTC trading in stocks listed on the exchanges. Until recently, commissions were always based on the cost of trading in round lots. The charges for 300 shares were three times that for a 100-share order. For 3,000 shares, the multiple was 30. As trading by large institutional investors, such as mutual funds, increased, there arose considerable discontent over this type of proportionate charging. Some brokerage firms responded by rebating part of the commission on large orders to the institutions.[13] Other firms who were not exchange members began seeking out large investors and arranging trades without the benefit of the exchanges. They charged lower commission rates for this service. Some nonmember firms also maintained inventories of listed stocks, and they often bought and sold these securities for their own accounts. Several firms dealing in the third market are oriented to small investors and offer them substantial discounts on commissions. Any investor, large or small,

[13] This procedure was known as the *give-up*. It was abolished in 1968.

is advised to always check the net price on orders. This will help assure the individual that lower commissions do indeed represent savings. Third market trading activity in 1974 was almost $7 billion and accounted for about 5 percent of all shares bought and sold on the NYSE.[14]

Some references identify a *fourth market* as trading of listed securities that occurs directly between institutions without the use of a broker.[15] Bypassing of the agent, of course, saves commissions. Several services that use computers to match buy and sell orders have been organized and have stimulated the fourth market activity.

The OTC is a marketplace for virtually every investor, offering an abundant variety of security types and grades of risk. This variety should not discourage investor participation but should rather serve to open new investment opportunities.

The Central Market

During the 1960s the increasing ownership of securities by pension funds, insurance companies, mutual funds, and so on, led Congress to direct the SEC to study the impact of this trend on the public interest. The report, which was completed in 1971, stated:

> . . . our objective is to see a strong central market system created to which all investors have access, in which, all qualified broker-dealers and existing market institutions may participate in accordance with their respective capabilities, and which is controlled not only by appropriate regulation but also by the forces of competition.[16]

Subsequent studies and discussions have supported this position which was written into a federal law which was passed in mid-1975. This encouraged plans that were being formulated for a system capable of reporting price and volume of all trades and identifying where each trade took place, for example NYSE, AMEX, a regional exchange, or OTC. In addition to this information on a common tape, the system will have the capacity to indicate quotes from all markets. Except for this feature the system closely resembles an expanded NASDAQ.

---

[14] NYSE *1975 Fact Book*, p. 16.

[15] As institutions focus more on commission savings, this market is likely to prosper. See R. F. Rustin, "Fourth Market Swells Sharply Following End of Fixed Brokerage Rates," *Wall Street Journal*, May 5, 1975, p. 5.

[16] *Institutional Investor Study of the Securities and Exchange Commission*, Letter of Transmittal (Washington, D.C.: U.S. Government Printing Office, March 10, 1971).

Other features of the proposed central market include a nationwide operation for clearing and settling all securities transactions. It is too early to tell just what the shape of the central market will eventually be but it is hoped that it will evolve into a hybrid combination of the best characteristics of the exchanges and OTC markets.

REGULATION OF SECURITY MARKETS

Conduct of the financial community is overseen by many state, federal, and industry organizations. The purpose of this surveillance is to provide protection for the public from dishonest practices by members of the securities industry. Trust in transacting business is a cornerstone of this industry. This confidence has been fostered by the formation and operation of agencies to regulate savings institutions and the investment community. Statutes and regulatory operations of the securities industry are discussed in this section.

Federal Regulation

After the skyrocketing stock prices in the 1920s and the subsequent stock market crash, comprehensive federal legislation was enacted to regulate the securities industry. Excessive speculation and outright fraud influenced the writing of the statutes. Before the first federal act was passed in 1933, the concept of *caveat emptor* (let the buyer beware) prevailed in the investment business. The legislation modified this principle by requiring disclosure of information about security issues, by banning fraudulent practices, and by providing surveillance of trading activities.

The Securities Act of 1933. This law, also called the truth-in-securities act, was passed to provide full and fair disclosure of information about companies selling securities to the public. The logic behind this act is not to prevent investors from losing money but instead to make it possible for them to evaluate new issues on an informed and realistic basis. The burden is on the investor to select securities, some of which certainly do become valueless. The law merely assures that investors have access to complete and accurate information on which to base decisions. The information is filed with the Securities and Exchange Commission in a *registration statement* and is made available to investors in a *prospectus.* This document contains relevant details about the offering and the issuer.

The cover page and the table of contents of a prospectus for an

FIGURE 3–5
Illustration of a Prospectus

PROSPECTUS

1,000,000 Shares

Ingersoll-Rand Company

COMMON STOCK

($2 par value)

The Company's Common Stock is listed on the New York Stock Exchange.

THESE SECURITIES HAVE NOT BEEN APPROVED OR DISAPPROVED BY THE SECURITIES AND EXCHANGE COMMISSION NOR HAS THE COMMISSION PASSED UPON THE ACCURACY OR ADEQUACY OF THIS PROSPECTUS. ANY REPRESENTATION TO THE CONTRARY IS A CRIMINAL OFFENSE.

PRICE $76 A SHARE

	Price to Public	Underwriting Discounts and Commissions	Proceeds to Company(1)
Per Share	$76.00	$2.85	$73.15
Total	$76,000,000	$2,850,000	$73,150,000

(1) Before deduction of expenses estimated at $135,000.

The Shares are offered by the several Underwriters named herein, subject to prior sale, when, as and if accepted by the Underwriters, and subject to approval of certain legal matters by Davis Polk & Wardwell, counsel for the Underwriters. It is expected that delivery of the Shares will be made on or about May 7, 1975 at the office of Morgan Stanley & Co. Incorporated, 140 Broadway, New York, N. Y., against payment therefor in New York funds.

MORGAN STANLEY & CO.
Incorporated

MERRILL LYNCH, PIERCE, FENNER & SMITH
Incorporated

SMITH, BARNEY & CO.
Incorporated

April 29, 1975

No person is authorized in connection with this offering to give any information or to make any representations not contained in this Prospectus, and any information or representation not contained herein must not be relied upon as having been authorized by the Company or any Underwriter.

TABLE OF CONTENTS

AVAILABLE INFORMATION

The Company is subject to the informational requirements of the Securities Exchange Act of 1934 and in accordance therewith files reports and other information with the Securities and Exchange Commission. Information, as of particular dates, concerning directors and officers, their remuneration, options granted to them, the principal holders of securities of the Company and any material interest of such persons in transactions with the Company is disclosed in proxy statements distributed to shareholders of the Company and filed with the Commission. Such reports, proxy statements and other information can be inspected at the principal office of the Commission at Room 6101, 1100 L Street, N. W., Washington, D. C. 20005, where copies of such material can be obtained at prescribed rates. Such material can also be inspected at the offices of the New York Stock Exchange, Inc., 11 Wall Street, New York, N. Y. 10005.

IN CONNECTION WITH THIS OFFERING, THE UNDERWRITERS MAY OVER-ALLOT OR EFFECT TRANSACTIONS WHICH STABILIZE OR MAINTAIN THE MARKET PRICE OF THE COMMON STOCK OF THE COMPANY AT A LEVEL ABOVE THAT WHICH MIGHT OTHERWISE PREVAIL IN THE OPEN MARKET. SUCH TRANSACTIONS MAY BE EFFECTED ON THE NEW YORK STOCK EXCHANGE OR IN THE OVER-THE-COUNTER MARKET. SUCH STABILIZING, IF COMMENCED, MAY BE DISCONTINUED AT ANY TIME.

2

offering of Ingersoll-Rand, Inc., common stock are shown in Figure 3–5. A general statement about the role of the SEC in the offering always appears on the front page of the prospectus along with basic details of the issue and the name of the managing underwriter(s). The main purpose of the disclaimer for the SEC is to make certain that investors do not have the impression that the federal government has endorsed or passed on the merits of the securities being sold. The range of information indicated by the Table of Contents illustrates the full disclosure concept of the 1933 Act. The 28-page pamphlet includes a rather thorough description of the current state of company operations, management's plans for use of the money raised from the offering, and other details of the underwriting. Financial statements, attested to fairness and accuracy by an independent certified public accounting firm, appear at the end.

When a registration statement is filed with the SEC, a preliminary prospectus or *red herring* is usually prepared to inform potential buyers about a forthcoming offering. This unusual name is derived from the red lettering used for the following statement appearing on the cover:

> A registration statement relating to these securities has been filed with the Securities and Exchange Commission, but has not yet become effective. Information contained herein is subject to completion or amendment. These securities may not be sold nor may offers to buy be accepted prior to the time the registration statement becomes effective. This prospectus shall not constitute an offer to sell or the solicitation of an offer to buy nor shall there be any sale of these securities in any State in which such offer, solicitation or sale would be unlawful prior to registration or qualification under the securities laws of any such State.

The prospectus shown in Figure 3–5 is a final copy, so the above statement does not appear on it.

The SEC examines the registration statement for compliance with the full and fair disclosure provisions of the statutes. In this examination, errors of omission and commission are identified. An example of incomplete disclosure appeared in a proposed offering by Republic Cement Corporation.

> . . . the registrant had failed to disclose that its proposed output of gray cement combined with that of a presently producing plant in its market area would far exceed any past or present market demand and that the existing plant had not been operating at full capacity. It further found that the registrant's proposed output of white cement exceeded

> 25 percent of the annual consumption of that product in the entire United States. The company's plant construction cost figures were determined to be much lower than those of its competitors because certain installations which are normally part of a cement plant were to be eliminated, and the registrant had not provided for sufficient storage capacity for its finished product. The Commission also found that despite the representation in the prospectus that the registrant had on its properties 1,851,300,000 tons of limestone suitable for the production of cement, only the most rudimentary type of exploration had been performed on the properties, and no systematic core drilling or sampling was used to test the continuity, depth, and quality of the limestone.[17]

When the examination process is completed, the SEC notifies the underwriter that registration has become effective. A final prospectus is then printed, including any amendments, and used to offer the issue to the public.

Certain types and sizes of issues are exempted from the registration provisions of the Securities Act. For example, bonds of federal and municipal governments and nonprofit organizations need not be registered with the SEC. Issues sold entirely to residents of the state in which a company conducts the major part of its business are also exempted from federal registration. These are intrastate offerings; even secondary trading across state lines is prohibited until at least one year after the issue has been sold.

Issues of $500,000 or less do not have to meet full registration requirements. These small issues are known as Regulation A, or Reg. A issues for short. The SEC still oversees this group of offerings, but it only requires the filing of an abbreviated disclosure report. This results in substantial savings to the company of both time and money. Reg. A offerings, like those using the full registration, may be sold in as many states as the issuer obtains clearance from the state authorities to do so.

The Securities Exchange Act of 1934. This law was passed to extend federal regulation of the securities industry to include security trading. The act empowered the SEC to regulate trading procedures and practices of most stock exchanges in the U.S.[18] A major accom-

---

[17] Securities and Exchange Commission, *23rd Annual Report* (Washington, D.C.: U.S. Government Printing Office, 1957), p. 46.

[18] It also established the Securities and Exchange Commission to administer the federal security statutes. The 1933 Act had been administered by the Federal Trade Commission.

plishment of the 1934 Act and the amendments added in 1964 was to require all corporations whose securities are listed on any stock exchange and other firms having at least 500 shareholders and $1 million in assets to periodically file up-to-date financial data with the SEC.

Another provision places restrictions on trading activities of corporate *insiders*. These are people who by virtue of their relationship with the company are privileged to know certain information which is not available to the public. Generally, insiders are usually defined as company officers, directors, and owners of 10 percent or more of the corporation's stock.[19] To discourage unfair use of confidential information, insiders must file monthly statements with the SEC, outlining their transactions in the company's securities.

The 1934 Act also makes the SEC responsible for regulating broker-dealer activities and the procedures used in bringing company business to shareholders for their approval.

Other Federal Legislation. Excessive abuses in many areas of investment activity led to additional remedial legislation. For example, the Public Utility Holding Company Act of 1935 was designed to correct improper practices in the public utility industry.

> There are three principal areas of regulation under the Act. The first includes those provisions of the Act which require the physical integration of public-utility companies and functionally related properties of holding-company financial structures of such systems. The second covers the financing operations of registered holding companies and their subsidiary companies, the acquisition and disposition of securities and properties, and certain accounting practices, servicing arrangements, and intercompany transactions. The third area of regulation includes the exemptive provisions of the Act, provisions relating to the status under the Act of persons and Companies, and provisions regulating the right of persons affiliated with a public-utility company to become affiliated with a second such company through the acquisition of securities.[20]

---

[19] The SEC has been quite active in regulating insider activities in the latter part of the 1960s. A landmark case involved stock purchases by officers and certain employees of Texas Gulf Sulfur Co. before the firm announced it had discovered a sizeable ore deposit in Canada. In another recent proceeding the SEC alleged that the brokerage firm of Merrill Lynch, Pierce, Fenner and Smith used "inside information" to warn some of their institutional clients that Douglas Aircraft was going to announce losses. These cases may serve to greatly extend the definition of insiders to include anyone who receives and acts upon inside information.

[20] Securities and Exchange Commission, *39th Annual Report* (Washington, D.C.: U.S. Government Printing Office, 1974), p. 109.

The *Maloney Act of 1938* made it possible to organize the National Association of Securities Dealers (NASD). This is a private organization which establishes fair trade practices and assures compliance to them by self-regulation. This industry group is discussed in a later section.

The *Bankruptcy Act of 1938* provides a procedure for reorganizing financially troubled firms. The SEC assists the courts to help assure soundness and fairness in the reorganization plans.

The *Trust Indenture Act of 1940* was passed to provide protection for bondholders by regulating the actions of the trustee as outlined in the bond indenture.

Congress enacted the *Investment Company Act of 1940* in an attempt to prevent improper practices of firms who invest in the securities of other organizations:

> . . . it provides a comprehensive framework of regulation which, among other things, prohibits changes in the nature of an investment company's business or its investment policies without shareholder approval, protects against loss, outright theft or abuse of trust, and provides specific controls to eliminate or to mitigate inequitable capital structures. The Act also requires that an investment company disclose its financial condition and investment policies; requires management contracts to be submitted to shareholders for approval; prohibits underwriters, investment bankers, or brokers from constituting more than a minority of the investment company's board of directors; regulates the custody of its assets; and provides specific controls designed to protect against unfair transactions between investment companies and their affiliates.[21]

Further discussion of this Act appears in Chapter 11.

The *Investment Advisors Act of 1940* was designed to protect the public against those who sell investment advice. The Act calls for registration of advisors and stipulates against certain practices.

In its role as the chief administrator of the federal securities statutes, the SEC becomes involved in a wide array of activities as illustrated in the clippings shown in Figure 3–6. The SEC's *1973 Annual Report* discussed the central market, automated trading information systems, the structure and level of commission rates, option market regulation, tax sheltered investments, and forecasts of company performance.

---

[21] Ibid., p. 124.

FIGURE 3–6
Activities of the SEC

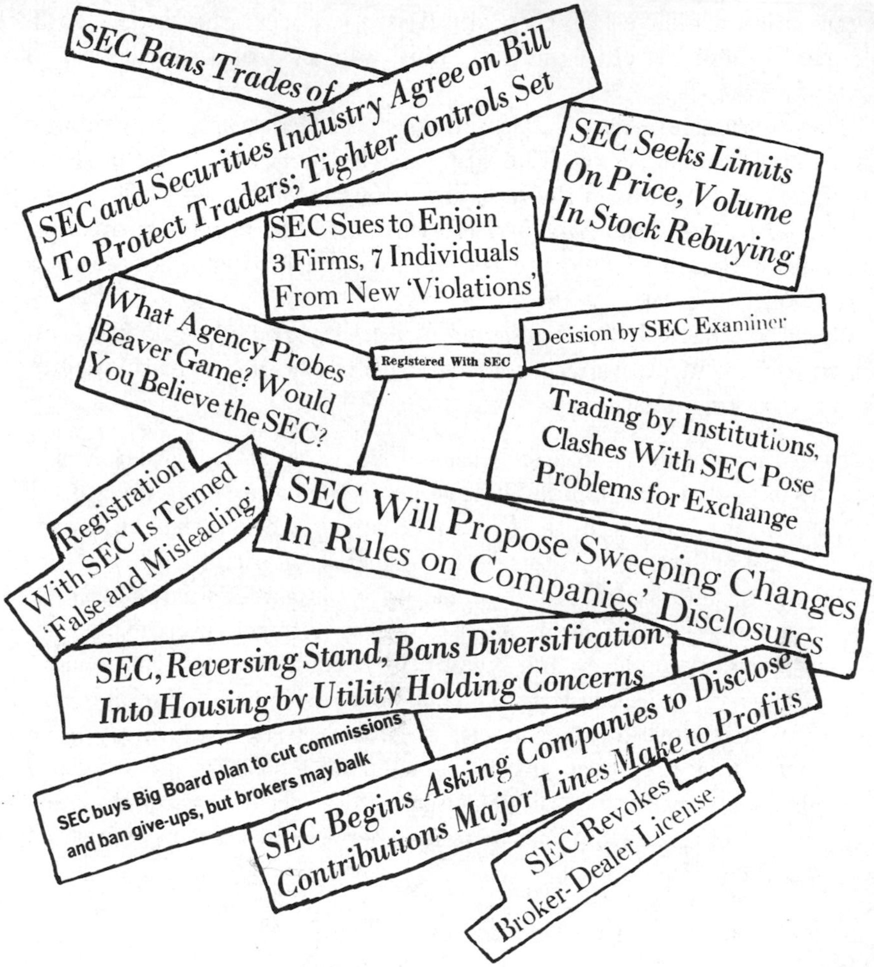

The function of the SEC is brought into perspective in a recent pamphlet:

> Securities are by their very nature much different from almost any other type of "merchandise" for which there are established public markets. A person who wishes to purchase a new car or household appliance—or for that matter, a peck of potatoes or a bag of beans—can pretty well determine from personal inspection the quality of the product and the reasonableness of the price in relation to other com-

peting products. But this is not so with respect to a bond or a share of stock.

An engraved certificate representing an interest in an abandoned mine or a defunct gadget manufacturer, for example, might look no less impressive than a "blue chip" security with a history of years of unbroken dividend payments. Beyond that all comparisons cease—and for the average investor to differentiate between the securities of little or no value and those offering at least reasonable prospect of a satisfactory return on his investment requires (1) a personal inspection of the properties and operations of the issuer (which for all practical purposes is generally impossible), or (2) that he place almost complete reliance on the oral and written representations and available literature about the company, its prospects, and the terms of its securities.

. . . It should be understood that the securities laws were designed to facilitate informed investment analyses and prudent and discriminating investment decisions *by the investing public*. It is the investor, *not* the Commission who must make the ultimate judgment of the worth of securities offered for sale. The Commission is powerless to pass upon the merits of securities; and assuming proper disclosure of the financial and other information essential to informed investment analysis, the Commission cannot bar the sale of securities which such analysis may show to be of questionable value.[22]

State Regulation

States enacted securities regulations more than two decades before comprehensive federal legislation was passed. The state statutes became known as Blue Sky Laws because they were designed to prevent sale of fraudulent securities by firms who were offering only a "piece of the blue sky" to investors. The current laws cover, for the most part, registration of persons and firms who buy and sell securities, registration of information on securities to be offered for sale, and prevention of fraudulent activities. The philosophy of the acts is to provide investor protection within each state, by requiring full disclosure of all pertinent facts surrounding securities offerings.[23] Some

[22] "The Work of the Securities and Exchange Commission," (Washington, D.C.: U.S. Government Printing Office, April 1974), p. vii.

[23] Many of the offerings registered with the SEC must also be filed within the state in which the issue is to be sold.

states have gone one step further and have provisions to permit the enforcing authorities to ban the sale of certain securities which they feel are objectionable. Usually the state administrators do not make economic judgments regarding the feasibility of a given project; rather they determine if the investors are receiving a "fair run" for their money. This, of course, requires a great deal of discretion and subjective judgment on the part of the administrators. Some states, notably New York, rely solely on antifraud provisions to deter any issuer from not giving the investor a "fair shake."

Industry Regulation

In addition to federal and state regulation, there are several private organizations which seek to oversee activities of their memberships.

National Association of Securities Dealers. The NASD is a self-regulatory body composed of most of the broker-dealer firms in the securities industry. Its stated purposes are

1. To promote the investment banking and securities business.
2. To standardize its principles and practices.
3. To promote high standards of commercial honor and to promote among members observance of federal and state securities laws.
4. To provide a medium through which the membership may consult with governmental and other agencies.
5. To cooperate with governmental authority in the solution of problems affecting this business and investors.
6. To adopt and enforce rules of fair practice in the securities business.
7. To promote just and equitable principles of trade for the protection of investors.
8. To promote self-discipline among members.
9. To investigate and adjust grievances between members and between the public and members.[24]

Regulation by the Stock Exchanges. Most of the exchanges carefully scrutinize the business of their memberships. They have rules to govern activities both on and off the trading floors. They fine or suspend members who are found guilty of infractions. This group has also contributed to minimizing dishonest practices in the securities industry.

---

24 "1974 Report to Members," National Association of Securities Dealers, p. 32.

Securities Investor Protection Corporation (SIPC). In 1970, Congress established a private, nonprofit corporation for the purpose of protecting customers of broker-dealer firms. This is accomplished by, in effect, insuring investors against loss due to failure of a brokerage firm. SIPC will pay up to $50,000 of each investor's claim caused by bankruptcy of a broker-dealer. It is important to note that this protection is not against losses investors may sustain from fluctuating security prices. Thus SIPC offers some investor protection and thereby promotes confidence in securities markets. The financial base of SIPC is derived from assessments of less than one percent of the gross revenues of the members which include essentially all of the broker-dealer firms in the industry.

Other Forms of Investor Protection. Most brokerage firms also maintain a vigilant watch over their individual operations. Many firms have a staff of lawyers, accountants, or former FBI men to guard against frauds.

Despite the massive efforts from many sources, improper practices in the investment community continue. Security price manipulations have all but disappeared, but other schemes and dishonest activities have developed and will continue to exist. Investors play a crucial role in the regulation process. They should carefully investigate situations before committing funds and report questionable practices. No one can protect an investor from making unwise decisions.

SUMMARY

Securities markets are a complex combination of people, customs, and regulations. The markets help make savings available to organizations so that they can use them to provide goods and services for the public. In addition to this economic function, securities markets provide a place where securities can be bought and sold at fair prices.

Governmental bodies and corporations often raise funds by exchanging stocks and bonds for money. These activities comprise *primary markets*. Assistance to the organizations seeking funds is provided by *investment bankers*. They offer advice on the type, terms, and timing of the issue. They buy the new securities from the issuer and then sell them to investors. This is known as an *underwriting*. Usually groups of investment bankers are formed to buy the offering, and if it is large, an additional *selling group* may be organized to help market the issue. Sometimes the securities are offered only to a small number of investors through a *private placement*. Investment bankers enter *competitive bidding* to underwrite securities of railroads, utilities, and governmental bodies.

After the securities are sold initially, they are traded in *secondary markets*. These include organized *stock exchanges* and *over-the-counter* markets. The New York Stock Exchange dominates trading. Its membership has an exclusive right to buy and sell securities through the NYSE facilities. Some members are *commission brokers* who execute orders for customers of their brokerage firms. *Floor brokers* assist commission brokers by handling orders in periods of heavy trading activity. *Specialists* are exchange members who are responsible for maintaining a fair and orderly market in one or more stocks. They set prices by buying and selling for their own account. Other classes of membership include *odd-lot dealers, registered traders,* and *bond brokers*. Investors may trade stock using *market orders,* which are executed immediately, or they may place price and time restrictions on their requests. *Commissions* vary somewhat at different brokers but always are a declining percentage as the transaction size becomes larger.

The American Stock Exchange, which is the other national exchange, lists stocks not traded on the NYSE. *Regional exchanges* list mainly stocks that are also traded in the NYSE or the AMEX. Any securities not listed on the exchanges are traded *over-the-counter*. The OTC marketplace exists in communities throughout the United States. Security prices are set by dealers who buy and sell for their own accounts. An automated information system, *NASDAQ* has greatly improved the OTC market and is a step toward an all inclusive *central marketplace*. Many financial institutions bypass the exchanges and trade large blocks of listed stocks in the *third market*.

Abuses and outright fraudulent practices by people in the securities industry led to the development of considerable regulatory activity. The *Securities Act of 1933* requires organizations seeking funds to disclose relevant information about the offering to potential investors. The other major piece of federal legislation was the *Securities Exchange Act of 1934* which provided regulation of trading in outstanding issues. Congress has passed several other acts to strengthen investor protection. States also regulate the securities industry by administering what are known as Blue Sky Laws. The industry itself engages in considerable self-policing activity through the *National Association of Security Dealers,* the exchanges, and compliance efforts within each brokerage firm. The *Securities Investor Protection Corporation* offers limited financial protection to customers of broker-dealer firms. Despite all rules and regulations, protection from loss remains largely the responsibility of individual investors.

PROBLEMS

1. Obtain a prospectus from a brokerage office or an investor. Write a two or three paragraph summary of the offering, being sure to include the nature of the issuer's business, the intended use of the proceeds from the offering, and other details which you feel are especially important.
2. Visit a local governmental agency and find out how they sell bonds to raise funds. You might try the city, county, or school district offices.
3. Calculate the spread on ten OTC stock quotations, using the formula:

$$\text{Spread} = \frac{\text{asked price} - \text{bid price}}{\text{bid price}} \times 100$$

   Why do you suppose the spreads differ?

QUESTIONS

1. What are the functions of securities markets?
2. Distinguish between *marketability* and *liquidity*.
3. Give an example of an asset that is marketable but is not very liquid.
4. Explain how security prices are influenced by supply and demand.
5. Using an analogy of new and used car dealers, distinguish between *primary* and *secondary markets*.
6. What is *investment banking*?
7. Why are services provided by investment bankers needed by governmental and corporate bodies?
8. Define the following terms:
   - *a.* Underwriting syndicate
   - *b.* Competitive bid
   - *c.* Dual listing
   - *d.* Margin
   - *e.* Best efforts offering
   - *f.* Private placement
   - *g.* Red herring
   - *h.* Central market
9. Briefly outline the major types of orders for securities listed on the New York Stock Exchange.
10. Describe the functions of each class of membership of the New York Stock Exchange.
11. Why has trading activity developed in the *third market*?

12. Explain the major provisions of the *Securities Act of 1933* and the *Securities Exchange Act of 1934.*
13. What is the purpose of a *prospectus?*
14. Why are restrictions placed on *insider trading?*
15. What is the role of the *NASD?*
16. Commission rates as a percent of transaction value decline as the order size increases. Why?
17. Tell what the following letters stand for and identify the terms: NYSE, AMEX, NASDAQ, SEC.

SELECTED READINGS

Brooks, John. *Once in Golconda: A True Drama of Wall Street, 1920–38.* New York: Harper & Row, 1969.

Dirks, Raymond L., and Gross, Leonard. *The Great Wall Street Scandal.* New York: McGraw-Hill, 1974.

Ellis, Charles D. *The Second Crash.* Westminister, Md.: Ballantine Books, 1974.

Friend, Irwin. *Investment Banking and the New Issues Market, Summary Volume.* Philadelphia: Wharton School of Finance and Commerce, University of Pennsylvania, 1965.

Galbraith, John K. *The Great Crash.* Boston: Houghton Mifflin, 1954.

Levine, Sumner N., ed. *Financial Analysts Handbook,* vols. 1 and 2. Homewood, Ill.: Dow Jones-Irwin, 1975.

Rolo, Charles J., and Nelson, George J., eds. *The Anatomy of Wall Street.* Philadelphia: J. B. Lippincott, 1968.

Securities and Exchange Commission. *Annual Report.* Washington, D.C.: U.S. Government Printing Office, published yearly.

Sobel, Robert. *The Big Board—A History of the New York Stock Exchange.* New York: Free Press, 1965.

4
Sources of Information

GENERAL MARKET INFORMATION

Occasionally investors have told brokers to "never mind all the data, just plug me into the action!" This is a dangerous approach. Much is to be gained by investigating before investing. Careful consideration of available information does not guarantee profits, but there are few, if any, successful investors who have not studied each situation before they made commitments.

There are three major inputs to any investment decision process. The first pertains to the capacity and limitations of the individual investor. The second involves characteristics of different types of securities. The third area consists of historical data about particular securities and the markets in which they are bought and sold. The first two inputs refer to knowledge about the investor, the investment alternatives, and their accompanying risks. Most of this book is devoted to discussions of these topics. Information about particular securities and markets is presented in this chapter.

Measures of Market Levels

Most comprehensive news broadcasts include a report of stock market activity. Even local newspapers carry some coverage of trading information. Mention is made in all these reports about what happened to stock prices in general as well as quotations on some individual securities. Investors want to know whether "the market" was up, down, or unchanged. They also want to know how far the general price movement proceeded.

A wide variety of measures have been developed to indicate the price performance for groups of securities. They range from relatively simple averages of a sample of stocks from a large population to carefully constructed indexes comprised of the entire list of stocks in a particular market. Some measures are calculated for individual industries. Others are developed for specific types and grades of securities such as high-grade public utility bonds. Each measure attempts to portray what happened to prices in the class of securities it represents.

Dow Jones Averages. The most widely known indicator of stock prices in this country is the *Dow Jones Industrial Average* (DJIA)[1] It dates back to 1885 when stocks of railroads dominated trading activity on the New York Stock Exchange. Over the years the sample has changed to reflect changes in trading activity of particular stocks. Since 1928 the list has included 30 firms which are, for the most part, widely known to investors. The group of stocks is listed in Table 4–1.

TABLE 4–1
Companies in the Dow Jones Industrial Average

Allied Chemical	Esmark	Owens-Illinois Glass
Alcoa	Exxon	Procter & Gamble
American Brands	General Electric	Sears, Roebuck
American Can	General Foods	Standard Oil of Calif.
American Tel. & Tel.	General Motors	Texaco
Anaconda	Goodyear	Union Carbide
Bethlehem Steel	International Harvester	United Technologies
Chrysler	International Nickel	U.S. Steel
Du Pont	International Paper	Westinghouse
Eastman Kodak	Johns-Manville	Woolworth

Source: *The Wall Street Journal,* May 19, 1975, p. 23.

The DJIA is computed by adding the prices of each of the 30 stocks in the group and dividing by a number which reflects stock splits and stock dividends over the years. Adjustments to the divisor have been necessary to minimize distortions. For example, if a stock were split two for one, the price would fall about one half. If the divisor were not changed, the DJIA would decline just because the split had occurred.[2]

---

[1] Evidence of the widespread public acceptance of this measure may be found in several songs and the Broadway musical "How Now Dow Jones." Also, Get Well Dow Jones greeting cards have been offered in periods of market decline.

[2] These adjustments have caused a minor complication in interpreting the DJIA. The closing figure on May 23, 1975 was 831.90. This was not the actual average price of the 30 stocks but instead indicated the price level of the stocks if no splits had ever occurred.

Dow Jones & Co. also publishes a transportation average of 20 firms, a utility average of 15 companies, a composite average of the 65 stocks in the three individual averages, and a number of averages for different types of bonds.

Standard & Poor's Indexes. Standard & Poor's Corporation publishes measures of stock price movements which are more refined than the Dow Jones Averages. These are *indexes* of stock prices. They have the advantage of indicating relative changes compared to a base period of the years 1941–43. Furthermore, the indexes are constructed so as to reflect the "importance" of each stock used. This is done by a weighting procedure which incorporates the number of shares outstanding for each company. A price change in a firm with millions of shares has more impact on the index than an identical price change in a firm having fewer shares. Standard & Poor's publishes four major common stock price indexes: the industrial with 425 stocks, the rail with 25 stocks, the utility with 50 stocks, and a composite of all 500 stocks. In addition, it calculates indexes for numerous other groupings, such as airline stocks, preferred stocks, and a wide variety of bonds.

New York Stock Exchange Indexes. The most comprehensive measure of stock price movement was begun in 1966 by the New York Stock Exchange. The NYSE Common Stock Index is a composite of all common stock issues traded on the exchange.[3] This can be compared to the samples of 65 stocks in the Dow Jones and 500 in the Standard & Poor's market indicators. The index is constructed in a manner similar to the Standard & Poor's indexes in that they both reflect changes in market values of outstanding shares. The base was set at 50.00 as of December 31, 1965. The index has been calculated back to 1939 so historical comparisons can be made. The NYSE also supplies finance, industrial, transportation, and utility indexes.

Other Market Measures. Several other organizations calculate their own market indicators. The *New York Times* averages, published in that newspaper, are similar to the Dow Jones averages. *Barron's*, a weekly publication of Dow Jones and Company, computes several measures, including a "Low Priced Stock Index" and a "Most Active Stock Average." *Moody's Investors Service* supplies indicators for broad groupings as well as for small categories, such as gas transmission firms, large life insurance companies, and savings and loan associations. The *American Stock Exchange* publishes its own index. Several organizations compute measures of OTC price movements. The

[3] At the end of 1974 there were 1,543 stocks listed.

most well known indexes are supplied by NASDAQ. They include measures of groups such as industrials, transportation, and banks, as well as a composite index for all of the approximately 2,600 stocks listed in the NASDAQ system.

A broad measure of stock price movements is prepared by *Value Line,* an investment advisory service. This average consists of 1,100 actively traded stocks selected from the New York Stock Exchange, the American Stock Exchange, regional stock exchanges, Canadian stock exchanges, and the OTC market. The broadest market measure of all is published by O'Brien Associates, Inc. It is an index computed weekly of the total market value of all stocks listed on the NYSE, the AMEX, and those actively traded OTC. The index was 765.188 billion dollars on May 23, 1975.[4]

Comparisons of Market Measures. The preceding discussion identified many of the indicators of security price movements which are available. The question often arises as to which measure is the "best." The answer depends upon the purpose for which the indicator is to be used. If a measure is needed to serve as a benchmark for evaluating price performance in a particular portfolio, then the "best" indicator would probably be one that is composed of similar securities. For example, if an investor has been holding bonds, a measure of bond price performance would be chosen. Furthermore, if the investor owned mainly municipal bonds, an index of municipal bonds would be the logical yardstick for comparison purposes. If the major portion of investments were in unlisted securities, the OTC index would be used. A portfolio of the well-established firms listed on the New York Stock Exchange would best be measured against the Dow Jones Industrial Average or the Dow Jones Utility Average if this particular industry were the main one represented in the list of stocks. The point is to avoid comparing apples and oranges and to choose instead a measure which represents the securities similar to those whose performance is being evaluated.

Several indicators purport to measure price movements in the same group of securities. Historical data for three of the best-known barometers of the New York Stock Exchange are plotted in Figure 4–1. Note that the price patterns are very similar in all cases. This means that, for many purposes, any one of the particular NYSE measures would be acceptable. However, there are times when the

---

[4] *Barron's,* May 26, 1975, p. 67.

FIGURE 4–1
Indicators of Price Movements on the New York Stock Exchange

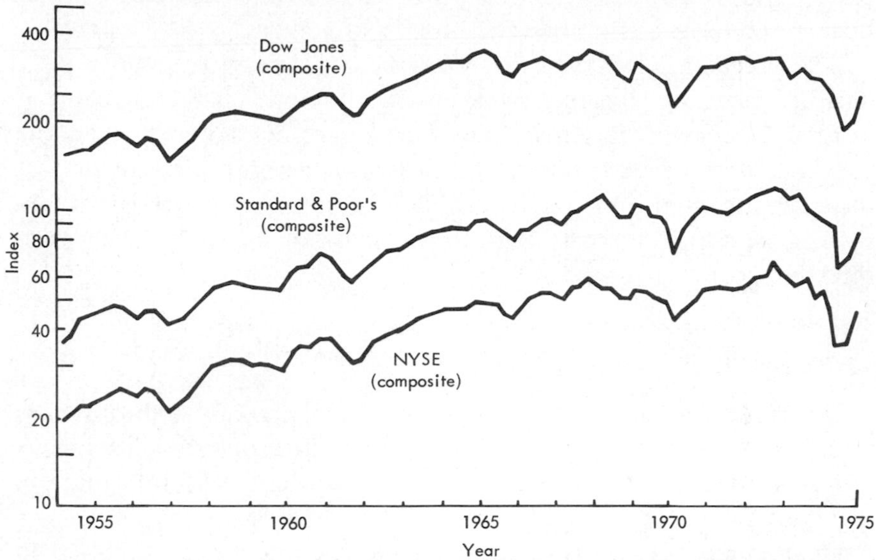

Source: Dow Jones Composite, taken from *Barron's*, various issues; Standard & Poor's Composite from *Standard & Poor's Trade & Securities Statistics*, 1974; and NYSE from *Federal Reserve Bulletin*, various issues.

choice of a barometer is quite important. A careful examination of the historical changes in the indexes and averages will reveal differences in the patterns. Some measures indicate wider swings than others. Some may be slower to show a price change. These differences are due to the differences in the securities that are used in the measure and also to the various ways in which the prices are combined —the weighting. The composite indicators for Dow Jones, Standard and Poor's, and the NYSE registered declines during the first five months of 1975 of 24, 30, and 31 percent, respectively. These data illustrate that while the directions of price movements may all be similar, the amount of the movement may vary, depending on which measure is used.

Another reason for choosing one measure over another is based on practical considerations rather than statistical grounds. This factor is the general availability of the measure. Some barometers have been calculated back into the late 1800s. Others have a much more limited history, such as the NYSE indexes, which only go back to 1939. Some measures are figured once a week. Others are figured daily, hourly, or by the minute. The Dow Jones Averages are quoted in most daily papers and over many broadcasts, whereas considerable effort might be required to stay current on the Moody's Averages.

The preceding discussion has described a variety of security price measures that are available, each having different characteristics and historical behavior patterns. The "best" barometer depends on the user and the purpose for using the yardstick. Several different market measures are cited throughout this book to help familiarize the reader with them and to indicate that, in most instances, they can be used interchangeably.

Price Quotations

A major advantage of securities is that they are being continuously traded at prices which are made known to the investing public. A wide variety of methods are used to disseminate this information, and it is wise for the investor to know about these sources.

Stock Prices. Reports of individual stock prices are published in most daily newspapers. Some accounts are quite abbreviated. One of the most thorough reports appears in *The Wall Street Journal.* A partial listing of the New York Stock Exchange quotations appears in Figure 4–2. The first two columns of numbers represent the highest and lowest prices at which each share of stock has traded during the current year. The name of the company that issued the stock appears next, followed closely by the dividend information. Because there are many variations in the ways dividends are paid, footnotes, indicated by letters, are often used for further explanation. The next column is the price-earnings ratio. It is computed by dividing the current earnings per share into the closing market price per share. The P/E ratio indicates how much investors are willing to pay for the earnings of a firm. The ratio is not computed if the company is currently losing money or if the particular issue is a preferred stock. Further discussion of the P/E appears in Chapters 2, 6, and 10.

The last five columns present information about trading that took place during the day preceding the publication of the paper. First, the volume of trades is shown. This is recorded in hundreds of shares. High and low prices achieved during the day and the price of the last trade are tabulated in the next three columns. The last entry is for the change from the closing price on the preceding day compared to the closing price on the day being recorded.

Note that fractions are used rather than decimals. There is a long-

FIGURE 4–2
Examples of Stock Price Quotations

New York Stock Exchange Transactions

Thursday, May 15, 1975

1975 High	1975 Low	Stock Div.	P.E. Ratio	Sales 100s	High	Low	Close	Net Chg.
39¼	23	Dentsply .80	18	73	35⅛	34¾	34⅞	+ ⅝
16	5¾	Deseret .25	20	60	14⅝	14	14	− ⅜
7⅜	5⅜	DeSotoIn .40	..	23	7⅛	7	7	.....
13⅜	8⅜	DetEdis 1.45	8	119	11½	11¼	11⅜	.....
67¾	50½	Det E pf7.45	...	z100	59¼	59¼	59¼	..
55¼	42⅜	Det E pf5.50	...	12	48¾	48⅜	48¾	+ ¼
14¾	7⅞	Dexter .36	9	8	13⅝	13⅝	13⅝	...
11	6⅜	Dial Finl .54	7	28	9¾	9½	9½	+ ⅛
34¼	24⅜	DiamInt 2	7	48	32⅞	32¼	32½	− ⅛
45⅞	21¾	DiamSh 1.60	7	1018	44	42⅝	43	+ ¾
52¼	27	Dia Sh pfC 2	...	20	50	49¼	49¼	− 1
22¾	14	Dia pf D1.20	...	104	21¾	21¼	21⅜	.....
10¼	6½	DickAB .40	9	38	9¾	9½	9½	− ⅛
11¾	7½	Dictaphn .60	7	94	8¼	8	8	− ¼
19¾	12½	Diebold .40b	8	44	15	14⅛	14¼	− ½
5¼	3⅜	DiGiorg .08p	...	73	4⅛	4⅛	4⅛	+ ⅛
112⅜	45⅜	Digital Eqpt	29	283	109⅝	107	107	− 3
8¾	4⅝	Dillingm .40	6	36	8	7¾	7¾	− ¼
34¾	24	Dillon 1.20b	13	67	36	34¾	36	+ 1⅜
55¼	21¼	Disney .12b	29	868	55⅝	53	53⅛	− 1⅝
8½	5¼	Disston .12	5	25	7¾	7⅜	7⅜	.....
3⅜	1⅝	Diversfd In	19	230	3⅛	2⅞	3	+ ⅛
3¼	1⅛	DivMtg .88e	...	26	1¾	1⅝	1¾	+ ⅛
15⅛	7	DrPeppr .30	28	759	14½	13⅞	13⅞	− ⅛
56½	41⅜	DomeM .80a	14	95	49	48	48¼	− 1
4⅞	2⅜	DonLuf Jen	...	2	3⅝	3⅝	3⅝	...
24¾	17¼	Donnelly .56	15	572	23½	22⅝	22¾	− ¾
13½	6¼	DorOliv .10e	8	39	13⅜	12⅞	13	....
6⅛	3⅝	Dorsey .10	9	52	6¼	6	6⅛	+ ⅛
47½	25⅝	Dover 1.20	9	48	44¼	43⅝	44	+ ¼
92½	53¾	DowCh 1.40	13	632	92⅞	89⅝	89¾	− 1⅝
5	3	DPF Inc	...	22	5	4⅞	5	+ ⅛
39¾	26¾	Dravo 1.80	8	6	39½	39¼	39¼	− ⅜
59¾	38⅝	Dresser 1.40	9	229	59¼	57	58¾	+ 2
60½	40¾	Dres pf 2.20	...	65	60	58	59¼	+ 2½
54¼	36½	Drssr pfB 2	...	8	54	53	54	+ 3
17⅜	14¾	DrexBd 1.44	...	1	15⅝	15⅝	15⅝	− ⅛
8	3¾	Dreyfus .45e	10	6	6¾	6¾	6¾	+ ⅛
15	10¾	Duk Pw 1.40	8	2160	13¾	13⅛	13⅜	− ⅜
89	74	Duke pf8.70	...	z230	79	78¾	78⅞	− ⅛
71¼	55⅞	Duke pf6.75	...	3	63½	62¾	63½	+ ½
25⅜	24⅜	Duke pf2.69	...	12	24½	24¼	24¼	− ⅝
30¼	18¾	DunBrad 1	19	557	28¾	28¼	28¾	+ 1
2⅞	1⅛	Duplan Cp	...	18	2½	2⅜	2⅜	− ⅛
133½	87⅛	duPont 5.50e	21	257	133	129¼	129¼	− 2¾
62	57	duPnt pf4.50	...	1	58¾	58¾	58¾	+ ¼
50	44	duPnt pf3.50	...	2	44¾	44¾	44¾	+ ¾

1975 High	1975 Low	Stock Div.	P.E. Ratio	Sales 100s	High	Low	Close	Net Chg.
16⅞	15	GtWn pf1.88	..	26	16¾	16½	16½	− ¼
19⅞	13⅝	GrGiant 1.08	7	23	18½	18	18½	+ ½
13½	10½	Greyhd 1.04	10	155	12⅞	12⅝	12⅝	.....
2⅛	1⅜	Greyhnd wt	...	133	2	1⅞	2	......
3¼	1	Grolier Inc	...	65	2⅞	2⅝	2¾	.....
18¾	10	Grumm .60	6	47	18½	18	18⅛	− ⅛
12	6¼	GuarIn .10e	9	20	9½	9⅛	9½	+ ⅜
4⅜	2⅜	Guard Mtg	...	60	2½	2¼	2⅜	....
8¾	6¼	GlfLfHld .50	7	80	8	7⅝	7¾	+ ⅛
4	1⅞	GulfMtg Rlt	...	12	2½	2½	2½	− ⅛
22	17⅝	GulfOil 1.70	4	1526	19⅞	19⅝	19¾	− ⅛
20½	11⅜	GlfRes .50e	3	434	19¾	19⅛	19⅛	− ⅜
30½	17	GlfR pfA.20	...	4	29	28⅝	28⅝	− ¾
24¾	15⅛	GfR pfB1.30	...	22	24¼	23⅞	24	− ¼
13⅜	10⅝	GlfStUt 1.12	7	389	12¼	12⅛	12¼	.....
53½	48½	GlfSU pf4.40	...	z70	52	51½	52	+ 2
36⅝	23½	GlfWtn 1.10	5	112	36	35½	35½	......
5¼	3⅜	GlfWInd wt	...	57	5	4¾	4¾	− ⅛
64	45	GlfW pf 3.87	...	6	62⅞	62½	62⅞	+ ⅞
4¼	1⅝	Gulton Ind	16	139	4⅜	4⅛	4⅜	+ ¼
		— H-H-H —						
29¾	20½	Hack W 2.48	12	3	27¾	27½	27¾	......
18½	10½	HallFB .50	15	21	18⅝	18⅜	18⅜	− ⅛
16¼	11	HallPrt .80a	6	4	16	16	16	......
171	115	Hallibtn 1.32	19	291	163	159¾	160¼	− 1
16¾	12⅛	HamrlP 1.20	4	159	17¼	16½	17¼	+ ½
5¼	3⅞	Hammond	7	19	4⅝	4⅝	4⅝	......
7⅞	3⅛	Handlmn .40	18	105	7⅝	7¼	7¼	− ⅛
25¾	20¼	HandH .80a	4	17	23¾	23¼	23¾	+ ¼
11	6¼	HanesCp .68	...	9	9¾	9½	9½	......
47¾	24½	Hanna 1.35	13	18	44⅞	44⅜	44⅝	+ ⅛
29⅜	14⅜	HarBrJ 1.20	9	480	29½	28¾	29¼	+ ¼
5⅞	3	Hardees	23	151	5¾	5¼	5¼	− ⅜
43¾	25⅞	Harnisf 1.80	6	108	44	43¼	43⅝	+ ⅝
16⅛	8	Harrahs .22	9	20	14⅛	14	14	− ¼
21⅞	14½	Harris 1.20	...	71	20¼	19¾	20¼	+ ⅛
16⅞	10	Harsco 1b	4	114	16⅜	15½	15½	......
9⅛	5½	HartSMx .60	7	78	8¾	8⅜	8½	......
17½	6¼	HarteHk .30	11	36	17	16⅞	17	......
17⅛	14¾	HattSe 1.44a	...	29	15⅝	15¼	15¼	− ⅜
22⅛	16½	HawiiEl 1.68	8	53	22	21¾	22	+ ⅛
10¾	7½	HayesAlb 1	6	13	9⅞	9¾	9⅞	− ⅛
4¼	2¼	Hazeltine	...	3	3⅞	3¾	3¾	+ ⅛
17½	5¾	HCA M .50e	9	116	17¾	16¾	17⅛	− ⅜
14⅞	5½	Hecks .12	8	34	14	13¾	13⅞	+ ⅛
20¾	13½	HeclaM .50t	17	89	18¾	18⅛	18⅝	+ ¼
12½	6⅝	Heilem .48a	9	64	12¾	12	12⅛	......
56	38½	HeinzH 1.28	13	366	55	54¾	55	+ ¾

EXPLANATORY NOTES

(Footnotes apply to New York, American and Pacific exchanges)

z—Sales in full.

Unless otherwise noted, rates of dividends in the foregoing table are annual disbursements based on the last quarterly or semi-annual declaration. Special or extra dividends or payments not designated as regular are identified in the following footnotes.

a—Also extra or extras. b—Annual rate plus stock dividend. c—Liquidating dividend. e—Declared or paid in preceding 12 months. h—Declared or paid after stock dividend or split up. k—Declared or paid this year, an accumulative issue with dividends in arrears. n—New issue. p—Paid this year, dividend omitted, deferred or no action taken at last dividend meeting. r—Declared or paid in preceding 12 months plus stock dividend. t—Paid in stock in preceding 12 months, estimated cash value on ex-dividend or ex-distribution date.

cld—Called. x—Ex dividend. y—Ex dividend and sales in full. x-dis—Ex distribution. xr—Ex rights. xw—Without warrants. ww—With warrants. wd—When distributed. wi—When issued. nd—Next day delivery.

vj—In bankruptcy or receivership or being reorganized under the Bankruptcy Act, or securities assumed by such companies.

Year's high and low range does not include changes in latest day's trading.

Where a split or stock dividend amounting to 25 per cent or more has been paid the year's high-low range and dividend are shown for the new stock only.

Source: *The Wall Street Journal*, May 16, 1975, pp. 23–24.

standing practice to quote prices in dollars or *points* and fractions thereof with the smallest increment usually being ⅛ of a point, or 12.5 cents. The row circled in Figure 4–2 serves as an example for this discussion. The information indicates that 868 hundred or 86,800 shares of Walt Disney Productions common stock changed hands on Thursday, May 15, 1975. The top price paid was $55⅝ and the lowest trade was at $53. The stock closed at $53⅛ which was down $1⅝ from the close on Wednesday, May 14. Dividing the closing price by the current earnings indicates investors paid $29 for each dollar of Disney earnings. These shares have traded in the range from $21¼ to $55¼ from the beginning of 1975 up through May 14. All this information presents a rather complete picture of daily transactions in each listed stock. Many newspapers publish just a portion of the entire NYSE list and cite closing figures only.

The Wall Street Journal also publishes prices of stocks on the American Stock Exchange, the regional exchanges, two Canadian exchanges, and a rather extensive group of OTC securities. The information for listed stocks is in a format similar to the NYSE quotations, although it is somewhat more abbreviated. The OTC data are somewhat different. The prices quoted do not represent actual transactions nor does the information cover one day of activity. Instead, the OTC section reports only the bid and asked prices quoted by dealers as of a certain time. A sample of these quotes appears in Figure 4–3. Note the quotation that has been circled for American Express. The asked price for this stock was $40⅞ per share and the bid price was $40⅜. These are "wholesale" prices that dealers quote to each other, so adjustments for commissions would have to be made to arrive at retail prices.[5] The last column in the section tells that the bid price on May 15 was $1⅜ per share higher than the bid quote given at the same time on the preceding day.

Over 50,000 unlisted issues have some degree of trading activity. *The Wall Street Journal* publishes daily quotations for around 1,500 OTC securities. The majority of OTC prices must be found elsewhere. Many OTC firms are of regional interest only; prices of their stock are published in newspapers in those areas. Other quotes can be obtained from several financial publications.[6]

Investors also ask brokers for stock price information. Their sources

[5] See the discussion of commissions in Chapter 3.

[6] See *Barron's, The Commercial and Financial Chronicle* and *The O-T-C Market Chronicle.*

FIGURE 4–3
Price Quotations

Over-the-Counter Markets

4:00 p.m. Eastern Time Prices, Thursday, May 15, 1975

All over the counter prices printed on this page are representative quotations supplied by the National Association of Securities Dealers through NASDAQ, its automated system for reporting quotes. Prices don't include retail markup, markdown or commission. Volume represents shares that changed ownership during the day. Figures include only those transactions effected by NASDAQ market makers but may include some duplication where NASDAQ market makers traded with each other.

Stock & Div.	Sales 100s	Bid	Asked	Net Chg.
—A A—				
Acady I nsGrp	28	1⅝	2⅛	− ⅛
Aceto Chemicl	18	17	18½	+ 1
ACMAT Corp	10	2⅝	3⅛	...
Acushnet C .60	1	11½	13	− ½
AddWesley .40	1	8¾	9⅛	+ ⅛
Advance Ross	58	1⅜	1⅝	...
Advan Mry Sy	47	3⅞	4⅜	...
Advan MicroD	270	10⅜	10⅞	+ ¼
Advent Corp	2	10½	12½	...
Affil Bnksh .80	3	10¾	11¾	...
AgMet Incorp	24	14½	15¼	...
Agnico Eagle	98	5½	5¾	...
AlaBancp 1.32	6	21½	22½	...
AlaTennN 1.20	2	10⅜	10⅞	...
Alaska Itl .05b	71	16¼	17¼	+ ¼
AldrichCh .20b	3	58	61	+ 1
AlexandrA .90	155	36⅛	36⅝	− ¼
Alex Bald 1.60	51	19⅜	19⅞	− ¼
AlicoIncp .12d	16	7¼	7¾	− ⅛
AllCity Ins .15	15	4½	5	− ¼
Allergan Phar	45	14½	15¼	− ¼
Allied Leisure	2	2¾	3½	...
Allied Tel .40	16	10⅞	11⅜	+ ⅛
Allyn Bacn .35	26	4¾	5⅛	− ⅛
Alton Box .40	4	12¼	12¾	+ ⅛
Amarex Incor	15	8⅛	8⅝	...
Amer Apprasl	23	3⅞	4¼	+ ⅛
AmBkr Ins .20	107	4¾	5⅛	− ½
AmBkTrPa 1g	4	15¾	16¾	− ¼
AmBkrAs .20g	10	8¼	9	− ¼
Am Beef Pack	7	1½	1⅞	− ⅛
AmCmwl Fncl	6	4⅝	5⅛	...
Am Exprss .80	1270	40⅜	40⅞	+ 1⅜
AmFidelLf .08	2	4½	5¼	...
AmFltrona .52	12	8⅜	8⅞	...
AmFinancl .04	44	12½	12⅞	...
AmerFncl pf 1	104	7⅝	7 13-16	...
AmFncl 80wts	20	2⅛	2⅜	...
AmFletch 1.16	19	18¾	19½	...
Am Furniture	4	3¼	3⅝	...
Am Greetg .25	629	13	13½	+ ¼
A GuarFcl 10k	14	2⅞	3¼	...
Am Heritg .32	35	9⅝	10⅛	+ ⅛
AmIntlGrp .24	98	59	60	− 2
AmIntlRes .14	220	43	44½	− ½
Am Microsys	84	12	12½	− ⅛
AmNatlFcl .42	11	7½	7⅞	...
AmNucler Cp	5	3⅜	3¾	...
Am Quasr Pet	44	11	11½	− ⅛
Am Reins .60	124	18	18½	+ ⅛
Amer Reserve	177	1½	2	...
Am SecTr 2.40	14	35¾	36¼	...
Am Telecomu	75	6¼	6¾	− ¼
ChrisSec 1.32b	167	124	128	− 3
ChubbCrp 1.40	293	37½	38	...
Chur FrCh .40	130	12	12⅜	...
Cinn FclC .60g	8	12	12½	− ¼
Circle Inc .60b	2	14¼	14¾	...
CitzSthnCp .88	2	14½	15½	+ ¼
CitSoNBGa .52	421	6⅝	6⅞	− ⅛
CitznFidel 1.40	20	21	23	− ½
CitzUtil B 1.88	4	25⅝	26⅛	+ ¼
CitzUtilA 8.45i	33	28⅝	29⅛	+ ½
ClarkJL Mf 1a	1	28	29	...
Clevepak .60	13	10	11	+ ½
ClevTrust Rlt	4	2⅞	3⅜	...
CocaCB La .74	214	16¾	17⅛	− ¼
CocaCBLapf 2	5	34	35½	− 1
CoCBtCons .40	4	9½	10¼	...
CoburnOp .08b	8	15¾	16½	− ¼
Cobe Labrator	60	17	18	− 1¼
CoastalSCp .27	1	4	4½	...
Coast Catama	20	2¾	3¼	− ⅛
Clow Corp .68	6	9	9½	...
Clinton Oil Co	556	2 1-16	2 3-16	...
Clevetrust 2.40	23	39¾	40¾	+ ¼
CoCBtlMia .20	28	13¼	14	...
CCBtlMidA .20	32	8¼	8¾	+ ¾
CocaCMdw .48	1	11	12	...
Codex Corp	97	34¾	35¾	− ¾
College Un .14	6	7⅛	7⅝	...
Coherent Rad	84	11	11¾	...
Coleman Amr	2	5½	6	...
ColLifeAcc .26	20	7⅝	8	− ⅛
ColoNtlBks .92	8	12	12¾	...
Cblumbia Crp	14	4⅜	4¾	+ ½
ComShare Inc	7	4	4½	+ ⅛
Combndlns .60	742	12	12¼	− ⅜
ComrcBkshr 1	7	19¼	20¼	− ¼
Com ClHo .16b	75	14¼	15¼	+ ¼
ComlShrg .60g	9	25	26½	...
ComTNJ 1.30a	1	21	21¾	...
CwthNtGs 1.62	1	15¼	16¼	− ¼
CmwTlPa 1.90	1	23¾	24½	...
Comunc In .28	30	13⅛	13⅝	− ⅛
Commun Prop	19	2⅝	3	− ⅛
Compuscan In	25	8⅛	8⅝	− ⅛
Computr Auto	149	7½	8	− ½
Comptr El Sys	21	5⅛	5⅝	...
Comptr Mach	64	1⅜	1¾	...
Comptr Usage	10	2⅝	3⅛	− ¼
Cmptrvisn Cp	26	5¼	5¾	− ⅛
Comtech Labs	41	8¾	9¾	+ ¼
Comten Incp	29	4⅝	5⅛	+ ¼
ConceptInc .07	1	5¼	6	...
ConnFincl 1.40	3	13	13¾	...
Conn Gen .96	377	42½	43	
1stTennNtl .44	87	7¾	8¼	− ¼
1st TexFin .40	x8	10⅝	11⅛	+ ⅛
1stUnionCp .92	9	11¾	12¼	...
1st UnInc 2.60	29	30¾	31½	+ ¼
1st UtdBnc .60	20	16	17	...
First West Fin	76	1⅞	2⅛	...
FitchbGE 1.38	2	10½	11½	− ¼
FlagshpBk .72	35	9⅞	10⅜	...
Flexsteel .28	z50	6⅜	6⅞	...
Flickinger .70	21	16¾	17¼	+ ¼
FlaComBk .68	1	7⅜	8⅜	+ ⅛
Fla CypressIn	102	3¾	4	+ ¼
FlaGRltT .32b	2	9¾	10¾	+ ¼
Fla NtlBnk .24	75	9⅞	10¼	...
FlaMgMtl .12d	12	7¼	8	...
Floyd Ent .20d	10	4⅞	5⅝	+ ¼
Food Town .16	9	29½	30½	+ 1¼
Foodways Nat	4	5¼	6	+ ¼
Forest Oil .25b	189	9⅛	9½	− ⅝
FotomatC .03b	47	9⅛	9½	...
FounderF .05d	21	1⅞	2⅛	...
Frankln El .28	2	8⅝	9⅛	...
FranklinLf .84	215	17⅝	18	+ ⅜
Frnklin CpNY	z61	3	3⅜	...
FrasrMtg .62b	1	8¾	9½	...
FredHerr .12b	3	4	4½	...
FredkHol .10e	3	5¾	6½	...
Frndly Ice .06	65	24¾	25½	+ ¼
Froz FdEx .32	1	9½	9⅞	...
Fuller H B .40	18	13	13½	+ ⅛
Furrs Cafe .28	28	8¾	9¼	+ ⅜
—G G—				
Gates Learjet	7	5⅝	6⅛	...
GatewayTr .60	2	6	6¾	...
Gelco Fld .09b	19	11⅝	12⅛	...
Gelman Instr	28	5	5⅜	...
Gen Automatn	195	9⅜	9⅞	− ¾
GenAutoPt .60	25	23	24	...
Genrl Binding	42	15	16	+ ½
GenCare Corp	1	5	5½	...
GnlEnrgy .20b	98	15½	15⅞	− ⅜
GenFinSy .06b	76	4⅜	4⅞	+ ¼
Gen Hlth Serv	3	2⅝	3	...
Gen Reins .40	53	167	171	− 1
GenlShale .80g	13	10	10½	...
GenTlCal5pf 1	3	9¾	10¾	...
Genova Incp	z25	5	5½	...
GilbertAsc .60	37	17¾	18¾	− ¼
GilfordInst .13	10	4⅛	4⅝	...
Girard Co 3.24	26	37½	39	...
Globe Life .20	4	9⅞	10⅜	...
Golden St Fds	14	23¼	24¼	+ 1¼
GvEmpF .08b	8	10⅜	10⅞	...

EXPLANATORY NOTES

z-Sales in full.

a-Annual rate plus cash extra or extras. b-Declared or paid this year, no regular rate. c-Declared or paid since stock dividend or split, no regular rate. d-Declared or paid in 1974. e-Declared or paid in 1975 plus stock. f-Declared or paid in 1974 plus stock. g-Annual rate plus stock dividend. h-Paid this year, latest dividend omitted. i-Paid in stock in 1974. k-Percent paid in stock in 1975. r-Ex-rights. x-Ex-dividend. y-Ex-distribution. (z) No representative quote.

Source: *The Wall Street Journal*, May 16, 1975, p. 20.

are mainly from a vast network of telephone, teletype, and electronic communication systems which will be discussed in a later section.

Bond Prices. All bonds are issued with a stated face amount, or par value. This is the amount the owner will receive if the bond is held until it matures. The most common denomination is $1,000, although bonds between $100 and $1,000,000 are also sold. To avoid confusion in quoting prices, a standard of 100 is used. This means at a price of 95, a $1,000 bond would be $950 or $9,500 for a $10,000 par bond. Fractions rather than decimals are used in bond quotations; eighths for corporate bonds, and thirty-seconds or sixty-fourths for government issues. Examples of bond price information appearing in *The Wall Street Journal* are shown in Figure 4–4. The reporting treatment of listed corporate bonds is similar to that of listed stocks and includes price ranges during the year and data for the day's high, low, close, and change from the preceding day. The major difference lies in the description of the issue. Most firms have only one class of common stock and none or perhaps one issue of preferred stock. However, companies typically sell several bonds at different times, so it is important to distinguish between each issue. Particular features of each bond follow the name of the company. The interest rate and maturity date are given at this point in an abbreviated style. An issue of Dow Chemical is circled in Figure 4–4. The phrase "8½s 05" identifies this issue as bearing an interest rate of 8½ percent with a maturity date of 2005. The current yield of 8.8 percent is computed by dividing the interest rate by the closing price.

Figure 4–4 shows that government bond price reports differ considerably from the corporate bond information. The first three columns of the Treasury Bond section list the amounts of yearly interest and maturity dates. Figures for the bid and asked prices and net change that follow are similar to any other OTC security except for the use of decimal points. This is somewhat misleading because the decimal is just used to separate the dollar figures from the fractions, which in this case are thirty-seconds. The last column in the report indicates the *yield to maturity* for the bond. This is a percentage figure which is computed to include the interest paid and an allowance for the fact that the bond will be redeemed at maturity for par value even though it was purchased for a different price.[7]

The government bond discussion may be summarized by referring to the row circled in the Treasury Bonds and Notes section of Figure

[7] Details of the calculation procedure may be found in the appendix to Chapter 8.

FIGURE 4–4
Bond Price Quotations

New York Exchange Bonds

Thursday, May 15, 1975

Bonds	Cur Yld	Vol	High	Low	Close	Net Chg
DetEd 9⅞04	11.	5	84¼	82⅝	82⅝	−1⅜
DetEd 9s99	11.	1	75⅛	75⅛	75⅛	+ ⅛
DetEd 8.15s	11.	4	68⅝	68⅝	68⅝	.....
DetEd 7½03	11.	10	6	66	66	−1
DetEd 7s76	7.1	28	99	98½	98½	.....
DetEd 6s96	10.	6	55⅛	55⅛	55⅛	+1⅛
DetEd 3¼80	4.6	20	70½	70	70½	+ ½
DialF 8¼s89	10.	2	80	80	80	+1⅞
DiGior 5¾93	10.	6	55	55	55	+1
Dilling 9¾99	cv	2	95½	95½	95½	+ ½
Dilling 5½94	cv	11	55⅞	55½	55⅞	.....
Divers 9⅞91	16.	10	59½	59½	59½	.....
Divers 5⅞93	cv	10	43¼	42½	42½	− ½
Dow 8.9 2000	8.8	3	100½	100½	100½	+ ⅜
Dow 8⅞2000	8.9	45	100	99½	99½	+ ½
Dow 8½s05	8.8	5	96½	96½	96½	.....
DPF 5½87	cv	28	54½	54½	54½	.....
duPt 8.45s04	8.5	37	99½	98¾	99⅜	+ ⅝
duPont 8s81	7.9	127	101½	101	101	− ¼
DukeP 13s79	11.	46	109⅜	109	109¼	− ⅛
DukeP 9¾04	10.	31	96¾	94⅝	94⅝	−2⅛
DukeP 9½05	10.	10	93¾	93¾	93¾	+ ½
DukeP 7¾02	9.9	5	78	78	78	− ½
DukeP 7¾03	10.	5	77	77	77	+1
DukeP 7⅜01	10.	18	73	72	72	− ½
Dupin 5½94	cv	4	28½	28½	28½	+1½
Duq 8¾2000	9.1	7	96⅛	96	96⅛	+ ⅛
DuqL 8¼76	8.2	5	100½	100½	100½	.....
DuqL 2¾77	3.0	10	90⅛	90⅛	90⅛	+ ⅛
EasAir 5s92	cv	5	39⅛	39⅛	39⅛	.....
EaAir 4¾93	cv	18	39½	39¼	39¼	− ⅜
EGG 3½s87	cv	6	57⅝	57½	57½	+ ⅜
ElPa 8½95A	cv	3	95¾	95¾	95¾	− ¼
ElPas 8½95	cv	3	97	97	97	.....
EqtLf 6¾90	cv	5	70½	70	70	.....
vjEri 3⅛90f	..	25	13	11½	13	+2½
vjEr 3⅛sG f	..	5	13	13	13	+2
Estrne 6¼95	cv	2	52	52	52	.....
Evans 6¼94	12.	28	49½	49	49½	.....
Exxon 6½98	8.0	14	81¼	80⅝	80⅝	−1⅛
Exxon 6s97	7.8	40	76¾	76	76½	+ ½
ExxnP 9s04	8.8	41	102	100½	102	+ ¾
Fairch 4⅞92	9.6	30	47	45¼	45¼	−1½
LgIsLt 9¼82	9.1	27	100¾	100¾	100¾	.....
LouGs 9¼00	9.3	10	99	99	99	.....
LouN 7⅜93	10.	1	73⅜	73⅜	73⅜	.....
LTV 7½s77	cv	44	161	158¼	158¼	+ ¼
LT V5s88	10.	75	47⅜	46¾	47	.....
Lyk 11s2000	12.	2	91⅝	91⅝	91⅝	.....
LykeY 7½94	11.	6	67	67	67	.....
LykY 7½94n	11.	25	66½	66	66	− ⅞
MckF 9¾91	10.	21	93	92⅞	93	.....
MckF 9⅝90	10.	1	93	93	93	.....
MckF 8½77	8.5	10	99	99	99	.....
Macmil 4s92	cv	5	47⅜	47⅜	47⅜	.....
Macy 5s92	cv	1	71	71	71	.....
McyC 7⅜s77	7.5	23	97¾	97¾	97¾	− ¼
Macy 4¼90	cv	1	71⅛	71⅛	71⅛	+ ⅞
Mapco 11s75	1.	5	99⅞	99¾	99¾	.....
Marco 6½88	8.9	5	73	73	73	− ½
Marcor 5s96	cv	5	75½	75½	75½	−1
MarMa 6s94	cv	10	72¾	72¾	72¾	.....
MaMu 6¾90	cv	10	65	65	65	−6
MaMu 6¼91	cv	29	58	57	57	− ½
May D. 3¼78	3.6	13	89½	89½	89½	+3
MayRlt 5s77	5.4	3	92½	92½	92½	+1
Myr 7.85s96	9.8	5	80	80	80	.....
McCr 10½85	15.	6	70	70	70	.....
McCro 7¾95	19.	12	40	38⅝	39¾	+ ⅝
McCro 7⅝97	19.	77	38⅜	38¼	38¼	.....
McCro 7½94	19.	158	38½	38	38	.....
McCr 7½94n	19.	9	38⅜	38⅜	38⅜	+1⅜
McCro 6½92	cv	1	38½	38½	38½	.....
McCror 5s81	12.	15	41⅞	41½	41½	+1½
McDD 4¾91	cv	6	65¾	65⅛	65⅛	.....
Mellon 10s89	9.8	60	101⅜	101¼	101⅜	.....
MGM 5s93	cv	11	80¼	80	80¼	+ ¼
MGIC 8⅜88	10.	5	77	77	77	.....
MGI C5s93	cv	62	56	55	55½	+ ½
MichB 3⅛88	5.2	7	59	59	59	+2
Micr 10s2000	12.	4	77	77	77	− ⅜
MoPac 5s45f	..	56	40	39¾	40	.....
MPac 4¾30f		3	39¼	39¼	39¼	+ ¾
MoAl 8.45 05	8.7	10	96¼	96¼	96¼	− ⅛
Moh D 5½94	cv	26	24	24	24	.....
Mona 10¼75						

Government, Agency and Miscellaneous Securities

Thursday, May 15, 1975

Over-the-Counter Quotations: Source on request.

Decimals in bid-and-asked and bid changes represent 32nds (101.1 means 101 1-32). a-Plus 1-64. b-Yield to call date. d-Minus 1-64.

U.S. TREASURY BONDS & NOTES

Rate	Mat.	Date		Bid	Asked	Bid Chg.	Yld.
5⅞s,	1975	Aug	n	100.2	100.4	.....	5.27
8⅜s,	1975	Sep	n	100.30	101.2	− .2	5.35
7s,	1975	Nov	n	100.19	100.23	− .1	5.49
7s,	1975	Dec	n	100.20	100.24	− .1	5.75
5⅞s,	1976	Feb	n	99.24	99.28	− .2	6.05
6¼s,	1976	Feb	n	100.0	100.8	− .2	5.90
8s,	1976	Mar	n	101.15	101.19	− .2	6.09
5¾s,	1976	May	n	99.19	99.23	.....	6.04
6½s,	1976	May	n	100.8	100.12	− .2	6.10
6s,	1976	May	n	99.23	99.27	− .2	6.16
8¾s,	1976	Jun	n	102.16	102.20	− .3	6.28
6½s,	1976	Aug	n	99.31	100.3	− .3	6.42
7½s,	1976	Aug	n	101.4	101.8	− .1	6.44
5⅞s,	1976	Aug	n	99.6	99.10	.....	6.44
8¼s,	1976	Sep	n	102.5	102.9	− .1	6.48
6¼s,	1976	Nov	n	99.18	99.22	.....	6.47
7⅛s,	1976	Nov	n	100.20	100.24	− .2	6.60
7¼s,	1976	Dec	n	100.26	100.30	.....	6.63
8s,	1977	Feb	n	101.26	101.30	.....	6.80
6s,	1977	Feb	n	98.16	98.20	−1.1	6.83
6½s,	1977	Mar	n	99.6	99.8	.....	6.94
7⅜s,	1977	Apr	n	100.23	100.27	− .3	6.90
6⅞s,	1977	May	n	99.29	100.5	− .1	6.77
9s,	1977	May	n	103.24	104.0	.....	6.82
7¾s,	1977	Aug	n	101.14	101.22	− .2	6.93
7¾s,	1977	Nov	n	101.14	101.22	− .2	7.00
6¼s,	1978	Feb	n	97.22	97.30	− .1	7.09
7⅛s,	1978	May	n	99.11	99.24	− .11	7.21
7⅝s,	1978	Aug	n	100.20	100.24	− .6	7.34
8¾s,	1978	Aug	n	104.2	104.10	− .4	7.23
6s,	1978	Nov	n	96.1	96.9	− .2	7.22
7⅞s,	1979	May	n	101.10	101.18	− .4	7.42
6¼s,	1979	Aug	n	95.23	95.31	− .2	7.37
6⅝s,	1979	Nov	n	96.24	97.0	− .2	7.43
7s,	1979	Nov	n	98.12	98.20	.....	7.36
4s,	1980	Feb	....	86.0	87.0	− .2	7.28
6⅞s,	1980	May	n	97.6	97.14	− .2	7.50

EXPLANATORY NOTES

Yield is current yield. Volume is in $1,000 units.

vi—In bankruptcy or receivership or being reorganized under the Bankruptcy Act, or securities assumed by such companies. xi—Ex interest. ct—Certificates. st—Stamped. f—Dealt in flat. x—Matured bonds, negotiability impaired by maturity. xw—Ex warrants. fn—Foreign issue subject to interest equalization tax.

cv—Convertible bonds.

Source: *The Wall Street Journal,* May 16, 1975, p. 22.

4–4. The particular issue indicated is a note bearing an interest rate of 6⅝ percent and maturing in November 1979. The bid and asked prices are reported as "96.24" and "97.0." This means a $1,000 par value note is offered by dealers for purchase and sale for $967.50 and $970.00, respectively.[8] The next column indicates that the bid price fell that day by ²⁄₃₂ or $.625 for a $1,000 bond. The yield to maturity of 7.43 percent is the average annual return offered to investors who buy this note for $970, receive interest of $66.25 each year, and receive $1,000 when the note matures in 1979.

[8] These prices were quoted in 32nds, so 24/32 is equal to $.75 on a $100 basis or $7.50 for a $1,000 bond.

Other Price Quotations. Many financial reports also include special sections for prices of foreign securities, commodities, mutual funds, and call options. Details of mutual fund and call option quotations may be found in Chapters 11 and 12.

BROKERAGE SERVICES

Virtually all investors use professional assistance for their security transactions. This aid is available from thousands of stock brokerage offices located throughout the United States. The main function of these offices is to execute buy and sell orders for the investing public. The objective of this section is to describe a variety of other services offered by the brokerage firms and to discuss factors which are influential in the selection of a particular broker.

PORTFOLIO PLANNING AND REVIEW

A service offered by many brokerage firms involves an analysis and appraisal of an investor's security holdings. This examination might include a rather detailed review of the client's financial capacity as well as a study of each security owned. The purpose of this service is to see that the investors and their investments are properly matched.[9] If a person is just beginning to invest, this help involves mainly establishing goals for the investment program within the individual's financial constraints. If the investor already owns securities, an additional check will be made to see if the current holdings are properly aligned with the objectives and resources available to meet them. Most of this type of work is done in the research office of the brokerage firm with the registered representative acting to bring the investor and the portfolio analyst together. Recommendations are made which the investor can accept or reject. This service is usually performed at no charge, although some investors ask that the firm actually manage their account, buying and selling when the firm feels it is proper to do so. A management fee is typically charged in this arrangement. Several firms offer computerized portfolio analyses for individual investors. These programs provide an objective measure of the risks associated with the securities owned.

[9] Recall the discussion in Chapter 2 which emphasized the need to consider the individual investor's situation before selecting securities; what is appropriate for one person may not be at all suitable for another.

Research

Every brokerage firm is busy investigating securities so as to identify what should be bought or sold. The larger firms employ a staff of security analysts to perform this function. These are highly trained people who specialize in a specific area of analysis. Many of them have technical backgrounds in the industry in which they concentrate. For example, engineers and scientists are often hired away from their technical jobs to analyze the investment prospects of companies in their areas of expertise.

The rise of importance of research in the securities business has been accompanied by the development of a new professional group known as the Chartered Financial Analysts (CFA). To become a member, a person must demonstrate a high degree of knowledge of security analysis similar to the accounting expertise required to become a Certified Public Accountant (CPA). Almost 4,000 CFAs work in research positions in the securities industry.

Medium-size and small brokerage firms often buy research reports from a firm that specializes in security analysis. In addition to the "in-house" and external research, most individual brokers try to investigate situations which they feel may show promise for investors. The object of all these efforts is to provide a continuing stream of buy or sell recommendations. These reports lead to the lifeblood of the business. That is, they generate orders that mean commissions. Furthermore, brokerage firms want to keep their customers for repeat business. Hence, considerable efforts are made to uncover situations that will make money for clients.

Research information is distributed in a variety of ways. Lengthy reports are prepared for investors on the prospect of individual companies. Often booklets are written which discuss a specific industry and also the corporations within that grouping. Many brokerage houses distribute a *market letter* to their clients. This publication is usually one to three pages long and is issued at regular intervals, such as daily, weekly, or monthly. Titles of these reports are indicative of their contents: *Research Review, Market Interpretations, Current Selections, The Market Review, Investments for a Changing Economy, Financial and Business Review, Market Communique, New York Stock Market Comment,* and so on. The reports typically include a few paragraphs about each of a number of companies relating to prospects for earnings and sales, to any new developments, etc.

FIGURE 4–5
Important Data on Stocks

92 Gen-Gen — STANDARD & POOR'S CORPORATION

INDEX	Ticker Symbol	STOCKS NAME OF ISSUE (Call Price of Pfd. Stocks)	Market	Earns &Div Rank-ing	Par Val.	Inst. Hold Cos	Inst. Hold Shs. (000)	PRINCIPAL BUSINESS	PRICE RANGE 1960-73 High	1960-73 Low	1974 High	1974 Low	1975 High	1975 Low	Mar. Sales in 100s	March, 1975 Last Sale Or Bid High	Low	Last	% Div. Yield	P-E Ratio
1	GBND	General Binding	OTC	B+	25¢	15	278	Plastic binding eq, supplies	35½	1⅛	37	8½	15¾	9	962	15¾	11¼	14B	...	16
2	GBD	General Builders	ASE	B—	1	..	...	Condominium & single-family	14¼	⅞	1⅞	¾	1¾	⅞	100	1¾	1¼	1⅜B	...	d
3	GK	General Cable	NYS,Bo,MW,PB	B+	1	23	1099	Mfr wire & cable products	55¾	6⅜	10⅛	6¾	10¾	7¼	6438	10¾	9	10⅛	7.1	5
4	GCRE	General Care	OTC	NR	10¢	..	...	Health care facilities	12	2⅜	7½	4⅝	9⅜	4¾	177	9⅜	7¾	9⅜B	...	5
5	GCR	General Cigar	NYS	B+	1	7	76	2d lgst mfr, NYS dstr,Ex Lax	78¾	10⅝	15¼	9⅝	14	10½	233	13⅞	13¼	13⅜	9.0	7
6	GCN	General Cinema	NYS	NR	1	18	525	Theatre chain:soft drinks	55½	1½	14	5⅜	19½	7½	3138	19½	15⅝	19½	2.3	10
7	GDV	General Development	[1]NYS,Bo,MW,PB,PS	NR	1	4	2061	Florida real estate developm't	38⅛	3⅝	7⅝	2⅛	6½	2¾	1156	6½	4⅛	5⅞	...	5
8	GD	General Dynamics	[2]NYS,Bo,Ci,De,MW,PB	B—	1	25	2575	Aircraft/subs,bldg mater'ls	79	15⅝	28¾	13½	31⅞	19	3635	31⅞	26⅛	30½	...	6
9	GED	General Educational Sv	ASE,Bo,PB	B—	10¢	1	50	Book mfr:vocation schools	41	1½	2⅞	1¼	2½	1	164	2½	1¼	2B	...	4
10	GE	General Electric	NYS,Bo,Ci,De,MW,PB,PS	A+	2½	705	16872	Lgst mfr electrical equipment	75⅞	27⅛	65	30	49½	32⅜	19944	49½	43¼	46	3.5	14
11	JOB	Gen'l Employ Enterprises	ASE	B—	No	..	...	Personnel placement service	24¼	1½	2⅝	1⅝	2⅞	1¾	53	2⅛	1⅞	2⅛	‡14.1	6
12	GNLE	Gen'l Energy	OTC	NR	1	7	524	Coal mining	16⅞	1/16	17¼	7¼	15¼	10½	1740	14½	12⅛	14B	2.9	4
13	GEX	General Exploration	PS	C	1	2	42	Coal: oil & gas,US & foreign	18¼	3½	5⅛	2	5⅛	2⅜	159	4	3¼	3½	...	8
14	GF	General Foods	NYS,Bo,Ci,De,MW,PB,PS	A	1	195	3625	Leading mfr packaged foods	53⅞	21¾	28⅝	16	26	18⅜	6975	26	22¾	24⅜	5.7	10
15	GGP	Gen'l Growth Prop SBI	NYS	...	1	31	800	Real estate investment trust	27¾	6¾	18½	11	17⅝	12½	1355	17⅝	15½	17⅛	7.0	18
16	GHEL	General Health Serv	OTC	B	1	..	...	Acute gen'l hospitals: labs	36½	3	5½	1⅜	3⅛	1½	690	3⅛	2½	2½B	...	4
17	GHOB	General Hobbies	OTC	NR	1¢	1	3	Hobby mdse: model RR eq	10	3	4¾	¾	1⅛	⅝	78	1	⅝	¾B	13.3	9
18	GH	General Host	NYS,PB,PS	B	1	3	109	Meat packer, bakery,food sv	45⅜	5½	9⅝	4¼	9⅜	4⅞	1217	9⅜	7¾	7¾	5.2	1.
19	WS	Wrrt (Purch 1 com at $40)	PS	...	....	2	174	convenience foods & stores	12½	⅝	1	¼	¾	¼	1062	¾	⅜	¾	...	..
20	GHW	General Housewares	ASE	NR	33⅓¢	1	3	Cookware, giftware, leisure pr	20¼	1	2	¼	1¼	½	96	1	½	⅞	...	d
21	GRL	General Instrument	[3]NYS,Bo,Ci,De,MW	B	1	28	519	Electronic components & eq,	74⅞	8¼	16¾	4⅜	11⅛	5	9171	11⅛	8½	10⅝	s...	6
22	Pr	$3.00 cm Cv A Pfd ([57]63)vtg	NYS,MW,PS	B	No	13	35	data collect eq: CATV eq	72½	29½	36¾	23½	31½	24½	70	31	30	30	10.0	..
23	GIT	General Interiors[58]	ASE	B—	33⅓¢	3	64	Early Am, Colonial furniture	35½	3	7¼	3⅝	9⅜	6¾	803	9¼	8⅝	8⅞B	...	9
24	GMD	General Medical	NYS	B+	1	9	161	Dstr hospital & med supplies	49½	3⅜	16¾	4⅝	11½	6⅛	1022	11½	9⅝	10¾	†2.2	9
25	GIS	General Mills	NYS,Bo,De,MW,PB,PS	A	1½	113	2773	Consumer foods,apparel,toys	67⅝	10¾	59⅞	28⅛	48¾	40⅝	3798	48¾	44	45¾	2.6	13
26	GM	General Motors	[4]NYS,Bo,Ci,De,MW,PB,PS	A—	1⅔	727	14909	Largest mfr automotive prods:	113¾	40¼	55½	28⅞	45⅞	31¼	26204	45⅞	39⅜	41⅛	5.8	13
27	Pr B	$5.00 cm Pfd (120)	NYS,MW,PB,PS	AAA	No	71	318	cars, trucks, buses: diesel,	118¾	67½	71	55½	68⅜	59	138	68⅜	66	66¾	7.5	..
28	Pr A	$3.75 cm Pfd (100)	NYS	AAA	No	57	311	aircraft engines:appliances	95½	48½	52½	43½	51¾	45¾	29	51¾	50	51¼	7.3	..
29	GPT	Gen'l Portland	NYS,Bo,MW	B+	1	42	1527	Cement producer	42½	9	13⅜	4⅛	8⅜	4⅝	2850	8⅜	6½	7¼	11.0	28
30	GPU	General Public Util	NYS,Bo,De,MW,PB,PS	B+	2½	63	648	Util hldg co: N.J. & Penna.	40¾	16¾	20¼	9½	14⅜	10⅜	5059	14¼	13⅛	13⅞	12.1	6
31	GER	General Recreation	ASE	NR	1	..	...	Outdoor recreational prod	13½	1⅞	2⅞	1	2¼	1¼	102	2⅛	1⅞	1⅞B	...	4
32	GRX	Gen'l Refractories	NYS,PB	B	5	1	15	Fire-brick for steel industry	33¾	3¾	8¼	4⅜	10⅝	5⅞	765	10⅝	9	9⅞	4.1	4
33	GREI	General Reinsurance	OTC	...	2	52	563	Reinsurance exclusively	256½	11½	221	99	173	129	2341	157	136	137B	0.3	23
34	GRS	General Research	ASE,PS	B—	10¢	..	...	Systems research: tech: lab	29	3⅜	4¾	⅞	2	1⅛	83	2	1⅝	1¾B	...	d
35	GEN	General Resources	ASE	C	50¢	..	...	Mfr prefinished plywood:R.E.	24	⅞	2¼	⅜	1	½	97	1	⅞	1	...	d
36	GSHL	General Shale Prods	OTC	B+	No	1	13	Face brick & concrete blocks	29⅞	3¼	13⅛	7	10⅞	7⅜	62	10⅜	10	10¼B	s7.8	8
37	GSX	General Signal	NYS,PB,PS	B+	1	43	1126	Electrical & electronic prods	59¼	10⅝	53	17¼	37	23⅞	710	37	32½	36	2.1	13
38	GSI	General Steel Ind	NYS	B—	1	..	...	Metal process: constr:safety	32¾	2½	4⅛	1⅞	4⅞	2⅛	891	4⅞	3¾	4⅜	...	5
39	GTELO	Gen'l Tel Cal 4½%Pfd(23½)vtg	OTC	A	20	30	98	Largest sub Gen Tel system	20¼	10½	11½	8½	10½	8½	15	10½	9¼	9¼B	9.7	..
40	GLF.B	Gen Tel Fla $1.30cmB Pfd[64]	NYS([10])	A	25	17	43	Tel. service in Fla., Tampa	28⅛	15¾	17	12½	16	13	19	15½	14	14¼	9.1	..
41	Pr A	$1.25 cm Pfd (25½)	NYS([10])	A	25	21	176	largest community served	28	14¾	17	12½	15	12½	11	15	14	14½	8.6	..
42	Pr C	8.16% cm Pfd ([65]108.16)	NYS([10])	A	100	69	321		100	87	100	67	84	84	1	84	84	80B	10.2	..
43	GTE	General Tel & Electr	[5]NYS,Bo,Ci,De,Ho	A	3⅓	372	14431	2d lgst tel sys-TV sets,	55	18½	26⅝	16⅛	22⅞	16⅞	19703	22½	19⅝	19⅞	9.1	9
44	Pr	5% cm Cv Pfd ([67]55)vtg	NYS	BBB	50	16	52	tubes: elec control eq	58	30½	38	25¼	32⅞	25⅝	70	32⅞	30	31¾	7.9	..

Uniform Footnote Explanations—See Page 1. Other: [1]TS. [2]PS,MS. [3]PB,PS. [4]TS,MS. [5]MW,PB,PS. [51]□$5.85,'73. [52]®$3.63,'74. [53]®$0.41,'74.
[54]Incl.$0.0517 cap.gains,$0.8278'74 non-taxable. [55]®$2.86,'74. [56]Accum on Pfd. [57]To 8-31-75, scale to $60 in'77. [58]Vote Apr 17 on acquis.by General Mills. [59]®$0.85,'74.
[60]®$1.22,'73. [61]Estimate 13%,'74 non-taxable. [62]Subsid. Pfd. Stk.. [63]□$12.37,'72. [64]Callable at $26¼. [65]To 8-1-78:scale to $102.04 in'88. [66]®$2.04,'74. [67]To 6-30-77, then $52½.

COMMON AND PREFERRED STOCKS

INDEX	Some Divs. Ea. Yr. Since	DIVIDENDS — Latest Payment — Per $	Date	Ex. Div.	$ So Far 1975	Total Ind. Rate	$ Paid 1974	FINANCIAL POSITION — Mil-$ — Cash & Equiv.	Curr. Assets	Curr. Liabs.	Balance Sheet Date	CAPITALIZATION — Long Term Debt Mil-$	Shs. 000 — Pfd.	Com.	End	$ Per Shr—EARNINGS—$ Per Shr — Years — 1970	1971	1972	1973	1974	Last 12 Mos.	INTERIM EARNINGS OR REMARKS — Period	$—Per Share—$ 1973	1974	INDEX
1◆	.....	None Paid			....	Nil	....	1.82	29.1	12.6	12-31-73	8.89	...	5200	Dc	0.43	0.50	0.61	0.80	P0.90	0.90				1
2	.....	0.05	3-31-56	3-20	....	Nil	....	Equity per shr $4.38			12-31-73	7.02	...	1541	Dc	0.08	0.21	0.13	0.14	Pd0.32	d0.32				2
3	1951	Q0.18	4-1-75	3-10	0.34	0.72	0.53½	7.39	160.	85.7	12-31-74	78.4	...	14269	Dc	1.22	□1.30	1.07	□1.27	1.90	1.90				3
4	.....	None Since Public			....	Nil	....	5.02	7.78	3.47	4-30-74	13.5	...	560	Ap	□0.04	d0.15	•0.16	•0.32	△1.05	1.86	9 Mo Jan△	△0.65	1.46	4
5	1909	Q0.30	3-17-75	2-14	0.30	1.20	1.20	21.2	100.	65.7	12-29-73	26.2	...	2187	Dc	△3.01	2.43	□2.13	1.84	P1.98	1.98				5
6◆	1953	Q0.11	4-11-75	3-17	0.22	0.44	0.31	11.1	41.3	37.5	10-31-74	79.9	...	5498	Oc	•1.41	△•1.62	△1.75	•1.58	•1.93	2.00	3 Mo Jan△	•0.28	0.35	6
7◆	.....	2%Stk	6-27-72	5-22	....	Nil	....	Equity per shr $9.31			12-31-73	87.5	...	9230	Dc	0.66	0.90	0.96	ʃ1.03	P1.18	1.18				7
8	.....	0.25	6-10-70	5-5	....	Nil	....	17.3	599.	406.	12-31-73	115.	...	10464	Dc	d0.62	△1.96	□2.47	•3.81	P△4.94	4.94				8
9◆	.....	None Paid			....	Nil	....	0.84	13.2	8.06	3-31-74	14.6	p 22	p1656	Mr	1.01	□0.17	0.75	△□[51]0.36	....	0.46	9 Mo Dec	□0.45	•0.55	9
10◆	1899	Q0.40	4-25-75	2-28	0.80	1.60	1.60	294.	5306	4047	9-30-74	1197	...	182120	Dc	1.81	2.60	2.91	3.21	P3.34	3.34				10
11◆	1973	Q0.06	3-20-75	2-27	0.06	0.30	‡0.236	1.42	2.30	1.28	12-31-74	....	...	974	Sp	□0.47	□d0.65	d0.29	•0.30	•0.52	0.37	3 Mo Dec	•0.14	d0.01	11
12	1974	0.10	3-7-75	2-13	0.10	0.40	0.20	14.5	20.9	7.43	12-31-74	1.74	63	4314	Dc	d1.51	△d0.33	△0.01	△0.43	•[52]3.91	3.91				12
13	.....	None Since Public			....	Nil	....	6.17	14.3	17.2	p9-30-73	9.99	213	3728	Dc	□d1.01	□d0.33	△d1.27	△d0.37	P•[53]0.46	0.46				13
14◆	1922	Q0.35	3-5-75	2-10	0.35	1.40	1.40	102.	1218	688.	12-31-74	269.	...	49775	Mr	2.38	□2.26	2.21	2.40	....	2.44	9 Mo Dec	1.72	1.76	14
15◆	1971	0.30	4-15-75	3-21	0.59	1.20	[54]1.06	Equity per shr $5.52			12-31-74	156.	...	5675	Sp	□0.35	△0.40	0.55	0.77	0.93	0.96	3 Mo Dec	0.21	0.24	15
16	.....	None Paid			....	Nil	....	3.42	16.9	8.83	8-31-74	23.6	...	2005	Au	0.85	0.93	□0.90	0.87	0.90	0.71	3 Mo Nov	0.22	0.03	16
17	1974	0.05	5-1-74	3-26	....	0.10	0.05	....	25.4	17.7	7-31-74	4.05	...	2370	Jl	0.12	0.26	0.45	0.53	•0.50	0.08	6 Mo Jan△	0.67	0.25	17
18	1974	Q0.10	2-7-75	1-21	0.10	0.40	0.40	14.2	90.7	34.7	12-28-74	127.	...	1557	Dc	□d2.09	•△1.01	•△1.21	•1.79	•[55]5.87	5.87				18
19	.....	Terms&trad.basis should be checked in detail						Cash or 7% Deb '94				....	...	6636	Co can reduce pur price temp periods							Warrants expire 1-31-79			19
20	.....	None Paid			....	[56]Nil	....	0.33	24.1	13.2	12-31-73	13.8	168	1993	Dc	□0.48	□0.93	•△1.07	d0.64	....	d2.09	9 Mo Sep	0.07	■d1.38	20
21◆	.....	2%Stk	5-31-74	4-29	....	Stk	2%Stk	22.7	237.	64.9	2-28-74	143.	520	p7060	Fb	△0.47	△0.57	1.08	1.78	E1.75	1.90	9 Mo Nov	1.43	1.55	21
22	1967	Q0.75	3-14-75	2-25	0.75	3.00	3.00	Conv into 0.76½ shrs common				....	520	...	Fb	8.58	10.39	16.80	26.82	....	....				22
23	.....	None Paid			....	Nil	....	3.20	20.6	6.15	10-31-74	14.4	...	2367	Oc	□d3.83	□d1.62	□d1.07	•0.74	•[59]0.97	1.02	3 Mo Jan△	•0.18	0.23	23
24	1972	Q0.03½	2-3-75	1-14	0.03½	0.24	†0.24	0.54	49.8	11.2	12-31-74	14.8	...	2620	Mr	0.87	1.02	□1.15	ʃ[60]1.25	....	1.20	9 Mo Dec	0.90	0.85	24
25	1898	Q0.30	5-1-75	4-4	0.60	1.20	1.11	n/a	698.	429.	11-24-74	296.	...	23855	My	□1.88	1.98	□2.37	2.81	ʃ3.18	3.46	9 Mo Feb△	2.51	2.79	25
26	1915	0.60	3-10-75	2-6	0.60	2.40	3.40	1338	11645	6103	12-31-74	★1477	2836	287617	Dc	2.09	6.72	7.51	8.34	3.27	3.27				26
27	1930	Q1.25	5-1-75	4-1	2.50	5.00	5.00	...	...	...		....	1836	...	Dc	214.8	682.6	762.7	845.7	335.0	....				27
28	1947	Q0.93¾	5-1-75	4-1	1.87½	3.75	3.75	...				....	1000	...	Dc	214.8	682.6	762.7	845.7	335.0	....				28
29	1947	Q0.20	3-10-75	2-7	0.20	0.80	0.80	8.18	47.2	21.4	12-31-73	★56.4	...	6800	Dc	1.40	1.61	1.65	0.88	P0.26	0.26				29
30	1942	Q0.42	2-26-75	1-20	0.42	1.68	[61]1.68	55.6	233.	116.	12-31-74	1821	[62]362	★49658	Dc	1.80	2.08	2.21	2.25	△2.25	2.34	12 Mo Feb△	2.19	2.34	30
31	.....	None Paid			....	Nil	....	0.46	28.7	19.2	12-31-73	5.32	★200	1647	Dc	0.85	0.31	0.56	ʃ0.36	P0.44	0.44				31
32	1974	0.10	4-1-75	3-5	0.10	0.40	0.10	11.5	103.	43.9	12-31-73	22.7	52	3798	Dc	•1.08	□d0.01	•△0.28	•0.80	P•2.50	2.50				32
33◆	1934	Q0.10	3-28-75	3-14	0.10	0.40	0.40	Equity per sh $49.07			12-31-73	23.6	...	5445	Dc	3.85	□5.59	□6.09	□7.02	P□5.93	5.93				33
34	.....	None Paid			....	Nil	....	0.93	16.0	10.3	6-30-74	4.99	...	1068	Je	□0.38	□0.67	0.80	0.94	d1.40	d1.48	6 Mo Dec	0.07	d0.01	34
35	.....	0.01	9-10-73	8-27	....	Nil	....	0.55	...	...	10-31-73	2.70	180	3098	Oc	d0.75	□d0.69	△d0.40	0.06	Pd0.33	d0.33				35
36◆	1951	Q0.20	4-5-75	3-14	s0.39	0.80	s0.752	2.29	9.17	3.86	12-31-73	★5.62	...	1912	Dc	0.86	△1.23	1.75	1.81	P1.30	1.30				36
37◆	1940	Q0.19	4-1-75	3-4	0.38	0.76	0.70	16.0	260.	103.	12-31-74	56.1	...	7617	Dc	1.78	2.12	2.40	2.51	2.71	2.71				37
38	.....	0.10	9-30-70	9-14	....	Nil	....	3.76	27.8	11.4	12-31-74	15.9	...	2519	Dc	□d0.91	d3.46[63]	□d2.02	•0.60	•0.94	0.94				38
39	1945	Q0.22½	5-1-75	4-2	0.45	0.90	0.90	n/a	118.	106.	12-31-74	891.	2999	24500	Dc	15.13	17.60	20.04	21.35	25.70	....				39
40	1959	Q0.32½	5-15-75	4-21	0.65	1.30	1.30	4.82	69.2	52.8	10-31-74	★597.	±1280	12200	Dc	20.99	28.58	32.65	14.50	23.98	....				40
41	1961	Q0.31¼	5-15-75	4-21	0.62½	1.25	1.25	...	...	...		....	400	...	Dc	20.99	28.58	32.65	14.50	23.98	....				41
42	1973	Q2.04	5-15-75	4-21	4.08	8.16	8.16	Red restr (8.16%) to 8-1-78				....	400	...	Dc	....	....	....	14.50	....	....				42
43	1936	Q0.45	4-1-75	2-13	0.90	1.80	1.74	178.	2227	2770	12-31-74	4866	★6005	126442	Dc	□2.02	2.35	2.58	2.86	[66]2.13	2.13				43
44	1967	Q0.62½	4-1-75	2-13	1.25	2.50	2.50	Conv into 0.95 to '77,then 0.81				....	453	...	Dc	....	....	....	....	....	....				44

◆ **Stock Splits & Divs By Line Reference Index** [1]2-for-1,'71. [6]3-for-2,'71. [7]Adj to 2%,'72. [9]Vote on 1-for-7 reverse split. [10]2-for-1,'71. [11]Adj to 5%,'74. [14]2-for-1,'71. [15]2-for-1,'72. [21]Adj to 2%,'74. [33]5-for-2,'71:2-for-1,'73. [36]Adj to 5%,'75. [37]2-for-1,'71.

Source: Standard & Poor's Corporation, *Stock Guide*, April 1975, pp. 92–93.

FIGURE 4–6
Standard & Poor's Listed Stock Report—Page 1

GM[1] **General Motors** 978

Stock—	Price Mar. 21'75	Dividend	Yield
COMMON	43	[2]$2.40	[2]5.6%
$5 PREFERRED	67¾	5.00	7.4
$3.75 PREFERRED	51⅛	3.75	7.3

RECOMMENDATION: This giant, financially strong company normally accounts for slightly more than half of all the automobiles assembled in the U. S. Except in strike-distorted 1970, earnings had exceeded $5.50 a share in every year for more than a decade until 1974 profits fell 60% below the 1973 peak because of the gasoline situation, consumer recession-inflation concern, and a cost-price squeeze. Earnings will remain depressed in 1975, and the dividend has been reduced. Even so, the COMMON is attractively priced as an investment based on probable average earning power in the years ahead. The PREFERREDS are high-grade income issues.

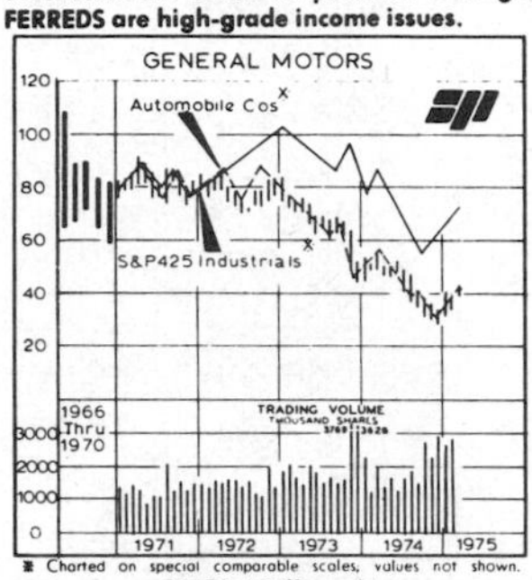

* Charted on special comparable scales; values not shown.

SALES (Million $)

Quarter:	1974	1973	1972	1971	1970
March	6,939	9,569	7,780	7,780	5,579
June	8,277	9,606	8,457	7,592	6,624
Sept.	6,938	7,608	5,378	5,624	3,592
Dec.........	9,396	9,015	8,820	7,268	2,957

Sales for 1974 fell 11.9% from those in 1973 on a 23% drop in worldwide sales of cars and trucks. Motor vehicle assemblies in the U. S. alone were down 29%. The lower unit volume, rapidly rising wage, materials, and other costs that were not nearly offset by price increases, and a greater percentage of less profitable small cars in the sales mix hurt results, more than offsetting benefits from cost-cutting measures and from reduced depreciation and tooling amortization charges. Pretax profits declined 63%. After taxes at 43.4%, versus 46.9%, net income was down 60%. For 1974's final quarter, profits were off 1.8%, year to year, on a 4.2% sales gain.

[3]COMMON SHARE EARNINGS ($)

Quarter:	1974	1973	1972	1971	1970
March	0.41	2.84	2.26	2.12	1.21
June	1.05	2.78	2.52	1.97	1.64
Sept.	0.05	0.92	0.41	0.75	d0.28
Dec.........	1.76	1.80	2.32	1.88	d0.48

PROSPECTS

Near Term—Dollar sales for 1975 appear likely to exceed the reduced $31.6 billion of 1974, even though industrywide domestic unit sales of automobiles and trucks should be below the depressed level of 1974. Price increases averaging 8.2% on cars and 10.9% on trucks on the 1975 models will boost dollar sales, and GM's share of the total U. S. automobile market may recover, helped by the introduction of several new luxury-type 1975-model subcompact cars. Overseas volume would respond to any improvement in the economies of major foreign countries.

A better balance between price increases and rising materials, wage, and other costs is expected during 1975 than that which prevailed in 1974, and the company will step up its efforts to raise operating efficiency. Accordingly, some recovery in 1975 profits may be attained from the depressed $3.27 a share of 1974. The interim dividend was reduced to $0.60, from $0.85, with the March 10, 1975, payment.

Long Term—Allowing for interim fluctuations, an outstanding trade position points to some long-range growth, assuming satisfactory gasoline supplies and prices.

RECENT DEVELOPMENTS

Capital expenditures rose to a new peak of $1.46 billion in 1974 and are expected to approximate $1.4 billion in 1975. Depreciation charges were $847 million in 1974 and should be moderately higher in 1975.

GM has postponed offering the Wankel rotary engine in one of its small cars.

DIVIDEND DATA

Payments in the past 12 months were:

Amt. of Divd. $	Date Decl.	Ex-divd. Date	Stock of Record	Payment Date
0.85...	May 6	May 10	May 16	Jun. 10'74
0.85...	Aug. 5	Aug. 9	Aug. 15	Sep. 10'74
0.85 Y-E	Nov. 4	Nov. 7	Nov. 14	Dec. 10'74
0.60...	Feb. 3	Feb. 6	Feb. 13	Mar. 10'75

[1]Listed N.Y.S.E.; com. & $5 pfd. also listed Midwest, PBW & Pacific S.Es.; com. also listed Detroit S.E. & traded Boston & Cincinnati S.Es. [2]Annual rate based on latest payment. [3]Based on avge. shs. d Deficit.

STANDARD N.Y.S.E. STOCK REPORTS STANDARD & POOR'S CORP.

Published at Ephrata, Pa. Editorial & Executive Offices, 345 Hudson St., New York, N.Y. 10014
Vol. 42, No. 60 Thursday, March 27, 1975 Sec. 12

Some firms publish several types of market reports. Research information is usually free for the asking to investors although a few houses have initiated charges recently. This trend will be discussed in a section on *Unbundling*.

Many firms also make available financial data which are assembled by other agencies. Some give out the Standard & Poor's *Stock Guide*.

FIGURE 4–7
Standard & Poor's Listed Stock Report—Page 2

978 GENERAL MOTORS CORPORATION

[1]INCOME STATISTICS (Million $) AND PER SHARE ($) DATA

Year Ended Dec. 31	Net Sales	[3]% Op. Inc. of Sales	[3]Oper. Inc.	Depr. Amort. & Obsol.	Net bef. Taxes	Net Income	Common Share ($) Data: [4]Earns.	*Funds Generated	Divs. Paid	Price Range	Price-Earns. Ratios HI LO
1975--	-----	---	----	----	----	----	---	----	0.60	45⅞-31¼	-----
1974--	31,550	7.6	2,403	846.6	1,677	950	3.27	6.60	3.40	55½-28⅞	17- 9
1973--	35,798	14.4	5,162	902.9	4,513	2,398	8.34	10.97	5.25	84⅝-44⅞	10- 5
1972--	30,435	16.3	4,960	912.4	4,223	2,163	7.51	10.36	4.45	84¾-71¼	11- 9
1971--	28,264	16.0	4,529	873.1	3,720	1,936	6.72	9.20	3.40	91⅛-73⅜	14-11
1970--	18,752	7.9	1,488	821.5	794	609	2.09	4.82	3.40	81⅜-59½	39-28
1969--	24,295	16.7	4,067	765.8	3,454	1,711	5.95	8.49	4.30	83⅜-65½	14-11
1968--	22,755	18.1	4,124	729.1	3,525	1,732	6.02	8.57	4.30	89⅞-72⅝	15-12
1967--	20,026	18.0	3,613	712.6	3,013	1,627	5.66	8.19	3.80	89⅜-67½	16-12
1966--	20,209	18.7	3,770	654.1	3,271	1,793	6.24	8.64	4.55	108¼-65⅝	17-11
1965--	20,734	21.6	4,483	556.7	4,092	2,126	7.41	9.47	5.25	113¾-91¼	15-12

[1]PERTINENT BALANCE SHEET STATISTICS (Million $)

Dec. 31	Gross Prop.	[2]Capital Expend.	[5]Cash Items	Inventories	Receivables	Current Assets	Current [5]Liabs.	Net Workg. Cap.	Cur. Ratio Assets to Liabs.	Long Term Debt	($) Book Val. Com. Sh.
1974--	17,626	1,458.5	1,338.4	6,404.7	3,000.8	11,644.8	6,102.8	5,541.9	1.9-1	876.56	43.01
1973--	16,197	1,163.4	3,046.1	5,176.9	3,082.5	12,166.5	5,969.7	6,196.9	2.0-1	756.52	43.00
1972--	15,469	940.0	2,946.9	4,200.2	2,806.2	10,538.5	4,973.7	5,564.8	2.1-1	790.88	39.85
1971--	14,939	1,013.0	3,342.1	3,991.6	2,724.2	10,536.7	6,006.3	4,530.4	1.8-1	615.62	36.70
1970--	14,528	1,134.2	394.1	4,115.1	1,725.7	6,491.9	3,224.4	3,267.6	2.0-1	281.22	33.39
1969--	13,211	1,043.8	1,824.4	3,760.5	2,112.7	7,697.6	3,345.6	4,352.0	2.3-1	316.99	34.64
1968--	12,422	860.2	1,898.2	3,423.3	2,013.9	7,335.4	3,105.2	4,230.3	2.4-1	284.28	32.96
1967--	11,761	912.6	1,802.5	3,210.4	1,833.6	6,846.5	2,840.1	4,006.4	2.4-1	344.83	31.17
1966--	11,012	1,188.1	1,951.0	3,103.3	1,657.5	6,711.8	3,105.8	3,606.0	2.2-1	287.46	29.27
1965--	9,982	1,322.0	1,387.2	2,986.5	1,538.7	5,912.5	2,227.6	3,684.9	2.7-1	231.66	27.47

[1]Data for 1973 as originally reported; data for each yr. prior to 1973 as taken from subsequent yr.'s Annual Report; incl. all subs. engaged in mfg. or wholesale marketing opers.; does not incl. G.M. Acceptance Corp. & Yellow Mfg. Acceptance or their subs. [2]Excl. additions for spec. tools. [3]Bef. depr., but aft. amort. of special tools & employee bonus. [4]Based on avge. shs. outstanding. [5]Aft. deducting gov't. sec. held for payment of taxes in 1965. [6]Note: During 1970 operations were affected by a 9 week strike.

*As computed by Standard & Poor's.

Fundamental Position

General Motors in 1974 derived 90.1% of U. S. sales from automotive products (including cars, trucks, buses, parts, and accesories) 8.5% from non-automotive products (including Frigidaire appliances, diesel and aircraft engines, locomotives, and earth-moving equipment), and 1.4% from defense and space work.

Chevrolet (including the Chevelle, Camaro, Nova, Monte Carlo, Corvette, Vega, and Monza), Buick (including Century, Apollo, Riviera, and Skyhawk), Cadillac (including the Eldorado), Oldsmobile (including Cutlass, Toronado, Omega, and Starfire), and Pontiac (including LeMans, Firebird, Grand Prix, Astre, and Ventura) accounted for 41.9% of total new U. S. registrations (including foreign-built cars) in 1974, compared with 44.3% in 1973. Comparable figures for Chevrolet and GMC trucks are 39.3% and 39.8%. General Motors has about 11,860 U. S. car dealers. Worldwide factory sales of cars and trucks in 1974 were 6,690,000 units, compared with 8,684,000 in 1973 and 7,791,000 in 1972. Domestic factory sales were 4,678,000, 6,512,000, and 5,741,000, respectively.

The company has about 169 plants, of which 111 are in the U. S., seven in Canada, and the remainder in 51 other countries. GM also has partial ownership of a number of companies with overseas plants. Before elimination of inter-company sales, GM in 1974 derived 73% of worldwide dollar sales and 89% (81% automotive and 8% other products) of total net income from the U. S., 10% and 11%, respectively, from Canada, and 17% and 0% from other foreign countries. Investments in non-consolidated subsidiaries, principally General Motors Acceptance Corp., totaled $1.42 billion at the end of 1974. GMAC earned $106 million in 1974.

Dividends, paid since 1917, averaged 71% of available earnings in the five years through 1974.

Employees (worldwide): 734,000. Shareholders (common and preferred): 1,348,000.

Finances

Giving effect to the March, 1975, sale of $300,000,000 of 8.05% notes due 1985 and $300,000,000 of 8⅝% debentures due 2005 for working capital, special tools, and other capital expenditures, capitalization was 10.5% long-term debt and 89.5% shareholders' equity.

CAPITALIZATION

LONG TERM DEBT: $1,476,564,000, incl. $754,000,000 foreign subsidiary debt.

$5 CUM. PREFERRED STOCK: 1,835,644 shares (no par); redeemable at $120.

$3.75 CUM. PREFERRED STOCK: 1,000,000 shs. (no par); redeemable at $100.

COMMON STOCK: 287,617,041 shs. ($1 2/3 par).

Incorporated in Del. in 1916. **Office**—3044 W. Grand Blvd., Detroit, Mich. 48202. **Chairman & Chief Exec Officer**—T. A. Murphy. **Pres**—E. M. Estes. **Secy**—C. Thomas. **Treas**—F. A. Smith. **Dirs**—T. A. Murphy (Chrmn), E. N. Beesely, H. Branch, Jr., C. B. Cleary, J. T. Connor, E. M. Estes, W. A. Fallon, C. T. Fisher, III, R. C. Gerstenberg, R. S. Hatfield, R. R. Jensen, H. H. Kehrl, J. R. Killlan, Jr., O. A. Lundin, J. A. Mayer, E. J. McDonald, W. E. McLaughlin, H. J. Morgens, E. C. Patterson, J. M. Roche, S. L. Sibley, G. A. Sivage, R. B. Smith, L. H. Sullivan, R. L. Terrell, C. H. Townes. **Transfer Agents**—Company's Offices—767 Fifth Ave., NYC; 3044 W. Grand Blvd., Detroit, Mich. **Registrar**—Chase Manhattan Bank, NYC.

Information has been obtained from sources believed to be reliable, but its accuracy and completeness, and that of the opinions based thereon, are not guaranteed. Printed in U. S. A.

This monthly publication is one of the broadest compilations of security information available. Figure 4–5 shows a sample page from this source. Copies of this pamphlet are found in most offices. Standard & Poor's also publishes *Listed Stock Reports* and *O-T-C Reports*. These materials provide a summary of financial histories and current developments of thousands of firms. They are updated several times a

FIGURE 4–8
New York Stock Exchange Ticker Quotations

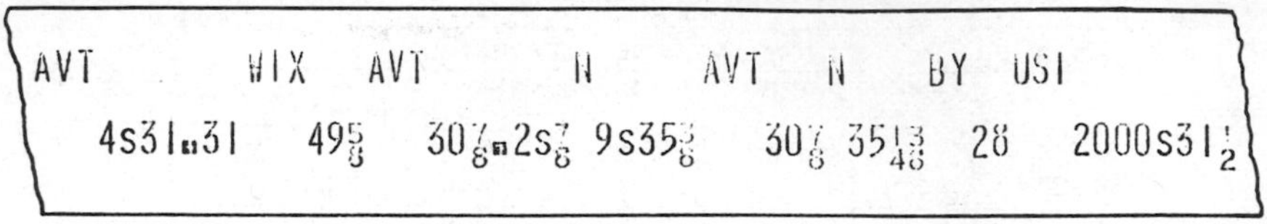

year and are available in many brokerage offices. A sample of one of these reports is shown in Figures 4–6 and 4–7.

Price Quotations

Another important function of brokerage firms is to provide current price information. This service yields up-to-the-minute quotations by a variety of methods.

Ticker Tapes. Offices of firms who are members of one or more stock exchanges usually have a "ticker" to receive trading data. The information is printed on a paper tape. A sample from the NYSE is reproduced in Figure 4–8. Abbreviations of the companies whose stock has been traded appear in the top row—AVT, WIX, N, BY, and USI are symbols for Avnet, Inc., The Wickes Corporation, International Nickel Company, Bucyrus-Erie Co., and U.S. Industries, respectively. One- to three-letter abbreviations are assigned to each issue listed. Usually the name of the company is obvious from the symbol used, but there are many exceptions, for example X stands for U.S. Steel. The bottom row on the tape indicates the number of shares and the prices at which they were traded. For example, 4s31.31 means 400 shares of Avnet exchanged hands at $31 per share followed immediately by a 100-share trade also at $31 per share. By convention, only the prices of 100-share transactions are shown. Also odd-lot trades are not recorded on the tape. The next activity in Avnet was 100 shares at $30⅞ followed by 200 shares at the same price. The second transaction recorded for International Nickel involved two round lots at prices of $35¼ and $35⅜, respectively. The largest trade shown in Figure 4–8 was 2,000 shares of U.S. Industries at $31½.

Most brokerage offices have equipment called *Transjet, Teletrade,* and so on, which projects the ticker tape data onto a large screen that can then be seen by many people simultaneously. Brokers and some investors watch this data so they can be current on trading activity.

FIGURE 4–9
Electronic Quotation Machine

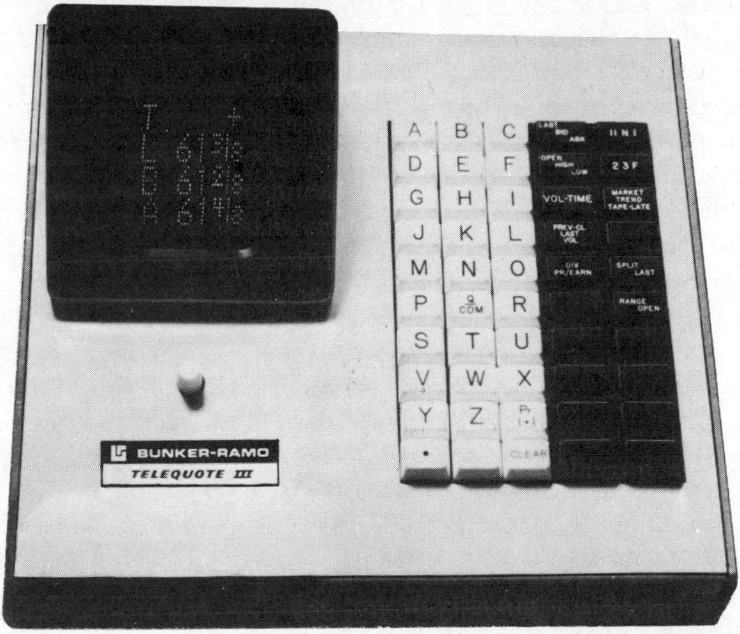

Courtesy of the Bunker-Ramo Corporation.

Quotation Devices. Several electronics firms offer equipment to provide trading information at the fingertips of brokers around the country. An example of one device is shown in Figure 4–9. This desk-top machine makes available on a TV-like screen up-to-the-second market information on thousands of different issues, both listed and OTC. Brokers press letter keys for the stock symbol and one of several other buttons for information on stock price, volume, earnings, and dividends. They can also get market averages and other statistics such as the ten stocks which have advanced, declined, or traded most actively up to the time when the inquiry is made. Some brokerage offices have a service known as *Market Decision System* 7. This information retrieval machine offers, in addition to all the features described above, capability to supply material from an extensive statistical data base containing most of the facts and figures influencing the value of all types of securities. The user can access news from leading financial publications. Detailed records on commodities are also available instantly. Applications of the electronics age make the information retrieval systems in the securities business very impressive indeed.

Other Services

A trip to almost any brokerage office will quickly reveal the emphasis placed on service to investors. In addition to research provided by the firms, most offices have a library of data sources and a room where the investor can do analysis work. Many financial publications are much too expensive for the average investor to purchase. Access to them and a vast array of other data can be highly beneficial to individuals who like to do their own research.

Most brokerage firms will store securities for their clients if this is desired. Some brokers offer free aid in transferring stock in the settlement of estates. They will also arrange to collect dividends and interest and redistribute them to an investor upon request. Loans for buying securities can be arranged through brokerage firms.[10] Interest is charged on the money borrowed, but until recently this is just about the only service outside of buying and selling securities for which a fee is collected.

Unbundling. The securities industry faced many challenges in the first part of the 1970s. One of the responses has been a recognition that fees for brokerage services should be adjusted to better reflect actual costs. This has resulted in brokerage firms offering a variety of plans under which they will transact business for their clients. One arrangement involves trading on a "no frills" basis. In these instances, investors' orders are executed for lower commissions but they are not entitled to other services without paying for them directly. Other plans include a package of services such as research reports, tax advice, and so on, and perhaps some discount on commissions. Investors pay a regular fee for these plans. One of the extensive-type programs available includes the right to receive discounts on car rentals. Investors should be aware of the existence of these options and determine just what services they do and do not need. This knowledge will help them be assured that they are not paying for more than they need.

Choosing a Broker

In many ways the task of choosing a broker is more difficult than selecting a personal physician. Doctors usually practice individually or

---

[10] The procedures involved in borrowing money for the *margin* accounts are discussed in Chapter 3.

they join with several others in a clinic. Brokers are almost always a part of an organization which may be nationwide and have thousands of employees. The problem of choosing a broker is really twofold. First, a firm must be selected and then a particular registered representative with that firm's office is chosen.[11]

Selecting a Brokerage Firm. There are around 3,500 different brokerage firms in the United States.[12] These vary considerably in their organization, clientele, and services offered. For example, some firms concentrate on OTC issues. They are usually not members of any exchange, although they can buy and sell listed securities through correspondent relationships with member brokerage firms. The OTC houses, or regional houses as they are often called, may do considerable research into small companies located within their areas. Some firms, both those having exchange memberships and those who do not, do a relatively large amount of underwriting. This means investors interested in new issues would be likely to do business with them. A few firms avoid underwriting activities because they feel they can better serve their clients if they act strictly as agents and do not try to sell issues that they own themselves.

Some firms do a considerable business in mutual funds and in buying and selling commodities futures. Others do not handle these forms of investments. Some firms will not place orders for low-priced, speculative issues, while others make this an important part of their business. A few firms discourage small accounts, while others actively solicit business regardless of the financial capacity of the investor. Policies of the firms can be learned by talking to an office manager or to one of the brokers.

In addition to types of securities which are handled, the services offered by the firms and the amounts and ways of charging for them vary considerably. A complete line of services like those described in this chapter would require a central office staff of several hundred people. Many firms employ the required personnel and have a hundred or more offices with thousands of brokers scattered throughout

---

[11] In many cases brokers "find" investors rather than the reverse. This often happens when a broker is aggressively seeking new customers and is out soliciting their business. This section describes the situation of an investor searching for a broker.

[12] The National Association of Security Dealers had 3,166 member firms at the end of 1974. Recall that the NASD is the self-regulatory body of the securities industry. Its membership includes the vast majority of the industry. Only a few, usually local and newly formed firms, are not NASD members. The NASD includes all members of the New York Stock Exchange, which had 508 member organizations as of the end of 1974.

the world. Many investors do not need all of the services offered by a large firm and choose to do business with a small brokerage house. For example, a library of financial information is a must for some investors but is rarely used by others.

Perhaps a factor of dominant influence in the selection of a brokerage firm is its accessibility to the investor. It is often desirable to be able to personally visit the office so one that is conveniently located may be of major importance. However, many individuals do all of their business by phone, and proximity to the office is not necessary. In fact, some investors deal with firms hundreds or thousands of miles away. Virtually every section of the United States is served from about 10,000 brokerage offices staffed with over 200,000 registered representatives.

Finding a Broker. After a securities firm has been selected, the investor must decide on a particular broker in that office. Personalities often play a large role in this decision. A major factor is that the investor should have the same kind of confidence in a broker as in other professional people such as a doctor, dentist, or lawyer. Age of the professional is important to some individuals. Some like older brokers who have lived through many market ups and downs. Others prefer youthful vigor, especially when it represents the new ideas and thoughts of "Wall Street." A conservative investor might seek a broker who has similar views.[13]

The training of brokers varies considerably among different firms and to a much lesser extent within the same firm. Some brokerage houses require their representatives to take part in a formal training program that lasts for six months or longer. Other firms have a much less ambitious program and rely heavily on the individual to develop the required background independently. All securities sales personnel must be licensed by the state and also by the federal authorities if the firm does interstate business. The licensing procedure usually involves demonstration of character and passing an examination covering the securities business.

After a firm and a particular registered representative have been selected, the investor may become dissatisfied for one reason or another such as losing money. A common solution is to switch brokers,

---

[13] An interesting study of psychological factors involved in the broker-client relationship indicated that retiring and conservative investors often want strong-willed brokers. One firm tried using personality tests to avoid mismatching customers and brokers after the study showed that 30 percent of investors sampled were unhappy with their brokers. See *The Wall Steet Journal*, June 24, 1970, p. 19.

but this may not solve the problem.[14] No securities firm or broker can consistently advise when to buy securities at their lowest points and to sell them at their highest prices, just as no baseball player can hit a home run every time at bat. Much of the anxiety and unhappiness caused by making poor investments can be avoided by realizing that brokers, for the most part, are trying to do the best possible job they can. They want nothing more than to help their clients make money.

On the other hand, since brokers earn commissions whenever securities are bought or sold, they have an incentive to urge greater investment activity than might be the case if they were paid on some other basis, such as a straight salary. This is one of the reasons why many organizations sell advice to investors but do not engage in any brokerage business. These firms point out that by separating the advising and brokerage functions their recommendations will never be influenced by the amount of commissions which might be forthcoming. Advisory services are discussed in the next section.

Brokers categorically deny any undue pressure to advise buying or selling just to generate commissions, but the investor should be aware of the incentive and reward system under which registered representatives earn their livings. The profession of selling securities is like any other; unethical or questionable practices are sometimes committed.

After repeated experiences of buying and selling too soon or too late, or if it appears that a broker is applying undue pressure to urge greater trading activity, it may be wise to seek another broker. However, the investor is cautioned that frequent switching will not insure success. Displeasure because of personality clashes can be minimized by discussion with registered representatives before a choice is made.

To be sure, some investors may be well served by simply looking for a firm in the yellow pages, walking into an office, and choosing the broker with the loudest clothing. However, most investors will be better off by considering carefully what they want from a firm and its employees before they make a commitment.

INVESTMENT SERVICES

Brokerage firms still make most of their money by offering free advice and then charging commissions on security transactions. There

---

14 A reportedly true and definitely sad story tells how one investor tried unsuccessfully to reverse his losses by seeking new investment ideas. Perhaps the major reason for the continual drop in his portfolio value was his frequent hopping from one broker to another. See Anonymous investor, *Wiped Out.*

FIGURE 4–10
Investment Advisory Services

are thousands of other organizations which do not buy and sell securities but instead provide information, advice, and other investment services for a fee. The purpose of this section is to describe the variety of services that the investor can purchase.

Information and Advisory Services

Many organizations sell investment information and advice. Sources of data offered by such firms as Standard & Poor's and Moody's have been discussed. These firms also have advisory services that can be subscribed to. Hundreds of other companies offer buy and sell recommendations which are sold by subscription.[15] Figure 4–10 illustrates the nameplates from a number of these services. Some of them concentrate on providing data—such as charts of stock prices—leaving interpretation of the graphs to the investor. Most of the services assemble the information, analyze it, and make recommendations to buy or sell. Often these selections are made in a relative manner, with stocks classified into groups according to their likely performance in the future. Typical titles of advisory reports and the excerpts from advertising used for them are shown in Figure 4–11. This information indicates the wide variety of approaches and objectives used by the advisors. Most of them can be identified as *fundamental* or *technical* services.

Fundamental Advisory Services. These services rely on selecting securities based on the present financial status and likely future developments of the firm. Emphasis is placed on company sales, earnings, dividends, and stock price. An example of this type of report is prepared by Arnold Bernhard & Company and is depicted in Figure 4–12. The page shown includes a considerable amount of information about Safeway Stores. Historical data on financial characteristics and a brief discussion of current news and expected developments are presented. The company is rated on several criteria, and by following instructions provided, anyone can determine how suitable an investment this stock would be at the time the report was published.[16]

Value Line offers a regular review of essentially the same group of better known companies. They also write up "Special Situations" which arise on an intermittent basis. This type of recommendation is used by many investment services offices. That is, the advisor follows a large group of stocks but reports only on those which warrant buy

---

[15] One publication gives brief descriptions of over 500 investment services. See Select Information Exchange, *1975 Investment Sources and Ideas* (New York: George H. Wein, 1975).

[16] Details of this procedure are found at the beginning of each report. They are not reproduced here because this example is used for illustration purposes only. The *Value Line Investment Survey* is published weekly. This service evaluates 1,400 of the best-known common stocks, and the report for each company is updated and distributed four times a year.

FIGURE 4–11
Advisory Services Reports

or sell action. These publications are quite similar to market letters issued by brokerage firms.

Advisory Services Using Technical Analysis. Another approach to recommending security purchases or sales is used by a group called *technical analysts*. They believe that the key to investing profits can

FIGURE 4–12
Value Line Stock Report

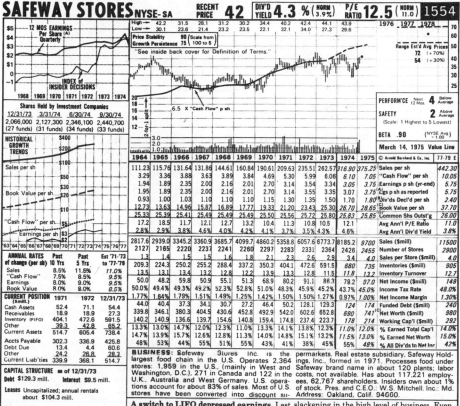

SAFEWAY STORES NYSE-SA | RECENT PRICE **42** | DIV'D YIELD **4.3** % (NORM 3.9%) | P/E RATIO **12.5** (NORM 11.0) | **1554**

High →	42.2	31.5	28.1	31.2	30.2	34.4	40.2	42.4	44.1	43.9
Low →	30.1	23.6	21.4	23.2	23.5	22.1	32.1	34.0	27.3	29.6

Price Stability 90, Growth Persistence 75 (Scale from 100 to 5)

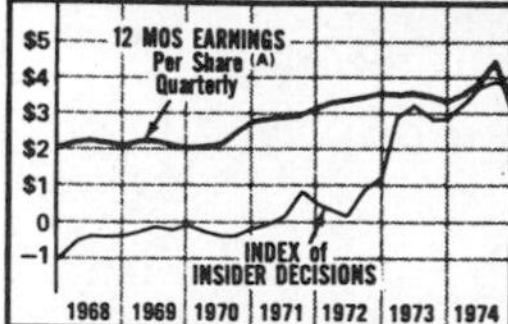

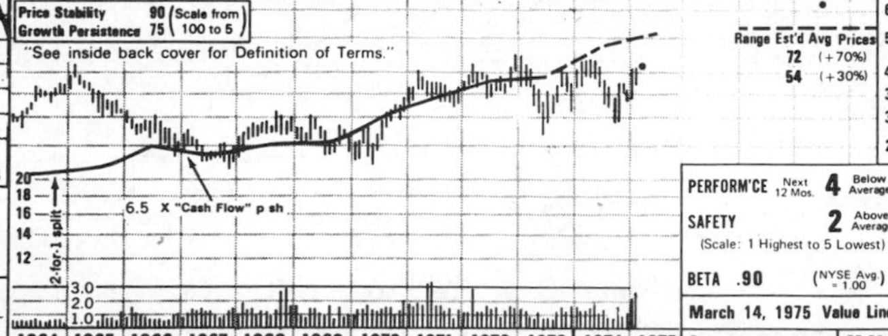

Shares Held by Investment Companies

12/31/73	3/31/74	6/30/74	9/30/74
2,066,000	2,127,300	2,346,100	2,440,700
(27 funds)	(31 funds)	(34 funds)	(33 funds)

PERFORM'CE Next 12 Mos. **4** Below Average
SAFETY **2** Above Average
(Scale: 1 Highest to 5 Lowest)
BETA **.90** (NYSE Avg. = 1.00)
March 14, 1975 Value Line

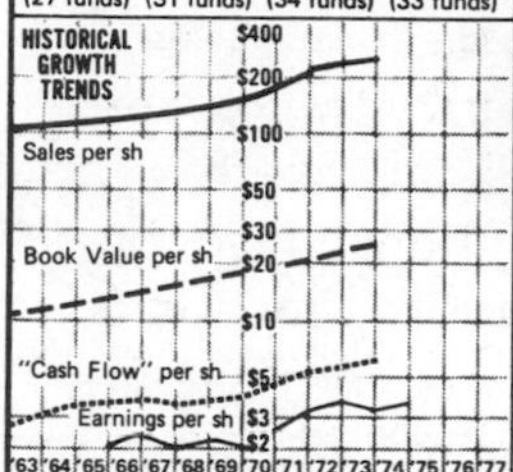

1964	1965	1966	1967	1968	1969	1970	1971	1972	1973	1974	1975	© Arnold Bernhard & Co., Inc.	77-79 E
111.23	115.76	131.64	131.86	144.61	160.84	190.61	209.63	235.51	262.57	*316.90*	*375.25*	Sales per sh	*442.30*
3.29	3.36	3.88	3.63	3.89	3.84	4.69	5.30	5.99	6.06	*6.10*	*7.05*	"Cash Flow" per sh	*10.05*
1.94	1.89	2.35	2.00	2.16	2.01	2.70	3.14	3.54	3.34	*3.05*	*3.75*	Earnings p sh (yr-end)	*5.75*
1.95	1.89	2.35	2.00	2.16	2.01	2.70	3.14	3.55	3.35	3.07	*3.75*	(A) Egs p sh as reported	*5.75*
0.93	1.00	1.03	1.10	1.10	1.10	1.15	1.30	1.35	1.50	1.70	*1.80*	(B) Div'ds Decl'd per sh	*2.40*
12.73	13.63	14.96	15.87	16.89	17.77	19.33	21.20	23.43	25.30	*26.70*	*28.65*	(C) Book Value per sh	*37.70*
25.33	25.39	25.41	25.49	25.49	25.49	25.50	25.56	25.72	25.80	*25.83*	*25.85*	(D) Common Shs Outst'g	*26.00*
17.2	18.5	11.7	12.1	12.7	13.2	10.4	11.3	10.8	10.5	12.1		Avg Ann'l P/E Ratio	*11.0*
2.8%	2.9%	3.8%	4.6%	4.0%	4.2%	4.1%	3.7%	3.5%	4.3%	4.6%		Avg Ann'l Div'd Yield	*3.8%*
2817.6	2939.0	3345.2	3360.9	3685.7	4099.7	4860.2	5358.8	6057.6	6773.7	8185.2	*9700*	Sales ($mill)	*11500*
2127	2165	2220	2237	2241	2260	2297	2283	2331	2364	2426	*2455*	Number of Stores	*2900*
1.3	1.4	1.5	1.5	1.6	1.8	2.1	2.3	2.6	2.9	3.4	*4.0*	Sales per Store ($mill)	*4.0*
209.3	224.3	250.2	255.2	288.4	337.2	350.3	404.1	472.6	591.5	*680*	*735*	Inventories ($mill)	*905*
13.5	13.1	13.4	13.2	12.8	12.2	13.9	13.3	12.8	11.5	*11.8*	*13.2*	Inventory Turnover	*12.7*
50.0	48.2	59.8	50.9	55.1	51.3	68.9	80.2	91.1	86.3	78.2	*97.0*	Net Income ($mill)	*149*
50.0%	49.4%	49.3%	49.2%	52.3%	52.8%	51.0%	48.3%	45.9%	45.2%	43.7%	*45.0%*	Income Tax Rate	*48.0%*
1.77%	1.64%	1.79%	1.51%	1.49%	1.25%	1.42%	1.50%	1.50%	1.27%	0.97%	*1.00%*	Net Income Margin	*1.30%*
44.0	40.4	37.3	34.1	30.7	27.2	46.4	50.2	128.1	129.3	*124*	*174*	Funded Debt ($mill)	*240*
339.8	346.1	380.3	404.5	430.6	452.8	492.9	542.0	602.6	652.8	*690*	*741*	(C) Net Worth ($mill)	*980*
140.2	140.9	136.6	139.7	154.6	140.8	159.4	174.8	237.4	223.7	*178*	*214*	Working Cap'l ($mill)	*292*
13.3%	13.0%	14.7%	12.0%	12.3%	11.0%	13.3%	14.1%	13.8%	12.3%	*11.0%*	*12.0%*	% Earned Total Cap'l	*14.0%*
14.7%	13.9%	15.7%	12.6%	12.8%	11.3%	14.0%	14.8%	15.1%	13.2%	*11.5%*	*13.0%*	% Earned Net Worth	*15.0%*
48%	53%	44%	55%	51%	55%	43%	41%	38%	45%	55%	*48%*	% All Div'ds to Net Inc	*42%*

ANNUAL RATES of change (per sh)	Past 10 Yrs	Past 5 Yrs	Est '71-'73 to '77-'79
Sales	8.5%	11.5%	*11.0%*
"Cash Flow"	7.5%	8.5%	*9.5%*
Earnings	8.0%	9.0%	*9.5%*
Book Value	8.0%	8.0%	*8.5%*

CURRENT POSITION ($mill.)	1971	1972	12/31/73
Cash Assets	52.4	71.1	54.4
Receivables	18.9	18.9	27.3
Inventory (FIFO)	404.1	472.6	591.5
Other	39.3	42.8	65.2
Current Assets	514.7	605.4	738.4
Accts Payable	302.3	336.9	425.8
Debt Due	13.4	4.4	60.6
Other	24.2	26.8	28.3
Current Liab'ties	339.9	368.1	514.7

CAPITAL STRUCTURE as of 12/31/73
Debt $129.3 mill. **Interest** $9.5 mill.
Leases Uncapitalized; annual rentals about $104.3 mill.

Pension Liab'ty None
Pfd Stock None **Pfd Div** None

Common Stock 25,797,225 shares

Cal-endar	QUARTERLY SALES ($ Millions) Mar. 31	June 30	Sept. 30	Dec. 31	Full Year
1971	1173	1217	1261	1708	5359
1972	1326	1375	1423	1934	6058
1973	1469	1520	1615	2170	6774
1974	1731	1835	1950	2669	8185
1975	*2050*	*2200*	*2350*	*3100*	*9700*

Cal-endar	EARNINGS AS REPORTED (per sh) Mar. 31	June 30	Sept. 30	Dec. 31	(A) Full Year
1971	.56	.72	.76	(E) 1.10	3.14
1972	.70	.81	.80	1.24	3.55
1973	.70	.85	.64	1.16	3.35
1974	.57 (F)	.73 (F)	.86 (F)	.91	3.07
1975	*.75*	*.85*	*.95*	*1.20*	*3.75*

Cal-endar	QUARTERLY DIVIDENDS PAID Mar. 31	June 30	Sept. 30	Dec. 31	(B) Full Year
1971	.325	.325	.325	.325	1.30
1972	.3375	.3375	.3375	.3375	1.35
1973	.35	.35	.40	.40	1.50
1974	.40	.40	.45	.45	1.70
1975	.45				

BUSINESS: Safeway Stores Inc. is the largest food chain in the U.S. Operates 2,364 stores: 1,959 in the U.S., (mainly in West and Washington, D.C.), 271 in Canada and 122 in the U.K., Australia and West Germany. U.S. operations account for about 83% of sales. Most of U.S. stores have been converted into discount supermarkets. Real estate subsidiary, Safeway Holdings, Inc., formed in 1971. Processes food under Safeway brand name in about 120 plants; labor costs, not available. Has about 117,221 employees, 62,767 shareholders. Insiders own about 1% of stock. Pres. and C.E.O.: W.S. Mitchell. Inc.: Md. Address: Oakland, Calif. 94660.

A switch to LIFO depressed earnings. Last month Safeway's management decided to value 56% of its inventory on the more conservative last-in, first-out basis to more truly reflect profits in an inflationary period. The switch was retroactive to the beginning of 1974 and reduced full-year earnings by $42.3 million or $1.64 a share. As a result of this accounting change, Safeway's profits dropped 8% to $3.07 a share. Volume, though, was very strong, climbing 21% to a record $8.19 billion. . . .Excluded from LIFO were nongrocery inventories and all inventories in Canadian and overseas supermarkets. Foreign subsidiaries are not eligible for the tax benefits resulting from a changeover to LIFO. . . . Our 1974 quarterly earnings figures in the box at the left have been restated to reflect the revised profit figures as provided by the company. . . . We have lowered these high-quality shares' ranking to Below Average for year-ahead relative market Performance.

Earnings could rebound in 1975. Worldwide, management has seen no slackening in the high level of business. Even in areas of the U.S. suffering from serious unemployment, Safeway's sales have remained strong, which may suggest that the company is carving out a larger slice of the consumer market. Safeway President Mitchell recently predicted 1975 sales could hit the $10 billion mark. Adopting a more conservative stance, we estimate volume will reach $9.7 billion, up about 18% from 1974. To be sure, a good chunk of the increased sales will be caused by inflation, currently still running well into double digits in England and Australia. A net increase of about 30 stores worldwide, population growth and increased market share also were factored into our 1975 volume estimate. The investment tax credit will decline from $6.4 million in 1974 to $5.2 million this year, probably resulting in a slightly higher overall tax rate. The after-tax profit margin might widen slightly, resulting in earnings of about $3.75 a share. *W.A.W.*

CASH POSITION	5-Year Av'g	12/31/73
Current Assets to Current Liabilities:	153%	143%
Cash & Equiv's to Current Liab'ties:	16%	11%
Working Capital to Sales:	3%	3%

(A) Based on avg. shs. outstanding. Excludes extraordinary gain: '69, 13¢. (B) Next div'd meeting about April 24. Goes ex about May 23. Div'd payment dates: last Friday of Mar., June, Sept., Dec. (C) Excludes intangibles of $4.8 million, 19¢ a sh. in '72. (D) In millions, adjusted for stock splits and div'ds. (E) Includes investment tax credit for full year, 12¢ a sh. (F) Reported EPS adjusted for switch to LIFO.

Source: *The Value Line Investment Survey,* Arnold Bernhard & Company, March 14, 1975, p. 1554.

be found by the analysis of stock price and volume data. They graph this information, which is discussed in Chapter 14, to provide them with buy or sell signals. Their interpretations of these charts are published in newsletters. Again, investors need only to read recommendations on particular issues which the advisor feels have displayed buy or sell signals and then place their orders.

Computers have been used to analyze stocks, both from technical and fundamental approaches. A number of advisors offer "Computerized Stock Selections."

Other Approaches of Advisory Services. Sometimes advice is sold on investments in particular geographic areas. Market letters for Australia, the Bahamas, or California are examples. Some reports are written for certain clients only, such as the institutional investors (banks, insurance companies, mutual funds). Subscriptions to reports on a specific type of investment can be bought. Examples of these include recommendations on commodities, bonds, convertible securities, life insurance stocks, growth stocks, low-priced stocks, income stocks, and mutual funds.

Costs of the Service. The wide variety in advisory services is matched by the broad range of their costs. Some offer occasional reports for as low as $1 each. Others sell service by the year at prices up to $5,000 or more. Many offer special inducements to begin a subscription, such as free trials or books as a bonus. No one has attempted a thorough appraisal of the predictive abilities of a significant number of advisory services because of the vast array offered and for many other reasons. Some recommendation services have been in business many years. People can be found who swear by and swear at most of the services.

Personal Investment Counsel

Another type of assistance is offered by organizations which will completely handle an individual's investments. These groups usually do no brokerage business and receive their income solely from fees charged to manage money for investors. Like the advisory services, they feel it is best to separate the influence of commissions from the investment decision. Another point cited in their behalf is that the investment counselor is a trained professional who is studying and managing investments full-time, whereas most individuals are part-time investors.

Some managers offer a special philosophy and approach to investing, but most of the services do not make a commitment to any specific technique. They all begin by establishing goals of the program that they feel are appropriate to the specific situation of each investor.

People who turn their accounts over to investment managers usually have one or more of several characteristics. Many people are simply too busy to personally invest their own funds. Others are untrained in investment opportunities. Some have no inclination to learn or desire to be bothered with the tasks of investing. Most of them share a common quality, namely, wealth. Substantial efforts are required just to set up and supervise a managed account. These efforts are in part independent of the size of the fund being established. In other words, fixed costs are involved that would necessitate prohibitive charges on small portfolios. In fact, many management firms establish minimums of $10,000 or more for accounts that they will accept. Fees are based on a percentage of the fund size. Typical annual charges are 2 percent for the first $50,000 with the percentage declining to 0.1 percent on amounts over $1 million.

Many large banks, in addition to their trust and regular investment management services, will invest small amounts by combining the funds with other small accounts. These are called *common trust funds,* or comingled accounts. They are somewhat similar to mutual funds that are described in Chapter 11 in that individual attention is not paid to each account.[17] In the process of pooling accounts the identity of the investor is lost.

Many people are do-it-yourself types and wish to handle their own investments. Others feel full-time professional management and freedom from the investment activity are worth the fees charged as long as the portfolio returns are high.

Stock Market Courses

Numerous organizations offer programs designed to educate investors so they can better invest on their own. These efforts include sessions sponsored by brokerage firms, investment courses at colleges and universities, and correspondence instruction offered by organizations similar to or in conjunction with advisory services. Some of these courses are free and others cost several hundred dollars.

---

[17] Most of the collective funds at banks are established to serve trusts. For example, money is often set aside for the education of children by using a bank-managed trust arrangement. This money can be combined with other trust accounts in a common trust fund. Banks have been seeking legislation to allow them to sell and operate mutual funds. As of this writing, congressional approval has not been granted.

The programs that are free are usually short and often cover introductory material only. The home-study courses may be quite rigorous and include lessons at advanced levels. Most of them teach "How to Invest" according to the "XYZ Institute." That is, the organization has developed techniques which it feels will enable students to achieve financial success in their personal investments. The following statements illustrate these approaches. "The stock market is talking to you. Are you listening? We can help you understand what it is saying." Another course is based on "The Laws of Supply and Demand and Cause and Effect."

The study of investments is a rewarding one, both in terms of personal satisfaction and in potential financial gain. If it were otherwise, this book would never have been written. The stock market courses offer an organized learning experience as opposed to self-taught approaches that tend to be disorganized and as a result often leave out important parts of a well-rounded education. Costs of instruction are in most instances well spent, although investors should be aware that some courses concentrate on very specialized techniques. In those instances, an outside effort should be made to supplement the training received to achieve a broad background in addition to knowledge in a specific area.

OTHER EDUCATIONAL ACTIVITIES

One quality common to most investors who have been successful over a long period is their quest for knowledge. This educational process is accomplished in ways which have been previously outlined and by other possibilities yet to be discussed.

Investment Literature

In addition to sources of data, hundreds of books have been written on investment topics. Some of them are nothing more than get-rich-quick techniques which have allegedly worked well for the author. Many millionaires have shared their secrets, but one wonders (1) if they have written *everything* which led to their success and (2) if the environment has changed since their fortunes were accumulated, making a repetition of their experience difficult. The stories are interesting reading, but investors are cautioned against feeling that they can follow in the author's exact footsteps.

Certain books are held in high regard throughout the investment community. Many of these sources are listed at the end of each chapter. Investors are encouraged to read in them as much as possible. The value of *The Wall Street Journal* for data is illustrated in this and other chapters. Much can be gained by reading other parts of this paper, such as the feature articles on companies, managements, and product developments. Other sections include dividend and earnings reports, examples of which are shown in Figure 4–13. Financial sections of newspapers and many magazines such as *Forbes, Fortune,* and *Business Week* publish articles relevant to investors. Publications such as the *Financial Analysts Journal* and the *Institutional Investor* are read by experienced individuals.

Investment Clubs

Several million people have been introduced to and/or educated about securities through investment clubs. In early 1975, there were an estimated 32,000 of these organizations in the U.S.[18] They consist of a group of people who meet regularly to invest small sums that are contributed by each member. The purpose of these clubs is to learn by doing, or in other words, to become educated about investing by investing.

Typical clubs have 10 to 20 members who each contribute $10 to $15 monthly. Everyone participates in security selections. They each analyze companies and present reports to the membership. The studies are discussed and votes are taken to buy or sell. Most clubs have tended to outperform the market averages in bull markets and in periods of moderate declines. However, in severe down markets, such as 1973 and 1974, the clubs, as a group, fall more than the averages. These associations offer a good educational opportunity for investors. Information about starting an investment club can be obtained at most brokerage offices or from the National Association of Investment Clubs.[19]

SUMMARY

Considerable amounts of information are available to investors. Study of this data does not guarantee profits, but few investors have

[18] For a discussion of the investment club movement see Margaret D. Pacey, "Make a Mint—Dow 2001: Investment Clubs Are Still Raring to Go." *Barron's,* April 7, 1975, pp. 3 ff.

[19] The National Association of Investment Clubs is located at 1515 East Eleven Mile Road, Royal Oak, Michigan 48067.

FIGURE 4–13
Reports of Earnings and Dividends

Digest of Earnings Reports

BRITISH PETROLEUM CO. (N)

Quar Mar 31:	1975	1974
Sales	$4,269,600,000	$4,114,200,000
Net inco	97,800,000	671,500,000
Shr earns:		
Net inco	.25	1.74

Computed at the pound's current rate.

COATS PATONS LTD. (F)

Year Dec 31:	1974	1973
Sales	$1,038,900,000	$960,800,000
Income	57,000,000	61,700,000
Extrd chg	2,500,000	....
Net inco	54,500,000	61,700,000

The above figures have been computed at the pound's current rate.

COURTAULDS LTD. (A)

Year Mar 31:	1975	1974
Sales	$2,628,400,000	$2,218,200,000
Net inco	206,500,000	194,900,000
Shr earns:		
Net inco	.76	.72

The above results have been computed at pound's current rate.

DCL INC. (A)

Quar Mar 31:	1975	1974
Revenues	$3,993,000	$5,037,000
Income	110,000	41,000
Extrd cred ...	11,000	....
Net income ...	121,000	41,000
Shr earns:		
Net income ..	.04	.01

ABBREVIATIONS

A partial list of frequently used abbreviations: loss dis op (loss from discontinued operations); inco bf dpr (income before depreciation); inco bf tax (income before taxes); inco cnt op (income from continuing operations).

(N) New York Stock Exchange (A) American Exchange (O) Over-the-Counter (Pa) Pacific (M) Midwest (P) PBW (B) Boston (D) Detroit (T) Toronto (Mo) Montreal (F) Foreign.

A "p" or "b" following exchange designation indicates company has only preferred shares, or bonds or debentures in public hands.

IOWA BEEF PROCESSORS (N)

26 wk May 3:	1975	1974
Sales	$811,902,000	$732,737,000
Net income ...	9,940,000	6,454,000
Shr earns:		
Net income ..	3.51	2.33

PAY'N SAVE CORP. (O)

Quar May 3:	1975	1974
Sales	$58,703,979	$45,265,575
Net income ...	1,483,295	1,125,774
Shr earns:		
Net income ..	.34	.26

SHAER SHOE CORP. (A)

6 mo Apr 30:	1975	1974
Sales	$2,556,364	$3,760,735
Net income ...	37,519	63,958
Shr earns:		
Net income ..	.04	.06

SYSTRON-DONNER CORP. (N)

Quar Apr 30:	1975	a1974
Sales	$14,367,000	$12,356,000
Inco cnt op ...	427,000	361,000
Loss dis op ...	....	54,000
Income	427,000	307,000
Extrd cred ...	....	b69,000
Net income ...	427,000	376,000
Shr earns:		
Inco cnt op ..	.26	.21
Income	.26	.18
Net income ..	.26	.22
9 months:		
Sales	42,118,000	35,411,000
Inco cnt op ...	1,195,000	1,335,000
Loss dis op ...	....	135,000
Income	1,195,000	1,200,000
Extrd cred ...	....	b173,000
Net income ...	1,195,000	1,373,000
Shr earns:		
Inco cnt op ..	.71	.79
Income	.71	.71
Net income ..	.71	.81

a-Restated. b-Principally from tax-loss carry-forward of acquired subsidiaries.

Dividend News

Dividends Reported May 29

Company	Period	Amt.	Payable date	Record date
AAV Cos	Q	c.07	7— 1—75	6—11
Acme-Cleveland Corp	Q	.12½	6—13—75	6— 9
Allegheny Pwr Sys Inc ...	Q	.38	6—30—75	6— 9
Am Home Prod $2 cvpf ...	Q	.50	7— 1—75	6—13
Ametek Inc	Q	.25	6—30—75	6—16
Babcock & Wilcox Co	Q	.20	7— 1—75	6—10
Banco Pop De PR	Q	.30	7— 1—75	6—13
Bendix Corp	Q	.45	6—30—75	6—10
Bendix Corp $3pfA	Q	.75	6—30—75	6—10
Beneficial Corp	Q	.31¼	6—30—75	6— 9
Beneficial Corp $4.50pf	S	2.25	6—30—75	6— 9
Beneficial Corp $5.50pf	Q	1.37½	7—31—75	7— 7
Beneficial Corp 5%pf	S	1.25	6—30—75	6— 9
Brewer C & Co Ltd	Q	.30	6—27—75	6— 9
BT Mtge Investors		.10	6—19—75	6— 9
Cato Corp	Q	.06¼	6—27—75	6—13
Cent Bancshres South ...	Q	.10	6—30—75	6—17
CIT Fincl Corp	Q	.55	7— 1—75	6—10
CIT Fin $5.50pf'67	Q	1.37½	7— 1—75	6—10
CIT Fin $5.50pf'70	Q	1.37½	7— 1—75	6—10
Coastal Ind Inc	Q	.05	7— 3—75	6—13
Craddock-Terry Shoe	Q	.10	7— 1—75	6—13
Empire Gas Corp	In	.05	10—15—75	10— 1
Excelsior Inc Shrs	M	.14	6—27—75	6—13
Fairchild Cam & Instr	Q	.20	6—23—75	6— 9
First Bancshrs Fla	Q	.13	6—27—75	6—19
First Nat St Bancorp	Q	.50	7— 1—75	6—13
First Mark Corp	Q	.06	7— 1—75	6—13
Floyd Enterprises	S	.10	7— 7—75	6—20
Guilford Mills Inc	Q	.05	6—19—75	6— 9
Heublein Inc	Q	.27½	7— 1—75	6—13
Interlake Inc	Q	.50	6—30—75	6—13

Source: *The Wall Street Journal*, May 30, 1975, pp. 16–18.

been successful without analyzing relevant information before making commitments.

Numerous indicators are published to tell what has happened to stock market prices. The *Dow Jones Averages* are the oldest and most widely quoted yardsticks, but other more comprehensive measures have been developed. There is no one best indicator, and the choice of a particular barometer depends on the user and his or her purpose.

Security prices are quoted in most newspapers. *The Wall Street Journal* offers a detailed listing, including price ranges, dividend and interest data in addition to the daily trading results. Up-to-the-second prices are available at brokerage offices on their electronic quotation machines.

Brokers offer many other services to clients at little or no charge. For example, through portfolio planning and review efforts, they attempt to match characteristics of investments with the needs of the investor. They also distribute research reports on industries and particular companies. Some firms have *unbundled* charges for services they offer. This separation has presented investors with an opportunity to choose from a range of plans and fees for brokerage services they use. Choosing a broker involves looking at the firm for such factors as reputation, specialization in types of securities and services offered, and accessibility. In selecting an individual registered representative, characteristics such as training, age, and personality all play a part. Investors who become dissatisfied with a broker should remember that rapid switching from one to another will not guarantee improvement.

Brokers are paid by commissions related to the amount of security trades they execute for their customers. Because of this type of remuneration plan, many services sell only information and advice to investors. They argue that separating the commission incentive from recommendations permits them to give unbiased counsel. Some of the services concentrate on providing data only; others make specific buy and sell recommendations. The advice may be based on *fundamental* or *technical* analysis and is sometimes offered for particular types of securities or geographic areas.

Complete investment management services are available as opposed to do-it-yourself investing. In the latter approach investors can take home-study courses, and read from a wide variety of books, magazines, and journals which concentrate on investment matters. An especially popular way of education has been through membership in investment clubs, which are located in most communities.

PROBLEMS

1. Visit or call several brokerage offices and ask how much they would charge to execute an order to buy 100 shares of a stock at $50/share. Compare the costs quoted. Why do you think these figures are or are not the same?
2. Suppose you wanted to compile detailed information about a company. Prepare an outline of headings which you would use. (Hint: Read reports of Moody's, Standard & Poor's, or a brokerage firm to see what kinds of information they consider to be relevant.)
3. Look up several measures of stock market activity and compare the percentage change in each measure over a period of several months or years. Why do the indicators not all show the same price changes?
4. Visit a brokerage office and see how they receive security price information.
5. Attend a meeting of a local investment club. (You may be able to find out when and where the meetings are held by asking a broker.)

QUESTIONS

1. Why are there so many measures of stock market activity?
2. What would cause someone to prefer one measure over another?
3. How do the price quotations for listed stocks differ from the OTC reports?
4. Outline briefly the major services provided by brokerage firms.
5. Why might an investor first choose a brokerage firm before selecting an individual broker?
6. Why do you suppose some investors do business with several brokerage firms?
7. Cite an argument used by advisory services as an advantage for using their recommendations as opposed to those given by brokerage firms.
8. Explain what is meant by *unbundling*.
9. Investors should seek to do business with the broker charging the lowest commissions. Do you agree or disagree?
10. Give reasons why some people use personal investment counselors.
11. What are the advantages and disadvantages of joining an investment club?
12. Why do you suppose there are so many more advisory services, in-

vestment counselors, and so on, offering assistance in security investments as compared to those involved in real estate investments?

SELECTED READINGS

Cohen, Jerome B., and Zinbarg, Edward D. *Investment Analysis and Portfolio Management*, rev. ed. Homewood, Ill.: Richard D. Irwin, 1973.

The Dow Jones Investor's Handbook. New York: Dow Jones, published yearly.

Financial Analysts Journal, published bimonthly.

Guide to Business and Investment Services. New York: George H. Wein, published periodically.

Industry Surveys. New York: Standard & Poor's, published periodically.

Investment Facts. New York: New York Stock Exchange, published periodically.

Levine, Sumner N., ed. *Financial Analysts Handbook*, vols. 1 and 2. Homewood, Ill.: Dow Jones-Irwin, 1975.

Moody's Handbook of Common Stocks. New York: Moody's Investors Service, published four times each year.

Moody's Manuals in Banking and Finance, Industrials, Municipal and Governments, Public Utilities, and Transportation. New York: Moody's Investor Services, published yearly.

Myer, John N. *Understanding Financial Statements*. New York: New American Library, 1970.

New York Stock Exchange Fact Book. New York: New York Stock Exchange, published yearly.

Stocks on the Big Board. New York: New York Stock Exchange, published periodically.

5

Analysis of Financial Statements

INTRODUCTION

Financial statements are issued periodically by all American and foreign corporations which have publicly traded securities. Annual statements are prepared by the company's mangement and are usually audited by an independent public accounting firm. Semiannual and quarterly statements are usually not audited. Through these statements interested parties may analyze the past operations of the company and make projections of future profits, sales, and other accounting measures which affect the value of the company's securities. Obviously, it is desirable for anyone interested in purchasing investment securities to have the ability to interpret and use financial statements.

This chapter has been designed to provide a basic understanding of financial statements, their construction, and their analysis. The meaning of the balance sheet and income statement are explained in the first part of the chapter. Each account of a "representative" company is examined and defined in this process. Persons who have taken a previous course in accounting may omit this portion, as they should be familiar with the material it contains.

The second part of the chapter examines financial statements by using some of the basic tools of financial analysis. The goal of this analysis is to discover weak or strong areas in a company's operations, and to rate its performance against certain norms. Persons having had a second accounting course, or a course in corporation or business finance, will probably be familiar with these techniques and may prefer to skip this chapter entirely. It should be emphasized that this chapter is *basic* in its scope. It will not turn readers into accountants or security analysts, but it should provide a basic understanding of corporate financial statements.

UNDERSTANDING CORPORATE FINANCIAL STATEMENTS

There are a variety of financial statements, the most common being balance sheets and income statements. Since every company prepares these two, our efforts will be directed to understanding them.

Financial statements of Levi Strauss & Co. have been chosen as the illustration around which this chapter is constructed. Hypothetical statements could have been prepared and used, but while it might have been easier to do this, the discussion would have been less realistic and interesting. Levi Strauss was chosen because (1) its financial statements are relatively straightforward and easy to read, (2) the business (clothing manufacturing) is easily understood and visualized, (3) the capital structure of the company is uncomplicated. This analysis is not undertaken to indicate that Levi Strauss is a "good" or a "bad" company, or that the stock of the company is a "good" or a "bad" buy. This company was chosen as an illustration entirely because of the usefulness of its financial statements.

Levi Strauss manufactures and markets apparel throughout the United States and much of the world. The domestic operations of the company are organized around product divisions—Jeans, Boyswear, Panatela Sportswear, and Levi's for Gals. International operations are organized geographically with three areas for Europe and one each for Asia-Pacific and the Americas.

The company is incorporated in Delaware; its executive offices are in San Francisco. Manufacturing plants are located in California and most of the southern states as well as in Canada, South and Central America, Europe, Australia, and the Philippines. Levi Strauss stock was first sold publicly in 1971. The stock is listed on the NYSE and its symbol is LSI.

Later in this chapter the financial ratios of Levi Strauss will be compared to those of similar manufacturing companies. This will be done in an attempt to learn how well this firm has done compared to its competitors.

The Balance Sheet

Levi Strauss' 1974 balance sheet is presented as Figure 5–1. Notes which accompany the financial statements are presented as Figure 5–2. The company's income statement is presented later as Figure 5–3. The balance sheet gives the bookkeeping value of the company's assets, liabilities, and capital *as of* November 24, 1974. It is as if the operation of the company had momentarily stopped at that date, and management had taken an inventory of the value of all things owned by the company (its assets), all things the company owed to others (its liabilities), and the ownership interest of its shareholders (stockholders' equity). The Notes to Consolidated Financial Statements provide additional information which is important to the understanding of the balance sheet but is not incorporated in it. Levi Strauss prepares its annual report at the end of each November because for accounting purposes its "year" ends then.[1] Quarterly and semiannual statements are also prepared, but these are in briefer form.

Consolidated and Unconsolidated Statements

The Figure 5–1 balance sheet tells us (top left-hand corner) that it covers Levis Strauss and *subsidiary companies*, and that it is prepared on a consolidated basis. This means that Levi Strauss owns other companies, known as subsidiaries, and that the financial statements of these companies are combined with that of the Levi Strauss company itself. This procedure is called *consolidation*.[2] Assets, sales, and net income from foreign operations are presented separately in a section of the annual report titled Notes to Consolidated Financial Statements.

To classify a company as a subsidiary the "parent" company must own controlling interest in the subsidiary company's common stock. If all the subsidiary company's stock is not owned, the financial state-

---

[1] Any yearly period (January 1 to December 31, May 5 to May 4 of the next year, July 1 to June 30, and so on) may be adopted as the yearly accounting period. Many businesses adopt a period which ends shortly after a seasonal peak in their business activity. Inventories then are probably low and more easily counted, and the business will at that time have completed a full yearly cycle of operation. For example, many retail trade companies use either February 1 or March 1 as the beginning date of their accounting period because this is a slack period in their activities.

[2] Most companies, including Levi Strauss, do not report earnings or expenses of subsidiaries separately. Recently there has been a movement on the part of investment advisors, investors, certain government agencies, and others to force companies to state income and expenses for each product line.

FIGURE 5–1

Consolidated Balance Sheets
Levi Strauss & Co. and Subsidiaries

	November 24, 1974	November 25, 1973
Assets:		
Current Assets:		
Cash and temporary cash investments	$ 23,737,000	$ 15,940,000
Trade receivables (less allowances for doubtful accounts—1974—$3,752,000; 1973—$3,335,000	116,909,000	101,764,000
Inventories	220,098,000	177,038,000
Other current assets	22,709,000	10,801,000
Total current assets	$383,453,000	$305,543,000
Property, Plant and Equipment—Net	82,272,000	68,010,000
Other Assets	4,637,000	9,106,000
	$470,362,000	$382,659,000
Liabilities and Stockholders' Equity:		
Current Liabilities:		
Current maturities of long-term debt	$ 4,946,000	$ 3,458,000
Due to banks under notes payable and overdraft agreements	53,747,000	53,688,000
Accounts payable and accrued liabilities	83,159,000	75,833,000
Salaries, wages and employee benefits	16,992,000	12,569,000
Taxes based on income	27,986,000	8,809,000
Dividends payable	1,306,000	1,306,000
Total current liabilities	$188,136,000	$155,663,000
Long-Term Debt—Less current maturities	$ 72,236,000	$ 48,110,000
Deferred Items	$ 3,985,000	$ 2,528,000
Stockholders' Equity:		
Common stock—$1.00 par value: 20,000,000 shares authorized; 10,880,080 shares outstanding (at stated value)	$ 48,960,000	$ 48,960,000
Additional paid-in capital	43,563,000	43,563,000
Retained earnings	113,482,000	83,835,000
Total stockholders' equity	$206,005,000	$176,358,000
	$470,362,000	$382,659,000

The accompanying accounting policies and notes to consolidated financial statements are an integral part of these balance sheets.

Source: Levi Strauss 1974 Annual Report.

ments probably would not be consolidated into those of the parent. The owning company's balance sheet could contain an asset called *Investments in Unconsolidated Subsidiaries* if a controlling but not complete interest in the subsidiary firm were owned. If the parent company owned less than a controlling interest, the cost of the partially-owned company would be contained in an asset account known simply as Investments. Since Levi Strauss' balance sheet contains neither of these accounts it can be presumed that all subsidiaries are wholly owned.

Assets

This balance sheet classification lists all things of value owned by the company. Quite commonly the assets category is broken into two parts: current assets, and long-term or fixed assets. Levi Strauss has chosen to use three asset subclassifications: current assets; property, plant and equipment—net; and other assets.

Current assets include cash and those which are expected to be converted into cash within one year after they are acquired in the normal course of the business. Examples of these are securities, inventory, accounts receivable, and notes receivable. *Long-term* or *fixed assets* are those which are expected to be held permanently in the business, and which are not readily converted into cash. Property, plant, and equipment are without question fixed assets (see Figure 5–1).

The cash and temporary cash investments account is made up of money on deposit in banks, currency held by the company, and very high-grade debt instruments. Firms having seasonal operations usually have temporarily unused idle cash balances at certain times of the year. Many companies buy Treasury securities and other liquid investments because they provide them with some return and the ability to turn them into cash immediately. These are entered in the books at what they *cost* the company. Such assets are valued at *cost* or *market* value, whichever is lower. More about this method of valuation when inventory is discussed.

Trade receivables are amounts *owed to* the company. For a firm of this type these assets would be mainly uncollected sales. As of November 24, 1974, Levi Strauss was owed $116,909,000 of trade receivables. The company expects to not be able to collect $3,752,000, or 3.2 percent of this total, and has made allowance for this anticipated loss by deducting this amount from trade receivables. This

$3,752,000 "loss" is an expense of doing business and has been charged against the revenue of the company.

Inventories are assets that the company had for resale to customers on the date of the balance sheet. These are listed "at lower of cost or market," which means that if the market price of inventory is for some reason less than its cost to the company, it is valued at this more conservative figure. Loss of value might be caused by deterioration, a decline in market price, obsolescence, style changes or any of several other events.

Inventory cost normally includes the price of raw materials and amounts spent to make raw materials into finished products. Manufacturing companies commonly record inventories as being either *raw materials, goods in process of manufacture,* or *finished goods.* These classifications describe how close to being marketable the inventory is. The Levi Strauss inventory is broken down into finished goods, raw materials, and work-in-process in Figure 5–2. Natural resource companies usually classify undeveloped resources—standing timber, oil, or minerals in the ground—as long-term assets. Once these resources have been "harvested," they become part of inventory, a current asset.

Other current assets are those that do not fit into any of the clearly defined current asset categories. This account is usually of an insignificant amount relative to other accounts.

Property, plant, and equipment are the fixed assets of this company. These assets are a permanent part of the business and are used in manufacturing, shipping, storing, and selling the company's products. For a manufacturing company these assets might be machinery, buildings, trucks, and other equipment; they would probably make up a large portion of the company's total assets. Levi Strauss, like many other companies, chooses to *lease* some of its assets. The balance-sheet effect of this procedure is to show a smaller amount of fixed assets. Levi Strauss uses and controls the leased assets—often for very long periods of time—but because they are owned by another party, they are not recorded on Levi Strauss' balance sheet as one of their assets.[3] Improvements to leased properties, furniture, fixtures, equip-

[3] Controversy over the method of recording lease liabilities has raged for several years. Lease payments are liabilities of the lessee company, but under current accounting practices the liability is stated as a footnote to the accounting statements or in the notes. Many people believe that the lease obligation should somehow appear on the balance sheet, but as yet no method of presenting this information exists which satisfies businesses, accountants, security analysts, and other interested parties.

ment, and land owned by this company are listed as assets. Whenever leased property is a substantial factor in the operation of a business, the terms of important lease agreements are presented as notes (in this case the note titled Leases) which accompany the financial statements. Annual lease fees of $16,225,000 in 1974 are operating expenses of the company.

Depreciation, *amortization*, and *depletion* are three ways in which an asset may be used up, or otherwise reduced in value. A company typically pays for a fixed asset when it is purchased, but uses it for many years. To charge this total payment as an expense of doing business *when it is incurred* is unrealistic and misleading. It violates the principle of matching income and expenses to each other when they occur. For example, assume that a company purchased an asset that cost $3,000 and had an expected useful life of three years. If the company charged the entire $3,000 against the income of the period in which the purchase took place, that period's income would be *reduced* by the full $3,000. In the following two periods income would be *increased* from the use of the asset (presuming that it was a profitable investment of funds), but there would be no cost associated with this increased income. Stated income would be "too low" in the first period and "too high" in the next two. Depreciation charges are a method of spreading the cost of a fixed asset over its productive life. In the above example, when the asset was purchased it would be entered on the books of the company as a fixed asset having a value of $3,000. At the end of the first year of ownership the value of the asset would be lowered by $1,000, the amount (one third of the price) that had been consumed during this year of use. A corresponding charge (the depreciation charge) would be levied against the income of the company for that period. The asset would then be valued at $2,000 after the first year of use, and the company's income for that period would be reduced by $1,000 rather than the full $3,000.

Next year the same $1,000 depreciation charge would be levied against income, and the asset's value would be reduced by an additional $1,000, to $1,000. In the third year an identical charge and deduction would be made. At the end of this year the asset would have no recorded value—it would have been completely depreciated and presumably would have no use for the company. Expenses and revenues have thereby been matched. This is an example of *straight-line* depreciation. Under this type of schedule it is assumed that an asset loses value or wears out an equal amount each year of its life. *Accelerated depreciation schedules* are often used to charge off more of an asset's value during its early life because this is the way some assets lose value.[4] Levi Strauss has chosen to use accelerated depreciation on some of its assets and straight-line depreciation on others. Their method of computing depreciation is discussed under Accounting Policies in Figure 5–2.

Assets may lose value for reasons having nothing to do with their use. Improvements made on leased property belong to the owner of the property when the lease period ends—regardless of the duration of their useful life. The usual method of recording the eventual loss of leasehold improvement value is to reduce the original cost of the improvement on a piece of property by whatever fraction of its value is "lost" each year. For example, a $10,000 leasehold improvement on a piece of property that was leased for five years should be reduced in value by $2,000 per year because at the end of five years the asset will cease to be owned by the purchaser. This charge, and other similar ones, are called *amortization charges* and have the same effects as depreciation charges on a company's balance sheet and income statement.[5]

Depletion is used to record the actual physical consumption of what are known as *wasting assets*. These are such things as oil deposits, standing timber, gravel in a gravel pit, coal in a mine, or other assets of this type. The recording procedure is exactly the same as in the above two examples. Neither amortization nor depletion charges are identified on the financial statements of Levi Strauss company.

Normal accounting procedure is to list the cost of all assets that are to be depreciated, amortized, or depleted, and to deduct from this figure the appropriate charges. The 1974 balance sheet illustration records Levi Strauss as having property, plant and equipment valued at $82,272,000 net of depreciation. The Property, Plant and Equipment note in Figure 5–2 contains a more complete statement of depreciation amounts. A total of $43,172,000 in depreciation charges have been written off against assets in use in the business. In 1974, $9,707,000 in depreciation charges were counted as an expense of doing business. Land cannot be used up and under normal circumstances cannot be depreciated. As the previous discussion indicated,

---

[4] For example, an automobile loses more of its value the first year after purchase than the second, and more the second than the third, and so on. To depreciate such an asset an equal amount each year would not record the true loss of value.

[5] Amortization charges may be levied against any assets which suffer a periodic loss of value but are not depreciated. Such assets are patents, copyrights, certain purchase or sale options, and so on. The amortization schedule may, like depreciation schedules, be accelerated.

FIGURE 5–2

Accounting Policies

Principles of Consolidation
The consolidated financial statements include the accounts of the Company and all subsidiaries. Intercompany accounts and transactions have been eliminated in consolidation.

Translation of Foreign Currencies
The accounts of the Company's operations outside the United States are maintained in other currencies. These accounts have been translated into U.S. dollars as follows:

Monetary assets and liabilities (including long-term debt) have been translated at current exchange rates at the respective year-ends.

Non-monetary items, principally inventories and property and equipment (and related reserves) have been translated at the exchange rates in effect at the time such assets were acquired. Stockholders' equity, except for the current year's results, have been translated at appropriate historical exchange rates.

Income and expenses, other than depreciation and cost of goods sold which have been translated at the historical exchange rates that apply to the related assets, have been translated at a weighted average exchange rate for the year. In 1974 and 1973, exchange adjustments including gains and losses on foreign exchange contracts (all of which have been realized) resulted in losses of $1,575,000 and $450,000 before giving recognition to the favorable impact on income resulting from translating cost of goods sold at historical exchange rates.

Inventory Valuation
Inventories are valued substantially at the lower of average cost or market.

Depreciation Methods
For financial reporting purposes, straight line depreciation methods are used on approximately 59% of depreciable assets including all current additions. Accelerated methods are used on the remaining depreciable assets. Rates are based on the estimated useful lives of the assets.

Amortization of Intangibles
Intangibles, primarily trademarks and trade names, are amortized over periods of expected benefit, normally five years. In addition, in 1974, intangibles of approximately $1,900,000 were determined to have lost their future economic usefulness and were written off to current operations.

Retirement Plans
The pension costs for the year include the cost of current service and the amortization, over ten years, of past service costs and actuarial gains or losses. Pension costs are funded as accrued.

Income Taxes
Deferred income taxes are provided for all significant timing differences between financial and tax reporting. The Company does not provide for taxes which would be payable if the net cumulative undistributed earnings at November 24, 1974 of its foreign subsidiaries ($27,873,000) were remitted to the Company. The Company intends to permanently re-invest such earnings in the operations of the subsidiary companies.

The Company reduces the provision for federal income taxes currently for the investment tax credit on qualified property additions.

Net Income Per Share
Earnings per share are calculated on the basis of the average number of common shares outstanding for the period. The exercise of stock options granted would not have a dilutive effect on net income per share.

FIGURE 5–2 (*continued*)

Consolidated Statement of Changes in Financial Position

Levi Strauss & Co. and Subsidiaries

	Year (52 Weeks) Ended November 24, 1974	Year (52 Weeks) Ended November 25, 1973
Working Capital Provided by:		
Operations:		
Net income	**$34,869,000**	$11,856,000
Add items not currently involving working capital:		
Depreciation and amortization	**11,420,000**	9,836,000
Other items, net	**4,643,000**	1,251,000
Working capital provided by operations	**$50,932,000**	$22,943,000
Proceeds from long-term debt	**28,460,000**	24,984,000
Working capital provided	**$79,392,000**	$47,927,000
Working Capital Used For:		
Additions to property, plant and equipment	**$24,334,000**	$28,812,000
Cash dividends declared	**5,222,000**	5,222,000
Reductions in long-term debt	**4,334,000**	14,617,000
Excess of purchase price over net assets of subsidiaries acquired	**750,000**	2,353,000
Other transactions, net	**(685,000)**	1,182,000
Working capital used	**$33,955,000**	$52,186,000
Increase (decrease) in working capital	**$45,437,000**	($ 4,259,000)
Increase (Decrease) in Working Capital:		
Cash and temporary cash investments	**$ 7,797,000**	$ 968,000
Trade receivables, less allowances	**15,145,000**	27,960,000
Inventories	**43,060,000**	22,553,000
Other current assets	**11,908,000**	1,677,000
Current maturities of long-term debt and due to banks	**(1,547,000)**	(21,297,000)
Accounts payable and accrued liabilities	**(7,326,000)**	(36,216,000)
Other current liabilities	**(23,600,000)**	96,000
	$45,437,000	($ 4,259,000)

The accompanying accounting policies and notes to consolidated financial statements are an integral part of this statement.

FIGURE 5–2 (continued)

Notes to Consolidated Financial Statements

International Operations

The Consolidated Financial Statements include the following amounts for international operations:

	1974	1973
Assets	$186,907,000	$156,363,000
Net Sales	292,978,000	217,354,000
Net Income (Loss)	10,195,000	(4,590,000)

Inventories

Inventories consist of:

	1974	1973
Finished Goods	$124,523,000	$ 96,166,000
Raw Materials and Work-in-Process	95,575,000	80,872,000
	$220,098,000	$177,038,000

Property, Plant and Equipment

Property, plant and equipment stated at cost less accumulated depreciation consists of:

	1974	1973
Land	$ 3,688,000	$ 3,123,000
Buildings and Leasehold Improvements	53,490,000	34,443,000
Machinery and Equipment	64,343,000	52,842,000
Construction in Progress	3,923,000	12,566,000
	$125,444,000	$102,974,000
Less accumulated depreciation	43,172,000	34,964,000
	$ 82,272,000	$ 68,010,000

Depreciation for fiscal years 1974 and 1973 amounted to $9,707,000 and $8,302,000 respectively. Property, plant and equipment includes $14,900,000 and $9,600,000 for 1974 and 1973 resulting from the capitalization of leases, less accumulated depreciation.

Income Taxes

The provision for taxes on income consists of:

1974	Federal	State	Foreign	Total
Current	$27,627,000	$3,678,000	$9,504,000	$40,809,000
Deferred	(3,344,000)	—	397,000	(2,947,000)
	$24,283,000	$3,678,000	$9,901,000	$37,862,000
1973				
Current	$14,305,000	$1,666,000	$4,753,000	$20,724,000
Deferred	(29,000)	—	1,257,000	1,228,000
	$14,276,000	$1,666,000	$6,010,000	$21,952,000

The provision or credit for deferred income taxes results from timing differences in the recognition of income and expense for tax purposes and for financial statement purposes. The principal sources of these differences and the tax effect of each were as follows:

	1974	1973
Accelerated depreciation taken for tax purposes	$ 905,000	$ 332,000
Provisions for inventory write-downs not deductible currently for tax purposes	(3,355,000)	(204,000)
Accrued pension expense not deductible currently for tax purposes	(203,000)	(328,000)
Deferred taxes provided on a portion of the income of the DISC not currently taxable	1,085,000	566,000
Inter-company profits in inventories of foreign subsidiaries recognized currently for tax purposes but upon ultimate sale of merchandise for financial reporting purposes	72,000	1,070,000
State franchise tax deductible for federal tax purposes when paid	(497,000)	28,000
Other, net	(954,000)	(236,000)
	($2,947,000)	$1,228,000

FIGURE 5–2 *(continued)*

In 1974, the Company provided for federal income taxes at 48% on both current earnings ($1,693,000) and undistributed prior years' earnings ($1,451,000) of its Domestic International Sales Corporation (DISC).

The provision for taxes on income for 1974 and 1973 as shown above differs from the amounts computed by applying the U.S. federal income tax rate (48%) to income before taxes. The principal reasons for this difference are:

	1974	1973
Tax computed at 48%	$34,911,000	$16,228,000
Increases (reductions) in taxes resulting from:		
Losses on foreign operations where the benefits cannot be currently utilized	2,501,000	7,103,000
State taxes, net of federal income tax benefit	1,913,000	862,000
Differences in income tax rates between the United States and foreign countries	(2,451,000)	(699,000)
Indefinite deferral of the tax liability on a portion of the DISC income	—	(566,000)
Other, net	988,000	(976,000)
Actual tax provision	$37,862,000	$21,952,000

At November 24, 1974, certain foreign subsidiaries had cumulative losses of about $14,100,000 which are available to reduce the future taxable income of those subsidiaries. Of these losses $4,525,000 are available indefinitely, $1,800,000 to 1979 and most of the remainder to 1978. These losses are subject to review and possible adjustment by the tax authorities of the countries involved.

Long-Term Debt

Long-term debt is summarized below:

	1974	1973
Secured by properties:		
Notes payable, 4% to 9⅜% in 1974 and 4% to 9¾% in 1973, due in installments through 1992	$ 10,093,000	$ 8,361,000
Capitalized leases due through 1993 of $15,155,000 in 1974 and $14,880,000 in 1973 less unexpended construction funds held by trustees of $1,809,000 in 1974 and $5,079,000 in 1973	13,346,000	9,801,000
Other indebtedness, 5% to 9⅝% in 1974 and 6% to 13% in 1973	558,000	692,000
	$ 23,997,000	$18,854,000
Unsecured:		
Notes payable to an insurance company, 8¾% in 1974 and 7⅝% in 1973 due in annual installments of $2,960,000 commencing 1975	$ 50,000,000	$27,800,000
Other indebtedness, 4¼% to 12½% in 1974 and 3% to 12¼% in 1973	3,185,000	4,914,000
	$ 77,182,000	$51,568,000
Less current maturities	4,946,000	3,458,000
	$ 72,236,000	$48,110,000

At November 24, 1974 and November 25, 1973 the original cost of properties pledged to secure indebtedness was $32,590,000 and $26,557,000, respectively.

In July, 1974, the Company entered into a seven and one-half year loan agreement (Loan Facility Agreement) with six banks. The Agreement includes a commitment by the banks to lend and to relend to the Company, when so requested a maximum of $100,000,000, of which up to $33,000,000 may be borrowed in foreign currencies. The maximum loan amount decreases to $85,000,000 on January 1, 1979, $65,000,000 on January 1, 1980 and $35,000,000 on January 1, 1981. Under certain conditions, the maximum loan commitment may be reduced by additional unsubordinated long-term borrowings after the date of this agreement. Through November 24, 1974 the Company incurred an additional $22,200,000 of such unsubordinated debt, thereby reducing the maximum commitment under this agreement to $77,800,000.

Interest on the outstanding loan balance is currently 1.15 times the bank prime rate. The Company is charged a commitment fee of 1/2 of 1% per annum on the unused amount of this commitment. The Company may at any time reduce or terminate the commitment amount. At November 24, 1974, there were no outstanding borrowings under this agreement.

FIGURE 5–2 (*continued*)

The Company's principal debt agreements, among other things, limit the declaration of dividends (other than stock dividends) and the redemption of its capital stock after July 1, 1974 to $10,400,000 plus Consolidated Net Income earned after November 25, 1973. Under the Agreements, retained earnings at November 24, 1974, not so restricted, amounted to $42,658,000. In addition, the Company must maintain 1) net working capital of at least $125,000,000 through December 31, 1976 and $150,000,000 thereafter, and 2) Stockholders' Equity (less intangible assets) of at least $165,000,000 through November 30, 1975 and in increasing amounts each year thereafter.

The aggregate long-term debt maturities for the next five years are:

Year	Principal Payments
1975	$3,433,000
1976	3,547,000
1977	3,582,000
1978	4,991,000
1979	3,632,000

Short-Term Debt and Lines of Credit

In addition to the $100,000,000 Loan Facility Agreement the Company and its subsidiaries had available at November 24, 1974, unused credit lines from domestic and foreign banks totaling $67,000,000 and $56,000,000, respectively. The domestic lines provide for borrowings on renewable short-term notes at bank prime interest rates. The average domestic short-term borrowings for the year were $20,023,000 at an average rate of 9.7%. The foreign lines provide for borrowings on both renewable short-term notes and on an overdraft basis at varying rates. The average foreign short-term borrowings for the year were $55,252,000 at an average interest rate of 11.6%.

Maximum short-term borrowings outstanding during the year, based on month-end balances, were $91,933,000. Short-term borrowings outstanding at November 24, 1974 (which totaled $53,747,000) were all from foreign lenders at an average rate of 12.2%.

The most common terms of the credit lines with domestic banks include an average annual compensating balance requirement of 10% of the line of credit or 20% of the amount borrowed, whichever is greater. These compensating balances, which are not legally restricted, are available to the Company for operating purposes and as compensation to the banks for other bank services. Credit arrangements with foreign lenders generally have no compensating balance requirements.

Stock Options

Under the Plan in effect, stock options to purchase up to 500,000 shares of the Company's common stock may be granted to eligible employees until November 1, 1980. Options may be granted at prices not less than 100% (qualified stock option) and 85% (non-qualified stock option) of the quoted market price on the date of grant. Such options become exercisable in cumulative installments of up to 20% during each of the second and third years and 30% during each of the fourth and fifth years after grant. Options expire five years after the date of grant in the case of qualified options and ten years in the case of non-qualified options. The maximum number of shares for which options may be granted to any one employee under the Plan is 15,000.

During 1973, options were granted on 119,850 shares at $20.25 per share and on 2,500 shares at $23.00 per share. In 1974, options were granted on 10,000 shares at $16.00 per share, 158,050 shares at $16.75 per share, and on 42,500 shares at $19.00 per share. Also during 1974, options were cancelled on 15,000 shares at $37.88 and 11,300 shares at $20.25.

Options outstanding on November 24, 1974 were:

Shares	Price
10,000	$16.00
158,050	16.75
42,500	19.00
108,550	20.25
2,500	23.00

Under the Plan, 178,400 shares are available for subsequent grants.

Retirement Plans

The Company and certain of its subsidiaries have contributory profit sharing and non-contributory pension and employee retirement plans which provide retirement benefits for their employees except those covered by union plans. At November 24, 1974, unfunded past service costs of the pension plans approximated $966,000 and the assets of those plans exceeded the actuarially computed value of vested benefits.

Prior to 1974, the Employee Retirement Plan (formally the Factory Savings Plan) provided for voluntary contributions by participating employees up to 5% of wages, not to exceed $600 for any employee annually, with the Company matching employee contributions. In 1974, the Plan was amended to discontinue employee contributions and to provide for Company contributions of 5%, 10% or 15% of covered wages, depending on

FIGURE 5–2 (concluded)

length of employee service. Forfeitures due to termination before vesting reduce the Company's required cash contribution to the Plan.

Subject to certain limitations, the Profit Sharing Plan requires minimum annual contributions of 1.95% of net income before provision for income taxes and contributions to the Plan. Participating employees may make voluntary contributions of up to 10% of their earnings, and may designate up to one-half of their contribution to be invested in Company stock. Also, unless there is a net loss, the Company and the participating subsidiaries make an additional contribution of 50% of employee contributions designated for purchase of Company stock. The additional Company contribution is also invested in Company stock. Stock acquired under this Plan is acquired in the open market. In 1973, the Company did not attain a sufficient level of profit to permit any contribution to the Profit Sharing Plan. In 1974, the Company made a normal contribution pursuant to the terms of the Plan.

The aggregate cost of these Plans for 1974 and 1973 totaled $4,387,000 and $1,368,000, respectively.

The Company is revising its retirement Plans to comply with the provisions of the Pension Reform Act of 1974. In management's opinion, changes to comply with the Act will not significantly affect the cost of the Plans.

Leases

The Company and its subsidiaries are obligated under long-term leases for real estate (office space, warehouses, plants and other facilities) and equipment, primarily truck fleet and computers. At November 24, 1974, the minimum commitments under these leases were:

	Year Ending November					Five Years Ending November			
	1975	1976	1977	1978	1979	1984	1989	1994	Total
	(In Thousands of Dollars)								
Real Estate	$ 9,232	$7,135	$6,670	$6,424	$5,873	$20,067	$15,822	$13,941	$85,164
Equipment	3,375	1,955	1,389	1,098	831	892	—	—	9,540
	$12,607	$9,090	$8,059	$7,522	$6,704	$20,959	$15,822	$13,941	$94,704

In general, leases relating to real estate include renewal options up to twenty years. Some leases contain escalation clauses relating to increases in the operating costs.

The Company has no significant "financing leases" that have not been capitalized.

Total rental expenses including those related to long-term leases were $16,225,000 and $11,600,000, in 1974 and 1973, respectively.

Commitments and Contingent Liabilities

The estimated cost to complete construction and renovation projects in progress or committed for at November 24, 1974 is approximately $1,700,000.

In 1969, a defendant in a lawsuit instituted by the Company filed a countersuit claiming unpaid royalties under a license agreement and damages for patent infringement and restraint of trade. This case has been settled out of court and resulted in no income or expense to the Company.

The Company has agreed with the trustees of the trusts established under the Profit Sharing Plan and the Employee Retirement Plan to purchase, if so requested, the Company's common stock held in trust while such stock is restricted against public sale. Such shares would be acquired at the market price. At November 24, 1974, 241,600 shares held in trust were so restricted.

Report of Independent Public Accountants

To The Stockholders and Board of Directors of Levi Strauss & Co.:

We have examined the consolidated balance sheets of Levi Strauss & Co. (a Delaware corporation) and subsidiaries as of November 24, 1974 and November 25, 1973 and the related consolidated statements of income, stockholders' equity, and changes in financial position for the years then ended. Our examination was made in accordance with generally accepted auditing standards, and accordingly included such tests of the accounting records and such other auditing procedures as we considered necessary in the circumstances.

In our opinion, the accompanying financial statements present fairly the financial position of Levi Strauss & Co. and subsidiaries as of November 24, 1974 and November 25, 1973, and the results of their operations and the changes in their financial position for the years then ended, in conformity with generally accepted accounting principles consistently applied during the periods.

ARTHUR ANDERSEN & CO.

San Francisco, California
January 20, 1975

Source: Levi Strauss 1974 Annual Report.

resources above and below ground may be *depleted* if they are actually being consumed.

Liabilities

A company's liabilities—what it owes to others—are usually classified as current and long-term liabilities. *Current liabilities* are those which are to be paid within the next accounting period, while *long-term liabilities* are expected to remain on the company's books for at least one year. Bonded debt might remain as a liability for 30 or more years. Levi Strauss' liability accounts (Figure 5–1) are representative of liability accounts in general, except that this company has sold no bonds. These accounts probably are more self-explanatory than are the asset accounts.

Current maturities of long-term debt is the portion of the company's long-term debt (largely notes payable) which was outstanding on November 24, 1974 and which is expected to be repaid during the next year. A fuller explanation of this account is contained in Figure 5–2 under the heading Long-Term Debt.

Due to banks under notes payable and overdraft agreements are the amounts of short-term credit that were outstanding at year end 1974 and which are expected to be repaid during the 1975 year. Information contained under the heading Short-Term Debt and Lines of Credit, in Figure 5–2, reveals that the entire liability of $53,747,000 is debt owed to foreign lenders.

Accounts payable and accrued liabilities are amounts owed to other businesses. Levi Strauss grants credit to its customers and is granted credit by the companies from which it buys things. Accounts payable is often a large liability for merchandising companies because they purchase on credit nearly everything that they sell. A typical manufacturing company purchases less from others, and as a consequence accounts payable are relatively less important for these firms.

Salaries, wages, and employee benefits are amounts owed employees. Since companies commonly pay twice or even once per month, earned but unpaid salaries are a liability of the company until paid. Employee benefit liabilities for insurance, retirement, and so on are a part of this account.

Taxes based on income are taxes which are *currently owed* to the federal government and are expected to be paid within the coming year. Corporations pay these taxes four times during the year; the current year taxes have been mostly paid by the time the balance sheet is constructed. This company's tax position is complicated by its overseas operations. At several places in the Notes presented as Figure 5–2 the company's income tax liabilities and method of calculation are discussed.

Dividends payable are dividends to common or preferred shareholders which have been declared but which are not yet paid. This and the previous five accounts constitute the current liabilities of the company.

Long-term debt less current liabilities is $72,236,000 of promissory notes owed to insurance companies and others—probably banks. Figure 5–2 provides information on the payment schedule of this debt and certain of its other characteristics.

Deferred items is an account set up to provide for future income tax or other liabilities which the company will eventually incur. The deferred items account usually arises because a company has lowered current income taxes by using accelerated depreciation on its assets. At a later time, when the benefit from accelerated depreciation has been exhausted, tax payments will increase. The liability of these increased future tax payments is recorded as a deferred credit. Almost all companies presently have such an account because they use accelerated depreciation. Recent changes in the income tax law have the effect of reducing this advantage.

Stockholders' Equity

The *capital accounts* identify the interest that shareholders have in the company. These are probably the most difficult accounts to understand because there is a natural tendency to try to equate the dollar values of the various accounts to the market price of the stock or to the amount available for stockholders in the event that the corporation is liquidated. These accounts have practically no relationship to either value except in very unusual situations. Market price is largely determined by the profitability of the company; the liquidated value of a common share (later identified as book value) is dependent upon the sale price of a company's assets and the amount of its liabilities.

The typical corporation's capital account contains at least three different subaccounts. These are the *common stock account,* the *paid in capital account,* and the *retained earnings account.* Companies issuing preferred shares (discussed in Chapter 9) have a *preferred stock account*. Some corporations have separate capital accounts for treasury stock, partially paid stock, and other accounts. Any standard financial accounting text will detail the meaning of these accounts.

Common stock may have a par value or be no par stock. A company having *no par stock* usually has only one capital stock account. The amount of this account is the amount received from the sale of common stock. The common stock account usually states how many of the *authorized shares* have been sold (usually listed as outstanding shares). No more than the authorized number may be sold. A company which has common stock with a par value will normally have two common stock accounts: the common stock account and a *capital surplus account*. The capital surplus account (sometimes called premium on sale of common stock) is the amount stockholders paid to the company *above* the par value of the stock.[6] An example may clarify this procedure. A hypothetical company is organized with 3,000 authorized shares of $10 par common stock. Only 2,000 of these shares are sold, but they are sold at a price of $15 each. The capital stock account would list the par value of total shares sold (2,000 shares × $10 = $20,000). The premium of $5 per share would be recorded as capital surplus (2,000 shares × $5 = $10,000). The capital section of this company's balance sheet would appear as below, assuming the company had just begun operations and had no other capital accounts.

Capital stock:	
3,000 shares authorized, 2,000 issued. Par value $10.	$20,000
Capital surplus.	10,000
Total.	$30,000

Retained earnings (often called *earned surplus*) are the amounts that the company has reinvested in the business over the years. This is a cumulative figure. A newly organized company would usually have no retained earnings. If, during its first year of operation after-tax profits were $100,000 and no dividends were paid, the retained earnings account would contain $100,000. Assume now that in the second year of operation, profits were again $100,000, but $25,000 of dividends were paid to stockholders. The retained earnings account would contain $175,000, calculated as follows:

[6] Shares are seldom sold below their par value because shareholders become liable for the difference between what they paid for the stock and its par value in case the company goes bankrupt.

Retained earnings at end of first year		$100,000
Net profit for second year	$100,000	
Less dividends paid	25,000	
Addition to earned surplus		75,000
Retained earnings at end of second year		$175,000

Losses would be *deducted* from retained earnings.

Levi Strauss' capital account contains the information that of the 20 million shares of common stock authorized, 10,880,080 have been sold. The statement further reveals that the stock has a par value of $1. Under the accounting procedures outlined above, the common stock account should contain $10,880,080 ($1 par times 10,880,080 shares outstanding). Levi Strauss has chosen to assign a value of $4.50 to each common share. Because of this the common stock account contains $48,960,000, rounded to the nearest $1,000 ($4.50 assigned value times 10,880,080 shares outstanding) rather than the smaller amount.

The reasons for the use of assigned value rather than par value are complex and beyond the scope of this book to discuss. The result of using $4.50 rather than $1 as the value of the stock is easy to explain, however. If the $1 par value had been used, the paid in capital account would contain an additional amount equal to $3.50 per share times the number of outstanding shares. The common stock account would have been reduced by this amount. The total stockholders' equity account would have remained the same at $206,005,000. *Use of assigned rather than par value has had no effect upon the company or the shareholder.*

The Income Statement

The *consolidated statement of income,* which is also called *statement of profit and loss* or *earnings report,* presents the revenues and costs obtained and incurred by the business *over a certain period of time.* This statement is related to the company's balance sheet in that the balance sheet lists the assets, liabilities, and capital of the company as of the end of a revenue period, and the income statement tells how much profit the company made *during this period.* Levi Strauss' balance sheet described the financial condition of that company as of November 24, 1974; their income statement covers the period from November 26, 1973 to November 24, 1974.

The title of Levi Strauss' income statement notifies readers that income and expenses of subsidiary companies are presented together in this statement. If this company had unconsolidated subsidiary companies, the income from these companies would be stated separately.

All income statements follow the same general format. Revenue is listed first, and expenses are deducted from revenues to produce profits. Most companies arrange their statements to produce a "profits before taxes" computation and then deduct taxes from this amount. Dividend and interest payments are usually stated as separate expenditures to make it easier to use these figures in analyzing the financial position of the company. This point will become clearer as the company's operations are evaluated by using the tools of financial analysis.

Sales and Other Revenue. The title of this account reflects the company's main source of revenue. It might be called *operating revenue* for a utility, railroad, or bank; an insurance company might call it *premium income;* for most manufacturing and merchandising companies it is titled *sales. Net sales* are total sales made during the income period less the price of goods sold but returned. This is the revenue generated through the normal operation of the business. Interest and other income is also revenue; it is listed separately because it is not produced from the normal operation of the business. Companies sometimes receive large amounts of revenue from the sale of assets or from another nonrecurring source. These amounts are identified separately as *extraordinary items* so that persons reading the income statement will recognize that they were not produced from the regular operation of the business and that they are not likely to be repeated.

Costs and Expenses. These are the costs directly associated with the production of revenue. *Cost of goods sold* is the direct payments made to suppliers for merchandise and raw materials. *Marketing, general, and administrative expenses* are those incurred in operating the business: sales commissions, salaries, rent, electricity, depreciation, and other costs of this type. Some individual expenses, depreciation, for example, are often listed separately if the account has particular importance.

Operating income is net sales less cost of goods sold and other major expenses of doing business. This equation typically excludes interest income and expense and other income and expense.

Interest expense is the interest paid on the company's debt.

Other expense is the net of income and expenses that are not a normal part of doing business.

Income before taxes is a preliminary profit figure obtained by sub-

FIGURE 5–3

Consolidated Statement of Income
Levi Strauss & Co. and Subsidiaries

	Year (52 Weeks) Ended November 24, 1974	Year (52 Weeks) Ended November 25, 1973
Net sales	**$897,696,000**	$653,042,000
Cost of goods sold	**622,214,000**	468,650,000
Gross profit	**$275,482,000**	$184,392,000
Marketing, general and administrative expenses	**186,175,000**	139,179,000
Operating income	**$ 89,307,000**	$ 45,213,000
Interest expense	**13,675,000**	10,133,000
Other expense (net of other income)	**2,901,000**	1,272,000
Income before taxes	**$ 72,731,000**	$ 33,808,000
Provision for taxes on income	**37,862,000**	21,952,000
Net income	**$ 34,869,000**	$ 11,856,000
Net income per share	**$ 3.20**	$ 1.09
Average number of shares of common stock outstanding	**10,880,080**	10,880,080

Consolidated Statement of Stockholders' Equity
Levi Strauss & Co. and Subsidiaries

	Common Stock		Additional	
	Shares	Stated Value	Paid-in Capital	Retained Earnings
Balance, November 26, 1972	10,880,080	$48,960,000	$43,563,000	$ 77,201,000
Net income				11,856,000
Cash dividends declared ($0.48 per share)				(5,222,000)
Balance, November 25, 1973	10,880,080	$48,960,000	$43,563,000	$ 83,835,000
Net income				34,869,000
Cash dividends declared ($0.48 per share)				(5,222,000)
Balance, November 24, 1974	**10,880,080**	**$48,960,000**	**$43,563,000**	**$113,482,000**

The accompanying accounting policies and notes to consolidated financial statements are an integral part of these statements.

Source: Levi Strauss 1974 Annual Report.

tracting costs and expenses of obtaining revenue from the revenue obtained.

Provision for taxes on income lists the amount of income taxes paid or incurred by a firm during the entire accounting period under examination. Total federal income taxes are expected to be $37,862,000 for the entire income period that ended November 24, 1974. The liability for income taxes of $27,986,000 which appears on the balance sheet, is the amount not yet paid.

Net income is the final computation on some income statements. It represents the amount of revenues remaining after all expenses have been paid. Levi Strauss had $34,869,000 of net income in 1974, up from $11,856,000 in 1973.

Net Income per Share. Income as well as dividends are usually recorded on a per share basis. Stating these amounts in this way is accomplished by dividing the total amount of each item by the average number of shares outstanding for the year.

$$\text{Net income per share in 1974} = \frac{\text{Total net income}}{\text{Average number of common shares outstanding during the year}}$$
$$= \$34{,}869{,}000/10{,}880{,}080$$
$$= \$3.20$$

Dividends per share are usually stated as the total amount paid on each share during the year. Dividends are usually paid quarterly. Shares issued during the year will therefore usually not receive the entire yearly dividend. Levi Strauss paid dividends of $0.48 per share in 1973 and1974.

Fully diluted earnings per share is the preferred way of stating earnings. Companies having securities which are convertible into the common stock of the company, and companies having stock option plans which may result in an addition to outstanding common stock, prepare earnings per share figures on a "fully diluted basis." This figure is often presented separately and tells what earnings per share would be if all convertible securities were converted and all stock options were exercised. Because additional common shares are presumed outstanding in this calculation, amounts stated in "per share" terms are lowered. Such computations serve to notify shareholders of the potential for lower per share earnings if conversion does take place. Stock option plans usually add so few shares of stock that dilution from this source is minor. Since Levi Strauss has no outstanding convertible securities, per share data do not need to be adjusted to reflect potential dilution.

Summary of the Income Statement. This accounting statement simply lists *revenues* for the period under consideration and *expenses* associated with these revenues. Extraordinary items are listed separately since they either do not pertain to the normal operation of the business, or they are not expected to recur. Expenses are deducted from revenues to produce a measure of the company's profits for the period under consideration. Profits are usually presented in terms of earnings per share.

The Auditor's Report

All companies whose stock is listed on the American or the New York Stock Exchange, and all unlisted companies having $1 million or more of assets and 500 or more shareholders, must supply audited financial statements. An independent accounting firm is employed by the company to prepare audited financial statements. Almost all companies prepare some kind of financial statements, but they are not always audited.

The auditor's report appears as a part of the financial statement. If the report is *unqualified,* the company's statements have satisfied the auditors of their reasonableness. The company's accounting procedures have also met the standards of the American Institute of Certified Public Accountants and the Financial Accounting Standards Board. If the statements do not meet these standards, the auditor's report is *qualified.* The reasons for qualification are stated as part of the report. Levi Strauss' 1974 financial statements were audited by Arthur Anderson & Co., whose statement appears as a part of Figure 5–2. The report is unqualified.

ANALYZING FINANCIAL STATEMENTS

This part of the chapter presents several commonly used methods of examining financial statements. Levi Strauss' statements are used as examples, but the techniques are generally applicable to other companies and other financial statements. Many companies present a *performance record* or *summary of operations* as a regular part of their annual report. These statements provide much financial information. Financial reporting companies and brokerage houses often prepare more detailed analyses of company operations. Investors seldom have to make these computations on their own, but they should know how they are made and how to interpret their meaning.

Ratios are used almost exclusively in this type of analysis so that the performance of one company can be compared directly to that of another. The measures may be divided into three general classifications:

1. *Liquidity ratios*, which measure the firm's ability to pay short-term obligations, and thereby to remain in business.
2. *Profitability ratios*, which attempt to measure the relative profitability of the firm.
3. *Financial ratios*, which measure the equity and debt contributions to the financing of the firm, and the return to investors.

A ratio is created whenever one quantity is divided into another to create either a percentage or a magnitude relationship. If quantity *A* is 30 and *B* is 100, the relationship of one to another may be stated in one of two generally accepted ways: *B* is 3.33 times as large as A ($B/A = 100/30 = 3.33{:}1$) or A is 30 percent of *B* ($A/B = 30/100 = 0.30$ or 30 percent). To be useful in financial analysis, ratios must be constructed of variables that are related to each other in such a way that the ratios produced have meaning.

Banks and other businesses construct and use ratios largely to predict the creditworthiness of potential customers. Several companies provide average ratios—called composite ratios—of firms in various identifiable industries. These ratios may be used as benchmarks against which ratios of similar companies being analyzed can be compared. Figure 5–4 is a portion of a list of manufacturing industry ratios prepared by Dun & Bradstreet, a company which provides credit information on companies and individuals for a fee.[7] It should be noted that the average ratios of different types of manufacturing firms differ greatly—even though all firms are in the general category of manufacturing. Ratios vary even more between firms in different industries. For example, electric utilities (because they cannot store electricity) have practically no inventory. Consequently, when inven-

[7] The Robert Morris Associates (also known as The National Association of Bank Loan and Credit Officers) presents a great deal of industry ratio information in its publication *Annual Statement Studies* (Robert Morris Associates, Research Department, Philadelphia National Bank Building, Philadelphia, Pennsylvania). Trade associations often publish financial ratios of member companies, and many banks prepare their own norms for ratio analysis. A publication which presents financial ratios taken from federal income tax statements is *Almanac of Business and Industrial Financial Ratios* (Englewood Cliffs, N.J.: Prentice-Hall, published annually).

FIGURE 5–4

Dun & Bradstreet's Key Business Ratios

Manufacturing

Line of Business (and number of concerns reporting)	Current assets to current debt	Net profits on net sales	Net profits on tangible net worth	Net profits on net working capital	Net sales to tangible net worth	Net sales to net working capital	Collection period	Net sales to inventory	Fixed assets to tangible net worth	Current debt to tangible net worth	Total debt to tangible net worth	Inventory to net working capital	Current debt to inventory	Funded debts to net working capital
	Times	Per cent	Per cent	Per cent	Times	Times	Days	Times	Per cent	Per cent	Per cent	Per cent	Per cent	Per cent
2337 Suits & Coats,	2.85	3.77	20.23	25.21	9.54	9.86	32	19.3	2.6	52.4	143.5	32.9	92.8	26.1
Women's & Misses'	**1.95**	**1.47**	**11.82**	**13.58**	**6.55**	**6.78**	**45**	**11.0**	**6.5**	**99.2**	**242.7**	**78.9**	**141.7**	**69.9**
(62)	1.56	0.71	4.55	4.80	4.56	5.18	63	4.8	13.9	176.7	403.4	116.5	247.5	102.7
2311 Suits, Coats &	3.02	3.25	14.49	16.27	5.89	6.91	34	7.9	3.4	41.7	74.2	61.4	63.9	7.6
Overcoats, Men's &	**2.29**	**1.82**	**8.06**	**8.61**	**4.49**	**4.71**	**58**	**4.5**	**9.1**	**73.6**	**140.9**	**91.1**	**80.5**	**20.2**
Boys'(86)	1.72	0.43	2.28	2.31	3.19	3.20	81	3.6	21.1	133.4	217.9	129.2	127.8	38.2
3841-42-43 Surgical,	4.80	7.38	17.00	24.93	2.80	4.96	50	6.2	16.7	18.1	41.2	53.3	53.7	14.3
Medical & Dental Instru-	**2.98**	**4.79**	**11.51**	**14.76**	**2.25**	**3.14**	**62**	**4.7**	**31.3**	**33.4**	**66.1**	**67.0**	**69.6**	**31.6**
ments (59)	2.44	2.41	5.91	8.44	1.85	2.35	74	3.7	57.3	55.1	111.4	92.7	92.6	73.8
3942-44-49 Toys,	3.38	6.01	20.35	24.00	4.39	5.12	41	6.0	17.8	38.8	66.2	66.8	65.1	23.5
Amusement & Sporting	**2.40**	**3.89**	**11.90**	**10.07**	**3.17**	**3.96**	**56**	**4.6**	**39.4**	**61.3**	**107.4**	**85.7**	**85.9**	**42.1**
Goods (65)	1.78	1.42	4.06	5.45	2.37	2.97	79	3.5	61.4	109.8	160.7	117.1	137.0	70.6
2327 Trousers, Men's	3.31	2.42	13.94	15.53	7.13	7.37	34	10.9	3.0	39.5	69.1	40.9	70.4	8.8
& Boys'	**2.15**	**1.37**	**6.91**	**8.33**	**4.44**	**4.78**	**48**	**6.8**	**9.3**	**78.6**	**111.3**	**72.6**	**98.0**	**20.0**
(58)	1.85	0.56	2.81	3.25	3.34	3.47	65	3.8	29.6	106.8	159.0	125.4	173.6	48.1
2341 Underwear &	3.34	3.48	11.45	15.48	7.56	9.09	36	9.3	4.8	41.1	47.6	56.9	69.0	13.9
Nightwear, Women's &	**2.09**	**1.38**	**7.46**	**8.78**	**5.32**	**5.92**	**46**	**6.4**	**12.0**	**70.0**	**114.6**	**92.9**	**97.7**	**37.1**
Childrens's (65)	1.69	0.49	3.05	3.62	3.49	3.93	72	4.2	31.7	139.3	185.9	132.8	137.2	73.3
2511-12 Wood House-	4.16	4.65	15.55	25.10	5.25	6.59	32	9.0	23.7	23.0	38.2	57.1	48.3	9.7
hold Furniture &	**2.92**	**3.18**	**11.32**	**16.03**	**3.17**	**4.95**	**44**	**6.2**	**39.2**	**36.1**	**69.4**	**82.7**	**70.3**	**36.8**
Upholstered (120)	1.87	1.72	7.38	10.15	2.46	3.57	54	4.2	71.0	72.3	143.4	129.0	97.8	78.8
2328 Work Clothing,	5.69	5.02	16.01	19.05	5.31	6.54	37	6.3	8.1	17.7	38.1	54.0	37.8	3.4
Men's & Boys'	**3.19**	**2.60**	**8.44**	**9.57**	**3.29**	**3.65**	**53**	**4.6**	**17.2**	**46.8**	**89.1**	**84.9**	**64.4**	**29.3**
(39)	1.62	0.88	2.99	4.02	2.47	2.79	71	3.3	35.0	110.4	148.6	129.0	104.3	47.7

Note: See Figure 5–5 for a discussion of how the ratics are constructed.
Source: Reprinted with the special permission of *Dun's Review*, November 1974.

FIGURE 5–5
Explanation of Dun & Bradstreet's Ratio Computations
How the Ratios are Figured

In the ratio tables each group of ratios in each industry carries three sets of figures. The top figure is the upper quartile, the center figure is the median, and the bottom figure is the lower quartile. They are calculated as follows: Year-end financial statements are selected from a sampling of corporations whose tangible net worth, with few exceptions, exceed $35,000. The financial statements are those appearing in the Dun & Bradstreet credit reports on these businesses. Ratio figures are arranged so that the best ratio figure is at the top, the weakest at the bottom. The figure which falls just in the middle of this series becomes the median for that ratio in that line of business. The figure halfway between the median and the highest term of the series is the upper quartile; and the term halfway between the median and the bottom of the series is the lower quartile. The purpose of these interquartile ranges is to show an upper and lower limit area without reflecting the extremes either at the top or the bottom of the series. After the first of the "14 Ratios" has been compiled for a particular industry, the identical process is followed for the remaining 13 ratios in this industry group, and then for remaining industry groups.

CURRENT ASSETS TO CURRENT DEBT
Current Assets are divided by total Current Debt. Current Assets are the sum of cash, notes and accounts receivable (less reserves for bad debt), advances on merchandise, merchandise inventories, and Listed, Federal, State and Municipal securities not in excess of market value. Current Debt is the total of all liabilities falling due within one year. This is one test of solvency.

NET PROFITS ON NET SALES
Obtained by dividing the net earnings of the business, after taxes, by net sales (the dollar volume less returns, allowances, and cash discounts). This important yardstick in measuring profitability should be related to the ratio which follows.

NET PROFITS ON TANGIBLE NET WORTH
Tangible Net Worth is the equity of stockholders in the business, as obtained by subtracting total liabilities from total assets, and then deducting intangibles. The ratio is obtained by dividing Net Profits after taxes by Tangible Net Worth. Tendency is to look increasingly to this ratio as a final criterion of profitability. Generally, a relationship of at least 10 per cent is regarded as a desirable objective for providing dividends plus funds for future growth.

NET PROFITS ON NET WORKING CAPITAL
Net Working Capital represents the excess of Current Assets over Current Debt. This margin represents the cushion available to the business for carrying inventories and receivables, and for financing day-to-day operations. The ratio is obtained by dividing Net Profits, after taxes, by Net Working Capital.

NET SALES TO TANGIBLE NET WORTH
Net Sales are divided by Tangible Net Worth. This gives a measure of relative turnover of invested capital.

NET SALES TO NET WORKING CAPITAL
Net Sales are divided by Net Working Capital. This provides a guide as to the extent the company is turning its working capital and the margin of operating funds.

COLLECTION PERIOD
Annual net sales are divided by 365 days to obtain average daily credit sales and then the average daily credit sales are divided into notes and accounts receivable, including any discounted. This ratio is helpful in analyzing the collectibility of receivables. Many feel the collection period should not exceed the net maturity indicated by selling terms by more than 10 to 15 days. When comparing the collection period of one concern with that of another, allowances should be made for possible variations in selling terms.

NET SALES TO INVENTORY
Dividing annual Net Sales by Merchandise Inventory as carried on the balance sheet. This quotient does not yield an actual physical turnover. It provides a yardstick for comparing stock-to-sales ratios of one concern with another or with those for the industry.

FIXED ASSETS TO TANGIBLE NET WORTH
Fixed Assets are divided by Tangible Net Worth. Fixed Assets represent depreciated book values of building, leasehold improvements, machinery, furniture, fixtures, tools, and other physical equipment, plus land, if any, and valued at cost or appraised market value. Ordinarily, this relationship should not exceed 100 percent for a manufacturer, and 75 percent for a wholesaler or retailer.

CURRENT DEBT TO TANGIBLE NET WORTH
Derived by dividing Current Debt by Tangible Net Worth. Ordinarily, a business begins to pile up trouble when this relationship exceeds 80 percent.

TOTAL DEBT TO TANGIBLE NET WORTH
Obtained by dividing total current plus long term debts by Tangible Net Worth. When this relationship exceeds 100 percent, the equity of creditors in the assets of the business exceeds that of owners.

INVENTORY TO NET WORKING CAPITAL
Merchandise inventory is divided by Net Working Capital. This is an additional measure of inventory balance. Ordinarily, the relationship should not exceed 80 percent.

CURRENT DEBT TO INVENTORY
Dividing the Current Debt by Inventory yields yet another indication of the extent to which the business relies on funds from disposal of unsold inventories to meet its debts.

FUNDED DEBTS TO WORKING CAPITAL
Funded Debts are all long term obligations, as represented by mortgages, bonds, debentures, term loans, serial notes, and other types of liabilities maturing more than one year from statement date. This ratio is obtained by dividing Funded Debt by Net Working Capital. Analysts tend to compare Funded Debts with Net Working Capital in determining whether or not long term debts are in proper proportion. Ordinarily, this relationship should not exceed 100 percent.

Source: Reprinted with the special permission of *Dun's Review,* November 1974.

tory is used as a part of a financial ratio, the utility's ratio will probably be very different in value from that of a firm which holds inventory. Some companies—grocery stores, liquor stores—sell only for cash. Their accounts receivable ratios will be very different from those of department stores, which grant credit freely to customers.

When comparing financial ratios of one company to those of another or a group of companies, the analyst must make certain that the companies are similar enough in their operation to be compared. Comparing the financial ratios of Levi Strauss to those of U.S. Steel will produce little meaningful information. Levi Strauss, because it is primarily a manufacturer of men's work clothing, probably most closely resembles the classification presented as category 2327 in Figure 5–4. A brief statement prepared by Dun & Bradstreet to explain how the ratios are computed, and what they indicate, is included as Figure 5–5.

These ratios have been constructed primarily for use in determining whether certain companies are good credit risks, not necessarily whether they are good investments. Some of the ratios are useful in both capacities, however. Levi Strauss will now be "analyzed" by constructing and comparing several of its more relevant ratios to those of the discount industry.

Liquidity Ratios

The Current Ratio. This is sometimes referred to as the working capital ratio. It is a good one to begin with because it shows clearly how data may become more meaningful when presented as a ratio.

Working capital is computed by subtracting current liabilities from current assets; this measure is always presented as a certain number of dollars. Working capital is considered to be that available for use in the day-to-day conduct of the business, as opposed to the fixed capital represented by fixed assets.[8] Levi Strauss' net working capital at the end of 1974 was

Current assets	$383,453,000
Less current liabilities	188,136,000
Equals working capital	$195,317,000

This amount can be compared to working capital for previous years—$149.8 million in 1973, $154.2 million in 1974, and so on as calculated in Figure 5–6—but it cannot be compared meaningfully to working capital of other firms, unless the other firms happen to be of the same size as Levi Strauss. Stating the same figures as a *ratio* of current assets to current liabilities makes similarly derived ratios of other companies more readily comparable.

---

[8] Dun & Bradstreet uses two terms, *net working capital* and *tangible net worth*, which require explanation. Companies sometimes assign dollar values to intangible things such as goodwill, trademarks, organization costs, patents, and copyrights—assets which may have no definite market value. The amount of these items is deducted from assets when computing certain ratios. *Net* working capital differs from working capital by the amount of the intangible assets. The term *tangible* net worth notifies the reader that intangible assets have been deducted from total assets in the construction of this ratio. Levi Strauss has no intangible assets, so its working capital may be considered "net," and its net worth "tangible."

$$\text{The current ratio} = \text{Current assets/Current liabilities} = \$383{,}453{,}000/\$188{,}136{,}000 = 2.0{:}1.$$

To determine whether this ratio of $2 of current assets to each dollar of current liabilities is "good," the ratio must be compared to that for other firms in the same line of business. Looking down the column titled current assets to current debt (Figure 5–4) to the Trousers, Men's and Boy's classification reveals three average ratios. The center number, 2.15, indicates that half the 58 firms examined had current ratios greater than this number and half had lower ratios. The top number, 3.31, is the lower limit of the upper quartile: 25 percent of the firms examined had ratios greater than this. The lower number identifies the upper limit of the lower quartile. Comparing Levi Strauss' current ratio to that of 58 other trouser manufacturers reveals that its current ratio is slightly less than average.

Inventory to Net Working Capital. This is another liquidity ratio which indicates the proportion of net working capital that is tied up in inventory. A low ratio is desirable in this case. Levi Strauss' 1974 ratio is

$$\text{Inventory to net working capital} = \text{Inventory/Net working capital} = \$220{,}098{,}000/\$195{,}317{,}000 = 1.127 \text{ or } 112.7\%.$$

Column 13 of Figure 5–4 reveals that this ratio is bettered by over half of the trouser manufacturers under examination. There are other liquidity ratios that might be computed (current debt to net worth, current debt to inventory, the "acid test ratio," which is current assets less inventories divided by current liabilities), but these ratios are more relevant to short-term lending decisions than investment decisions and are omitted from this discussion.

Profitability Ratios

These ratios attempt to measure the relative profitability of the firm.

Net Profits to Sales. Often called the net operating margin, this ratio is derived by dividing net sales into net profits.[9] In 1974 Levi Strauss had the following ratio:

[9] Net profits are usually adjusted for the effects of extraordinary expenses or revenues. Some analysts also deduct interest expense to remove the effect that different types of financing (debt versus equity) have on this ratio.

Net profits to sales = Net profit/Net sales
= $34,869,000/$897,696,000
= .0388 or 3.9%.

Compared to the Dun & Bradstreet averages (column 3 of Figure 5–4), Levi Strauss performed excellently in this area.

Net Profits on Net Worth. This measures the company's profitability on net worth. Net worth is assets less liabilities, which is the company's stockholder equity of $206,005,000.

Net profits on net worth = Net profits/Net worth
= $34,869,000/$206,005,000
= 0.1692 or 16.9%.

Levi Strauss' performance is much above the average of other trouser manufacturers (column 4 of Figure 5–4).

Net Profits on Working Capital. This measure relates income to working capital.

Net profits on working capital = Net profits/Working capital
= $34,869,000/$195,317,000
= 0.1785 or 17.9%.

This figure, when compared to those in column 5 of Figure 5–4, indicates that Levi Strauss is considerably above average in this measure of profitability.

Gross Operating Margin. This widely used ratio relates net sales to gross profit from sales. Gross profit from sales is net sales less cost of goods sold.

Levi Strauss' 1974 net sales	$897,696,000
Less cost of goods sold	622,214,000
Equals gross profit	$275,482,000

Gross operating margin = Gross profit/Net sales
= $275,482,000/$897,696,000
= 0.3068 or 30.7%.

This ratio indicates that Levi Strauss' average price markup is about 30 percent above what it cost to produce this merchandise. Gross margin varies greatly between different kinds of businesses. Those having large, slow-moving inventories (furniture stores, hardware stores) usually have high gross margins. Grocery stores and service stations have smaller, more rapidly sold inventories, but lower price markups. Dun & Bradstreet does not list this ratio as one of its "key ratios." Standard & Poor's does provide industry ratios of gross operating margin in its *Industry Surveys: Basic Analysis.*

There are many profitability ratios which are unique to certain industries. Net profits per ton-mile is a common measure of the profitability of a railroad; net profits per seat-mile is commonly used in the airline industry.[10] An advertising firm might use gross billings to profits.

Financial Ratios

These are of more importance to the investor because their emphasis is on the financial position of the company. Many of these measures are concerned with the company's capitalization, and they relate debt to net worth or some other measure. As debt increases, financial risk increases because interest payments must be made or the company becomes insolvent. However, debt is not automatically "bad." A company which can earn more on borrowed funds than it costs to borrow them can increase common stockholders' earnings and make the company more profitable by borrowing some of its capital. Stability of income is the main factor which controls a company's ability to go into debt safely. Utilities have very constant income and can borrow large proportions of their funds. The income of most manufacturing companies is variable, and as a consequence they can borrow less. A well-managed company will borrow as much as it can, with safety, to increase the company's profitability. This amount varies greatly between individual firms and between firms in different industries.

Debt to Net Worth. Several ratios equate debt to net worth or debt to total assets. Total debt to total assets, current debt to total assets or net worth, long-term debt to total assets or net worth, and fixed assets to net worth are those most often used. Debt to net worth is the most common of these ratios. Levi Strauss' ratio for 1974 is

$$\begin{aligned}\text{Debt to net worth} &= \text{Total debt/Net worth}\\ &= \$264{,}357{,}000/\$206{,}005{,}000\\ &= 1.283 \text{ or } 128.3\%.\end{aligned}$$

Column 12 of Figure 5–4 shows that in relation to other trouser manufacturers, Levi Strauss' ratio is somewhat high. It should be

[10] A ton-mile is one ton shipped one mile. It is the product of total tonnage shipped times total miles traveled by the trains.

remembered that Levi Strauss has *leased* some of its assets. Had they borrowed to purchase them, the ratio would undoubtedly have been higher because more long-term debt would have been incurred.

Current Debt to Net Worth. This ratio (or its complement, the ratio of long-term debt to net worth) measures the importance of current (or long-term) debt in the company's capital structure. Dun & Bradstreet considers a ratio of 0.8:1, or 80 percent to indicate financial difficulties, but this figure differs greatly with the industry. Levi Strauss' 1974 ratio is 91.3 percent, slightly higher than the industry average.

$$\text{Current debt} = \text{Net worth}$$
$$\text{Current debt to net worth} = \$188{,}136{,}000/\$206{,}005{,}000$$
$$= 0.9132 \text{ or } 91.3\%.$$

Productivity of Assets. The ratio of net profits after taxes plus interest payments to total assets measures the rate of return on assets. It is often called the *return-on-investment* ratio. Interest expense is added to net profits to compensate for the effect of borrowed funds (the more borrowed, the higher the interest payments) and makes this ratio more applicable to all companies. Levi Strauss' ratio is computed below.

Levi Strauss' 1974 net income.	$34,869,000
Plus interest payments	13,675,000
Equals adjusted income	$48,544,000

$$\text{Net income to assets} = \text{Adjusted income/Assets}$$
$$= \$48{,}544{,}000/\$470{,}362{,}000$$
$$= .1032 \text{ or } 10.3\%.$$

This ratio is also prepared on a before-taxes basis. Dun & Bradstreet does not present this ratio as one of its "key ratios."

Horizontal and Vertical Analysis. Examining ratios or other data over time is sometimes called *horizontal analysis.* Another type is *vertical,* or *common size,* analysis. In this kind of computation, all balance sheet items are presented as a percent of total assets, and all income statement items are stated as a percent of total sales or revenue. The value from this form of presentation is the same as that from using other ratios: It allows the financial statements of different firms to more easily be compared one to another. A slightly abbreviated form of the Levi Strauss 1974 income statement is presented in this fashion in Table 5–1. Such data can be prepared "horizontally"

FIGURE 5–6

10 Year Financial Summary
Levi Strauss & Co. and Subsidiaries
(Dollar Amounts in Millions Except Per Share Data)

	1974	1973	1972
Net Sales	**$897.7**	$653.0	$504.1
Gross Profit	**275.5**	184.4	160.3
Income Before Taxes (1)	**72.7**	33.8	48.1
Provision for Taxes on Income	**37.9**	22.0	23.0
Net Income	**34.9**	11.9	25.0
Earnings Retained in the Business	**29.6**	6.6	20.9
Cash Flow Retained in the Business (2)	**41.1**	16.5	28.0
Income Before Tax as % of Sales	**8.1%**	5.2%	9.5%
Net Income as % of Sales	**3.9%**	1.8%	5.0%
Net Income as % of Beginning Stockholders' Equity	**19.8%**	7.0%	16.8%
Current Assets	**$383.5**	$305.5	$252.4
Current Liabilities	**188.1**	155.7	98.2
Working Capital	**195.3**	149.8	154.2
Ratio of Current Assets to Current Liabilities	**2.04/1**	1.96/1	2.57/1
Long-Term Debt (3)	**$ 72.2**	$ 48.1	$ 37.6
Stockholders' Equity	**206.0**	176.4	169.7
Capital Expenditures	**$ 24.3**	$ 28.8	$ 17.6
Depreciation & Amortization	**11.4**	9.8	7.1
Property, Plant & Equipment—Net	**82.3**	68.0	48.0
Number of Employees	**30,141**	29,141	25,137
Per Share Data:			
Net Income (4)	**$ 3.20**	$ 1.09	$ 2.30
Cash Dividends Declared	**.48**	.48	.38
Book Value (on Shares Outstanding at Year End)	**18.93**	16.21	15.60
Market Price Range	**12½-22⅜**	49¾-16⅝	59¾-40⅜
Shares Outstanding (4)	**10,880,080**	10,880,080	10,880,080

(1) Net of minority interest in net income of consolidated subsidiaries.
(2) Net income plus depreciation and amortization minus dividends declared.
(3) Excludes current maturities.
(4) Based on weighted average of shares outstanding during the year.

for several years. Presented in this way it sometimes reveals trends that have taken place over time.

Many firms prepare summaries of their operations as a part of their annual report. Figure 5–6 is Levi Strauss' ten-year summary. Several of

FIGURE 5–6 (*continued*)

1971	1970	1969	1968	1967	1966	1965
$432.0	$349.5	$269.0	$213.5	$176.5	$164.3	$136.5
129.6	112.0	86.0	68.2	50.7	46.3	44.7
35.7	37.7	31.7	26.6	14.8	15.5	15.3
16.0	19.1	17.1	14.5	6.9	7.5	7.7
19.7	18.6	14.7	12.1	7.8	7.9	7.6
16.3	15.7	12.0	10.4	5.8	5.8	5.1
21.9	20.1	14.9	12.8	8.0	7.4	6.2
8.3%	10.8%	11.8%	12.5%	8.4%	9.4%	11.2%
4.6%	5.3%	5.5%	5.7%	4.4%	4.8%	5.6%
23.2%	26.8%	25.6%	25.8%	19.0%	23.2%	26.4%
$202.8	$169.0	$131.0	$ 94.9	$ 78.0	$ 71.4	$ 48.7
67.9	87.9	57.5	29.6	23.3	21.3	20.3
134.9	81.1	73.5	65.3	54.7	50.1	28.4
2.99/1	1.92/1	2.28/1	3.21/1	3.35/1	3.35/1	2.40/1
$ 28.4	$ 25.4	$ 22.6	$ 22.2	$ 22.1	$ 22.2	$ 1.8
148.8	85.0	69.3	57.4	46.9	41.0	34.0
$ 15.6	$ 14.5	$ 6.9	$ 2.4	$ 3.9	$ 4.5	$ 2.4
5.6	4.4	2.9	2.4	2.2	1.6	1.1
39.6	29.2	19.4	15.4	14.6	13.5	8.8
21,383	18,900	16,466	14,067	12,527	13,738	9,340
$ 1.86	$ 1.92	$ 1.50	$ 1.23	$ .79	$ .81	$ .78
.32	.30	.28	.18	.21	.21	.20
13.68	8.66	7.07	5.85	4.79	4.20	3.49
64¼-33¼	—	—	—	—	—	—
10,586,000	9,661,000	9,754,000	9,809,000	9,791,000	9,771,000	9,756,000

Management's Discussion and Analysis of the Summary of Operations

Levi Strauss & Co. manufactures and markets apparel throughout the United States and in a large number of foreign countries. Financial data required by the Securities and Exchange Commission for this summary of the last five fiscal years' operations is included in the 10-year financial summary above with the exception of interest expenses which were: 1970, $4,356,000; 1971, $4,358,000; 1972, $4,328,000; 1973, $10,133,000; 1974, $13,675,000. The company's sales have had an uninterrupted growth during those years as it broadened its product line and diversified geographically, both internationally and through increased emphasis on U.S. markets outside the Western region where the company was founded. Growth in net income was interrupted in 1973 when a fourth-quarter loss, due primarily to losses by the company in Europe, brought about a 53 per cent decline in earnings for the year. The company's historic growth pattern was restored in 1974 and record sales and earnings were achieved, as discussed throughout this annual report.

Levi Strauss & Co. had its first public offering of stock March 3, 1971. During recent years there has been a continuing gap between consumer demand for Levi's products and the company's production capacity to meet that demand. The figures for capital expenditures and the increasing value of property, plant and equipment reflect the steps taken to expand that capacity. Historically the company was organized functionally but in 1971 the domestic business was reorganized into four product divisions—Jeans, Boyswear, Panatela Sportswear and Levi's for Gals—for better management and improved responsiveness. The International group is organized geographically with three areas for Europe and one each for Asia-Pacific and the Americas.

Source: Levi Strauss 1974 Annual Report.

the ratios constructed earlier are a part of this summary, and several measures not previously explained are also used.

Most data in Figure 5–6 except book value and stock dividends should be self-explanatory. Book value is simply the company's assets less its liabilities, or in other words, its net worth. Book value per share is this amount divided by the number of shares outstanding at the time book value was computed. Some people regard book value as a rough indication of the worth of a share of stock. Book value is re-examined in Chapter 10.

In general terms, the summary of operations shows that the company's sales have been increasing at an increasing rate in recent years; earnings as a percent of sales declined greatly in 1973 but improved in 1974; the current ratio is improved from last year but, relative to other firms, is still below average. A fairly obvious trend is the increase of long-term debt and stockholders' equity to finance increased capital expenditures. It should be remembered that this firm has much "debt" in the form of leases. A big advantage to presenting financial data over time is that it makes it easier to identify trends and temporary abnormalities in company operations.

TABLE 5–1
Percentage Distribution of Levi Strauss' 1974 Income Statement (dollars in thousands)

Net Sales	$897,696	100.0%
Cost of goods sold	622,214	69.3
Gross Profit	$275,482	30.7%
Marketing, general and administrative expenses	186,175	20.7
Operating income	$ 89,307	9.9%
Interest expense	13,675	1.5
Other expense (net of other income)	2,901	.3
Income before taxes	$ 72,731	8.1%
Provision for taxes on income	37,862	4.2
Net income	$ 34,869	3.9%

Summary of Ratio Analysis. This type of analysis is used to compare various operating and financial characteristics of one company to another or to a group of companies. Used this way, the ratios show the relative performance of the company. Table 5–2 is a summary of the ratios examined in this chapter and, where available, the Dun & Bradstreet industry average ratios.

TABLE 5-2
Key Ratios of Levi Strauss Compared to Those Calculated by Dun & Bradstreet

		Dun & Bradstreet's Industry Ratios		
Ratio and Calculation	*Levi Strauss' 1974 Ratio*	*Top Quartile*	*Median*	*Low Quartile*
Current ratio = Current assets ÷ Current liabilities	2.01	3.31	2.15	1.85
Inventory to working capital = Inventory ÷ Working capital. . .	112.7%	40.9%	72.6%	125.4%
Net profit to sales = Net profit ÷ Sales	3.9%	2.42%	1.37%	0.49%
Net profit to net worth = Net profit ÷ Net worth	16.9%	13.94%	6.91%	2.81%
Net profits on working capital = Net profit ÷ Working capital. . .	17.9%	15.53%	8.33%	3.25%
Gross operating margin = Gross profit ÷ Net sales	30.7%	NA	NA	NA
Debt to net worth = Total debt ÷ Net worth	128.3%	69.1%	111.3%	159.0%
Current debt to net worth = Current debt ÷ Net worth	91.3%	39.5%	78.6%	106.8%
Productivity of assets = Net income ÷ Total assets.	10.3%	NA	NA	NA

NA = not available.

Levi Strauss compares favorably to the manufacturers which are presumed similar to it in operation. On balance, the company seems more profitable than others, but it is carrying more debt and inventory than the average firm.

Earnings per Share and Cash Flow

These two measures differ from the ratios cited earlier in two important ways. First of all, these ratios cannot be interpreted in the same way that the current ratio, for instance, can. A current ratio of 2:1 is "better" than one of 1.5:1, all other things being equal. Earnings or cash flow of $10 per share is a practically meaningless ratio because unless the price of the stock is known, it is impossible to tell whether $10 of earnings per share is "good."

The previously studied ratios have some meaning of and by themselves. Earnings or cash flow per share almost always must be examined over time and in the context of ratios of other similar companies to be interpreted meaningfully. For these reasons these two ratios have been treated separately. There are no "industry average ratios" of these two measures.

Earnings per Share. This is unquestionably the most widely used measure of investment profitability. It will be examined in great detail in Chapter 10, so at this time discussion is limited to defining the measure and stating its meaning.

Earnings per share is a ratio of total earnings to the number of common shares outstanding. It tells how many dollars of after-tax profits were "earned" by each share of common stock. Levi Strauss' earnings per share figure for the year ended November 24, 1974 is

$$\begin{aligned}\text{Earnings per share} &= \text{Total net income/Number of shares}\\ &= \$34{,}869{,}000/10{,}880{,}080\\ &= \$3.20.\end{aligned}$$

This figure is larger than it was in any other year (see Figure 5–6), but it cannot be related directly to earnings per share figures of other firms, even those in the same industry.

Cash Flow and Cash Flow per Share. The term *cash flow* refers to the cash available for use of a business during a period of time. Most analysts define cash flow as net income after taxes plus any noncash–using expenses such as depreciation, depletion, and amortization. It will be remembered that these expenses were deductions from profits in determining net profit, but they were "noncash expenses" in that no money was actually paid out to cover them. A simple bookkeeping entry reduces profits by the amount of the yearly charges, but the cash that would have paid these expenses, if they were the regular kind, remains in the business to be used by management for expansion, to repay debt, or even to pay dividends.

Emphasis on cash flow began in the early 1950s, and many financial analysts grasped it as being a better measure of future profitability than earnings. Most analysts reported cash flow per share figures alongside earnings per share. Cash flow data are regularly recorded by many companies and financial services. Few analysts would now accord it equal importance to earnings because cash flow is largely influenced by how noncash expenses are accounted for. For example, a firm using accelerated depreciation would have a larger cash flow and lower profits than an identical firm depreciating the same assets on a straight-line basis. Cash flow analysis is a tool that should be used with caution. Cash flow for Levi Strauss during 1974 would be computed as follows:

Net income	$34,869,000
Plus depreciation, amortization, and other items (from Consolidated Statement of Changes in Financial Position)	16,063,000
Equals cash flow during 1974	$50,932,000

Cash flow per share = Total cash flow/Number of shares outstanding
= $50,932,000/10,880,080
= $4.68.

SUMMARY

Every investor should be familiar with the use and interpretation of at least the most common techniques of financial analysis. *Ratio analysis* is the relating of various accounting data by dividing one measure into another. In this way common performance measures from different companies can be compared more easily. Ratios may be divided into three general classifications: *liquidity ratios,* which measure the firm's ability to pay short-term obligations and thereby to remain in business; *profitability ratios,* which measure the relative profitability of the firm; and *financial ratios,* which measure the equity and debt contributions to the financing of the firm and the return to investors. These ratios are often compared to those of other similar companies or to ratios of groups of similar companies. Industry average ratios vary widely because of the way different industries operate. A high debt ratio may be normal in one industry but abnormal in another.

Financial data and ratios are often presented in sequence for a period of years. This so-called *horizontal analysis* makes it easier to see how the business's operation has changed over time. It makes trends and temporary fluctuations easier to identify. *Vertical analysis* refers to the use of percentage distributions of balance sheet and income statement items to show the relative importance of each component of these accounts. Data presented in this form allow easy comparison between different firms.

Earnings per share and *cash flow per share* are two ratios commonly used as measures of present and future profitability. Such ratios must be interpreted differently than other financial ratios because it is impossible to determine whether a given earnings per share or cash flow per share ratio is good without obtaining additional information about the company involved.

There are many more ratios and techniques of financial analysis than were surveyed in this chapter. Some will be covered in later chapters, but most are left to the investor to examine and evaluate as need dictates. As a guide to doing this, it should be remembered that there is a potentially huge number of different ratios. Use only those that logically relate two variables that are meaningful in the context of the information being sought.

This chapter has used only the amounts and ratios contained on financial statements as the basis for the analysis of a company. These statements are often misleading in that they do not identify the most important assets that a company owns. For example, what is the true value of the Coca-Cola trademark, IBM's basic computer patents, Kodak's research and sales organization? These assets have been responsible for much of the profitability of these firms, but because of accounting convention they are stated as having little or no value on the company's financial statements.

Conventional financial analysis usually cannot identify one company as being a better *investment* than another. Whether an investment is good or bad is largely dependent upon how much one must pay for its securities relative to the returns that are expected from owning them. Analysis of the factors important to this type of evaluation are covered under the heading *security analysis.* They will be examined in the next chapter.

PROBLEMS

1. Hypothetical financial statements of Jones Corporation are presented below.
   a. Construct the ratios listed below from the data in these statements.
   b. This firm sells suits and coats (line number 2337 of Dun & Bradstreet's "Key Ratios in 125 Lines," Figure 5–4). Compare the ratios of Jones Corporation with those of the average firm in category 2337 to answer these questions:
      (1) Is the company financially sound?
      (2) Is the company profitable?

JONES CORPORATION
Balance Sheet
12/31/75

Assets		**Liabilities**	
Cash	$ 15,000	Accounts payable	$23,000
Accounts receivable	40,000	Notes payable	9,000
Inventory	97,000	Other current liabilities	13,000
Total current assets	$152,000	Total current liabilities	$45,000
Buildings and land (net of depreciation)	200,000	Mortgage	41,000
		Total liabilities	$86,000
		Capital	
		10,000 shares of no par stock authorized, 5,000 shares issued	$ 65,000
		Retained earnings	201,000
Total assets	$352,000	Liabilities and Capital	$352,000

JONES CORPORATION
Income Statement
For the Year Ended 12/31/75

Net sales		$475,000
Cost of goods sold	$350,000	
Operating expenses	92,500	442,500
Profit before taxes		32,500
Taxes		13,500
Profit after taxes		$ 19,000

1. Working capital.
2. Sales to working capital.
3. Current assets to current liabilities.
4. Net profits to total assets.
5. Current debt to net worth.
6. Net profit to sales.
7. Debt to net worth.
8. Earnings per share.

2. This question requires consultation with either the annual reports of a company, Moody's *Industrials Manual* or the Standard & Poor's *Industrial Manual*. Choose any large, well-known industrial company (to assure that data are available). Construct the following ratios from its financial statements for each of the past five years.

a. The current ratio.
b. Debt to net worth.
c. Sales to net worth.
d. Sales to assets.
e. Profits to sales.
f. Profits to net worth.
g. Earnings per share.

Use these ratios (and any others you feel are important) to determine whether the company is performing better or worse than it was five years ago.

QUESTIONS

1. Are composite industry ratios always a good basis of comparison when using ratio analysis to determine the performance of a firm?
2. Which of the ratios presented in Figure 5–4 are useful to the investor and which are useful to the banker or other lender? Justify your choices.
3. What advantage does trend analysis (horizontal analysis) have over simple one-year ratio analysis?
4. Would it be possible for a company to have a high current ratio and still go bankrupt?
5. What is *cash flow*? What does it indicate?
6. Why are there no composite earnings per share ratios for different industries?
7. Is it possible for the debt to net worth ratio of a company to be "too good"?
8. Why is depreciation called a "noncash expense"?
9. What does a balance sheet show?
10. What does an income statement show?
11. What determines whether an asset is recorded as a current or a long-term asset? Can long-term assets ever become current assets?
12. Levi Strauss' balance sheet does not list one particular asset which is of very great value to the company. What is this asset and why is it valuable?

SELECTED READINGS

Bernstein, Leopold, A. *Financial Statement Analysis: Theory, Application and Interpretation.* Homewood, Ill.: Richard D. Irwin, 1973.

Christy, George A., and Clendenin, John C. *Introduction to Investments,* 6th ed. New York: McGraw-Hill, 1974.

Cohen, Jerome B.; Zinbarg, Edward D.; and Zeikel, Arthur. *Investment Analysis and Portfolio Management,* rev. ed. Homewood, Ill.: Richard D. Irwin, 1973.

Graham, Benjamin; Dodd, David L.; and Cottle, Sidney. *Security Analysis: Principles and Technique.* New York: McGraw-Hill, 1962.

"How to Read a Financial Report." New York: Merrill Lynch, Pierce, Fenner, and Smith. Copies may be obtained from Merrill Lynch brokerage offices.

Mauriello, Joseph A. *Accounting for the Financial Analyst.* C. F. A. Monograph Series, rev. ed. Homewood, Ill.: Richard D. Irwin, 1971.

Vaughn, Donald E. *Survey of Investments,* 2d ed. New York: Holt, Rinehart and Winston, 1974.

6
Analysis of Individual Securities, Industries, and Securities Markets

INTRODUCTION

Analysis of individual securities is performed to identify securities which are priced relatively high or low—compared to a calculated value. The methodology of the analysis used with each type of security is discussed in the chapters which follow, after there is clear understanding of the investment characteristics associated with each type of security. At this point it is sufficient to state that while the concept of identifying relative value is common to all types of analysis, the factors which are analyzed differ with each security. For example, the two most important considerations in analyzing savings accounts, bonds, and straight preferred stocks are the amount of expected returns and the certainty with which interest and dividends are anticipated to be paid. The *coverage ratio* is the most widely used tool of analysis for these fixed income investments. This ratio simply compares the amount of funds available to pay interest and preferred dividends to the amounts that must be paid. If the coverage ratio is high there is little risk that these payments will not be made. Such investments are analyzed as being of high grade; they usually pay the lowest returns. Fixed return investments which have low coverage ratios are more risky because returns from these investments might not be forthcoming. Investors require, and usually obtain, higher returns from these investments to compensate for the risk of nonpayment of interest or dividends.

Convertible securities are those which may under certain circumstances be traded for securities of a different type. The analysis of this type of security is made difficult because the relative value of one security is dependent upon the relative value of the security for which it may be traded. The purpose of the examination of these securities remains the same as before, even though the techniques of analysis differ. The analysis of such securities is discussed in Chapter 9.

Common stock analysis is based upon growth rates, earnings per share, and dividends per share. Computation of the relative value of these securities is somewhat less precise than that performed on fixed income securities, and yet it is widely performed by security analysts and individual investors. A large portion of Chapter 10 is devoted to this topic.

The analysis of investment companies follows the established pattern of equating risk and return characteristics to determine the relative value of the shares of individual companies. Investment companies are somewhat easier to analyze than either convertible securities or common stocks because investors are provided with information about the investment policies of each investment company. While investment company managers are not always able to meet the goals set for their companies, potential investors at least know what these goals are. Such information allows investors to assign a likely amount of risk and return to each type of investment company. The analysis of investment companies is presented in Chapter 11.

Warrants, puts and calls, and rights are discussed and analyzed in Chapter 12 along with several other types of speculative investments. Warrants, puts and calls, and rights have potential value only because they may be used to acquire other securities. Analyzing warrants, puts and calls, and rights is exceptionally difficult because it requires that one be able to predict the future value of the security which can be acquired with them. In most respects the analysis of these securities follows the format used when examining convertibles.

The purpose of these brief paragraphs on the analysis of individual types of securities is to prepare the reader for the chapters which follow in Part 3, Types of Investments, and to introduce the concept of *relative value*. While different techniques are used to determine this value, in all cases it is based upon the risk and return characteristics of the security under examination. Before proceeding further it is advisable to discuss how corporate financial statements may be adjusted to give the security analyst a more accurate indication of the true financial condition of a company, and how industries and securities markets may be analyzed.

FINANCIAL STATEMENT ANALYSIS REVISITED AND REFINED

Without a great deal of training or difficulty, one can compute the various measures of financial analysis which were outlined in Chapter 5. This is a necessary first step in investment decision-making, but before final inferences and conclusions can be drawn, an intermediate step must be undertaken. This step involves an examination of and appropriate adjustments to the raw data in the financial statements. Omitting this stage might cause one to be misled by these reports and make unwise investment decisions.

The necessity for close scrutiny of the balance sheet and income statement numbers can be illustrated by recalling a children's story about the blind men from India. Each of these men "observed" an elephant by feeling a part of the animal. One touched a leg and said, "The elephant is like a tree." Another grasped the tail and remarked, "The elephant is like a snake." A third blind man caught an ear and used a fan in his description and so on. While every observation was partially accurate, each individual's concept of a total picture was vastly distorted. This is a danger in security analysis as well. A cursory ratio analysis can result in a partial view. While the analyst can "see" all the numbers, erroneous conclusions may be drawn because a close look behind the figures was omitted. Confidence in one's judgment can only be achieved if the process includes a study of the numbers themselves. A few illustrations will indicate that "things are not always as they appear to be."

INVENTORY ACCOUNTING

Gross profits are measured by the difference between net sales and the cost of the items being sold. For firms offering tangible items such as soft drinks, clothing, and so on, this profit calculation involves keeping track of the direct costs of preparing the items for the inventory.[1] Accounting procedures for this task are fairly straightforward and are not of concern in this discussion. However a problem of cost calculation develops when the costs of the items being sold are changing, as in a period of rapid inflation. As an example, imagine that after

[1] The following discussion is written for a manufacturing type firm. The situation for retailing and wholesaling firms is quite similar.

the items to be sold are produced, they are stocked in a large room. Suppose that the goods made most recently cost more than the earlier production. The shipping clerk who receives an order from the sales personnel will select one of the units from the inventory in the room. If the first one stored were chosen, the gross profit would be higher compared to the amount that would be calculated if the order had been filled with one of the recently produced items. This happens because the difference between the cost of this item and its sale price is greater than it would be if a new, higher-cost item were sold. For the most part, accounting systems are not set up to identify which item was actually sold out of the inventory. Instead, the typical convention is to keep track of production costs and then to assume, for reporting purposes, that sales are either taken off the "top" or from the "bottom." These systems are referred to as *Fifo* (first in, first out) and *Lifo* (last in, first out). During a period of cost stability, both methods result in the same gross profits. However, when costs are rising rapidly, the choice of Lifo rather than Fifo will lower reported profits. Particularly affected will be companies which have large inventories that are relatively slow to turn over. Lack of uniform inventory accounting can cause difficulty for the analyst who is attempting to (1) compare one firm with another and/or (2) appraise a trend in profits over time. While firms always specify the basis for inventory accounting in the footnotes to the financial statements, it is perfectly acceptable to change the basis from time to time. In the mid-1970s when costs increased rapidly, many firms switched their accounting practice from Fifo to Lifo.

These changes were made so that current sales could be matched with current costs of production. This results in a more accurate gross profit report. Under a Fifo system the older and lower production costs would be used and current profits would be overstated. An example of the significance of this type of change is illustrated in the 1974 Du Pont Annual Report. This statement revealed that the switch from Fifo to Lifo accounting resulted in a $145 million reduction in 1974 profits! Earnings per share declined from $11.22 to $8.02. While this change from Fifo to Lifo probably did not make shareholders happy, most persons would agree that it was necessary to accurately reflect Du Pont's current earning power.[2]

[2] If prices were to decline substantially, a shift back to Fifo reporting might be justified because the company would have the older and higher cost inventory on the books. Continuance of Lifo reporting would result in overstating the current market value of the inventory and understating profits.

Shifts in inventory accounting procedures can present a problem to the analyst. Much of the effort in appraising share values depends on comparing one firm with others. If all companies are not reporting income and costs on the same basis, meaningful comparative analysis is made more difficult. Changing inventory accounting procedures causes distortions in year-to-year profit calculations of individual firms. Profits may be abnormally high or low in years when such shifts are made. Recognition of the distortions and educated guesses as to their magnitudes are the only practical solutions to these problems. A careful reading of annual report footnotes will provide the analyst with a better grasp of the firm's "true" profitability.

NONOPERATING INCOME AND EXPENSE

Firms often have income and expense items which are not directly related to their normal experience in doing business. For instance, a company may invest in securities of other corporations or of the U.S. Government. Such investments may result in gains or losses; but, in either case, they have nothing to do with the company's basic profitability. Accounting practice calls for identifying any of these items so that a clearer picture of past operations may be developed. Typically these items are listed on financial statements as *extraordinary* or *nonrecurring gains or losses,* so as to indicate their special or transitory nature. The 1974 Annual Report for Dart Industries identifies two such losses suffered by this firm, whose products include Tupperware, Rexall Pharmaceuticals, and West Bend Cookware. Not related to these or other lines of its business were its investments in common and preferred stocks of other firms. The 1974 stock market decline resulted in Dart's reporting a loss on its marketable securities of over $16 million. In addition, the Company sold a resort development project at more than a $21 million loss. These transactions were nonrecurring and are separately identified in the company's financial statements. The analyst should adjust the reported earnings figure to eliminate the distortion caused by these extraordinary items.

OTHER TYPES OF FINANCIAL STATEMENT ADJUSTMENTS

The list of items in the financial statements needing careful interpretation is a lengthy one. Depreciation and depletion accounting policies vary among firms and require close scrutiny. Taxation provisions are another troublesome area. Sometimes there may be clouds on the horizon. An example is pending litigation. The 1974 Annual Report for American Brands (Pall Mall, Sunshine Biscuits, Jergens Lotion, and others) stated it is a defendent in a $2.5 billion law suit. Detailed explanation of these and other examples cited above is beyond the scope of this discussion—references at the end of this chapter present the most widely used source materials for the interested reader. Suffice it to say that analysis of individual firms is indeed complex. One need not be a full-time professional to do a good job; everyone should carefully review the statements and footnotes *before* making investment decisions.

MARKET ANALYSIS

Many years ago a reporter asked the eminent financier J. Pierpont Morgan to predict what the stock market would do in the future. Mr. Morgan's reply, "Stocks will continue to fluctuate," is as true today as it was then. It is one of the few statements about the future which always seems to be true. The sections of this chapter on market and industry analysis attempt to show how it is possible to tell when stock prices in general or prices of stocks of companies in specific industries have fluctuated "too much" in one direction or another. Techniques of analysis which are directed toward individual securities, options, and other types of investments appear in later chapters which are devoted to these specific investments.

Market analysis attempts to determine whether security markets in general are relatively high or relatively low. This type of study focuses on the markets for common stocks, bonds, preferred stocks, or commodities such as coal, plywood, wheat, and so on. Different variables are examined in the evaluation of each market, but the question to be answered is always the same: Is the market for common stocks, bonds, or other securities relatively high or low?

Because this book emphasizes common stock investments, discussion of market analysis will be centered around the markets for these securities. From earlier chapters we know that there are several securities markets: The New York Stock Exchange, the American Stock Exchange, the regional exchanges, and the over-the-counter-market. We also know that much statistical information is available on each of these markets. The exchanges construct their own indexes or averages of security prices, as do independent organizations such as Standard & Poor's, Moody's, the New York Times, and others. The composition of each index is slightly different, but with minor variations they all move in the same direction at the same time. Any of the indexes would be suitable for the purpose of determining whether the market for common stocks was relatively high or low in the spring of 1975. Because readers are already familiar with the Dow Jones Industrial Average (it was discussed in Chapter 4) this average will be examined with the purpose of determining whether the current level of stock prices is relatively high or low.

Figure 6–1 presents the DJIA over the past 15 years. One can tell from this graph that market prices were higher in 1966 than they were in 1962. One can also see that prices varied greatly over this period. While this information is interesting and may provide the observer with a rough idea of when this market is relatively high and low, our preference is to not use this or any other stock index by itself to

FIGURE 6–1
Price, Earnings, and Dividends per Share of the Dow Jones Industrial Average

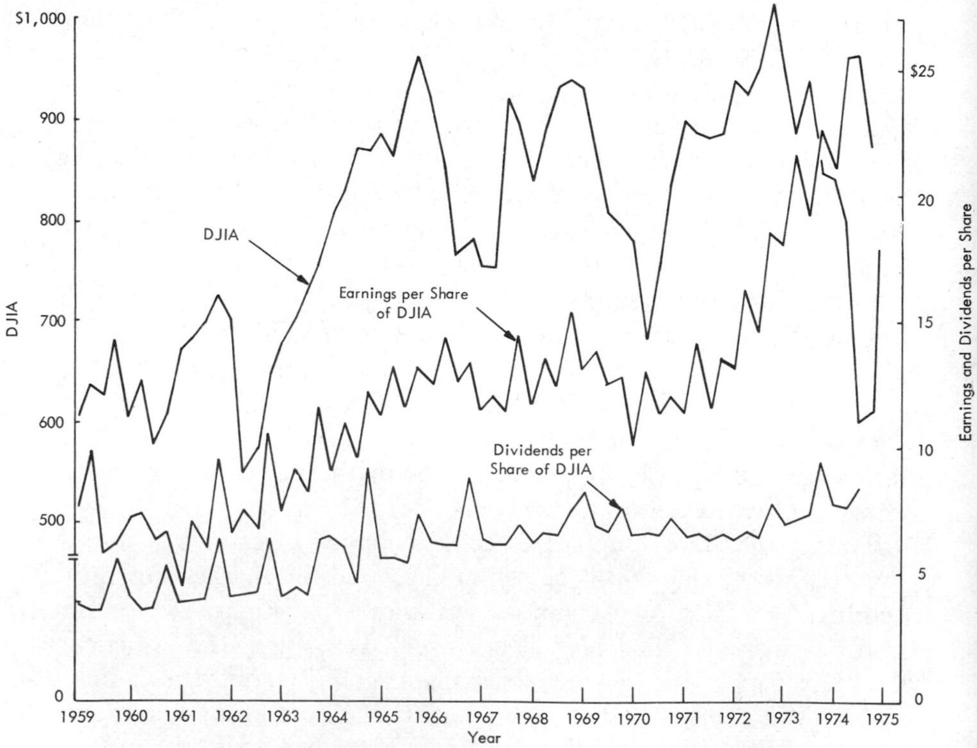

Source: *The Dow Jones Investor's Handbook—1975* (Chicopee, Mass.: Dow Jones Books, 1975), pp. 14–16.

analyze relative market conditions because the index only reveals current security *prices*.[3]

The prices of any investment—a single security or a market average—are meaningless figures unless they can be equated to the current and expected returns from owning the investment. For example, at one time an investment may sell at $10 and have a current and future expected return of $2 per year. At another time it may sell at $20 and have a current and future expected return of $5 per year. Without making use of the earnings information the investment at $10 appears to be a better buy because its price is lower; in reality it is not. It is a better buy at $20 because earnings, when related to price, are relatively greater.

SECURITY EARNINGS AND THEIR EFFECT UPON SECURITY MARKET PRICES

Brief mention was made in Chapter 5 of the fact that it is earnings and dividends which provide value for stocks. (Interest payments have the same relationship to bond prices.) There is no question but that over the long run, prices of individual stocks are related to the earnings and dividends expected to accrue to the owners of the securities. The same logical relationship holds for stock indexes and the dividends and earnings of the firms making up the index.

While one might expect the amount of dividends to have the stronger influence upon security prices, a brief examination of Figure 6–1 shows that this is not the case. Of the two earnings-associated measures presented in Figure 6–1, annual dividends are the least closely related to security prices. The graph of quarterly earnings (Figure 6–2) more closely resembles changes in market prices in that when earnings decreased so did the market price index, and vice versa.[4] It is seldom that average earnings and market prices move in different directions.

---

[3] Several types of market analysis attempt to use indexes and individual stock prices directly to determine future stock market prices. These methods are commonly grouped together under the heading of Technical Analysis, a topic which is examined in Chapter 14.

[4] In constructing the DJIA and the averages of dividends and earnings, adjustments have been made which attempt to take into account the stock splits and dividends which have occurred through the years. These adjustments have resulted in some difficulty in interpreting the DJIA because its price at any time cannot be determined by summing the prices of the 30 stocks making up the average. However, these same adjustments have been made in the dividends and earnings of securities in the average. These measures are directly related to the DJIA and it is logical to equate them to the price averages.

FIGURE 6–2
Dow Jones Industrial Average Price Earnings Ratios (quarterly data)

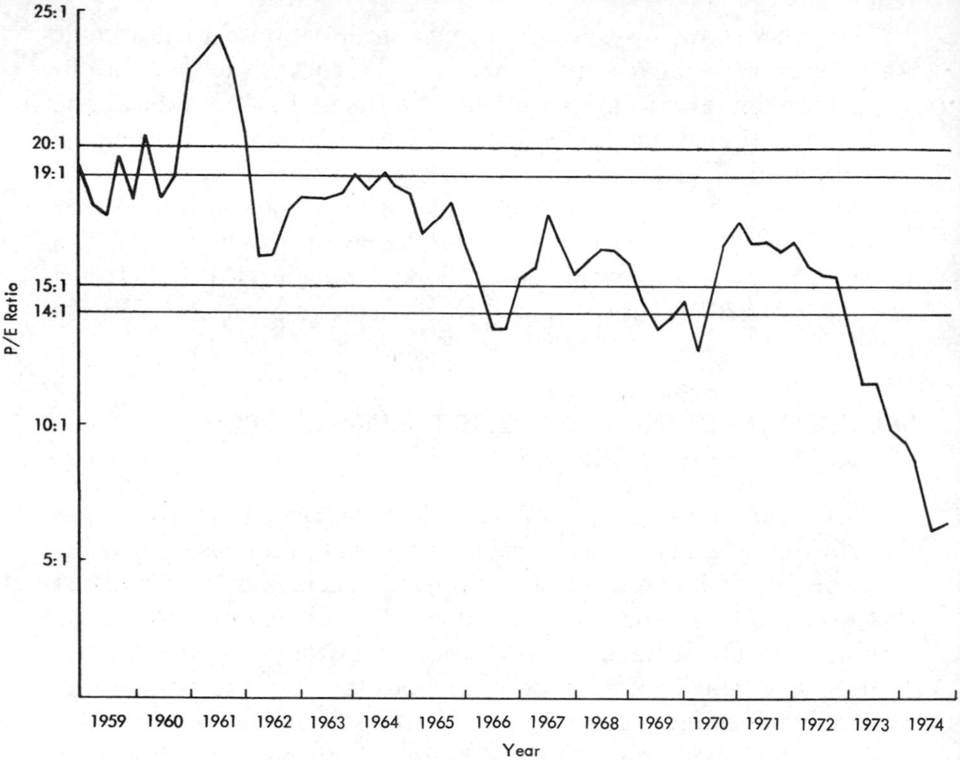

Source: *The Dow Jones Investor's Handbook—1975* (Chicopee, Mass.: Dow Jones Books, 1975), pp. 14–16.

Figure 6–2 presents the price-earnings (P/E) ratio of the DJIA. This ratio is computed in much the same way as it was for individual securities—by dividing the index price by the annual earnings per share of the securities making up the index. For example, if the index were at 800 and annual earnings were 40, the P/E ratio at that time would be 20:1. These ratios tell us how much investors were willing to pay for the earnings of securities making up the DJIA at different points in time. In the first quarter of 1961 investors paid $676.63 (the price of the index) for annual earnings of $29.54. In the first quarter of 1974 they paid $846.68 for $89.12 of earnings. In the first example the P/E ratio was 23:1; in the second it was about 10:1. Is it possible to identify either of these ratios as being relatively high or low?

Over the 15 years studied, the DJIA price-earnings ratio has varied between 6.2:1 and 24.2:1. If one assumes that the "normal" P/E ratio of the index lies within a range of values of from 14:1 to 20:1 during the period covered in Figure 6–2, the P/E ratio would have been "normal" about 72 percent of the time. Obviously, if a narrower range of values (15:1 to 19:1 for example) were defined as the normal range, the P/E ratios would have been outside the range (abnormally high or low) a larger proportion of the time. More sophisticated techniques may be used to measure the average P/E ratio, and to calculate the normal range more precisely. The purpose of these calculations is simply to provide analysts and investors with an indication of when security market prices are high or low, relative to a stated norm.

Assuming that the normal range of the DJIA price-earnings ratio is between 14:1 and 20:1, the ratios that prevailed in 1973 and 1974 clearly were abnormally low. At this time investors were extremely pessimistic and refused to pay what they had paid in the past for earnings. The question of whether the market prices of the index were relatively high or low in early 1975 can now be answered: Prices appeared to be relatively low, based upon historical P/E ratios.

A RELATIVE VALUATION FORMULA

There are other methods of identifying whether the stock market is relatively high or low. One such technique relates relative average stock prices to three main factors: earnings, the historical growth rate of stock prices, and the interest rate on high-grade bonds. Statistical techniques, which because of their complexity cannot be explained in this text, were used to determine the mathematical relationship that the above three variables had to stock prices.[5] These relationships are presented in this formula:

$$\text{Value} = \text{Earnings} \times \frac{37.5 + 8.8G}{\text{Aaa bond rate}}$$

where

Value = Expected (intrinsic) value of the DJIA.
Earnings = Average annual earnings per share of the stocks making up the DJIA.

[5] Variations of this formula are in common use by security analysts. A discussion of this particular formula appears in Benjamin Graham, "The Decade 1965–1974: Its Significance for Financial Analysts," from *The Renaissance of Value* (Charlottesville, Va.: Financial Analysts Research Foundation, 1974), pp. 1–2. A much more detailed discussion of the analysis of security market prices is presented in Benjamin Graham, David L. Dodd, and Sidney Cottle, *Security Analysis: Principles and Techniques,* 4th ed. (New York: McGraw-Hill, 1962).

G = Historical growth rate of the DJIA.
Aaa bond rate = Current interest rate on long-term corporate bonds rated Aaa grade.

The numbers 37.5 and 8.8 are constants which were derived through statistical techniques. These constants will not change in value unless the relationships between value, earnings, growth, and the Aaa bond interest rate change.

In early 1975 annual earnings of the DJIA are estimated at $88, the historical growth rate of the DJIA is 4.5 percent, and the Aaa bond interest rate is 9 percent. These figures are entered into the valuation equation which is solved below.

$$\begin{aligned} \text{Value} &= \$88 \times \frac{37.5 + 8.8\,(4.5)}{9} \\ &= \$88 \times 8.75 \\ &= \$754 \end{aligned}$$

Early in 1975 the DJIA should have had a value of $754, based upon the conditions and relationships stated in the formula. Its actual value was about $100 less. Analysts basing their estimates of intrinsic value either upon the formula presented above or upon the P/E analysis presented earlier would have concluded that in early 1975 stock price averages were well below their intrinsic values and offered investors the chance to buy securities at relatively low prices.

There are many variations of this and the previous type of analysis. Different averages, more sophisticated mathematical techniques, and longer or shorter periods of analysis, are all used for the purpose of measuring relative value. The strength of this type of analysis lies in the ease with which it is understood and performed and the fact that it has given reasonably good answers in the past. The main weakness is that the analysis deals with past relationships. A primary assumption in the P/E analysis, for example, is that if the "normal" P/E ratio in the past were 16:1, this ratio will continue to be normal in the future. The formula type valuation is also based entirely upon historical relationships. It is assumed that the mathematical constants 37.5 and 8.8 will continue to cause the formula to produce correct answers, and that earnings, the growth rate, and the Aaa bond rate continue to be as important in the calculation as they once were. The relationships of all these variables are historical. If some underlying condition changes these relationships, the formula must be altered to record this change or it will produce faulty answers. The analyst really needs to know what P/E ratio will be normal in the future, what the future growth rate will be, and how the variables of the relative value formula will interact in the future. Obviously none of this information is available. Analysts are therefore forced to rely upon historical data as the basis for much of their work. This must be done with caution, however. Whenever the techniques of analysis that worked well in the past cease to produce good results, one must examine all the historical assumptions and relationships contained in the analysis to see if they still hold true.

Another weakness is one that is common to the use of indexes and averages. At any time, some stocks in the DJIA will be increasing in price while others are decreasing. The use of an average hides the performance characteristics of the individual stocks that make up the average. It should be remembered that whenever averages such as the Dow Jones, the Standard & Poor's, or others are used as tools of analysis, that they only show very broad trends and relationships. However, single industries and companies may be examined separately. The tools to do so are presented later in this book.

INDUSTRY ANALYSIS

Investors who call their brokers for information often begin the discussion by asking, "What did the market do today?" Attention may then focus on the price action of industry groups and finally on individual stocks of interest. Such a sequence is quite logical—it begins with the general and moves to the specific. A number of studies have supported this approach.[6] One in particular has found that, on average, price change of market and industry or similar groupings explained about four-fifths of the price changes in common stocks.[7] The belief of a strong industry price influence is shared by most securities research departments. They typically have their analysts become specialists in one or two groups such as chemicals, airlines, paper, and so on.

RELATIVE VALUE

A technique used by industry analysts that is identical to one discussed in the market analysis section involves the price-earnings ratio.

---

[6] Many are summarized in Richard A. Brealey, *An Introduction to Risk and Return from Common Stock* (Cambridge, Mass.: The M.I.T. Press, 1969).

[7] Ibid., pp. 59–61. More recent studies at the brokerage firm of Paine, Webber, Inc. have confirmed this result.

The historical pattern of this ratio indicates periods when investors placed high or low values on earnings. Subject to the weaknesses outlined previously, the P/E is most helpful in gaining perspective for relative values. Figure 6–3 illustrates this point. The data plotted are computed by calculating the average of P/Es for a sample of firms in a single industry. Included in the electronics average are such companies as Beckman Instruments, Raytheon, and Techtronix. Notice the wide swings of relative values for this group. In 1968, investors were so optimistic about the future of these firms that they were willing to pay up to $43 for each dollar of earnings. Contrast this amount with the situation in 1974 when a dollar of earnings was only valued at $21.

Having the past record available helps an investor to decide whether or not the industry as a group is overpriced or underpriced. As previously mentioned, P/E data must be carefully interpreted. A low P/E ratio does not always indicate an undervalued situation, but simply calls attention to a possible opportunity. Also, P/E ratios present only part of the picture, but they are a beginning.

FIGURE 6–3
Price/Earnings Ratios of the Electronics Industry and Standard & Poor's 425 Industrial Stock Index

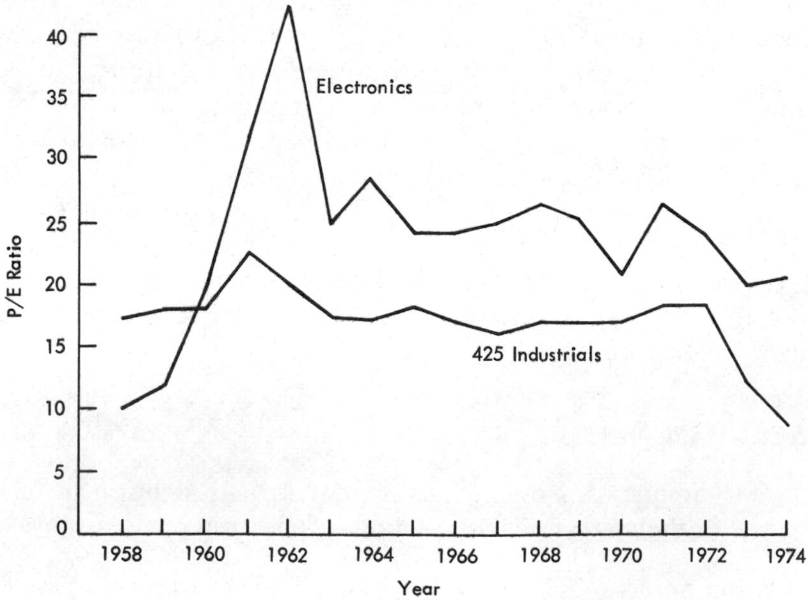

Source: Standard & Poor's *Industry Surveys, 1974.*

FIGURE 6–4
The Relative Strength Index of the Soft Drink Industry (ratio of industry to value line composite)

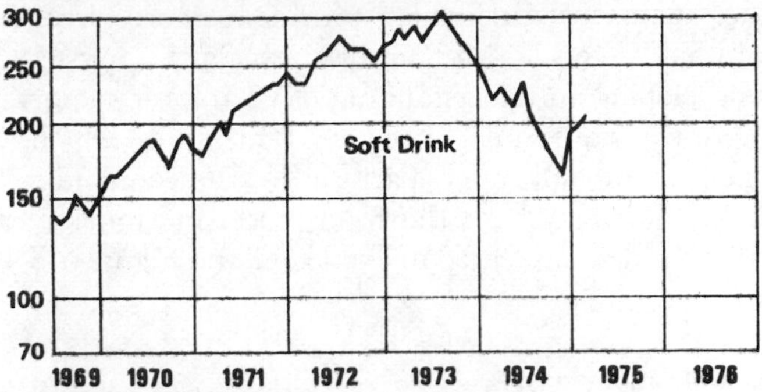

Index: June 1967 = 100
Source: *Value Line Investment Survey,* Edition 10, March 14, 1975, p. 1,516.

Another measure of relative value can be developed by dividing the industry price index by an average market price. This ratio provides an indication of how investors value a given industry relative to the entire market. Figure 6–4 shows that during a four year period ending in August 1973, soft drink companies were outperforming the market as a whole. Then, a sharp rise in sugar prices caused the bottlers to fall into disfavor in investors' minds. This shift is reflected in the steep decline on the graph. The trend was reversed in late 1974 when the outlook for soft drink firms picked up again and the industry outpaced the market's rise into 1975. Studying these ebbs and flows in investor expectations over time can help give the analyst an idea about the industry's investor appeal. A substantial rise in the ratio should make one cautious about the prospects for continuing relative strength of the industry under examination. A long period of decline in the measure serves to call attention to the industry as perhaps being in an attractive position.

One weakness of the relative strength ratio is that the indicator may be misinterpreted. Suppose the ratio points to an improving industry position relative to the market. This performance could occur during a falling stock market. Relative strength would be shown if the industry fell at a slower rate compared to the market. This would offer little consolation to investors using the relative strength measure, unless one could say they are only *relatively* unhappy.

ABSOLUTE VALUE

This shortcoming in the relative strength ratio points out the need for another approach.[8] One which provides a more direct indication of when to buy or to sell. Most industry analysts approach this challenge by developing an understanding of what basic factors make the industry prosper or decline. They seek measures which will help explain the demand and supply patterns for the companies' products. For instance, the analyst for the food processing industry would be interested in the data presented in Table 6–1 and Figure 6–5.

TABLE 6–1
Agricultural Products Data

	1974		*1975*	
	Plantings, Thousand Acres	*Output, Million Bushels*	*Planting Intentions, Thousand Acres*	*Indicated Output, Million Bushels*
Corn	76,500	4,651	76,100	6,621
Soybeans.	53,000	1,233	57,100	1,565
Spring wheat.	18,700	402	18,500	507
Winter wheat	52,400	1,391	55,500	1,854

Source: U.S. Department of Agriculture.

This information indicates a favorable outlook for the U.S. *supply* of grains and a strong worldwide *demand* for them. This and much other information would then be translated into a forecast for the industry.

Another example will further illustrate the industry analyst's approach. The apparel business is heavily dependent upon people's ability to spend. The correlation between spending power and purchases of clothing and accessories is shown in Figure 6–6. Since most of the points plotted lie very close to the line drawn, there is a strong indication that disposable income is a reliable measure of demand for the industry's products.

The careful reader will note that these steps still do not provide an answer to industry outlook. The analyst must still forecast grain

[8] Strictly speaking, all values are relative. The term absolute value, while not totally satisfactory, is used to differentiate several other techniques of value analysis from those outlined in the relative value analysis section.

FIGURE 6–5
Statistics on World Grain Production, Consumption, and Reserves

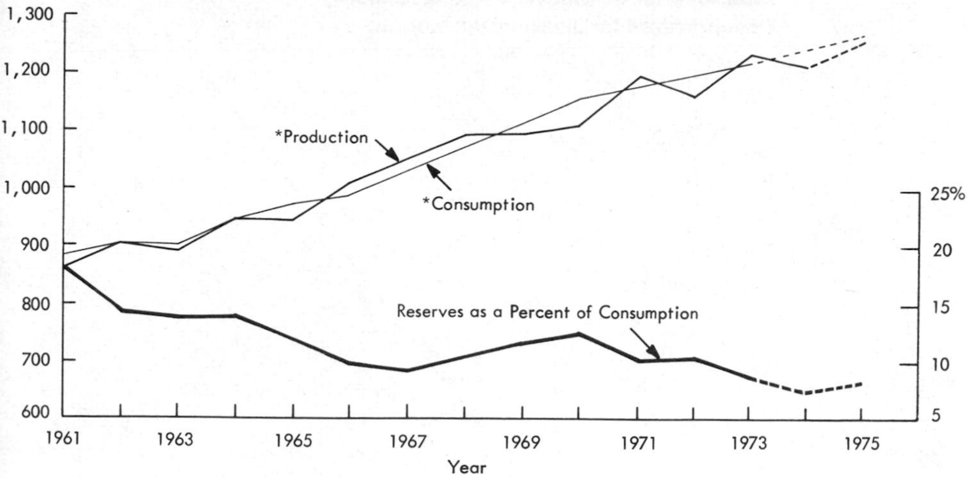

* Millions of metric tons
Source: Historic data, The Conference Board, "Food and Population: The Next Crisis"; chart, *Value Line Investment Survey,* Edition 10, March 14, 1975, p. 1,453.

supply and demand and disposable income. These intermediate procedures do not really beg the question because one can predict grain production from plantings, and disposable income from other economic forecasting techniques. The idea is that it is easier to project some items than others. Few analysts would attempt to only estimate, for example, next year's apparel sales without studying what caused sales to rise and decline. For this reason most forecasts are based on a careful investigation of what makes the industry "tick." Having a better understanding of this identifies the projections needed to make a complete study of the industry.

The industry experts become knowledgeable by reading a multitude of magazines, reports, and other data. For instance, an aerospace analyst would pour through such periodicals as *Aerospace International, Air Force and Space Digest, American Aviation, Aviation Daily,* and *Aviation Week and Space Technology* to name but a few.

The general topic of security analysis can be completed by studying individual companies. Market and industry factors are major influences on the behavior of individual securities. Understanding the characteristics of different types of investments facilitates the analysis process. For this reason, further treatment of security analysis will be delayed to Chapter 10.

FIGURE 6–6
Relationship of Clothing and Accessory Expenditures to Disposable Income

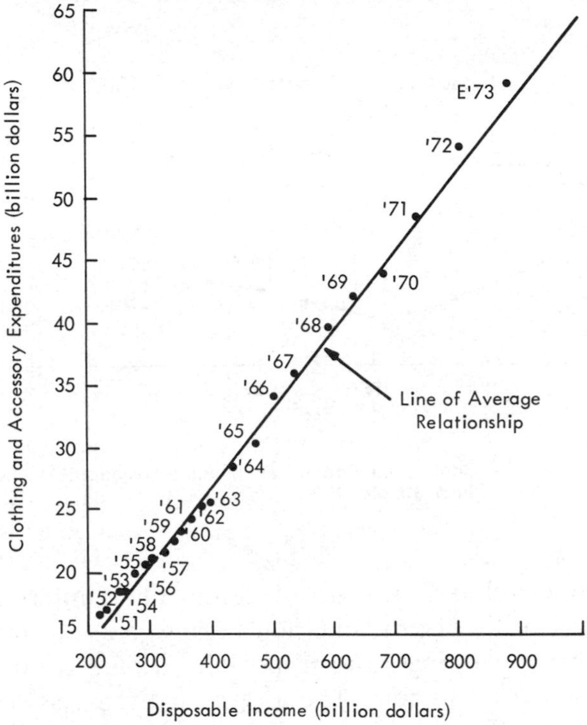

Source: *Industry Surveys*, Standard & Poor's Corporation, June 20, 1974, p. A 102.

SUMMARY

This chapter presented several ways in which industries, security markets, and to a lesser extent individual securities could be analyzed to determine whether their current values were relatively high or low. The presumption is that the normal market price of these investments is determined by historical relationships and that these relationships can be identified and measured to produce an estimate of the price that an investment or group of investments should have. A further presumption is that security prices are likely to fluctuate up and down more than they logically should, given known security market conditions. When security prices have fluctuated upward to the point where they are abnormally high it is time to sell. When they have fluctuated downward an abnormal amount it is time to buy. Successful investing then is dependent merely upon one's ability to tell when prices are relatively high or low.

A company's earnings and dividends are the main factors that give value to a company's securities. Earnings may be increased or decreased in any given time period by the way that the company accounts for its income and expenses. A necessary first step to any analysis that is based upon a company's earnings, requires that the company's financial statements be examined for the purpose of identifying any accounting practices that might cause income to be overstated or understated.

Examples of such practices are *last in, first out* (Lifo) and *first in, first out* (Fifo) accounting for inventory. Each procedure has the ability to understate or overstate income depending upon whether the cost of the inventory is rising or falling.

Nonoperating expenses and income are defined as income and expenses which are not normal to the business. If a company has income from a source (sale of real estate for example) which is expected to be nonrecurring, the analyst usually adjusts the company's profits downward by the amount of this extra income. By the same logic, the income statement would be adjusted upward if a company experienced extraordinary nonrecurring losses. There are other reasons for adjusting a company's financial statements; the purpose in making these adjustments is to obtain a more accurate estimate of what the company's earnings would have been under normal conditions of operation.

Market analysis attempts to identify when the market price for securities, commodities, or other investments is too high or too low. The central concept in this type of analysis is that there is some *normal* (intrinsic) *value* at which an investment should sell. The normal value is based upon many factors—historical investment prices, relationship of stock prices to bond yields, and the relationship of earnings to investment prices, to mention but the most obvious. Market analysis consists of using these relationships to answer the question of whether current prices are relatively high or low, based upon the factors studied. The relationship between security earnings and prices is examined in detail to determine the value of this ratio (the P/E ratio) as an indicator of relative price levels. A more complicated approach which uses earnings, price growth rates, and bond interest rates to arrive at an estimate of relative value is also explained. While these methods have produced fairly good relative value estimates in the past, there can be no assurance that they will continue to perform well in the future. Persons must constantly guard against using techniques of analysis which have become inaccurate because of changes in the underlying relationships of the factors that are used in the analysis.

Industry analysis makes use of techniques similar to those used to analyze security markets and individual securities. The concept of a *normal value* that is based upon what investments should sell for, given certain market and other considerations, is a central theme in this type of analysis. The use of price-earnings ratios in industry analysis is discussed as is the *relative strength index*. This index is constructed by dividing the industry security price index by an average security price. The resulting ratio tells how investors value the industry relative to all securities.

Absolute value analysis attempts to identify the factors most important to the profitability of a company and/or industry. For example, there is a strong relationship between the demand for lumber and housing starts. If housing starts are predicted to increase, then lumber manufacturers can be expected to sell more products. Profits should increase and so should stock prices of companies in the lumber industry. The demand for products of all companies is strongly controlled by relationships such as these. Absolute value analysis attempts to use these relationships to predict the expected future value of securities.

PROBLEMS

1. The profit and loss statement of XYZ Company appears below. How would you change it to make it more realistic so far as earnings are concerned?

XYZ COMPANY
Profits and Losses
For the Period Ended 12/31/1975

Sales		$1,000,000
Cost of goods sold		900,000
Gross profits		$ 100,000
Distribution expense	$50,000	
Administrative expense.	10,000	60,000
Profits before taxes.		$ 40,000
Sale of building		100,000
Total profits before taxes . . .		$ 140,000

2. A company has total after-tax earnings of $1 million. Dividends are $500,000. The company's stock is priced at $50 per share and there are 500,000 shares outstanding. What is the P/E ratio of this company?
3. Assume that the DJIA is growing at 4 percent per year, Aaa bonds yield 8 percent, average earnings of the DJIA are $95, and the money supply has been increasing at 10 percent per year. Use the valuation formula in the text to determine the probable value of the DJIA under these conditions.

QUESTIONS

1. What are the most important factors in the analysis of fixed income securities?
2. What are the most important factors in the analysis of common stocks?
3. A necessary first step to the analysis of the financial statements of a company is the "adjusting" of the raw data of the financial statements. What are the most important things to examine when making these adjustments?
4. What is the goal of *market analysis?*
5. The relative valuation formula presented in this chapter bases stock average values upon earnings, the growth rate of the DJIA, and the Aaa bond rate. List and defend two other variables which you believe are also related to stock prices.
6. What is the main difference between *industry* and *market* analysis?
7. What is the *relative strength ratio?* What does it tell the investor?
8. What is *absolute value analysis?* How does one perform such analysis?

SELECTED READINGS

Bolten, S. E. *Security Analysis and Portfolio Management.* New York: Holt, Rinehart and Winston, 1972.

Findley, M. Chapman, and Williams, Edward E. *Investment Analysis.* Englewood Cliffs, N.J.: Prentice-Hall, 1974.

Graham, Benjamin. "The Decade 1965–1974; Its Significance for Financial Analysts," in *The Renaissance of Value.* Charlottesville, Va.: Financial Analysts Research Foundation, 1974.

Graham, Benjamin; Dodd, David L.; and Cottle, Sidney. *Security Analysis: Principles and Techniques,* 4th ed. New York: MacGraw-Hill, 1962.

Levine, Sumner, N., ed. *Financial Analysts Handbook*, vols. 1 and 2. Homewood, Ill.: Dow Jones-Irwin, 1975.

Smith, Keith V., Eiteman, David K. *Essentials of Investing*. Homewood, Ill.: Richard D. Irwin, 1974.

Sprecher, C. Ronald. *Introduction to Investment Management*. Boston: Houghton Mifflin, 1975.

part three

Types of Investments

7
Investing in Savings

INTRODUCTION TO PART THREE

This chapter is the first of a series devoted to the characteristics of various investments.[1] The order of coverage roughly follows the plan of Table 7–1, which is a very informative table. It tells not only the dollar amounts of various classes of financial assets, but it also shows how different types of assets have changed in importance over a period of time. Each of the assets listed in the table is examined in the remaining chapters of this book. With certain exceptions, the amount of space devoted to each of the assets is in proportion to the importance this asset holds for individuals.

The exceptions to this statement are demand deposits and currency, mutual fund shares, life insurance reserves, and pension fund reserves. Mutual fund shares are given far more coverage than seems warranted because this form of investment has gained such great popularity in recent years. Demand deposits and currency, while comprising 8 percent of the financial assets of individuals in 1974, are not covered at all. They are omitted because very few people hold cash as an *investment*, although a few people do speculate by purchasing foreign currencies and gold.

Life insurance and pension fund reserves are discussed in Chapter 15 which emphasizes investment goals and strategies. These assets are not investments as the term is defined in this book. Insurance or pen-

[1] The chapters of Part Three have been written so that each chapter stands on its own; they may be read in any order. The exception to this statement is that persons not familiar with the meaning of yield and compound interest should read the next two parts of this chapter before going to the later chapters.

TABLE 7–1
Financial Assets of Individuals (dollar amounts in billions)

	1955		*1965*		*1974*	
Type of Asset	*Amount*	*Percent*	*Amount*	*Percent*	*Amount*	*Percent*
Demand deposits and currency	66.1	9.3	94.2	6.4	173.9	8.0
Savings accounts	106.3	15.0	287.5	19.6	694.7	31.8
at commercial banks	43.8	6.2	115.9	7.9	325.2	14.9
at savings institutions	62.5	8.8	171.6	11.7	369.5	16.9
U.S. government securities	68.9	9.7	81.8	5.6	118.2	5.4
State and local bonds	19.2	2.7	36.4	2.6	62.3	2.9
Corporate and foreign debt instruments	7.1	1.0	13.5	.9	59.1	2.7
Corporate stock (market value)	278.8	39.4	602.2	41.1	488.6	22.3
Investment company shares (market value)	7.8	1.1	35.2	2.4	36.6	1.7
Mortgages	22.4	3.2	34.3	2.3	38.9	1.8
Life insurance reserves	69.3	9.8	105.9	7.3	157.5	7.2
Pension fund reserves	50.4	7.1	153.8	10.5	313.7	14.5
Miscellaneous assets	12.3	1.7	19.5	1.3	39.7	1.7
Total	708.6	100.0	1,464.3	100.0	2,183.2	100.0

Note: Details may not equal totals due to rounding error. 1974 data preliminary.
Source: Special computer run of the Flow of Funds and Saving Section of the Board of Governors of the Federal Reserve System.

sion reserves may not be sold or used like any of the more conventional investments. In fact, from a technical viewpoint they are not directly owned by the policyholder or the owner of pension fund rights. Life insurance and retirement plans do have a bearing on an individual's investment policy because upon death or retirement they will provide the owner or the owner's heirs with money.

This chapter begins with a discussion of the general investment characteristics of savings accounts and the meaning of yield as it relates to savings-type investments. The operation of compound interest and its computation is described briefly. Savings investments in commercial banks, savings banks, savings and loan companies, and credit unions are next examined with the goal of describing the risk and return characteristics associated with savings investments in these *deposit financial institutions*.

INTRODUCTION TO SAVINGS ACCOUNTS

Savings accounts are by far the most common form of personal investment. Most people either have an account currently or have had one sometime in the past. Many children are given their first gifts in the form of a savings deposit at the local bank or savings and loan company, and they often keep these accounts for many years, perhaps for an entire lifetime. Studying savings accounts first allows one to look at debt contracts and yields in their simplest forms. Understanding the more complex types of investments should be easier after one has a good grasp of the basic concepts of interest and contractual debt obligations.

Each type of savings institution offers savers slightly different rates of return, withdrawal privileges, and degrees of safety and convenience. However, the main features of the agreement between the saver and the company accepting the savings are very similar. In all cases, the financial institution is obligated to pay upon request the amount deposited in a savings account plus any interest that has accumulated. Under certain conditions the company may refuse to make immediate withdrawal privileges available, but ultimately it must stand ready to repay these funds. This statement holds true even though the saver's legal position varies from that of a *creditor* in banks offering deposits to that of being an *owner* of savings shares in other institutions.

A second characteristic of all savings accounts is that the depositor must make application to withdraw money from an account. Checking accounts are *demand* accounts, not savings accounts. The institution offering this type of account must pay any part or the total amount of a demand account immediately upon request. By federal law no interest may be paid on these accounts. A recently introduced banking innovation, the *negotiable order of withdrawal,* for all practical purposes does allow interest to be paid on demand deposits. These NOW accounts, as they have come to be called, will be examined later in this chapter.

The contract between the saver and the institution holding the savings is usually contained in a passbook or upon a certificate which evidences the deposit or savings share purchases. This contract will state the conditions under which withdrawals may be made. Rule 6 of the passbook presented in Figure 7–1 is a typical statement on withdrawal procedure. Some institutions have more detailed regulations which provide for a longer notice of withdrawal period when large amounts of deposits are to be withdrawn.

State and federal laws force financial institutions that accept savings deposits to provide themselves with the *option* of not paying out deposits on demand. But as a practical matter savers can usually consider their regular savings accounts as payable upon demand. No savings

FIGURE 7–1
A Typical Passbook of a Commercial Bank

RULES AND REGULATIONS GOVERNING SAVINGS ACCOUNTS

DEPOSITOR AND BANK AGREE:

Rule 1. All savings deposits are received by United States National Bank of Oregon subject to rules and regulations as printed herein; as shown on Bank's deposit and other forms; and as changed from time to time by posting of notice in Bank's lobby. Acceptance of this passbook, and inscription of name by depositor or agent on signature card required by the Bank, shall be deemed and held to be a valid assent thereto.

(THE SAVINGS PASSBOOK)

Rule 2. A pre-numbered passbook shall be issued for each savings account. All deposits made by or for the account of the depositor will be entered in the passbook at the time they are made, or as soon thereafter as the passbook shall be presented for such purpose. The balance shown in the passbook to the credit of depositor is subject to correction to accord with the Bank's records.

Should the savings passbook be lost, destroyed or fraudulently obtained from any depositor, immediate notice must be given the office of the Bank at which the account is carried. After such notice, if satisfactory explanation be made and bond of indemnity be given in a form approved by the Bank's officers, the amount to the credit of the depositor will be paid to such depositor, or a new book will be issued therefor.

(ASSIGNMENT OF ACCOUNT)

Rule 3. No assignment of the depositor's passbook or account, or any part thereof, shall be valid unless made in writing, and shall not bind the Bank until it has been filed with the Bank in writing.

(DEPOSITS)

Rule 4. Deposits will be received of any sum from one dollar to such maximum amount as may from time to time be designated by the Bank.

Items are credited conditionally at time of deposit and may be forwarded on next business date after receipt. Bank may charge back any item before ultimate payment, including items drawn on this Bank; it is not liable for losses in transit; and it may decline to honor withdrawals against conditional credits. Depositor is bound by all clearing house and/or Federal Feserve collection rules and practices.

The Bank may decline to receive any deposit and at any time may require depositor to withdraw all or part of the funds on deposit. Notice thereof will be mailed to the depositor by first-class mail at his last address on file with the Bank. Interest shall cease on such deposit or part of deposit for which withdrawal is required after thirty days from date of such notice.

(DEPOSITS OF MINORS)

Rule 5. Deposits made by any person or persons for or in the name of any minor shall be made and received upon the express condition that the Bank may pay out such deposit or part thereof only upon the written order of the minor.

Deposits made by any person or persons in trust for any minor shall be made and received upon the express condition that the Bank during the lifetime of the depositor may pay out such deposit or part thereof only upon the written order of the person or persons who made the deposit in trust for the minor.

(WITHDRAWALS)

Rule 6. The passbook must be presented to the Bank when a withdrawal is made.

Withdrawals may be made personally, the depositor being required to sign a receipt for the amount of the withdrawal, or by order in writing satisfactorily authenticated, or by power of attorney, duly authenticated.

It is understood and agreed that the Bank may require, whenever in the opinion of any of the officers it may be deemed advisable, written notices of the intention of any depositor to withdraw as follows:

Thirty days' notice to withdraw any sum up to $100; sixty days' notice to withdraw any sum from $100 to $500; ninety days' notice to withdraw any sum from $500 to $1,000; four months' notice to withdraw any sum from $1,000 to $3,000; six months' notice to withdraw any sum over $3,000.

A second notice of withdrawal will not be accepted until the first notice has expired or been cancelled. Failure to demand payment at the Bank within five days after the expiration of the notice shall be constituted a waiver of such notice and a new notice may be required.

(INTEREST)

Rule 7. Interest will be allowed and paid on savings accounts on such terms and conditions and at such rates and on such balances as may, from time to time be designated by the Bank or as limited by the Federal Reserve Board or other legally constituted authority.

(SERVICE CHARGES)

Rule 8. All savings accounts, whether active or inactive, shall be subject to service charges now or hereafter in effect.

(AMENDMENTS)

Rule 9. These rules, conditions and regulations may be altered or amended, and new ones made by the Bank at any time, but no alterations or amendments or new rules, regulations or conditions shall be in force until notice thereof shall have been posted in the Bank lobby for at least thirty days. Such posting shall be held to be a personal notice to each depositor.

Source: U.S. National Bank of Oregon, Portland, Oregon. (This statement was in effect on March 22, 1975.)

institution will willingly fail to honor a deposit withdrawal request, unless a specified delay is required under the savings account contract. Even though the company is legally entitled to withhold money, to do so would suggest that it is insolvent. As soon as this information became known, as it certainly would, many savers would attempt to withdraw their money "to see if the bank is sound." Very few savings institutions keep enough cash on hand to satisfy exceptionally large withdrawal requests because deposits are either lent out or invested. Since it would be difficult to liquidate assets to obtain cash, they are very careful to do nothing which would cause depositors to lose faith in the institution, and thus to test it.

A final characteristic of savings accounts is that interest or savings dividends (both terms are used for technical reasons discussed later) of a specified amount are paid on all *principal* which is on deposit. These payments are legal liabilities of the company; they must be paid when due.

INVESTMENT CHARACTERISTICS OF SAVINGS ACCOUNTS

In Chapter 2 an attempt was made to explain the nature of the several types of risk encountered in almost all investments and how these characteristics are related to the return that is expected from any given investment. This discussion will now come alive as the risk and return properties of savings accounts are examined. The key to understanding investments lies in one's ability to classify the many different types of investments by their risk and return characteristics. These are the common denominators of investments which allow logical comparison of one type of investment against another. Unless this approach to selecting investments is used, it is nearly impossible to choose the investments most suitable to the individual investment situation. Yield is one of the most important attributes of all investments.

Measuring Yield

The yield of an investment refers to the amount received during a certain period of time over and above the amount originally placed into the investment. The simplest way to explain yield is by looking at the accumulation of money in a savings deposit. Yields from bonds, common stocks, and preferred stocks are computed somewhat differently. These methods will be discussed in the chapters devoted to each specific type of investment.

Computation of Savings Deposit Yields. The *yield* of a savings deposit is the amount of interest that the institution will pay for the use of deposited money. Normally the yield is identified as a percentage of the amount deposited—5 percent for example—and this means that the institution will pay the depositor $5 for every $100 that are on deposit at the institution over a stated period of time. The percentage amount is identified in the contract—written or unwritten—that the depositor has with the institution.

Of further interest to the depositor is *when* the interest is to be paid and what is to be done with the interest when it is paid. By convention and law, interest rates are stated on an *annual simple interest* basis. Simple interest is the percentage of the amount on deposit that would be earned by allowing the deposit to remain in the institution for a full year accumulating interest. Under this calculation the interest is assumed to be paid to the depositor as it is earned.

Most financial institutions compute interest payments on a semiannual or quarterly basis. Some make this computation over even shorter time periods—months, weeks, or days. If $100 were deposited at the beginning of the year in a savings account which paid 5 percent annually, interest to be computed semiannually, $2.50 would be received on the last day of June, and $2.50 would again be received at the end of the year. This assumes that the interest payments are paid directly to the depositor and not retained in the savings account. If interest were computed quarterly, four payments of $1.25 would be paid to the depositor every three months. The important point is that over the year $100 of principal was on deposit and $5 was paid during the year as a return to this investment. Measuring the yield on any investment is done by dividing the amount earned over the period by the amount invested at the beginning of the period, and adjusting the answer so that it is in terms of an annual rate of interest.

$$\$5/\$100 = 0.05, \text{ or } 5\%.$$

In this example the time period is one year so the answer is automatically presented as an annual rate. While most depositors have the option of receiving interest on their deposits on a monthly, quarterly, semiannual, or annual basis, in practice they usually allow their interest payments to remain in the account to be added to the amount of money that they have on deposit. This action provides for *compound interest*. It means that every time interest is calculated it is calculated on the interest that has been paid *and left in the account* as well as on the original principal. Interest paid and retained in the account becomes principal.

For example, if $100 were on deposit in a savings account which paid 5 percent annually and which computed interest payments semiannually, at the end of six months the deposit account would contain $100 of principal plus $2.50 of interest. At the end of the full year the semiannual interest computation would be made on the basis of a principal amount of $102.50. The interest for this second period would be

$$\text{Principal} \times \text{Interest rate} = \text{Dollar amount of interest}$$
$$\$102.50 \times 0.025 = \$2.56.$$

In this formula the interest rate has been reduced to one half the annual rate (5%/2 = 2.5%) to take into account the fact that the principal will earn interest for only half a year. Total interest paid on this deposit for the entire year would be $5.06. This can be seen from the illustration below. If the interest had been computed quarterly or more often, the amount of interest earned per year would have been slightly higher.

Principal on deposit at beginning of year.	$100.00
Interest paid for six months	2.50
Equals amount in account at beginning of second six-month period	102.50
Interest paid during next six months	2.56
Total amount in account at year end	$105.06

The true annual interest rate on this account is 5.06 percent per year.

$$\$5.06/\$100 = 0.0506 = 5.06\%$$

Some financial institutions advertise the simple interest rate, "5 percent per year on savings accounts," and others use the true annual rate, "5.06 percent per year compounded semiannually." A general rule is that the more often interest is compounded during a given time period, the greater is the true annual rate of interest. But even when interest is compounded daily, as it increasingly is, the difference between the true annual rate and the simple interest rate is small. Daily compounding of 5 percent interest results in a true annual yield of about 5.13 percent.[2]

The Power of Compound Interest. Over a short period of time, modest differences in the true rate of interest on savings investments are not very important. This is particularly true when the amount of

---

2 There are many different methods in current use for determining interest payments on savings accounts. A study by the American Bankers Association recorded over 100 different ways to do essentially the same thing. See American Bankers Association, *Methods and Procedures in Computing Interest on Savings Deposits*. Also see "How to Pick the Best Saving Account," *Consumer Reports*, February 1975, pp. 90–97.

TABLE 7–2
Accumulation of Interest and Principal at Various Rates of Compound Interest

Original Principal	Rate of Interest	Principal and Accumulated Interest After		
		10 Years	20 Years	30 Years
$100	3%	$134.39	$180.61	$ 242.73
100	6	179.08	320.71	574.35
100	9	236.72	518.61	1,265.20

principal is small because the dollars of yield are often insignificant. But over many years of compounding, differences in interest rates have very important effects upon the amount of accumulated savings, even when the principal is small. Table 7–2 shows how much $100 would accumulate to in 10, 20, and 30 years under three different interest rates. Interest is compounded annually and allowed to remain in the account.

At 6 percent compounded annually money doubles in amount in slightly less than twelve years; at 8 percent it doubles in slightly over nine years; at 10 percent doubling occurs in just over seven years. Over very long periods of time, the increase in amounts of money due to compound interest is truly staggering.

In 1626, Peter Minuit, an official of the Dutch West Indies Company, purchased Manhattan Island for about $24 in trinkets. This purchase is widely acclaimed as one of the best real estate investments on record because of the tremendous increase in the value of the island. However, the original $24 if left at annual compound interest at 6 percent for the 349 years between 1626 and 1975 would have shown a rather large increase on its own. It would have been worth about $16.3 billion at the end of 1975!

Grace Days and Other Savings Account Features. Over the long run the account offering the highest rate of interest with the highest number of compounding periods will produce the highest yield. Persons having relatively inactive savings accounts should seek such accounts. Persons who expect to make frequent deposits or withdrawals from their savings accounts must consider grace days and other features of savings accounts because they may materially affect the yield from a given savings account.

Deposit *grace days* refer to the practice of many savings institutions of crediting interest from the first of the month on deposits received before a given date. The 10th and 15th of the month are common grace dates. Withdrawal grace dates are the number of days before the end of a month or other accounting period within which depositors are allowed to make withdrawals and still have interest on the deposit credited to the end of the period. In general, withdrawal grace dates are fewer in number than deposit grace dates; three days of withdrawal grace being common.

Some savings institutions levy *maintenance fees* on accounts which have been inactive for a given period of time. Some institutions levy charges for withdrawals of over a certain number during a given time period. Some institutions pay interest only on accounts of a minimum size. Often the minimum size is calculated as the smallest amount on deposit during the interest computation period. Under such a rule, no interest would be paid on an account, no matter how large the amount deposited, if the account were drawn down to a zero balance before the end of the interest computation period.

In a recently published series of articles dealing with savings, four hypothetical savings accounts were compared to determine which gave the highest interest. The same amounts were deposited and withdrawn on the same dates in each account. Each account paid the same rate of interest, credited deposits, and compounded interest in the same manner. The only difference in the accounts was in the way interest was computed.[3] Figure 7–2 presents these calculations in the form of passbook savings account statements. The "best" account paid 68 percent more interest than the "worst."

Risk and Return Characteristics of Savings Accounts

The general relationship between risk and return described in Chapter 2 holds true for savings accounts. The yield on these investments is relatively low and constant; the principal is usually extremely safe. In another part of this chapter risk and return characteristics of savings deposits held at different financial institutions are examined, but at this time several general statements can be made on risk and return relationships.

Most of the companies engaged in the business of holding the savings of others are tightly regulated by federal or state laws, or both. These institutions are forced to meet certain financial tests in order to remain in business. Most of the institutions have chosen to have their deposits insured by either the Federal Deposit Insurance Cor-

---

[3] "How to Pick the Best Savings Account," *Consumer Reports*, February 1975, pp. 90–97.

FIGURE 7–2
Example of Saving Account Interest Calculations

These four banks all pay the same interest rate—yet interest payments range from $44.93 to $75.30.

There are many ways of computing interest, as the text of our report indicates. Here are four passbooks showing the identical deposits and withdrawals (made on the same days), with explanations of how the interest has been computed under four common methods. All four assume a six per cent interest rate and quarterly crediting and compounding.

IN ACCOUNT WITH

	DATE	WITHDRAWAL	DEPOSIT	INTEREST	BALANCE	TELLER
1	JAN-1		**1,000.00		**1,000.00	
2	JAN10		**2,000.00		**3,000.00	
3	FEB-6		**1,000.00		**4,000.00	
4	MAR-3	*1,000.00			**3,000.00	
5	MAR20	**500.00			**2,500.00	
6	MAR30	**500.00			**2,000.00	
7	APR-1			*14.79	**2,014.79	
8	JUL-1			*30.14	**2,044.93	
9						
10						

LOW BALANCE
Under this method, interest is paid only on the smallest amount of money that was in the account during the interest period. Despite a balance that reached $4000 during the first quarter, this account earned interest only on $1000—the lowest balance during that period. (There are no withdrawals during the second quarter, so the low-balance formula is not important there.) This method, which tends to discourage deposits, is the most punitive to savers. Yet 30 per cent of commercial banks still use it, according to a study last year by the American Bankers Association.
Interest: $44.93

IN ACCOUNT WITH

DATE	WITHDRAWAL	DEPOSIT	INTEREST	BALANCE	TELLER
JAN-1		**1,000.00		**1,000.00	
JAN10		**2,000.00		**3,000.00	
FEB-6		**1,000.00		**4,000.00	
MAR-5	*1,000.00			**3,000.00	
MAR20	**500.00			**2,500.00	
MAR30	**500.00			**2,000.00	
APR-1			*22.19	**2,022.19	
JUL-1			*30.25	**2,052.44	

FIRST-IN, FIRST-OUT (FIFO)
With this method, withdrawals are deducted first from the starting balance of the interest period and then, if the balance isn't sufficient, from later deposits. This erodes the base on which your interest is figured and means you automatically lose interest on withdrawals from the start of the interest period rather than from the dates on which the withdrawals were actually made. Another variation of this method is to apply the first withdrawal to the first deposit, rather than to the beginning balance; this would earn $53.93. About 16 per cent of commercial banks use the FIFO methods, according to the ABA.
Interest: $52.44

IN ACCOUNT WITH

DATE	WITHDRAWAL	DEPOSIT	INTEREST	BALANCE	TELLER
JAN-1		**1,000.00		**1,000.00	
JAN10		**2,000.00		**3,000.00	
FEB-6		**1,000.00		**4,000.00	
MAR-5	*1,000.00			**3,000.00	
MAR20	**500.00			**2,500.00	
MAR30	**500.00			**2,000.00	
APR-1			*28.10	**2,028.10	
JUL-1			*30.34	**2,058.44	

LAST-IN, FIRST-OUT (LIFO)
Under this plan, withdrawals are deducted from the most recent deposits in the quarter and then from the next most recent ones. This method, which does not penalize savers as much as the two FIFO methods, is used by about 5 per cent of commercial banks.
Interest: $58.44

IN ACCOUNT WITH

DATE	WITHDRAWAL	DEPOSIT	INTEREST	BALANCE	TELLER
JAN-1		**1,000.00		**1,000.00	
JAN10		**2,000.00		**3,000.00	
FEB-6		**1,000.00		**4,000.00	
MAR-5	*1,000.00			**3,000.00	
MAR20	**500.00			**2,500.00	
MAR30	**500.00			**2,000.00	
APR-1			*44.71	**2,044.71	
JUL-1			*30.59	**2,075.30	

DAY-OF-DEPOSIT TO DAY-OF-WITHDRAWAL
Under this arrangement, the bank pays you interest for the actual number of days the money remains in the account. This method, which is sometimes called daily interest, instant interest, or day-in day-out, is the fairest to consumers. It is used by almost 50 per cent of commercial banks and 60 per cent of insured S&Ls (there are no industry figures for savings banks). It yields the greatest return.
Interest: $75.30

Source: Excerpted by permission from *Consumer Reports*, February 1975.

poration (FDIC), The Federal Savings and Loan Insurance Corporation (FSLIC), or one of several state-operated insurance plans.

The importance of deposit insurance cannot be overestimated. In mid-1975, deposits of most financial institutions were insured to a maximum of $40,000 per deposit.[4] This means that if an insured institution has financial difficulties, depositors will receive the amount of their account to a maximum $40,000 per account. A saver may sacrifice some liquidity by depositing money in an account which precludes withdrawing money from it for a minimum period of time (this usually increases the yield on the deposit), but deposit insurance has practically eliminated the loss of liquidity that a depositor might experience due to the financial embarrassment of the institution holding the savings account.

Since the safety and liquidity characteristics of savings account investments are so high, it is not surprising that the average yields from these types of investments are relatively low. Figure 7–3 shows annual average yields paid by commercial banks, mutual savings banks, and savings and loan companies on savings deposits. As the chart indicates, over the years the savings and loan companies have paid the highest returns on savings and the commercial banks the lowest. Mutual savings banks have usually paid rates between these two institutions. In recent years the differential between these companies has narrowed appreciably, and during 1973 and 1974 commercial banks actually paid higher rates. Many savings institutions, attempting to attract and hold savings accounts, have paid the maximum rates of interest which they are legally entitled to pay. During recent years savers found rates at these three institutions to be very competitive.

Purchasing Power Risk. Savings accounts provide investors with very little protection against purchasing power risk. As Figure 7–3 indicates, rates on savings deposits are somewhat sensitive to economic conditions. They rise when interest rates are high, and they become lower when the opposite condition prevails. Yield rates on many savings accounts may be adjusted upward or downward by the savings institution at any time upon suitable notice to depositors. This means that these investments provide more protection against loss of purchasing power than do any of the long-term debt contracts that will be examined in the following chapters. Regardless of this fact, however, in recent years the increase in savings account yields has not kept pace with the increase in the cost of living. There is no reason to believe that these investments will ever provide substantial purchasing power protection.

---

[4] Exceptions are credit unions, of which only about 67 percent are insured, and a very small number of other financial institutions which are uninsured because they either cannot qualify for insurance or for some other reason have chosen not to be insured.

FIGURE 7–3
Average Yields on Savings Accounts

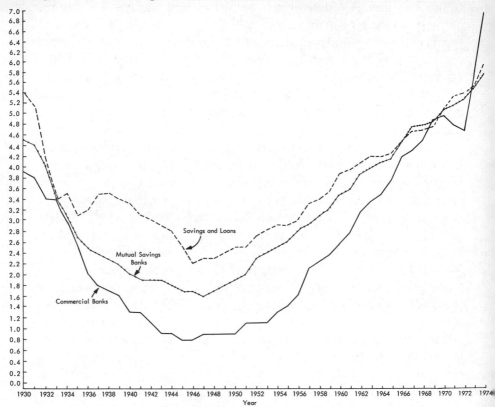

Source: United League of Savings Associations, *Fact Book,* Chicago, Ill., various issues.

RELATIVE IMPORTANCE OF DIFFERENT TYPES OF SAVINGS

Table 7–3 lists the dollar amount of savings of various types for selected years. In 1974 these savings amounted to about 40 percent of the total financial assets of households. The largest amount of savings were held in commercial banks, followed by those held in savings and loan institutions. Table 7–3 shows that over the years shifts have occurred in the way that people save. Prior to 1960 more savings were held in mutual savings banks than in savings and loans. During that year savings and loans held nearly the same dollar amount of deposits as did commercial banks. In 1950 savings bonds still were the most important single medium of saving—a legacy from the

TABLE 7–3
Financial Savings in the United States (dollar amounts in billions)

	1940		*1950*		*1960*		*1974*	
Method	*Amount*	*Percent*	*Amount*	*Percent*	*Amount*	*Percent*	*Amount*	*Percent*
Commercial bank time deposits . . .	15.4	41.2	34.9	27.3	66.8	30.5	417.7*	48.9
Mutual savings banks	10.7	28.6	20.0	15.6	36.3	16.5	98.6	11.5
Savings and loans	4.3	11.5	14.0	11.0	62.1	28.3	242.9	28.4
Credit unions	0.2	0.5	0.9	0.7	5.0	2.4	27.6	3.2
Savings bonds	6.1	16.3	57.5	45.0	47.2	21.5	63.8	7.5
Cash value of life insurance . .	0.7	1.9	0.6	0.4	1.6	0.8	3.8	0.5
Total . .	37.4	100.0	127.9	100.0	219.0	100.0	854.4	100.0

* Preliminary

Note: Most of these savings may be considered to be owned by individuals. The greatest exception to be found is in the area of commercial bank time deposits. In 1974 approximately 80 percent of commercial bank time deposits were owned by individuals. The remainder was owned by corporations, governments, and other institutions.

Source: National Association of Mutual Savings Banks, United States League of Savings Associations, The Institute of Life Insurance, and the *Federal Reserve Bulletin*.

financing of World War II. During the past 15 years, commercial banks have again become the largest holders of savings.

Cash Value of Life Insurance Policies

The cash value of life insurance policies narrowly fits within the traditional definition of savings. Cash value is the amount that a policyholder could obtain immediately from the insurance company by either canceling a policy or by borrowing against it.[5] This is the only part of the contract which can be considered "savings" because this is the only portion of the funds held by the insurance company over which the policyholder has any control. The cash value of insurance policies can be looked at exactly as any other savings deposit except that it is usually a little more difficult to "withdraw" funds. A letter is usually required to do this. Relative to any of the other forms of savings investments covered in this chapter, life insurance cash values are unimportant.

[5] Life insurance reserves and cash value of life insurance policies are two entirely different things. Reserves are important to the insured because they provide financial support for all policies, but these reserves are owned by the company. They cannot be directly acquired by the insurance policy owner in the normal course of business. The cash value can be so acquired.

SAVINGS ACCOUNTS IN COMMERCIAL BANKS

At the beginning of 1975 all American commercial banks were empowered to offer two main types of deposit accounts—demand deposits and time deposits. By law no bank can pay interest on its demand deposits, but all may pay interest on their time deposits. "Demand deposits" is the terminology that banks use to describe checking accounts. Most banks have several different kinds of checking accounts, but the accounts differ mainly in the charges the bank makes for writing checks and other services the banker may provide. Checking accounts are not classified as investments because there is no return paid on this kind of an account. In fact, bankers normally charge depositors for the service of using a checking account. (The Negotiable Order of Withdrawal account discussed later may bring great changes in this area.)

Types of Commercial Bank Savings Accounts

Banks which are members of the Federal Reserve System are governed so far as savings deposits are concerned by the System's Regulation Q, titled "Payment of Interest on Deposits." State chartered banks which are not members of the Federal Reserve System are governed by the laws of the state in which the bank is chartered, or if they are insured banks, by the Federal Deposit Insurance Corporation. Most state laws closely follow rules of the Federal Reserve System in regard to the type of deposit accounts which may be offered and the amount of interest payable on these accounts.

Deposits upon which banks may pay interest are defined by the Board of Governors of the Federal Reserve System as (1) savings deposits, (2) multiple maturity time deposits, (3) time deposits—open account and, (4) time certificates of deposit. Banks seldom use these titles in describing their various deposit plans, but the accounts are always classified as one or another of these types by regulating authorities. Classification is important because the maximum amount of interest which may be paid differs with the type of account. In recent years regulatory authorities have followed a philosophy of allowing higher rates to be paid on large deposits and on deposits which provide less liquidity to the owner. Regular savings deposits are the most liquid and pay the lowest interest. Time certificates of deposit pay the highest yields to depositors. These deposits will not be redeemed by the bank until a certain amount of time has passed.

TABLE 7–4
Maximum Rates Payable on Time and Savings Deposits at Member Commercial Banks

Type and Size of Deposit	*Effective Date* Nov. 27, 1974	Dec. 23, 1974
Savings deposits	5	5
Other time deposits (multiple- and single-maturity):		
Less than $100,000:		
30–89 days	5	5
90 days to 1 year	5½	5½
1–2½ years	6	6
2½ years or more	6½	6½
Minimum denomination of $1,000:		
4–6 years	7¼	7¼
6 years or more	(4–6 years and 6 years or more together)	7½
Governmental units	7½	7¾
$100,000 or more	(*)	(*)

* There is no maximum rate on single-maturity time deposits of over $100,000.

Note: Maximum rates that may be paid by member banks are established by the Board of Governors under provisions of Regulation Q; however, a member bank may not pay a rate in excess of the maximum rate payable by state banks or trust companies on like deposits under the laws of the state in which the member bank is located. Beginning Feb. 1, 1936, maximum rates that may be paid by nonmember insured commercial banks, as established by the FDIC, have been the same as those in effect for member banks.

Source: *Federal Reserve Bulletin*, February 1975, Table A 10.

Table 7–4 shows recent structures of maximum interest rates that banks could pay.

Savings deposits refer to deposits which are left in the bank on an indefinite basis. These deposits are usually evidenced by a passbook, but some banks merely keep records (statements) of the deposits in the bank. In either case, the depositor may withdraw money from this account at any time. Although the bank has the option of waiting as long as 30 days—or even longer in some cases—to pay the withdrawal, for the reasons explained earlier in this chapter, it is very unusual for this option to be taken. The depositor usually looks at these deposits as "ready cash" which earns a modest amount of interest. The maximum rate of interest which may be paid on these accounts is the lowest of any savings deposit account, 5 percent as this book is being written. Remember, however, this is the *maximum* rate which may be paid. Individual banks may pay less than this, and all banks may change the interest paid on this type of deposit at their option, with suitable notice to the depositor.

Multiple maturity time deposits are deposits which are (1) payable at the depositor's option on more than one date and (2) either payable only after written notice of withdrawal, or automatically renewable as the deposit matures. These accounts take many forms and carry different names at different banks. The characteristic which most clearly distinguishes them from regular savings deposits is the limited withdrawal privilege and the potential for higher interest payments. At this time maximum rates of from 5 to 7½ percent may be paid on this type of deposit, depending upon the time to maturity and the amount of the account.

Time deposits—open account closely resemble savings deposits except that there is in force a written contract between the bank and the depositor which *requires* the depositor to request in writing a withdrawal from this type account. Depositors *must* wait at least 30 days to receive this money; they *might be required* to wait at least 30 days to obtain a withdrawal from a regular savings account. The depositor may add money to this type of account at any time. These deposits are classified as single maturity deposits in Table 7–4.

Time certificates of deposit are a special kind of single maturity deposit. The difference between these and the time deposits—open account is that such deposits are evidenced by a certificate which states on its face the amount of the deposit payable to the owner of the certificate. The certificates may be negotiable or nonnegotiable, at the option of the bank. They may be issued with a specific maturity date, or they may be issued in a form which requires the owner of the deposit to make a written request for withdrawal and then to wait at least 30 days before redemption takes place.

The rate schedule does not limit the rate of interest that may be paid on deposits of over $100,000. Interest rates also increase as maturities lengthen. As it now stands, the larger single maturity certificate time deposits (these are commonly abbreviated "CDs" for certificate of deposit) provide more liquidity to depositors than do the smaller ones. This additional liquidity comes from the fact that the large CDs, those of over $100,000 in face amount, are often negotiable. To the bank these deposits seem nonliquid because the bank knows they will not be withdrawn before a certain date; to the owner, the CDs have great liquidity because they can be sold to another investor at any time before they mature. Early redemption of CDs usually results in a substantial sacrifice of interest.

Insurance of Bank Deposits

As of October 30, 1974 there were 14,423 commercial banks in the United States; 14,188 of these banks were "insured banks," which means their depositors were insured against loss up to a maximum of $40,000 for each separate deposit in the bank. All banks which are members of the Federal Reserve System are *required* by law to be insured. Nonmember banks *may be* insured if they meet the requirements of the insuring agency, the Federal Deposit Insurance Corporation. The FDIC, as it is usually called, estimates that in recent years about 99 percent of all accounts in insured banks were completely covered by deposit insurance. One reason for the very high coverage comes from the way insurance is granted, on each separate account regardless of its ownership. Large-scale savers can increase their insurance coverage by placing deposits of no more than $40,000 each in *different* insured savings accounts. These accounts may be in separate insured banks, or they may be held in the same institution, but under different titles.[6] For example, a husband and wife might increase the insurance coverage of bank deposits in a single bank this way:

Type of Account	*Maximum Insurance*
Individual account of John Doe	$ 40,000
Individual account of Mary Doe	40,000
Joint account of John and Mary Doe	40,000
Revocable trust account with John and Mary Doe as trustees for son Thomas	40,000
Irrevocable trust account established by John Doe with Mary Doe as beneficiary	40,000
Total Insured Deposits	$200,000

Any imaginative lawyer or bank trust officer could increase the total deposit insurance coverage of this couple to a very large amount, at least to $400,000 in a single bank. Other insured accounts could be placed in different banks practically without limit.

Investment Characteristics of Bank Savings Accounts

From an investment viewpoint, the strongest characteristics of bank savings deposits are their safety and convenience. Since most

[6] To qualify for separate insurance, ownership of each savings account in the same bank must be *legally different*. A single saver having $40,000 in a checking account and another $40,000 in a savings account at the same bank would only have $40,000 of insurance because both accounts have the same legal owner.

savings accounts are insured, and since it is so easy to obtain insurance far above the $40,000 maximum set by law, these accounts are among the safest investments obtainable in the United States.

Saving at a commercial bank is usually very convenient. Banks or banking offices are located in almost every city and town in the country. For persons located in a town without banking facilities, banking by mail provides nearly the same convenience. In some cases it is possible for deposits to be made automatically, directly from each paycheck.

Regular time deposits provide savers with immediate liquidity, even though the bank has the option of not making payment before 30 days. There is some sacrifice in liquidity when deposits are made in any of the multiple maturity or certificate accounts. In many cases even these accounts may be withdrawn on an emergency basis, although there is usually a loss of interest return. Negotiable certificates of deposit may, of course, be sold to provide liquidity.

In return for this convenience, liquidity, and safety, the depositor sacrifices some yield. Even the maximum yields paid on the longest maturity certificates of deposit are less than a saver could obtain by placing money in other investments having similar investment characteristics. But all in all, savings in commercial bank time deposits are ideally suited to the needs of the individual, and most investors have at least a portion of their financial assets in the form of deposits at either a commercial bank or one of the other deposit-type financial institutions. Bank savings accounts, like other savings accounts, provide little protection against purchasing power risk.

SAVINGS ACCOUNTS IN MUTUAL SAVINGS BANKS AND SAVINGS AND LOANS

From the viewpoint of the saver, mutual savings banks and savings and loan companies have more similarities than differences. For this reason they can be discussed at the same time.

Organization and Operation

All mutual savings banks and savings and loan companies (hereafter referred to as MSBs and S&Ls) accept money from savers, invest this money, and pay interest to the persons who provided the funds. Their operation closely resembles that of a commercial bank with the following exceptions.

Organization. All commercial banks are organized as corporations.[7] All MSBs and about 85 percent of all S&Ls are organized as mutuals.

Mutual organizations are *owned* by the persons they serve. With the exception of MSBs, the owners elect trustees or directors who operate the organization in the best interests of the members. Some MSB trustees are elected and some appointed, but in no case are all *elected.* S&Ls which are not mutuals are organized as corporations. Ownership of these companies, like the ownership of a commercial bank, is vested in the common stockholders. From a purely practical viewpoint, the form of organization is not very important because members of mutuals almost never exercise their right to change the management of their companies even when management is doing a less than satisfactory job. In this respect they resemble common stockholders of large corporations, a group noted for its lack of interest in voting its stock. Savers are affected little by the different forms of organization except that a saver at a commercial bank or MSB is classed as a *creditor* of the organization. Savers at S&Ls and certain other companies which accept savings may legally be *owners.* The difference is largely meaningless so long as savings are insured. Savers having uninsured accounts would probably receive less in the event of financial failure if they were owners rather than creditors, but this is not normally an important consideration.

Services. Few commercial banks, MSBs, or S&Ls require that persons be depositors before they can obtain the services of the institution. Banks, for example, generally do not require that a person have a savings deposit before they will grant them a consumer loan. Nevertheless, people tend to be both savers and borrowers, and they often transact all their financial business with a single institution. For this reason it is necessary to understand the type of services offered by each savings institution so that a better decision can be made regarding where to save.

MSBs and S&Ls invest most of their funds in mortgage loans by convention and by law. MSBs are not so rigidly regulated as S&Ls and have in recent years been attempting to broaden their services to depositors and other customers. Some MSBs now offer a limited amount of consumer credit, they provide bill paying services and cashier's checks, and sell life insurance and mutual funds to depositors. But for all this, they cannot offer the wide variety of loans and other

---

[7] This is not completely true. There are still a handful of private banks which are organized as partnerships or sole proprietorships. These companies are unimportant for purposes of this discussion.

services provided by commercial banks. Only a small proportion of their assets are in nonmortgage loans.

Until recent years, there was little desire on the part of S&L managers to make other than mortgage loans. Housing was being constructed at such a rapid rate that between 1940 and 1973 the S&L industry grew faster than any other financial institution except credit unions. Credit unions had a larger *rate of increase* because they had so few assets at the beginning of the period, but in terms of absolute dollars they are still relatively unimportant. In recent years, housing construction has slowed and so has growth of S&Ls. The members of this industry are now seeking legislation which would allow them to make other loans and thereby provide higher earnings and more services to attract savers.

Regulation and Insurance

MSBs are regulated by the state in which they operate. These institutions are located primarily in the eastern part of the United States. Nearly three quarters of the 500 or so MSBs in operation in 1974 were located in the states of Massachusetts, New York, and Connecticut. In two of these states their assets are nearly as large as those of commercial banks. Throughout the East Coast area MSBs are very important as savings institutions.

Over 99 percent of all mutual savings banks have deposit insurance of one type or another. Nearly 67 percent of all mutual savings banks belonged to the Federal Deposit Insurance Corporation at the end of 1974. The deposits in these institutions are insured up to a maximum of $40,000 per account, as they are in commercial banks. Insurance coverage can be increased in the same way as was explained earlier. Deposits of MSBs located in certain states are also insured by state insurance agencies. Such deposits may be insured for more than $40,000.

There are over 5,000 S&Ls spread throughout the United States. These organizations may be mutuals or stock corporations and may be regulated by either the state in which they operate, or by the Federal Home Loan Bank System. S&Ls are more tightly regulated than MSBs in that they may not invest in the variety of assets open to MSBs, but this does not necessarily indicate they are safer.

Savings accounts at S&Ls are known as *savings shares* rather than *deposits*. The difference between a deposit and a savings share is a legal one: a depositor is a creditor of an institution, while the owner of a savings share has equity in the organization. This means that if an S&L had financial difficulties, and was uninsured, savers would not have as strong a legal claim against the company as they would if they were depositors.

Over 95 percent of all S&L savings accounts were insured to $40,000 in 1974. For all federally chartered and most state chartered S&Ls, insurance is provided by the Federal Savings and Loan Insurance Corporation (FSLIC). In all important respects this insurance resembles that provided by the FDIC. In some states—Massachusetts, Ohio, and Maryland—agencies of the state or private insurance companies provide insurance for state chartered S&Ls. A few state chartered institutions are uninsured. As a practical matter, individuals should have little preference as to whether savings are legally classified as deposits or as savings shares—so long as they are insured. If their accounts do not exceed $40,000 they will be reimbursed for the amount of their savings accounts in the event that the financial institution becomes insolvent.

Types of Savings Accounts

Savings accounts are of two general types—regular (passbook) accounts and special accounts. The first type closely resembles the commercial bank savings account. Each account is evidenced by a passbook, and deposits and withdrawals may be made upon presentation of the passbook. As was the case with commercial banks, these institutions have the right to hold up withdrawals for at least 30 days; like commercial banks, they seldom avail themselves of this privilege.

Special accounts may be classified as *notice, certificate,* or *bonus accounts.* Notice accounts most nearly resemble commercial bank open account time deposits. This account differs from the regular account in that the saver *must* give notice of intent to withdraw funds and then must wait a specified period before receiving the withdrawal. These accounts pay higher returns than regular accounts.

Certificate accounts most nearly resemble commercial bank certificates of deposit. These accounts are issued in fixed minimum amounts—usually $1,000—and have fixed maturities of six months to two years. Many of the large commercial bank CDs are negotiable, but few of those issued by MSBs or S&Ls are. The liquidity for this type of account lies in the willingness of the issuing institution to redeem it before maturity. Some companies allow early redemption but only at a lowered rate of return. Often certificates may be used

FIGURE 7–4
Savings and Loan Certificate of Deposit

Cascade Federal
Savings and Loan Association

Interest Rate________ Class________
Term________

CERTIFICATE OF DEPOSIT

VOID

This certifies that________

has opened a certificate of deposit in the initial principal sum of________

________and for the initial term ending________

________as adjusted as to principal and term from time to time and recorded in this evidence of account in Cascade Federal Savings and Loan Association, subject to its charter and bylaws, to the Rules and Regulations for the Federal Savings and Loan System, to the Regulations for the Federal Home Loan Bank System, to the laws of the United States of America, and to the rules established by its board of directors for this deposit classification consistent with said charter, bylaws, rules, regulations and laws.

This sum shall bear interest at the rate of________% per annum, payable on December 31, March 31, June 30, and September 30 of each year, provided the account is not reduced below the minimum principal established by the association to be eligible to receive the stated rate. If the rate or term or both is adjusted in connection with a change in the account balance, such rate and term shall be as indicated in this evidence of account.

This certificate of deposit shall be automatically and successively renewed at the conclusion of each term at the last applicable rate paid on this certificate and for the term established at that time by the association for this class of account, except that at least fifteen days prior to a maturity date the association may give written notice to the depositor that this certificate will be renewed at a different rate and/or a different term, or will not be renewed and will revert to the status of a regular savings deposit and earn interest at the rate paid on regular savings deposits.

In the event of any withdrawal from this account during the first three months (90 days) of the term, no earnings shall be paid on the amount withdrawn. In the event of any withdrawal thereafter, prior to the conclusion of the term, earnings on the amount withdrawn shall be paid at the then current rate on regular savings deposits for the period since issuance or renewal of the account, less three months. To the extent necessary to comply with these requirements, deductions shall be made from the amount withdrawn. In the event the term of this certificate is extended by reason of an additional deposit, the withdrawal penalty provision applicable during the original term will also apply to any withdrawal during the extended term.

Determination of earnings is subject to the rules established by the association for this class of account.

CASCADE FEDERAL SAVINGS AND LOAN ASSOCIATION

VOID

Date________ BY________
Authorized Signature

Courtesy of Cascade Federal Savings and Loan Association, Corvallis, Ore.

as collateral for loans and in this way can provide owners with some liquidity.

Figure 7–4 is a certificate which evidences a single payment certificate account at Cascade Federal Savings and Loan Association. The terms are clear enough so that they require no further explanation. Note the penalties associated with early withdrawal. Large denomination commercial bank CDs are usually "bearer instruments," which means that the person who has possession of them is presumed to be the legal owner. This type is more easily negotiable.

Bonus plans are systematic savings plans under which the participant agrees to save a certain amount of money periodically until a savings program goal is reached. If the savings program is completed as planned, the account is paid a bonus yield. If the plan is not completed, savings are rewarded at the lower rate of regular accounts.

Maximum interest rates payable by MSBs are set by the FDIC and state banking commissions and are fairly uniform from state to state. S&L rates are set by the Federal Home Loan Bank Board, which allows different maximum rates to prevail in different parts of the country. Higher rates are usually allowed where demand for housing is high so that more capital is attracted into these areas. Maximum rate settings are also based upon the competing rates of other savings institutions. Although the regulation of maximum interest rates of all financial institutions is accomplished by several agencies (the Federal Reserve Board, the Federal Home Loan Bank Board, and various state banking commissions), the effect has been to set a fairly uniform structure of maximum interest rates. This regulation has traditionally allowed S&Ls and MSBs to pay slightly higher rates than commercial banks. Table 7–5 lists recent maximum allowable rates on the most common types of savings accounts. It should be emphasized that these are *maximum* rates.

TABLE 7–5
Maximum Allowable Rates on Various Types of Savings Accounts

Type of Account	*Commercial Banks*	*MSBs and S&Ls*
Regular savings	5 %	5¼%
90-day	5½	5¾
1 to 2½ years	6	6½
2½ to 4 years	6½	6¾
4 to 6 years (minimum deposit $1,000)	7¼	7½
6 years or over (minimum deposit $1,000)	7½	7¾

Note: Rates effective early in 1975.

Negotiable Order of Withdrawal (NOW) Accounts. Competition between commercial banks and other financial institutions is regulated by the federal government so that "cutthroat" competition will not develop. Commercial banks were the only institutions allowed to offer checking accounts, but they were prohibited from paying interest on these accounts. Other financial institutions were allowed to pay slightly higher interest rates on savings accounts so that they could compete against the commercial banks. The more aggressive MSBs and S&Ls have for many years sought permission to offer more financial services. Until recently their requests have not been met.

Now, however, S&Ls and MSBs in two states have been allowed to offer NOW accounts, which for practical purposes are checking accounts. If these accounts prove successful, and if savings institutions throughout the United States are allowed to offer them, each saver will be profoundly affected. Commercial banks and other savings institutions will more closely resemble each other because they will provide more similar services; competition between these institutions for the saver's dollar will probably increase. Because interest may be paid on NOW accounts it is likely that commercial banks will be allowed to pay interest on their checking accounts.

NOW accounts are savings accounts which could require 30 to 90 days notice prior to withdrawal of funds. Since prior notice is not required by savings institutions and since the negotiable order operates much like a check, NOW accounts effectively provide savers with the convenience of a checking account which earns savings account interest.

At year end 1974, 151 mutual savings banks, 81 savings and loan companies, and 63 commercial banks located in the states of Massachusetts and New Hampshire offered NOW accounts. Over $312 million was invested in these accounts and there were 317,175 separate NOW accounts in existence. The average interest paid on these accounts was just under 5 percent, which is the maximum interest rate allowed on these accounts at this time.[8] NOW accounts, like other accounts, may be insured.

NOW accounts are offered only by institutions in Massachusetts and New Hampshire because no other states have (as of January 1976) passed legislation which would enable savings institutions located within their boundaries to offer such accounts. However, there has been much discussion of the desirability of such accounts both at the state and federal levels. A legislative package has been submitted to the Congress which would allow all commercial banks and thrift institutions in the United States to offer interest-bearing demand deposit accounts. This legislation has not yet been passed, but if the experience of Massachusetts and New Hampshire is judged to be good it is

---

[8] The Federal Reserve Bank of Boston is monitoring institutions offering NOW accounts. Information on these accounts is available by request from the Research Department of this bank.

likely that federal-level permission to offer such accounts will soon be granted.

The advent of NOW accounts provides persons with yet another choice of what to do with their investible funds. On the surface it would appear that a person would always be benefited by transferring all of his or her checking account to a NOW account because this account would provide additional interest which was not available under the standard checking account. However, a number of NOW accounts charge up to 15 cents for each negotiable order of withdrawal, while many checking accounts provide unlimited free checks so long as a minimum balance remains in the account. For some individuals it is likely that the charges for the writing of each withdrawal will be larger than the interest received on the NOW account. These persons may be better off to continue to use a standard checking account for their checking needs while placing savings in a standard saving account.

Investment Characteristics of Mutual Savings Bank and Savings and Loan Accounts

The overriding characteristic of MSB accounts is their safety. In several states no MSB depositor has lost any money—principal or interest—since the beginning of the 20th century. Neither commercial banks nor S&Ls can match this record. However, now that deposit insurance is so widely used by savings accounts, the safety advantages of MSBs have largely disappeared. With very minor distinctions, all insured accounts are equally safe. Savers should be certain that they place money only in insured institutions. While nearly all commercial and mutual savings banks are insured, there are still a significant number of small state-chartered S&Ls which are not. Since uninsured and insured institutions pay nearly the same rates, there can be little gain from saving at an uninsured institution—and there is the possibility of great loss.

MSB and S&L accounts provide about the same liquidity as those of commercial banks. Regular accounts provide ready cash, while certificate or notification accounts may not be withdrawn or redeemed for a stated period of time. NOW accounts, of course, provide maximum liquidity. All savings accounts are good collateral for loans and may be "borrowed against" to provide ready cash.

No savings accounts provide good protection against purchasing power loss. Rates may be, and commonly are, adjusted upward as interest rates rise. But in recent years they have not risen enough to offset price inflation. They are, however, slightly better at protecting against purchasing power loss than are long-term bonds. Bond interest rates are fixed until the bond matures. Savings accounts do not lose market value due to rising interest rates as do long-term bonds. These accounts are always redeemable at the amount deposited plus accumulated interest.

SAVINGS IN CREDIT UNIONS

By number, credit unions are the largest single type of financial institution. At the end of 1974 there were approximately 22,900 credit unions in the United States; membership was about 29.4 million persons.[9] These institutions are mutuals, like mutual savings banks and most savings and loan companies. They have been formed as cooperative associations to accept savings from and make consumer loans to their members only. Savers at credit unions do not have a creditor position since they are technically the owners of the company. Membership in these organizations is limited to persons who belong to whatever group has formed the association. In theory, the membership can be made up of practically any grouping of people; in practice most credit unions are organized by groups of workers who are members of the same trade union or who are employees of the same company. The numbers of credit unions are very impressive, but because these institutions are so small, they hold a nearly insignificant proportion of the savings of persons in the United States. This proportion is increasing slowly, but in 1974 only about 3 percent of U.S. personal savings were held in credit unions.

Regulation of Credit Unions

These institutions may have either state or federal charters, neither of which is difficult to obtain if the low minimum requirements for organization can be met. Once the association is operating, state and federal laws require that reserve or guarantee funds be established and annual audits be conducted. Aside from these restrictions, credit unions have wide discretion in the investment policies they pursue and in the rates of interest they pay savers.

---

[9] Personal correspondence with the Credit Union National Association, Inc., Madison, Wisconsin.

Accounts may be insured to $40,000 through the National Credit Union Association. In early 1976 about two thirds of all credit unions were insured. Safety also comes from the fact that all key employees are heavily bonded (in effect this insures the credit union against loss due to theft or misappropriation of funds by these persons), and the boards of directors are required to oversee periodic audits of the companies.

Savings Accounts at Credit Unions

There is little variety in the savings plans offered by credit unions as only one class of saving shares is sold. In many cases these shares may be purchased in installments, and in this way systematic savings may be accumulated. The rates at which interest is paid on these accounts varies greatly between institutions. In 1975 some paid savers as much as 7 percent, while others paid very low rates. Credit unions may legally withhold withdrawals, but they seldom do so.

Most credit unions which are organized around occupational lines, where members share the same employer, are equipped to accept savings through payroll deduction procedures. If this is not done, there is no great loss in convenience since the credit union itself is usually conveniently located for the members. However, payroll deduction is a feature nearly unique to these institutions.

Many credit unions provide free life insurance for owners of savings accounts. Usually there is an upper limit on the amount of insurance provided, but some companies provide insurance equal to each saver's total account. Credit unions must be considered less safe, on the average, than other savings institutions. The fact that substantial numbers of these institutions have no insurance, and because most credit unions are organized around an occupation or a company, contributes to this lack of safety. When adverse economic conditions strike a particular occupation or company, the entire membership of the credit union is affected. Savers turn into borrowers rapidly and often strain the capacity of the organization.[10]

The probable reasons why credit unions have continued to grow so rapidly is that they are convenient places to do business and they

---

[10] Liquidation or failure of a financial institution which holds savings does not necessarily mean that savers will lose money. Many of these institutions go out of business each year, are liquidated, and every creditor or owner of saving shares receives every dollar that is owed. In contrast to this, when a corporation is liquidated, it is usually liquidated because of bankruptcy. Creditors' claims may be satisfied, but common shareholders usually lose money.

pay reasonably high yields. Saving there may be attractive to people who want their savings to be used to provide loans for fellow members. Many people probably purchase shares in these associations in anticipation of borrowing at a later time because loans are made only to members. Although cooperative businesses have never been particularly popular in America, it is anticipated that these mutual institutions will continue to increase in size and importance.

OTHER SAVINGS ALTERNATIVES

Many states allow businesses other than those just described to accept savings accounts. They are usually engaged in the consumer loan business and accept savings accounts from borrowers and others. Common names for these companies are "Thrift and Loan," "Consumer Thrift," "Credit Thrift," "Industrial Bank," and "Morris Plan Bank." From the standpoint of dollar amount of deposits these institutions have very little importance. They are usually small in size and local in operation.

These organizations are state chartered and state regulated, usually by the state banking commissioner. Regulation and supervision vary with the state, but it is usually less intense than that imposed upon commercial banks. Industrial banks are eligible to join the FDIC and thereby obtain share insurance if they can meet the standards of membership. Insured banks would provide the depositor with the same safety as any other insured savings organization. Uninsured savings institutions are to be avoided in favor of those which are.

In recent years a substantial number of investment companies have developed investment policies which make ownership of their shares attractive to savers. These funds invest in bonds, money market instruments, and mortgages to provide the saver with returns potentially higher than could be obtained through savings deposits. These investments are discussed in Chapter 11.

Government securities have many characteristics that cause them to have appeal for savers. These investments will be examined in the next chapter.

SUMMARY

This chapter was an introduction to the most popular types of saving account investments. Yield and methods of computing yields were discussed first since these computations are common to all debt securities. The relationship of risk and return, first developed in Chapter 2, was applied to debt investments.

Savings investments in different financial institutions were next examined and compared one to another. The main thrust of this comparison was that (1) all insured accounts are nearly identically safe; (2) yield can be increased by investing in less liquid accounts—certificate or notice accounts; (3) the difference in yields between uninsured and insured institutions is not great enough to cause an investor to save at an uninsured institution; and (4) some savings institutions provide more services to depositors than others.

Investment characteristics of all savings accounts are low financial risk, low interest rate risk, good liquidity, and high purchasing power risk. Yields are lower than those available on nearly any other investment.

APPENDIX TO CHAPTER 7

Compound Interest

The effects of compound interest are considerations which are of prime importance to most financial decisions. The compound interest formula is the basis for future value as well as present value calculations of all types. This formula is simple to derive and to use.

Assume that interest is paid at 6 percent per year on a \$100 bank account. Interest is computed once at the end of the year, and the original principal and interest remain on deposit for two years.

Let

P = Principal, the amount on deposit.
i = Interest rate stated on a per annum basis.
n = Number of periods over which the principal is on deposit receiving interest.

$P_1, P_2, \ldots, P_n$ = Principal at end of 1st, 2d, . . . , nth periods.
$I_1, I_2, \ldots, I_n$ = Interest for 1st, 2d, . . . , nth periods, respectively.

Then,

$$I_1 = P \times i = Pi \qquad \$100(0.06) = \$6$$
$$P_1 = P + I_1 = P + Pi = P(1 + i) \qquad \$100 + \$6 = \$106$$

$I_2 = P_1 \times i = P(1+i)i$ $\$106(0.06) = \$6.36$

$P_2 = P_1 + I_2 = P(1+i) + P(1+i)i$ $\$106 + \$6.36 = \$112.36$

Factoring $P(1+i)$ from this equation,

$$P_2 = P(1+i)(1+i)$$
$$P_2 = P(1+i)^2$$

The future value of P, for n periods of compounding interest at i interest rate is given by the general formula

$$P_n = P(1+i)^n$$

Interest rates are usually stated as annual rates, but interest is more often compounded semiannually or quarterly. An annual 6 percent rate of interest compounded semiannually would be compounded twice as many times per year at half the yearly interest rate.

$$P_n = P(1+i/2)^{n \times 2}$$

This formula may be generalized. If t is the number of times per year that interest is compounded, then

$$P_n = P(1+i/t)^{n \times t}$$

Compound interest tables have been published which give values of $(1+i)^n$ for various rates of interest and compounding periods. Figure 7–6 is a page from one of these tables. To solve the problem of what will be the value of $100 in two years if 6 percent annual interest is compounded semiannually, first determine i and n values. In this case $i = 0.06/2 = 0.03$, and $n = 2 \times 2 = 4$.

The table gives factors of $(1+i)^n$ for values of $i = 1$ through $i =$ 20 percent and n from 1 to 50 periods. Other tables cover different interest rates and time periods. To use this table to determine the value of $100 which has been compounded semiannually at an interest rate of 6 percent, simply locate the intersection of the n row and the i column. In this case the factor for $(1+0.03)^4$ is 1.1255.

The value of P_2 under the above conditions of compounding is

$$P_2 = \$100 \times 1.1255$$
$$= \$112.55$$

This amount is slightly larger than that obtained in the initial example due to the fact that the number of compounding periods has been doubled. The interest rate has been halved, from 6 to 3 percent, but the effect of the additional compounding periods outweighs the reduction in the compounding rate and results in a very slight increase

TABLE 7–6
Compound Sum of $1 $P = (1 + i)^n$

Value of $1.00 n Periods Hence with Interest Rate i per Period
$S(i, n) = (1 + i)^n$

n	1%	2%	3%	4%	5%	6%	8%	10%	15%	20%
1	1.0100	1.0200	1.0300	1.0400	1.0500	1.0600	1.0800	1.100	1.150	1.200
2	1.0201	1.0404	1.0609	1.0816	1.1025	1.1236	1.166	1.210	1.322	1.440
3	1.0303	1.0612	1.0927	1.1249	1.1576	1.1910	1.260	1.331	1.521	1.728
4	1.0406	1.0824	1.1255	1.1699	1.2155	1.2625	1.360	1.464	1.749	2.074
5	1.0510	1.1041	1.1593	1.2167	1.2763	1.3382	1.469	1.611	2.011	2.488
6	1.0615	1.1262	1.1941	1.2653	1.3401	1.4185	1.587	1.772	2.313	2.986
7	1.0721	1.1487	1.2299	1.3159	1.4071	1.5036	1.714	1.949	2.660	3.583
8	1.0829	1.1717	1.2668	1.3686	1.4775	1.5938	1.851	2.144	3.059	4.300
9	1.0937	1.1951	1.3048	1.4233	1.5513	1.6895	1.999	2.358	3.518	5.160
10	1.1046	1.2190	1.3439	1.4802	1.6289	1.7908	2.159	2.594	4.046	6.192
11	1.1157	1.2434	1.3842	1.5395	1.7103	1.8983	2.332	2.853	4.652	7.430
12	1.1268	1.2682	1.4258	1.6010	1.7959	2.0122	2.518	3.138	5.350	8.916
13	1.1381	1.2936	1.4685	1.6651	1.8856	2.1329	2.720	3.452	6.153	10.699
14	1.1495	1.3195	1.5126	1.7317	1.9799	2.2609	2.937	3.797	7.076	12.839
15	1.1610	1.3459	1.5580	1.8009	2.0789	2.3966	3.172	4.177	8.137	15.407
16	1.1726	1.3728	1.6047	1.8730	2.1829	2.5404	3.426	4.595	9.358	18.488
17	1.1843	1.4002	1.6528	1.9479	2.2920	2.6928	3.700	5.054	10.761	22.186
18	1.1961	1.4282	1.7024	2.0258	2.4066	2.8543	3.996	5.560	12.375	26.623
19	1.2081	1.4568	1.7535	2.1068	2.5270	3.0256	4.316	6.116	14.232	31.948
20	1.2202	1.4859	1.8061	2.1911	2.6533	3.2071	4.661	6.727	16.367	38.338
21	1.2324	1.5157	1.8603	2.2788	2.7860	3.3996	5.034	7.400	18.821	46.005
22	1.2447	1.5460	1.9161	2.3699	2.9253	3.6035	5.437	8.140	21.645	55.206
23	1.2572	1.5769	1.9736	2.4647	3.0715	3.8197	5.871	8.954	24.891	66.247
24	1.2697	1.6084	2.0328	2.5633	3.2251	4.0489	6.341	9.850	28.625	79.497
25	1.2824	1.6406	2.0938	2.6658	3.3864	4.2919	6.848	10.835	32.919	95.396
26	1.2953	1.6734	2.1566	2.7725	3.5557	4.5494	7.396	11.918	37.857	114.475
27	1.3082	1.7069	2.2213	2.8834	3.7335	4.8223	7.988	13.110	43.535	137.370
28	1.3213	1.7410	2.2879	2.9987	3.9201	5.1117	8.627	14.421	50.065	164.845
29	1.3345	1.7758	2.3566	3.1187	4.1161	5.4184	9.317	15.863	57.575	197.813
30	1.3478	1.8114	2.4273	3.2434	4.3219	5.7435	10.063	17.449	66.212	237.376
35	1.4166	1.9999	2.8139	3.9461	5.5160	7.6861	14.785	28.102	133.175	590.668
40	1.4889	2.2080	3.2620	4.8010	7.0400	10.2857	21.725	45.259	267.862	1469.771
45	1.5648	2.4379	3.7816	5.8412	8.9850	13.7646	31.920	72.890	538.767	3657.258
50	1.6446	2.6916	4.3839	7.1067	11.4674	18.4202	46.902	117.391	1083.652	9100.427

in the true annual rate of interest over what it would have been under conditions of less compounding periods.

PROBLEMS

1. What are the current rates of interest being paid on savings deposits of various types? (Obtain this information from local savings institutions.) Considering all investment characteristics, which account offers the best combination of risk and return?
2. How much interest would be received over a one-year period on a $1,000 deposit under the following conditions?
   a. Interest is paid once at the end of the year at a rate of 5 percent.
   b. Interest is compounded semiannually and paid at the end of the year at a rate of 6 percent.
3. What is the future value of $100 invested as follows?
   a. $100 invested at 10 percent, interest compounded annually for seven years.
   b. $100 invested at 20 percent per annum compounded semiannually for five years.
4. You have the choice of saving $100 at a bank which offers interest of 6 percent compounded annually, or at a saving and loan company which pays interest at a rate of 4 percent compounded quarterly. How much interest will accumulate on these deposits in four years if no interest or principal is withdrawn?

QUESTIONS

1. What are the main differences between *time deposits* and *demand deposits?*
2. How do savings and loan companies differ from commercial banks so far as safety, liquidity, and convenience are concerned? Adopt the viewpoint of a depositor.
3. What are the most important investment characteristics of saving accounts?
4. As a saver, which of the institutions described in this chapter has the most appeal to you? Why?
5. Credit unions are usually seen as being less safe places to save than commercial banks. Is this a justified criticism?
6. From the viewpoint of a saver, what are the advantages to be obtained from saving in a stock S&L rather than a mutual one?

7. What are NOW accounts? How do they aid savers?
8. What are *grace days*? How do they aid savers?
9. "All banks pay the same time deposit rates. It does no good to shop around for the best deal." True or false? Discuss.

SELECTED READINGS

"Early History and Initial Impact of NOW ACCOUNTS," *New England Economic Review*. Published by the Federal Reserve Bank of Boston, January–February 1975.

"Finance Facts Yearbook." Washington, D.C.: National Consumer Finance Association, published yearly, free upon request.

"International Credit Union Yearbook." Madison, Wisc.: CUNA International, published yearly, free upon request.

Kendall, Leon T. *The Savings and Loan Business*. U.S. Savings and Loan League for the Commission on Money and Credit. Englewood Cliffs, N.J.: Prentice-Hall, 1962.

Meyer, Martin J., and McDaniel, Joseph M., Jr. *Don't Bank on It*. Lynbrook, N.Y.: Farnsworth Publishing, 1970.

"Mutual Savings Banking: Annual Report of the Executive Vice-President, National Association of Mutual Savings Banks." New York: National Association of Mutual Savings Banks, published each year, free upon request.

"Savings and Loan Fact Book." Chicago: U.S. Savings and Loan League, published yearly, free upon request.

8

Investing in Debt Securities

INTRODUCTION

Debt security investments comprise about 12.8 percent of the financial assets of individuals. These investments are of less importance than savings accounts or corporate stock but are more important than any other type of financial asset.

Debt contracts take many forms—bonds, notes, certificates, and mortgages are the general types of debt contracts. These contracts differ in many ways, but they have some common characteristics. In all cases, one party lends money to another and is compensated for the loan by payment of interest from the borrower. Usually the principal of the loan (the par value of debt securities) must be repaid at a certain time.

Debt security investments are much more formal than the savings deposit agreement one has with a bank or other financial institution. The additional formality is necessary because the agreement is usually expected to last for many years. While savings may be left with a single financial institution for an equally long period of time, the agreement between the institution and the depositor can usually be changed at the option of either party upon suitable notice. Owners of debt contracts are usually prohibited from redeeming these securities before they mature or before the company wishes to retire them. For this reason many of these financial instruments are sold, perhaps several times, before they mature. Very few bonds, except U.S. savings bonds, are held until maturity by the person who originally acquired them.

Because of the long-term nature of bond contracts, and because the final owners of these investments may not have purchased them originally, every aspect of the debt agreement is set down in a carefully worded statement which is legally binding on the borrower. This statement, the bond *indenture,* lists each and every thing that the issuer promises to do. The indenture remains in effect until the bonds are matured or otherwise retired, and anyone purchasing a bond, whether it be purchased from the issuer or from another party, receives all the protection and benefits that are described in the indenture. Once an issue of bonds has been sold the indenture cannot be changed except by agreement of a certain proportion of the bondholders. In practice it is very unusual for an issuer to ever effect change in a bond indenture, even if the change is advantageous to the bond owners.

Federal, state, and local statutes exist to outline the types of bond agreements that these governments and other issuing agencies can enter into. These statutes serve the same purpose for these instruments as indentures do for privately issued bonds; they outline the liability of the issuer. Government issued securities have fairly uniform characteristics, although there are many different instruments. Corporations are not nearly so restricted in the types of debt agreements they may make. Corporate bond indentures are very complex, written in legal terminology, and difficult for the layperson to interpret. The average owner of a corporate bond cannot read the bond indenture with enough understanding to tell whether or not the corporation is meeting its obligations as they are stated in the indenture. For this reason the corporation appoints a *trustee* (usually a bank or other large financial institution) to oversee that the corporation is meeting the conditions set forth in the indenture. The trustee may also handle the payment of interest on the bonds and the recording of ownership of the securities. Should the corporation fail to live up to the indenture agreement, the trustee will bring legal action to bear to protect the interest of the bondholders.

Bond owners may obtain a copy of the indenture if they desire one. However, the main features of the bond issue are contained in the *prospectus,* which is provided to all original purchasers of securities. People buying bonds in secondary markets usually obtain information of the type contained in the indenture from financial reporting services such as Moody's or Standard & Poor's.

CLASSIFICATION AND IDENTIFICATION OF DEBT SECURITIES

There are a bewildering variety of debt securities. They may be classified and identified in several ways, but the most common method of doing this is on the basis of *issuer* and *security*. The issuer, of course, is the organization which originally sold the security. Security refers to either the collateral behind the bond or the source of payment of interest and repayment of principal. The outline presented below is designed to classify debt securities by these characteristics, but it should be understood that classification by other characteristics (maturity, legal standing, grade, and so on) is both proper and common.

Classification of Debt Securities

I. By issuer
   A. Securities issued by governments
      1. Treasury securities
      2. Agency securities
      3. Municipals
         a Full faith and credit bonds
         b Revenue bonds
         c Assessment bonds
   B. Securities issued by corporations
      1. Utilities
      2. Railroads
      3. Industrials
II. By security or source of repayment
   A. Mortgage bonds
   B. Collateral trust bonds
   C. Debenture bonds
   D. Equipment trust certificates
   E. Guaranteed bonds

Classification by Issuer

Bonds issued by governments are generally identified as *governments* while those issued by corporations are called *corporates*. The broad classification of government issued debt securities is usually broken into three subclassifications: *Governments* or *treasuries* are those issued directly by the U.S. Treasury; agency securities, usually referred to as *agencies*, are issued by such federal organizations as the

Federal Home Loan Bank, the Federal National Mortgage Association, the Federal Land Bank, and other federal agencies; state and local government bonds are called *municipals* whether they are issued by a state, a city, a sewer district, or some other taxing district or agency.

The general term *corporates* refers to any bond issued by a private corporation. *Utilities*, *railroads*, and *industrials* are easily identified sub-classifications, and as one would anticipate, there are further unlisted sub-subclassifications.

Classification by Security or Source of Repayment

Governments and Municipals. The security behind the debt of governments is the willingness and ability of the issuer to pay interest and principal when due. Specific assets are almost never pledged as collateral for federal securities. Interest payments and repayment of principal on this type debt are usually made from general tax revenues.

State and municipal bonds are usually classified as being *full faith and credit bonds, revenue bonds, assessment bonds*, or combinations of these three. Full faith and credit bonds are those which are unconditionally backed by the full taxing power of the issuer. These securities are usually the most highly regarded of the municipals because the payment for these bonds may come from many different tax sources. Full faith and credit bonds seldom go into default.

The payment for revenue bonds comes from the income generated by the facility which was paid for by the issuance of the bonds. Examples of such facilities are toll roads, toll bridges, municipal waterworks, transit systems, electric power departments, pollution control facilities, and other state and municipally owned enterprises. The usual procedure is for the issuing agency to build the facility and to charge fees for its use. The fees provide the revenue for the agency to pay off the debt incurred in financing it. Often the borrowing agency is granted a monopoly in offering this particular service, such as a toll bridge, transit system, or a utility distribution system. Occasionally the revenue from one of these projects is not adequate to satisfy the claims of the bondholders, but on the whole these securities have very little financial risk.

Assessment bonds are issued to finance the costs of improvements such as sewers, streets and sidewalks. Voters direct the assessment district to make the designated improvements. Charges—assessments—are then levied against the property owners of the district to pay for this debt. Of the three types of municipal bonds discussed in this chapter, these are probably the most risky. Even here the risk of nonpayment of interest or principal is very low.

Corporates. Interest and principal payments on corporate debt normally come from the income of the company. Corporate bonds are commonly identified by the security that is pledged against the bond, even though bondholders seldom anticipate that they will have cause to take over the security.

Mortgage bonds are securities which are backed by real property—land or buildings or both. Mortgage bonds were once thought to be the safest of all corporate securities because in case of default one could always obtain the real assets which were pledged as collateral for the bonds. In theory this was correct. However, many bondholders who took over the collateral of defaulted issues found that the real property which they received did not have as much value as it had when it was being used by the company which issued the bonds.

On the other hand, while the mortgaged property may have had little value for the bondholder, it often was necessary to the operation of the business. Consequently, corporations usually do everything possible to keep mortgage bonds from going into default because the bondholders may then claim a specific piece of property which the company must control in order to operate.

Collateral trust bonds are backed by collateral—bonds or other securities. The collateral is often the bonds or common stock of subsidiary corporations, or sometimes it is the security investments of the company issuing the bonds. The market value of the collateral is of importance because this asset can easily be taken over by bondholders in case of default. It is usually more marketable than real estate or other fixed assets, and its market value is usually more easily determined.

Debenture bonds have no specific assets pledged as collateral. Bond owners are classified as general creditors of the company and have as collateral for their debt all the assets of the company not already pledged. All Treasury, agency, and most municipal bonds are debentures. The largest and most financially sound corporations often issue these bonds because their debt is so secure that there is no reason to pledge specific assets against it. Weaker companies may sell debentures because they have no assets which they can pledge. It is impossible to judge whether a bond is "good" or "bad" solely on the basis of whether it is a debenture.

Subordinated debentures are debenture bonds which hold a creditor position *beneath* that of general and other specified senior creditors. Many of the subordinated debentures currently issued are convertible into the common stock of the issuing company. Subordinated debentures are sometimes issued by companies which have recapitalized due to bankruptcy. These securities contain substantial amounts of financial risk.

Equipment trust certificates are unique securities which are designed to allow companies having poor credit ratings to borrow at low rates of interest. Security for this obligation is personal property —a piece of equipment of some type. Several different ways are used to pledge the equipment.[1] The unique ingredient of this financing device is that the collateral has a known value and a wide market. These debt instruments usually have low financial risk.

Guaranteed bonds, as their name implies, are debt securities which are backed by another party. All agency securities are implicitly guaranteed by the federal government in that the federal government would probably never allow an agency issue to default. Strong corporations often guarantee the securities of a weaker organization so that the credit rating of the second company is higher. This guarantee is specifically stated. Such securities are becoming more common as larger companies acquire control over smaller firms.

Joint bonds are issued and guaranteed by two or more companies. Their most usual use is that of financing the building of commonly used facilities—railroad terminals, docks, and so on.

Figure 8–1 is a picture of a bond issued by Bell Telephone Company of Pennsylvania. It is a debenture bond, paying semiannual interest of 8⅝ percent per annum. The bond is registered in the name of the owner, and interest payments are mailed by the company to this person. In case of loss or destruction, registered securities are much easier to replace than bearer securities since the company has no knowledge of who the bearer (the owner) is. This bond was issued July 1, 1970, and matures in 36 years.

NOTES AND BILLS

Notes and bills are not bonds. They have many of the characteristics of bonds, but their maturities are usually shorter. The traditional defi-

[1] See any business law or corporation finance text for a complete discussion of the legal attributes of these securities.

FIGURE 8–1
Bell Telephone Company Bond

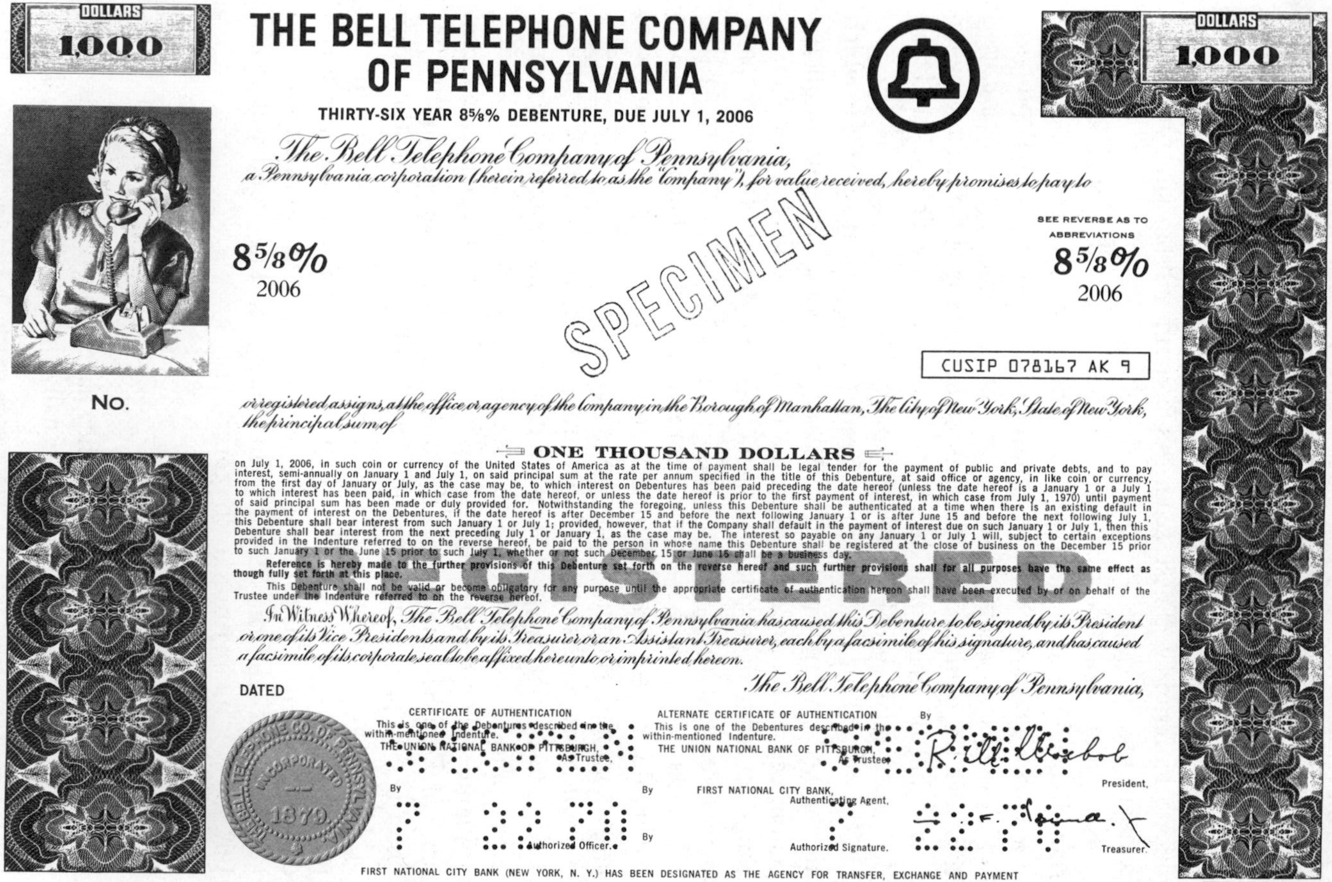

DOLLARS 1,000

THE BELL TELEPHONE COMPANY OF PENNSYLVANIA

THIRTY-SIX YEAR 8⅝% DEBENTURE, DUE JULY 1, 2006

The Bell Telephone Company of Pennsylvania, a Pennsylvania corporation (herein referred to as the "Company"), for value received, hereby promises to pay to

$8\frac{5}{8}\%$ 2006

SPECIMEN

SEE REVERSE AS TO ABBREVIATIONS

$8\frac{5}{8}\%$ 2006

CUSIP 078167 AK 9

NO.

or registered assigns, at the office or agency of the Company in the Borough of Manhattan, The City of New York, State of New York, the principal sum of

ONE THOUSAND DOLLARS

on July 1, 2006, in such coin or currency of the United States of America as at the time of payment shall be legal tender for the payment of public and private debts, and to pay interest, semi-annually on January 1 and July 1, on said principal sum at the rate per annum specified in the title of this Debenture, at said office or agency, in like coin or currency, from the first day of January or July, as the case may be, to which interest on Debentures has been paid preceding the date hereof (unless the date hereof is a January 1 or a July 1 to which interest has been paid, in which case from the date hereof, or unless the date hereof is prior to the first payment of interest, in which case from July 1, 1970) until payment of said principal sum has been made or duly provided for. Notwithstanding the foregoing, unless this Debenture shall be authenticated at a time when there is an existing default in the payment of interest on the Debentures, if the date hereof is after December 15 and before the next following January 1 or is after June 15 and before the next following July 1, this Debenture shall bear interest from such January 1 or July 1; provided, however, that if the Company shall default in the payment of interest due on such January 1 or July 1, then this Debenture shall bear interest from the next preceding July 1 or January 1, as the case may be. The interest so payable on any January 1 or July 1 will, subject to certain exceptions provided in the Indenture referred to on the reverse hereof, be paid to the person in whose name this Debenture shall be registered at the close of business on the December 15 prior to such January 1 or the June 15 prior to such July 1, whether or not such December 15 or June 15 shall be a business day.

Reference is hereby made to the further provisions of this Debenture set forth on the reverse hereof and such further provisions shall for all purposes have the same effect as though fully set forth at this place.

This Debenture shall not be valid or become obligatory for any purpose until the appropriate certificate of authentication hereon shall have been executed by or on behalf of the Trustee under the Indenture referred to on the reverse hereof.

REGISTERED

In Witness Whereof, The Bell Telephone Company of Pennsylvania has caused this Debenture to be signed by its President or one of its Vice Presidents and by its Treasurer or an Assistant Treasurer, each by a facsimile of his signature, and has caused a facsimile of its corporate seal to be affixed hereunto or imprinted hereon.

DATED

The Bell Telephone Company of Pennsylvania,

CERTIFICATE OF AUTHENTICATION
This is one of the Debentures described in the within-mentioned Indenture.
THE UNION NATIONAL BANK OF PITTSBURGH, As Trustee,
By
Authorized Officer.

ALTERNATE CERTIFICATE OF AUTHENTICATION
This is one of the Debentures described in the within-mentioned Indenture.
THE UNION NATIONAL BANK OF PITTSBURGH, As Trustee
By
FIRST NATIONAL CITY BANK, Authenticating Agent,
By
Authorized Signature.

By
President,
Treasurer.

THE BELL TELEPHONE CO. OF PENNSYLVANIA INCORPORATED 1879

FIRST NATIONAL CITY BANK (NEW YORK, N. Y.) HAS BEEN DESIGNATED AS THE AGENCY FOR TRANSFER, EXCHANGE AND PAYMENT

FEDERATED BANKNOTE COMPANY.

Courtesy of American Telephone and Telegraph.

nition of a bond is a debt security having an original maturity of at least five years.

The largest classification of nonbond debt is notes of one type or another. Businesses and individuals issue notes, which are simply promises to pay a stated sum of money at a specified future date. Few of these ever come into the possession of the average investor, however, because they are usually payable to banks or other businesses. The U.S. Treasury had outstanding nearly $130 billion of notes at the end of 1974. Maturities of these securities ranged from one to seven years. Notes having the longest maturities might well be confused with bonds since the main difference between them and bonds is their name. These securities pay interest periodically and are freely negotiable. Individuals hold substantial amounts of them.

Treasury bills are noninterest bearing securities having maturities of one year or less. They are sold at a discount from their redemption, or par, value. The difference between what is paid for the security and its maturity value is the return to the investor. Almost $120 billion of these securities were outstanding at the end of 1974. Treasury bills are auctioned each week through the Federal Reserve banks, and are purchased by investors seeking the ultimate in financial safety and liquidity. The minimum purchase of these securities is $10,000. The most popular maturities are three and six months, although there are occasional issues of shorter or longer maturity. Some businesses issue securities with very short maturities (commercial paper), but these are usually sold only in very large dollar amounts. They are seldom purchased by individuals.

SAVINGS BONDS

These Treasury securities are sold only to U.S. citizens or residents. Two series of bonds, E and H, are currently offered. At the end of 1974 slightly over $63 billion of these securities were outstanding.

Series E savings bonds are sold at a discount from their maturity values. Maturity values begin at $25 and advance in $25 increments to $100; larger bonds are available in amounts of $200, $500, $1,000, and $10,000. Purchase prices are $18.75 for the $25 bond, $37.50 for the $50 one, and so on to $7,500 for the largest denomination. At the present time, these securities mature in five years from date of purchase, which provides investors with a yield of 6 percent—if the bonds are held to maturity. Series E bonds may be redeemed at any time after they have been held for two months; they may be held longer

FIGURE 8–2
Yield on Series E Savings Bonds Held for Various Time Periods

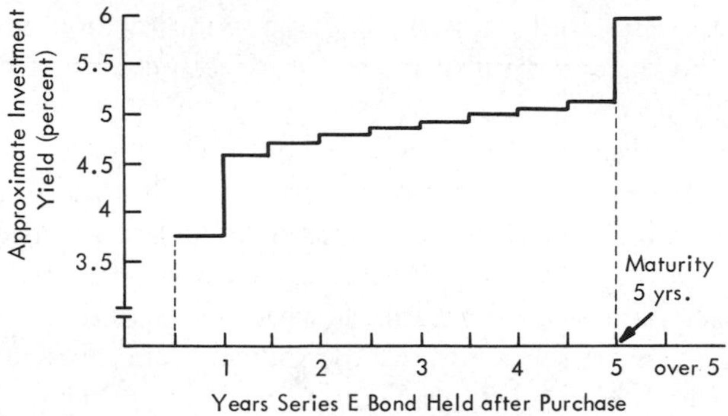

Source: U.S. Department of the Treasury, Series E Bond Redemption Tables.

than five years. Early redemption means less yield. Figure 8–2 shows the approximate yield on Series E bonds held for various maturities.

Series H bonds are sold in denominations of $500, $1,000, $5,000, and $10,000. They currently yield 6 percent and mature in ten years. These bonds may be redeemed at any time after they have been held for six months. The difference between Series E and H savings bonds is that interest is paid semiannually on Series H, while it is taken as a discount on the Series E. Series H bonds have more appeal for persons desiring constant interest income.

Savings bonds are sold only in *fully registered form.* The name and address of the legal owner is imprinted on the face of the bond and recorded at the Treasury. If stolen, lost, burned, or otherwise destroyed, duplicate securities can easily be issued. Savings bonds cannot be sold to a third party. This means that their market value is always the current redemption value. Regardless of what happens to market rates of interest, these securities always have a known value. Investment characteristics of savings bonds closely resemble those of certificate accounts of savings institutions.

The investor has a choice of when taxes are paid on Series E bond interest. The total tax may be paid when the security is redeemed, or taxes may be paid yearly on the amount of interest which accrues each year. Taxes on the income of these securities may be deferred for many years. How this is accomplished is discussed in Chapter 13, titled Tax Aspects of Investments.

GRADING DEBT SECURITIES

The *grade* of a debt security refers to the likelihood that the issuer will be able to make the interest and principal payments called for in the bond indenture or other debt financing agreement. It is a measure of financial risk. U.S. Treasury securities are rated highest of any securities because of the ability of the Treasury to levy taxes to make these payments. Other borrowers, whether they be states, local governments, or corporations, do not have the same taxing powers. There is usually some risk, however small, that the issuer of these bonds will not be able to live up to the contract which was made with the purchasers of the bonds. Financial analysts attempt to measure this risk and to indicate their assessment of its amount by assigning a grade to each individual issue of the bonds of better known corporations and state and local governments.

The degree of risk is seen as being determined mainly by the amount and constancy of the issuer's income or tax revenue. The key relationship in this analysis is the ratio of the amount of funds available to pay interest and principal, to the amount which is required to make these payments. If a corporation issued an amount of bonds which was small enough so that there was practically no doubt that the corporation would be able to make the interest and principal payments which were called for, there would be very little risk that the company could not meet its obligations. Such a bond would be rated as being a very high-grade security. Another issue of bonds of a different company, or an issue of bonds from the same company which were junior or subordinated to the first issue, might have less interest and principal payment coverage. These securities would have a lower grade than the first issue. Rating of bonds is done by the companies which publish financial information for the investment community. Moody's and Standard & Poor's ratings are probably the most widely used, although several other companies publish their own bond ratings.[2] The descriptions of ratings in Figure 8–3 are indicative of what the rating services look to when devising a specific rating for a bond issue.

Treasury bonds are not graded. They are the standard against which all corporate and municipal bonds are measured. The grade of corporate and municipal bonds may change after the security has been sold, due to changes in the financial condition of the issuer. Changes

---

2 Moody's uses the symbols Aaa, Baa, etc., for their ratings; Standard & Poor's uses AAA, BBB, etc. The grades identified by the two types of symbols are for all practical purposes identical.

FIGURE 8–3
Moody's Bond Rating System

Aaa Bonds which are rated Aaa are judged to be of the best quality. They carry the smallest degree of investment risk and are generally referred to as "giltedge." Interest payments are protected by a large or by an exceptionally stable margin and principal is secure. While the various protective elements are likely to change, such changes as can be visualized are most unlikely to impair the fundamentally strong position of such issues.

Aa Bonds which are rated Aa are judged to be a high quality by all standards. Together with the Aaa group they comprise what are generally known as high grade bonds. They are rated lower than the best bonds because margins of protection may not be as large as in Aaa securities or fluctuation of protective elements may be of greater amplitude or there may be other elements present which make the long term risks appear somewhat larger than in Aaa securities.

A Bonds which are rated A possess many favorable investment attributes and are to be considered as higher medium grade obligations. Factors giving security to principal and interest are considered adequate but elements may be present which suggest a susceptibility to impairment sometime in the future.

Baa Bonds which are rated Baa are considered as lower medium grade obligations, i.e., they are neither highly protected nor poorly secured. Interest payments and principal security appear adequate for the present but certain protective elements may be lacking or may be characteristically unreliable over any great length of time. Such bonds lack outstanding investment characteristics and in fact have speculative characteristics as well.

Ba Bonds which are rated Ba are judged to have speculative elements; their future cannot be considered as well assured. Often the protection of interest and principal payments may be very moderate and thereby not well safeguarded during both good and bad times over the future. Uncertainty of position characterizes bonds in this class.

B Bonds which are rated B generally lack characteristics of the desirable investment. Assurance of interest and principal payments or of maintenance of other terms of the contract over any long period of time may be small.

Caa Bonds which are rated Caa are of poor standing. Such issues may be in default or there may be present elements of danger with respect to principal or interest.

Ca Bonds which are rated Ca represent obligations which are speculative in a high degree. Such issues are often in default or have other marked shortcomings.

C Bonds which are rated C are the lowest rated class of bonds and issues so rated can be regarded as having extremely poor prospects of ever attaining any real investment standing.

Source: *Moody's Transportation Manual* (New York: Moody's Investors Services, 1974), p. viii.

in grade are important to investors because there is a definite relationship between the grade of a bond and its yield.

The Relationship Between Bond Rating and Yield

As financial risk rises, it is logical that a purchaser of a fixed income security would demand a higher return from the investment to offset the additional risk. This is in fact what happens. At any point in time, the yield of a Baa rated security will be higher than the yield on an Aaa security of similar maturity. As the market rate of interest moves up and down over time in response to the supply of and demand for credit, the yields of the different grades of securities will *all* move up and down. Figure 8–4 shows this relationship clearly.

A somewhat closer viewing of Figure 8–4 indicates that at certain times the relationship between the different grades of securities changes. For example, the spread between long-term Treasury bonds and Baa rated corporate bonds averaged 107 basis points during 1962. During 1965, this spread declined to about 66 basis points. In 1974 it averaged an exceptional 251 basis points.[3]

Historically, the spread in yield between different grades of bonds is greatest when interest rates are rising rapidly and least when interest rates have been constant for some time. Persons who make their living by managing large portfolios of bonds are aware of these relationships and often follow an investment strategy which calls for them to shift from one grade of bonds to another when the basis point differential between the two issues becomes more than or less than a predetermined amount.

Characteristics other than grade help determine the yield of a given debt security. Such characteristics are coupon rate, maturity date, sinking fund provisions, convertibility, legality for investment, and amount outstanding to mention only the most influential. However, it is the grade that most strongly determines yield because financial risk is the most important consideration for most persons investing in debt securities.

REPAYMENT OF BONDS

A unique feature of debt is that it must someday be repaid.[4] When bonds are to be repaid and how the repayment is to be financed are of importance to the owner of debt securities.

---

[3] A basis point is one one-hundredth of a percentage point. The difference between a yield of 3 percent and a yield of 4 percent is therefore 100 basis points.

[4] This statement is not completely true. There are several examples of debt securities which have been issued with no maturity date. It is expected that these securities will remain outstanding indefinitely. The British government has issued these bonds, called consols, and several private corporations have also issued them. Other bonds have maturity dates so far in the future that they certainly must have seemed to be perpetual bonds to their original purchasers. The New York Central 4½s series A of 2007, issued in 1913; the Missouri Pacific General Income B 4¾s of 2030, issued in 1956; and the Duquesne Light Company Debenture 5s of 2010, issued in 1960 are examples of bonds with extremely long maturities. The dollar amount of bonds having maturities of 50 years and over is much larger than the dollar amount of perpetual bonds which have been issued. The amounts of both are insignificant when compared to the amounts of shorter term bonds.

FIGURE 8–4
U.S. Treasury Bond, Aaa Corporate, and Baa Corporate Bond Interest

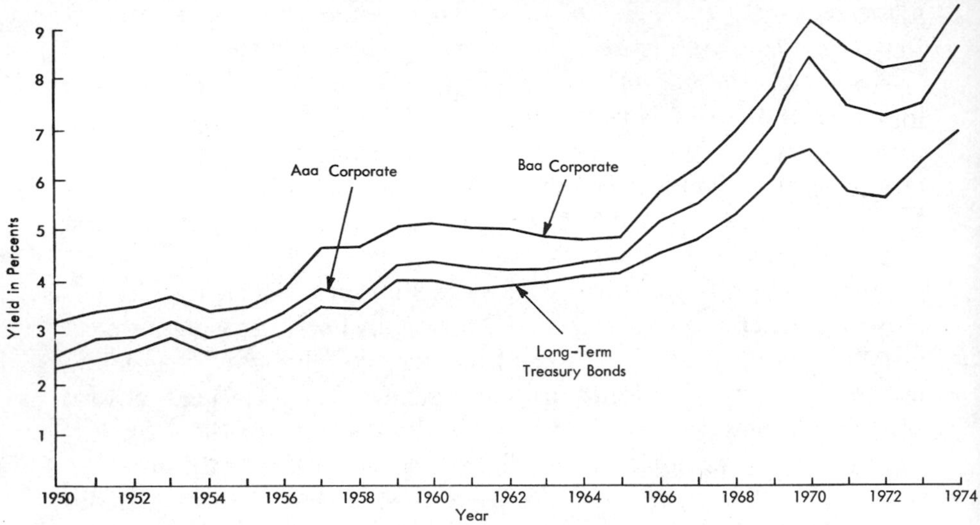

Source: *Federal Reserve Bulletin*, various issues.

Callable Bonds

Most corporate bonds and some Treasury and state and local bonds have a feature which allows the issuer to redeem the bond before the stated maturity date of the security. This feature is known as *callability,* and it means that the issuer may redeem the bond at any time after a certain date, up to the maturity date of the security. It can be assumed that the bond will not be called unless it is advantageous for the issuer to do so. If it is advantageous to the issuer, it is usually harmful to the security owner. Inclusion of a call feature in a debt contract tends to raise the interest rate buyers require because these securities are less attractive as investments.

To make callable securities more marketable at lower yield rates, two devices are commonly used to provide some protection for the purchaser. These are *call protection* and the *call premium.* Call protection simply means that the company issuing the securities agrees not to call them until a certain time period has elapsed *after* their issue. Currently, most nonconvertible bonds have five to ten years of call protection.

The call premium provides the owner of a called bond with extra compensation for having had the security called. The premium is normally less than 10 percent of par, and it is usually highest when the bond first becomes callable, decreasing in amount as time passes to the point where it disappears. Table 8–1 is the call premium schedule of an issue of bonds of American Hospital Supply Corporation.

TABLE 8–1
Call Premium Schedule of American Hospital Supply Corporation (5¾ percent convertible subordinated bonds due 1999)

Redemption

The Debentures are to be redeemable, at AHSCs option, as a whole or in part, on at least thirty days' notice given as provided in the Indenture, on any date prior to maturity at the following redemption prices (expressed as percentages of principal amount) plus accrued interest to the redemption date, if redeemed during the twelve-month period beginning December 1 of the years indicated below:

1974	105.750%	1984	102.875%
1975	105.463	1985	102.588
1976	105.175	1986	102.300
1977	104.888	1987	102.013
1978	104.600	1988	101.725
1979	104.313	1989	101.438
1980	104.025	1990	101.150
1981	103.738	1991	100.863
1982	103.450	1992	100.575
1983	103.163	1993	100.288

and thereafter at 100 percent of the principal amount thereof.

Source: American Hospital Supply Corporation, *Prospectus*, November 26, 1974, p. 17.

A recent innovation in the area of call protection is seen in the 10¾ percent Pacific Power and Light bond issue which was sold in April 1975. These securities provide *owners* with the option of cashing in the bonds at par on May 1, 1985 or holding them until May 1, 1990. The advantage to this feature lies totally with the holder. If market interest rates on similar securities are higher than 10¾ in May 1985, the bonds will be surrendered for their par value. If market interest rates are lower, the bonds will be held until 1990. Pacific Power and Light made this agreement because they believed that it would allow the issue to be sold at a higher price than could be obtained if a typical call contract agreement were used.

Sinking Funds

An agreement which has as its purpose the gradual reduction of either the amount of outstanding bonded debt or the amount of the liability of the outstanding debt issue is called a *sinking fund agreement.* Such an agreement is seen as being advantageous to bondholders because it forces the corporation to begin making arrangements to repay the issue before it matures. The corporation is bound to its sinking fund agreement as tightly as it is bound to its agreement to pay interest. If the terms of the sinking fund are not met, the bond issue is in default, and the bondholders may take legal action against the company. Over half of the bonds issued recently have had some form of sinking fund agreement in their indentures.

FIGURE 8–5
Sinking Fund Provisions of American Hospital Supply Corporation (5¾ percent convertible subordinated bonds due 1999)

SINKING FUND

The Debentures will be redeemable through the operation of a sinking fund on December 1, 1985, and on December 1 in each year thereafter to and including December 1, 1998, upon at least thirty days' notice given as provided in the Indenture, at a sinking fund redemption price equal to 100% of the principal amount thereof and interest accrued thereon to the redemption date. On December 1 of each of the years 1985 to 1998, inclusive, AHSC will pay to the Trustee, for a mandatory sinking fund, cash sufficient to redeem on such December 1, Debentures in the aggregate principal amount of $4,125,000; provided that Debentures converted, acquired or redeemed otherwise than through the sinking fund may be used, at the principal amount thereof, to reduce the amount of any mandatory sinking fund payment. AHSC, at its option, may make an optional sinking fund payment in cash in any year in an amount equal to the mandatory sinking fund payment. Such optional right of payment shall not be cumulative and no optional sinking fund payment shall operate to reduce the amount of any mandatory sinking fund payment. Cash payments for the sinking fund (subject to carryover of amounts less than $25,000) are to be applied to redeem Debentures. (*Article IV*)

Source: American Hospital Supply Corporation, *Prospectus*, November 26, 1974, p. 17.

Figure 8–5 presents the sinking fund agreement for the convertible bonds of American Hospital Supply Corporation. While the issue is immediately callable—as are most convertible issues—no bonds will be purchased to meet sinking fund requirements before 1985. As a careful reading of Figure 8–5 reveals, no cash sinking fund payments may ever become necessary for the principal amount of converted securities may be used to offset the sinking fund liability.

Serial Repayment Provisions

Sinking funds are used almost exclusively with corporate bonds. Treasury and federal agency bonds are usually refunded with a new issue when they mature; state and municipal securities and equipment trust certificates are usually retired *serially*. When an issue of serial bonds is sold, it is divided up into portions which mature in various amounts at various times. Serial repayment means that each year a certain portion will be retired, at par. Figure 8–6, an announcement of a recent equipment trust issue, shows how this is done. Purchasers of these securities have a choice of maturity, and to a lesser extent a choice of yield.

TAXABILITY

Interest payments on all bonds except those issued by state and municipal governments are taxed as ordinary income to the recipient. Nontaxability is a definite advantage to the investor because all of the interest can be spent: none goes for taxes. Implications of this feature so far as the investor is concerned are covered in Chapter 13, Tax Aspects of Investments.

Lack of taxability is also important to the issuer because it allows the sale of debt securities at a lower yield cost. Investors appraise bonds primarily on factors of grade, maturity, and yield. If two bonds have identical grade and maturity characteristics, yield becomes the factor which determines the security to buy. Investors having taxable income relate the *after-tax* yield of the taxable bond to that of the untaxed security. Obviously, taxable securities will have to yield more in order to have comparable yields—when the yield is computed after taxes. Recently (January 1975) tax exempt bonds of about 20-year maturity were being sold at an interest cost of from 6 to 7 percent for issues of various grades. Southwestern Bell had to pay about 9 percent to sell a recent bond issue which was rated Aaa. As Figure 8–7 shows, the highest grade municipal bonds have yields lower than even Treasury securities.

FIGURE 8–6
Announcement of a New Serial Bond Issue

New Issue / May 14, 1975

$15,000,000

(Third Installment)

The Atchison, Topeka and Santa Fe Railway Company

Equipment Trust, Series J

8⅜% Equipment Trust Certificates

Non-Callable

To be dated December 15, 1974. To mature in 15 annual installments of $1,000,000 on each December 15 from 1975 to 1989.

Issued under the Philadelphia Plan with 20% original cash equity

MATURITIES AND YIELDS

1975	6.00%	1979	7.90%	1983	8.25%	1987	8.70%
1976	7.15	1980	8.00	1984	8.35	1988	8.75
1977	7.50	1981	8.10	1985	8.50	1989	8.75
1978	7.75	1982	8.20	1986	8.60		

These certificates are offered subject to prior sale, when, as and if issued and received by us, subject to approval of the Interstate Commerce Commission.

Salomon Brothers

Blyth Eastman Dillon & Co.
Incorporated

Drexel Burnham & Co.
Incorporated

Source: *The Wall Street Journal,* May 14, 1975, p. 18.

FIGURE 8–7
Yields on Long-Term U.S. Treasury Bonds and Aaa Municipal Bonds (average yields)

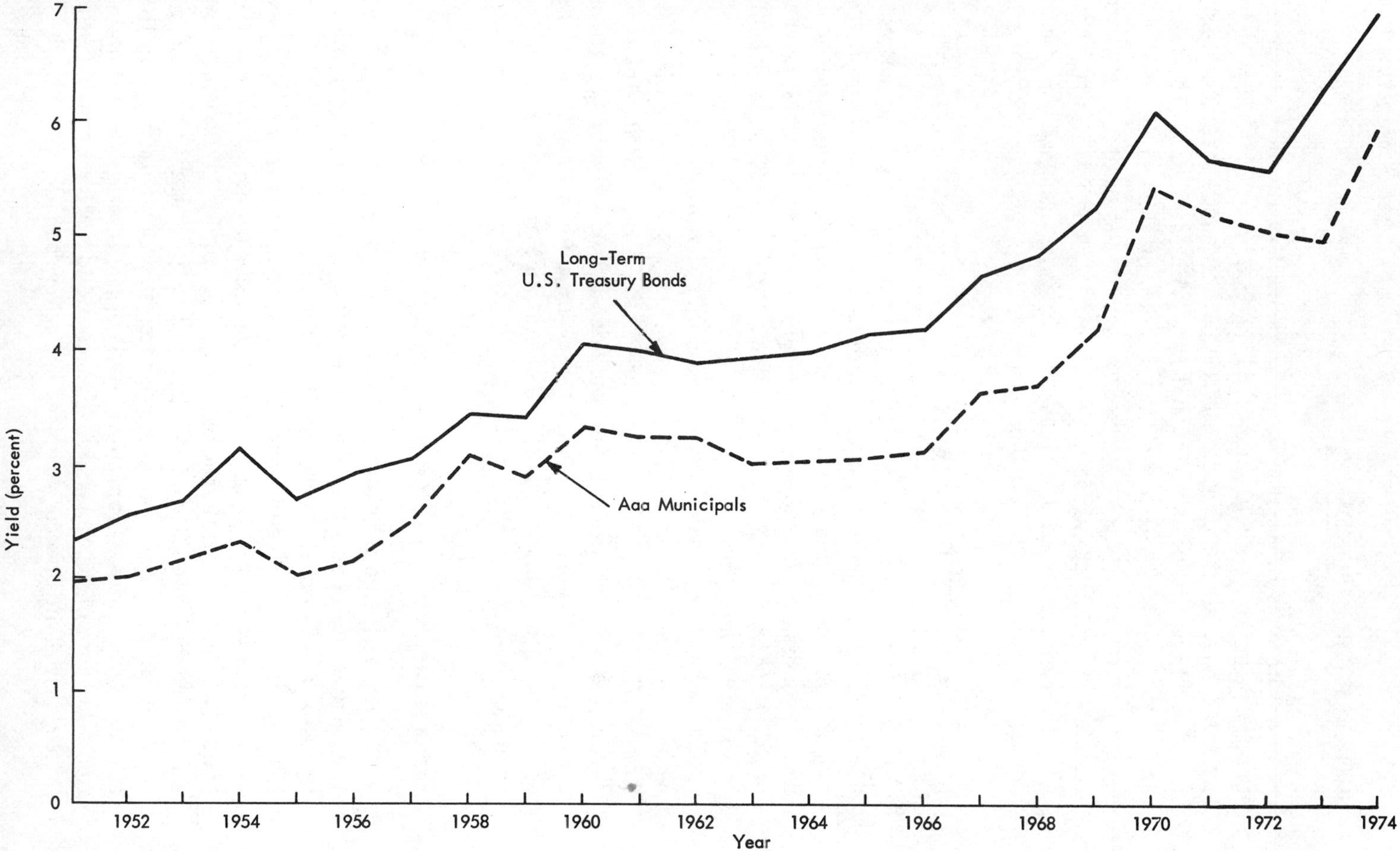

Source: *Federal Reserve Bulletin*, various issues.

CONVERTIBLE BONDS

In recent years between 2.5 and 22 percent of the new corporate bonds sold in the United States have been *convertible*. These debt securities have all the characteristics of other bonds—callability, par value, coupon rate of interest, maturity date, and so on—and the ability to be exchanged for common stock of the company which issued them. Because of this feature, these bonds lie somewhere between debt and equity securities so far as their investment characteristics are concerned. For this reason they are discussed along with convertible preferred stock in Chapter 9.

PRICES AND YIELDS OF BONDS

Calculation of the yield of a bond may be difficult to understand because the term has a number of different meanings. However, the material in this section should help the reader to understand bond yields and should provide knowledge sufficient to make yield calculations. Prior to showing these procedures, it is necessary to explain bond yield terminology.

The discussion of yields and prices will be tied in with Figure 8–8, which is a series of corporate bond price quotes as they appeared in *The Wall Street Journal* on January 14, 1975. Price listings of U.S. Treasury bonds were discussed in some detail in Chapter 4. Quotes of corporates are similar except that prices are quoted in 8ths or 16ths of a point rather than in 32ds, and more price and sales volume information is given.

Prices of Bonds

It will perhaps be valuable to review several definitions which have appeared in earlier chapters. *Par value* is the face amount—the maturity value of a bond. By far the most common par value is $1,000, but some bonds are $500 and even $100 par. All bonds listed in Figure 8–8 have par values of $1,000. The *market value* or *market price* of the bond is seldom the same as the par value. Exceptions to this statement can be found in bonds that will mature in the near future and in bonds which happen to pay a rate of interest which is identical to the current market rate of interest on bonds of the same grade and maturity. The current market value of each bond in Figure 8–8 is the "close" price—the price at which the last sale was made.

FIGURE 8–8
Price Quotes of Corporate Bonds (Monday, January 13, 1975)

Bonds	Cur Yld	Vol	High	Low	Close	Net Chg
ReyTob 7s89	8.4	6	83	83	83	.....
RocIn 4⅞87	cv	30	58⅝	58⅝	58⅝	+2⅛
RocIn 4¼91	cv	12	55	55	55	− ¼
Rohr 5¼86	cv	20	54⅞	54⅞	54⅞	.....
Rydr 11½90	11.	45	96	95⅞	96	+ ⅛
StL SF 5s06f	..	4	45½	45½	45½	+1
StLSaF 4s97	8.6	1	46¼	46¼	46¼	....
StRPa 4⅞97	cv	80	75	74	74	+ ¾
SaF In 6¼98	cv	14	94	93⅞	93⅞	− ⅛
SaulRl 8½80	14.	18	60	60	60	....
SCM 5½s88	cv	51	60¾	60½	60⅝	+ ⅝
Searl 8.7s95	8.7	10	99¾	99¾	99¾	.....
Searle 7½80	7.6	2	98⅛	98⅛	98⅛	....
Sear R 8⅝95	8.4	28	102	101	102	+1
Sear R 8⅛76	8.0	47	101¾	101	101	− ⅞
Sear R 6⅜93	7.7	2	82¼	82¼	82¼	.....
Sear R 4¾83	5.8	3	81	81	81	.....
Sears A 5s82	6.1	4	82	82	82	+2
Sear A 4⅝77	5.0	20	91¼	91¼	91¼	− ¾
Seatrin 6s94	cv	36	28¼	28	28¼	+ ¼
Singer 8¼76	8.4	40	97¾	97¼	97¾	+ ¼
Singer 8s99	10.	4	75⅜	75⅜	75⅜	−7⅝
Skell 8.15s76	8.0	9	101⅞	100½	101⅞	+1⅜
Skil Cp 5s92	cv	22	40	40	40	.....
SmK 8.15s84	8.0	86	101	101	101	−1⅞
SoCBll 10s14	9.2	67	107⅞	107¼	107⅞	+ ½
SoC Bl 8¼04	8.6	40	95¼	94⅝	95¼	+ ½
SoCBl 8¼13	8.7	12	95	94¾	94¾	...
SBIT 9.05s03	8.8	21	102½	102	102	− ½
SBelT 7.6s08	8.6	5	88	88	88	+1⅛
SoBIT 7⅜10	8.6	8	85½	85¼	85½	+3
SoBIT 6½79	6.9	5	93¾	93¾	93¾	−2
SoBelT 3s79	3.6	12	83⅜	83⅜	83⅜	+3⅜
SoBIT 2¾85	4.6	5	59½	59½	59½	+ ½
SoCG 10¼81	9.7	1	104⅞	104⅞	104⅞	+ ⅞
S CG 8.85s95	9.4	13	93⅝	93¼	93¼	
SoNGs 9⅛76	9.0	10	101¼	100¾	100¾	−1¼

Note: The abbreviation "cv" means the bond is convertible; "s" stands for percent.

Source: *The Wall Street Journal*, January 14, 1975, p. 26.

Yields of Bonds

The purchase of a bond gives its owner the right to receive interest payments of a certain amount over a known period of time.[5] The owner also is entitled to receive the par value of the security when it

[5] This and the following statements are directed to interest bearing, freely marketable debt securities. Excepted from this discussion are noninterest-bearing debt securities —Treasury bills and other discount securities—and nonmarketable securities such as Series E and H savings bonds. Yield on discount securities is the difference between the market price and the redemption price computed as a percent of the current market price of the security and adjusted for the time to maturity. Changes in the market rate of interest have a direct effect on the market prices of such securities. Since relatively few small-scale investors hold these securities, and since we hope to keep this book to a readable length, computation of yields on these securities will not be discussed.

matures. The current market price of a given bond is determined by several factors: (1) the par value of the bond, (2) the rate of interest paid on the bond, (3) the grade of the security, (4) the time remaining to maturity, (5) the current rate of interest paid on bonds having similar characteristics as the one being examined, and (6) the tax status of the interest payments. These are the most important considerations, but there are others which are sometimes of equal force. At this time, however, it is probably desirable to work toward simplifying this discussion of yield rather than making it more complex.

Three assumptions will make it possible to reduce the number of variables which must be considered. Assume that all par values are $1,000, that all bonds are of the highest possible grade, and that all bond interest is taxed as income for the purpose of computing income taxes. The maturity date of the security, the coupon rate of interest paid on the bond, and the current rate of interest being paid on similar bonds are now the only important variables which determine the market price of the security. Even with this simplification, there are several types of yield.

Coupon Yield. The *coupon* or *nominal* yield of a bond is the yearly dollar amount of interest paid divided by the bond's par value. This computation does not take into consideration either time to maturity or the yield on similar bonds. The coupon rate may be stated in dollars of interest to be paid (per year), or as is more common, it may be stated in percents. The Reynolds Tobacco Company bonds (first line, Figure 8–8), maturing in 1989, have a coupon yield of 7s, or 7 percent. The yield amount is $70 per year since 7 percent of $1,000 is $70. The coupon rate does not change unless the company issuing the bond experiences a financial reorganization.

Current Yield. The *current yield* is the dollar amount of interest received each year divided by the market price of the security. A bond paying $70 interest each year would have a *coupon yield* of 7 percent regardless of the market price of the security. If this bond had a market price of 83 ($830), it would have a current yield of,

$$\frac{\text{Yearly interest}}{\text{Market price}} = \frac{\$70}{\$830} = 0.084337 \text{ or } 8.43\%.$$

Coupon yield tells how much, in dollars, one can expect to receive from a bond investment each year; current yield tells in percentage terms the yearly return *on the purchase price* of the bond. This computation will equal the yield to maturity on a bond investment only if the bond were purchased at par or if the bond is a consol.[6] In all other cases this formula does not consider the fact that if the market price of the security is either more or less than the par value of the bond, the person holding the security to maturity will have either a capital loss or gain when the bond is redeemed at par. For example, the purchaser of the Reynolds Tobacco 7s of 89 will have a $170 capital gain if the bonds are held until redemption. The Sears Roebuck 8⅝s of 1995 would provide an investor with a capital loss of $20, the amount of the premium on the bond. The gain or loss on this transaction either adds to, or subtracts from, the investment's current yield.

Yield to Maturity. The *yield to maturity* calculation takes into account the relationship between the maturity value, the time to maturity, the current price, and the coupon yield of a bond. This yield calculation allocates the bond premium or discount over the life of the security. For example, if a bond were purchased for $100 less than its par value and if this security had ten years remaining until it matured, the yield to maturity calculation would allocate $10 of this capital gain to each of the remaining years to maturity. If a bond were purchased at a price greater than par, the capital loss would likewise be spread equally over the remaining life of the security. The yield to maturity is the true annual yield that an investor would receive on a bond if it were held to maturity. An approximate form of this calculation is the following.

Let

Y = Yield to maturity
C = Coupon yield in dollars per year
P = Par value of the bond
M = Market value of the bond
N = Number of years to maturity

Then

$$Y = \frac{C + \dfrac{P - M}{N}}{\dfrac{P + M}{2}}$$

[6] This calculation is used to compute the yield on consols—perpetual bonds which do not mature. It is also modified and used to compute the yield on preferred stocks.

In the case of the Reynolds Tobacco 7s, the yield to maturity would be computed as follows. As of 1975, 14 years remain to maturity.

$$Y = \frac{\$70 + \dfrac{\$1{,}000 - \$830}{14}}{\dfrac{\$1{,}000 + \$830}{2}}$$

$$= \frac{\$70 + \dfrac{\$170}{14}}{\dfrac{\$1{,}830}{2}}$$

$$= \frac{\$82.14}{\$915}$$

$$= 0.08977, \text{ or } 9.0\%$$

This formula provides an approximate yield figure only. A more accurate and far quicker way to calculate yield to maturity is to use a book of bond value tables.[7] These tables provide yield calculations which consider all the factors mentioned earlier except the grade of the security. A portion of a page from one of the tables is reproduced in Figure 8–9. The 7 percent figure at the top of the page indicates that this part of the book is devoted to bonds having coupon rates of this amount. This particular page covers the price and yield relationships for bonds having a 7% coupon maturing from 10½ to 14 years into the future. The yield to maturity for the Reynolds Tobacco bond is determined by looking down the 14-year maturity column until one comes to the amount closest to the bond's current market price. In this example the market price was $830. Look now to the yield column and read out the yield to maturity figure—between 9.1 and 9.2 percent in this case—which is listed on the same line as the bond's price. This figure is different by about 0.15 percentage points (15 basis points) from that derived by using the approximate formula listed earlier. It is more accurate because of the way the yield is computed, and it is far quicker to use the tables than to work through the formula.[8]

[7] *Bond Value Tables* (Boston, Mass.: Financial Publishing Co., 1958) and *Supplementary High Rate Bond Values* (Boston, Mass.: Financial Publishing Co., 1966).

[8] The appendix to this chapter contains a derivation of the formula used to construct these tables.

FIGURE 8–9
Page from a Bond Value Table

7%	YEARS and MONTHS							7%
Yield	18-6	19	19-6	20	20-6	21	21-6	22
4.50	131.17	131.70	132.23	132.74	133.24	133.73	134.22	134.68
4.60	129.68	130.19	130.68	131.16	131.64	132.10	132.55	132.99
4.70	128.22	128.69	129.16	129.61	130.06	130.49	130.91	131.33
4.80	126.78	127.22	127.66	128.08	128.50	128.91	129.30	129.69
4.90	125.36	125.77	126.18	126.58	126.97	127.35	127.72	128.08
5.00	123.96	124.35	124.73	125.10	125.47	125.82	126.17	126.50
5.10	122.58	122.95	123.30	123.65	123.99	124.32	124.64	124.95
5.20	121.22	121.56	121.89	122.22	122.53	122.84	123.14	123.43
5.30	119.89	120.20	120.51	120.81	121.10	121.38	121.66	121.93
5.40	118.57	118.86	119.15	119.42	119.69	119.95	120.21	120.45
5.50	117.28	117.54	117.81	118.06	118.31	118.55	118.78	119.01
5.60	116.00	116.25	116.48	116.72	116.94	117.16	117.38	117.58
5.70	114.74	114.97	115.18	115.40	115.60	115.80	115.99	116.18
5.80	113.51	113.71	113.90	114.10	114.28	114.46	114.64	114.81
5.90	112.29	112.47	112.64	112.82	112.98	113.15	113.30	113.46
6.00	111.08	111.25	111.40	111.56	111.71	111.85	111.99	112.13
6.10	109.90	110.04	110.18	110.32	110.45	110.58	110.70	110.82
6.20	108.73	108.86	108.98	109.10	109.21	109.32	109.43	109.54
6.30	107.58	107.69	107.80	107.90	108.00	108.09	108.18	108.27
6.40	106.45	106.54	106.63	106.72	106.80	106.88	106.96	107.03
6.50	105.34	105.41	105.48	105.55	105.62	105.68	105.75	105.81
6.60	104.24	104.30	104.35	104.41	104.46	104.51	104.56	104.61
6.70	103.15	103.20	103.24	103.28	103.32	103.36	103.39	103.43
6.80	102.09	102.12	102.14	102.17	102.19	102.22	102.24	102.27
6.90	101.04	101.05	101.06	101.08	101.09	101.10	101.11	101.12
7.00	100.00	100.00	100.00	100.00	100.00	100.00	100.00	100.00
7.10	98.98	98.97	98.95	98.94	98.93	98.92	98.91	98.90
7.20	97.97	97.95	97.92	97.90	97.87	97.85	97.83	97.81
7.30	96.98	96.94	96.91	96.87	96.84	96.80	96.77	96.74
7.40	96.00	95.95	95.91	95.86	95.81	95.77	95.73	95.69
7.50	95.04	94.98	94.92	94.86	94.81	94.75	94.70	94.65
7.60	94.09	94.02	93.95	93.88	93.82	93.75	93.69	93.64
7.70	93.16	93.07	92.99	92.92	92.84	92.77	92.70	92.63
7.80	92.23	92.14	92.05	91.96	91.88	91.80	91.72	91.65
7.90	91.32	91.22	91.12	91.03	90.93	90.85	90.76	90.68
8.00	90.43	90.32	90.21	90.10	90.00	89.91	89.81	89.73
8.10	89.55	89.42	89.31	89.19	89.09	88.98	88.88	88.79
8.20	88.67	88.54	88.42	88.30	88.18	88.07	87.97	87.86
8.30	87.82	87.68	87.54	87.42	87.29	87.18	87.06	86.95
8.40	86.97	86.82	86.68	86.55	86.42	86.29	86.17	86.06
8.50	86.14	85.98	85.83	85.69	85.56	85.43	85.30	85.18
8.60	85.31	85.15	85.00	84.85	84.71	84.57	84.44	84.31
8.70	84.50	84.33	84.17	84.02	83.87	83.73	83.59	83.46
8.80	83.70	83.53	83.36	83.20	83.05	82.90	82.76	82.62
8.90	82.92	82.73	82.56	82.39	82.23	82.08	81.93	81.80
9.00	82.14	81.95	81.77	81.60	81.43	81.28	81.13	80.98
9.10	81.37	81.18	80.99	80.82	80.65	80.48	80.33	80.18
9.20	80.62	80.42	80.23	80.04	79.87	79.70	79.54	79.39
9.30	79.87	79.67	79.47	79.28	79.11	78.93	78.77	78.62
9.40	79.14	78.93	78.73	78.53	78.35	78.18	78.01	77.85
9.50	78.41	78.20	77.99	77.80	77.61	77.43	77.26	77.10
9.60	77.70	77.48	77.27	77.07	76.88	76.70	76.52	76.36
9.70	76.99	76.77	76.55	76.35	76.16	75.97	75.80	75.63
9.80	76.30	76.07	75.85	75.64	75.45	75.26	75.08	74.91
9.90	75.61	75.38	75.16	74.95	74.75	74.56	74.38	74.20

Source: *Supplementary High Rate Bond Values*, p. 87.

It is possible to substitute the market rate of interest (the yield to maturity of similar securities) for the yield to maturity rate and to solve this yield problem for the appropriate market price of a bond. If, for example, the market rate of interest on bonds maturing in 12½ years were 8 percent, and if a bond having a coupon rate of 7.0 percent and a maturity of 12½ years were offered for sale, its current price should be about 92.19 or $921.90. At this price (determined by working through the table backwards) the yield to maturity of the security would be the same as the current market rate of interest—8 percent. If the actual market price of the bond were less than $921.90 the bond would yield *more* than the market rate of interest; it would be a *better buy* than a new bond of equal grade and maturity having a coupon rate and yield of 8 percent.

The importance of the yield to maturity calculation cannot be overemphasized. All Treasury bonds are sold on the basis of yield to maturity. High-grade corporate and municipal securities are also sold on this basis, but the yield to maturity calculation is not normally stated in the financial press. Persons buying or selling such securities make these calculations on their own, however, and it is yield to maturity which is the most important determinant in deciding which bond or bonds to purchase. For securities which are callable, yield is usually calculated on the basis of the first call date.

Qualitative Factors. Grade, taxability, legality for investment, and other qualitative characteristics of bonds are also important. As the grade of a bond declines, the yield on the security must increase because lenders require a higher return to induce them to accept additional financial risk. Bonds having interest payments which are fully or partially tax exempt yield less than taxable bonds, because tax exemption is an advantage which makes the bonds worth more to some investors. Bonds which qualify as *legal investments*—for savings banks, trusts, and other financial institutions—yield less than those not qualifying because the demand for these bonds is greater. Small size bond issues of the less well-known companies may provide higher yields than bonds of other companies which have outstanding securities that are identical in every respect, except for the size of the company or bond issue. These companies usually pay a premium for being small and unknown, because these bonds are not as marketable as others. The important point of this discussion is that while bond yields are affected by many qualitative factors, in choosing between bonds having essentially the same qualitative features, it is the yield to maturity which determines which bond is the better investment.

RELATIONSHIP BETWEEN BOND PRICES AND INTEREST RATES

When the market rate of interest rises, the market price of outstanding bonds declines. When the market rate of interest declines, the price of outstanding bonds rises. This relationship was initially discussed in Chapter 2, but because it is so confusing to many persons it bears repeating here.

Imagine yourself to be a potential purchaser of one bond. To simplify things, assume that your choice is between the outstanding 7 percent bond previously examined and another one which is to be issued today to mature in 1989 and which carries a coupon rate of 8 percent. The only difference in these securities is their coupon rates, and this difference can be traced to the fact that the market price of interest has risen since the 7 percent bonds were first sold. Would anyone buy the 7 percent bond if they could instead buy the one yielding 8 percent? Certainly not! Persons wishing to sell these 7 percent bonds will find that they must price them at a *discount*, below par, or no one will purchase them. The market price of the 7 percent bond will decline in a competitive market until the yield to maturity of both issues of bonds is about 8 percent. To accomplish this, its price would be about $916.70. (Figure it out on your own using thc bond valuc table.)

What would happen to the price of the 8 percent bond if in the future the market rate of interest *declined?* Its market price would *increase* above par because this security would then pay *more interest* than was being paid on new bonds of the same type and grade. Remember, when market rates of interest increase, prices of outstanding bonds decrease; when market rates of interest decrease, prices of outstanding bonds increase.

It is the highest grade bonds, the "interest rate" securities as they are called, which are most affected by changes in market rates of interest. These securities have practically no financial risk and a high degree of marketability. Because of this, the market prices of these securities are determined almost completely by the increases and decreases in the market rate of interest. Bonds of lower grade are less affected by movements in the market rate of interest because investors look at these securities largely in terms of their financial risk characteristics.

INVESTING IN MORTGAGES

Mortgages and other debt contracts are commonly purchased by the more well-to-do members of communities. Often the purchaser of a mortgage (this person may originate the contract or purchase an outstanding one) takes on some sort of risk that the financial institutions which ordinarily provide mortgage financing hesitate to accept. Perhaps the mortgage is on a property for which there is no ready market. Maybe the title to the property is not completely legally clear. Possibly the title to the property is not insurable. At any rate, many persons purchase these mortgages. Such investments may provide a relatively high rate of return because of their special risk characteristics.[9]

Some financial institutions will not purchase *second* or *junior mortgages*. Such a mortgage is one which receives its interest payments only after the interest payments due on the first mortgage are paid. If the mortgagor defaults on the first mortgage, the owner of the second mortgage will receive no compensation until the first mortgage has been completely paid off. Second mortgages are often created when a piece of real property is sold before the original mortgage on the property can be paid off. If the value of the property is at least as much as the amount of the remaining outstanding first mortgage plus the amount of the second mortgage, there is no reason not to invest in such a mortgage—given that it is otherwise a good investment.

Today, most mortgages are *amortized*. Under this type of contract the mortgagor agrees to periodically pay interest and some principal. The contract is usually written so that the payments are constant in amount. In the early years of the contract much of the payment will be for interest. As principal is repaid, the mortgage becomes "safer" because although part of the loan has been repaid, the total mortgaged property is still security for the loan.

Mortgage contracts have traditionally been straight debt contracts. Recently, however, many lenders have been writing agreements into

---

[9] Yields on mortgages are measured in the same general way that yield to maturity is calculated for bonds in that the cost of the mortgage is related to yearly interest and principal payments. This can be done by modifying the present value formula presented in the appendix to this chapter. A simpler way is through the use of tables prepared especially to measure mortgage yields. All real estate offices have such tables.

their mortgage contracts which allow them to obtain an investment return over and above the interest payment. On mortgages which finance apartment buildings the mortgagee may demand that the mortgagor pay a percent of the gross rentals of the apartments in addition to the customary interest payment. (A percent of gross sales may be obtained on mortgage contracts which finance stores or other income-producing property.) As prices rise, gross rentals and sales should also increase; income from this source may keep pace with inflation. Borrowers are naturally reluctant to make these contracts, but in a time of tight credit and very high interest rates, lenders can demand and obtain concessions of this type.

INVESTING AND SPECULATING IN DEBT

Debt securities can be used for both investing and speculation. To understand how they can be used in two seemingly contradictory ways, it is first necessary to look to their investment characteristics.

Investment Characteristics of Debt

High-grade bonds and other debt contracts provide the investor with several things unique to these investments. They have great financial safety and marketability, but they perform poorly so far as purchasing power risk and interest rate risk are concerned.

Financial Risk. Payment of principal and interest on high-grade debt issues will be made as specified. It is true that many bond issues went into default in the 1930s, and several have recently defaulted, but these were not high-grade issues. Treasury securities and the first two grades of municipal and corporate securities—the Aaa and Aa rated bonds—are almost completely safe from financial risk. Mortgages cannot usually be graded so accurately as bonds, but very high quality mortgages do exist and may be purchased.

Investors sometimes "reach" for yield by purchasing low-grade bonds. They reason that the difference in yield between high-grade and low-grade bonds, although it is seldom more than 2½ percent, is "worth the risk." Such a strategy can only be pursued effectively if the investor is able to purchase so many different low-grade bonds that they are not all affected by the same economic events. Losses will doubtlessly be experienced on a few securities, but they will be more than covered by the increased yield from the other bonds. Individuals who are purchasing just a few bonds cannot hope to obtain this average experience and must therefore forgo the premium yields of low-grade securities. The additional yield cannot offset the potential loss.

Marketability. All high-grade bonds are easily *marketable*, but they are not necessarily *liquid*. Marketability refers to the ability to sell or buy large amounts of a given security in a short period of time without causing large fluctuations in market prices. All high-grade bonds have this characteristic.

To be *liquid* a security must be marketable, but it must also be marketable at a price near to its purchase price or par value. All short-term high-grade debt instruments—Treasury bills and notes, commercial paper, bonds soon to mature—are marketable and liquid. Because maturity is never far in the future, and because par value will be paid at maturity, market values stay near to par value. Owners of these securities know they can market them at a price very near to what they originally paid.

Lower grade debt securities may be neither marketable nor liquid, even though they are short-term in duration. The previous caution deserves to be repeated: Low-grade debt securities are not "investment-grade" securities. They cannot and will not provide the investment characteristics that most investors want from debt securities.

Purchasing Power Risk. One of the greatest disadvantages to debt securities is the loss of purchasing power experienced by owners during times of price inflation. Interest will be paid and securities will be redeemed as specified in the contract, but each dollar received purchases less goods and services.

It is true that inflation strikes at all incomes—common stock dividends, the market price appreciation of art objects, the appreciation of land values—all lose purchasing power through price inflation. However, the returns to these investments are not *limited* by contract. They may rise in value at a faster rate than that at which inflation occurs. Debt contracts seldom have such protection.

In a time of price *deflation* high-quality debt contracts become excellent investments. Not only is the income from these investments relatively secure, but it will purchase more during each period in which deflation continues. The United States has not experienced a period of sustained deflation since the depression years of the 1930s. This is over 40 years in the past. During the ensuing period we have had years of relatively stable prices and several years of great price inflation, but there is little question of the direction in which prices are moving. There has been, and there will probably continue to be, at least moderate price inflation. Every investor should consider this important fact when formulating a personal investment strategy.

Interest Rate Risk. One of the often-cited strengths of high-grade debt instruments used to be their great market price stability. The recent period of rapidly rising market interest rates has caused all outstanding marketable, long-term debt securities to decrease in price greatly and has caused investors to reappraise the value of bonds in this regard.

The Reynolds Tobacco Co. 7s of 1989 were issued in 1969, at approximately par. Six years later they are quoted at 83; a loss in market value of about 17 percent. The grade of the bond has not changed (it is still A grade), and it is no more or less marketable than before. Market rates of interest have simply raised, forcing these bonds to lose much market value.

All high-grade bonds are affected by interest rate changes. If rates declined, bond prices would rise. But so long as interest rates remain high, holders of debt securities who purchased them when rates were lower are "locked in." They cannot sell their securities without taking a capital loss.

The individual who cannot afford to accept interest rate risk but who wishes to invest in long-term securities should give consideration to either Series E or H savings bonds. These securities provide less yield than other bonds, but rcdcmption values are known at all times.

Collateral for Loans. High-grade marketable debt investments make good loan collateral. Treasury securities are such good collateral that during period of easy credit many banks will lend up to 95 percent of their market value. Under this arrangement, if you had $100,000 market value of these securities, you could borrow $95,000 against them. Banks cannot now lend more than $50,000 on listed common stocks having the same market value.[10] Mortgages may also make good collateral, but since there is not normally a good market in these contracts, their use as collateral is limited compared to high-grade bonds. U.S. savings bonds may not be used as collateral.

Summary of Investment Characteristics. High-grade bonds have many obvious disadvantages during a period of rising prices and interest rates. However, many individuals (and some professional investors) have such a natural aversion to financial risk that they willingly accept

---

[10] Legal lending limits on stock and securities convertible into stock are set by the Federal Reserve Board. Limits fluctuate with economic conditions. In early 1976, margin requirements were 50 percent for stocks and convertible bonds. Treasury securities do not come under Federal Reserve Board margin requirements. A bank could theoretically lend 100 percent of their market value.

all these disadvantages to obtain what they believe to be safety in their investments. High-grade debt securities do have a place in many investors' portfolios, but it must be realized that financial safety is acquired at a high cost in terms of purchasing power and interest rate risk. Convertible securities have helped to overcome some of the deficiencies of straight debt. These securities are discussed in the next chapter.

Speculating in Debt

Speculation may be defined as the act of taking on more investment risk in the hope of higher than normal returns. This can be done in any of several ways using bonds or other debt contracts as the vehicle for speculation.

Low-Grade Securities. One may purchase the debt contracts of financially embarrassed companies or individuals. When one makes such a speculative investment, the security behind the contract becomes of extreme importance, for the issuer of the security is often facing bankruptcy. However, even bankruptcy need not always be feared, for if the claims of the debt security holders are strong enough, they may be paid quickly and in full. During periods of economic recession the grade of many debt securities becomes lowered. Companies do not have earnings high enough to maintain the required coverage ratios to keep their bonds of Aaa, Aa, or A rating. Lowering of the grade of a security will almost always cause its market price to decline, and as institutions and individuals hurry to sell these securities, market prices are driven down even further. At some point such bonds become very reasonable investments for persons who can accept this kind of investment risk. Studies have shown that nearly all bonds are eventually redeemed at par by their issuers. In many instances it is just a matter of being able and willing to wait until this happens.

Speculation through Financial Leverage. It is also possible to speculate in "money rate bonds." These are the high-grade securities whose market prices are almost completely determined by the current market rate of interest. Speculation in these securities becomes possible when interest rates are relatively high and are expected to decrease. One may simply purchase long-term Treasury bonds and wait for their prices to rise as interest rates decline. There is not very much speculative risk, or profit, involved in this kind of investment because it would take a very large change in the market rate of interest to cause a substantial change in the price of these very high-grade securities. Such changes usually take much time.

To maximize the potential return from this type speculation the maximum amount of money should be borrowed at the lowest possible rate. The collateral for the loan would be the debt securities purchased. Depending upon capital market conditions the speculator may be required to pay cash for between 5 and 25 percent of the total amount of securities purchased. Interest costs of the loan will also be determined by the availability of credit. The cost of holding this investment is the interest paid on the loan, plus the amount of return that is lost by not investing the cash portion of the investment in a higher-yielding investment (this cost is known as *opportunity cost*), plus brokerage and other fees. From this total the amount of interest received from holding the securities is deducted. The net figure represents the cost associated with holding the investment.

The investor will always incur a cost to hold this investment because interest received will be less than interest paid out and other costs. Each period that passes without a decline in the market rate of interest adds to these costs. If interest rates decline as expected, the increase in the market price of the bonds provides the speculator with a trading profit which can be used to pay these costs and provide a profit on the speculation.

There are two main problems associated with this type of speculation. One is obtaining the necessary financing on advantageous terms; the other is accurately predicting interest rate movements. It should be obvious that if interest rates rise rather than decline, the speculator incurs a paper loss on the transaction. The lender will probably ask for more cash to be placed against the declining market value of the bonds. This, of course, results in a most unfavorable situation for the speculator. Even when interest rates do not rise the speculator is harmed. The costs of holding this investment accrue so long as the securities are held. If interest rates do not decline within a reasonable period of time the costs of holding the securities may be larger than the profits, even though declining interest rates eventually cause the securities prices to rise. For the above reasons these speculations are short-term in nature.

SUMMARY

All debt contracts are similar in that the borrower receives the use of funds belonging to others and pays interest for their use. This agreement is formalized in the bond indenture, or mortgage contract.

Bonds may be classified by their security or the source from which their repayment is expected, in the following manner.

Classification of Debt Securities

I. By issuer
   A. Securities issued by governments
      1. Treasury securities
      2. Agency securities
      3. Municipals
         a Full faith and credit bonds
         b Revenue bonds
         c Assessment bonds
   B. Securities issued by corporations
      1. Utilities
      2. Railroads
      3. Industrials
II. By security or source of repayment
   A. Mortgage bonds
   B. Collateral trust bonds
   C. Debenture bonds
   D. Equipment trust certificates
   E. Guaranteed bonds

Notes, bills, and *savings bonds* resemble traditional bond investments but are generally of shorter maturity. An added difference in savings bonds is that they are nonmarketable.

Corporate and *municipal* bonds are graded by their financial risk characteristics. *Treasury* bonds are not graded because they are seen as being of the highest possible grade. Yields and grades of bonds are related in that the highest grade securities have the lowest yields, and lower graded securities offer higher yields. An exception to this rule are *municipal* bonds. Interest on these bonds is not taxed as income to its recipients. Consequently, these securities have lower market yields, per given grade, than any other bond. But because of the tax free interest they may yield more to investors in the high income tax brackets than other debt securities of similar grade.

Coupon yield, current yield, and *yield to maturity* are three different ways of computing yields. Only the yield to maturity calculation provides a mathematically correct statement of true yield. A formula for computing the approximate yield to maturity is given in the chapter. The appendix to this chapter is used to develop the mathematically correct formula used to compute yield to maturity of debt instruments.

Debt securities of high grade have these investment qualities: (1) negligible financial risk, (2) very high liquidity, and (3) a high degree of purchasing power and interest rate risk. Most debt securities, mortgages included, are good loan collateral.

High-grade debt instruments are usually purchased as investments to provide financial safety for a portfolio. Such securities may become vehicles for speculation if financial leverage is used to increase the profits (or losses) from holding these securities. Low-grade debt contracts are usually classified as speculative securities.

APPENDIX TO CHAPTER 8

Computation of Bond Values

The basic formula behind all bond value tables, present value tables, future value tables, and special tables which make use of a variant of these calculations is the compound interest formula $P_n = P\ (1 + i)^n$, which is derived in the appendix to Chapter 7.

A bond obtains its value from the two promises of the company issuing the security: (1) the promise to redeem the security at some time in the future for its par value, and (2) the promise to pay periodic interest of a known amount to the owner of the bond. Other determinants of the value of a bond are the grade of the security, and the current yield that is obtainable from bonds having similar grade and maturity characteristics to the one under analysis. To simplify the problem of valuation, assume that the bond to be analyzed is riskless or that other alternate investments have identical risk characteristics.

The first step in developing a *current* or *present theoretical market value* for a bond—the terms mean the same thing—is to break the promises of the bond issuer into two separate problems. These are the problems of arriving at present values for (1) a sum of money (the par value) which will be paid at a future date, and (2) the periodic payments of interest received over the remaining life of the bond.

The present value of a sum of money to be paid at some time in the future is dependent upon how much an investor could earn on money owned *now* on the next best alternative investment having similar risk characteristics. For purposes of this example assume that the bond to be valued matures in exactly ten years and that it pays $50 in interest each year at the end of the year. Its par value is the customary $1,000. Assume further that a current annual return of 4 percent can be obtained from other bonds of like grade and maturity. The first part of the valuation problem, that of determining how much one should pay *now* for a contract which promises $1,000 in ten years, can be stated simply as how much money would one need to invest now, at 4 percent compounded annually, to have $1,000 of principal and accumulated compound interest at the end of ten years. The value P_n of the compound interest formula, $P_n = P(1 + i)^n$, is a *future value*. This is the amount that a present sum of money, P, would accumulate to at a given rate of compound interest. Solving this formula for P tells what amount would be necessary to invest now so that the amount P_n would result in n time periods through the working of compound interest.

$$P_n = P(1 + i)^n$$

$$P = P_n \left[\frac{1}{(1 + i)^n}\right]$$

Inserting the numbers of the problem, we get

$$P = \$1{,}000 \left[\frac{1}{(1 + 0.04)^{10}}\right]$$
$$P = \$1{,}000(0.67556)$$
$$P = \$675.56.$$

If $675.56 were invested now for ten years at 4 percent interest compounded annually, its value would be $1,000 in ten years. Therefore, the present value of the $1,000 par value of the bond is $675.56. Tables of present value factors for various interest rates and time periods are readily available, although no examples of these tables are presented in this text.[11]

The valuation of interest payments is more complex because these payments will be received $50 at a time at the end of each year for ten years.[12] However, the valuation of their present worth is done exactly as above. The $50 interest payment to be received at the end of

[11] Thomas M. Simpson, Zareh M. Pirenian, Bolling H. Crenshaw, *Mathematics of Finance*, 3d ed. (Englewood Cliffs, N.J.: Prentice-Hall, 1951); Paul M. Hummel and Charles L. Seebeck, Jr., *Mathematics of Finance*, 2d ed. (New York: McGraw-Hill, 1956); Robert Cissell and Helen Cissell, *Mathematics of Finance*, 2d ed. (Boston: Houghton Mifflin, 1964).

[12] In actuality bond interest is usually paid semiannually or quarterly. Annual interest payments have been assumed here to keep the problem as simple as possible.

the first year is equal to an amount now which if invested at 4 percent compound interest would increase to $50 at year end,

$$\begin{aligned} P &= \$50\left[\frac{1}{(1+0.04)^1}\right] \\ &= \$50(0.96153) \\ &= \$48.08 \end{aligned}$$

The present value of the first year's interest payment is $48.08 because if this amount were invested at 4 percent per annum it would be worth $50 at the end of one year, when the interest payment is to be received. Another way of stating this is that an investor who has alternative investments which will yield 4 percent should be willing to pay $48.08 *now* for the right to receive $50 in one year. This is logical because no more than this amount could be earned on any other investment having similar risk characteristics. To value the ten-year stream of interest payments it is necessary to sum the ten present value amounts derived from ten separate calculations which differ only in the n values of each term. Written mathematically, the question for the present value of future interest payments would be:

$$\begin{aligned} P = \$50 &\left[\frac{1}{(1+0.04)^1} + \frac{1}{(1+0.04)^2} + \frac{1}{(1+0.04)^3} + \cdots \right. \\ &\left. + \frac{1}{(1+0.04)^{10}}\right] \\ &= \$50(8.11089) \\ &= \$405.55 \end{aligned}$$

Total interest payments have a present value of $405.55 because if one had this amount accumulating interest at 4 percent per annum, one could remove $50 from this fund at the end of each year for ten years. The last $50 withdrawal would exhaust the fund.

Tables of present values of annuities of I amount received for n periods are available and were used to solve the above problem. They are not widely used in investments because these tables give only the present value of a series of interest payments. Of concern is the total present value of both parts of the bond contract: the promised par value payment and the promised interest payments. Stated mathematically, using the following abbreviations, we find the formula is as follows:

Let

P = Present value of the total contract
i = Current yield obtained from investments having similar risk and maturity characteristics

$n =$ Number of time periods to maturity
$I =$ Interest in dollars per period
$M =$ Maturity value of the bond

$$P = I\left[\frac{1}{(1+i)^1} + \frac{1}{(1+i)^2} + \frac{1}{(1+i)^3} + \cdots + \frac{1}{(1+i)^n}\right] + M\left[\frac{1}{(1+i)^n}\right].$$

Bond value tables, a sample page of which was presented previously, are no more than completed problems of the above form which have been worked out for a variety of values of P, I, n, and i. M, the par value of the security, is assumed to be $1,000. The values given in these tables are accurate only if the purchase of the bond is made on a day which begins an interest payment period. In practice it is rare for the date of purchase to occur on this date, so extrapolation is used to obtain an approximate value for the bond. Computer programs are available which calculate prices more accurately than do the bond value tables. Such programs are used at some companies which do large volumes of bond trading.

The market price of the above bond, from the bond value tables, is $1,081.80. Summing the present values of interest and principal as they were computed ($675.56 + $405.55) produces a value of $1,081.11. The difference in calculations of $0.69 is the result of rounding error.

PROBLEMS

1. From Moody's, Standard & Poor's, the *Federal Reserve Bulletin*, or any other source, obtain current yields of Aaa municipals, Treasury long-term bonds, and corporate Aaa and Baa bonds.
   a. Determine the basis point yield difference between each grade using the bonds with the lowest yield as the standard against which the others are measured.
   b. Explain why the differences are what they are.
2. Compute the *approximate* yield to maturity of bonds having the following characteristics:
   a. Twenty-five years remain to maturity, coupon yield is 6 percent, par value is $1,000, current market price is 85.
   b. Twelve years remain to maturity, coupon yield is 9 percent, par value is $1,000, current market price is 105.
3. Record the yearly market price of a soon-to-mature Treasury bond each

year for the past ten years. (Be certain you choose a bond that had at least a ten-year maturity when issued.) Explain why these market prices have differed from par and why they are now near par.

QUESTIONS

1. Bonds are identified as very *formal* financing agreements. Why are they formal and how is this formality accomplished?
2. Bonds issued by municipalities, federal agencies, or the U.S. Treasury seldom, if ever, have indentures. Why is this true?
3. How are debt securities usually classified? Is this a reasonable method of classification?
4. "Debenture bonds are often of the highest grade, even though there is no collateral pledged for the bond." Explain this statement.
5. Why is it that collateral trust bonds can be sold by companies of poor credit rating at such a low interest cost?
6. How do Series E savings bonds differ from corporate bonds? To what kind of investor do they have the most appeal?
7. What is meant by *yield to maturity?* Why is this yield calculation more accurate and meaningful than *current yield?*
8. "Bond investing is not for me. I'm always looking for capital gains." Agree or disagree with this statement, basing your answer on your knowledge of bond price movements.
9. What are the most important differences and similarities in the investment characteristics of mortgages and bonds?
10. What are the most important investment characteristics of debt contracts?
11. What is *call protection* for a bond purchaser?
12. What is a *call premium?*
13. How is it possible to speculate in bonds?

SELECTED READINGS

"Annual Review of the Bond Market." New York: Salomon Brothers & Hutzler, published annually.

Ascher, Leonard W. "Selecting Bonds for Capital Gains," *Financial Analysts Journal,* March–April, 1971.

Comprehensive Bond Values Tables, 4th desk ed. Boston: Financial Publishing Co., 1958.

Graham, Benjamin; Dodd, David L.; and Cottle, Sidney. *Security Analysis: Principles and Techniques,* 4th ed. New York: McGraw-Hill, 1962.

"Handbook of the Securities of the United States Government." New York: First Boston Corp., published annually.

Homer, Sidney, and Leibowitz, Martin. *Inside the Yield Book: New Tools for Bond Market Strategy.* Englewood Cliffs, N.J.: Prentice-Hall, 1972.

Sauvain, Harry C. *Investment Management,* 4th ed. Englewood Cliffs, N.J.: Prentice-Hall, 1973.

Sherwood, Hugh C. *How to Invest in Bonds.* New York: Walker & Co., 1974.

9

Investing in Preferred Stock and Convertible Bonds

INTRODUCTION

When compared to either bonds or common stock, the amounts of preferred stock in the hands of individual investors is very small. No one knows exactly how much preferred stock is outstanding or who owns it, but records are kept on the amounts of these securities that are sold each year. As Table 9–1 indicates, the amounts of newly issued preferred shares have increased greatly since 1961 but are still small when compared to either new issues of common stock or bonds.

The New York Stock Exchange lists 502 preferred issues for trading, and the American Stock Exchange lists 83[1]. At the end of 1974, the market value of preferred shares on the NYSE was about $20 billion; those on the AMEX were valued at about $1.3 billion. While this is a large amount of money, it is a very small percentage of the total market value of the equity securities listed on the exchanges: about 3.3 percent of those on the NYSE and 5.5 percent of those on the AMEX. Preferred shares are also sold OTC. No accurate figures are available on the amount of preferred stock traded in this market or on the regional exchanges, but there is no reason to presume that it would be more or less important than it is on the two largest exchanges.

Before the days of high corporate income taxes, preferred stock was sold by a large proportion of American corporations. It was an important part of their financial structure, and it was widely held by indi-

[1] Data obtained from the New York and American Stock Exchanges.

TABLE 9–1
New Issues of Corporate Securities Sold in Recent Years (millions of dollars)

Year	*Preferred Stock*	*Common Stock*	*Bonds*
1974	2,254	4,050	31,567
1973	3,375	7,655	21,022
1972	3,340	10,723	25,825
1971	3,670	9,291	32,123
1970	1,390	7,240	30,315
1969	682	7,714	18,347
1968	637	3,946	17,383
1967	885	1,959	21,954
1966	574	1,939	15,561
1965	725	1,547	13,720
1964	412	2,679	10,865
1963	343	1,011	10,856
1962	422	1,314	8,969
1961	450	3,294	9,420

Source: *The Federal Reserve Bulletin* (various issues) and the Securities and Exchange Commission.

vidual investors. Most of these securities were not convertible into common stock. From the early 1900s until the present time straight (nonconvertible) preferred shares have continued to become less important as a financing device, except for utilities. The explanation for this decline in use appears in the next section of this chapter. Ownership of straight preferred stock has over time fallen into corporate hands; a discussion of this phenomenon appears later in the section that follows, titled Ownership of Preferred Stock.

To this point there appears little justification for studying preferred stock. However, in recent years convertible preferred stock has come into much wider usage. This type of security, because of its special characteristics, is often suitable for the individual investor. This fact provides the justification for this chapter.

LEGAL CHARACTERISTICS OF PREFERRED STOCKS

Definition of Preferred Stock

Preferred stock is an *equity* security, which differs from the *common stock* of the corporation in that it receives some sort of preferential treatment. The rights and privileges of any preferred stock issue are described in the articles of incorporation of the company and often on the reverse side of the stock certificate. The most important of these rights and privileges are listed by several financial reporting services.[2] Preferred stocks legally may have practically any sort of preference over the common shares. But most preferred stocks receive preference only in that their dividends are paid before any dividends may be paid on the common, and they receive preferential treatment if the corporation is liquidated. In return for this, the owners of preferred shares receive a limited dividend return. Under normal conditions they may not vote to elect the board of directors of the corporation. However, some corporations allow preferred shareholders to elect a small proportion of the board if preferred dividends have not been paid for some stated time period. In a still smaller number of cases, preferred shareholders have full voting rights.

The preferred shareholders' dividend is often confused with bond interest. Like bond interest, it is paid periodically and is usually a stated amount. The resemblance ends here, however. Bond interest payments are a legal liability of the company, while preferred dividends are not. Not paying bond interest may force a company into bankruptcy. Passing a preferred dividend has no such result because this dividend is seen as a return to the equity owner and not as a liability of the company.

Legally, bonds are debt. Bond interest payments are a cost of doing business and are therefore deductible from income when computing income taxes. Preferred stock is ownership capital, and preferred dividends are not a cost of doing business for most companies. These dividend payments are paid "after taxes" and are more expensive than an equal dollar amount of bond interest. The effect of this different tax treatment can be seen in Table 9–2. This is a situation in which one company has financed with bonds while another has financed with preferred stock. Operating income and financing expenses are the same for each company, but there is a large difference in the earnings available to common shareholders.

When income tax rates are low it makes little difference whether a company pays interest or dividends as its cost of obtaining financing. But when income tax rates are high, as they have been for many years, the method of financing has an important impact on profits. The natural result of this "tax disadvantage" has been an increase in the use of bonded debt and a decrease in the use of preferred stock. There

[2] Moody's and Standard & Poor's publish information of this type for most corporations having preferred stock issues.

TABLE 9–2
Earnings Available to Common Shareholders under Two Types of Financing

	Company A Bond Financing $100 of Interest	*Company B Preferred Stock Financing $100 of Dividends*
Operating income	$300	$300
Less bond interest	100	-0-
Taxable income	200	300
Income tax @ 50% rate	100	150
After-tax income	100	150
Less preferred dividend	-0-	100
Available to common shareholders	$100	$ 50

are two exceptions to this statement: (1) Utility companies have continued to issue preferred stock because preferred stock dividends are classified as an expense of doing business for the purpose of setting their rates. It is not surprising that a large proportion of the straight preferred shares listed on the exchanges is utility shares. (2) Convertible preferred stock has been issued in substantial amounts in years when common stock prices are relatively high. The securities are often issued by companies who might have had difficulty in selling convertible debt securities because of low or fluctuating earnings.

Types of Preferred Stock

There are not nearly as many types of preferred stock issues as bond issues. Most of them can be classified under one of the following headings, which identify them by the different claims they hold on dividends.

1. Straight preferred.
2. Cumulative preferred.
3. Participating preferred.
4. Convertible preferred.

Straight preferred stock is preferred stock which has a fixed annual dividend payment. If the corporate directors declare this dividend it is paid; if they do not make this declaration it is not paid. The decision of whether or not to pay a dividend rests entirely with the board of directors of the company. A dividend not paid in any year is not carried over to the next year as a liability of the company. The only advantage that this security has over the common shares is that no dividends may be paid on the common until the *current* preferred dividend has been paid. This may be very small advantage indeed! A company could pass the dividends on both the preferred and common stock for one year and in the next year pay the regular preferred dividend and a "double" common dividend. Because of this possibility most preferred stocks have dividends which are cumulative.

Cumulative preferred stock is identical to the straight preferred except that when a preferred dividend payment is not made, the company continues to owe this amount to the preferred shareholder. This *dividend arrearage,* as it is called, is not a *liability* of the company in the same sense that interest payments are a liability. However, since no dividends may be paid to the common stock until all preferred dividend arrearages have been paid, the cumulative shareholder is in a somewhat stronger position than is the owner of straight preferred stock. If the corporation wishes to pay dividends on common shares, it must either pay the entire amount of preferred dividends in arrears or in some way dispose of the claims of this class of owners.

There are many examples of preferred stocks which have accumulated large dividend arrearages. One might expect these stocks to be valued at the amount of the dividend arrearage plus the investment value of the security, but in fact this is seldom the case. The usual solution to a problem of large dividend arrearages is for the corporation to reach an agreement with the preferred shareholders whereby it either purchases the preferred stock from them or satisfies the arreage claims with a payment of something less than the total amount of the claim.

Participating preferred shares receive a stated dividend before any dividend may be paid on common stock. If this and the common stock dividend are paid, and if earnings are high enough that further common dividends are justified, the participating feature allows the preferred shares to also receive additional dividends. Such an arrangement gives the preferred shareholders the best of two worlds. They receive preferential treatment on dividend payments, and they also may share in any large profits that the company obtains. Moody's Manuals indicate that there are only about 84 participating preferred issues now outstanding.

There is an even rarer type of preferred stock, the *cumulative participating* preferred stock. This issue is a decided curiosity; Moody's lists less than ten of these issues.

Convertible Preferred Stock

The outstanding characteristic of this type of security is the fact that it may be converted into the common stock of the company which has issued it. Convertible preferred stock may have any of the characteristics described above, but in practice most convertible preferred is cumulative. All the pertinent information on the convertibility features of these stocks is stated in the records of the corporation and usually on the stock certificates. Summaries of this information are prepared by several of the financial reporting services.

Conversion is normally at the option of the shareholder. However, most convertible preferred is callable so that the company can either retire the issue or force its conversion.

The investment characteristics of convertible stocks and convertible bonds are very similar. A discussion of convertible bonds is presented at the end of this chapter, rather than in the preceding one, because of this similarity.

The discussion of convertible preferred is limited at this point because nearly everything stated later about convertible bonds pertains to these securities.

Callability Features

While there are more noncallable preferred stock issues than issuers of perpetual bonds (securities which they closely resemble), the modern trend is definitely toward callability. Modern corporations do not usually issue securities, other than common stocks, which cannot somehow be retired. A survey of 493 issues of nonconvertible preferred stock indicated that about 95 percent of these issues either were presently callable or would become callable at some future date.[3] Almost all convertible preferred is callable.

The callability feature of these stocks holds the same potential disadvantage for the owner as does the callability feature of bonds. While there is almost always a call premium associated with preferred stock issues, it is seldom that a call will not cause financial harm to the owner of these shares. The callability feature also acts to limit the possible price appreciation of these securities when interest rates fall. Investors hesitate to pay more than the call price for preferred stocks because

---

[3] *Preferred Stock Guide, 1970* ed. (New York: Salomon Brothers & Hutzler, 1970).

of the possibility that the stocks may be called at less than they paid for them.

Sinking Fund Features

While most corporate bond issues have sinking fund agreements, few preferred stocks do. It is believed that this device is used so seldomly because (1) for most corporations the preferred stock is a very small proportion of the total capitalization of the company. There is no need for the corporation to guarantee repayment of the issue by some certain date or over a certain time period because the financial obligation of the issue is unimportant. (2) It is assumed that convertible preferred stocks will be converted into common, rather than being redeemed or retired in some other way.

Some preferred issues (most of these are issued by utilities) do have sinking fund agreements. This agreement probably has some slight value to the owners of these securities because purchases of the securities for the sinking fund provide demand for these shares that might not otherwise exist. Such an advantage is probably very small. Yields on sinking fund preferreds are very close to yields of other preferreds of like grade.

OWNERSHIP OF PREFERRED STOCK

Most nonconvertible preferred stock is owned by corporations rather than individuals. This is because of the way that corporations are taxed on the dividend income they receive. If the company meets certain conditions, it is taxed on only 15 percent of its total dividend income. For example, if $100 of dividends were received, only $15 would be seen as taxable income for purposes of computing federal income taxes.[4]

All bond interest—except that on municipal bonds—is taxable at regular income tax rates, so certain corporations purchase high-grade

---

[4] The dividend offset is designed to reduce what would be triple taxation. Without it taxes would be levied as follows: Corporation A would be taxed on its earnings, a portion of which were paid to Corporation B as dividends on the stock of A held by B. Corporation B would then be taxed on these dividends because they are income to it. When B declares dividends, B's shareholders will next be taxed.

The companies which can most easily and advantageously make use of the dividend offset are companies which hold large amounts of high-grade equity securities as investments. In practice these companies are property and casualty insurance companies, life insurance companies, and to a lesser extent other financial corporations.

preferred stock issues as investments rather than bonds of an equally high grade. Because of the 85 percent income tax offset, preferred stocks provide corporations with high *after-tax* yields. A corporation paying taxes of 50 percent on regular income would pay only 15 percent of this amount, or 7.5 percent, on dividend income. As a consequence of this, preferred dividends are *more valuable,* after income taxes have been paid, than an equal amount of interest. For many corporations, the tax deductibility feature outweighs the extra financial risk characteristics associated with preferred stock. Demand for these shares causes the yields of high-grade preferred shares to be lower than those on high-grade corporate bonds, even though the financial risk characteristics of bonds are more desirable. For example, the after-tax "profit" of $100 of interest versus $100 of preferred dividends for a corporation paying 50 percent federal income taxes can be seen in Table 9–3. An equal dollar amount of dividends will provide

TABLE 9–3
After-Tax Income of Bond Interest versus Preferred Stock Dividends

		Bond Interest	*Preferred Dividends*	
Total income		$100		$100.00
Taxable income		100	0.15($100) =	15.00
Tax	0.50($100) =	50	0.50($ 15) =	7.50
After-tax income		$ 50		$ 92.50

far more after-tax income than will bond interest. Stated another way, substantially lower before-tax preferred yields will provide higher after-tax yields to corporations which qualify for the 85 percent dividend offset. These securities have no such value for individuals.

Convertible preferred shares are another matter entirely. Many corporations own convertible preferred issues, and many of them benefit from the special taxation of their dividends. However, much of the convertible preferred stock is of such a low grade that it is not purchased for investment by the same companies that purchase the high-grade straight preferred shares. Furthermore, dividends on convertible preferred shares are relatively low because of the convertibility feature of the securities. This makes them less appealing to companies seeking high, constant returns. It is believed that the vast majority of convertible preferred shares are owned by individuals. This argument is examined in the next section.

ANALYSIS OF PREFERRED STOCK

Grading Preferred Securities

Formal grading of preferred stocks is much less common than it is for bonds. Standard & Poor's Corporation provides such a rating for most preferred issues, while Moody's makes no attempt to do so. It is logical to assume that investors do assign some sort of a quality rating to preferred shares that they consider for purchase and that this quality grading is directly related to the price they are willing to pay. However, the covenants of preferred stock issues are far less uniform than those of bond issues, and it is therefore more difficult to grade these securities. Grading, for bonds as well as preferred stock, deals mainly with the probability that interest or dividends will continue to be paid. Since dividend payments are far harder to predict than bond interest for securities of the same company, grading of preferred stock is simply more difficult and perhaps less meaningful. This is particularly true for convertible securities; the most important feature of this type of security is whether or not the price of the common stock will rise. Grading makes no attempt to determine this important consideration.

Price and Yield Considerations

Preferred stocks are considered to be equity securities, but they are most like bonds. They differ from the common stock of the company only in the various privileges they receive and in the lack of voting power that they usually have. Companies issuing preferred stocks often designate this stock as Class A common stock and the regular common stock as Class B common, or vice versa. In normal usage these securities are referred to as simply the "common" and "preferred" of the company.

For some corporations, utilities in particular, preferred stock is an important source of financing. These companies often have several series of preferred stock outstanding at the same time. Different series are usually designated by letters—Series A, Series B, and so on—although many companies identify the different issues as First Preferred, Second Preferred, and so on. Since these different issues will probably have been sold at different times and under different interest rate conditions, it is normal for the coupon yields of each issue to be different. For example, Long Island Lighting has outstanding four separate issues of $100 par preferred stock. All are listed on the NYSE, all are callable, none has sinking fund protection, and all are rated A by Standard & Poor's. Table 9–4 lists the important investment characteristics of these securities.

TABLE 9–4
Yield and Dividend Rate on Four Long Island Lighting Preferred Stock Issues

Issues	*First Issued*	*Currently Callable at*	*Dividend Rate*	*Par Value*	*Price 2/19/75*	*Yield 2/19/75*
LIL Series "B" . . .	1952	101	5.00%	100	48	10.4
LIL Series "E" . . .	1954	102	4.35	100	40	10.8
LIL Series "J". . . .	1971	115	8.12	100	75	10.8
LIL Series "K" . . .	1971	115	8.30	100	81	10.2

Source: Standard & Poor's *Stock Guide,* March 1975. Price quotes as of February 19, 1975.

Note several important things in Table 9–4: Dividend rates are low—4.35 and 5 percent—on the first two issues because they were sold when money rates in general were low. The dividend rates for the "J" and "K" issues are much higher because these securities were sold when market rates of interest were high. Preferred stock dividend rates and interest rates move up and down together because they are both determined by the supply of and demand for credit.

At any one time, dividend rates tend to be made uniform by the action of the market. This does not mean that every preferred stock of a given grade will yield exactly the same rate. These investments have other characteristics which make one issue more or less desirable than another, and yields mirror these differences. Markets for many preferred shares are relatively inactive, and the number of shares in each issue is often small. Market participants are often corporations, who buy and sell in large quantities. Recent trades of specific issues will often knock these yields temporarily "out of line."

Computation of Preferred Yields. The yield on preferred stock is computed somewhat differently from that on bonds. Most bonds have a maturity date and a stated par value because it is expected that they will be redeemed sometime in the future. While most preferred stocks are callable, the time at which they will be called is unknown; the securities may remain outstanding indefinitely. Because of this, the yield to maturity calculation used in Chapter 8 is inappropriate.

The usual yield calculation is simply one of dividing the annual dividend by the current market price. For example, a preferred stock paying $5 per year in dividends, having a market price of $65 would yield 7.69 percent.

$$\$5/\$65 = 0.0769, \text{ or } 7.69\%.$$

So long as this security continues to pay $5 per year in dividends, it will yield 7.69 percent to the person who purchased it at $65.

The yield calculation for preferred stock is certainly simple enough to perform, but even so, tables have been prepared which provide investors with approximate yields "at a glance." Figure 9–1 is a portion of such a table. The market price and dividend are "lined up" by looking down the appropriate dividend row and across the appropriate price column to determine the yield.

While the par value of bonds is nearly always $1,000, the par or stated amount of a preferred share may be practically any amount. The most common value is $100, followed by $50, $25, and $20. This value carries the same meaning for preferred shareholders as it does for bondholders. If either security is redeemed, the owner will receive this amount, plus any call premium for early redemption. When a company is dissolved, preferred shareholders and bondholders receive only the par value of their securities. Yield calculations are somewhat complicated by the fact that preferred dividends are sometimes stated as a percent of par and sometimes as a flat dollar amount. In the above example, the par value of this security can be *assumed* to be $100 since its yield is then reasonable in light of current market conditions. However, it could have been $50. Then the stated dividend rate would be $\$5/50 = 0.010$ or 10 percent. Par values are listed by most financial reporting services.

Financial Risk

Straight preferred stocks closely resemble bonds so far as financial risk characteristics are concerned. There is practically no doubt that dividends on the higher graded securities will be paid for the foreseeable future. Lower graded or nongraded securities have more financial risk, as would be expected, and yields reflect the difference in risk. Table 9–5 shows this relationship by listing price and yield data of several utility preferred issues. All investment characteristics other than grade are nearly identical.

FIGURE 9–1
Portion of a Preferred Stock Yield Table

Price	3.50	3.60	3.70	3.80	3.90	4.00	4.10	4.20	4.30	4.40	4.50	4.60	4.70	4.80	4.90	5.00	5.10	5.20	5.30	5.40	Price
	DIVIDEND																				
	Yield																				
$50	7.00	7.20	7.40	7.60	7.80	8.00	8.20	8.40	8.60	8.80	9.00	9.20	9.40	9.60	9.80	....	....	....	....	....	$50
52	6.73	6.92	7.12	7.31	7.50	7.69	7.88	8.08	8.27	8.46	8.65	8.85	9.04	9.23	9.42	9.62	9.81	....	....	....	52
54	6.48	6.67	6.85	7.04	7.22	7.41	7.59	7.78	7.96	8.15	8.33	8.52	8.70	8.89	9.07	9.26	9.44	9.63	9.81	....	54
55	6.36	6.55	6.73	6.91	7.09	7.27	7.45	7.64	7.82	8.00	8.18	8.36	8.55	8.73	8.91	9.09	9.27	9.45	9.64	9.82	55
56	6.25	6.43	6.61	6.79	6.96	7.14	7.32	7.50	7.68	7.86	8.04	8.21	8.39	8.57	8.75	8.93	9.11	9.29	9.46	9.64	56
57	6.14	6.32	6.49	6.67	6.84	7.02	7.19	7.37	7.54	7.72	7.89	8.07	8.25	8.42	8.60	8.77	8.95	9.12	9.30	9.47	57
58	6.03	6.21	6.38	6.55	6.72	6.90	7.07	7.24	7.41	7.59	7.76	7.93	8.10	8.28	8.45	8.62	8.79	8.97	9.14	9.31	58
59	5.93	6.10	6.27	6.44	6.61	6.78	6.95	7.12	7.29	7.46	7.63	7.80	7.97	8.14	8.31	8.47	8.64	8.81	8.98	9.15	59
60	5.83	6.00	6.17	6.33	6.50	6.67	6.83	7.00	7.17	7.33	7.50	7.67	7.83	8.00	8.17	8.33	8.50	8.67	8.83	9.00	60
61	5.74	5.90	6.07	6.23	6.39	6.56	6.72	6.89	7.05	7.21	7.38	7.54	7.70	7.87	8.03	8.20	8.36	8.52	8.69	8.85	61
62	5.65	5.81	5.97	6.13	6.29	6.45	6.61	6.77	6.94	7.10	7.26	7.42	7.58	7.74	7.90	8.06	8.23	8.39	8.55	8.71	62
63	5.56	5.71	5.87	6.03	6.19	6.35	6.51	6.67	6.83	6.98	7.14	7.30	7.46	7.62	7.78	7.94	8.10	8.25	8.41	8.57	63
64	5.47	5.63	5.78	5.94	6.09	6.25	6.41	6.56	6.72	6.88	7.03	7.19	7.34	7.50	7.66	7.81	7.97	8.13	8.28	8.44	64
65	5.38	5.54	5.69	5.85	6.00	6.15	6.31	6.46	6.62	6.77	6.92	7.08	7.23	7.38	7.54	7.69	7.85	8.00	8.15	8.31	65
66	5.30	5.45	5.61	5.76	5.91	6.06	6.21	6.36	6.52	6.67	6.82	6.97	7.12	7.27	7.42	7.58	7.73	7.88	8.03	8.18	66
67	5.22	5.37	5.52	5.67	5.82	5.97	6.12	6.27	6.42	6.57	6.72	6.87	7.01	7.16	7.31	7.46	7.61	7.76	7.91	8.06	67
68	5.15	5.29	5.44	5.59	5.74	5.88	6.03	6.18	6.32	6.47	6.62	6.76	6.91	7.06	7.21	7.35	7.50	7.65	7.79	7.94	68
69	5.07	5.22	5.36	5.51	5.65	5.80	5.94	6.09	6.23	6.38	6.52	6.67	6.81	6.96	7.10	7.25	7.39	7.54	7.68	7.83	69
70	5.00	5.14	5.29	5.43	5.57	5.71	5.86	6.00	6.14	6.29	6.43	6.57	6.71	6.86	7.00	7.14	7.29	7.43	7.57	7.71	70
71	4.93	5.07	5.21	5.35	5.49	5.63	5.77	5.92	6.06	6.20	6.34	6.48	6.62	6.76	6.90	7.04	7.18	7.32	7.46	7.61	71
72	4.86	5.00	5.14	5.28	5.42	5.56	5.69	5.83	5.97	6.11	6.25	6.39	6.53	6.67	6.81	6.94	7.08	7.22	7.36	7.50	72
73	4.79	4.93	5.07	5.21	5.34	5.48	5.62	5.75	5.89	6.03	6.16	6.30	6.44	6.58	6.71	6.85	6.99	7.12	7.26	7.40	73
74	4.73	4.86	5.00	5.14	5.27	5.41	5.54	5.68	5.81	5.95	6.08	6.22	6.35	6.49	6.62	6.76	6.89	7.03	7.16	7.30	74
75	4.67	4.80	4.93	5.07	5.20	5.33	5.47	5.60	5.73	5.87	6.00	6.13	6.27	6.40	6.53	6.67	6.80	6.93	7.07	7.20	75
76	4.61	4.74	4.87	5.00	5.13	5.26	5.39	5.53	5.66	5.79	5.92	6.05	6.18	6.32	6.45	6.58	6.71	6.84	6.97	7.11	76
77	4.55	4.68	4.81	4.94	5.06	5.19	5.32	5.45	5.58	5.71	5.84	5.97	6.10	6.23	6.36	6.49	6.62	6.75	6.88	7.01	77
78	4.49	4.62	4.74	4.87	5.00	5.13	5.26	5.38	5.51	5.64	5.77	5.90	6.03	6.15	6.28	6.41	6.54	6.67	6.79	6.92	78
79	4.43	4.56	4.68	4.81	4.94	5.06	5.19	5.32	5.44	5.57	5.70	5.82	5.95	6.08	6.20	6.33	6.46	6.58	6.71	6.84	79
80	4.38	4.50	4.63	4.75	4.88	5.00	5.13	5.25	5.38	5.50	5.63	5.75	5.88	6.00	6.13	6.25	6.38	6.50	6.63	6.75	80
81	4.32	4.44	4.57	4.69	4.81	4.94	5.06	5.19	5.31	5.43	5.56	5.68	5.80	5.93	6.05	6.17	6.30	6.42	6.54	6.67	81
82	4.27	4.39	4.51	4.63	4.76	4.88	5.00	5.12	5.24	5.37	5.49	5.61	5.73	5.85	5.98	6.10	6.22	6.34	6.46	6.59	82
83	4.22	4.34	4.46	4.58	4.70	4.82	4.94	5.06	5.18	5.30	5.42	5.54	5.66	5.78	5.90	6.02	6.14	6.27	6.39	6.51	83
84	4.17	4.29	4.40	4.52	4.64	4.76	4.88	5.00	5.12	5.24	5.36	5.48	5.60	5.71	5.83	5.95	6.07	6.19	6.31	6.43	84
85	4.12	4.24	4.35	4.47	4.59	4.71	4.82	4.94	5.06	5.18	5.29	5.41	5.53	5.65	5.76	5.88	6.00	6.12	6.24	6.35	85
86	4.07	4.19	4.30	4.42	4.53	4.65	4.77	4.88	5.00	5.12	5.23	5.35	5.47	5.58	5.70	5.81	5.93	6.05	6.16	6.28	86
87	4.02	4.14	4.25	4.37	4.48	4.60	4.71	4.83	4.94	5.06	5.17	5.29	5.40	5.52	5.63	5.75	5.86	5.98	6.09	6.21	87
88	3.98	4.09	4.20	4.32	4.43	4.55	4.66	4.77	4.89	5.00	5.11	5.23	5.34	5.45	5.57	5.68	5.80	5.91	6.02	6.14	88
89	3.93	4.04	4.16	4.27	4.38	4.49	4.61	4.72	4.83	4.94	5.06	5.17	5.28	5.39	5.51	5.62	5.73	5.84	5.96	6.07	89
90	3.89	4.00	4.11	4.22	4.33	4.44	4.56	4.67	4.78	4.89	5.00	5.11	5.22	5.33	5.44	5.56	5.67	5.78	5.89	6.00	90
92	3.80	3.91	4.02	4.13	4.24	4.35	4.46	4.57	4.67	4.78	4.89	5.00	5.11	5.22	5.33	5.43	5.54	5.65	5.76	5.87	92
94	3.72	3.83	3.94	4.04	4.15	4.26	4.36	4.47	4.57	4.68	4.79	4.89	5.00	5.11	5.21	5.32	5.43	5.53	5.64	5.74	94
96	3.65	3.75	3.85	3.96	4.06	4.17	4.27	4.38	4.48	4.58	4.69	4.79	4.90	5.00	5.10	5.21	5.31	5.42	5.52	5.63	96
98	3.57	3.67	3.78	3.88	3.98	4.08	4.18	4.29	4.39	4.49	4.59	4.69	4.80	4.90	5.00	5.10	5.20	5.31	5.41	5.51	98
102	3.43	3.53	3.63	3.73	3.82	3.92	4.02	4.12	4.22	4.31	4.41	4.51	4.61	4.71	4.80	4.90	5.00	5.10	5.20	5.29	102
104	3.37	3.46	3.56	3.65	3.75	3.85	3.94	4.04	4.13	4.23	4.33	4.42	4.52	4.62	4.71	4.81	4.90	5.00	5.10	5.19	104

Source: *Preferred Stock Guide, 1970 ed.* (New York: Salomon Brothers and Hutzler, 1970), p. 43.

TABLE 9–5
Grade and Yield of Selected Utility Preferred Stocks

Issues	*Standard & Poor's Rating*	*Dividend*	*Yield 1/31/1975*
Northern States Power "G"	AA	$4.56	9.0%
Long Island Lighting Series "B".	A	5.00	10.4
Niagara Mohawk Power "G"	BBB	5.25	11.5
Consolidated Edison "C"	BB	4.65	12.1

Note: No AAA or B ranked public utility preferred stocks having investment characteristics similar to those above could be identified in January 1975.
Source: Standard & Poor's *Stock Guide*, February 1975.

Purchasing Power Risk

Purchasing power risk affects straight preferred issues exactly like it affects straight bonds. Dividends on outstanding shares do not increase, so in a period of price inflation each dividend purchases less goods and services. Everything previously stated about how debt investments are affected by inflation pertains to these securities and does not warrant repeating.

Interest Rate Risk

Preferred shares are seldom redeemed and therefore resemble consol bonds so far as interest rate risk is concerned. In practical terms this means that prices of these securities vary *even more* than those of bonds. Most bonds will be redeemed at some time in the future, at par, and market prices will return to near par as this time approaches. Preferred shares do not have this characteristic. So long as market dividend rates remain above coupon rates of outstanding preferred shares, prices of these securities will be below par.

Table 9–6 shows the effects of interest rate risk on straight preferred stocks of different grades. All these securities are listed on the NYSE. Two are industrial companies and three are utilities, but the investment characteristics of all securities are similar except for grade. On average these securities sold 44 percent *below* their 1967 prices in 1975. Over the same period of time long-term Treasury bonds declined only 11 percent in price.

Current yield rates on high-grade preferred stocks are far more closely related to the movements in interest rates of long-term bonds than to the dividend rates on common shares. Figure 9–2 shows this

TABLE 9–6
Prices of Selected Preferred Stocks at Three Different Dates

Security	*Standard & Poor's Rating*	*Dividend*	*Close or Bid 1/31/1975*	*Close or Bid 1/30/1970*	*Close or Bid 1/31/1967*
General Motors $5.00 cumulative preferred . . .	AAA	$5.00	$64	$72 1/2	$99 1/4
Kansas City Power & Light 4.5% cumulative preferred	AA	4.50	48	59	84 3/8
Long Island Lighting 4.35% cumulative preferred series "E" . .	A	4.35	40	55 1/2	82
Virginia Electric & Power 4.2% cumulative preferred	BBB	4.20	40 1/2	56	81
Armour & Co. $4.75 cumulative preferred . . .	BB	4.75	47	57 1/2	79 1/2

Source: Standard & Poor's *Stock Guide,* February 1967, 1970, and 1975.

relationship clearly. This figure also shows that, in the eyes of recent investors, high-grade preferred stocks *appear* to have lower risk characteristics than do the highest grade debt securities—because they have had lower yields than bonds in most years since 1963. The explanation for this illogical relationship lies in the fact that the dividends on preferred stocks, so far as most corporations are concerned, are taxed at only 15 percent of the amount of the dividend, while all interest income is taxable. This topic was examined previously under the heading Ownership of Preferred Stock.

INVESTING IN PREFERRED STOCK

With rare exception, straight preferred stocks are not attractive investments for the average individual. Their yields are lower than can be obtained on bonds, and bonds usually offer less financial and interest rate risk. If financial risk is not an overpowering consideration, the investor should consider investment in common stock, for in this type of investment one can benefit directly from gains in earnings that are made by the company.

Convertible Preferred

These securities resemble straight preferred stock except that they may be exchanged for (converted into) common stock of the same company. Owners of these securities have the financial safety of the

FIGURE 9–2
Yields on High-Grade Debt Securities, Preferred and Common Stock

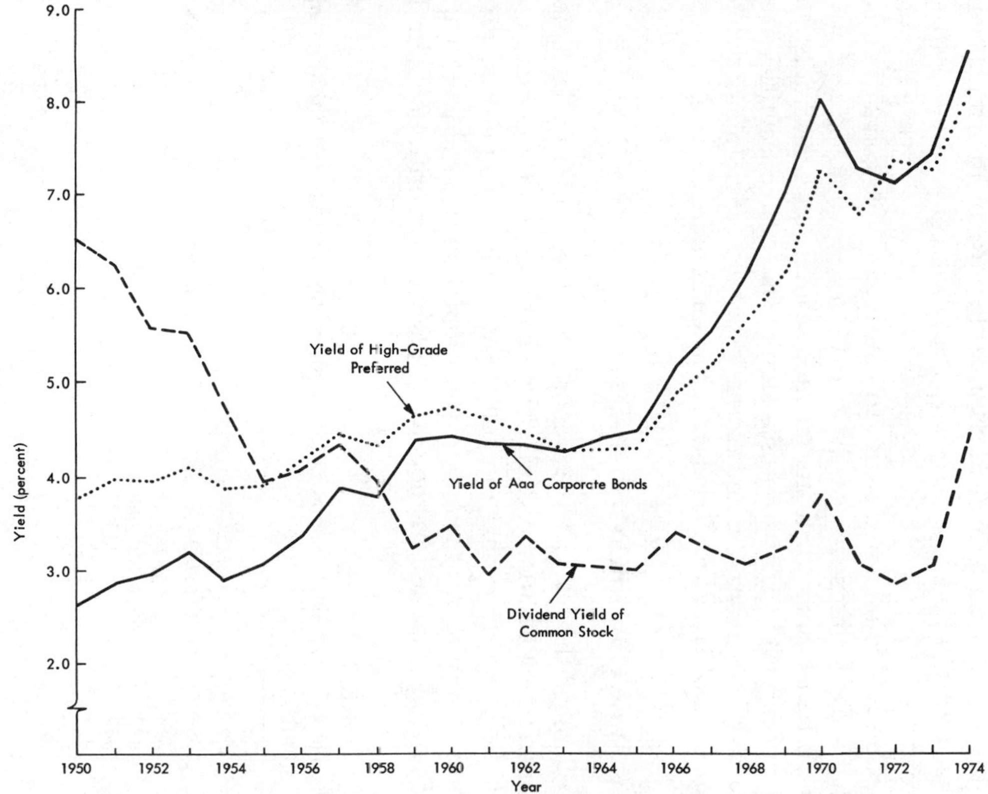

Source: Yield of Aaa Corporate Bonds taken from *Federal Reserve Bulletin;* Yield of High-Grade Preferred from *Moody's Industrial Manual:* Dividend Yield of Common Stock from *Standard & Poor's 500 Stock Index.*

preferred dividend and an ownership position, and they also have the possibility of substantial market price gains—if the price of the company's common stock rises.

Yields on convertible preferred shares are lower than those on straight preferred of the same grade, and few of these securities are rated highly so far as financial risk is concerned. Purchasers of these securities sacrifice yield and financial safety for the possibility of capital gains from a rise in market price. Because of their financial risk characteristics and low dividend yields, few corporations own these securities.

Convertible preferred shares so closely resemble convertible bonds that separate discussion of the two securities would be repetitive in the extreme. Since there are far more convertible bonds outstanding than convertible preferred, discussion of convertible securities has emphasized bonds. At the end of this discussion, investment characteristics of convertible preferred will be again examined.

CONVERTIBLE BONDS

Through the years a large proportion of the debt securities issued by American corporations have been convertible into the common stock of the company issuing the bonds. As Table 9–7 indicates, there is great year-to-year variability in the proportion of total debt which is convertible. Because of the advantages these securities offer to both

TABLE 9–7
New Convertible Bonds Offered for Cash (amounts in millions of dollars)

Year	*Total Corporate Debt Issued*	*Amount Convertible*	*Percent of Total Convertible*
1974	$31,567	$ 482	1.5
1973	21,022	567	2.7
1972	25,825	2,192	8.5
1971	32,123	3,678	11.4
1970	30,315	2,654	8.8
1969	18,347	4,041	22.0
1968	17,383	3,281	18.9
1967	21,954	4,475	20.4
1966	15,561	1,872	12.0
1965	13,720	1,264	9.2
1964	10,865	425	3.9
1963	10,856	357	3.3

Source: Securities and Exchange Commission, *Statistical Bulletin*, various issues.

issuers and buyers it is anticipated that they will continue to be an important type of investment security.

The Conversion Agreement

Convertible bonds closely resemble other corporate bonds in that they usually have a $1,000 par value, they pay a fixed amount of interest per annum, they have a fixed maturity date, and they are almost always callable. Most are debenture bonds, and their interest payments and other claims are often subordinated to those of other debt holders. The most important feature of these securities is that they can be exchanged for a certain number of shares of common stock in the company which issued them. This conversion agreement takes various forms. In one case a bond may be convertible until its maturity at a fixed number of shares of common stock. Another bond may be convertible into a fixed number of shares of stock of the company for some period after it is issued, and then convertible into a lesser number of shares after that date. The agreement might be written so that the bond cannot be converted until some time period has passed after the issue date. Like all other covenants of a bond issue, the description of the convertibility agreement will appear in the bond indenture and prospectus. The conversion agreements are normally protected against changes in the conversion value of the bond which would arise if the capital structure of the company were altered.

The actual conversion agreement may be written in two ways. The bond indenture may state that each bond is convertible into a certain number of shares of common stock, or it might say that the bond is convertible into common stock at a certain dollar value per share. The meaning of both statements is identical so long as the par value of the bond remains unchanged.

The conversion statement from the prospectus of American Hospital Supply Corporation is presented as Figure 9–3. In this example the statement describes the convertibility as being at a conversion price of $29.50 per share of common stock. The statement might have read "convertible into 33.8983 shares of common," because dividing the par value of the bond by this number of shares gives a conversion price of $29.50 per share.

$$\frac{\text{Par value of bond}}{\text{Number of shares of stock into which bond is convertible}} = \text{Conversion price}$$

$$\frac{\$1{,}000}{33.8983} = \$29.50.$$

FIGURE 9–3
Conversion Statement

$75,000,000

AMERICAN HOSPITAL SUPPLY CORPORATION
5¾% Convertible Subordinated Debentures Due 1999

The Debentures are convertible, unless previously redeemed, into Common Stock of American Hospital Supply Corporation at a conversion price of $29.50 per share, subject to adjustment in certain events. On November 25, 1974, the reported closing sales price of the Common Stock on the New York Stock Exchange was $26.125 per share.

Beginning on December 1, 1985, the Debentures are entitled to an annual sinking fund in installments of $4,125,000, which is calculated to retire at least 77 percent of the issue prior to maturity. AHSC also has the noncumulative option to increase any sinking fund payment by an amount not exceeding the mandatory payment. The sinking fund redemption price is 100 percent of the principal amount plus accrued interest. Interest is payable June 1 and December 1.

The Debentures are redeemable at AHSC's option, in whole or in part, at any time on 30 days' notice, at 105.75 percent of the principal amount, plus accrued interest, if redeemed prior to December 1, 1975, at decreasing premiums thereafter, and without premium on and after December 1, 1994.

Source: American Hospital Supply Corporation, *Prospectus*, November 26, 1974, p. 1.

The Value of Convertibility

Convertible bonds offer advantages to both the buyers and issuers of these securities. The security is expected to provide the purchaser with interest income up to the time it is converted. This interest will probably be at a lower rate than that available from a conventional nonconvertible bond of a company having financial characteristics similar to those of this firm. However, the advantage of potential price appreciation far in excess of that found in conventional debt securities works to offset the lower interest yield. This potential results from the fact that the price of the common stock of the company may increase an unlimited amount. So long as the market price of the common stock of American Hospital Supply Corporation is less than $29.50,

FIGURE 9–4
Theoretical Value of a Convertible Bond of American Hospital Supply Corporation Corresponding to Different Market Prices of the Common Stock of the Company

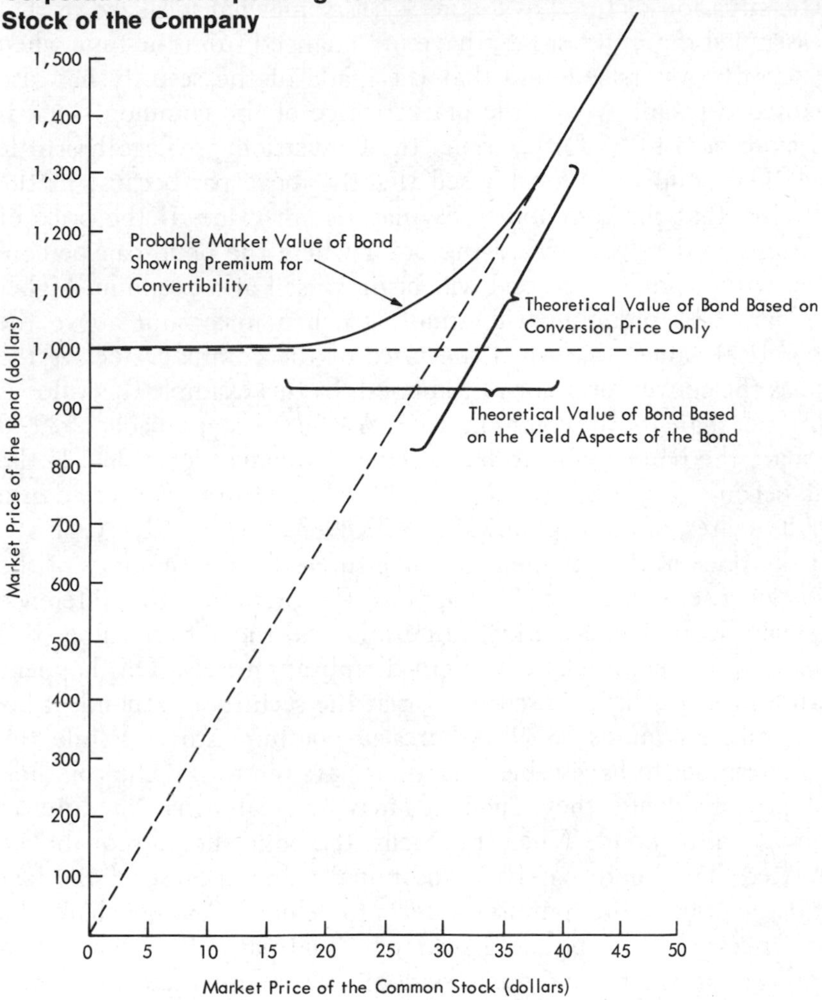

Note: Par value of the bond is $1,000; bond is convertible into common stock at $29.50 per share.

the bond will *theoretically* be valued on the basis of its yield, grade, and maturity—just like conventional bonds. But as the price of the common stock increases toward the bond conversion price, the market price of the bond will increase. A convertible bond which has any potential for profitable conversion will almost always sell at a premium over nonconvertible securities, even when the price of the common stock is far below the conversion price of the bond. Figure 9–4 shows the theoretical relationship of stock and convertible bond prices of American Hospital Supply Corporation.

The situation pictured in Figure 9–4 is somewhat idealized in that it is assumed that interest rates have not changed from the time when this security was issued, and that the grade of the security has also remained constant. When the market price of the common stock is low, from zero to $5 for example, the conversion privilege has little value. The bond will probably sell slightly above par because of the possibility that the common stock may rise in value. If the price of the common does rise toward the point where the bond can be converted with a profit, the bond will begin to sell at a premium higher than par. This premium will usually reach a maximum above the "theoretical value" line when the price of the common stock is the same as the conversion value of the bond. In this example this value is $29.50 per share for the common stock. As the stock approaches $29.50 per share the bond begins to be priced at its conversion value. If the stock becomes worth $35 per share and the bond can be converted into 33.8983 shares, the conversion value is 33.8983 × $35 = $1,186.44.

If the price of the common stock continues to rise, the price of the bond will rise with it. As this happens, the premium, the difference between the probable market value and the theoretical value, will decrease to the point where it might disappear entirely. This happens because investors have ceased to look at the security as a bond; it becomes in their minds 33.8983 shares of common stock. While the bond continues to have value because it pays interest, if the common stock pays dividends, these dividends may be greater than the interest payment on the bond. When this occurs the bond should probably be converted. The bond may have additional value because of the fact that if the price of the common retreats to below $29.50 per share, the bond price will probably hold near par. The par value often sets a "floor" under which bond prices seldom sink unless interest rates rise or the grade of the security declines. Prices of convertible preferred stock are controlled by the same factors.

Investment Characteristics of Convertibles

Convertibility usually allows a company to sell securities at a lower than normal interest or dividend cost. In some cases, because of the risk characteristics of the company issuing them, securities which could probably be sold only at very high yield rates, if at all, may find a willing market if they are convertible. A further advantage of issuing convertibles is that the company is really selling common stock in disguise. Almost all convertible securities are callable so that the management of the company can force the owners to trade their senior securities for common if equity security prices rise.

Convertible securities are usually at least mildly speculative in character. A person buying such securities usually accepts a lower yield payment and a less firm creditor position in exchange for the possibility of above average profits. In 1973–74 there was a great decline in the amount of convertible securities issued. This decline is the result of the relatively low market prices of common stocks during these years. Most corporations do not sell convertible securities when this condition prevails.

When analyzing a convertible security with the intention of purchasing it, one must determine whether the price of the common stock can be expected to rise, and when. If this event cannot be anticipated with a reasonable degree of certainty, then the convertible security is probably not a good investment. Even if market conditions indicate an increase in stock prices, there are other things which must be examined before putting in a buy order. Is the market price of the common stock so far below the conversion price that it is unlikely that the conversion feature will ever have any value? A bond convertible into 20 shares of common will have little convertibility value until the price of the common is near $50 per share. If the market price of the common stock is $25, an investor might have to wait many years before reaping any benefit from the convertibility feature of the bond. In this case one might be better off to purchase the common stock if its price is expected to rise.

Many securities have conversion ratios which decline over time. Initially the bond might be convertible into 30 shares of common. After five years the conversion might be into 25 shares, and after another five years into 20. Under such a situation the market price of the common must not only rise, it must rise relatively soon because the conversion privilege becomes less valuable as time passes. It is possible to pay more in reduced yield and increased financial risk than the conversion privilege is worth.

Risk Characteristics of Convertibles. At various times there has been such a demand for convertible securities that many companies of really poor financial character have been able to sell these securities. Persons buying them apparently believe that because these securities are not common stock they are relatively safe investments. This is not true. Persons purchasing convertible securities should examine them

FIGURE 9–5
Share of Convertible Preferred Stock

INCORPORATED UNDER THE LAWS OF THE STATE OF OREGON

NUMBER PB–4460

SHARES

BAZA'R, INC.

SPECIMEN

THIS CERTIFIES THAT

is the owner of fully paid shares of Series B $2.75 Cumulative Convertible Preferred Stock, without par value, of BAZA'R, INC., transferable only on the books of the Corporation in person or by duly authorized attorney upon surrender of this certificate properly endorsed.

A statement of the designations, preferences, limitations and relative rights of the shares of Common Stock and of the shares of Cumulative Preferred Stock which the Corporation is authorized to issue, of the variations in the relative rights and preferences between the shares of each series of said Cumulative Preferred Stock so far as the same have been fixed or determined and of the authority of the board of directors of the Corporation to fix and determine the relative rights and preferences of the series of said Cumulative Preferred Stock is set forth in Article III of the Articles of Incorporation, as amended. A copy of said Article III, as amended, is printed upon the back hereof, and this certificate and the shares represented hereby are issued and shall be held subject to all the provisions of said Article III, to all of which the holder by the acceptance hereof assents.

Witness the facsimile seal of the corporation and the facsimile signatures of its duly authorized officers.

Dated:

BAZA'R, INC.

Registered: FIRST NATIONAL BANK OF OREGON Registrar By Authorized Signature

Countersigned: UNITED STATES NATIONAL BANK OF OREGON Transfer Agent By Authorized Signature

Ronald R. Holman, Secretary

W. 2. Trupeett, Jr, President

BAZA'R, INC. CORPORATE SEAL OREGON

SERIES B $2.75 CUMULATIVE CONVERTIBLE PREFERRED STOCK WITHOUT PAR VALUE

© GOES 840

Courtesy of Baza'r Corporation.

carefully to see that interest payments will be made while they wait for the convertibility feature of the security to have some value. Convertibles are probably more speculative in character than most investors realize, and yet these securities do provide the investor with the potential for sharing in the profits of the company, in a way which is impossible with a straight debt or preferred stock investment.

Convertibles and the Small Investor. Convertible preferred stock should have special interest for the small investor who is willing to spend some time looking for bargains. Many preferred issues are small in size and therefore likely to escape the attention of the large security houses. With no one to place them on a "recommended list," they may often sell at less than their intrinsic or true, value.

Figure 9–5 is a picture of the front side of a share of the Baza'r series B, $2.75 preferred stock. The conversion agreement and other information on this issue is printed on the back of the share.

SUMMARY

This chapter examined the investment characteristics of *preferred stock* and *convertible bonds.* Straight preferred stock has investment characteristics which make it resemble debt more than equity. Dividend payments are usually fixed and are paid before common dividends. If the corporation is dissolved, creditors are paid off first, then preferred shareowners. Preferred stock is classified as equity capital for purposes of computing a company's earnings, but preferred shareowners may seldom vote for directors.

Most straight preferred stock is owned by corporations because they pay income taxes on only 15 percent of income they receive as dividends. For this reason, and others, yields on high-grade straight preferred stocks are lower than yields on bonds of similar grade.

Investment characteristics of straight preferred stock are low financial risk (depending upon grade), fair liquidity, high purchasing power risk, and extremely high interest rate risk. In this last respect they are more risky than bonds. Straight preferred stock is not considered a suitable investment alternative for most people because these securities have all the worst investment characteristics of bonds, along with more financial risk and less yield.

Convertible preferred stock and convertible bonds were discussed together because these securities bear such close resemblance to each other. Their most distinguishing feature is that these securities may be converted into a certain number of shares of the common stock of the company which has issued them. This feature makes possible a large rise in the market price of these senior securities—if the price of the common rises above the conversion price. When common prices are lower than this amount, the convertible securities are priced upon the basis of yield and grade, the determinants of price for nonconvertible bonds and preferred stocks.

Investment characteristics of convertible securities are (1) fairly high financial risk (2) low interest rate and purchasing power risk because of their potential for vastly increasing prices, and (3) possibly low liquidity, depending upon the individual issue.

PROBLEMS

1. An issue of preferred stock has a par value of $25 per share, a coupon dividend of 8 percent, and a current market price of $22 per share. This security has no call or maturity date. What is the current dividend in dollars, and the current yield?
2. If the security described in Problem 1 were convertible into two shares of common stock, and the common had a current market price of $16 per share, what would be the approximate theoretical market price of each preferred share? What if the common sold for $10 per share; what would be the market price of the preferred then?
3. A bond is convertible into 50 shares of common stock. What price will the stock have to attain before it becomes profitable to convert the bond? (Assume a $1,000 par, which is the price at which the bond is selling.)
4. You have the choice of purchasing either the convertible bonds of a company or its common stock. The bonds are priced at $1,100 and pay a coupon of 8 percent; each bond is convertible into 40 shares of common stock. The common sells for $27.50 per share and pays a dividend of $2 per share. Would you purchase the common directly or the bonds? Give reasons for your choice.

QUESTIONS

1. List the advantages and disadvantages of owning straight preferred stock.
2. What are the different types of preferred stocks and their legal characteristics?

3. What investment advantage does a cumulative preferred stock offer investors over common stock? What disadvantages?
4. What advantages do convertible securities offer investors and the companies which issue them?
5. Most straight preferred stock is owned by corporations. Why is this?
6. Convertible bonds are sometimes described as "equity investments with the risk removed." Explain the meaning of this statement.
7. Changes in market rates of interest affect which security most—noncallable high-grade straight preferred stock, or a typical high-grade corporate bond which is also noncallable?
8. Look through a common stock guide and note the market prices, coupon (stated) yields, and yields to maturity of preferred issues of any large utility. The market prices and coupon yields of securities of different issues will usually differ, perhaps greatly, but yield to maturity of all issues will be nearly identical. Why is this true?

SELECTED READINGS

"Annual Review of the Bond Market." New York: Salomon Brothers & Hutzler, published annually.

Christy, George A., and Clendenin, John C. *Introduction to Investments*, 6th ed. New York: McGraw-Hill, 1974.

Cohen, Jerome B.; Zinbarg, Edward D.; and Zeikel, Arthur. *Investment Analysis and Portfolio Management*, rev. ed. Homewood, Ill.: Richard D. Irwin, 1973.

D'Ambrosio, Charles A. *A Guide to Successful Investing*. Englewood Cliffs, N.J.: Prentice-Hall, 1970.

Sauvain, Harry C. *Investment Management*, 4th ed. Englewood Cliffs, N.J.: Prentice-Hall, 1973.

Walter, James E., and Que, Agustin V. "The Valuation of Convertible Bonds," *Journal of Finance*, June 1973.

10
Investing in Common Stock

INTRODUCTION

The New York Stock Exchange calculated that in 1975 there were about 25 million shareholders of public corporations. There is some double counting in these figures because many people own shares of several different companies, but there is little doubt that a very large number of Americans own equity securities. Table 10–1 presents share ownership data for 1965 and mid-1975. While the number of shareholders has increased about 25 percent during this ten-year period, the 1975 totals are approximately 5 million shareowners less than in 1970. This reduction is a result of the very poor market for equity securities experienced during the 1973–74 period.

A completely accurate tally of shareholders cannot be established in any event because the appropriate information does not exist. The NYSE study attempts to count only shareholders who own common stocks directly. Many more people own these securities indirectly. Over 100 million people own shares in private pension funds, savings institutions, insurance companies, and other organizations which invest some of their funds in common stocks. These investments make each pension fund member, savings share owner, or policyholder, an indirect owner of common stock. Common stocks have gained very wide acceptance by investors, and an understanding of their legal and investment characteristics is imperative.

LEGAL CHARACTERISTICS OF COMMON STOCK

The ownership in a corporation is vested in the common stock shareholders. While many corporations issue bonds, and a lesser

TABLE 10–1
Total Shareholders of Public Corporations (by types of issues owned)

	1965		*Mid-1975*	
Types of Issues Owned	*Number of Shareholders*	*Percent of Total*	*Number of Shareholders*	*Percent of Total*
New York Stock Exchange*	12,430,000	62.0%	17,910,000	71.4%
Other stock exchanges†	1,285,000	6.4	1,000,000	4.0
Over-the-counter‡	3,130,000	15.6	3,292,000	13.1
Investment companies only	3,205,000	16.0	2,890,000	11.5
Subtotal	20,050,000	100.0%	25,092,000	100.0%
Shareholdings in nominee names only (not classified by type of issue)	70,000	—	114,000	—
Total	20,120,000		25,206,000	

* Includes some persons who also own issues other than those listed on the New York Stock Exchange.
† Includes some persons who also own over-the-counter issues, investment company shares, or both.
‡ Includes some persons who also own investment company shares.
Source: New York Stock Exchange, *Shareownership U.S.A.*, 1975 Census of Shareowners.

number issue preferred stock, all corporations must issue common stock. The contractual relationship between a corporation and a person owning its bonds is spelled out in the bond indenture agreement.

Stock ownership is evidenced by the stock certificate. A copy of a stock certificate of Richard D. Irwin, Inc., is presented as Figure 10–1. This document is representative of most common stock certificates. On its face it contains a serial number to identify it, a space to record the number of shares it evidences, the name of the registrar and transfer agent (if both are used), the par value of the stock (if a par value is stated), and usually a statement indicating that the shares are fully paid and nonassessable. This statement means that regardless of what happens to the company (for example bankruptcy, reorganization, or merger) the purchaser has no legal liability to provide more money to it.

The back of the certificate is usually an assignment statement which the shareholder fills out to transfer ownership of all or a portion of the certificates. Transfer may be made to another individual directly (no brokerage commissions on this kind of transaction), or the certificate may be sold through a broker to an unknown party. In the first case, if John Doe were selling these securities to Richard Roe, Richard Roe's name would be entered in the blank space after the statement, . . . "hereby sell, assign and transfer unto." John Doe would sign and date the security in the appropriate places, and give

FIGURE 10–1
Share of Common Stock

NUMBER
C0000

SHARES
100

RICHARD D. IRWIN • INC.

INCORPORATED UNLER THE LAWS OF THE STATE OF DELAWARE

This Certifies that SPECIMEN is the owner of

SEE REVERSE FOR CERTAIN DEFINITIONS

ONE HUNDRED

FULL PAID AND NON-ASSESSABLE SHARES, OF THE PAR VALUE OF FIFTY CENTS ($.50) EACH, OF THE COMMON STOCK OF RICHARD D. IRWIN • INC., transferable on the books of the Company by the holder hereof in person or by duly authorized attorney upon surrender of this certificate properly endorsed. This certificate is not valid unless countersigned by the Transfer Agent and registered by the Registrar.

In Witness Whereof, said Company has caused this certificate to be signed in facsimile by its authorized officers and its corporate seal to be affixed in facsimile.

Dated

RICHARD D. IRWIN, INC. CORPORATE SEAL DELAWARE

SPECIMEN SECRETARY.

SPECIMEN PRESIDENT.

COUNTERSIGNED:
AMERICAN NATIONAL BANK AND TRUST COMPANY OF CHICAGO,
TRANSFER AGENT,
BY
AUTHORIZED SIGNATURE.

REGISTERED:
CONTINENTAL ILLINOIS NATIONAL BANK AND TRUST COMPANY OF CHICAGO
REGISTRAR,
BY
AUTHORIZED SIGNATURE.

FIGURE 10–1 (*continued*)

The following abbreviations, when used in the inscription on the face of this certificate, shall be construed as though they were written out in full according to applicable laws or regulations:

TEN COM	— as tenants in common	UNIF GIFT MIN ACT — .... Custodian .... (Cust) (Minor) under Uniform Gifts to Minors
TEN ENT	— as tenants by the entireties	
JT TEN	— as joint tenants with right of survivorship and not as tenants in common	Act .... (State)

Additional abbreviations may also be used though not in the above list.

For value received, ________ *hereby sell, assign and transfer unto*

PLEASE INSERT SOCIAL SECURITY OR OTHER IDENTIFYING NUMBER OF ASSIGNEE

PLEASE PRINT OR TYPEWRITE NAME AND ADDRESS OF ASSIGNEE

________ *Shares of the Common Stock represented by the within Certificate, and do hereby irrevocably constitute and appoint* ________

Attorney to transfer the said stock on the books of the within-named Company with full power of substitution in the premises.

Dated, ________

NOTICE: THE SIGNATURE TO THIS ASSIGNMENT MUST CORRESPOND WITH THE NAME AS WRITTEN UPON THE FACE OF THE CERTIFICATE, IN EVERY PARTICULAR, WITHOUT ALTERATION OR ENLARGEMENT, OR ANY CHANGE WHATEVER.

THIS SPACE MUST NOT BE COVERED IN ANY WAY

Courtesy of Richard D. Irwin, Inc., Homewood, Ill.

the certificate to Richard Roe. Roe would send the document to the transfer agent; in a few weeks a new certificate would be mailed to him. Mr. Roe would then be recorded as the owner of these shares on the books of the corporation. The only charge for this transaction is a very small transfer fee.

If the sale is through a broker, the securities are usually transferred by naming the broker's firm as the "attorney," and dating and signing the certificate as above. These securities are surrendered to the broker, who may sell them to a third party, Jane Poe for example, by inserting Ms. Poe's name in the "assign and transfer unto" space, and then sending the shares to the transfer agent. The same end may be accomplished by preparing a separate legal document, a *stock assignment*, and mailing this to the broker separately. The stock assignment method is a safe way to transfer securities because the certificates need not be signed. The assignment and the certificates may be mailed in separate envelopes, making theft of the securities even more difficult.

The corporate bylaws and charter contain detailed statements of the rights of shareholders. Because these statements appear there, rather than on the stock certificate, the certificate remains simple and uncluttered. Corporate bonds and preferred shares usually contain much "fine print" which attempts to set down the main contractual obligations of the company. These obligations usually vary from issue to issue and are not recorded in the charter or bylaws except in the most general terms.

The ownership of all common shares is recorded at the offices of the registrar and the corporation. In this sense these securities are registered. However, if they are lost or destroyed, the procedure for obtaining replacement certificates is involved, time-consuming, and somewhat expensive. Shareholders should keep all securities in a place safe from theft or fire; they should never be endorsed until just before they are sold. Most people use registered mail when mailing certificates.

Rights of Common Stockholders

The legal characteristics of common shares are more uniform than they are for other types of securities because, under common law, all equity owners receive several important rights. Certain of these rights may be canceled, but only through the agreement of the shareholder.

The most important of these are listed and are examined below to determine their significance to the common stock investor.

Voting on Matters Important to the Corporation. Common shareholders evidence their ownership by voting for the directors of the corporation, one vote for each share owned. Presumably, the directors operate as a group to promote the best interests of the owners in the long run. Directors who do not satisfy the majority of shareholders may be replaced with persons who are expected to do a better job. As a practical matter it is difficult to replace an established board, unless they do such a poor job that a large proportion of shareholders desires change. Most shareholders in large public corporations take little managerial interest in their company. They prefer to sell their securities when profits sag rather than attempt to effect change in the management of the company. Most shareholders never vote their shares directly. Unless they attend the annual meeting in person, they vote through a *proxy* or not at all. A proxy is a legal document which allows a person to select someone, also called a proxy, to vote the shares. By law, shareholders must be allowed to vote by proxy, but many shareholders never avail themselves of this right.

Figure 10–2 is a *proxy card*, which if signed and returned, allows the shareholder to vote for or against several proposals presented by the company's management. A *proxy statement* accompanied this proxy card and explained management's proposals for the election of directors. Shareholders may vote by proxy, and also attend the meeting. At the meeting shareholders may cancel previously submitted proxy votes and vote differently on one or all of the issues.

It is often justifiably stated that the boards of directors of most large corporations are self-perpetuating organizations because of the lethargy of shareholders. However, common shareholders do have the right to elect directors, and they are the only class of security holders which has this right as a matter of common law. In some cases preferred shareholders and even bond holders may vote for directors, but only if the company has in some way violated its contract with these classes of security owners. Shareholders may also vote on several other matters. The selection of the accounting firm to audit the books of the company, stock option plans for employees, and merger plans are common examples of other areas of shareholder control.

Some corporations issue two classes of common stock, voting and nonvoting shares. This practice is far less common than it once was. In 1957 the New York Stock Exchange stopped listing shares of com-

FIGURE 10–2
Proxy Card of Evans Products Co.

MANAGEMENT PROXY

EVANS PRODUCTS COMPANY

ANNUAL MEETING OF SHAREHOLDERS, MAY 21, 1975

The undersigned hereby appoints MONFORD A. ORLOFF, J. KENNETH BRODY, and SAMUEL J. ROBINSON, and each of them, with power of substitution to each, proxies of the undersigned, to vote or act with respect to all shares of stock of Evans Products Company standing in the name of the undersigned at the close of business on April 11, 1975, at the Annual Meeting of Shareholders of Evans Products Company to be held on the 21st day of May, 1975, and at all adjournments thereof, with all the powers the undersigned would possess if personally present, including (without limiting the general authorization hereby given) the authority to vote,

(1) Upon the election of directors of the Company,

(2) In their discretion upon such other matters as may properly come before the meeting.

A majority of such proxies who shall be present and shall act at said meeting (or if only one shall be present and act, then that one) shall have and exercise all the powers of said proxies hereunder. The undersigned hereby revokes any proxy or proxies heretofore given to vote or act with respect to the shares held by the undersigned and hereby ratifies and confirms all that said proxies, their substitutes, or any of them, may lawfully do by virtue hereof.

(Continued and to be SIGNED on Reverse Side)

The undersigned hereby acknowledges receipt of the Notice of Annual Meeting of Shareholders dated April 21, 1975, the Proxy Statement furnished therewith, and the Annual Report of the Company for 1974 heretofore furnished.

Dated: ...., 1975 ....

Signature

....

Signature

Please sign exactly as name appears at left. If the shares are registered in the name of two or more persons, each should sign. Executors, administrators, trustees, guardians, attorneys, and corporate officers should add their titles.

PLEASE SIGN, DATE AND MAIL THIS PROXY IN THE ENCLOSED ENVELOPE, WHICH REQUIRES NO POSTAGE IF MAILED IN THE UNITED STATES.

Courtesy of Evans Products Company.

panies having more than one class of common stock when the voting rights differed from one class to another. Some such shares are listed on the American Exchange or traded over the counter. The usual intent behind the issuance of two classes of stock is to maintain control over a company with a minimum amount of investment.

Receive Dividends on a Prorata Basis. The board of directors is under no legal obligation to declare dividends to common shareholders. However, if a dividend is declared, each shareholder by law receives an equal amount per share. Although shareholders have brought legal suits against boards of directors to force them to declare dividends, the suits are seldom successful. Under normal circumstances a shareholder who is unhappy with the dividend policy of a corporation has two alternatives: the securities can be sold or an attempt can be made to elect a new board of directors. While it is difficult to replace directors, it should be noted that few things will unite shareholders into a powerful cohesive force more rapidly than omitted or lowered dividends. Directors know this and usually declare dividends if earnings are sufficient for them to do so.

Buy New Shares of Stock When Issued. Under common law shareholders are allowed to maintain their proportion of ownership in a company. This means that if a company offers new common stock for sale, shareholders are entitled to purchase enough of it so that their interest in the company is not diminished. As an example, if a company were selling 10 percent more stock than it presently had outstanding, a person owning 200 shares would be entitled to purchase 20 additional shares.

This right is known as the *preemptive right,* and it extends to the sale of securities, bonds, or preferred stock, which are convertible into the common stock of the company. In its strictest form it gives shareholders great protection against dilution of their interests through issuance of more common stock. However, the preemptive right may be denied in the corporate charter or bylaws. A person purchasing securities of such a company loses this right partially or entirely. Normally, the preemptive right is of less importance to the shareholder in the large corporation than to persons owning shares in a corporation that is small and closely held. Maintaining a proportionate ownership in General Motors, a company with over 285 million common shares outstanding and nearly 1.3 million stockholders, is certainly unnecessary so far as control is concerned. The largest shareholder probably owns less than 1 percent of the stock.

Some corporations follow a policy of selling new common stocks through a *rights offering* to existing shareholders whether or not they have the preemptive right. These offerings and stock warrants are examined in Chapter 12.

Receive a Prorata Share of the Business if It Is Dissolved. Common shareholders are often called residual owners. This term reflects the fact that they can receive no dividends until bond interest, preferred dividends, and other expenses have been paid. The term also reflects their legal position in the event that the firm ceases operation. When this happens all the creditors are paid, the preferred shareholders receive the par or stated value of their shares, and then, if anything remains from the sale of the corporation's assets, each common shareholder receives a prorata share of what is left. Corporations may cease operations for a reason other than bankruptcy, and when this happens there is often a residual amount (a liquidating dividend) paid to shareholders. Bankrupt firms may also pay this type of dividend. However, there is seldom anything of value left for the common shareholder because the firm will normally have used up all its assets or pledged them as collateral for loans in an attempt to continue operating.

Common shareholders have other rights which are of lesser importance for the average small investor. They may, through relatively costly legal procedures, obtain the list of stockholders of the company, examine the books of the company, and bring suit against the directors of the company when it can be proved that the directors have knowingly acted against the best interest of the corporation. Some states allow a form of voting for directors—cumulative voting—which may enable a minority group of shareholders to elect at least one director.

Maturity of Common Shares

Most bonds have a definite maturity date, a time at which the corporation agrees to redeem these securities. With the exception of *treasury stock*, common stock is never redeemed.[1] Its life is that of the corporation. Since most modern corporations operate under perpetual charters, for all practical purposes the life of common shares is indefinite, ending only when the corporation is dissolved or otherwise ceases to exist.

Stated Par and No Par Stock

Unsophisticated investors often attach the same meaning to the par value of a stock as they do to that of a bond. But there is absolutely no similarity in these two values. Bond owners can rightly expect their securities to be redeemed at the par value, but common shares are not expected to be redeemed. If the company is liquidated and the common shareholders are compensated in this liquidation, the amount of the liquidating dividend will be a prorata share of whatever remains after all liabilities are paid and all assets sold. This amount has nothing to do with the par value of the security.

[1] Treasury stock is stock that has been issued and then reacquired by the company. These shares may be resold, issued as stock dividends, used in mergers, or otherwise be returned to general ownership. While they are held as treasury stock, they receive no dividends, nor can they be voted.

Many years ago stocks were assigned high par values (often $100 per share) to indicate to investors that these shares were valuable in the par amount. Apparently it was believed that a high par value made it easier to sell common stocks. However, investors who purchased securities at less than par value could be assessed the difference between what they paid for the stock and its par value in case the company became financially insolvent. This is a type of liability which most investors do not wish to assume. Today, about half of the newly incorporated firms issue no par stock and the other half issue shares having a nominal value. The debate over the desirability of no par versus low par is largely a legal one, best excluded from a book of this nature. Older corporations have lowered the par value of their shares through stock splits (explained later in this chapter) to the point that the par value has no relationship to the normal market value of their stock. For example, the present par value of Du Pont is $5, Ford Motor Co. is $2.50, Ford Motor Co. of Canada is no par, Richard D. Irwin is $0.50, and Capehart Corporation is $0.10. The recent market prices of these firms are many times greater than the par value of their shares.

INVESTMENT CHARACTERISTICS OF COMMON STOCK

The most important investment characteristics of fixed income securities were found to be yield, grade, and maturity. These variables are easily identified and measured for fixed income securities. While the grade and yield characteristics of common stocks continue to be of primary importance, because of the residual nature of stockholder claims the identification and measurement of grade and yield becomes extremely difficult. The next section of this chapter looks to valuation techniques. These techniques have as their points of emphasis dividends and the grade of the security. Since the grade of a common stock security is largely determined by the past and future performance of the company, a thorough understanding of dividends and dividend payment procedures is a necessity.

Common Stock Dividends

The usual dividend is a payment of cash from the corporation to each shareholder. Dividends are normally paid quarterly but may be paid more or fewer times per year. The amount of the dividend is determined by the board of directors. As it was previously explained, directors have nearly complete discretion over the amount and frequency of dividend payments, with the exception that they may not pay dividends if their payment would result in the insolvency of the corporation. Since the laws of dividend payments originate in 50 separate states, there is understandably some lack of uniformity in what corporate directors may do. The intent of all this legislation is to protect the creditors of the corporation from too generous dividend payments which would cause financial harm to the company.

Dividends are of obvious importance to all investors. Announcements of declared dividends are carried in the financial press in a format similar to that of Figure 10–3.

Stock Dividends. Most dividends are cash dividends, but they may take the form of products of the company, other assets of the company, or the stock of the company. The most common form of divi-

FIGURE 10–3
Dividends Reported January 22, 1975

Company	Period	Amt.	Payable date	Record date
Acme Electric Corp	Q	.05	3–10–75	2–10
Alison Mtge Inv Trust			Omitted dividend	
Alpha Portland Indus	Q	.18	3–10–75	2–14
AMP Inc	Q	c.09¼	3– 3–75	2– 3
Anchor Coupling Co	Q	.54	2–28–75	2– 7
Anchor Income Fund		h.12½	2–18–75	2– 6
Anheuser Busch Inc	Q	.15	3– 7–75	2– 6
Arkansas Western Gas	Q	c.27½	2–20–75	2– 5
Baker Oil Tools Inc	Q	.09⅜	2–25–75	2– 3
Blessings Corp			Omitted dividend	
Burroughs Corp	Q	c.15	5– 7–75	4– 9
California Water Co	Q	c.55	2–15–75	2– 3
Castle AM & Co new	Q	.20	2–19–75	2– 3
Central Ill Light Co	Q	.40	3–20–75	2–21
Cent Ill Lt $2.875pfA		.71875	4– 1–75	3– 7
Cent Ill Lt 4½%pf	Q	1.12½	4– 1–75	3– 7
Citation Cos	Q	.10	3– 3–75	2– 3
Contl Copper & Stl Ind	Q	.20	3– 1–75	2–13
Doremus & Co	Q	.10	2–20–75	2– 4
Doremus & Co	E	.04	2–20–75	2– 4
Downey Sav&Loan Asso ..		.30	3– 1–75	2– 3
Dreyfus Corp	Q	.10	2–25–75	2– 4
Electronics Corp Amer ...	Q	.25	2–26–75	2– 5
Essex Chemical Corp ...	In	.03	2–18–75	2– 3
Finc'l Security Group	Q	.08	3–27–75	3– 7
First Utd Bancorp	Q	.15	3–31–75	3–17
Faodarama Supermkts ..	Sp	.15	2–18–75	1–31
GAF Corp	Q	.13	2–20–75	2– 3
GAF Corp $1.20pf	Q	.30	2–20–75	2– 3
Gen'l Tire&Rubb Co	Q	.27½	2–28–75	2– 3
Gen'l Tire&Rubb Co	Stk	2%	4–25–75	2– 3
Green Giant Co	Q	.27	3–15–75	2–22
Her Majesty Ind cl A	Q	.12	2–25–75	2– 6
Hughes Tool Co	Q	.12½	2–28–75	2– 4

c-Increased dividend. d-Reduced dividend. h-From income. j-From capital gains. b-Payable in Canadian funds. A, annual; Ac, accumulation; E, extra; F, final; G, interim; In, initial; Liq, liquidation; M, monthly; Q, quarterly; R, resumed; S, semi-annual; Sp, special.

Source: *The Wall Street Journal*, January 23, 1975 p. 16.

dend payment after cash dividends is stock dividends. When a stock dividend is declared, it is usually stated as a percent dividend: 2 percent, 10 percent, and so on. This means that each shareholder will be issued a certain percentage more stock than was owned when the dividend was declared. An investor holding 100 shares of General Tire and Rubber Co., a company which paid a 2 percent stock dividend April 25, 1975, would have owned 102 shares after the dividend.

There is much misunderstanding over the value of a stock dividend. Most investors see it as being favorable to their individual position, but a close examination of what takes place when this type of dividend is declared shows that this is not true. A straight stock dividend can have no value to any single shareholder because every shareholder has received a proportional increase in the number of shares owned. The value or earning power of the corporation has not changed; simply stated, each shareholder just has more pieces of paper which evidence ownership in the company. No one owns more of the company.

The following example illustrates this point. Assume a corporation which has outstanding 100 shares of common stock held by ten people each owning 10 shares. The corporation earns $50 per year, all of which it pays out in dividends, $0.50 per share. The company declares a 20 percent stock dividend so that each of the shareholders now owns 12 shares; the corporation then has a total of 120 shares outstanding. Total dividend payments remain at $50, which lowers the dividend per share to $50/120 shares = $0.4167 per share. Dividends paid to each share are lower, but each shareholder has 20 percent more shares. The dividend return to each investor remains the same as it was before the stock dividend, $0.4167 × 12 shares = $5. If the market price of the stock is related to the dividend per share, as we shall assume it to be, then the market price of each share must also have declined. However, the total value of each shareholder's securities remains constant. Studies have shown that stock dividends neither lower nor raise the value of shareholder's holdings.

Corporations may issue stock dividends while continuing to pay the same cash dividend per share. The effect of this action is to increase *total* dividend payments by the percent of the stock dividend. This would happen if General Tire and Rubber continued to pay dividends at the current rate (27½¢ per share) after the stock dividend. In this situation the market price of the stock—old as well as newly issued stock—would theoretically remain constant at the price it held before the stock dividend because dividends per share would not have changed. Shareholders would obtain a real increase in the market value of their investments, but the increase would result from the increased cash dividend payout rather than the stock dividend.

Stock Splits. The major difference between a stock split and a stock dividend stems from the way that the dividend or split is accounted for on the books of the corporation. If the newly issued stock amounts to a small proportion of the total outstanding stock, the dividend is paid in stock of the company. This stock will have been authorized in the corporate charter but is as yet unissued; most corporations have this type of stock in generous amounts. If the dividend is to be a substantial proportion of the total amount of outstanding stock, this event is seen as being a recapitalization of the company.[2] This recapitalization is recorded by reducing the par value of the stock by the same proportion that the stock dividend had to the total stock outstanding.

A company having a two-for-one stock split would give each shareholder twice the number of shares held before the split, and on the books of the corporation the par value of each share would be halved. Dividend payments would possibly be halved, and so would the market price of each share. Corporations usually split their stock to put its market price into what the company considers to be its "best" trading range. Many companies believe this to be between $20 and $50 per share. When the market price of the stock of such a company climbs above $50 the company may declare a two-for-one or three-for-one stock split. The shareholders all have more stock, but the market price of each share will be back into the "best" trading range. A less common type of stock split is one where the number of outstanding shares is reduced. This usually occurs when the market price of a corporation's stock has dropped to the point where the directors believe it is "too low." In a reverse split, or "split up" as it is sometimes called, shareholders exchange their shares for a proportionately fewer number. Par value and market price are adjusted upward by a proportionate amount.

Perhaps the most compelling argument that one could use to prove that neither stock dividends nor splits have any value or cost for the individual shareholder is this: the Internal Revenue Service does not tax either stock dividends or splits as income, while any other type of dividend is so taxed. A company paying a cash and a stock dividend,

[2] The American Institute of Certified Public Accountants states that a company should recapitalize (use a stock split) when the transaction promises to "materially affect" the market price of the stock. They suggest that this event is likely to happen when the dividend is over 25 percent, and unlikely to happen when the dividend is less than 20 percent. A dividend between 20 and 25 percent may be recorded either way.

as some do, would cause each shareholder to assume a tax liability on only the cash portion of the dividend.

The following companies are a few of the many having stock dividends during 1974. A complete listing of stock dividends and splits can be obtained from Standard & Poor's *Annual Dividend Record* or Moody's *Dividend Record.*

Commonwealth Oil Refining . . .	5%
Dart Industries	3%
Frigitemp Corporation	2%
Peabody Galion Corporation . . .	3%
Ronson Corporation	4%
Sun Oil Company	10%

Payment of Dividends. The dividend on common and preferred stocks is always paid to the person who owns the security at the time the dividend payment becomes effective. Bond interest is paid on a prorata basis. A person owning a bond for three months will receive 3⁄12 of the yearly interest payment; ownership for six months entitles the owner to 6⁄12, or ½, of the yearly interest.

The dividend payment procedure is usually spread over many weeks and follows this sequence: The directors meet and *declare* a dividend of a stated amount which is to be paid at a certain time in the future. This dividend is payable to persons listed as *holders of record* on a certain date. The holder of record is the person recorded by the corporation as owning its stock.

There is some difficulty in knowing exactly who owns shares in a company as of a certain date. A person could have sold shares just before the holder of record date, and the company might not have received notice of this transaction until after the holder of record date had passed. To simplify the ownership problem this rule is followed: Dividends remain with the stock until four business days *before* the date of record. On the fourth day preceding the date of record, the stock begins selling *ex-dividend.* This means that the dividend will be received by persons owning the stock on the fifth business day preceding the dividend record date; persons purchasing the stock at that time will not receive the current dividend but will receive future dividends if they continue to own the stock. The dividend payment is often announced publicly, especially if the dividend is being increased or if the company has been paying dividends for a long time. The announcement, shown in Figure 10–4, was published in *The Financial Analysts Journal.* The dividend was declared on July 10, 1975; stocks

FIGURE 10–4
Announcement of a Stock Dividend

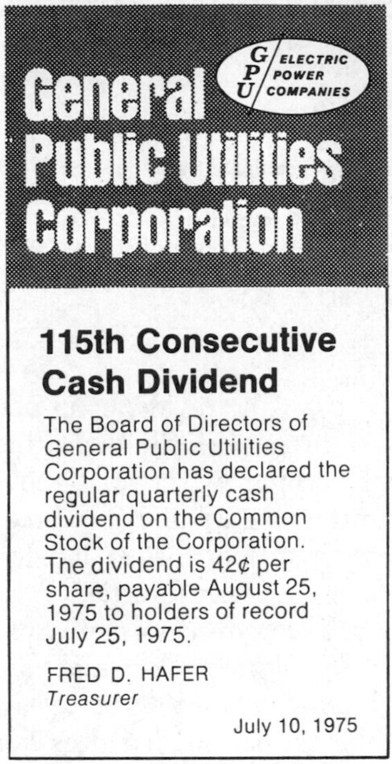
General Public Utilities Corporation

G/P/U ELECTRIC POWER COMPANIES

115th Consecutive Cash Dividend

The Board of Directors of General Public Utilities Corporation has declared the regular quarterly cash dividend on the Common Stock of the Corporation. The dividend is 42¢ per share, payable August 25, 1975 to holders of record July 25, 1975.

FRED D. HAFER
Treasurer

July 10, 1975

Courtesy of General Public Utilities Corporation.

went ex-dividend on July 21, 1975, four business days before the July 25, 1975 date of record. The financial press notifies investors of the fact that a stock has gone ex-dividend by placing an "x" immediately after the dividend column in the stock quote section of the newspaper.

Grading of Common Stocks

Several investment advisory services publish ratings of common stocks. Although these ratings are quantitative in their origin and resemble the grade assignments awarded to bonds, they do not have the same clear and definite meaning as does the grade of a bond.

Both Standard & Poor's and Value Line prepare these rating measures, as do several less well-known firms. But while the basis for a

TABLE 10–2
Common Stock Rating Systems

*Standard & Poor's**		*Value Line†*	
Symbol	*Symbol Meaning*	*Symbol*	*Symbol Meaning*
A+	Highest	A+ and A.	Highest
A	High	A– and B+.	Above average
A–	Above average	B	Average
B+.	Average	B– and C+.	Below average
B	Below average	C and C–.	Lowest
B–	Low		
C	Lowest		
D	In reorganization		

* Standard & Poor's, *Stock Guide,* February 1975, p. 4.
† *The Value Line Investment Survey* (New York: Arnold Bernhard & Co.).

bond's grade is its financial risk, the ratings prepared by these companies are based mainly upon stability of earnings and stock prices and growth in earnings and dividends. The rating symbols of Standard & Poor's and Value Line are listed in Table 10–2.

The following words of caution are supplied by the Standard & Poor's Corporation along with the description of how they compute their common stock earning and dividend rankings. The statement should keep investors from attaching too much meaning to formal grading techniques for common stocks.

> These scorings are not to be confused with bond quality ratings, which are arrived at by a necessarily altogether different approach. Additionally, they must not be used as a substitute for market recommendations; a high graded stock may at times be so over-priced as to justify its sale, while a low score may be attractively priced for purchase. Rankings based upon earnings and dividend records are no substitute for analysis. Nor are they quality ratings in the complete sense of the term.[3]

ANALYSIS OF COMMON STOCK

This discussion builds upon materials presented in Chapter 6 which attempted to show how security markets and industries could be analyzed for the purpose of identifying intrinsic values and likely price movements. The goal of common stock analysis is the same as it was for industries and markets. That is, the analysis of common stocks has

[3] Standard & Poor's *Stock Guide,* January 1975, p. 4.

as its goal the identification of securities which have market values different from their intrinsic values. The most often quoted statement defining the relationship between intrinsic value and market value follows.

> A general definition of intrinsic value would be "that value which is justified by the facts, e.g., assets, earnings, dividends, definite prospects, including the factor of management." The primary objective in using the adjective "intrinsic" is to emphasize the distinction between value and current market price, but not to invest this "value" with an aura of permanence. In truth, the computed intrinsic value is likely to change at least from year to year, as the various factors governing that value are modified. But in most cases intrinsic value changes less rapidly and drastically than market price, and the investor usually has an opportunity to profit from any wide discrepancy between the current price and the intrinsic value as determined at the same time.[4]

The investor is constantly seeking securities which have intrinsic values larger than present market values. To be successful at this type of analysis one must be aware of the things that give value to a share of common stock. Although there are nearly as many theories of security analysis as there are security analysts, almost all valuation theories are ultimately based upon future earnings and dividends expected to be obtained by the common shareholders. Without dividends and earnings, or the promise of these in the future, it is seldom that common stock can have more than a speculative value.

There is a minimum of uncertainty associated with investment in fixed income securities. The valuation of these securities is concerned with determining the grade of the security and what price the security should have to allow the purchaser to obtain a yield near to the current market yield of interest for securities having similar investment characteristics. Most of this analysis is quantitative, being based upon various ratios taken from the company's financial statements. Valuing common stocks is not only a quantitative procedure, but one that also requires many qualitative judgments on the part of the security analyst or the person who uses the analyst's computations. Several things make common stock valuation most difficult: (1) Common stock earnings and dividends are a residual, and because of this they may vary greatly in amount from year to year; (2) The corporation is under no legal obligation to pay common stock dividends; (3) In-

[4] Graham, Dodd, Cottle, *Security Analysis.*

vestor psychology can cause common stock prices to fluctuate wildly, particularly in the short run.

As a practical matter, the average investor seldom makes intensive analyses of securities. However, all the major brokerage firms and investment advisors publish such studies. It is necessary that each investor understand the basis upon which these analyses are made because they will probably provide the background for many investment decisions.

Book Value. Logically, the things that determine the value of a common stock are its expected future earnings and dividends. With certain exceptions, the book value of a company has little direct relationship to these measures. However, book value per share is such a common measure of value that an examination of its meaning is necessary.

The book value, or net asset value, of a company is determined by subtracting its liabilities from its assets. The remainder is book value. The balance sheet provides the information for this calculation, but most annual reports and stock fact sheets present the dollar amount directly. Usually the information is presented as "book value per share," which means that the total book value has been divided by the number of shares of common stock outstanding.

This amount is not very useful in determining the intrinsic value of a share of common stock for several reasons; (1) It has little or no direct effect on future earnings or dividends; if book value per share doubled, earnings might increase or they might decrease; (2) It does not usually give a realistic market value of the business because most assets are carried on the books at their original cost less accumulated depreciation, not their present market value; (3) Some of the productive resources and liabilities of the business do not appear on the balance sheet. Leased productive facilities are not necessarily recorded as assets, and lease payment liabilities are not always recorded as liabilities. These may be important considerations for some companies.

There are some instances where book value does have meaning. The shares of mutual funds and other trust type investments are usually sold and redeemed on the basis of net asset value (book value) per share. In this case, book value and market value are identical except for sales or redemption charges.[5]

Book value may also have meaning when a company's earnings are exceptionally low or high. Valuing stock on the basis of earnings under

[5] Chapter 11 examines these investments and computes the net asset value of a mutual fund share.

either of these conditions is likely to result in an erroneous assessment of worth. It might be better to look at book value as the base from which profits flow and to reason that if similar firms earned 10 percent on book value over the long run, this firm should do the same. The stock could then be valued on the basis of these assumed long-run earnings.

Logically, book value should have meaning for natural resource companies because profits are tied directly to assets held in the form of oil, timber, copper ore, and so on. The difficulty in using book value is that for these companies it is invariably too low. Assets are recorded at *cost*, and balance sheet valuations of natural resource assets are usually far below the present or future market value of the assets. Security analysts often attempt to assign market values to natural resource type assets, "to see what the company is really worth." This approach has some merit, but huge reserves of oil, timber, or copper ore do not necessarily guarantee future profits. Costs of drilling, mining, logging, transporting or otherwise preparing the asset for sale may be so high that exploitation is uneconomical. A more explicit example of the difficulty of translating book values into future profits is found in the Weyerhaeuser Company annual reports. Weyerhaeuser's 1974 annual report valued its timber lands at $452.8 million. Responsible estimates of the current market value of this timber are somewhere over $3 billion. However, it will take many years to turn this timber into profits. How much is it really worth to a Weyerhaeuser shareholder today?

Liquidating value refers to the amount that would remain if a company ceased operations, paid off all creditors, sold its assets, and divided whatever was left among the common stockholders. The calculations for book value and liquidating value are identical except that in computing liquidating value, assets are priced at market value rather than at their balance sheet amount. Some companies, especially those owning large amounts of real estate which is carried on their books at its original cost, may have a liquidation value per share far greater than either book value or current market value per share. These companies may be "better dead than alive." Book value may be looked at as the amount *put into* a company by common shareholders, while liquidating value is the amount that may be *taken out* if the company is liquidated.

Capitalization of Earnings and Dividends. When valuing common stocks, which is more important, earnings per share or dividends per share? Presently the earnings per share (EPS) measure is far more widely accepted as "the" key measure of company performance; not so many years ago dividends were more important. This shift in emphasis is important enough to warrant further examination.

There can be no single year identified as the year when this shift took place, but there is little doubt that it has. Until the 1940s and even later, investment in common stock was seen as being much the same as investment in bonds, with the exception that dividend payments on stock were somewhat less certain. At that time investors made direct comparisons between interest rate yield and dividend yield. They used common stock cash dividends the same way they used bond interest, as the basis for the intrinsic value of the security. For example, a person contemplating the purchase of a long-term bond would assign it an intrinsic value based upon its grade and yield to maturity.

Common share owners judged equity securities in much the same manner. The grade of the common stock was determined largely by the dividend payment history of the company. If the company had been able to continue paying dividends through bad years and good, the stock was classified as being high grade. Poorer dividend performance identified a stock as being of lower grade. The investor *capitalized dividends* in the same way that interest payments were capitalized.

Capitalization is most easily explained by using a bond interest illustration. Assume that an investor owns a 4 percent perpetual bond (neither perpetuals nor corporate stocks have maturities). The investor would reason that if debt securities having similar investment characteristics were yielding 5 percent this investment should yield about the same amount. Since this bond had a yearly coupon interest payment of 4 percent—\$40—it should have a market value of approximately,

$$\frac{\$40}{0.05} = \$800.$$

The logic of this valuation procedure is that 5 percent of \$800 is \$40. Forty dollars per year indefinitely, capitalized at a rate of 5 percent is *worth* \$800.[6]

The only difficulty in applying this valuation procedure to common shares is that of introducing the risk of lowered future dividends into the equation. This has traditionally been accomplished by increasing the capitalization rate as the risk of the security increased. Dividends

[6] If this procedure is still unclear, see the discussion of current yield in Chapter 8.

TABLE 10–3
Capitalization Rate Calculations

Estimated Average Dividends	*Capitalization Rate*	*Computed Market Price of Stock*
$2.	6%	$33.33
2.	8	25.00
2.	10	20.00

on the very highest grade common stocks might be capitalized at 6 percent, while those of poorer securities would be capitalized at 8, 10, or even greater percentages. Capitalizing the same yearly dividend payments at different capitalization rates has the effect of lowering the market price one would pay for the security. (see Table 10–3.)

The computations in Table 10–3 and the logic of this kind of analysis are based upon the assumption of constant future dividends. If dividends are expected to increase over time, the capitalization rate is lowered below the "normal" rate. The market prices that investors are willing to pay for these "growth" securities then increase. From a mathematical standpoint this reasoning is not correct because it does not consider the timing of increased or decreased dividend payments; however, this is in fact one of the methods used to determine the intrinsic value of common stock. For many years the rule of thumb was that "a good stock yields 6 percent." Or in our terms, dividends on good common stocks were capitalized at a 6 percent rate.

By the late 1940s and early 1950s it was becoming apparent that our nation was not sinking into the post-World War II depression that had been widely anticipated. Rather the economy was expanding at an unparalleled rate. To participate in this great economic boom the common stock investor sought shares in companies which were growing, not necessarily in those which paid constant dividends. In fact many investors looked upon companies which paid "good" dividends with some suspicion. Would it not be more profitable for the company to retain its earnings, reinvesting them back into the business, rather than paying them out as dividends? With the adoption of this line of reasoning the time-hallowed 6 percent capitalization rate became defunct, and investors began analyzing common stock securities on the basis of earnings, and particularly *growth* in earnings.

This change in investor logic as it relates to stock valuation is reflected in the downward shift in the dividend yield of common stock over the last 25 years. As Figure 9–2 shows, immediately after World

War II ended, capitalization rates on common stock dividends decreased.[7]

Valuation Based upon Capitalization of Earnings. A capitalization rate on dividends which is less than that on high-grade fixed income securities can be logically defended only if the value of the security is based upon something other than current dividends. This is what has happened. Investors now place more emphasis upon earnings per share and the future growth prospects of the company than upon dividends per share. The argument for this measure is easily understood. Companies which have good growth prospects *should* pay low dividends; capital which would normally go to shareholders is thus retained in the business. The shareholder benefits from this action because the earnings of the company increase over time, and may increase future dividends. Since the company is financing its expansion through retained earnings rather than new stock issues, the number of common shares remains constant. Increased company earnings are evidenced by increased EPS, and as EPS increase, so should the stock's market price. The method of valuation on the basis of dividends alone largely overlooked increased market prices of stock as a source of value.

Investors still arrive at an intrinsic value approximation through the process of capitalization, but what they now capitalize is earnings. This is done through the use of the earnings/price, or E/P, ratio computed as follows. International Business Machines had EPS of $12.47 during 1974. Its average market price was $202.25 per share over the same year. Earnings therefore were capitalized at an average rate of 6.2 percent.

$$\$12.47/\$202.25 = 0.062 = 6.2\%$$

The more common way of stating this ratio is by reversing it,

$$\$202.25/\$12.47 = 16.22{:}1$$

The analyst would say that IBM sold for 16 times earnings.[8]

Relative price/earnings measures are used to analyze individual stocks in much the same manner as they were used to analyze industries and markets, except that the company's performance is usually measured against firms in the industry or against security markets in

[7] The dividend yield in Figure 9–2 is really the average capitalization rate on common stocks. It is computed by dividing average yearly dividends by average market prices.

[8] This ratio becomes meaningless when earnings are nonexistent, or when the company experiences a loss, because the resulting ratio is infinitely large.

general. Industry and market analyses were performed in Chapter 6; at this time an individual company's performance will be examined using the same analytical framework as before. IBM's EPS will be compared to the Standard & Poor's 425 Industrial Stock Price Index to determine how IBM's performance compares with the "average" industrial stock.

Figure 10–5 presents the average yearly P/E ratio for the S&P Industrial Stock Price Index with the average P/E ratio of IBM. From this chart one can tell several things: (1) IBM stock has been valued on the basis of a higher P/E ratio than the average industrial stock over the period studied; (2) In 1974 IBM's P/E ratio was at a 10-year low. Figure 10–5 is useful to the analyst because it puts IBM's current P/E ratio into historical perspective and relates this ratio to the benchmark of the average industrial company stock. Studying a company's P/E ratio in this manner points up any changes in value that investors have made in IBM stock relative to the average share value.

IBM's P/E ratio declined drastically during 1973 and 1974. Since changes in either earnings or stock prices could have caused the ratio to change in this manner one must look into the composition of the ratio (earnings per share and share prices) to obtain a clearer understanding of what has happened. IBM had earnings per share of \$7.13 in 1970, \$7.50 in 1971, \$8.83 in 1972, \$10.79 in 1973, and \$12.47 in

FIGURE 10–5
Average Yearly P/E Ratios of IBM and the Standard & Poor's 425 Industrial Stock Price Index

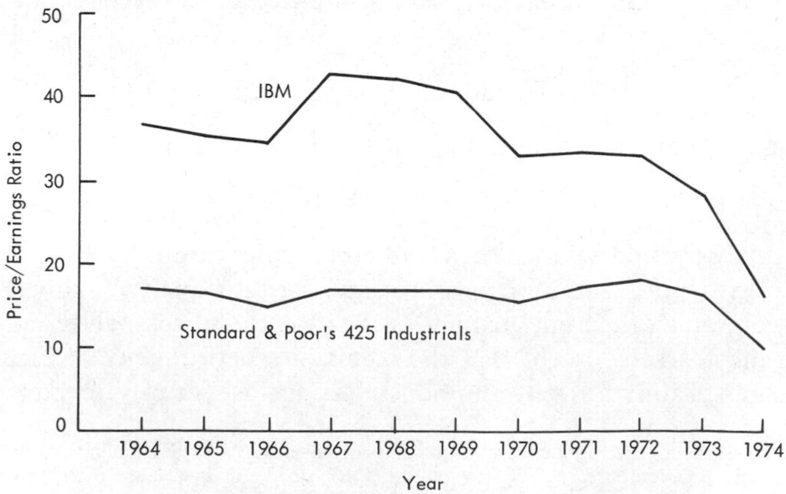

Source: Standard & Poor's, *Listed Stock Reports,* February 4, 1975, sec. 12, p. 1, 210.

1974. In fact, earnings per share of this company have increased each year for many many years. Over the past ten years they increased at a 15 percent annual compound rate. As earnings increased average stock prices also increased, which caused the P/E ratio to remain fairly constant at an average of between 34 and 43. The relationship between EPS and the price of IBM common is graphed in Figure 10–6. This set of graphs clearly presents the historical relationship between earnings and stock prices for this company. The graphs also point up the fact that the lowered P/E ratio of 1973 was the result of slightly lowered share prices and a substantial rise in EPS. Increased EPS in 1974 was responsible for part of the lowered EPS ratio, but the main cause was the 33 percent decline in the average stock price.

The analyst must now attempt to determine why share prices declined so much. All common stock price indexes dropped drastically during 1973 and 1974. This depressed market for equity securities doubtlessly had an adverse effect upon the price of IBM stock. It explains part of the reason for the price decrease. The analyst must now seek to identify any other factors that might have caused IBM stock prices to drop. For example, investor expectations of IBM's future

FIGURE 10–6
Earnings per Share and Average Stock Price of IBM (1964 through 1974)

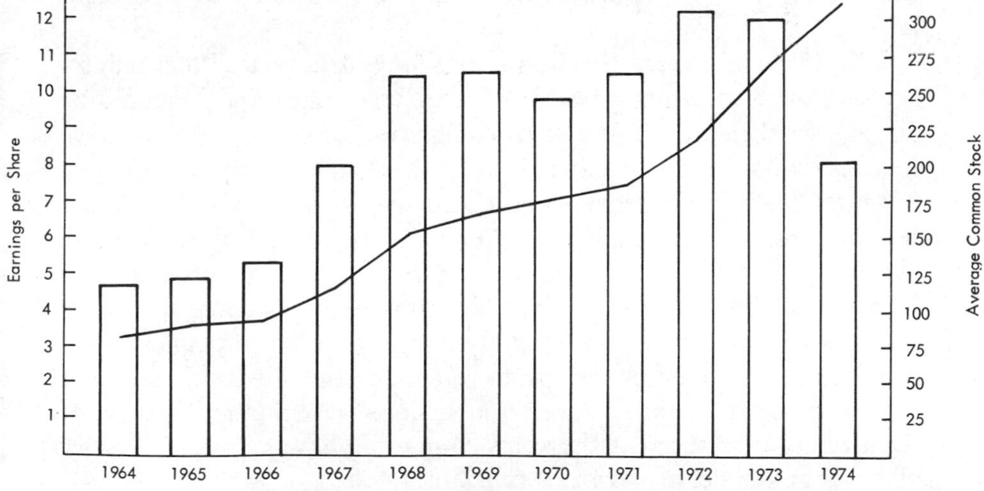

Note: The line graph shows earnings per share (use the left-hand scale); the bar graph shows average common stock prices (right-hand scale). Average stock prices are calculated as the midpoint of the high and low price for each calendar year.

Source: Standard & Poor's, *Listed Stock Reports*, February 4, 1975, sec. 12, p. 1, 210.

growth prospects may have been lowered. If no reasons for the price drop can be identified, the assumption is that the stock will again sell at the "normal" P/E ratio (compiled from 1964 to 1972) of between 34 and 43. In early 1975 IBM common stock is identified as having a market price *less* than its intrinsic value. Under the terms of the type of analysis now being performed, IBM common is seen as a "good buy."

Would IBM be a poor buy at a price of 50 times earnings? That question cannot be answered without more information. However, on the basis of the P/E ratios of the past ten years, that price for IBM appears relatively high. Many conservative investors would never purchase a security priced so high as a matter of principle, on the grounds that the risk of market price decline is too great.

Does this mean that stocks selling *below* their normal P/E ratios hold little or no risk of price decline? Certainly not. There is no reason why securities selling at low P/E ratios cannot go even lower. As a general statement, however, there is usually less risk associated with a stock selling at an exceptionally low P/E ratio—if the company has reasonably good future prospects—than there is in the company selling at an extraordinarily high P/E ratio. The low P/E ratio company can produce just average dividends and earnings and still be a reasonably good investment. The high P/E company must continue its above average performance into the future to justify the high price paid for the security. Few companies can generate above average earnings over long periods of time.

The Growth Factor in Common Stock Analysis. Potential for future growth in earnings per share does have value, and it should be an ingredient in all intrinsic value calculations. Security analysts have many methods for introducing growth into their valuation procedures, but there is no single generally accepted way of doing it. The analyst usually assigns an earnings multiplier to a stock which is based upon the things considered most important to the determination of the intrinsic value of the stock. Since the computer has come into wide usage as a stock market tool of analysis it is possible to employ many variables in complex equations to calculate the intrinsic values of thousands of securities. Different equations have held the favor of security analysts through the years, but none has performed well at all times and under all market conditions.

As an example of how one valuation formula may be used to assess common stock intrinsic values—not necessarily to recommend it above all others—we now return to the formula presented in Chapter 6:

$$\text{Intrinsic value} = \text{Normal earnings} \times \frac{37.5 + 8.8\ (\text{growth rate})}{\text{Aaa Bond interest rate}}$$

This formula was then used to calculate the intrinsic value of security indexes. It will now be used to assign an intrinsic value to the shares of IBM under conditions prevailing in early 1975. Assume normal earnings per share to be the amount earned in 1974—\$12.47. The growth rate of IBM earnings per share over the past ten years has averaged 15 percent per year; in the equation "G" is therefore 15. The Aaa bond rate in early 1975 was about 8.5 percent. Inserting these values in the equation results in the following intrinsic value for the IBM common shares:

$$\begin{aligned}\text{Intrinsic value} &= \$12.47 \times \frac{37.5 + 8.8\ (15)}{8.5}\\ &= \$12.47 \times \frac{169.5}{8.5}\\ &= \$12.47 \times 19.9\\ &= \$249.\end{aligned}$$

IBM shares sold well below this amount in early 1975 and would have been considered a possible bargain issue by analysts who used the above formula to derive intrinsic values of securities.

But during the early part of 1975 a very large number of securities appeared to be bargains under this formula. Certainly few persons could have purchased even a single share of stock of all the companies which would have been identified through the above procedure as selling below their intrinsic values. Further analysis is in order in this situation. The analyst responsible for the above formula recommends great caution in its use. It is suggested that persons using the type of analysis which is recommended, use it only for companies which meet specific criteria of financial strength (modest use of debt, fairly steady earnings, firms having assets over some minimum amount, and so on). Furthermore, it is believed that it is prudent to limit purchases to shares selling well below (three-fourths, two-thirds, or even one-half) the computed intrinsic value. The analyst's position is that the equation will currently identify so many firms which pass both the financial strength and the intrinsic value investment tests that it is possible and desirable to add an additional "margin-of-safety" into the analysis procedure by the use of this last investment criterion.[9]

[9] Benjamin Graham, "The Decade 1965–1974: Its Significance for Financial Analysts," from *The Renaissance of Value* (Charlottesville, Va.: Financial Analysts Research Foundation 1974), p. 11.

This example is designed to indicate in only the most general terms how analysts value growth stocks. Many of these "stock value models" are complex, incorporating additional factors in the analysis. Complexity does not necessarily mean that the derived prices are accurate, however. Many of these models are based upon *assumed* future growth rates and security prices. They are only as reliable as the predicted values that go into them. Investors must use caution when using or interpreting these models because it is easy to accept them as being scientific and therefore infallible. Security valuation always has been, is, and will probably continue to be an art rather than a science. Analytical tools are valuable aids to analysis, but investors must recognize their limitations.

SUMMARY

Equity share ownership has increased dramatically in recent years. The New York Stock Exchange calculates that in 1975 about 25 million Americans owned corporate shares directly; many more persons own these securities indirectly through investments in pension funds and ownership in life insurance companies.

Common shareholders own the corporation. They elect directors to represent their interests and to oversee the management of the company. Stock ownership is evidenced by shares of stock, which may have a par or no par value. Since these shares are not redeemed in the normal course of business, par value of common stock does not have the same meaning as does the par value of a bond or a preferred share. Stock is voted and dividends are paid on the basis of one vote and one dividend per share. Management is under no legal compulsion to pay common dividends, nor may shareholders force payment of dividends under normal circumstances.

Under common law, shareholders have the right to maintain their prorata share in the company by being allowed first choice to purchase new shares of common stock, or senior securities convertible into common stock. In practice most companies have abridged this *preemptive right* by denying it in the corporate charter. When a corporation is dissolved, common shareholders receive what remains after the claims of creditors and senior security owners are satisfied.

Common dividends may be in cash, or practically anything else. Companies may pay *stock dividends,* which result in each shareholder owning a larger *number* of the company's shares; proportion of ownership remains unchanged. Unless cash dividends per share remain the same or are increased, a stock dividend has no value to the shareholder.

Common stocks are graded by several firms, but the grading is not as accurate or as meaningful as it is for bonds. Grading is performed mainly on the history of the company so far as amount and constancy of dividends is concerned. It does not usually attempt to measure future dividends.

Analysis of common stock is directed toward determining what is the *intrinsic* value of the share. This value is that justified by the "facts"—earnings, assets, dividends, and future prospects. At one time or another *book value* or *liquidation value* may be a good indicator of intrinsic value. Analysts often use sophisticated *stock value models* and other analytical techniques to determine a stock's intrinsic value. A stock selling for more than this amount is overpriced; one selling for less is underpriced.

Investors often try to evaluate a security's *relative price* through the use of the earnings-per-share/price-per-share ratio. This ratio varies with changes in either earnings or price, of course, but it provides a benchmark to use in identifying which of a group of similar securities are relatively overpriced and which are relatively underpriced. Many analysts assign *basic price multipliers* to stocks on the basis of factors they believe to be most important in determining stock prices. An example of a simple price multiplier model is presented at the end of the chapter. A more sophisticated present-value stock value model is presented in the appendix to this chapter.

APPENDIX TO CHAPTER 10

The Present Value Approach to Common Stock Valuation

The logic of common stock valuation follows that for bonds. A share of stock is worth the present value of future dividend payments plus the present value of whatever the stock can be sold for at some future date. This is exactly the same reasoning presented in the Appendix to Chapter 8. However, in using the present value formula

$$P = I\left[\frac{1}{(1+i)^1} + \frac{1}{(1+i)^2} + \cdots + \frac{1}{(1+i)^n}\right] + M\left[\frac{1}{(1+i)^n}\right]$$

to value common stocks, we have the problem of assigning values to fluctuating yearly dividends and an unknown future market price.

These are formidable problems, and there are different ways of handling them.[10] The following example has been prepared to illustrate one way that the present value technique may be used to value common stock, and to clarify the concept of this type valuation. It will not provide the reader with a general formula into which data can be inserted to derive investment decisions.

The example carries the following assumptions:

1. Dividends are currently \$2 per share. They are paid annually and are expected to increase by 5 percent per year.
2. The present market price of the stock is \$40 per share. It is assumed to increase by 8 percent per year.
3. If the stock is purchased it will be purchased at the beginning of the year, after it has gone ex-dividend. It will be sold at the end of three years, receiving the third-year dividend.
4. Other securities of equal risk characteristics are currently discounted at a rate of 4 percent.

The first task is to determine yearly dividends over the three-year holding period:
Let

$$D_0 = \text{Beginning dividend of \$2.}$$
$$D_1, D_2, \text{ and } D_3 = \text{Dividends received for years 1, 2, and 3.}$$
$$r = \text{Yearly increase in dividends.}$$

The formula for determining the future dividends is

$$D_n = D_0(1+r)^n$$

Time	*Cash Dividend*
Year before purchase	\$2
1st year	D_1 = \$2(1 + 0.05)^1 = \$2.10.
2d year.	D_2 = \$2(1 + 0.05)^2 = \$2.20.
3d year.	D_3 = \$2(1 + 0.05)^3 = \$2.32.

Next is computed the future value of the security based upon an expected increase in its market price of 8 percent per year for three years. The same formula is used except that D_0 is now \$40 and r becomes 8 percent. Under these conditions it is but a simple matter to

$$P_n = \$40(1+0.08)^3 = \$50.40$$

[10] See W. Scott Bauman, "Investment Returns and Present Values," *Financial Analysts Journal*, 25, no. 6 (November–December 1969): 107 ff., for a good description of several of the newest techniques of present value analysis.

determine that the present value, or intrinsic value, of this security is the present value of future dividends plus the future value of the security. These values are discounted at 4 percent.

$$P = \frac{D_1}{(1+i)^1} + \frac{D_2}{(1+i)^2} + \frac{D_3}{(1+i)^3} + \frac{P_3}{(1+i)^3}$$

$$P = \frac{\$2.10}{(1+0.04)^1} + \frac{\$2.20}{(1+0.04)^2} + \frac{\$2.32}{(1+0.04)^3} + \frac{\$50.40}{(1+0.04)^3}$$

$$= \$2.02 + \$2.04 + \$2.06 + \$44.80$$

$$= \$50.92.$$

This amount, $50.92, represents the current intrinsic value of this stock under the conditions defined above. Since the current market value is $40, it is a good buy. This example is oversimplified so that the analogy between common stock valuation and bond valuation can be seen more easily. The obvious difficulties in using this approach are not the mathematics (computers can solve these problems with ease) but rather those of determining future dividend payments and a future sale price. There is naturally some error in making these judgments. However, most all investment decisions are of necessity based upon judgments.

The above present value model can be used in several different ways. One could assume that the market price of the stock was expected to advance only 6 percent per year, or that dividends would remain constant at $2, or that they would decline. One could assume a longer holding period. As the basic assumptions change, the intrinsic or present value will change. These models are often used by assuming the worst possible future events and the best possible future events; this results in a high and low present value for the stock and gives the investor a somewhat better idea of the relative current price of the stock based upon different future expectations.

PROBLEMS

1. As a project, consult Standard & Poor's *Annual Dividend Record* and obtain names of several firms which paid stock dividends during the preceding year. Devise a test to determine whether the stock dividends had an effect on the market price of the securities chosen.
2. What would be the value of a common stock that promised to pay a dividend of $3 per year for the foreseeable future if the next best investment alternative yielded 9 percent per year?

3. In 1974, the XYZ Company earned $5 per share. Stocks of similar companies are selling at P/E ratios of 15:1. What is the maximum amount per share you would pay for this security on the basis of the above facts? What other important things would you wish to consider?
4. Choose two companies in different industries. From newspapers or investment manuals compute the P/E ratios for these companies over the past several years. Try to relate changes and absolute differences in these P/E ratios to such things as the degree of risk (grade) of each security, the growth in profits of each company, and any other factors considered important. Is one security a "better buy" than the other? If so, why?
5. Use the valuation formula contained in this chapter to derive an intrinsic value for a common stock under the following conditions. The normal earnings per share are $2 per year. Earnings have increased at a rate of 5 percent and are expected to increase at that rate into the foreseeable future. The current Aaa bond interest rate is 8 percent. The company traditionally pays dividends of 20 cents per quarter.

QUESTIONS

1. Compare the important characteristics of bonds and common stock.
2. What legal rights do most states grant owners of common stock?
3. What is the meaning of *par value* as it relates to common stock?
4. What is the usual dividend payment procedure?
5. What value does a stock dividend have for shareholders?
6. What are the main differences between *stock dividends* and *splits?*
7. Why cannot common stocks be graded as accurately as bonds?
8. What is the difference between *market value* and *intrinsic value?*
9. Under what conditions would book value be a good approximation of market value?
10. How is the capitalization rate related to the grade of a stock?
11. "Stocks selling at above average P/E ratios should never be purchased by the cautious investor." Discuss this statement.
12. How do *market factors* cause stock prices to change?
13. Why is the present value approach to stock valuation an improvement over any other method?
14. What cautions are in order when using any stock valuation model?

SELECTED READINGS

Christy, George A. and Clendenin, John C. *Introduction to Investments,* 6th ed. New York: McGraw-Hill, 1974.

Cohen, Jerome B.; Zinbarg, Edward D.; and Zeikel, Arthur. *Investment Analysis and Portfolio Management,* rev. ed. Homewood, Ill.: Richard D. Irwin, 1973.

D'Ambrosio, Charles A. *A Guide to Successful Investing.* Englewood Cliffs, N.J.: Prentice-Hall, 1970.

Fisher, Lawrence, and Lorie, James H. *Rates of Return on Investments in Common Stocks.* Chicago: University of Chicago, Graduate School of Business, Center for Research in Security Prices.

Francis, J. C. *Investments: Analysis and Management.* New York: McGraw-Hill, 1972.

Graham, Benjamin. *The Intelligent Investor.* New York: Harper & Row, 1973.

Graham, Benjamin; Dodd, David L.; and Cottle, Sidney. *Security Analysis: Principles and Techniques,* 4th ed. New York: McGraw-Hill, 1962.

"New York Stock Exchange, 1974 Census of Share Owners." New York Stock Exchange, 1975.

Sauvain, Harry C. *Investment Management,* 4th ed. Englewood Cliffs, N.J.: Prentice-Hall, 1973.

Shade, Paul A. *Common Stocks: A Plan for Intelligent Investing.* Homewood, Ill.: Richard D. Irwin, 1971.

Vaughn, Donald E. *Survey of Investments,* 2d ed. New York: Holt, Rinehart and Winston, 1974.

Wendt, Paul F. "Current Growth Stock Valuation Methods," *Financial Analysts Journal,* March–April 1965.

11

Investing in Investment Companies

INTRODUCTION

An *investment company* is any of several types of companies which are formed for the purpose of acquiring and managing a portfolio of investment securities. Owners of the investment companies provide the capital to purchase these securities and receive the benefit of their ownership. There are two main types of investment companies in the United States. By any measure, the more important of these is the *open-end investment company,* or *mutual fund* as they are usually called. Second in importance is the *closed-end investment company.* Other kinds of investment companies exist, but compared to these two they are relatively unimportant. Figure 11–1 shows the growth in assets of investment companies since 1940.

CLOSED-END INVESTMENT COMPANIES

Closed-end investment companies first appeared on the American investment scene in the 1920s. These early investment companies closely resembled regular industrial corporations in that the capital structure of the company was often made up of bonds, preferred stock, and common stock. The term *closed-end* refers to the fact that, like a regular corporation, once the capital structure of the company was set, it could only be changed by issuing or retiring securities, or retaining earnings. While it was legal to change the size of these companies through these methods, in practice this was rarely done. Conse-

FIGURE 11–1
Growth in Investment Company Assets

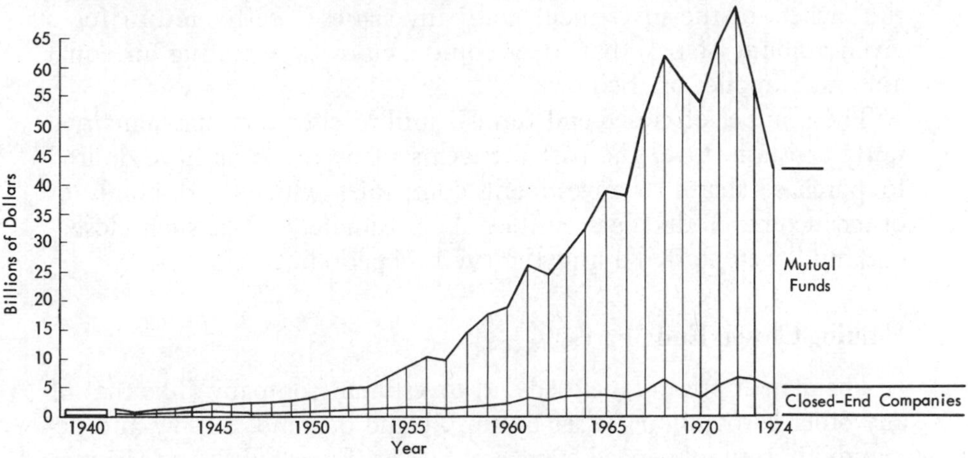

Source: *Arthur Wiesenberger Financial Services*, New York, 1975.

quently, these companies were closed-ended in that they were not expected to increase the amount of their capital stock from what it was when the company was organized. Table 11–1 presents a simplified balance sheet of Lehman Corporation, a large closed-end investment company representative of thc type first organized in this country.

In a conventional company, profits come from the difference between sales revenues and the costs incurred in obtaining these revenues. Closed-end investment company profits can come only from the interest, dividends, or capital gains on the securities that this

TABLE 11–1
Lehman Corporation Balance Sheet December 31, 1974 (amounts rounded to thousands)

Assets	
Cash in bank, receivables, other assets	$ 1,892
Short-term securities	46,250
Investment in other securities	324,571
Total Assets	$372,713
Liabilities, Capital, and Surplus	
Liabilities	$ 35,165
Capital stock (31,353,275 shares of $1 par stock outstanding, 40,000,000 shares authorized.)	31,353
Surplus	306,195
Total liabilities, capital, and surplus	$372,713

Source: The Lehman Corporation 1974 Annual Report.

company holds. Managing these closed-end investment companies consists of purchasing and selling securities which will hopefully give the owners of the investment company shares a better return for a given amount of risk than they could obtain by investing an equal amount of money on their own.

The number of closed-end funds, until recent years, has remained fairly constant. Over the past few years many investors have desired to purchase shares of investment companies which held bonds or other income producing securities. Approximately 40 of such closed-end funds were started during the 1970–74 period.

Valuing Closed-End Shares

The market price of a closed-end investment company (like that of any other corporation) is set by supply and demand. Supply and demand is in turn influenced by several factors. Expected future earnings and dividends are of great importance, but net asset value per share is also a determinant of market price.

Net asset value of investment companies is computed by summing the market price of all assets and by deducting all liabilities from this amount. The remaining amount is divided by the number of outstanding common shares to provide *net asset value* per share. The net asset value of Lehman Corporation shares is

$$\begin{aligned} \text{Net asset value} &= \text{Assets less liabilities/Shares outstanding} \\ &= \$372{,}713{,}000 - \$35{,}165{,}000/31{,}353{,}000 \\ &= \$10.77 \end{aligned}$$

Since securities are not continuously redeemed, shareholders of closed-end investment companies cannot obtain the net asset value of their shares unless the company is liquidated. Nevertheless increases and decreases in this value have an effect upon the market prices of all closed-end shares. Over the long run, market prices seem to increase when net asset value increases and vice versa. At any given time, market prices may be above or below net asset value. These premiums and discounts are caused by current security market conditions, expected future earnings of the company, and the many other things which affect stock values.

OPEN-END INVESTMENT COMPANIES

As Figure 11–1 indicates, open-end investment companies have nearly dominated the scene so far as investments of this type are concerned since 1940. While these companies closely resemble closed-end companies, there are differences in their operations which readily explain why this type of company has become so important. Table 11–2 shows a simplified balance sheet of Eaton and Howard Balanced Fund, a large, well-known open-end investment company. One can see that this balance sheet looks much like that of the Lehman Corporation. The company's capital ($102,847,000) has been provided by the shareholders or through additions to surplus due to profitable operations.

TABLE 11–2
Eaton and Howard Balanced Fund Balance Sheet for December 31, 1974 (dollar amounts rounded to thousands)

Assets	
Cash in bank, receivables, other assets	$ 1,971
Investments at market value	101,591
Total assets	$103,562
Liabilities and Shareholders' Equity	
Liabilities	$ 715
Net assets applicable to outstanding capital shares (14,778,924) shares of $0.50 par value outstanding)	102,847
Total liabilities and shareholders' equity	$103,562

Source: *Eaton and Howard Balanced Fund 43rd Annual Report 1974.*

The most important difference in these companies cannot be seen by looking at a single balance sheet. The closed-end investment company is restricted in the amount of its capital stock to the initial amount authorized and sold. The open-end company may increase its capitalization by selling more shares of its capital stock. This is an extremely important difference because it enables the company to become larger as more persons purchase its shares.

Net Asset Value of Mutual Funds

The net asset value of a share of stock in a mutual fund is of far more importance to the investor than is the net asset value of a share in a closed-end company. This is because these companies offer to sell or buy their shares on the basis of current net asset value. This value is computed in the following way for the Eaton and Howard fund.

Market value of all assets 12/31/1974	$103,561,704
Less all liabilities	– 714,911
Equals the net asset value of the company	$102,846,793

Net asset value per share = Net asset value/Number of shares outstanding
= \$102,846,793/14,778,924
= \$6.96 per share.

On the date of this balance sheet, this company offered to sell its shares on the basis of the net asset value per share—\$6.96—plus commissions, or to buy its shares at \$6.96.

The thing to be emphasized is that it is *net asset value* rather than supply and demand factors which determines the market price of mutual fund shares. In fact, shares of mutual funds are not traded on the securities exchanges. These firms sell new shares directly to investors and repurchase all shares offered for sale.

Investment policies, even the individual investments, of a closed-end and open-end company might be identical. However, the open-end company has the ability to sell and redeem its shares. These companies provide shareowners with a wide variety of services and accounts not provided by the closed-end companies. This is one reason for the rapid growth of these funds. Another very important reason is that there is incentive for these companies to continue to market their securities in a most aggressive fashion. As will be explained later, the managers of mutual funds, like those of closed-end funds, receive a fee for managing the assets of the company.

Regulation of Investment Companies

Investment companies which have chosen to be regulated under the terms of the Investment Company Act of 1940 are known as *regulated investment companies*. These companies are also regulated under the Securities Act of 1933 and the Securities Exchange Act of 1934, as are all corporations which sell securities publicly to residents of at least two states. These laws affect investment companies mainly in that they require them to register issues of their stock with the SEC. Registration of these securities may be blocked by the SEC if it is determined that the company has made erroneous, misleading, or incomplete statements about itself. Investment companies, like other corporations, must provide prospectuses to persons interested in purchasing new issues of their shares.

The Investment Company Act of 1940 was designed specifically to cause changes in the way investment companies were managed. Companies were required to include outside (presumably independent) persons on their boards of directors. Each board was then required to pass upon contracts which the company made with certain other businesses or individuals. The purpose of this legislation was to keep the investment companies from giving management, brokerage, or other contracts to persons or firms which did not fully warrant receiving the contracts. The regulation also forced companies to provide a certain minimum amount of diversification of assets. No more than 5 percent of a regulated company's assets may be invested in the securities of a single company. Finally, the act limited the maximum amount of leverage that a regulated investment company could have in its capital structure. Regulated open-end companies could have no financial leverage. Regulated closed-end companies were allowed to issue only limited amounts of bonds or preferred stock.

Most investment companies choose to become regulated under the 1940 act because of the special tax advantages offered to regulated companies. While the law is complex, the theory it follows is simple. Regulated investment companies are seen as being *conduits* through which income passes to their shareholders. So long as the investment company meets certain minimum tests as stated in the act, it pays no income taxes. However, dividends received by investment company shareholders are taxed as income.[1]

An investment company that is regulated is not necessarily a "safe" or a "good" company. The regulation, like other security laws, is designed to provide investors with enough facts to make intelligent decisions and to protect them from fraud. Managers of investment companies can still make poor investment decisions; shareholders can and do lose money on these investments. There is no doubt, however, that investment company shares are much safer now than they were before this federal legislation was passed. Figure 11–2 is a copy of a mutual fund share. Note how closely it resembles a regular common stock certificate.

OPERATION OF A MUTUAL FUND

As was indicated previously, there are two different types of investment companies. They operate in a very similar manner except for the way their shares are sold and repurchased. This section emphasizes the operation of a mutual fund because the shares of these organizations are owned by such a large number of investors.

[1] Tax treatment of mutual fund dividends is examined later in this chapter.

FIGURE 11–2
A Share of Mutual Fund Stock

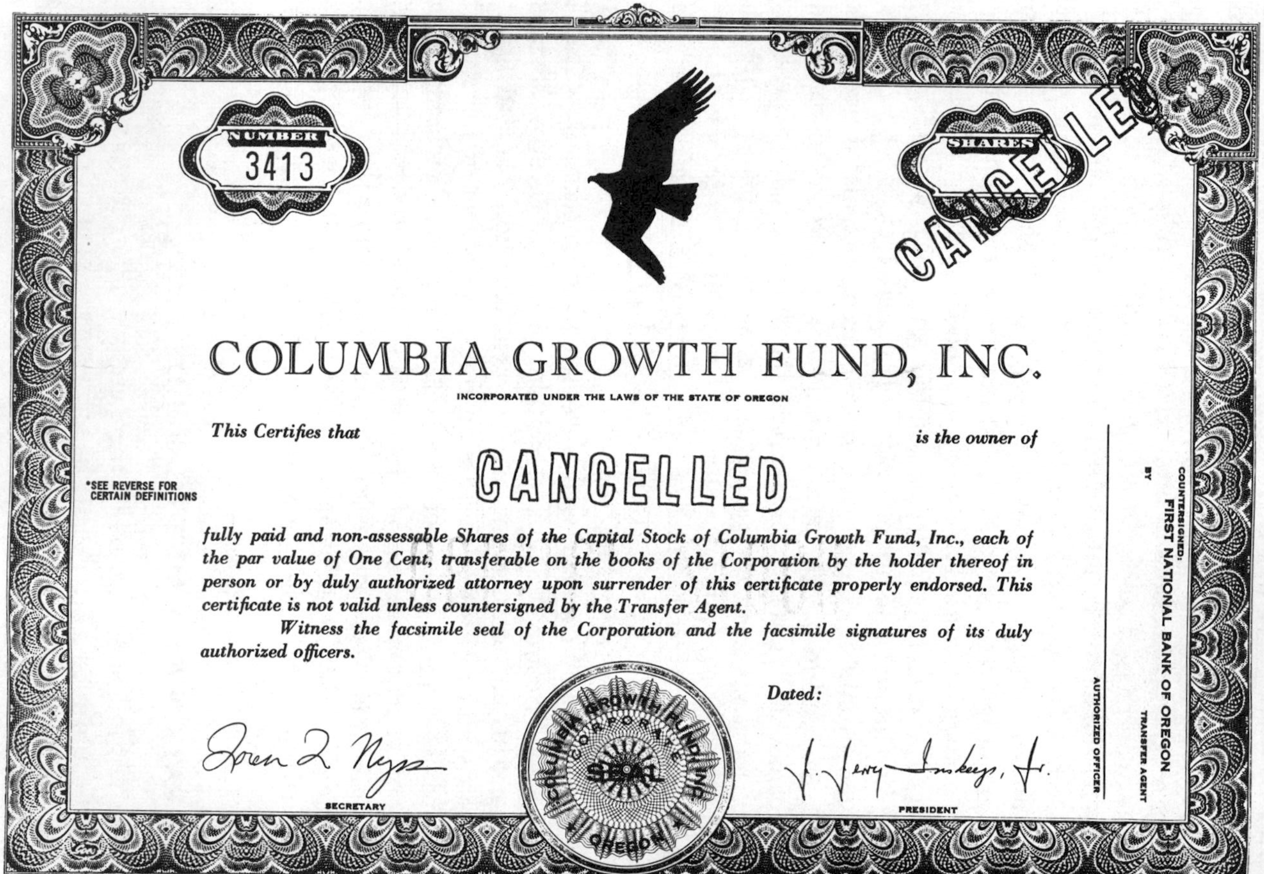

Courtesy of Columbia Growth Fund, Inc.

Custodian, Transfer Agent, and Registrar

These institutions perform the same services for the mutual fund (or the closed-end investment company) as they do for other corporations. The *custodian* holds the assets of the company, which are mainly in the form of investment securities, and guards them against theft or loss from any other cause.

The *transfer agent* accounts for the changes of ownership in the company's shares and makes certain that the shares it transfers are genuine.

The *registrar* is an officer of a trust company or commercial bank which is independent of the investment company and the transfer agent. This person's job is to make certain that the transfer agent's efforts have been diligent and that no unauthorized stock is issued by the investment company.

Investment Advisor

In order for an investment company to be successful over the long run, it must be able to invest its owners' money in a more productive fashion than they themselves could do. Excellent investment management can do this, or so we are told by the managements of all mutual funds. The investment advisor provides the advice which determines which securities the mutual fund will purchase and sell. The advisor is paid a fee for this service.

Often the advisor company (usually another corporation) is controlled by the same persons who manage or control the mutual fund. It is sometimes difficult to determine where a given person's responsibilities end as a fund manager and where they begin as an investment advisor. The investment advisor company is employed by contract, a contract which has been passed upon by the stockholder owners of the mutual fund. This contract can be terminated if the management of the mutual fund is sufficiently unhappy with the advice it has been receiving.

Securities Broker

The broker enters into the mutual fund scene at several points. Some of the very large funds have representatives who sell their securities exclusively, but the majority of mutual fund shares are sold by brokers who have wide discretion as to which fund's shares they sell.

In theory the independent broker merely takes orders for the securities which a customer wishes to purchase, for the broker has no financial stake in the transaction other than receipt of a commission.

As a practical matter, most of the large brokerage houses have agreements (formal or informal) to sell the shares of certain mutual funds. The ties between brokerage and investment companies are the result of two things: Many brokerage companies underwrite and distribute the shares of selected mutual funds. While their companies may be allowed to sell the shares of other mutual funds, their sales effort will usually be directed toward "their" company or companies. The shares of these companies may not have the most appropriate investment characteristics for a given investor, but they may be purchased because of ignorance of alternatives.

A less formal tie is created between brokerage houses and investment companies because mutual fund companies generally are not members of stock exchanges. This forces the mutual fund to place buy and sell orders with brokers who execute these orders for them.

The commission income generated by a large mutual fund is enormous. Since the fund's management has complete discretion as to which broker it will use when trading securities, and since each brokerage house has great discretion over which mutual fund shares it will sell most aggressively, the stage is set for a system of mutual accommodation. The broker sells the shares of certain mutual funds, and in return, is awarded some of the security purchase and sale orders of these companies. There is nothing illegal in this arrangement, but it may not result in the lowest brokerage costs for the fund. Of perhaps more importance to the investor is the inability to obtain objective advice about mutual funds from a broker whose company is emphasizing the sale of securities of a limited number of funds.

The Mutual Fund

The fund itself is the corporation in which the purchaser of mutual fund shares invests money.[2] This corporation is the legal owner of the investment securities and other assets which are purchased through the sale of its shares to the public. Managers of mutual funds spend much time marketing their company's securities. This effort includes preparation of promotional literature, hiring and instructing sales

---

[2] Some mutual funds are organized in the legal form known as a Massachusetts trust. From the investor's viewpoint there is no significant difference between this and the corporate form.

personnel, making sales agreements with brokerage companies, and devising mutual fund plans which have appeal for large numbers of investors. These companies must also handle the many details of share reinvestment, dividend payments, investment policies, and all the record keeping involved in operating this kind of business. The fund receives a great amount of aid from the investment advisor, accountants, the trustee, and all the other related parties, but it is the management of the fund which is responsible for the operation of the company and its success or failure.

ADVANTAGES AND DISADVANTAGES OF PURCHASING INVESTMENT COMPANY SHARES

For many investors there are definite advantages to be obtained from investment company shares. In this part of the chapter we shall look carefully at the individual characteristics of investment company shares and examine them under the general format of risk and return. In this way these investments may be judged against the alternative investment opportunities discussed elsewhere in this book.

Professional Investment Management

At the time of this writing there are in operation about 600 mutual funds and about 50 actively traded closed-end funds. All these companies are supposedly operated so as to attain a specific goal or goals for their owners, and all companies list professional management as one of their strengths.

Professional management implies that the investment company can manage the investor's money better than the individual, assuming that the goals of each are similar. Making any sort of scientific test of whether investment companies are in fact more successful investors than individuals is very difficult. An investment company having very successful investment performance in the past will not necessarily have the same success in the future, and one which has done poorly in the past may have great success in future years. The topic of measuring performance will be examined in detail later in this chapter. At this point it is sufficient to state that for the person who knows little about investments, or has limited time to manage them, the professional management offered by the investment company is probably valuable.

Diversification

A diversified investment company is one which spreads the risk associated with the purchase of investments among many different holdings. It is difficult for an individual to do this unless substantial money is available to invest. If a person had $10,000 to invest, and wanted to invest it in such a way as to obtain the same amount of diversification as would be provided through purchase of shares in a regulated investment company, at least 20 different securities would have to be purchased. A maximum dollar amount of $500 could be invested in each security, as no more than 5 percent of the total investment could be in any one form. These purchases would probably be of odd lots of securities, and commission charges would be high. Perhaps of more importance is the problem of managing 20 different investments. This large number of different securities would take a great deal of time—if they were adequately managed. Few people have the necessary time to devote to this task.

Diversification may take many forms. Bonds, preferred stocks, and common stocks may be purchased to provide diversified types of securities. Diversification may be by industry. To do this, investments are made in several different industries, perhaps in accordance with some predetermined formula for spreading investments among the companies of certain industries. Diversification may be geographical; investments are purchased in companies located in many different parts of the United States or the world. Diversification may be performed by purchasing securities of many different companies which are in the same type of business.

There are other ways that diversification can be carried out, but the goal is the same in every case: It is to spread risk over a large number of different investments so that it becomes nearly impossible for the investor to have exceptionally poor investment results. Diversification usually does protect the investor against worse than average investment experience. But while it is protecting against loss, it is also "protecting" the investor against better-than-average experience. Because of this, a well-diversified investment company has great difficulty in performing much better than the stock market averages, even though the company has professional investment management.

In the late 1960s a new concept of investment company appeared. These companies were formed to provide investment *performance*, not diversification and safety. The strategy was to not diversify, but rather to concentrate investments in a relatively few companies which have great growth potential. The professional management of these companies supposedly offsets the risk that one takes when investments are not diversified. More will be said about this type of fund when we discuss some of the different types of investment policies followed by various investment companies.

PURCHASES AND SALES OF INVESTMENT COMPANY SHARES

Closed-End Companies

Recall that the price of closed-end shares is set by supply and demand, with some regard to the net asset value of the stock. *The Wall Street Journal* reports the weekly closing price of these securities each Monday in the format shown in Figure 11–3. Other financial news services carry the same information.

The *net asset value* of these companies is always published (N.A. Value), but the price at which stock is traded is listed in the third column under the abbreviation "Stk Price." Commission charges would be added to this amount if you were buying these securities; if you were selling, the commission would be deducted from the price. Commissions are computed in exactly the same way that they are computed for any other common stock because these securities are sold through brokers like any other stock. The percent-difference column tells the percentage that the stock price differs from the stock's net asset value.

Mutual Fund Shares

Mutual fund shares are not sold like other securities. The mutual fund company agrees to redeem shares in the company on any business day. At least twice each business day the net asset value of the company's shares is computed. It is at this net asset value that the shares are redeemed. Some mutual funds charge a modest amount for the privilege of redemption, but this is unusual.

Mutual fund share prices are quoted by nearly every newspaper in the United States because so many people own these investments. The list in Figure 11–4 contains only a part of the several hundred shares which are reported on a daily basis in *The Wall Street Journal*.

Mutual Fund Commissions. The *net asset value* (NAV) listed in Figure 11–4 is the value per share at the close of trading. The *offering*

FIGURE 11–3
Closed-End Fund Prices

Closed-End Funds

January 17, 1975

Following is a weekly listing of unaudited net asset values of closed-end investment fund shares, reported by the companies as of Friday's close. Also shown is the closing listed market price or a dealer-to-dealer asked price of each fund's shares, with the percentage of difference.

	N.A. Value	Stk Price	% Diff
Diversified Common Stock Funds			
bAdmExp	10.57	8¾	−17.2
Advance	9.24	8½	− 8.0
Carriers	12.80	10¾	−16.0
CentSec	5.73	3½	−38.9
GenAInv	9.98	8⅛	−18.4
IntlHold	11.14	7	−37.2
Lehman	10.62	9½	−10.5
Madison	10.84	7⅞	−27.4
NiagaraSh	11.48	12	+ 4.5
OseasSec	3.29	2¼	−46.2
Tri-Contl	18.86	17	− 9.9
United	8.79	6½	−26.1
US&For	15.88	13⅜	−15.8
Specialized Equity and Convertible Funds			
AmGenCv	15.36	16⅛	+ 5.0
ASA	z	z	z
BakerFen	40.04	19	−52.6
BancrftCv	16.59	12¾	−23.1
BayrckUt	10.43	9	−13.1
Castle	15.76	12¾	−19.1
ChaseCvB	8.72	8½	− 2.6
CLIC	(−5.99)	15	.....
Diebold	6.70	2⅛	−68.2
DrexelUt	15.32	15⅛	− 1.8
Japan	9.19	6⅝	−27.9
KeysnOTC	6.34	4½	−29.2
NatlAvia	13.50	9⅜	−30.6

	N.A. Value	Stk Price	% Diff
NewAmFd	9.65	5⅜	−44.3
bPetroCp	18.18	17	− 6.5
REITIncC	1.35	2	+48.1
S-GSecInc	1.11	2	+80.2
Source	14.00	7¾	−44.6
StdSh	18.10	11⅝	−35.8
VtLnDvCp	4.59	1½	−67.3
Bond Funds			
AmGnBnd	20.90	23⅞	+14.2
BunkerHill	20.80	21	+ 1.0
CNAIncSh	11.78	11½	− 2.4
aCurrentI	11.44	11	− 3.9
bDrexelBd	16.99	16¾	− 1.4
bExcelsior	19.42	18¼	− 6.0
FtDearInc	15.03	14¾	− 1.9
INAIncS	18.12	17¾	− 2.0
IndSqls	16.77	17¼	+ 2.9
JHanI	20.12	20½	+ 1.9
bJHanSc	15.40	16⅞	+ 9.6
Hatteras	15.45	16⅞	+ 9.2
MMIncInv	12.03	11¾	− 2.3
MntgSt	20.96	21¾	+ 3.8
MuOmaha	14.32	15	+ 4.7
bPacAmI	13.16	13¼	− 6.8
StPaulS	11.27	11⅜	+ 0.9
StateMSec	11.17	11	− 1.5
S-PIncS	20.08	22½	+12.1
USLIFE	8.58	9¾	+15.6

a-As of 1-14-75. b-Ex-dividend. z-Not Available.

Source: *The Wall Street Journal*, January 20, 1975 p. 17.

price (Off. Prc.)—is the price at which the company offers shares for sale. The difference between the NAV and the offering price is the amount of the maximum commission. It is usually between 7½ and 8½ percent of the NAV.

The mutual fund industry has come under criticism for these seemingly high commissions. While most funds have a scale of commission charges which is graduated down from the maximum rates, the graduation usually begins with purchases of $10,000 or $15,000. Of particular objection to many persons is the way commissions are assessed on contractual plans. These mutual fund purchase plans obligate the purchaser to buy shares over an extended period of time. The purchaser usually pays for the shares each month and does not obtain full ownership of the plan until all payments are made. A

FIGURE 11–4
Mutual Fund Prices

Mutual Funds

Friday, January 17, 1975

Price ranges for investment companies, as quoted by the National Association of Securities Dealers. NAV stands for net asset value per share; the offering includes net asset value plus maximum sales charge, if any.

	NAV	Off. Prc.	NAV Chg.
Ad Gwth	3.11	3.41–	.02
Adm Incm	2.91	3.18	...
Adm Insur	5.84	6.40–	.06
Adviser Fd	3.38	3.69+	.01
Aetna Fnd	5.25	5.74–	.04
Aetna InSh	11.16	12.20	...
Afutur (v)	5.05	5.05–	.02
AGE Fund	3.61	3.68–	.05
Allstate	7.03	7.56–	.10
Alpha Fnd	8.03	8.78–	.10
Amcap Fd	3.24	3.54	...
Am Birthrt	9.86	10.84	...
AmDiv Inv	6.27	6.85–	.06
Am Equity	3.39	3.72–	.04
American Express Funds:			
Capital	4.39	4.80–	.08
Income	7.08	7.74–	.02
Invest	6.09	6.66–	.04
Spec Fnd	4.20	4.59–	.06
Stock Fd	5.14	5.62–	.07
Am Grwth	3.62	3.96–	.02
Am Ins Ind	3.67	4.01+	.02
AmInv (v)	3.57	3.57–	.04
Am Mutual	6.70	7.32–	.05
AmNat Gw	1.71	1.87–	.01
Anchor Group:			
Daily Inc	1.00	1.00	...
Growth	4.98	5.46–	.09
Income	5.90	6.47–	.02
Reserv	10.04	11.00	...
Spectm	3.00	3.29–	.04
Fund Inv	5.09	5.58–	.08
Wa Natl	7.42	8.13–	.15
Audax Fnd	4.58	5.01	...
Beacnl (v)	7.83	7.83–	.05
Berksh Gw	2.37	2.59–	.04
BndFd Am	13.88	15.17	...
Bondsk Cp	3.51	3.84–	.03
Bos Found	7.06	7.72–	.09
Brown Fnd	(z)	(z)	(z)
Burnm (v)	7.62	7.62–	.05
Calvin Bullock Funds:			
Bullock	9.25	10.13–	.07
Canadn	8.34	9.13–	.03
Div Shrs	2.38	2.61–	.02
Ntwide	7.70	8.43–	.02
NY Vent	8.24	9.02–	.10
C G Fund	6.81	7.36–	.09
CG Inc Fd	7.41	8.01–	.03
Cap Presv	94.02	94.02+	.02
Century Sh	8.51	9.30–	.08
Chalng Inv	7.13	7.79–	.05
Channing Funds:			
Amercn	.95	1.04–	.01
Balanc	7.53	8.23–	.05
Bond Fd	7.52	8.22+	.02
Eqty Gth	5.22	5.70–	.08
Eqty Prg	1.89	2.07–	.02
Fnd Amr	5.14	5.62–	.08
Growth	3.25	3.55–	.05
Income	5.49	6.00–	.01
Prov Inc	2.96	3.23–	.01
Special	1.09	1.19–	.01
Venture	4.99	5.45–	.08
Charter Fd	7.77	8.49–	.08
Chase Group of Boston:			
Fnd Bost	4.75	5.19–	.04
Front Cp	3.04	3.32–	.03

z—Quote not available. v-Net asset value. x-Ex-dividend. r-Ex-rights. d-Ex-Distribution a-Funds redemption price.

Source: *The Wall Street Journal,* January 20, 1975 p. 18.

disproportionate share of the total sales commissions may be collected from the early payments. This procedure is called the front-end load.

Commissions decline in the second, third, and later years of the plans. The higher commissions of the early years are offset by the lowered commissions of later years. A problem arises when a person starts one of these plans and then drops out (as one legally may). In this situation as much as 20 percent of the first year's investment may go to sales commissions.

Some mutual fund companies sell several different funds. Many of these companies allow owners of shares in one fund to trade these shares for an equal dollar amount of one of the other funds. Most companies allow this type of switch without any commission charge, or with a small "bookkeeping" charge.

Some mutual funds charge lower commissions to persons who sign a letter of intent to buy a substantial dollar amount of securities over a specified period of time. These purchasers pay commissions at the rate that they would have paid if they had purchased the total amount of securities all at one time. This way, the total commission on the purchase may be lower than it would have been if the securities had been purchased piecemeal. These and other features of mutual fund purchase plans may serve to lower the commission charge for some purchasers, but on the whole these charges remain substantial.

For several years the Securities and Exchange Commission has sponsored legislation which would lower mutual fund commission charges and do away with the front-end loading of commissions. In addition, suggestions have been made for a maximum commission of 5 percent, with lower rates on larger purchases. While no legislation has been passed which limits mutual fund commissions, there are more funds being sold which charge no commissions. Recent changes in the commission structure of common stock purchases and sales have generally acted to increase the commissions on small trades. For example, under the newest commission schedules it costs about $60 or 6 percent to buy and sell $1,000 of common stock. The narrowing of the commission charges between mutual fund shares and small purchases of common stock will probably cause some persons to shift from direct stock investments to mutual funds.

No-Load Funds

Some mutual funds charge no sales commissions—Afutur and American Investing for example (see Figure 11–4). These are *no-load funds,* and the bid and ask prices of these securities are identical. No-load funds are usually sold directly to the purchaser by the fund. The sales effort of these companies is not at all aggressive, and for this reason these funds have not expanded in size nearly so rapidly as those which sell through brokers and charge commissions on all securities sold. To purchase these securities, the investor must usually use some personal initiative. The best sources of information on these companies are *Investment Companies*, *FundScope*, *Forbes*, and the financial press.

Most no-load funds do not offer the wide variety of purchase options and accounts commonly available at other funds. They all do allow an investor to start off with 100 percent of his or her money invested, which should result in a larger return on the total amount invested—all other things being equal.

All other things are seldom equal, of course, and it is impossible to say whether an investor is better advised to purchase a no-load or another company. An interesting study recently conducted by *Fund-Scope*, a company which publishes investment company news, concluded that there was no correlation between commission charges or lack of charges and fund performance.[3] Their advice was to buy shares on the basis of the fund's objective and its past performance.

INCOME FROM MUTUAL FUND SHARES

Mutual funds usually do not pay taxes on their income. They pass it through the company to the fund's owners in the form of dividends. Recipients must report the dividends as income on their federal and state income tax forms. Taxes are paid on these dividends in the year they are declared, even if all dividend payments are retained in the funds and used to purchase additional shares.

Dividends are usually paid quarterly. At the end of the year, the mutual fund is required to present each shareholder with a statement, such as that presented in Figure 11–5, which tells the amount and type of dividends the investor has received during the year.

Gross dividends are the total dividends that have been paid to the shareholder. *Dividends qualifying for exclusion* are those paid from income that came to the investment company in the form of dividends from other corporations. Taxpayers should list these dividends along with other dividend income on their tax returns. The "qualifying for exclusion" phrase refers to the fact that $100 of dividend income is currently exempted from federal income taxes. This amount may be as high as $200 for married persons filing joint returns.[4]

Dividends not qualifying for exclusion are dividends on income

[3] "No Load Funds vs. Load Funds," *FundScope*, 18, no. 1 (January 1975), p. 33 ff.

[4] See Chapter 13, Tax Aspects of Investments, for a fuller explanation of the taxation of dividend income. Dividends entered in Figure 11–5 are carried through the tax recording procedure to the final income tax form in this chapter.

FIGURE 11–5
Income Tax Form for Reporting Mutual Fund Dividends

Statement for Recipients of
Dividends and Distributions 1974

XYZ Mutual Fund

Copy B
For Recipient

Type or print PAYER'S Federal identifying number, name, address and ZIP code above.

1 Gross dividends and other distributions on stock (Total of boxes 2, 3, 4, and 5)	2 Dividends qualifying for exclusion	3 Dividends not qualifying for exclusion	4 Capital gain distributions	5 Nontaxable distributions (If determinable)	6 Foreign tax paid (Applicable only to taxes eligible for foreign tax credit)
$200.00	$100.00	-0-	$100.00	-0-	-0-

RECIPIENT'S identifying number ▶

7 Foreign Country or U.S. Possession

If this form shows two or more recipients, the recipient whose Federal identifying number is shown should file Form(s) 1087–DIV with the Internal Revenue Service for each of the other recipients and provide them with copies. However, a husband or wife is not required to file a Form 1087–DIV to show payments for the other.

This information is being furnished to the Internal Revenue Service and appropriate State officials.

Type or print RECIPIENT'S name, address and ZIP code above.

An "X" in the upper left corner indicates this is a corrected form.

Form **1099–DIV** ☆ GPO:1973—O-500-091 25-1116272 Department of the Treasury—Internal Revenue Service

that is taxable at ordinary rates. Income from interest payments and short-term security transactions are examples of this form of income. As the name indicates, these dividends are not eligible for exclusion under the dividend exemption.

Capital gain distributions are dividends from income generated by the sale of capital assets held for more than six months. This type of income is taxed at a lower rate than other income and is reported on a special schedule in the federal tax form.

Nontaxable distributions are dividends paid to the mutual fund from income that was not taxable. No one pays any tax on this income, but it must be reported.

The *foreign tax paid* column records the share of foreign taxes paid that are allocated to each shareholder.

Because of the several types of dividend distributions, it may seem that ownership of mutual fund shares has somehow complicated the tax position of the investor. This is not true. Ownership of these shares does not cause the investor to pay more or less taxes or have more or fewer types of income than would be the case if money had been invested directly in the same investments as were held by the fund. In fact, the records provided to investors by all mutual funds at year end actually simplify income tax preparation for most investors.

Taxation of closed-end investment company dividends usually follows the procedure outlined above. However, special benefits through ownership of shares of certain funds may be available to persons in the highest income tax brackets. These are special situations beyond the scope of this text.

TYPES OF MUTUAL FUND ACCOUNTS

In marketing their products, managers of mutual funds have followed the examples set by the life insurance industry. They offer prospective buyers many different payment plans and several choices of dividend distributions. In sharp contrast to this, purchasers of closed-end investment company shares normally pay cash for their shares and have no option on dividend distributions. These investments most nearly resemble the regular mutual fund account which pays out all dividends as they are obtained.

The Regular Account

This is the least complicated account sold by the mutual fund industry. Purchasers of these shares invest a certain amount of money (some funds have a minimum dollar amount of shares that they will sell) and receive a certain number of shares of stock in the fund. Investors make no agreement to purchase more shares of the fund, and dividends are disbursed periodically as they are realized. Income dividends are usually paid quarterly, and capital gains dividends annually.

Accumulation Plans

These plans are of two types—voluntary and contractual. Under a *voluntary accumulation plan* the investor begins by purchasing some modest dollar amount of investment company shares. This may be as low as $100; the minimum amount varies among mutual funds. At the time of this purchase the investor declares an intent to make future periodic purchases of a minimum amount. The regular commission is charged on each future purchase and the number of shares purchased is credited to the investor's account. These plans allow persons to acquire shares in small amounts as money becomes available. Many plans allow the purchase of fractional shares in this way. The investor has no legal liability to make the purchases he or she has agreed to make, and the account may be canceled and shares may be redeemed at their net asset value at any time.

The *contractual plan* differs from this one in that the agreement between the buyer and the mutual fund is much more formalized. When opening one of these plans the purchaser agrees to buy a certain dollar amount of mutual fund securities over a given period of time. Most of these plans run at least two years, often much longer. A popular investment goal is $10,000. The buyer signs an agreement to purchase a certain dollar amount of securities monthly, quarterly, or semiannually until the goal is reached.

There are many variations on this general type of investment. Some companies sell plan completion insurance which completes the plan as scheduled if the plan owner dies. Most of the plans allow the purchaser to have all dividends reinvested in additional shares of stock in the mutual fund. All these plans may be canceled by the purchaser at any time. Purchasers are allowed to miss payments or to make larger than agreed upon payments. Incentive to stay with the plan is provided by the fact that the commission charge on the entire plan is paid out of early payments. In return for this feature, some mutual funds charge a commission that is based upon the total dollar amount of the plan—if it is completed as scheduled. This commission may be at a lower rate than it would have been if the person had purchased the same dollar amount of shares in a voluntary accumulation plan. These are the most popular plans being sold.

Accounts with Automatic Dividend Reinvestment

The preceding discussion of types of mutual fund accounts was centered on *when* the purchaser paid for the shares and *whether* an agreement was made to purchase more of them in the future. Many, if not most, of these accounts have the feature of automatic dividend reinvestment and might well be classified with these plans in Figure 11–6.

Automatic dividend reinvestment means that the income or capital gain dividends of the fund, or both, are reinvested immediately in additional shares of stock of the mutual fund. The benefit from automatic reinvestment is similar to that received from compound interest. No dividends are received currently, but the new shares that are purchased with the reinvested dividends in turn receive dividends. Persons who do not need to receive current income from their mutual fund investments can accumulate more shares in the fund by reinvesting dividends.

Reinvestment of dividends may allow the investor to acquire more shares without paying the normal commissions. Reinvested income

FIGURE 11–6
Types of Shareholder Accounts (mutual funds 1960–74)

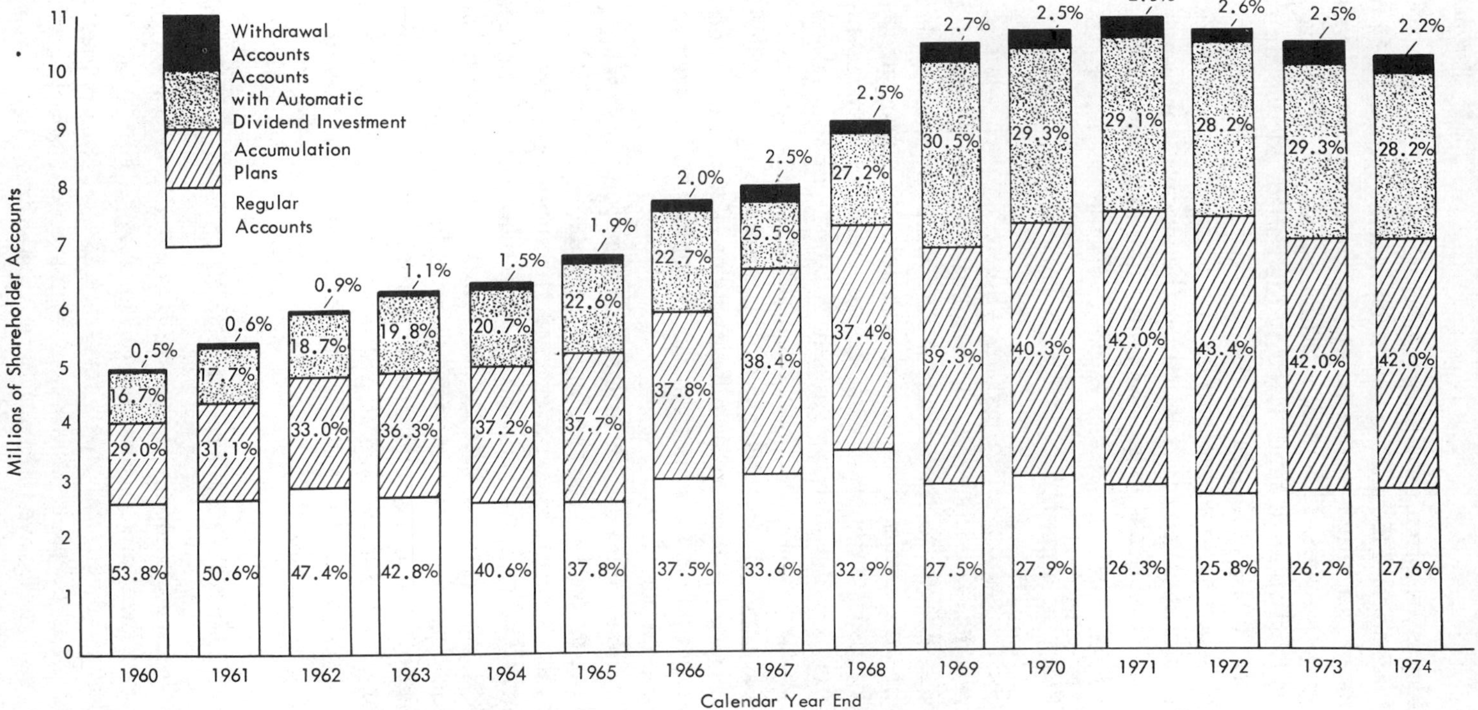

Source: *Arthur Weisenberger Financial Services*, New York, 1975.

dividends are often used to purchase additional shares at the current *offering price*. This price includes commission charges. Capital gains dividends are often reinvested at the current *net asset value* of the company's shares. This price includes no commission. The procedure varies from fund to fund. Even though all dividends are reinvested, they are taxed as income in the period in which they are declared. Later, when the investor redeems the account and takes possession of these securities, no tax is levied on the amount that was reinvested. No-load fund accounts usually allow automatic dividend investment.

Withdrawal Accounts

These plans appeal to persons who wish to receive a certain sum of cash regularly from their investments. Savings accounts which pay interest directly to the account holder and annuities sold by life insurance companies most nearly resemble this investment.

The usual withdrawal plan begins when an investor purchases a minimum dollar amount (usually $10,000) of mutual fund shares. These are normally purchased in a single transaction, although most mutual funds allow other types of accounts to be changed into withdrawal plans if they are of sufficient size. The mutual fund agrees to make periodic payments from the account to its owner or to other designated persons.

Payments will be made as long as the account has value. If the beginning amount of the account was large and the withdrawals small, or if the investment experience of the fund were exceptional, payments could be made indefinitely. This is usually not the case. Withdrawal payments are first made from dividend income, and if the dividends do not cover the withdrawal, the additional amount is obtained by redeeming fund shares. If a mutual fund has very poor investment experience, and if withdrawal payments are large relative to the size of the investment, the principal of the investment might be rapidly used up.

INVESTMENT POLICIES OF INVESTMENT COMPANIES

Investment company shares are purchased for a variety of reasons. Some of them are convenience of purchase, ability to sell shares immediately, diversification of investments, and professional management. It is probably professional management which attracts most people to these investments. There is widespread belief that management of money by a professional will produce greater returns than could be obtained if the investor had invested directly in securities. Whether or not professional management does provide greater profits is a topic for later discussion. The important thing now is to realize that investment companies, like individual investors, have different goals. The investor should first determine his or her own investment objectives. Then, if the purchase of investment company shares is desired, the shares of a company having an investment goal which parallels that of the investor should be purchased.

There were 431 open-end companies selling 586 different mutual funds and about 50 actively traded closed-end funds being sold in the United States as of year end 1974. These funds had a wide variety of investment objectives and policies. Every firm makes a statement of these policies and goals in its offering prospectus, a document easily obtained from the company or a broker. Classification of investment companies by stated objectives is done by several financial reporting services. Most all investment companies may be classified as one of the following types, although many of them have unique features. Table 11–3 shows the importance of these different types of funds.

Balanced Funds

The investment objective of these funds is long-term growth of both capital and income through purchase of bonds, preferred stocks, and

TABLE 11–3
Investment Companies Classified by Investment Objective (as of December 31, 1974)

Type of Fund	*Number of Funds*	*Combined Assets (000 omitted)*	*Percent Total*
Balanced	23	$ 4,014,400	10.4
Bond and/or preferred stock	27	1,212,800	3.1
Money market	19	2,384,600	6.2
Income	65	3,576,400	9.3
Tax-free exchange	14	547,200	1.4
Common stock:			
Specialized	26	530,600	1.4
Growth	170	10,754,100	28.0
Growth and income	103	11,845,400	30.7
Maximum capital gain	139	3,680,000	9.5
Total	586	$38,545,500	100.0

Note: These classifications were made by *Arthur Wiesenberger Financial Services* on the basis of the stated investment objectives of the funds.
Source: *Arthur Wiesenberger Financial Services*, New York, 1975.

common stocks. The term "balanced" comes from the policy followed by some of these companies of trying to "balance" portions of their investment portfolios among these different securities in some fairly constant proportions. While there is wide diversity in the performance of these funds, they are usually managed so that they offer shareholders both capital gains and dividend income. Price fluctuations of the net asset values, or market values in the case of closed-end companies, are usually less than most types of funds.

Bond and Preferred Stock Funds

As the name implies, the investments of these funds are all in senior securities. The specific investment objective of these funds varies mainly in its emphasis upon income and price stability. One could not reasonably expect anything but very modest capital gains distributions from this type fund. Share value should be fairly constant, except when changes in market interest rates cause changes in prices.

Money Market Funds

Money market or *liquidity* funds have greatly increased in number during recent years. These funds invest in short-term liquid debt securities—Treasury bills, bankers acceptances, commercial paper, and other such securities. They provide investors with a return that may be very high in periods when short-term interest rates are high. During such times these investments are more attractive than savings accounts because they pay a higher yield. Of course, as short-term interest rates decline the returns to these funds will also decline. Many of these funds are more liquid than savings accounts in that they allow owners to write checks against their accounts, or in other ways to quickly obtain funds. Money market fund securities cannot be expected to pay even modest capital gains dividends.

Income Funds

These funds emphasize liberal current income. This objective may be realized through purchase of bonds, preferred stock, or common stock. Most of these funds hold a variety of investments. One could expect greater than average price stability in the shares of these companies, high yearly income dividends, and low capital gains distributions. Neither this type nor the bond and preferred stock funds are very important when compared to the growth or capital gains oriented common stock funds. Many withdrawal plans are income funds.

Tax-Free Exchange Funds

Prior to 1967 investors had the opportunity to exchange shares of common stock for shares of these funds without paying capital gain taxes on the price increase of the stock. As an example, an investor having a large gain in common stock investments would be taxed upon these profits if the stock were *sold;* if the stock were *traded* for these mutual fund shares, no taxes would be levied until the mutual fund shares were sold. These funds had lists of shares acceptable for trading and were an important type of fund until these types of exchanges became taxable. The fund's shares are still sold and identified as tax-free fund shares even though they have no special tax features for investors purchasing them today.

Common Stock Funds

These funds invest only in common stocks or securities which are convertible into common stocks. This general classification includes the largest number of funds and is far and away the most popular kind of investment company in existence today. The objectives of these firms vary in the degree to which they seek dividend income or capital gains growth and in the way they go about attaining their investment objectives. Their shares would typically have less price stability than the shares of balanced funds, income funds, or those holding senior securities.

Specialized Common Stock Funds. These funds were organized with the objective of purchasing common stocks of firms engaged in a certain industry. They are offered as a way for investors to participate in the growth and profits of such industries as electronics, air travel, oceanography, and chemical. What diversification there is in the investment company's portfolio comes from purchasing the shares of different companies in a given industry.

Several funds invest only in the shares of companies located in certain countries, for example the Japan Fund. They diversify investments among different types of companies, but the companies are located in the same country. The philosophy of this type investment is to participate in the economic growth of a certain country. Investments may be in bonds or stock, although stock investments are emphasized.

Growth, Growth Income, and Capital Gains Funds

These titles serve to indicate that the investment objective of the fund is capital growth. The usual vehicle for this growth is investment in common stocks of smaller, less well-known companies. Some of these companies seek modest financial leverage by borrowing money to increase the fund's ability to purchase securities. Some of the funds diversify their investments, and some do not. It is very difficult to draw a line between this class of funds and the even more speculative ones next discussed. One should not expect much price stability in the shares of these companies or hardly any income dividends. Some of these funds have performed very well in rising markets; most of them have suffered substantial losses in share values in declining markets.

Hedge Funds, Special Situations Funds, and Others

Many of these companies were first organized as private investment trusts and were unregulated by the SEC or the 1940 Investments Company Act. Several are now public funds and generally available to all persons. They vary greatly in their investment objectives and in the way they are operated.

One thing that these companies have in common is that the investment manager has very wide discretion over the type of investments that the company purchases. Borrowing is often used to obtain financial leverage. Put and call options may be sold or purchased and securities may be sold short. (See Chapter 12 for a discussion of these kinds of investments.) Normally this type of company would have very little diversification in its investment portfolio. Investors in these funds could expect to receive income dividends only by accident, as the company will not be investing in securities of companies which emphasize payment of dividends or interest. The company may do a great amount of short-term trading of securities. Sometimes the fund's investment management contract specifies that the compensation of the manager is to be based upon the performance of the fund—low performance, low management fee, and high performance, high management fee. Persons investing in these companies must be willing to accept a great amount of price variability in their shares. Sharp losses or large gains may be incurred. During the 1973–74 market slump, securities of these funds performed far worse than average.

FIGURE 11–7
Prices of Dual Purpose Fund Shares

Dual Purpose Funds

Friday, January 17, 1975

Following is a weekly listing of the unaudited net asset values of dual-purpose, closed-end investment funds' capital shares as reported by the companies as of Friday's close. Also shown is the closing listed market price or the dealer-to-dealer asked price of each fund's capital shares, with the percentage of difference.

	Cap. Shs. Price	N.A. Val Cap. Shs.	% Diff.
Am DualVest	3	3.86	−22.2
Gemini	6⅞	8.83	−22.1
Hemisphere	1⅜	0.03	+4483.3
Income and Cap	3½	4.86	−28.0
Leverage	5¼	6.37	−17.7
Pegasus Inco&Cap	5⅛	0.98	+422.9
Putnam Duo Fund	2¾	3.08	−10.7
Scudder Duo-Vest	4⅝	6.02	−22.3
Scudder D-V Exch	14	17.85	−21.6

Lipper Analytical.

Source: *The Wall Street Journal*, January 20, 1975 p. 17.

Dual Purpose Funds

Another type of fund is the *dual purpose fund* (see Figure 11–7). The purpose of this closed-end fund is to provide a single investment opportunity for two different types of investors. To do this the fund sells two types of investment shares—income shares and capital shares. Income shares are purchased by persons seeking current investment income. The owners of these shares receive *all* the income from the entire investment portfolio. They are guaranteed a certain minimum annual dividend payment, and they normally receive the right to all income over this minimum that the company may earn. Holders of capital shares receive no dividends of any type. As the company realizes capital gains in its investment portfolio, these gains are reinvested in more assets.

The leverage in this investment comes from the fact that income and growth shares are initially sold in *equal dollar amounts*, but one class of shareholders obtains *all* the capital gains and the other *all* the income. As the asset value of the fund increases, the market price of both classes of stock should increase, although not necessarily at the same rate. However, the shares of capital stock are not redeemable at their net asset value until after the income shares have been called in. These funds began operations with a stated life of between 12 and 18 years. The market price of both classes of shares will be set by supply and demand over these years. Market prices may be above or below net asset values, depending upon how investors assess future prospects for the shares of the investment company.

Seven of the nine dual purpose funds listed in Figure 11–7 were started in 1967. Both classes of securities are callable, a feature which is necessary so that the funds can be liquidated and all the shareholders paid off at one time. The usual procedure will be to call both classes of stock and sell the assets of the fund at the same time. A specified amount (usually the par value) will next be paid to the owners of income shares—if there are sufficient assets to do this. Money remaining after this payment will be divided up and distributed to the owners of capital shares. The fund will cease to exist after this distribution because all its assets will have been paid out. Since practically all of these securities have traditionally sold at discounts from their net asset values, these may be good investments to buy and hold until the shares are called.

ANALYSIS OF INVESTMENT COMPANY SHARES: MEASURING PERFORMANCE

Performance of a given investment company should be measured against the stated objectives of the company. If the investment policy of the fund is to produce maximum current income, then this is the main factor to be measured. If the objective is to obtain capital gains with little or no emphasis on dividend income, then this is the important thing to measure. Unfortunately, many mutual fund shares are sold on the basis of their past performance with little regard to what were the investment objectives of the company. Mutual fund sales representatives often emphasize the growth performance of their funds to the exclusion of other investment characteristics which may be more important to the investor in the long run. Unsophisticated investors often buy shares in these companies without fully understanding that this dramatic growth may be obtained by assuming a very high degree of market price instability—something the investor may wish to avoid. Investment company shares which increase more than average in value during rising stock markets usually decrease more than average in declining markets.

Performance of a mutual fund—and most closed-end funds—is measured by summing the effect of three different things: (1) changes in the net asset value of mutual fund shares, or the market value of shares of closed-end companies, (2) the amount of income dividends paid, and (3) the amount of capital gains dividends paid. This information is often presented by yearly periods as an index of performance. This index may be compared to the Dow Jones or other stock averages, or to the index of performance of other investment companies.

Several companies present investment company performance information in varying degrees of detail. Figure 11–8 is a portion of the information of the Eaton and Howard Balanced Fund presented in *Investment Companies*. The data are given in a form that makes it easy to see how this company has performed over a ten-year period. This is but a portion of the information that *Investment Companies* gives on this and other funds. Most annual reports and prospectuses present similar information, as do several other financial publishing companies.[5]

Investment company shares can provide investors with certain unique advantages. Diversification, special purchase and withdrawal plans, and professional management are commonly cited examples. However, all investment companies cannot perform better than the security market averages all the time. This was rather dramatically shown in a study prepared for the SEC several years ago. This study was directed toward all facets of the industry, and performance was but one of many topics covered. This study's summary statement on fund performance is most interesting because it should serve to indicate to investors that they must be as selective in purchasing shares in a mutual fund as they are in making any other investment.

> With respect to the performance of mutual funds, it was found that on the average, it did not differ appreciably from what would have been achieved by an unmanaged portfolio consisting of the same proportions of common stocks, preferred stocks, corporate bonds, Government securities, and other assets as the composite portfolios of the funds. About half of the funds performed better, and half worse, than such an unmanaged portfolio.[6]

---

[5] *Investment Companies: Mutual Funds and Other Types* (New York: Arthur Wiesenberger Financial Services); *FundScope* (Los Angeles, Cal.: FundScope, Inc.); *Barron's National Business and Financial Weekly* (New York: Dow Jones and Company); *Forbes* (New York: Forbes, Inc.); *Financial World* (New York: Guenther Publishing Co.). These publications and others, as well as the financial pages of most city newspapers, provide much information of interest to buyers of investment company shares.

[6] Irwin Friend, et al., A *Study of Mutual Funds.* Prepared for the SEC by the Wharton School of Finance and Commerce. (Washington, D.C.: U.S. Government Printing Office, 1962, pp. x, xi.

FIGURE 11–8
Performance Information

THE EATON & HOWARD GROUP OF FUNDS

24 Federal Street, Boston, Massachusetts 02110

This group is composed of five funds, the oldest of which, Eaton & Howard Stock Fund, was organized in 1931. The Balanced Fund came into being the following year. The Income Fund was organized as General Investors Trust in 1932 and came under the management of the Boston investment counseling firm of Eaton & Howard, Inc., in 1966. In 1968 two new funds were launched: the Growth Fund and the Special Fund. The total net assets of the five funds at the close of 1974 amounted to $271.7 million.

Special Services: The voluntary *accumulation plan* also serves for *automatic dividend reinvestment.* There is no minimum or subsequent investment requirement. Income dividends are invested at offering price, except that dividends on Income Fund are invested at asset value less a 30-cent service charge. Arrangements may be made for plan payments to be made through bank drafts on the investor's checking account. The Income, Balanced and Stock Funds have a provision for the payment of income dividends on a monthly basis; if this option is elected, capital gains must be reinvested and cannot be included in monthly payments. A periodic *withdrawal plan,* on a level payment or variable payment (liquidation to be effected in not less than ten years) basis, is available without charge; annual withdrawals may not exceed 10% of the total amount deposited. Shares may be *exchanged* at asset value for those of other Eaton & Howard funds for a $5 service charge. A *Keogh Plan* custody agreement, master corporate profit-sharing and pension plans and *Individual Retirement Account* plans are available.

EATON & HOWARD BALANCED FUND

The Balanced Fund is managed as if it were "the entire investment program of a prudent investor." Current income is an important objective, as well as reasonable growth of both principal and income. Balance among bonds, preferred stocks and common stocks is maintained at all times, with a maximum limitation of 75% for any single type of security.

At the end of 1974, the fund had 57% of assets in common stocks, of which a major proportion was concentrated in five industry groups: consumer goods & services (11.3% of assets), oil & gas (10.2%), construction & farm equipment (6.8%), paper & publishing (5.2%), and transportation (5.1%). Exxon, at 5.6% of assets, was the fund's largest common stock investment, followed by Dow Chemical (3.2%), Union Pacific (3%), and American Home Products and Deere & Co. (each 2.6%). The rate of portfolio turnover during the year was 10.8% of average assets. Unrealized appreciation was 1.2% of year-end assets.

Statistical History

Year	Total Net Assets	Number of Share-holders	Cash & Equiva-lent (% of Assets in)	Bonds & Pre-ferreds (% of Assets in)	Common Stocks (% of Assets in)	Net Asset Value Per Share	Offer-ing Price	Yield	Income Divi-dends	Capital Gains Distribu-tions	Expense Ratio	Offering Price High	Offering Price Low
	AT YEAR-ENDS								ANNUAL DATA				
1974	$102,846,793	18,464	6%	37%	57%	$ 6.96	$ 7.61	5.2%	$0.417	$0.35	0.66%	$10.05	$ 6.72
1973	142,448,003	18,960	5	34	61	9.50	10.38	3.8	0.414	0.652	0.64	11.29	9.91
1972	166,555,144	19,834	3	30	67	10.99	12.01	3.3	0.416	0.45	0.62	12.03	10.72
1971	159,267,777	20,769	6	32	62	10.40	11.37	3.9	0.458	0.36	0.63	11.38	10.38
1970	158,596,884	21,298	9	33	58	10.10	11.04	4.1	0.47	0.50	0.64	10.92	8.86
1969	166,808,244	21,747	9	29	62	10.51	11.49	2.5	0.30	0.60	0.59	13.57	11.25
1968	197,806,114	22,860	4	32	64	12.52	13.54	3.4	0.455	...	0.57	14.17	11.71
1967	190,563,730	23,737	1	29	70	11.31	12.23	3.5	0.44	0.50	0.58	13.22	12.02
1966	198,836,807	24,771	2	36	62	11.47	12.40	3.3	0.425	0.35	0.57	14.06	11.87
1965	224,825,285	25,455	5	30	65	12.89	13.94	2.8	0.403	0.40	0.56	14.75	13.78
1964	232,404,713	25,921	9	25	66	13.31	14.39	2.6	0.3875	0.35	0.56	15.09	13.64

An assumed investment of $10,000 in this fund, with capital gains accepted in shares, is illustrated below. The explanation on page 190 must be read in conjunction with this illustration.

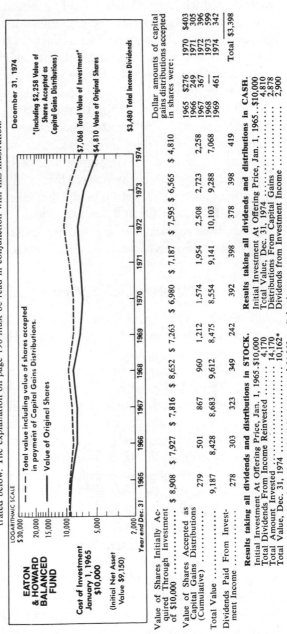

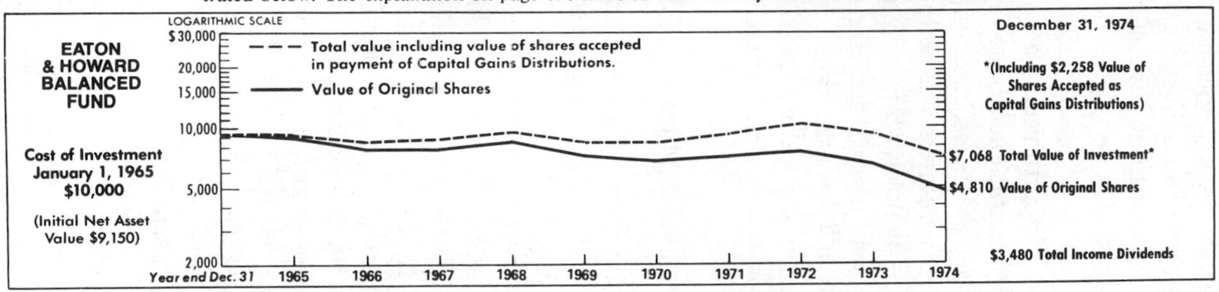

	1965	1966	1967	1968	1969	1970	1971	1972	1973	1974
Value of Shares Initially Acquired Through Investment of $10,000	$ 8,908	$ 7,927	$ 7,816	$ 8,652	$ 7,263	$ 6,980	$ 7,187	$ 7,595	$ 6,565	$ 4,810
Value of Shares Accepted as Capital Gains Distributions (Cumulative)	279	501	867	960	1,212	1,574	1,954	2,508	2,723	2,258
Total Value	9,187	8,428	8,683	9,612	8,475	8,554	9,141	10,103	9,288	7,068
Dividends Paid From Investment Income	278	303	323	349	242	392	398	378	398	419

Dollar amounts of capital gains distributions accepted in shares were:

1965	$276	1970	$403
1966	249	1971	305
1967	367	1972	396
1968	—	1973	599
1969	461	1974	342
		Total	$3,398

Results taking all dividends and distributions in STOCK.

Initial Investment At Offering Price, Jan. 1, 1965	$10,000
Total Dividends From Income Reinvested	4,170
Total Amount Invested	14,170
Total Value, Dec. 31, 1974	10,162*

*Includes value of shares received in payment of $4,065 capital gains.

Results taking all dividends and distributions in CASH.

Initial Investment At Offering Price, Jan. 1, 1965	$10,000
Total Value, Dec. 31, 1974	4,810
Distributions From Capital Gains	2,878
Dividends from Investment Income	2,900

Source: *Arthur Wiesenberger Financial Services*, New York, 1975.

While the past performance of a fund should not be completely disregarded when purchasing fund shares, such information should be interpreted cautiously. It seems logical to assume that if in fact a given investment company does have superior investment management, this company will perform consistently better than others. It also seems reasonable to assume that certain investment companies that have performed well in the past will continue to do so. However, the facts are that the best performers one year may be be the poorest during the next. *The Institutional Investor*, a magazine directed toward professional money managers, rates mutual fund performance on a monthly and yearly basis. Reports of performance, current as well as historical, are prepared by several financial services and publishers. Of particular interest are the reports prepared by Arthur Wiesenberger, *Forbes*, *The Institutional Investor*, and *FundScope*. When reading performance reports it is interesting to note how few mutual funds are listed as top performers over any appreciable length of time.

Investment Characteristics of Mutual Funds

There is such a wide variety of mutual fund companies that it is possible to buy securities having many different investment characteristics. Companies stating their investment goals as being "above average profits" or "capital gains through special situations," and so on, sell securities that have great amounts of financial risk. Potential for high profits is matched by potential for large losses.

The more conservatively managed funds have less financial risk, but they are sometimes (depending upon the proportion of fixed-income securities in their investment portfolios) open to interest rate risk. Purchasing power risk is not nearly so much of a problem as it is for fixed-income securities, although "bond funds" may suffer losses in purchasing power during inflationary periods.

Marketability has not been a problem for mutual funds, to date, but it is enough of a potential problem that it warrants some discussion. Marketability for closed-end companies is provided by the security markets, and for most of these firms it is fairly good. Marketability for open-end fund shares comes from the fund's ability and willingness to repurchase any shares offered to it for redemption. In normal times this procedure poses no problems. The fund is constantly selling more securities than are being redeemed so that, in effect, cash from new shareowners is transferred to those wishing to redeem shares. The company does not have to sell investments to provide cash for refunded shares, nor does it have to keep great amounts of cash on hand to provide for repurchase of shares. If the sort of panic selling of securities that took place during the 1929 market crash occurred again, mutual fund shares might not be so marketable. Funds could only obtain cash by selling their investments, and under these conditions redemption prices would be low. Shares might remain marketable, but because of potential losses from redemptions, they would not be very liquid.

The fund's statement of investment objective found in every prospectus is a guide to what sort of investment characteristics, and risks, can be expected. These statements are not infallible, but when considered along with the fund's past performance, they provide the best method of determining what to expect in the way of investment risk and return.

Mutual Fund Insurance

Since 1970 it has been possible for mutual fund investors to *insure* their accounts against loss. At the current time insurance is available on only a few selected mutual fund accounts. If investors react with favor toward the concept of fund insurance it is expected that coverage for a wide variety of plans will soon become available.

The Insured Mutual Fund Redemption Value program works this way: Persons investing in funds which offer the insurance feature (the more stable, income oriented funds) purchase a policy which guarantees that at the end of the policy period they will receive *at least* what was paid for the mutual fund. Policy periods are from 10 to 15 years and the insurance premium is about 0.6 percent of the amount insured.[7]

The policy may be canceled at any time prior to its expiration, but unless the policy is held until maturity the investor receives no compensation for loss. If share prices rise, investors may wish to cancel an existing insurance policy and buy a new one which is effective at the higher share price. In this way profits can be "locked away." Insurance of mutual fund accounts acts to remove the financial risk from this type investment.

---

[7] See Armon Glenn, "Guarantee against Loss: More Mutual Funds Have Begun to Offer One," *Barron's*, June 30, 1975, pp. 5 and 22.

SUMMARY

An *investment company* is a company formed for the purpose of purchasing and managing a portfolio of investment securities for its shareholders. These companies are of two main types: *open-end*, or *mutual funds*, and *closed-end* funds. Shares of open-end companies are sold and redeemed by the mutual fund and through brokers. Shares of closed-end companies are sold like those of any other corporation. Except in the case of dual purpose funds, shares of closed-end companies remain outstanding indefinitely. Mutual funds are of far more importance than closed-end funds. At the end of 1974, mutual fund assets were $38.5 billion while those of closed-end companies stood at $5.3 billion.

Mutual fund shares are priced on the basis of *net asset value per share*. Net asset value is determined by subtracting the company's liabilities from its assets. Dividing this remaining amount by the number of outstanding shares restates the amount as net asset value per share. Mutual funds buy and sell their securities for net asset value adjusted for commissions. Commissions vary from nothing on no-load funds, to 8½ percent on certain other shares. Lower commissions may often be obtained on purchases made under a *contractual purchase plan*.

Most investment companies are regulated under the Investment Company Act of 1940, and various rules of the SEC and certain state agencies. Regulation has been directed mainly toward providing investors with information which they may use to make intelligent decisions, although some regulation controls certain of management's actions. Investment companies regulated under the 1940 Act pay no taxes themselves, passing income through to their shareholders.

Investment companies offer shareholders two important things—*diversification* of investments and *professional investment management*. Diversification is defined as the spreading of investment risks by purchasing a large number of different kinds of investments. Professional management is somewhat more difficult to define, but it means management by a person—a professional—who can be expected to produce better investment profits over the long run than the "average investor." Diversification is "good" in that it spreads investment risk; a well-diversified investment portfolio should not experience exceptionally large losses. However, diversification also keeps the portfolio from experiencing above average profits. Really aggressive investment portfolios are seldom diversified, emphasizing instead careful selection of a limited number of securities that are expected to perform well. Some mutual funds are not diversified, seeking large profits from relatively few investments.

It is difficult to measure the worth of professional management. Studies of mutual fund performance indicate that the average mutual fund performs about as well as the stock market averages. It is impossible to meaningfully rank mutual funds by performance because the funds have widely differing investment goals and therefore cannot be expected to perform identically.

Balanced funds are those invested in a balanced amount of common stock and fixed-income securities. These funds do not usually show great changes in market value over time.

Bond, preferred stock, and income funds are similar in that they seek high, constant returns. Shares of these companies should not show great market price changes.

Money-market funds invest in short-term highly liquid debt securities. These investments allow the small investor to obtain the high interest returns that are normally available only to persons or companies able to purchase large amounts of Treasury bills, commercial paper, and other high-yield debt instruments.

Common stock funds take a variety of forms, but all are invested in common stocks. The growth and income funds are probably the least risky, so far as financial risk is concerned, while those emphasizing maximum capital gains are probably most risky. Some are unregulated trust-type funds which are formed to drill for oil, trade commodities, and engage in other highly speculative activities.

Mutual funds offer investors many different ways of paying for plans and of receiving benefits from them. The *regular account* is simply a single purchase of shares with no agreement or obligation to purchase more. *Accumulation plans* are those under which an investor agrees to purchase a certain minimum number or dollar amount of shares over a given period of time. These plans are of a *voluntary* or *contractual* nature. Many plans allow for *dividend reinvestment.* Capital gain or regular dividends or both are automatically reinvested in additional shares of the fund's stock. *Withdrawal accounts* are those which pay out to their owners a certain specified amount per period. The minimum dollar amount of this type account is usually $10,000. These accounts are often purchased by retired persons.

Investment characteristics vary greatly from fund to fund. As a general statement, the performance-oriented funds usually offer the most financial risk, while those invested in fixed income securities offer the least. Marketability of fund shares has remained good, but in a market downturn such as that experienced through 1973–74, most mutual fund shares that were redeemed were redeemed at a loss. Stated another way: Marketability is high, but liquidity is no better than that of other common shares. The only funds that are liable to interest rate risk are those invested in fixed-income securities. Over the long run, inflation affects fixed-income security funds more than others.

PROBLEMS

1. Go to the latest copy of *Investment Companies* and outline the investment objectives of the Income Fund of Boston and the Research Equity Fund. These funds would appeal to what kinds of investors? (Any two funds having different objectives may be used.)
2. In *Investment Companies,* or any of the other information sources on mutual funds, look up and record the investment performance of the above two funds over the last year. Have these companies performed as you would expect them to have performed given their stated investment goals?
3. The Thornton Fund has $125,600,000 of assets, $2,200,000 of liabilities, and 12,591,800 shares of stock outstanding.
   a. What is the net asset value of this company?
   b. What is the net value per share?
   c. If this company charged a 7 percent commission on all securities sold, what would be the price of 100 shares of Thornton Fund stock?
4. From an investment company's annual report, or from any of the financial services, obtain the performance data for a common stock fund over the past ten years. Compare this information to that of one of the stock market indexes. Rate the company's performance as good, average, or poor on the basis of this comparison and the company's stated investment policy (assume no reinvestment of dividends).

QUESTIONS

1. How does the operation of an investment company differ from that of an industrial corporation?
2. What are the main differences between open-end and closed-end investment companies?

3. Why have mutual funds become so much more important than closed-end companies?
4. Why is the *net asset value* of a mutual fund share more important than the *book value* of a regular corporate stock?
5. Purchasing shares in a *regulated* investment company provides investors with certain safeguards. What are they?
6. What is the *investment advisor*, and what does this person or firm do for the investment company?
7. What is a *no-load fund?* What advantages may be had from purchasing shares of one of these companies?
8. What are the most important advantages to the purchase of investment company shares?
9. Regulated investment companies pay no income taxes on their earnings. Is this "fair" tax treatment?
10. How do *accumulation plans* differ from so-called *regular* accounts?
11. To what kind of an investor would a *withdrawal account* have the most appeal?
12. What is a *liquid asset* or *money market* fund? What advantage does it hold for small-scale investors?

SELECTED READINGS

Duke, Edward E. *Selecting Your Mutual Funds: A Professional Program for Producing Perpetual Profits.* Jericho, N.Y.: Exposition Press, 1972.

Friend, Irwin; Blume, M.; and Crockett, J. *Mutual Funds and Other Institutional Investors: A New Perspective.* New York: Twentieth Century Fund, 1970.

Friend, Irwin, et al. *A Study of Mutual Funds.* Prepared for the SEC by the Wharton School of Finance and Commerce. Washington, D.C.: U.S. Government Printing Office, 1962.

"Forbes Mutual Fund Survey," *Forbes Magazine.* An annual performance study usually presented in the August issue of the magazine.

Investment Companies, Mutual Funds and Other Types. New York: Arthur Wiesenberger Financial Services, published annually.

Management Investment Companies. Prepared for the Commission on Money and Credit by the Investment Company Institute. Englewood Cliffs, N.J.: Prentice-Hall, 1962.

Mutual Fund Fact Book. Washington, D.C.: Investment Company Institute, published annually.

Potts, W. George. *Understanding Investments and Mutual Funds*. New York: Arco Publishing Co., 1973.

Watkins, A. M. *Making Money in Mutual Funds*. New York: Hawthorn Books, 1973.

12
Investing in Speculative Investments

INTRODUCTION

The preceding chapters of this book have been devoted to the description and analysis of the more common types of investments. This chapter examines several forms of investments which are somewhat lesser known and therefore held by fewer investors. Justification for including them in a basic book comes from the fact that these investments are finding ever wider usage by all investors, large as well as small.

Several of the special investments included in this chapter are *options* of one type or another. An option is simply a contract to purchase or sell something for a known value over a known period of time, at a price agreed upon when the option contract was originated. Rights and warrants and puts and calls are this type of contract. Short sales, new issue purchases, and investment in special situations are entirely different.

RIGHTS AND WARRANTS

From the viewpoint of the investor, rights and warrants have nearly identical investment characteristics. They both give their owners the legal right to purchase a limited number of additional shares of common stock of the company which has issued the rights or warrants, at a fixed price, until some designated future time. Rights are designed to raise capital quickly and usually expire within 30 days after they are issued. Warrants have much longer maturities.

Valuing Rights

Rights are usually issued to a company's shareholders to get them to purchase additional shares of stock in the company. Firms having a preemptive right provision in their charter or bylaws *must* offer new shares to existing shareholders. Other companies may choose to sell new securities this way. The shareholders may either exercise their rights and purchase new shares of stock, or they may sell the rights to others, who may then exercise or sell them. The issuance of rights, like the issuance of a stock dividend, cannot increase or decrease the value of the shareholder's investment. Typically, rights are issued on the basis of one right for each share of outstanding stock.

An example of a hypothetical rights offering may help to make the procedure more clear. Sunnyfuture Co. has decided to sell additional shares of common stock through a rights offering. Several weeks before the offering takes place all shareholders, the financial press, and the SEC are notified that the company intends to issue new shares. Terms of the issue are (1) all stockholders of record on July 15, 1975, will receive one right for each share of common then held, (2) rights will be issued on August 1, 1975, and will be exercisable at any time until August 31, 1975, (3) four rights and $40 enable an investor to purchase one new share of stock at any time prior to and including August 31, 1975, (4) until August 15, 1975, the rights will "trade with the stock" or the stock will sell "rights on," which means that if shares are sold, the rights are sold with them. The following formula may be used to determine the theoretical value of a right when the stock is still selling "rights on."

Where

$R =$ Value of a single right
$P_1 =$ Market price of one share with its right still attached
$S =$ Subscription price of an additional share
$N =$ Number of rights necessary to buy an additional share

$$R = \frac{P_1 - S}{N + 1}$$

Sunnyfuture's outstanding stock was selling for $50, and additional shares cost $40 and four rights. Under these conditions each right had the following value.

$$R = \frac{\$50 - \$40}{4 + 1}$$
$$= \$2$$

After the 15th of the month, when the stock goes ex-rights, the value of a right is computed by this formula.

$$R = \frac{P_2 - S}{N}$$

P_2 is the market value of the stock *after* the stock and the rights trade separately; the other symbols stand for the same things as before. Theoretically, when the stock began trading ex-rights, each share provided security owners with a two-part investment made up of the market price of a share with no right attached to it, and the value of one right. Unless some other factor has changed the market price of the company's stock, the value of the right plus the market value of the stock can be no more or no less than it was before the stock began selling ex-rights. Since our stock had a market value of \$50 with rights attached, it must have a value of

$$\$50 - \$2 = \$48$$

when the rights are sold separately. This result may be checked by using the second valuation formula.

$$R = \frac{\$48 - \$40}{4} = \frac{\$8}{4} = \$2$$

The important point to all this is that the shareholder receives no additional value from a rights offering. The market price of the company's stock might increase or decrease while the rights are outstanding, and thereby increase or decrease the value of each right, but this change in value can be traced to the change in the market value of the stock, not to the rights offering.

Valuing Warrants

Warrants have investment characteristics similar to those of rights in that they too give their owners the ability to purchase shares of stock at a certain price for a stated period of time. The main difference between warrants and rights, from the viewpoint of the investor, is the time each remains outstanding. Rights are designed to raise new capital quickly. They usually expire within a month after their issue to insure that the company obtains this new capital by a certain date. Warrants are often issued along with bonds or preferred stock to enable the company to sell these senior securities at a lower interest or dividend cost. Warrants are also issued in mergers and to underwriters in an effort to provide equity participation in the company.

The theoretical value of a warrant is determined by a formula similar to the second one presented above. Warrants are almost always sold separately from the common stock, and they usually allow the holder to buy one share of common stock for each warrant. Theoretically, then, a warrant is worth the difference between the subscription price and the market price of the security it entitles the holder to purchase. In 1975 Alleghany Corporation had warrants outstanding which allowed their owners to buy the common stock of this company at $3.75 per share. Alleghany common stock recently had a value of $8. The theoretical value of the warrant was $4.25 ($8 —$3.75), but its market price was $4.87. The difference between the theoretical and actual value of a warrant is known as a *premium*. It is caused by the willingness of investors to pay more than the theoretical value of the warrant. Persons reason that the warrant is worth more because if the common stock rises in price, the warrant will rise in price even more rapidly. This calculation is presented in the next section.

TABLE 12–1
Warrant Exercise Prices, Market Prices, and Premiums for Selected Companies (prices as of January 27, 1975)

Company	*Warrant Exercise Price*	*Common Stock Price*	*Theoretical Warrant Price*	*Actual Warrant Price*	*Premium*
Alleghany Corp. . . .	1 common @ $3.75	$ 8	$4 1/4	$4 7/8	15%
Moly Corp.	1 common @ $15	20	5	9 1/2	85%
AMAX	1 common @ $47.50	36 1/8	0	4 3/4	Infinite
Atlantic Richfield. . .	1 common @ $127.50	86 1/2	0	7 1/4	Infinite
CMI Investment. . . .	1 common @ $31.75	8 1/4	0	4 3/4	Infinite

Source: Standard & Poor's *Stock Guide* and *The Wall Street Journal*, January 28, 1975.

Table 12–1 presents recent price data for several firms having regularly traded warrants. The determination of the theoretical value of the warrant was explained above. The premium is the difference in the theoretical and actual warrant prices presented in terms of the percent one is above the other. To complete the Alleghany example, the dollar premium is determined by subtracting the theoretical market price from the actual market price.

Actual price of warrant.	$4.87
Theoretical price of warrant.	4.25
Premium.	$0.62

Next, the premium is stated in terms of the percentage it is above the theoretical price.

$$\frac{\$0.62}{\$4.25} = 0.145 \text{ or } 15\%$$

These premiums are usually around 5 percent when the market price of the common is substantially above the warrant exercise price. When the market price of the stock drops near to the price at which the warrant entitles its owner to buy the common, the premium usually increases dramatically. This happens because even though the warrants have little theoretical value, they have enough speculative value that they are almost always priced above their theoretical value. The infinitely high premiums on the AMAX, Atlantic Richfield, and CMI Investment warrants are due to the fact that the theoretical warrant values are zero. Persons are willing to purchase these options in the hope that at some future time the stock price will increase causing the warrant values to rise.

Speculative Characteristics of Rights and Warrants

To account more fully for the warrant premiums it is necessary to look to the speculative value they offer investors. The following example pertains equally well to rights, but as rights do not remain outstanding very long, there is less chance for the market price of the outstanding stock to move upward. With less chance of a market price rise the rights have less speculative value.

Assume a situation where a company has common stock selling for $20 a share and warrants entitling owners to buy one share of common at $18. The warrant has a theoretical value of $2. Now assume that the common doubles in price, to $40 per share—a 100 percent increase. The warrant should now be worth $22.

$$\$40 - \$18 = \$22$$

The percentage increase of the warrant is

$$\$20/\$2 = 10 \text{ or } 1{,}000\%$$

In this example, an increase of 100 percent in the price of the common resulted in a 1,000 percent increase in the theoretical value of each warrant. The possibility of such large gains causes investors to bid up the price of warrants to premium levels and gives value to warrants even though the market price of the stock is below that at which the warrant holder can purchase it. When stock prices decline, warrant prices decline as rapidly as they increase.

Warrants may be used as part of an investor's total investment program. However, these securities are usually classified as speculative because of their potential for large price fluctuations. Furthermore, the warrant holder receives no dividends, nor can the warrants be voted since they do not evidence ownership in the company. Warrants may be perpetual, but most have an expiration or a call date at least several years in the future when they are issued. Some warrants have subscription prices which increase over time. Ownership of warrants is evidenced by a certificate resembling a common stock share. About 40 different warrants are traded on the American Stock Exchange, and many more are traded OTC. Only a few warrants are listed on the New York Stock Exchange. Rights are listed on exchanges and traded OTC. Information about warrants and rights can be obtained from either the company issuing them or Moody's, Standard & Poor's, or other companies providing financial information services.

Puts and Calls

A *put* is a contract which allows its owner to *sell* a specified number of securities, to a specified buyer, at a specified price, within a specified time period. A *call* allows its holder to *purchase* securities under the above conditions. Both contracts are called *options*.

Prior to the opening of the Chicago Board Options Exchange (CBOE) in April 1973 all options were bought and sold in the OTC securities markets. These contracts were privately negotiated between brokers acting for the buyer and seller. Since these contracts had no standard expiration date or exercise price they were difficult to transfer to a third party. Consequently, while it was legally possible to sell an option contract before it expired, in reality most contracts were held by the original parties until they matured.

The CBOE was designed to overcome the above problems associated with option trading. First of all, the CBOE is a national securities exchange. Like other exchanges its members make continuous auction markets in the securities that are accepted for trading on the exchange. Prices are set on the exchange floor and are quoted daily in the financial press. The list of companies against whose stock call options are written is being gradually expanded and currently includes the stock of 57 companies. CBOE options are standardized as to number of units involved, exercise price, and expiration date. Each trading unit includes 100 shares of the stock under option; exercise prices are stated only in round dollar amounts; expiration dates are the last business days of January, April, July, and October. Many persons were apparently looking for just these investment characteristics, for the volume on the CBOE has increased greatly. Option trading began on the American Stock Exchange in 1974 and on the Philadelphia-Baltimore-Washington Stock Exchange in 1975.

When option contracts were traded over the counter they were used almost exclusively by professional investors. Because of the ease with which options can now be traded on the CBOE, many individual investors have been drawn to these securities. Option contracts allow investors to hedge their investment portfolios in ways beyond the scope of this book to explain, but the primary reasons why individual investors buy options is because the option provides the potential for great gain, with a known maximum amount of loss.

How Put and Call Options Are Listed and Sold

Learning all the important investment characteristics of rights and warrants requires interested persons to consult various sources of information: Moody's, Standard & Poor's, company prospectuses, and so on, carry the relevant information. Because CBOE option contracts are uniform, complete information about each option can be printed in the financial press.

Figure 12–1 is a section from the *Wall Street Journal* of January 9, 1975 which displays prices of various call options sold by the CBOE on that day. The first column after the name of the firm lists the price at which the security can be called. Note that for most companies there are several call prices listed. The headings—Jan—,—Apr—, and —Jul— designate the months in which the call options expire. Options are also written to expire in October, but few if any of these options will be written until near the end of January. Options expire on the last business day of the month. Volume figures are in hundreds; "Last"

FIGURE 12–1
Chicago Board Options Exchange Price Quotes

Chicago Board Options Exchange

Wednesday, January 8, 1975

Closing prices of all options. Sales unit is 100 shares. Security description includes exercise price.

Option & price	— Jan — Vol.	Last	— Apr — Vol.	Last	— Jul — Vol.	Last	Stock Close
Alcoa .. 30	b	b	18	2⅝	3	3⅞	29
Am Tel ·50	144	1-16	b	b	b	b	46⅝
Am Tel 45	219	1¾	177	2⅞	96	3¾	46⅝
Am Tel 40	29	6⅜	19	7¼	b	b	46⅝
Atl R .. 90	357	2	194	6	8	9¼	89½
Atl R .. 80	436	9	15	12	15	18	89½
Avon 35	145	⅛	513	1¾	b	b	29¾
Avon .. 30	507	15-16	220	3½	27	5	29¾
Avon .. 25	184	4¾	45	6⅜	52	8	29¾
Avon .. 20	62	9⅝	25	10¾	3	11½	29¾
Beth S ..30	83	1-16	102	⅝	68	1 5-16	26⅜
Beth S ..25	208	1⅜	127	2⅛	40	2⅞	26⅜
Beth S ..35	1	1-16	b	b	b	b	26⅜
Bruns .. 15	15	1-16	26	¼	b	b	9½
Bruns .. 10	210	5-16	341	1 3-16	223	1⅝	9½
Citicp .. 35	43	1-16	b	b	b	b	28¾
Citicp .. 30	151	½	55	2¼	37	3¾	28¾
Citicp .. 25	40	3¾	22	5½	6	6⅞	28¾
Delta .. 25	b	b	24	4¼	a	a	26¾
Delta .. 30	b	b	38	2¼	6	3¾	26¾
Dow Ch 50	b	b	a	a	1	10	54½
Dow Ch 60	b	b	40	2⅜	3	5½	54½
Eas Kd 100	1	1-16	3	⅛	b	b	63⅜
Eas Kd 90	a	a	167	7-16	b	b	63⅜
Eas Kd 80	118	1-16	137	1⅛	31	3½	63⅜
Eas Kd 70	213	3-16	198	3⅛	24	6⅝	63⅜
Eas Kd 60	335	3⅞	111	8	18	11¼	63⅜
Exxon .. 80	1	1-16	66	⅞	b	b	66½
Exxon ..70	102	⅜	161	2⅞	20	4½	66½
Exxon ..60	38	6⅜	35	7⅞	8	9⅝	66½
F N M 15	b	b	17	4½	30	5¼	18¾
F N M 20	b	b	205	1 11-16	122	2½	18¾
Ford 45	a	a	5	⅜	b	b	34¾
Ford 40	4	1-16	69	¾	b	b	34¾
Ford 35	128	¾	102	2⅜	15	3⅜	34¾
Ford 30	36	4⅞	23	5⅞	6	6¾	34¾
G M 30	b	b	109	5⅝	64	6⅝	35½
G M 35	b	b	213	2	69	3⅜	35½
Gen El 30	b	b	11	5¾	13	6⅝	33¾
Gen El 35	b	b	145	2⅝	73	4	33¾
Glf Wn 25	188	½	155	2⅛	41	3	24⅜
Glf Wn 20	109	4¼	63	5⅛	2	6¾	24⅜
Gt Wst . 20	15	1-16	b	b	b	b	15¼
Gt Wst 15	421	¾	409	2	119	⅞	15¼
Gt Wst 10	80	5	139	5¾	51	5⅞	15¼
I B M 220	73	1-16	291	1¾	b	b	163¼
I B M 200	213	⅛	427	3⅞	82	9	163¼
I B M 180	528	⅝	347	8½	137	15⅛	163¼
I B M 160	446	6¾	186	17¾	67	25½	163¼

a—Not traded. b—No option offered.

Source: *The Wall Street Journal*, January 9, 1975, p. 19.

refers to the final price per share at which an option was sold. The final column lists the closing price of the common stock of the company against which the call options are written. Deciphering the first line of price information from Figure 12–1 tells us this: Call options for Alcoa common are currently traded on the CBOE. The single option available is priced at $30. No January option exists. Eighteen 100-share call contracts expiring in April were traded on January 8, 1975. The last price was $2⅝ per share, or $262.50 per 100-share call contract. Only three of the July contracts were sold at a price of $3⅞. Alcoa common stock closed at $29 on the same date.

Put options are the reverse of call options. A put option allows its owner to *sell* a specified number of securities, to a specified buyer, at a specified price, within a specified time period. It is the stated intention of the CBOE to list put options in early 1976. All put options currently available are sold in the OTC market.

Leverage Advantages from Call Options

Warrants and rights have investor appeal largely because of the financial leverage that they offer. Call options offer exactly the same advantages and disadvantages as these securities. The owner of an average call option will make a larger rate of return on investment from the option than from holding the stock, if the stock price rises by enough to compensate for brokerage charges and the premiums associated with the call option. Like warrants and rights, call options have theoretical values which can be easily computed, and actual values which reflect the premium that investors grant to these contracts because of the potential that they hold for large gains.

The theoretical value of the Avon $20 call option is the difference between the call price, $20, and the market price, $29¾, on January 8. On this date the theoretical value was $9¾; the market value was $9⅝ for the January contract, $10¾ for the April contract, and $11½ for the July contract. The January contract is due to expire within a few weeks and therefore does not have a great deal of profit potential remaining—hence the low price. The premium of market price over theoretical value for the April call option is slightly over 10 percent and the July option premium is nearly 18 percent. These premiums reflect the fact that there is increasing time—three months—during which the price of the stock can rise.

The potential for financial leverage is obvious: If Avon moves from $29¾ to $31¾ an investor holding the shares outright would have a paper profit of $2 per share. Assuming that the premium remains at nearly the same percentage, an increase of $2 in the market price of the stock should increase the price of the call option by a like amount. The gain associated with owning the stock would be about 6.7 percent; the gain from owning the April option should be about 18.5 percent. However, if the stock has not risen during the period of the option the investor will probably be unable to dispose of the call contract for more than its cost. Declines in the market price of the optioned stock cause even greater decline in the call option value. This, of course, is the risk associated with all option contracts.

A *straddle* occurs when a person owns a put and a call option contract on the same stock. This type of investment costs more because two contracts must be purchased. But if the market prices moves far enough—either up or down—the investor will make money. Rising prices will make the call option valuable, and falling prices give value to the put. However, the amount of price movement in either direction must be substantial to make this investment profitable.

Risk Characteristics of Rights, Warrants, and Other Options

Rights, warrants, puts, and calls are speculative investments. Their market prices can be expected to fluctuate greatly, so these investments require constant attention. Option holders never receive dividends; therefore any profit on these investments must come entirely from rises in the price of the security that the option is written against. Marketability and liquidity depend upon the issue. Rights and warrants of large, well-known corporations may have excellent marketability and liquidity characteristics while similar securities of smaller or less well-known companies may score poorly so far as these characteristics are concerned. Options traded upon listed exchanges will probably have good marketability and liquidity characteristics. Option contracts have no interest rate risk because their prices are not related to interest rates. Their ability to protect against inflation depends entirely upon whether they increase in value.

Real Estate Investment Trusts

REITs, as they have come to be called, are companies formed to lend funds to the real estate construction industry. Some of these companies specialize in the financing of short-term construction contracts and others emphasize the purchase of long-term mortgages. The intent of all the trusts is the same. They seek to obtain capital from shareholders and lenders at rates that are lower than the returns from their real estate investments. Profits, often very high profits, may result from this arrangement. During the credit crunch of 1969–70 the number of REITs grew very rapidly because these companies were able to obtain financing for the rapidly expanding construction industry at rates which provided REITs with large profits.

Times have changed, however. Extremely tight credit, lowered construction activity, and failure of several large construction companies and other borrowers have caused several of the larger REITs to experience extreme financial difficulty. Prices of the stocks of most REITs are near their all-time lows because of this, even though many companies are financially sound.

For example, Chase Manhattan Mortgage, which at one time sold as high as $70 per share, was quoted at $3¾ in May 1975. Citizens and Southern is down to $3 from a high of $39¾. Not all of the 200 plus REITs have done so poorly, but the entire industry has been adversely affected by current economic conditions. And yet, the concept of the real estate investment trust has much to recommend it. If economic conditions change so that construction activity increases and financing for REITs becomes more readily available, many REITs can be expected to resume their profitability and investor appeal.

SHORT SELLING

People can make money in the stock market when it is rising *or* falling. Both opportunities are shown in Figure 12–2. The conventional way of making a profit is by buying at point A and selling at point *B*. Short sellers simply reverse this pattern, selling at point *B* and buying later at point C. The transaction is simple, relatively inexpensive, and may be performed with round- or odd-lots, or with bonds.

Short sellers sell stock which they normally do not own. Persons wishing to do this instruct their broker to sell short a certain number of shares of a particular stock. The shares are borrowed from those which the broker holds in margin accounts. A person who has a margin account agrees to this arrangement so the borrowing procedure is perfectly legal. When the sale is made, the amount of the transaction is held by the broker along with a like amount of money from the short seller. Thus, if an investor sold short $10,000 of stock, the broker

FIGURE 12–2
Short Selling Illustrated

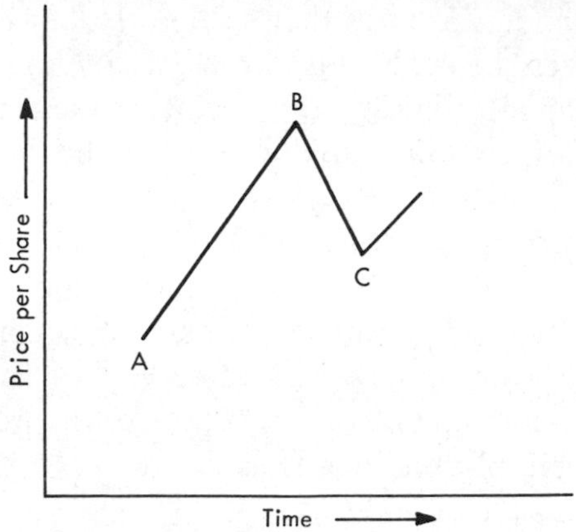

would credit this account with $10,000 from the sale of these securities plus $10,000 deposited by the short seller. In accordance with prevailing margin requirements, the short seller could borrow part of the $10,000 deposit.

The short position is *covered* by later buying the stock in the market. The broker uses the newly purchased shares to replenish the account from which they were borrowed. If the stock price had declined, the investor would make a profit. If the price had advanced, the result would be a loss.

Short sellers are likely to be somewhat nervous persons. On a *long* position investors can lose no more than their original investment; the potential loss on a short contract is immense. For example, a person who is *long* on a $20 stock can only lose $20 per share since the value of the stock cannot become less than zero. The person who *shorts* at $20 may buy back the stock at $40, $50, $80, or more. There is no upward limit on how high the price can go. Other disadvantages are that the short seller must pay any dividends declared to the person from whom the shorted shares were borrowed. Interest must also be paid on any money borrowed in a margin account.

SEC regulations forbid short sales at a price *below* the last preceding sale. The intent of this rule is to keep people from selling short a stock that is already moving downward, thereby increasing selling pressure and causing further price decline. This was a common tactic of the "bear raiders" of the pre-SEC days. Several people would secretly agree to sell shares of a certain company short, forcing the price to extremely low levels. At a prearranged signal they would cover their short positions, making large profits on the transaction.

Short Selling against the Box

The "box" in this phrase refers to a safe deposit box which holds the same shares that were sold short. In other words, in this transaction investors sell short shares of stock that they own. By doing this they are able to protect a profit that they already have in a stock. If the market price declines, the profit on the short sale offsets the loss on the long position. If prices rise, the gain from being long is offset by the loss on the short contract. The purpose of this transaction is usually to carry forward into the next tax year a gain on a security transaction.

Most short sales are made by professionals, but there is certainly no reason why the individual investor who can accept the inherent risk should not use this type of investment. Securities may be shorted in anticipation of an economic recession. Specific stocks may appear to be "too high" and due for a price drop. The rules often stated by professional investors, while quite general, are nevertheless relevant: (1) never short the stock of a strong company, (2) never short stock in a rising market.

Risk Characteristics of Short Selling

This type of investment is probably more speculative than warrants but less speculative than puts and calls. Because of the potential for high losses, these investments require constant attention. Interest rate risk and purchasing power risk have little meaning for short selling.

NEW ISSUES

Corporations have an almost continuous need for external financial assistance. Some funds are provided by bank loans. Other monies are acquired by selling securities. Bonds and stocks offered for the first time are known as *new issues*. From Chapter 3 it will be recalled that these original offerings make up the *primary market*. Once these securities are outstanding they are traded in *secondary* or *after markets*. This section focuses on primary offerings and on new issues of common stock.

There are periods when new issues are the "hottest thing around"; when investors stand in line to buy them, and then are allocated only a fraction of what they desire. At other times investors turn their backs on highly promising opportunities.[1]

In 1970, Standard Oil of New Jersey (now called Exxon) sold 8.6 million additional shares for nearly $500 million. "Jersey" has done this many times since its formation almost a century ago. In like manner American Telephone and Telegraph raised over $1.5 billion dollars also in 1970. Communications Satellite Corporation made its initial and much heralded public offering of 5 million shares in 1964. New issues are usually not so large nor do they often create so much attention.

Most offerings are more modest and are made by relatively unknown or even newly formed companies. Shortly after World War II a man named Henry Land perfected a device which he felt would find a ready market. The early investors and many others who followed them realized astronomical returns because in a relatively short time period Land's invention was successfully developed and marketed as the Polaroid camera. In 1966 the public was offered a chance to participate in a promising venture to sell cooked poultry. Phenomenal gains were realized by those who did invest since this emerging company was the Kentucky Fried Chicken Corporation.

Thousands of other innovations have followed this pattern. Indeed this is an essential element of the free enterprise system and has played a very important role in America's growth. Someone discovers a new way of doing things and proceeds to exploit this breakthrough. In countless instances these innovators themselves do not have sufficient financial resources. They turn to the public for aid, usually by selling new issues of common stock. The incentive to buy these original offerings is somewhat akin to a desire to "get in on the ground floor."

Investment results do not always require considerable patience. It has been possible to realize substantial gains in a few months, weeks, or, in many instances, in a matter of hours. For example, Educational Computer Corporation went public on March 7, 1968. Three and one-half months later the stock had soared almost 3500 percent. Before the brokers closed shop on the day which Friendly Ice Cream Corporation

[1] This section was originally written at the close of the 1960s when new issues were very appealing to investors. During the first half of the next decade these investments were not favored. No one can say what investor attitudes will be in the latter part of the 1970s. However, there is little doubt that a resurgence in the popularity of this vehicle will occur again just as it has many times in the past. Because interest in new issues has been very low recently, this section has not been rewritten, except for minor editorial changes. When new issues "rise again" the comments in this section will be especially appropriate.

sold shares in July 1968, the price rose 80 percent. While these results are phenomenal, there are hundreds of other examples of spectacular gains. Losses have also occurred, and this sobering action will be examined later. At this point it is sufficient to note that many investors have fared quite well, and it is highly appropriate to study new issues in greater detail.

Origination

Before any securities may be legally offered to the general public, applications must be filed with federal and/or state authorities. It should be recalled from the discussion in Chapter 3 that security laws provide three main methods for the "birth" of the new issue: (1) national offerings, which are usually in excess of $1 million and are offered by well-established firms and some new ventures, (2) Regulation A offerings, which are for $500,000 or less and as such are normally made by newer companies. (3) intrastate offerings, the average dollar size of which is between the two other categories. Securities in this class are typically offered by small firms or newly organized ventures.

Price Performance[2]

The opportunity to be in or near the start of a venture provides intuitive appeal for the new stock offerings. There is ample statistical evidence to substantiate this attraction. Studies of price patterns occurring during the first year of life for new issues show consistently larger increases compared to outstanding stocks—either listed or OTC. The superior performance is basically due to relatively small losses coupled with substantial gains. One researcher determined that the national offerings made in 1967 and 1968 had an average price increase of more than double in their first year of existence.[3] The study also revealed that a group of intrastate offerings exceeded this performance. These rises occurred during a period when the average price on the NYSE *declined* slightly.[4]

---

[2] This section presents historical price movements of new issues of common stock only as opposed to bond or preferred stock offerings. Furthermore the results described are on companies offering their stock to the public for the first time. New stock issues by fims like Ford, Exxon, and ATT are excluded.

[3] T. E. Stitzel, "Investor Experience with New Intrastate Stock Issues," *Journal of Financial and Quantitative Analysis*, January 1970, p. 705.

[4] Names of these companies are sometimes interesting, for example—A Trysting Place, Inc. One of the biggest gainers in 1968 was Weight Watchers International.

It is often difficult to purchase new issues. This is because of the method by which they are marketed and also because of the relatively small number of shares that are usually issued. There are several thousand brokerage offices scattered widely throughout the country. These businesses buy and sell virtually any stock in which secondary trading occurs. Primary markets are a different matter. A particular new issue is sold only by a small proportion of the brokerage firms. Their efforts are directed first toward their own existing clients. In many cases the new shares must be rationed. Investors usually do business with one or, at most, several brokerage firms. This means that only a few new issues will be available. For the majority of cases, the investor must wait until an after market begins. At this point anyone can buy. In fact there is some evidence to indicate even better performance can be achieved by purchasing only those stocks which have registered gains during their first month of existence.[5]

It has been emphasized throughout this book that risk and return go hand in hand. New issues are no exception. There are several flags of caution. First of all the after markets for many of the new issues are extremely thin. This means that orders for a few hundred shares or more can cause a significant price change. There is a story about an investor who bought a substantial block of a new offering at $10 per share. One week later the price had risen to $20. More shares were bought. At the end of the first month the quote was $35. Not wishing to be greedy, the investor decided to sell. The broker's reply in sickening conciseness was "sell to whom?" The registered representative was telling this client that getting out of the stock was not such a simple matter. Large buy and sell orders for the newly issued or "unseasoned" stock may take time for execution. If speed is of critical importance, the price realized may vary considerably from the current quote. This problem will be recognized as *marketability*, a concept which was discussed in Chapter 3.

Another problem concerns the possibility of a price decline which is known as *downside risk*. New issue increases of greater than 100 percent have been cited. This is an *average* figure and as such it hides important information. For example, an earlier cited study reported that while average price movements resulted in substantial gain, one out of every five new issues declined in price.[6] Further evidence in-

---

[5] Frank K. Reilly and Kenneth Hatfield, "Experience with New Stock Issues," *Financial Analysts Journal*, September–October 1969, p. 79.

[6] Stitzel, "Investor Experience," p. 704.

dicates that when stocks in general are declining, new issues prices may drop even faster.

Original offerings wax and wane in the eyes of the investor. The hot new issue activity during 1961 and 1968 is well remembered by the investment community. In the aftermath of these periods the general attitude toward this type of investment was one of downright apathy.

Finally, the investor should be cautioned to be extremely careful about buying new issues, putting them away, and forgetting about them. An SEC report provides some sobering evidence on this point.[7] Of 504 companies that went public between 1952 and 1962, 55 percent had been liquidated, placed in receivership, or could not be located. Another 26 percent were reporting losses, and only *one* in *five* could be considered successful when the study was made. This illustrates the most crucial point of all—*selectivity*. The search for companies offering new ideas is extremely demanding. There is no doubt that in the future many innovations will be developed by new firms that offer their stock to the public. Identifying the "acorns that will sprout" is not an easy task, but the potential of spectacular returns will attract the investor.

Risk Characteristics of New Issues

New issues of the younger firms are low grade with respect to financial and market risks. They are usually speculative investments, although some issues may be purchased for their long-run potential provided that periodic reviews are made of each situation. Marketability depends heavily on the size of the issue and whether or not it can be traded interstate. Interest rate and purchasing power risks are not critical considerations in new issues.

TURNAROUND SITUATIONS

"Many shall be restored that now are fallen and many shall fall that now are in honor."[8] This quotation is especially applicable to corporate activity. Most firms have ups and downs. Relatively few com-

---

[7] *Report of Special Study of Securities Markets, Part I,* Securities and Exchange Commission, 1963, pp. 550–59.

[8] Horace, *Ars Poetica* and cited in the introduction of Graham, Dodd, and Cottle, *Security Analysis.*

panies enjoy continuous prosperity. This fluctuating behavior presents an opportunity for investors.

Examples of a Turnaround

The term *turnaround* is applied to corporations which have done poorly in the recent past but are now expected to reverse the trend and "turnaround" and do better. Several developments might cause this recovery. The most common reasons are improvement in general economic conditions, development of a new product, discovery of a mineral deposit, receipt of a new contract, and new management. Examples of these changes in company fortunes are legion. Most manufacturers of cars, major appliances, and other durable goods realize improvements as the economy picks up after a period of slowdown. Texas Gulf Sulfur shares rose substantially when the company discovered a vast ore body. A similar price movement was triggered when Natomas struck oil in Indonesia. Ups and downs by major government contractors such as Boeing, General Dynamics, and Lockheed are "normal" patterns. Most of the above situations are difficult to predict reliably. The stock prices of these firms may soar when the developments are proclaimed, but it is usually not possible for the general public to anticipate these announcements. Timing is critical, and when the individual investor decides to purchase the stock, much, if not most, of the price rise may have occurred.

Management as a Factor

In the examples just cited, the new developments were rather dramatic. The stock market reactions tended to coincide with the news. Another cause of turnaround—a change in top management—often creates a delayed price rise. Firms often shuffle their leaders in an effort to turn red ink operations into the black. The purpose is to breathe new life into the company. Improvements in these cases do not occur overnight, and stock price movements generally lag the management changes. This allows investors time to analyze the situation.

There are many instances where a new aggressive chief executive has transformed an old, established, and conservative company into an exciting, dynamic moneymaker. Scovill Manufacturing Company presents just such a case. This firm has been an important name in manufacturing for over one and one-half centuries. While it sells some home appliances through the Hamilton Beach Division, its reputation is mainly as a manufacturers' manufacturer. Scovill primarily converts raw materials into components for use by other firms. In the early 1960s it became evident that the company was not keeping pace with changing patterns of business in markets it served. New leadership was urgently needed. Malcolm Baldridge, president of an iron foundary operation, was brought in to infuse new vigor into Scovill. He took decisive action and trimmed costs, acquired new companies, and expanded sales. The response of earnings and stock price is shown in Figure 12–3.

This basic pattern has occurred over and over—a declining business, new executives, sweeping changes, and subsequent improvements. The 110-year-old American-Standard Co. began the 1970s attempting to scrap its dowdy image by installing new leadership. Twentieth Century–Fox was saved from financial disaster by a new chairman who replaced the father-son dynasty that had run the film company for 38 years. Some firms stress this action in announcements. For example, Allis-Chalmers, since the hiring of a new president advertised repeatedly of a "Turnaround at Allis-Chalmers." The new officers usually have held responsible jobs in other firms. Litton Industries has the distinction of training several dozen men who have been respon-

FIGURE 12–3
Turnaround at Scovill Manufacturing Co.

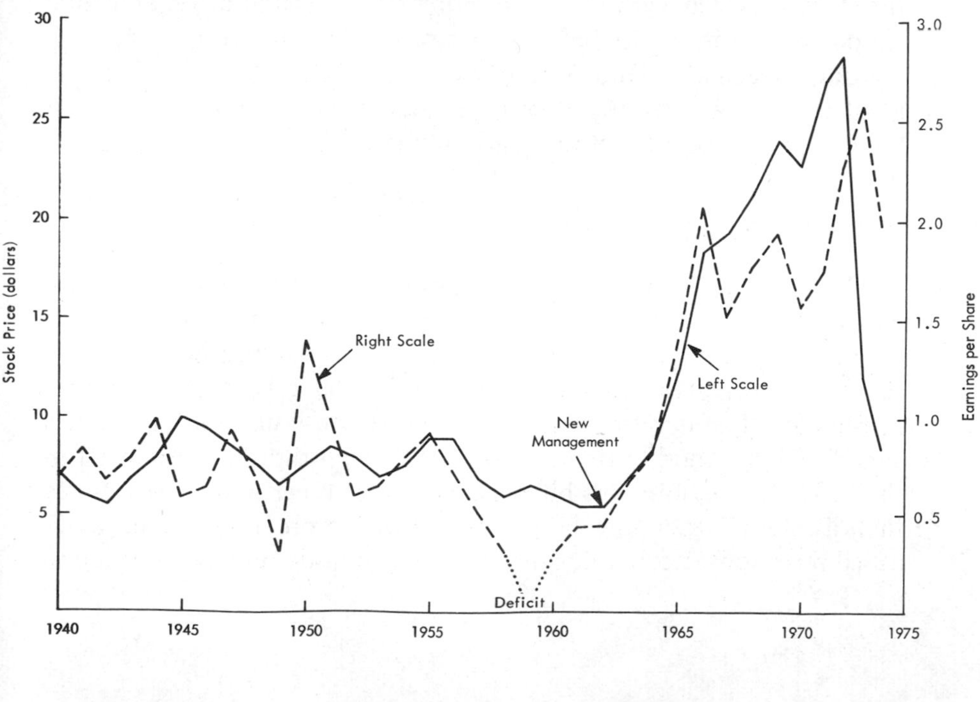

sible for turnaround situations, for example, Boise-Cascade, City Investing, and Walter Kidde.

It must be emphasized, however, that new management is by no means an assurance of *subsequent and continued improvement* in company performance. In some instances, it would be difficult for even a Deity to accomplish the change. Studebaker Corporation and Montgomery Ward tried numerous chieftans to no avail. Boise-Cascade, after a promising start, faltered badly and another new leader was installed. Nonetheless, there have been so many cases of turnaround caused by new management that the investor is well advised to take notice of companies that select new heads. Excellent sources of this information are found in the Management section of *Business Week* and the Who's News column in *The Wall Street Journal.* Once a list of potential investments has been compiled, the investor may carefully analyze the prospects of success for the corporation's recovery and then make selections.

The preceding discussion can be readily summarized by paraphrasing Horace's quotation, "Many firms shall be restored by new management."

Risk Characteristics of Turnaround Situations

It is difficult to assign risk grades to turnaround situations because they vary so widely with respect to potential gains and losses and time periods which must pass before improvement occurs. In general, they are quite speculative and offer considerable exposure to market and financial risks. As with the other investments discussed in this chapter, the importance of interest rate and purchasing power risk is not great.

TREND BUCKERS

The 1960s were unique in U.S. history in that this period encompassed the longest sustained economic growth on record. The next decade began with a slowdown in business activity. Sessions of expansion and contraction, called business cycles, have been characteristic of the past. The duration and frequency of these ups and downs has varied widely. Another depression of the magnitude that occurred in the 1930s is a remote possibility according to most economists. Since that disaster the economy has progressed with more moderate declines, called recessions. Economic growth rates will undoubtedly continue to fluctuate in the future. These changes present an opportunity for the investor.

"It is always a good time to buy," This advice is often given by brokers because at *any* point in time the prospects for certain industries and individual companies are very favorable. Even when most firms' activities are declining there are those who are setting record highs. These companies that continue growing in periods of economic slowdown are known as *trend buckers*.

The reasons for these "exceptional" industries can be largely attributed to two factors. Some types of economic activity are given timely boosts by developments such as new products, cost reductions, or changes in consumer buying habits. These developments are irregular and not limited to expansion periods. In a dynamic economy, invention and innovation are continuous. Because of this, breakthroughs will occur in slack as well as in boom periods. The exceptional industry in one cycle may not perform similarly in the next.

The second major reason for counter-trend behavior is that some lines of business just react differently to economic declines. Consumers will cancel or at least postpone purchases of durable goods such as new cars and appliances. Other products remain in demand regardless of the economic circumstances of the buying public. Industries offering these items are said to be recession resistant.

Examples of Trend Buckers

A recession resistant industry is typified by food chain stores. Many purchases can be delayed, but not food. Furthermore as people reduce expenditures they do more entertaining and dining at home. The food retailing business is thus one of the least affected by economic downturns.

Some industries do not feel the effects of a slowdown for some time. For example when overtime is cut and layoffs begin many people undertake do-it-yourself home projects. Thus the portable power tool industry does well in the early stages of a recession. If the downtown persists, this line of business will eventually be hurt, but when general declines are modest, these firms should prosper.

Several industries produce items that are almost considered as necessities by their consumers. Both the brewing and soft drink businesses are in this category. They represent habit patterns that are relatively inexpensive and are hard to alter. Traditionally they have been among the last to feel the pinch of a slowdown. Cosmetics are no longer a luxury for many women. They are almost as essential to the psychological health of the average woman as a balanced diet is to her physical well-being.

Shakespeare wrote, "Ill blows the wind that profits nobody." This is another way of expressing the effect of moving counter to the crowd. The downward trend need not be in the general economy. Things happen that create problems in some industries while benefitting others. An example is the oil crisis that occurred in 1973. This situation caused trouble for such industries as the automobile manufacturers, tourism, some oil firms, and chemical companies. On the other hand, the event aided coal companies, insulation manufacturers, and a part of the oil industry—especially those firms connected with well drilling and secondary recovery operations. Pollution control device manufacturers have benefitted by new air quality standards. Opportunities for profit are available to investors who can discover the *silver lining* in the clouds of change and trouble.

There are several points of caution that should be made with respect to the trend buckers. First, it is difficult to imagine that any industry is truly recession-proof. If bad times continue, the decline will eventually be felt by virtually all companies. Secondly, the fact that certain lines of business can run counter to downturns does not mean that all firms in that industry will enjoy this experience. The investor must be careful to select only the most promising ventures. Finally, and perhaps most importantly, investors need to remember that growth in earnings of a company does not mean that the stock will necessarily rise. Recall from Chapter 2 that the overall market movement has a substantial effect on the price behavior of any individual stock. When the price averages are declining this will have a restraining influence on the share prices of firms that are performing well. This requires investors to remain patient and realize that the market will eventually reflect superior earning power.

It is always appropriate to look for new trends, products, and companies—even in periods of general gloom—because some trend buckers are present.

Risk Characteristics of Trend Buckers

Investments in these situations are usually short term and hence speculative in nature. The potential gains and losses are less than the other special types of investing discussed earlier in this chapter. Because of the relative price stability they are, in most cases, high grade with respect to market risk. Financial risk is usually little and the other investment risks are not of crucial importance.

COMMODITIES

Each year thousands of individuals undertake a new type of activity known as *trading commodity futures.* This term refers to the buying and selling of, mainly, foodstuffs and metals. Beginning with apples and ending with zinc, the list includes frozen pork bellies and foreign exchange, mercury and molasses, platinum and plywood, oats and orange juice—about three dozen types in total. This compares with many thousands of common stocks. Several criteria must be met by any commodity if it is to be traded. First of all, there has to be a substantial supply and demand. Second, the item must be definable in terms of quality and grade. A third criterion, and perhaps the most important qualification for trading interest, is a history of fluctuating prices. This acts as the encouragement for participants.

How to Trade Commodities

Most assets are delivered at or soon after the time of purchase. For example, you can walk onto a used-car lot, buy a car, and drive it away. Commodities can be handled similarly. This is known as the *cash* or *spot* market. Commodities can also be bought and sold for delivery at later dates. This is known as the *futures* market. A *futures contract* involves the purchase or sale of a commodity at a price agreed upon when the contract is made. Delivery of the goods is to be at a future time which is spelled out when the agreement is drawn. The contract is also the minimum trading unit with actual quantity determined by the particular commodity. For example, one contract represents 112,000 pounds of sugar, 100 troy ounces of gold, or 40,000 board feet of lumber. An example of commodity price quotations is shown in Figure 12–4. Contracts are traded in formal markets in many cities throughout the world. The Chicago Board of Trade and the Chicago Mercantile Exchange are the largest commodity exchanges in the U.S. Orders may be placed with a number of brokerage houses. Some firms handle commodities activity exclusively; others offer their clients stock and bond brokerage services as well.

A typical transaction is illustrated by the following example: Suppose in September someone is interested in eggs. Production and con-

FIGURE 12–4
Commodity Price Quotations

Futures Prices

Wednesday, May 21, 1975

	Open	High	Low	Close	Change	Season's High	Season's Low
CHICAGO—WHEAT							
July	320	326	316	324½-323½	+5¾to4¾	509	306½
Sept	326	330	321	329	+4¾	513	311
Dec	333	339¾	331	338½-339	+4¾to5¼	523	319
Mar 76	343	347	339½	346¼	+4¼	392½	326
CORN							
July	275¼	282	273	281-280	+6to5	411	254¾
Sept	264½	271¾	262	269-268	+4½to3½	388½	246¼
Dec	250	254¾	247½	253-253½	+2¾to3¼	355	234
Mar 76	255¾	260¼	253	259¼	+3¼	358	239
May	258	263	256½	262¼	+3¼	283	248
OATS							
July	158	161½	156¼	161½	+5	198½	123½
Sept	145	150	144¾	148½-149	+3½to4	178	122¼
Dec	145½	149¼	144½	148½	+3¼	188	126½
Mar 76	146	150	146	150	+3½	160	136½
SOYBEANS							
July	521	536	518½	530-533	+10to13	972½	493
Aug	513	527	509½	523½	+11½	961	488
Sept	504	518	501½	517	+12¾	945	485
Nov	502	516	499½	513-515	+10¼	869	485
Jan 76	509	522	506	521	+12	860	492
Mar	516	530	513½	528	+12½	620	498
May	522½	537	521	533½	+11¾	579	505
July	525½	539	525	539	+13½	582	511
Aug	527½	542	527½	542	+14½	546½	514
SOYBEAN OIL							
July	22.60	23.53	22.36	23.40-.50	+ .87to.97	45.12	21.35
Aug	21.80	22.75	21.55	22.65	+ .90	44.30	21.00
Sept	21.15	22.10	20.90	21.85	+ .75	43.70	20.60
Oct	20.50	21.30	20.25	21.20	+ .75	32.75	19.95
Dec	20.05	20.80	19.80	20.55-.50	+ .55to.50	30.90	19.50
Jan 76	19.70	20.30	19.45	20.10	+ .62	28.50	19.10
Mar	19.30	19.85	19.10	19.65	+ .57	24.50	18.80
May	19.00	19.50	19.00	19.25-.50	+ .50to.75	21.20	18.00
July	18.80	18.90	18.70	18.75	+ .42	20.70	18.00
SOYBEAN MEAL							
July	127.50	128.00	125.00	127.50-127.	+1.5to1.0	212.50	112.00
Aug	128.00	128.00	125.50	127.50-127.	+1.0to.50	212.00	115.00
Sept	129.50	129.50	127.00	127.50b	− .30	211.00	118.00
Oct	129.50	130.00	128.00	128.50	....	170.00	121.10
Dec	132.00	132.00	129.50	130.5-129.5	+ .5to−.5	166.00	123.00
Jan76	135.00	135.00	131.50	131.50	−1.70	169.00	124.00
Mar	134.50	135.00	134.00	133.00b	−2.80	151.00	128.30
ICED BROILERS							
May	43.70	44.20	43.70	44.00	+ .20	46.65	36.60
June	43.10	43.45	43.05	43.40	+ .35	46.50	36.85
July	42.95	43.40	42.85	43.35-.40	+ .53to.58	46.50	37.05
Aug	40.65	41.10	40.65	41.10	+ .50	43.00	37.10
Sept	39.45	39.70	39.40	39.65	+ .35	42.50	35.75
Nov	36.75	36.75	36.60	36.60	+ .30	39.25	35.65
Jan 76	37.80	37.95	37.80	37.95	+ .20	37.95	36.95
PLYWOOD							
July	129.90	130.40	126.20	126.80	−6.40	150.00	102.00
Sept	131.00	133.00	129.30	129.70-.80	−6.6to6.5	151.50	104.50
Nov	131.20	132.30	129.50	130.50	−4.50	148.50	115.00
Jan 76	131.50	133.00	130.50	131.50	+4.00	150.00	126.00
Mar	135.00	135.00	132.50	132.50	−4.50	150.50	132.00
CHICAGO—SILVER							
May	466.50	475.00	466.50	468.00	+10.00	475.00	404.00
Aug	468.00	484.50	467.50	478.00477.	+12.7to11.7	563.50	402.00
Oct	474.50	491.50	474.50	484.00	+11.80	570.00	405.00
Dec	483.00	498.50	482.00	491.50	+13.00	574.00	410.00
Feb76	485.50	504.00	485.50	498.00	+13.50	506.00	428.00
Apr	491.90	510.50	491.90	504.00	+13.50	512.00	432.00
June	497.00	517.50	497.00	511.00	+13.50	517.50	441.00
Aug	512.50	523.00	512.50	517.00	....	523.00	473.30
KANSAS CITY—WHEAT							
July	326½	334	325¼	329330	+1¼to2¼	509¾	315
Sept	331	339	329¾	334	+1¾	489	319½
Dec	340	346	337	342½	+3	409	327½
MINNEAPOLIS—WHEAT							
July	370	376	368	374375	+4to5	560	356
Sept	357	360	353	359	+2	453	342
Dec	359	362	355	361	+2½	408	345
WINNIPEG—RAPESEED (VANCOUVER)							
June	623	638	619½	638b	+15	974	524
Sept	599½	616	594¾	615b	+16	930	520
Nov	585	595¾	583¼	595a	+16	705	510¼

	Open	High	Low	Close	Change	Season's High	Season's Low
POTATOES (IDAHO RUSSET)							
May 76	8.95	9.00	8.95	8.95	+ .06	9.00	8.80
Sales: 2 contracts.							
FROZEN PORK BELLIES							
May	74.60	74.70	73.80	74.35-.40	− .27to.22	76.85	36.25
July	74.75	74.95	74.05	74.50-.40	− .45to.55	77.10	38.25
Aug	73.50	73.50	72.75	73.10-72.95	− .52to.67	75.85	52.10
Feb 76	69.25	69.40	68.65	69.00-.15	− .67to.52	75.85	52.10
Mar	68.15	68.40	67.90	67.95	− .80	69.95	58.20
May	67.75	67.75	67.05	67.30a	− .60	68.90	63.30
Sales estimated at: 1,633 contracts.							
HOGS							
June	48.50	48.55	47.65	47.65-.70	− .87to.82	49.90	35.30
July	48.90	49.00	48.10	48.15-.20	− .85to.80	51.10	36.72
Aug	47.75	47.77	46.55	46.80-.65	−1.02to1.17	49.40	39.00
Oct	44.60	44.80	44.00	44.10-.20	− .77to.67	47.80	38.70
Dec	45.00	45.10	44.30	44.30	− .95	48.00	38.75
Feb 76	44.15	44.20	43.75	43.90	− .57	45.45	38.30
Apr	42.15	42.15	41.60	41.77b	− .68	43.50	38.00
Sales estimated at: 4,526 contracts.							
LUMBER							
July	147.90	147.90	144.00	144.00a	−5.00	168.00	111.00
Sept	154.90	154.90	150.70	50.70a	−5.00	164.90	127.50
Nov	151.10	151.10	147.50	147.50	−5.00	161.20	140.00
Jan76	152.20	152.20	149.80	149.80	−4.50	163.00	146.00
Sales estimated at: 1,255 contracts.							
NEW YORK—SILVER							
May	459.50	474.00	459.50	469.00	+10.30	657.00	342.90
June	467.10	472.50	467.10	469.70	+9.70	468.20	410.00
July	464.50	480.00	464.50	473.00	+10.00	659.40	400.00
Sept	471.60	486.00	471.50	479.50	+10.00	650.10	407.10
Dec	482.50	496.00	481.30	489.50	+10.40	568.00	417.00
Jan 76	483.00	498.50	483.00	492.50	+10.00	572.00	419.00
Mar	490.00	506.00	490.00	498.90	+0.50	576.00	431.00
May	507.00	511.50	507.0	505.20	+0.60	529.00	432.00
July	502.50	513.90	502.50	511.40	+10.70	508.70	441.20
Sept	514.80	521.00	514.80	517.60	+0.80	514.80	475.00
Sales estimated at: 6,905 contracts.							
COPPER							
May	55.50	56.30	55.50	56.20	+ .30	126.20	52.50
June	56.10	56.30	56.10	56.20	+ .30	59.70	54.80
July	56.20	56.90	56.20	56.70	+ .30	103.50	53.70
Sept	57.40	57.90	57.30	57.80	+ .30	96.00	55.00
Dec	59.10	59.60	59.10	59.50	+ .30	74.20	56.50
Jan76	59.60	60.20	59.60	60.10	+ .30	67.40	57.50
Mar	61.10	61.20	60.80	61.10	+ .30	68.30	58.50
May	61.60	62.20	61.60	62.10	+ .30	69.10	59.80
SUGAR (WORLD CONTRACT)							
July	17.50	17.65	16.85	16.95-.85	− .65to.75	60.05	10.20
Sept	17.00	17.00	16.20	16.20-.35	− .80to.65	56.05	10.40
Oct	16.50	16.85	16.05	16.12-.09	− .81to.84	53.55	11.95
Mar 76	15.90	16.10	15.40	15.50-.40	− .70to.80	45.45	15.30
May	15.25	15.50	15.15	15.20-.15	− .70to.75	28.65	15.05
July	15.00	15.20	15.00	14.95n	− .65	25.10	14.75
Sept	15.05	15.05	14.65	14.65	− .65	25.10	14.75
Sept	15.05	15.05	14.65	14.65	− .65	18.20	14.50
Oct	15.20	15.20	14.60	14.65-.60	− .65to.70	15.75	14.25
Sales estimated at: 4,406 contracts. Spot: 17.25n.							
COFFEE							
July	52.15	53.50	51.90	53.20b	+1.00	66.55	47.00
Sept	54.10	55.00	53.65	55.00	+ .60	63.55	48.30
Nov	55.15	55.25	55.15	55.50b	+ .20	63.50	49.70
Dec	55.45	56.30	55.00	56.20-.30	+ .45to.55	64.05	49.50
Mar 76	56.00	56.70	56.00	56.60	+ .30	56.70	50.00
May	56.40	56.90	56.40	57.10n	+ .40	57.00	51.80
Sales estimated at: 341 contracts.							
COCOA							
July	47.50	48.00	47.20	47.50	− .42	73.50	43.85
Sept	45.45	46.25	45.30	45.90	− .10	70.00	43.75
Dec	45.80	46.70	45.80	46.30	− .15	66.45	44.90
Mar 76	46.01	47.00	46.00	46.45	− .05	64.20	45.60
May	46.35	46.75	46.35	46.75	− .06	59.45	45.70
July	46.60	47.05	46.60	47.05	− .05	57.05	46.60
Sales estimated at: 820 contracts.							
WOOL FUTURES							
No sales. Spot: 134.0n.							
ORANGE JUICE (FROZEN CONCENTRATED)							
July	52.30	52.30	51.50	51.75	− .65	61.90	48.20
Sept	53.80	53.90	53.50	53.45b	− .65	63.00	50.15
Nov	55.40	55.50	55.30	55.20b	− .50	59.55	51.85

Source: *The Wall Street Journal*, May 22, 1975, p. 22.

sumption patterns have been studied. The price of eggs for delivery six months hence, for example March, is 50 cents a dozen.[9] Now suppose the prospective egg trader feels that eggs should sell for less next March. The step then would be to *sell* a futures contract. This would mean the trader is obliged to deliver eggs in six months for the price prevailing when this contract was sold, such as, 50 cents a dozen. If the investor was correct, the March futures contracts that are written at a later time would be for less than 50 cents a dozen. Suppose in December this quote is 45 cents a dozen, which the investor believes is as low as eggs will drop. The trader would back this judgment with a *purchase* of a March egg futures contract in December. This would result in a profit before commissions and taxes of 50 − 45, or 5 cents a dozen.

Notice what has happened. The commodity was bought at 45 cents a dozen and sold at 50 cents a dozen, only the sequence was reversed. Gains are made by buying low and selling high but not necessarily in that order. In this case the sale preceded the purchase but the profits were the same as if the opposite had occurred.

Another point of interest is that the participant in these trades need not be an egg farmer or processor. The actual physical delivery of the eggs was never contemplated when the contract was made that obliged the seller to make a March delivery. The commitment was satisfied by the futures purchase in December.

Reasons for Trading Commodities

Commodity trading also involves producers, manufacturers, and merchandisers. These groups may engage in an activity known as *hedging*. Here the objective is to minimize risk. The egg illustration resulted in a profit, but an opposite price movement would have caused a loss. Hedging is designed to prevent either from occurring. For example, a grain elevator operator buys wheat when it is harvested in June. This grain will be sold later during the year but at unknown prices. To prevent losses on the wheat which has been purchased, the operator might sell futures contracts and actually deliver the grain from storage when the contract so stipulates. There are many other methods and degrees of hedging but the general purpose is the same. The objective is to know in advance what the purchase or sale price of a commodity will be in the future and thereby minimize potential

[9] This is the March futures price. It may be higher, lower, or the same as the quote in the cash market.

losses due to unforeseen market declines. The existence of futures markets has made a positive contribution toward the efficient distribution of commodities into channels of use.

The "trading in tomorrows" appeals to people for various reasons. The basic attraction is the allure of quick and substantial profits. This in turn is made possible by two circumstances. The first is that price swings are often rapid. A freeze, strike, or East-West crisis can upset supply and demand and send prices plummeting or skyrocketing. Crop failures are almost regular even though unpredictable. The second circumstance is the fact that the price movements, even if small, can be greatly magnified by *leverage*. This involves using one's own funds *plus* credit to enlarge commitments in much the same manner as a house or car is bought with a small down payment. This amplification of resources is accomplished by *margin* trading. Margin is the amount required to be put up when something is purchased. For a used car it may be nothing. For common stocks in early 1976 it was 50 percent. For commodities it has ranged between 5 and 15 percent, depending on the particular type. With a 10 percent margin, the commodities trader will realize a gross return of 50 percent if the futures profits are 5 percent.[10] This multiplication results in fast action which entices many investors. The leverage also means total losses of funds can occur with equal rapidity if prices move the wrong way. Further attention is focused on commodities when bond and stock prices are sagging.

The dazzling profit potential attracts the speculator. In futures trading, prosperity may be enjoyed, but disaster is never far away. People who have been successful traders for long periods have died penniless. One oft-cited rule is, if you cannot afford to lose, you cannot afford to try to win.[11] Even proper monetary and psychological characteristics are not sufficient for futures trading. The activity is very demanding and ideally it requires omniscience so as to know the interrelationships of worldwide events. Clairvoyance would be helpful to foresee impending crop disasters in Spain, expropriations in Africa,

[10] If a contract was bought for $10,000 with a 10 percent margin, the investment would be $1,000 and the remaining $9,000 would be borrowed. A 5 percent price rise would result if this contract could be sold for $10,500. The gross return to the individual would be $10,500 – $9,000, or $1,500, which is $500 more than his original investment. The relative gross profit would be $500/$1,000, or 50 percent. Commission and other fees would lower this figure somewhat.

[11] Recall the discussion of types of return that investors seek; some are desirous of psychological benefits. The psychological makeup of the individual is a factor bearing on every investment program. Successful commodity traders are nonemotional in their decision-making. Furthermore, they fully realize that their commitments can be and sometimes actually will be wiped out overnight.

and so on. For mere mortals, then, the prime requisite for commodity futures trading is to study, study, study.

Investing in Gold

Before January 1, 1975 U.S. citizens could not legally own gold, other than gold coins, jewelry, artifacts, and so on. Since being permitted to own this precious metal, interest in the "gold market" has been heightened. A brief history of the evolution of gold as an investment is perhaps in order to place this development in perspective.

Prior to 1934 American citizens could own gold, and currency could be traded for gold at any bank. As part of the 1930's depression legislation U.S. citizens were prohibited from owning gold, except in the forms mentioned above. This prohibition remained in effect until 1975. From 1934 to 1971 the official price of gold was $35 an ounce. Rapid price inflation and continuing deficits in our balance of payments during the late 1960s and early 1970s caused the U.S. dollar to be devalued twice. The first devaluation occurred in 1971; the second in 1973. These devaluations were accomplished by changing the official price of gold from $35 to $38 and then to $42.22 per ounce.

Because of the rapid worldwide inflation of the 1960s and 1970s many persons strongly desired to own gold as protection against erosion of purchasing power. These people were willing to pay far more than the official gold price to obtain the metal. In March 1968 a free market in gold, where prices are set by supply and demand, was instituted to help satisfy this demand. Only non-U.S. citizens could buy gold in this market. Americans interested in "buying gold" could only do so by investing in gold coins, artifacts, jewelry, or other objects, or in stocks of companies which produced gold.

Shares of gold producing companies out performed all other industries during the 1973–74 market decline, as evidenced by Table 12–2. The market price of gold and gold futures prices have also increased over the same period. Whether the prices of gold and gold stocks will remain high is dependent upon demand and supply factors.

The supply of gold has increased only moderately in recent years because the easily attainable gold has for the most part already been recovered. The rise in the price of gold has made it profitable to process low-grade ore, to mine deeper, or to otherwise develop more costly sources of ore. Because of this the supply of gold is expected to increase modestly each year for the foreseeable future.

This increase in production will probably meet the industrial de-

TABLE 12–2
Performance of the 15 Best Industries 1973–74 (Standard & Poor's industry classifications)

Classification	*Price Change Percent*
Gold mining	+146.87
Sugar (beet refiners)	+ 66.00
Atomic energy	+ 40.65
Coal (bituminous)	+ 11.50
Oil (domestic integrated)	– 0.53
Steel (including U.S. Steel)	– 0.60
Building materials (heating and plumbing)	– 1.56
Oil well machinery and service	– 3.98
Steel (except U.S. Steel)	– 8.44
Lead and zinc	– 8.77
Forest products	–10.36
Foods (canned)	–11.59
Copper	–13.37
Chemicals (except Du Pont)	–14.44
Tobacco-cigarette manufacturers	–17.34

Source: *Business Week*, January 27, 1975, p. 51.

mand for gold and partially meet the demand for speculative or investment purposes. Demand from these sources cannot be accurately predicted, however. If inflation continues at a high rate, more persons will wish to purchase gold to protect themselves from price rises; the free-market price of gold will increase. If inflation becomes less of a problem the opposite situation will occur. Gold has also been desired through the years because its purchasing power is large in relation to its weight or size, and because it is easily exchanged for goods. Persons living in countries where the political situation is very uncertain (much of the Far East at this time) hold gold as protection against political developments which will make other assets valueless. One can only guess whether future demand of this type will increase or decrease.

Ownership of shares in gold companies poses no special problem for the investor. These shares are traded like any other stocks, and many of them pay dividends. Shares may be purchased in mutual funds which specialize in investing in gold-producing companies. Some limited partnership ventures are currently being formed to exploit existing or new mining claims.

Owning gold directly has several disadvantages in that it is expensive to transport, store, and insure. Of perhaps more importance is the fact that profits from holding gold can come only from price rises in the metal. There is probably as much risk in investing directly in gold as there is in investing in the shares of gold producing companies, and the costs may be greater. With the beginning of free ownership of gold in 1975, a U.S. gold futures market was started. This market has been in operation for too short a time to evaluate its performance. One can expect its contracts to have investment characteristics similar to those of other futures contracts.

Risk Characteristics of Commodities

This type of investment is highly speculative, especially because of the many unpredictable influences on prices. Market risk is of considerable importance, but the other risk concepts have little meaning for application to commodity investing. Constant attention is required because of volatile price action.

SUMMARY

Rights and Warrants

Rights and *warrants* are options to purchase securities for a known price over a limited time period. The value of these investments depends upon the difference between the subscription price (the price at which the owner of a right or warrant is entitled to purchase a security) and the security's market price. Rights are usually short term in nature, seldom remaining outstanding longer than 30 days, while warrants may have any maturity.

These securities have speculative value because if the market price of the security which they may purchase rises, the price of the option contract rises relatively more. Rights and warrants do not receive dividends or interest and do not entitle their owners to vote on corporate matters.

Puts and Calls

A *put* contract allows its owner to *sell* a certain number of securities, at a specified price, to a specified buyer, at any time during a specified time period. This contract has a market price which is dependent upon the market price of the security, the put price, and the time remaining before the contract expires.

A *call* contract is the opposite option. It allows its owner to *purchase* shares under the above conditions. In each case losses are limited to the cost of the option contract, while profits are theoretically unlimited. However, these contracts do not prove profitable for very many investors because security prices seldom fluctuate enough over the option period to offset the option's cost. Prior to the sale of options on the CBOE and other exchanges, these contracts were sold OTC. Most trading in these securities is now done through exchanges.

A *straddle* contract is one where an investor has a put and a call contract on the same securities. If prices increase or decrease *enough*, a profit is made.

Real Estate Investment Trusts

These investments allow persons of modest means to "own" real estate. While the entire REIT industry is currently experiencing financial difficulties, if economic conditions change these might again be profitable investments.

Short Selling

Short selling is the name given to sales of borrowed securities made in anticipation of a price decline. The "shorted" securities are borrowed from a broker, to be repaid at a later time. If the market price of the shorted stock declines, the transaction will be profitable because the investor will repay the stock loan with lower priced securities than were borrowed. If prices rise instead, the investor will suffer a loss when the short contract is repaid. There is more risk in shorting a security than in holding it directly because the potential loss is greater. A security purchased at $10 can cause a loss of only $10 because its price cannot become less than zero. A stock shorted at $10 may increase to any value, providing a large potential loss when the short sale is covered.

New Issues

The primary market for securities presents a special opportunity for investors. *New issues* of common stock are offered by a wide range of corporations—from billion dollar firms down to companies which are just beginning. The smaller and newly formed ventures are of particular interest because they offer an opportunity to "get in on the ground floor." Many investors have realized substantial gains by purchasing these new issues. In some periods few new offerings are made due to adverse stock market conditions.

Some offerings are distributed nationwide, while others are sold only to residents of one state. Because each issue is sold only by a relatively few firms, investors are not able to purchase most of the offerings until they become available in the secondary markets. This is not too late since some evidence indicates superior performance can be achieved by waiting a brief period before purchases are made.

The risk-return relationship is verified by price action in new issues. While many stocks increase substantially in value in relatively short time periods, many others decline or even become valueless. The high degree of price volatility should serve as both an incentive and caution to investors.

Turnaround Situations

Many corporations that have done poorly in past times reverse the trend, *turnaround*, and do better. Early recognition of forthcoming improvements in seemingly unattractive situations can provide investors with very favorable results. A major factor in creating the turnaround is a change in management. A pattern has been established in a considerable number of firms—a declining business, new executives, sweeping changes, and subsequent improvements. Considerable judgment is required to identify which situations can be reversed and those which are hopeless. Risks of not being successful in distinguishing the differences are commensurate with the potential rewards for correct analysis.

Trend Buckers

Trend buckers are companies whose growth does not decline when the general economy enters a slowdown period. They provide special opportunities for investors to buy securities when stock prices in general are falling. Firms in the food industry are quite recession-resistant. Companies that supply "do-it-yourself" products may actually prosper in the early stages of a downturn. Trend bucker companies can be identified in the likely industries, but very few of them can continue to grow if a recession persists or becomes severe.

Commodities

Thousands of investors trade in *commodity futures.* This involves buying and selling about three dozen types of foodstuffs and metals. Prices are established today for delivery in the future. Profits are realized if prices have changed in the appropriate direction when the deliveries are to be made. Commodity investors usually employ a high degree of leverage; so small price changes can result in large gains or *losses.* Risk is present due to the constant threat of hard-to-predict events such as floods, droughts, freezes, strikes, diseases, expropriations, and wars. Considerable effort is also required to stay abreast of other influences of supply and demand.

Investment in gold may take the form of futures contracts, holding the metal, or buying shares in companies which produce gold. Holding gold directly is relatively expensive because of storage and transportation costs, and because gold provides no returns except those from price rises. The price of free-market gold is controlled entirely by supply and demand conditions. Supply is limited in that the most easily accessible ore has already been mined and few new mines are being discovered. Demand for gold comes from industrial users and from speculators and investors. The industrial demand is increasing modestly each year. Demand for speculative and investment purposes is controlled largely by persons' desires to hold the metal as a protection against loss of purchasing power. It is demand for this purpose which causes most of the price fluctuations in this commodity.

PROBLEMS

1. A company just offered its shareholders the opportunity to purchase additional shares of stock on the basis of one new share for each four old shares held. The price of the new shares is $25 each; the outstanding common stock currently sells for $45.
   a. Assume that the rights sell with the stock for 14 days. What is the value of each right during this period?
   b. When the 14-day period expires and the rights begin selling separately from the stock, how much should the market price of the stock drop? (Assume no economic or other forces cause a price change.)
   c. If the market price of the stock increased to $60 after the stock began selling ex-rights, how much would each right be worth?

2. Look in a recent newspaper for price quotes on the selected stocks and warrants included in Table 12–1. The subscription price of these warrants may change over time, so check Moody's *Industrial Manual* to see whether this has happened.
   a. Compute new theoretical values for these warrants of the companies you have selected.
   b. Explain the logic of the premium.
3. From information contained in Figure 12–1 outline the conditions which must prevail (timing, stock price, and so on) in the market for Ford common in order for the person purchasing a Ford $30 April call option to have a profit from this speculation.
4. Shirley sold Safeway stock short at $22 per share. If she covers her short (buys the stock later) at $15 per share, what would be her gross profit on a 100-share transaction?
5. Test the stock price performance of trend buckers by comparing the average price change for three drug industry stocks with the change in the Dow Jones Industrial Average. Select a period during which stock prices fell substantially, such as 1966, 1969, 1973, or 1974.
6. Trace the stock price performance of a new issue by plotting month-end prices for one year. Select the new issue by looking in the "new issues" section of the *Commercial and Financial Chronicle* or ask a local broker.
7. Look up commodity futures prices for frozen pork bellies (bacon) in *The Wall Street Journal*. Based on the quotations, do you think bacon will cost more or less six months from now? State your reasoning.

QUESTIONS

1. What is a *put* contract? What must happen to stock prices to make it profitable?
2. What is a *call* contract? What must happen to stock prices to make it profitable?
3. What is a *short sale?* What must happen to stock prices to make it profitable?
4. If a company wanted to raise money quickly, would they be likely to use warrants or rights? Why?
5. Why do warrants usually sell at a premium over their theoretical value?
6. Why are short sales more speculative than a regular purchase of an equal number of shares?

7. Define the term *trend bucker*. Why are trend buckers of interest to investors?
8. What is a *commodity futures contract?* In what ways are these contracts similar to puts and calls?
9. What are *new issues?* Describe three different methods by which they are offered.
10. What is appealing about new issues to investors?
11. What are some problems associated with buying new issues?
12. What is a *turnaround situation?* How can potential turnarounds be discovered?

SELECTED READINGS

Carabini, Louis E., ed. *Everything You Need to Know Now about Gold and Silver*. New Rochelle, N.Y.: Arlington House, 1974.

Clasing, Henry. *The Dow Jones-Irwin Guide to Put and Call Options*. Homewood, Ill.: Dow Jones-Irwin, 1975.

Kassouf, Sheen T., and Thorpe, D. O. *Beat the Market*. New York: Random House, 1967.

Miller, Jarrot T. *The Long and Short of Hedging*. Chicago: Henry Regnery, 1973.

Prendergast, S. Lawrence. *Uncommon Profits through Stock Purchase Warrants*. Homewood, Ill.: Dow Jones-Irwin, 1973.

Rosen, Lawrence R. *When and How to Profit from Buying and Selling Gold*. Homewood, Ill.: Dow Jones-Irwin, 1975.

Schultz, Henry D. *Financial Tactics and Terms for the Sophisticated International Investor*. New York: Harper & Row, 1974.

Smyth, David, and Stuntz, Laurence F. *The Speculation Handbook*. Chicago: Henry Regnery, 1974.

Teweles, Richard J.; Harlow, Charles V.; and Stone, Herbert L. *The Commodity Futures Games: Who Wins? Who Loses? Why?* New York: McGraw-Hill, 1974.

part four

Managing Your Investments

13
Tax Aspects of Investments

INTRODUCTION

Income taxes concern everyone except the very poor and the very rich. The poor are not concerned because they have little or no income to tax; taxes are low and preparing the tax forms is easy. The wealthy may pay more taxes, but because they have large incomes, it almost always pays them to hire tax consultants to compute and minimize their taxes. For the large group of middle-income persons, income taxes are a terrible bother. The incomes of this group are not high enough to justify the use of expensive tax consultants, so the burden of tax record keeping and tax form preparation usually falls upon thc head of the household.

The United States government, like most modern governments, attempts to tax its citizens on their ability to pay. This philosophy of taxation results in a *progressive income tax structure.* Simply stated, as taxable income increases, each addition to income is taxed at a progressively higher rate. These rates currently begin at 14 percent and continue to a maximum of 70 percent. This does not mean that individuals in the "70 percent bracket" pay 70 percent of their income in taxes. It does mean that a single person earning over $100,000 or married individuals filing joint accounts and earning over $200,000 will pay taxes at a rate of 70 percent on taxable income over these amounts. The *marginal rate of taxes* is the rate at which each dollar of additional income is taxed. A single person earning taxable income of $12,000 will be taxed at a marginal rate of 29 percent on the next $2,000 of income.[1]

[1] See Table 13–1 for the 1974 tax rate schedules.

If our tax laws had no exceptions, and if all types of income were taxed at the same marginal rates, every citizen would be taxed proportionately on the basis of their income. However, there are several classes of income—each taxed at a different rate or not at all—and there are many ways to avoid taxes. Tax evasion is illegal, but tax avoidance is practiced by most people to the extent possible.

The purpose of this chapter is to identify the most important methods of minimizing the income tax bite and to outline a record keeping system that will simplify the unavoidable paperwork that accompanies investing. These are important aspects of all investment programs. It is self-defeating to invest wisely and profitably only to pay the highest possible taxes on profits. Adequate records of investment transactions must be kept for tax purposes; they should also be kept to provide important investment information.

First a word of caution: The laws of taxation change as courts reinterpret existing statutes and Congress passes new ones.[2] The investor must always be alert for subsequent changes in the tax law. Furthermore, the tax aspects of investments which will be examined are those which are expected to be of most importance and interest to the largest number of persons. Many special features of the tax laws are not covered. These may be valuable to certain investors, but the scope of this book does not allow examination of them.

Tax law is extremely complex, and any person having a modestly large income is probably well advised to obtain competent advice in setting up a program which will minimize taxes. Possible advisors are attorneys, bank trust officers, accountants, brokers, and investment advisors. The examples and illustrations to follow are general in nature and are routinely hedged with the statement "this is usually true," "normally this is the case," or other such statements. This must be done because there is hardly a portion of the tax code to which there is not somewhere an exception.

CAPITAL GAINS VERSUS ORDINARY INCOME

Ordinary income refers to the income received as salary, wages, interest payments, sales commissions, rent, and other normal sources of income. This type of income is taxed at the rates listed in Table 13–1. *Capital gain* income is defined as income resulting from the sale or

[2] This chapter contains the most up-to-date information that was available when the book was published.

TABLE 13–1
Federal Income Tax Schedules

1974 Tax Rate Schedules

SCHEDULE X—Single Taxpayers Not Qualifying for Rates in Schedule Y or Z

If the amount on Form 1040, line 48, is: / Enter on Form 1040, line 16:

Not over $500....**14% of the amount on line 48.**

Over—	But not over—		of excess over—
$500	$1,000	$70+15%	$500
$1,000	$1,500	$145+16%	$1,000
$1,500	$2,000	$225+17%	$1,500
$2,000	$4,000	$310+19%	$2,000
$4,000	$6,000	$690+21%	$4,000
$6,000	$8,000	$1,110+24%	$6,000
$8,000	$10,000	$1,590+25%	$8,000
$10,000	$12,000	$2,090+27%	$10,000
$12,000	$14,000	$2,630+29%	$12,000
$14,000	$16,000	$3,210+31%	$14,000
$16,000	$18,000	$3,830+34%	$16,000
$18,000	$20,000	$4,510+36%	$18,000
$20,000	$22,000	$5,230+38%	$20,000
$22,000	$26,000	$5,990+40%	$22,000
$26,000	$32,000	$7,590+45%	$26,000
$32,000	$38,000	$10,290+50%	$32,000
$38,000	$44,000	$13,290+55%	$38,000
$44,000	$50,000	$16,590+60%	$44,000
$50,000	$60,000	$20,190+62%	$50,000
$60,000	$70,000	$26,390+64%	$60,000
$70,000	$80,000	$32,790+66%	$70,000
$80,000	$90,000	$39,390+68%	$80,000
$90,000	$100,000	$46,190+69%	$90,000
$100,000		$53,090+70%	$100,000

SCHEDULE Y—Married Taxpayers and Certain Widows and Widowers
If you are a married person living apart from your spouse, see page 5 of the instructions to see if you can be considered to be "unmarried" for purposes of using Schedule X or Z.

Married Taxpayers Filing Joint Returns and Certain Widows and Widowers (See page 5)

If the amount on Form 1040, line 48, is: / Enter on Form 1040, line 16:

Not over $1,000 **14% of the amount on line 48.**

Over—	But not over—		of excess over—
$1,000	$2,000	$140+15%	$1,000
$2,000	$3,000	$290+16%	$2,000
$3,000	$4,000	$450+17%	$3,000
$4,000	$8,000	$620+19%	$4,000
$8,000	$12,000	$1,380+22%	$8,000
$12,000	$16,000	$2,260+25%	$12,000
$16,000	$20,000	$3,260+28%	$16,000
$20,000	$24,000	$4,380+32%	$20,000
$24,000	$28,000	$5,660+36%	$24,000
$28,000	$32,000	$7,100+39%	$28,000
$32,000	$36,000	$8,660+42%	$32,000
$36,000	$40,000	$10,340+45%	$36,000
$40,000	$44,000	$12,140+48%	$40,000
$44,000	$52,000	$14,060+50%	$44,000
$52,000	$64,000	$18,060+53%	$52,000
$64,000	$76,000	$24,420+55%	$64,000
$76,000	$88,000	$31,020+58%	$76,000
$88,000	$100,000	$37,980+60%	$88,000
$100,000	$120,000	$45,180+62%	$100,000
$120,000	$140,000	$57,580+64%	$120,000
$140,000	$160,000	$70,380+66%	$140,000
$160,000	$180,000	$83,580+68%	$160,000
$180,000	$200,000	$97,180+69%	$180,000
$200,000	....	$110,980+70%	$200,000

Married Taxpayers Filing Separate Returns

If the amount on Form 1040, line 48, is: / Enter on Form 1040, line 16:

Not over $500....**14% of the amount on line 48.**

Over—	But not over—		of excess over—
$500	$1,000	$70+15%	$500
$1,000	$1,500	$145+16%	$1,000
$1,500	$2,000	$225+17%	$1,500
$2,000	$4,000	$310+19%	$2,000
$4,000	$6,000	$690+22%	$4,000
$6,000	$8,000	$1,130+25%	$6,000
$8,000	$10,000	$1,630+28%	$8,000
$10,000	$12,000	$2,190+32%	$10,000
$12,000	$14,000	$2,830+36%	$12,000
$14,000	$16,000	$3,550+39%	$14,000
$16,000	$18,000	$4,330+42%	$16,000
$18,000	$20,000	$5,170+45%	$18,000
$20,000	$22,000	$6,070+48%	$20,000
$22,000	$26,000	$7,030+50%	$22,000
$26,000	$32,000	$9,030+53%	$26,000
$32,000	$38,000	$12,210+55%	$32,000
$38,000	$44,000	$15,510+58%	$38,000
$44,000	$50,000	$18,990+60%	$44,000
$50,000	$60,000	$22,590+62%	$50,000
$60,000	$70,000	$28,790+64%	$60,000
$70,000	$80,000	$35,190+66%	$70,000
$80,000	$90,000	$41,790+68%	$80,000
$90,000	$100,000	$48,590+69%	$90,000
$100,000		$55,490+70%	$100,000

Source: U.S. Internal Revenue Service, 1974 Income Tax Schedule.

exchange of a *capital asset*. Capital assets are those which are held for the production of income rather than for consumption or resale. In the United States, securities are classified as capital assets. The gain or loss from their sale is classified as a *long-term capital gain* or *loss* if the security has been owned for over six months.[3] This is an important distinction. The first $50,000 of long-term capital gains are taxed at a rate of one half the rate on ordinary income or 25 percent, which-

---

[3] A definition of what assets, other than securities, are classified as capital assets may be obtained from several sources. The Internal Revenue Service *Tax Code* is the most authoritative source and the most difficult to read. The current edition of *Your Income Tax* (Washington, D.C.: Internal Revenue Service) is a readable, condensed version of the *Code*. Other sources are the *U.S. Master Tax Guide* (Chicago: Commerce Clearing House) and J. K. Lasser's, *Your Income Tax* (New York: Simon & Schuster).

ever is the lesser.[4] Gains on securities held less than six months are taxed as ordinary income.

As an example of how long-term capital gains are taxed, assume that you sell stock which you owned for over six months for a profit of $2,000. This profit is computed by subtracting the purchase price and all brokerage fees, transfer taxes, and other direct expenses from the sale price. Other taxable income for the year amounts to $12,000, and you are a married taxpayer filing a joint return. From Schedule Y (Table 13–1) it can be seen that the tax on this $2,000 of marginal income would be levied at a rate of 25 percent if the profit were *ordinary income.*

However, this is a capital gain from the sale of an asset owned for over six months. The rate of tax on a long-term capital gain is one half the regular rate, or 12½ percent. The tax saving of $250 as shown in Table 13–2 is an important consideration for most persons. Note that the saving would have been even greater, $290, if the income belonged to a single taxpayer filing under Schedule X.

TABLE 13–2
Two Thousand Dollars of Income Taxed as Ordinary versus Capital Gain Income

Tax on ordinary income	$2,000 × 0.25 = $500
Tax on long-term capital gain income	$2,000 × 0.125 = 250
Difference in taxes	$250

COMPUTATION OF CAPITAL GAIN AND ORDINARY INCOME FROM SECURITY TRANSACTIONS

Almost all residents of the United States earning $750 or more must file a federal income tax return.[5] All persons now filing income tax returns use IRS Form 1040, and if they have gains or losses from the sale of securities, these transactions must be recorded on Schedule D, Form 1040 (see Figure 13–1).

[4] Capital gains, along with accelerated depreciation on real property, income from stock options, and several other forms of income or methods of reducing income are known as *tax preferences.* When tax preferences amount to over $15,000 for a single person, or $30,000 for two persons filing jointly (after various adjustments), an additional tax in an amount of 10 percent is levied against tax preferences in excess of the above amounts.

[5] There are exceptions to this rule. See the *Federal Income Tax Forms* (U.S. Treasury Department, Internal Revenue Service), or any of the many tax guides for these exceptions.

FIGURE 13–1
Schedule D (sales or exchanges of property)

SCHEDULE D (Form 1040)
Department of the Treasury
Internal Revenue Service

Capital Gains and Losses

(Examples of property to be reported on this Schedule are gains and losses on stocks, bonds, and similar investments, and gains (but not losses) on personal assets such as a home or jewelry.)
▶ Attach to Form 1040. ▶ See Instructions for Schedule D (Form 1040).

1974

Name(s) as shown on Form 1040 | Social security number

Part I Short-term Capital Gains and Losses—Assets Held Not More Than 6 Months **D**

	a. Kind of property and description (Example, 100 shares of "Z" Co.)	b. Date acquired (Mo., day, yr.)	c. Date sold (Mo., day, yr.)	d. Gross sales price	e. Cost or other basis, as adjusted (see instruction D) and expense of sale	f. Gain or (loss) (d less e)
1	100 shares of "W" Co.	2/6/74	4/11/74	2,000	3,000	(1,000.00)
	100 shares of "X" Co.	6/9/74	12/9/74	2,000	1,600	400.00

		Line	Amount
2	Enter your share of net short-term gain or (loss) from partnerships and fiduciaries	2	-0-
3	Enter net gain or (loss), combine lines 1 and 2	3	(600.00)
4(a)	Short-term capital loss component carryover from years beginning before 1970 (see Instruction G)	4(a)	(-0-)
(b)	Short-term capital loss carryover attributable to years beginning after 1969 (see Instruction G)	(b)	(-0-)
5	Net short-term gain or (loss), combine lines 3, 4(a) and (b)	5	(600.00)

Part II Long-term Capital Gains and Losses—Assets Held More Than 6 Months

	a. Kind of property and description	b. Date acquired	c. Date sold	d. Gross sales price	e. Cost or other basis	f. Gain or (loss)
6	200 shares of "Y" Co.	2/22/72	1/5/74	5,000	3,000	2,000.00
	$1M bond of "Z" Co.	1/9/74	7/10/74	1,000	500	500.00

		Line	Amount
7	Capital gain distributions	7	100.00
8	Enter gain, if applicable, from Form 4797, line 4(a)(1) (see Instruction A)	8	-0-
9	Enter your share of net long-term gain or (loss) from partnerships and fiduciaries	9	-0-
10	Enter your share of net long-term gain from small business corporations (Subchapter S)	10	-0-
11	Net gain or (loss), combine lines 6 through 10	11	2,600.00
12(a)	Long-term capital loss component carryover from years beginning before 1970 (see Instruction G)	12(a)	(-0-)
(b)	Long-term capital loss carryover attributable to years beginning after 1969 (see Instruction G)	(b)	(-0-)
13	Net long-term gain or (loss), combine lines 11, 12(a) and (b)	13	2,600.00

Part III Summary of Parts I and II

14 Combine the amounts shown on lines 5 and 13, and enter the net gain or loss here . . . . | 14 | 2,000.00

15 **If line 14 shows a gain—**
(a) Enter 50% of line 13 or 50% of line 14, whichever is smaller (see Part VI for computation of alternative tax). Enter zero if there is a loss or no entry on line 13. . . . | 15(a) | 1,000.00
(b) Subtract line 15(a) from line 14. Enter here and on Form 1040, line 29 . . . | (b) | 1,000.00

16 **If line 14 shows a loss—**
▶ If losses are shown on BOTH lines 12(a) and 13, omit lines 16(a) and (b) and go to Part IV. See Instruction H.
▶ Otherwise,
(a) Enter one of the following amounts:
(*i*) If amount on line 5 is zero or a net gain, enter 50% of amount on line 14;
(*ii*) If amount on line 13 is zero or a net gain, enter amount on line 14; or,
(*iii*) If amounts on line 5 and line 13 are net losses, enter amount on line 5 added to 50% of amount on line 13 . . . | 16(a) | -0-
(b) Enter here and enter as a (loss) on Form 1040, line 29, the smallest of:
(*i*) The amount on line 16(a);
(*ii*) $1,000 ($500 if married and filing a separate return—if a loss is shown on line 4(a) or 12(a), see instruction L for a higher limit not to exceed $1,000); or,
(*iii*) Taxable income, as adjusted (see Instruction K) . . . | (b) | (-0-)

Source: Internal Revenue Service, 1974 Income Tax Schedule D.

This schedule is used to record the sale of all types of capital assets —real property, livestock, and so on—but our discussion includes security transactions only. Schedule D has been designed so that the Internal Revenue Service can identify the assets sold, their period of ownership, and the amount of taxable loss or gain from their ownership. The form also makes it easy to separate short-term and long-term gains and losses.

Recording Capital Gains and Losses

In the normal process of filling out the form, short-term gains are first merged with short-term losses and long-term gains are merged with long-term losses. The purpose is to determine the two types of *net* gains and losses. Lines 2, 8, and 9 of Schedule D are not used when recording security transactions. The use of lines 4a, 4b, 7, 10, 12a and 12b will be explained later.

Figure 13–1 contains an example of *net* short-term and long-term capital gains. Investments in companies "W" and "X" were entered as short-term transactions because the securities were not held for *more than* six months. The gain on "X" was $400 and the loss on "W" was $1,000, for the net short-term loss of ($600).[6]

The holding time of "Z" is only one day longer than "X," but this is enough to qualify this gain as being long-term. Transactions in both "Y" and "Z" were profitable. The total long-term gain is $2,500; this amount is recorded on line 13 after combining this gain with those from any other sources. Line 14 is used to record the net gain or loss on all security transactions.

Directions for filling out lines 14 through 16b are self-explanatory, but the form is constructed in such a way that it is difficult to see exactly what is being done. The law requires that each taxpayer (1) identify short- and long-term capital gains and losses, (2) offset short-term gains against short-term losses, and long-term gains against long-term losses, and (3) pay income taxes on the short-term gains at the rate for regular income, and on the long-term gains at long-term capital gain rates. The law allows short-term capital losses to be offset against ordinary income on a dollar-for-dollar basis up to a maximum of $1,000 per year for persons filing joint returns, and $500 for persons filing separately. Up to $1,000 of long-term capital losses may be de-

[6] Numbers recorded in parentheses indicate losses.

ducted from ordinary income in any one year, but these losses may only be deducted on the basis of $2 of loss for each $1 of deduction. Losses which are larger than can be used in any tax year may be carried forward into future tax years. Changes in the tax code which limited the amounts of capital losses were effected by the Tax Reform Act of 1969. Losses incurred prior to 1970, when the act became effective, receive different treatment. Such losses are identified on lines 4a and 12a; losses incurred after 1969 which are carried forward are recorded on lines 4b and 12b of Schedule D.

Capital gains distributions, recorded on line 7, are the capital gains dividends paid by an investment company in which the investor owns shares. The investment company is required to inform each of its shareholders of the amount of long-term capital gains credited to their accounts each year. Dividend income and short-term capital gains of investment companies are taxed as ordinary income.

Line 10 of Schedule D is used to record the taxpayer's prorata share of certain income generated by Subchapter S corporations. Gains or losses as summarized on lines 15 or 16 are entered on line 29 of Form 1040. This entry appears on the back side of the 1974 Form 1040, where gains or losses recorded on Schedule D are merged with income and losses from other sources. The total of these revenues and expenses are brought forward and entered on line 12 of Form 1040. This example assumes no other income or expenses so the $1,000 of net long-term capital gain is entered on line 12 of Figure 13–3.

Recording Dividend and Interest Income

Income in the form of dividends and interest is *ordinary income* and must be recorded as such on Form 1040 and Schedule B of Form 1040. Figure 13–2 is a "filled in" Schedule B, and Figure 13–3 is a partially completed Form 1040. Part 1 of Schedule B lists dividend income; it must be filled out only if gross dividends are $400 or more. Regular dividends are listed on line 1 and totaled on line 2. On line 3 are listed capital gain distributions. Companies paying such dividends (mutual funds mostly) will identify which portion of their dividend is considered to be a capital gain. (See Chapter 11 for a review of how mutual funds report dividends.) On line 4 are recorded additional nontaxable distributions. Dividends listed on lines 3 and 4 are summed on line 5 and deducted from total dividends

FIGURE 13–2
Form 1040, Schedule B

Schedules A & B (Form 1040) 1974 **Schedule B—Dividend and Interest Income** Page 2

Name(s) as shown on Form 1040 (Do not enter name and social security number if shown on other side) | Your social security number

Part I Dividend Income

Note: *If gross dividends (including capital gain distributions) and other distributions on stock are $400 or less, do not complete this part. But enter gross dividends less the sum of capital gain distributions and non-taxable distributions, if any, on Form 1040, line 10a (see note below).*

1 Gross dividends (including capital gain distributions) and other distributions on stock. (List payers and amounts—write (H), (W), (J), for stock held by husband, wife, or jointly)

H Share of Smith Bros. Partnership	$175.00
H XYZ Mutual Fund	200.00
H R. D. Irwin, Inc.	60.00
W Ford Motor Co.	55.00
W General Motors Co.	30.00
2 Total of line 1	$520.00
3 Capital gain distributions (see instructions on page 13. Enter here and on Schedule D, line 7). See note below	100.00
4 Nontaxable distributions (see instructions on page 13)	-0-
5 Total (add lines 3 and 4)	100.00
6 **Dividends before exclusion (subtract line 5 from line 2).** Enter here and on Form 1040, line 10a	$420.00

Part II Interest Income

Note: *If interest is $400 or less, do not complete this part. But enter amount of interest received on Form 1040, line 11.*

7 Interest includes earnings from savings and loan associations, mutual savings banks, cooperative banks, and credit unions as well as interest on bank deposits, bonds, tax refunds, etc. Interest also includes original issue discount on bonds and other evidences of indebtedness (see instructions on page 13). (List payers and amounts)

Cloverleaf Bldg. and Loan	$16.75
State Savings Bank	574.28
U. S. Series E Bond ($100 bond) redeemed	25.00
Reynolds Tobacco Co. 8 1/8% Bonds (2M)	162.50
8 **Total interest income.** Enter here and on Form 1040, line 11	$778.53

Note: *If you received capital gain distributions and do not need Schedule D to report any other gains or losses or to compute the alternative tax, do not file that schedule. Instead, enter 50 percent of capital gain distributions on Form 1040, line 34.*

B

☆ U.S. GOVERNMENT PRINTING OFFICE: 1974—O-548-049 93—0151340

Source: Internal Revenue Service, 1974 Income Tax Schedule.

FIGURE 13–3
Form 1040

Form **1040** US Department of the Treasury—Internal Revenue Service **Individual Income Tax Return** **1974**

For the year January 1–December 31, 1974, or other taxable year beginning ...., 1974, ending ...., 19......

Please print or type

Name (If joint return, give first names and initials of both) | Last name | COUNTY OF RESIDENCE | Your social security number

Present home address (Number and street, including apartment number, or rural route) | Spouse's social security no.

City, town or post office, State and ZIP code | Occupation: Yours ▶ Spouse's ▶

Filing Status (check only one)

1 ☐ Single
2 ☐ Married filing joint return (even if only one had income)
3 ☐ Married filing separately. If spouse is also filing give spouse's social security number in designated space above and enter full name here ▶
4 ☐ Unmarried Head of Household (See instructions on page 5) ▶
5 ☐ Widow(er) with dependent child (Year spouse died ▶ 19)

Exemptions Regular / 65 or over / Blind

6a Yourself . . . ☐ ☐ ☐
b Spouse . . . ☐ ☐ ☐ Enter number of boxes checked ▶
c First names of your dependent children who lived with you .... Enter number ▶
d Number of other dependents (from line 27) . . . ▶
7 Total exemptions claimed . . . . ▶

8 Presidential Election Campaign Fund ▶ Do you wish to designate $1 of your taxes for this fund? . . Yes No
If joint return, does your spouse wish to designate $1? . . Yes No
Note: If you check the "Yes" box(es) it will not increase your tax or reduce your refund.

Please attach Copy B of Forms W–2 here

Income

9	Wages, salaries, tips, and other employee compensation (Attach Forms W–2. If unavailable, see instructions on page 3.) . . .	9	
10a	Dividends (See instructions on pages 6 and 13) $ 420.00, 10b Less exclusion $ 185.00, Balance ▶ (*If gross dividends and other distributions are over $400, list in Part I of Schedule B.*)	10c	$235.00
11	Interest income. [If $400 or less, enter total without listing in Schedule B / If over $400, enter total and list in Part II of Schedule B] .	11	778.53
12	Income other than wages, dividends, and interest (from line 38)	12	1,000.00
13	Total (add lines 9, 10c, 11, and 12)	13	
14	Adjustments to income (such as "sick pay," moving expenses, etc. from line 43) .	14	
15	Subtract line 14 from line 13 (adjusted gross income)	15	

- **If you do not itemize deductions and line 15 is under $10,000, find tax in Tables and enter on line 16.**
- **If you itemize deductions or line 15 is $10,000 or more, go to line 44 to figure tax.**
- CAUTION. If you have unearned income and can be claimed as a dependent on your parent's return, check here ▶ ☐ and see instructions on page 7.

Tax, Payments and Credits

16	Tax, check if from: ☐ Tax Tables 1–12 ☐ Schedule D ☐ Tax Rate Schedule X, Y, or Z ☐ Schedule G OR ☐ Form 4726	16	
17	Total credits (from line 54)	17	
18	Income tax (subtract line 17 from line 16)	18	
19	Other taxes (from line 61)	19	
20	Total (add lines 18 and 19)	20	
21a	Total Federal income tax withheld (attach Forms W–2 or W–2P to front)	21a	
b	1974 estimated tax payments (include amount allowed as credit from 1973 return)	b	
c	Amount paid with Form 4868, Application for Automatic Extension of Time to File U.S. Individual Income Tax Return	c	
d	Other payments (from line 65)	d	
22	Total (add lines 21a, b, c, and d)	22	

Please attach Check or Money Order here

Pay amount on line 23 in full with this return. Write social security number on check or money order and make payable to Internal Revenue Service.

Balance Due or Refund

23	If line 20 is larger than line 22, enter **BALANCE DUE IRS** . . . . ▶ (Check here ▶ ☐, if Form 2210, Form 2210F, or statement is attached. See instructions on page 7.)	23	
24	If line 22 is larger than line 20, enter amount **OVERPAID** . . . ▶	24	
25	Amount of line 24 to be **REFUNDED TO YOU** . . . . ▶	25	
26	Amount of line 24 to be credited on 1975 estimated tax. ▶	26	

If all of overpayment (line 24) is to be refunded (line 25), make no entry on line 26.

Sign here

Under penalties of perjury, I declare that I have examined this return, including accompanying schedules and statements, and to the best of my knowledge and belief it is true, correct, and complete. Declaration of preparer (other than taxpayer) is based on all information of which he has any knowledge.

▶ Your signature .... Date ▶ Preparer's signature (other than taxpayer) .... Date

▶ Spouse's signature (if filing jointly, BOTH must sign even if only one had income) .... Address (and ZIP Code) .... Preparer's Emp. Ident. or Soc. Sec. No.

Source: Internal Revenue Service, 1974 Income Tax Schedule.

listed on line 2. The amount remaining on line 6 is entered on line 10a of Form 1040.

Each taxpayer may exclude up to $100 of qualified dividend income from taxation. However, married persons filing joint returns are not automatically allowed to exclude $200 of dividend income. The exclusion applies to $100 of dividends *for each person.* In the example presented in Figure 13–2, the husband had total dividend income of $435, of which only $100 was excluded. The wife had only $85 of dividends. The total exclusion (line 10b, Form 1040) was $185. $100 of the XYZ Mutual Fund dividend of $200 was a capital gain dividend and is listed on line 3 of Schedule B; it was also listed on line 7 of Schedule D (shown in Figure 13–1).

Part II of Schedule B is used to report taxable interest income. All interest payments received throughout the year are recorded here and identified by their source if they amount to $400 or more. If less than this amount, the total only is reported on line 11 of Form 1040.

A Strategy for Capital Gains

The tax savings on long-term capital gains are so large and so obvious that many investors seek this kind of income to the exclusion of short-term gains. These investors reason that they can increase the after-tax return from their stock transactions by simply holding all investments until they qualify as long-term gains or losses. This policy is believed to be illogical and one that may actually *cause* losses.

Important factors in the decision to hold out for long-term treatment are (1) the time which remains to complete the six-month-and-one-day holding period, (2) the possible market price loss of the security over this period, (3) the marginal income tax rate paid by the investor, (4) already realized capital gains and losses, (5) the available investment alternatives. An example may illustrate how these factors are interrelated.

Assume that an investor has owned stock for one month and one day, and that it could be sold for a profit of $1,000. Further assume that the investor has no other capital gains or losses for this year and that taxes are levied at the marginal rate of 28 percent on additional income. To analyze this situation logically, the investor should compute the after-tax profit from this investment that could be realized through immediate sale. The following formula may be used to do this. As with most examples in this book, brokerage fees and other selling costs are omitted to simplify the calculations, and state income taxes are not included.

Let

I_a = Income after taxes
I_b = Income before taxes
T = Investor's marginal tax rate
t = Investor's long-term capital gain tax rate

Then

$$\begin{aligned} I_a &= I_b(1 - T) \\ &= \$1{,}000(1 - 0.28) \\ &= \$1{,}000(0.72) \\ I_a &= \$720 \end{aligned}$$

If the investor sells now, the after-tax profits will be $720. If the securities are held for five more months, the gain (if any) will be *long-term* and taxed at one half of 28 percent or 14 percent. The important question is how much of this present $1,000 gain could be lost over the next five months and still provide the investor with $720 of after-tax income. By substituting the long-term gains income tax rate of t = 14 percent into the above formula and solving it for I_b, one can determine the lowest price to which the investment can drop and still give the investor $720 of after-tax profit.

$$\begin{aligned} I_b &= I_a/(1 - t) \\ &= \$720/(1 - 0.14) \\ &= \$720/0.86 \\ I_b &= \$837.21 \end{aligned}$$

If the value of the investment did not drop to less than $837.21, the after-tax profit on the investment would remain the same. The investor should base the decision of whether to hold or sell partially on whether it is likely that the profit on the investment will be reduced by no more than this amount over the next five months. If it is unlikely that the market price will dip this low, after-tax profits can be increased by holding for the six-month period.

Of further consideration are the available alternative investment opportunities and the gains and losses on other capital investment transactions which already have taken place or which might take place. For example, if this person has available another investment which appears very profitable, it may be logical to sell this one to provide funds to buy it. In this case lowered taxes through long-term capital gains may not be an important consideration. If this investor already has a substantial amount of losses it may be prudent to establish this gain immediately, without regard to whether it is long-term or short-term. The already realized losses can be used to offset the gain from this investment regardless of its holding time.

Each investor should consider his or her own situation when making investment decisions. Long-term gains are usually preferable to short-term gains, but as it has often been said, "You cannot go broke taking a profit."[7]

The example of security trades in Figure 13–1 shows that if the investment in "X" company had been held one more day it would have qualified as a long-term capital gain. The natural reaction is to say it should have been held one day longer. However, had this been done, the taxes paid by this investor in the current year would not have been altered because total merged gains would still be $2,000. It is unlikely that an investment would suffer much loss in value in one day. However, if the additional period necessary to qualify the investment for long-term gains had been a week, a month, or longer, substantial price loss could have occurred. In the above example there was no tax-associated reason for accepting this risk. Investors should not blindly seek long-term capital gains; rather they should analyze each investment decision in light of its effect on their total tax burden.

TIMING OF INVESTMENT INCOME

Gains and losses on investments affect the income tax position of the person receiving them during the year in which these gains or losses are realized, except to the extent that losses can be carried forward. It is often desirable to shift investment profits or losses from one tax period to another to lower income taxes. Several of the more common methods of doing this are presented. It should be recognized that there are other, more complex, ways of obtaining the same results.

---

[7] While this statement is completely true, taking a profit *too soon* tends to lower the potential profit from the investment. Studies indicate that many small investors are unsuccessful because they sell profitable investments too soon and hold losing investments too long. The old stock market adage "cut your losses short and let your profits run" is as true today as it ever was.

Taking Losses or Gains in a Particular Year

The tax year for almost all individuals begins January 1 and ends December 31. To establish a *loss* during a given tax year an investment may be sold at any time during the year *up to and including* December 31. To establish a gain the proceeds from the transaction must be available by December 31. This usually means that an investor can take a gain in a given year only if securities are sold at least five business days before the end of the year. This rule is based on the current five-day delivery period allowed brokerage houses. Exceptions to it may be made for persons using an accrual accounting system and for securities sold for next-day delivery. *Paper profits* and *losses* are profits and losses that an investor has or has had from investment but which have not been realized through sale. A paper profit or loss has no meaning for tax purposes until it is realized through sale of the security.

Taxpayers should begin preparation of their personal income tax statements in December, if not earlier. Although all information necessary to complete the return will probably not yet be available, it can easily be determined whether to attempt to shift gains or losses into or out of the current tax year. If one waits until February, when all pertinent information is available, it will be too late to shift losses or gains.

The simplest kind of tax timing problem is one of determining whether to take gains or losses in the current tax year or in a later one. As a general statement, if current year income is higher than the expected income of next year, losses should be taken in the current year and gains postponed until later. If future income is expected to increase, the reverse strategy should be used. Since personal income tax rates increase as income increases, total taxes may be minimized by keeping any single year's income from becoming "too large."

It is not so obvious that it is possible to take investment *gains* in a given year and continue to own the investments. An investor who had a large gain in a security that was expected to rise in price might wish to do this. This security could be sold and repurchased immediately at the same price, plus brokerage charges of course. The sale would establish a profit in the year in which the investor wanted to take it, and the "new" securities that were purchased would provide a higher base from which to compute future capital gains.

An investor is not allowed to take a *loss* in a given year and still own the investment. One may not repurchase the identical securities sold or "substantially identical securities," or an option to purchase substantially identical securities, within 30 days before or after the sale of the security in question.[8] A transaction which violates this rule is called a *wash sale*. Losses from wash sales are not deductible losses.

There are several ways around this law. First, identical securities can be purchased 31 days before the "old" securities are sold. Investors may take losses this way, but they must own double the original number of shares for 31 days. Second, the investor can sell the securities and wait 31 days to repurchase them. But in the interim the price may go up or down, and this is exactly the risk that the investor wishes to protect against. Third, this investment can be exchanged for one having similar, but not identical, characteristics. This is easy to do if the securities are bonds, because bonds of like grade and maturity are very similar securities indeed. Finding a suitable exchange for common stock is difficult, and one always runs the risk that the new securities will not perform identically to those originally owned. Most of the large brokerage houses compile lists of securities which they believe would be good "tax exchanges." Figure 13–4 is an example of such a list. ACF Industries is seen as a good exchange for Pullman Inc. and vice versa, AMAX Inc. for Utah International, and so on down the list. If the exchange is into securities of a different company, there is no question that the loss will be allowed, but if the exchange is into another class of securities of the same company, the Internal Revenue Service may not allow the loss.

Gains can be protected by complicated transactions involving puts and calls, warrants, and/or convertible securities. It is suggested that investors obtain professional advice on these types of trades.

Tax Treatment of Debt Securities Sold at a Discount

Certain debt securities, most notably Treasury bills and Series E savings bonds, do not pay periodic interest. The yield on these securities is the difference between the current value and the maturity value of the security. Owners of these securities have the option of either paying taxes on the interest income each year as it accumulates or all at once when the security matures.

The longest Treasury bill maturities are one year. Consequently,

---

[8] The courts have defined "substantially identical securities" in various ways. Nonconvertible bonds and preferred stock are usually not identical to the common of the same company, but convertible bonds or preferred stock or warrants of the same firm generally are. Persons contemplating this sort of switch should seek competent professional advice *before* beginning the switch.

FIGURE 13–4
Tax Exchanges

Tax Exchanges

March 1975

Merrill Lynch Pierce Fenner & Smith Inc.

Securities Research Division

Stock Comment No. 6

The following exchange suggestions are presented for the use of investors who may wish to establish capital gains or losses. The exchanges in this first section are intended to be satisfactory in either direction; that is, exchanges may be made from stocks in the left-hand column into stocks in the right-hand column and vice versa, as the investor sees fit. It should be emphasized that these suggestions are being made for tax purposes.

I. SUGGESTED TWO-WAY EXCHANGES FOR TAX PURPOSES

Company	Price 3/18/75	Dividend†	Yield %	Company	Price 3/18/75	Dividend†	Yield %
ACF Industries	42	$2.60	6.2	Pullman Inc. (S)	44	$1.70	3.9
Amax Inc. (S)	40	1.75	4.4	Utah International (S)	55	1.00	1.8
Amax Inc. (S)	40	1.75	4.4	St. Joe Minerals	42	2.20	5.2
+Acushnet Co. (S)	13	0.60	4.6	Coleman Co., Inc. (S)	8 3/8	0.44	5.3
Air Products & Chemicals (S)	65	0.20b	0.3b	Big Three Inds. (S)	41	0.48	1.2
American Can	34	2.20f	6.5f	Continental Can (S)	27	1.80	6.7
American Hoist & Derrick (S)	11	0.70	6.4	Trinity Industries	16	0.80	5.0
American Home Products (S)	39	0.88	2.3	Squibb Corp. (S)	39	0.84	2.2
Ametek, Inc. (S)	14	1.00	7.1	+Kaman Corp. Cl. A	16	0.80	5.0
Armco Steel (S)	29	1.60	5.5	Republic Steel (S)	32	1.60	5.0
Δ+BankAmerica Corp. (M)	38	1.48	3.9	ΔWells Fargo & Co.	16	0.96	6.0
Baxter Laboratories (L)	44	0.19	0.4	Merck & Co., Inc. (L)	78	1.40	1.8
Bendix Corp.	34	1.80	5.3	ΔEaton Corp. (S)	27	1.80	6.7
Bethlehem Steel (S)	34	2.75c	8.1c	Lukens Steel Co. (S)	27	1.40	5.2
Blue Bell (S)	20	0.80	4.0	ΔV. F. Corp. (S)	21	1.00	4.8
Boeing Company (S)	21	0.80	3.8	General Dynamics (S)	31	Nil	–
Borden, Inc. (S)	24	1.30	5.4	Norton-Simon	19	0.40b	2.1b
CBS, Inc.	45	1.46	3.2	Walt Disney Productions (S)	44	0.12b	0.3b
CMI Investment (S)	10	Nil	–	MGIC Investment (S)	13	0.10	0.8
Carter Hawley Hale	22	0.80	3.6	Mercantile Stores	43	0.80	1.9
Cessna Aircraft Co.	16	1.00	6.3	Beech Aircraft Corp. (S)	11	0.60b	5.5
Chesebrough-Pond's (S)	62	1.36	2.2	Revlon Inc. (S)	68	1.20	1.8
ΔChrysler Corp. (S)	11	Nil	–	American Motors (S)	6 1/8	Nil	–
Colgate-Palmolive (S)	30	0.68	2.3	Eastman Kodak (L)	93	1.56f	1.7f
Collins & Aikman (S)	6 1/2	0.40	6.2	Bath Inds. (S)	10	0.40	4.0
Collins Foods International	4 3/4	Nil	–	Specialty Restaurants	4	Nil	–
Colonial Stores	20	1.25	6.3	Jewel Co's	24	1.20	5.0
Connecticut General Mtg. & Rlty. Inv.	15	1.45h	9.7h	Equitable Life Mortgage & Realty	18	1.85-1.90h	10.4h
Continental Illinois Corp.	34	2.20	6.5	First Chicago Corp.	18	0.90	5.0
Copperweld Corp. (S)	26	1.80	6.9	Colt Industries (S)	29	2.00	6.9

Source: Merrill Lynch, Pierce, Fenner, and Smith, Inc.

the maximum amount of time that the taxes on these investments can be deferred is from one year to the next. For example, the income from bills purchased during one year can be taxed in the next if the bills mature during the next year. Series E savings bonds offer investors better income tax deferral characteristics than most discount securities because these investments have longer maturities. Series E bonds may currently be held for up to 30 years past their stated maturity date. They continue to appreciate in price, thus providing owners with continued income at a 6 percent rate.

As we stated before, taxes on the income from these securities can either be paid as they accrue or when the securities mature. Many persons choose to hold Series E bonds until retirement. At this time their incomes are lower, and as a consequence income from the securities is taxed at a lower rate. Of further advantage is the ability to exchange Series E for Series H bonds. So long as the entire accrued value of the Series E bonds is converted into the other series no taxes are levied on the accrued income. Series H bonds pay semiannual interest to their holders and therefore have much appeal to retired persons living partially or wholly on income from savings. The periodic interest payments are taxed as ordinary income in the year they are received. When the Series H bonds mature, taxes must be paid on the amount of income on the Series E bonds which was converted into Series H bonds. Series H bonds currently have a maturity of ten years. They may be retained for an additional ten years, however. Investors may, through purchase of Series E and later conversion to H bonds, defer taxes on the Series E income for over 50 years.

Holders of notes, bills, and other debt securities which are sold at a discount and pay no coupon amount of interest are accorded the privilege of either paying taxes on the accrued amount of income earned yearly or paying taxes on all accrued income when the security is sold or matures. They do not have the option of further deferring taxes by extending these contracts past their maturity date or by exchanging them for other debt contracts.

INVESTMENTS PROVIDING TAX-FREE OR REDUCED-TAX INCOME

Municipal Securities

Interest on debt obligations of all states and political subdivisions of states are wholly exempt from federal income taxes. This broad class of securities includes the debt of toll road commissions, port and utility service authorities, and other bodies created to further public functions. The investment characteristics of these securities, which are all called municipals, have been examined in Chapter 8. At this time the tax treatment given these securities is our single concern.

Municipals have the greatest value for persons in the high income tax brackets. This can easily be seen by using a formula which tells how much a taxable security would have to yield on a *before-tax basis* in order to provide an after-tax yield equivalent to that of a municipal bond of a given grade and maturity. This formula is nearly identical to that derived in the previous section of this chapter. The formula works equally well using the yearly dollar amount of interest paid as I or by using the current yield as I. For reasons explained later, it is incorrect to use the yield to maturity rate.

Let

I_b = Interest payment before taxes
I_a = Interest payment after taxes, or tax-free interest
t = Marginal income tax rate of person receiving interest

Then

$$I_a = I_b(1 - t)$$

Assume that you are offered a municipal bond which has a current yield of 5 percent. How much yield would you have to receive on a corporate bond having the same grade and maturity in order to be indifferent to which security ycu purchased? Assume taxes are 36 percent of all taxable income.

$$\begin{aligned} I_b &= I_a/(1 - t) \\ &= 0.05/(1 - 0.36) \\ &= 0.05/0.64 \\ I_b &= 0.078 \text{ or } 7.8\% \end{aligned}$$

If you were taxed at a rate of 36 percent, a 7.8 percent current yield before taxes would just equal 5 percent after taxes. It should be obvious that as the tax rate increases, the tax advantage of municipal securities increases, and vice versa. At an income tax rate of 60 percent, a nontaxable current yield of 5 percent is equivalent to a taxable yield of 12.5 percent. At the lowest personal income taxe rate of 14 percent the equivalent before tax yield is only 5.8 percent. Because of this, municipals are owned mainly by businesses and persons in the very high income tax brackets.

Investors can use the above formula to determine whether they would be better off to invest in tax free or taxable bonds. This is done by comparing the current yield of a municipal bond to the current yield of a taxable bond having similar grade and maturity characteristics to see which provides the greater *after-tax* yield. Brokerage houses routinely prepare computations which equate taxable and nontaxable bond yields at various tax rates. Figure 13–5 is one of these tables.

FIGURE 13–5
Table Equating Nontaxable Municipal Bond Yields to Taxable Yields

TAX EXEMPT VS. TAXABLE YIELDS

Taxable Income			Following Yields (%) On Tax-Exempt Securities										
More Than	But Not Over	Tax % Rate	4.00	4.50	5.00	5.50	6.00	6.25	6.50	6.75	7.00	7.25	7.50
			Are Equal to Yields Below on Taxable Issues										
$4,000	$8,000	19	4.94	5.56	6.17	6.79	7.41	7.72	8.02	8.33	8.64	8.95	9.26
8,000	12,000	22	5.13	5.77	6.41	7.05	7.69	8.01	8.33	8.65	8.97	9.29	9.62
12,000	16,000	25	5.33	6.00	6.67	7.33	8.00	8.33	8.67	9.00	9.33	9.67	10.00
16,000	20,000	28	5.56	6.25	6.94	7.64	8.33	8.68	9.03	9.38	9.72	10.07	10.42
20,000	24,000	32	5.88	6.62	7.35	8.09	8.82	9.19	9.56	9.93	10.29	10.66	11.03
24,000	28,000	36	6.25	7.03	7.81	8.59	9.38	9.77	10.16	10.55	10.94	11.33	11.72
28,000	32,000	39	6.56	7.38	8.20	9.02	9.84	10.25	10.66	11.07	11.48	11.89	12.30
32,000	36,000	42	6.90	7.76	8.62	9.48	10.34	10.78	11.21	11.64	12.07	12.50	12.93
36,000	40,000	45	7.27	8.18	9.09	10.00	10.91	11.36	11.82	12.27	12.73	13.18	13.64
40,000	44,000	48	7.69	8.65	9.62	10.58	11.54	12.02	12.50	12.98	13.46	13.94	14.42
44,000	52,000	50	8.00	9.00	10.00	11.00	12.00	12.50	13.00	13.50	14.00	14.50	15.00
52,000	64,000	53	8.51	9.57	10.64	11.70	12.77	13.30	13.83	14.36	14.89	15.43	15.96
64,000	76,000	55	8.89	10.00	11.11	12.22	13.33	13.89	14.44	15.00	15.56	16.11	16.67
76,000	88,000	58	9.52	10.71	11.90	13.10	14.29	14.88	15.48	16.07	16.67	17.26	17.86
88,000	100,000	60	10.00	11.25	12.50	13.75	15.00	15.63	16.25	16.88	17.50	18.13	18.75
100,000	120,000	62	10.53	11.84	13.16	14.47	15.79	16.45	17.11	17.76	18.42	19.08	19.74
120,000	140,000	64	11.11	12.50	13.89	15.28	16.67	17.36	18.06	18.75	19.44	20.14	20.83
140,000	160,000	66	11.76	13.24	14.71	16.18	17.65	18.38	19.12	19.85	20.59	21.32	22.06
160,000	180,000	68	12.50	14.06	15.63	17.19	18.75	19.53	20.31	21.09	21.88	22.66	23.44
180,000	200,000	69	12.90	14.52	16.13	17.74	19.35	20.16	20.97	21.77	22.58	23.39	24.19
200,000 up		70	13.33	15.00	16.67	18.33	20.00	20.83	21.67	22.50	23.33	24.17	25.00
Corporation													
$25,000		22	5.13	5.77	6.41	7.05	7.69	8.01	8.33	8.65	8.97	9.29	9.62
25,000 up		48	7.69	8.65	9.62	10.58	11.54	12.02	12.50	12.98	13.46	13.94	14.42

Tax rates are for married taxpayers filing joint returns.

Source: Standard & Poor's, Inc.

Capital Gain Taxes on Municipals. Capital gain income from the sales of municipals—long-term as well as short-term—is *taxable,* and capital losses are *deductible.* A municipal purchased for $900 and held to maturity would cause its owner to pay taxes on the capital gain of $100. Such losses and gains must be recorded along with other capital losses and gains on Schedule D of Form 1040.

The yield to maturity calculation includes the capital gain or loss on bond investments as part of the yield.[9] Such yields are often presented by financial reporting services for both taxable and nontaxable

[9] This computation was explained in the appendix to Chapter 8.

securities. While these yields may be used for comparative purposes, the investor should realize that the portion of the yield to maturity that is due to the capital gain obtained from holding the security to maturity is taxable. The after-tax yield to maturity is somewhat less than indicated.

U.S. Estate Tax Bonds

Certain Treasury bonds, when owned as part of a decedent's estate are redeemable at par and accrued interest *if* they are applied against the decedent's federal estate tax liabilities. Persons having estates large enough that federal estate taxes will be levied against them may find these securities to be exceptionally good investments.[10] Table 13–3 lists Treasury issues which qualified for application against federal estate taxes in 1975.

TABLE 13–3
U.S. Treasury Bonds Eligible for Application against Federal Estate Taxes at Par

2 3/4s.	1975–80	April	4 1/4s.	1987–92	August
4 1/4s.	1975–85	May	4s	1988–93	February
3 1/4s.	1978–83	June	4 1/8s.	1989–94	May
4s	1980	February	3 1/2s.	1990	February
3 1/2s.	1980	November	3s	1995	February
3 1/4s.	1985	May	3 1/2s.	1998	November

Source: *Handbook of Securities of the United States Government and Federal Agencies, and Related Money Market Instruments*, 26th ed. (New York: The First Boston Corporation, 1974), p. 52.

In recent years any of the long-term bonds could have been purchased at substantial discounts. For example, the 3½s of 1990 could have been purchased at 74 during January 1975; $740 of these bonds would have paid $1,000 of estate taxes. Many wealthy investors (mostly older persons) try to hold enough of these securities to pay anticipated estate taxes. Investors obtain interest payments as long as they hold the securities, of course. But because of their desirable tax characteristics, demand for these securities has lowered their yield relative to other similar U.S. Treasury debt instruments. The amount

10 Federal estate taxes are levied against estates of over $60,000 in amount, after deduction of certain death expenses and a marital deduction. Tax rates vary from 3 percent on the first $5,000 of taxable estate to 77 percent on estates of over $10 million. See *U.S. Master Tax Guide* (Chicago: Commerce Clearing House 1974), pp. 31, 32.

of this premium can easily be determined by comparing the yield to maturity of any of the above listed "flower bonds," as they are called, to the yield on Treasury securities of similar maturity which cannot be used to pay federal estate taxes at par.

Investments in Assets Which Receive Preferential Tax Treatment

For many years the tax laws have allowed special treatment for certain types of investments such as cattle farming, oil and gas drilling, real estate, and so on. The intent has always been either to provide an incentive for investors to take the risks associated with a particular kind of investment—drilling for oil—or to lower income taxes for a particular group of people—farmers.

The Tax Reform Act of 1969 was specifically designed to reduce the tax advantages that certain investments traditionally held. There is little doubt that investments which were desirable largely because of the way they were taxed have been adversely affected by the changed tax laws, but how much or whether they will continue to be affected is anyone's guess. It is desirable that persons seeking investments having special tax characteristics obtain competent professional advice before purchasing them.

Retirement Plans Which Defer Taxes

For many years employees have received the benefit of deferred taxes from retirement plans which were paid for by employers. More recently, employees have been allowed to make contributions from their salaries into various retirement plans which also grant them tax advantages. Tax advantages of the employer-financed plans derive from the fact that the employee is not taxed upon the amounts of money the employer contributes to the employee's benefit plan. The retirement benefits are taxed as income as they are received, but when this happens most persons have lowered incomes and are therefore taxed at a lower marginal rate. If they have reached the age of 65 they receive additional tax concessions which act to decrease the amount of taxes paid. Employees normally do not have any control over the amount of employer contributions to these plans or the benefits attained because the plans must by law provide equal treatment for all classes of employees.

Employee contribution plans provide persons with the ability to purchase additional retirement benefits by making the contributions themselves. Portions of many of these contributions may be deducted from the taxable income generated in the year in which the contribution is made. Until recently, self-employed persons had only limited opportunity to create a retirement plan with contributions which were partially or totally tax deferred. Prior to December 31, 1975 Keogh plans (also known as HR–10 plans) allowed self-employed persons to contribute each year 10 percent of their earnings or $2,500, whichever was lesser, into a retirement plan. The contributions were deducted from gross income, thus lowering taxable income in the year of the deduction. When the person retired, income from the retirement plan was taxed at regular rates.

The Pension Reform Law of 1974 (which became effective January 1, 1975) increased the amount of retirement plan contributions that could be made by self-employed persons to 15 percent of taxable income or $7,500, whichever is lesser. It is expected that many persons who did not use the Keogh plan originally, because the maximum contributions were so small that they did not materially affect potential retirement income, will take advantage of the higher contribution limits to start these plans.

Advantages of the employee contribution plans are straightforward and for the most part obvious: Contributions made into any retirement plan which qualifies for tax deferred treatment of contributions allows the amount of the contribution to be deducted from gross income, thereby reducing the individual's taxable income. Plans in which all contributions are made by the employer work the same way if one assumes that these contributions, if not made by the employer, would be given to the employee in the form of additional wages—which would be subject to income taxation.

The amount of tax savings from retirement plan contributions can be computed by using a formula similar to the one derived earlier in this chapter.

Let

S = Tax saving
C = Contribution to a retirement program which is tax deferred
t = Marginal income tax rate of person making contribution

$$S = Ct$$

A person in the 40 percent income tax bracket who makes a contribution of $5,000 into a qualified retirement program will have a tax saving of $2,000, as calculated on the following page.

$$S = \$5,000\,(.40)$$
$$= \$2,000$$

Stated another way, the $5,000 contribution to the retirement fund only "cost" the taxpayer $3,000 in lowered current-year income because the contribution "saved" the taxpayer $2,000 in the form of reduced income taxes. True, when payments from the retirement fund are received by the taxpayer they will be taxed. But taxes will probably then be at a lower marginal rate. Even if tax rates remained the same it would still be beneficial to postpone payment of taxes, because the money not paid in taxes can be invested.

For example, tax deferred contributions allow a person to invest more money in a retirement account than could be invested if the contributions were not tax deductible. The ability to do this increases the total value of the account when the owner wishes to make use of it. Let us return to the above example, where the person making the contribution earned $5,000 which was put directly into a retirement plan. Had this contribution not been tax deductible, $2,000 of the $5,000 would have gone to taxes; only $3,000 could have been put into the retirement fund without lowering the person's after-tax income. A fund having contributions of $5,000 made to it will obviously accumulate to a larger amount than one receiving $3,000 contributions. Table 13–4 shows how great this difference can amount to over three different time periods.

The entire amount of the "tax-free" account will be subject to taxation as income is taken from the fund. Only the returns from the "taxable" fund, not the principal, will be taxed as it is used because taxes have already been paid on the principal part of this fund. Except in cases where the taxpayer will obtain more income after retiring

TABLE 13–4
Value of a Retirement Fund after Various Periods of Time* (yearly contribution is $5,000)

	After 10 Years		*After 20 Years*		*After 30 Years*	
Annual Rate of Return	*Tax Free Account*	*Taxable Account*	*Tax Free Account*	*Taxable Account*	*Tax Free Account*	*Taxable Account*
5%	$62,890	$37,734	$165,330	$ 99,198	$332,195	$199,317
6%	65,905	39,543	183,930	110,358	395,290	237,174
7%	69,080	41,448	204,975	122,985	472,305	283,383

* This example assumes that the contributor pays taxes at a rate of 40 percent while the fund accumulates, that the full $5,000 contribution was placed in the tax-free account but that only the after-tax amount of $3,000 was placed in the taxable account, and that lump sum payments of these amounts were made to each fund at the end of the year.

than while making contributions into a retirement fund, the ability to reduce current taxes through deductible retirement contributions is advantageous. Such programs should be considered by all persons who wish to build a retirement program in excess of that provided by their employer and Social Security. Retirement fund contributions can be placed in a variety of investments. Management of these funds is performed by life insurance companies, commercial banks, savings banks, mutual funds, and companies offering financial management or investment services. The investor might also in some cases purchase Treasury Series E or H bonds with the contributions. Of all areas of investment, this area is probably the most complex and difficult for the layperson to understand. An error in the preparation of a retirement program can have enormous long-run adverse effects. Competent advice should be obtained by anyone wishing to set up an individual retirement plan.

Investments Exempt from State Income Taxes

Most states levy their income taxes against the same income as does the federal government. The single most important exception to this statement is interest on certain bonds issued by the federal government. Some states exempt all or a portion of interest income on federal securities from their income taxes. They almost universally exempt the interest on debt issued by municipals located in the state. Interest income on the debt of municipals located in other states is sometimes taxed. Since state income taxes are always levied at a far lower rate than federal income taxes, the ability to avoid these taxes may seem unimportant. However, the alert investor can often increase after-tax investment returns by choosing securities that have tax benefits. When this can be done without sacrificing yield or some other desirable investment characteristic it should be done even though the gain seems small.

KEEPING RECORDS

Some people purchase investments, lock them away in a safe deposit box, and forget them. This practice minimizes the time spent in managing investments, but it also may minimize their profits. Investments should be followed closely, and records should be kept of price performance, dividend and interest income, and any other important changes in the fortunes of the company. Records may be kept in many different ways, depending upon the purpose of the record.

Keeping Records for Income Taxes

By law, U.S. taxpayers must keep records which will enable them to prepare an accurate tax return. Furthermore, these records and supporting documents—canceled checks, brokerage tickets, or other receipts—must be kept for as long as they may be material in administering any internal revenue law. This does not mean they must be kept forever. Rather, they must be kept until the *statute of limitations* has expired. Normally, this means that records supporting a given income tax return must be kept for three years from the date the return was filed, or two years from when the tax was paid. If securities were purchased and held for ten years, then sold, the records of that particular transaction would have been held by the investor for a total of 13 years to comply with the legal requirements for reporting taxes.

Because the holding period for an investment may span several income tax periods, it is usually desirable to keep investment records separate from other tax records. For purposes of recording capital gains and losses, the record form should identify the amount and type of investment, the date acquired and sold, the cost price and sale price, and a column to record whether the transaction was a long-term or short-term gain or loss. A form which would record this information is presented as Figure 13–6. Most brokerage houses have such forms available for the asking.

This sort of form is usually maintained throughout the year and examined closely while it is still possible to sell securities to take gains and losses within the current tax year.

For recording data on the prices, dividends or interest, and other characteristics of various security investments a form like the one presented in Figure 13–7 may be used. This form provides data of as

FIGURE 13–6
Form for Recording Capital Gains and Losses on Securities

No. of Shares or Bonds	Company	Date Acquired	Date Sold	Purchase Price	Sale Price	Short-Term		Long-Term	
						Losses	Gains	Losses	Gains

FIGURE 13–7
Investment Record Form for a Single Security

Name of company ____________________

Type of security ________ Number of shares or bonds ____________________

Purchase date and price ____________________

Sale date and price ____________________

Gain or loss on transaction ____________________

Dividend or interest payment dates:

	1st Quarter			2d Quarter			3d Quarter			4th Quarter		
Year	Declaration Date	Amt. Recd.	Date Recd.	Declaration Date	Amt. Recd.	Date Recd.	Declaration Date	Amt. Recd.	Date Recd.	Declaration Date	Amt. Recd.	Date Recd.

Price history of security:

Year	Jan	Feb	Mar	Apr	May	June	July	Aug	Sept	Oct	Nov	Dec

Other important information:

much detail as the investor may wish to prepare, while the form presented as Figure 13–6 is used mainly for income tax purposes.

Figure 13–7 allows the investor to anticipate dividend and interest payments. Such information is useful for persons who are obtaining a substantial portion of their income from interest and/or dividends. It allows them to plan for their arrival; and it also helps the investor to make certain that dividends or interest that are owed have in fact been paid. This is less of a problem when securities are held by the investor; dividends and interest are then mailed directly to this person. When securities are held in a street name at a brokerage house, dividends and interest payments are made to the brokerage house which then credits these amounts to the account of the owner. It is a wise precaution to keep track of these payments as they arrive even though the brokerage house provides you with a monthly statement. Mistakes are made, and without some sort of procedure for recording dividends and interest payments as they are received, it is difficult to detect when a payment has been missed. By February 15, all shareholders are supposed to be notified of the amounts of dividends, and interest they have been paid during the preceding year. This information is usually accurate, but it arrives too late to be useful in preparing an "early" tax estimation.

Many investors like to record the price history of their investments on a monthly, weekly, or even daily basis. Figure 13–7 is arranged for monthly compilations, but it would not be difficult to alter the form for weekly use. Several companies sell prepared charts for the recording of this type information.

Other important information that might be recorded would be stock splits and dividends, insider activity in the stock, or practically anything the investor decides is important.

The record keeping suggested above is probably the *minimum amount* that an investor should undertake. Obtaining profits from investments is a difficult and somewhat time-consuming task. The intelligent investor constantly examines all securities owned to see how they are performing and whether individual investments continue to live up to the expectations that prompted their purchase. This need not be a full-time occupation, except for persons having exceptionally large amounts of investments, but each investor must spend some time at this task. Investments do not take care of themselves.

SUMMARY

Taxes are the burden of modern man. Not only are they costly to pay and bothersome to compute, but under our *progressive* income tax structure, the more you earn, the larger the fraction of taxable income that is taxed away. Or so goes the theory of progressive taxation. In actuality it is possible to reduce and minimize taxes by perfectly legal means. This possibility is documented by data which show that as persons' incomes increase, their income taxes do not increase as much as tax rate schedules indicate they should. What happens is this. Wealthy persons are able to hire competent advisors who tell them how to minimize taxes. This chapter explains some of the simplest ways of minimizing taxes on investment income and how to keep the necessary records of investment transactions.

Ordinary income is income received as salary, wages, interest payments, rent, and so on. This income is taxed at regular income tax rates. *Capital gain* income is that received from the sale of a capital asset. *Short-term capital gains* are taxed as ordinary income; *long-term capital gains* are taxed at about one half these rates. The procedure for recording income received as capital gains is to offset short-term losses against short-term gains, and long-term gains against long-term losses. In this way, *net* short-term and long-term gains are computed and taxed at the appropriate rates. With few exceptions, the gain or loss from the sale of an asset owned over six months is classified as a long-term gain or loss; the transaction is short-term if the asset is held less than six months. It is usually, but not always, desirable to hold securities long enough to qualify them for long-term capital gain treatment since taxes are thereby appreciably lowered.

Capital gains and losses from security transactions are currently recorded on Schedule D of the Internal Revenue Service Form 1040. Dividend and interest income—if over $400 in amount—is recorded on Schedule B of Form 1040. Dividends on stocks are of three main types—regular, capital gain, and nontaxable distributions. Regular dividends are taxed as ordinary income, but each taxpayer is allowed to exclude up to $100 of dividend income from taxation. Nontaxable distributions are not taxed, but capital gain dividends are taxed at the low capital gain rate.

Timing of investment income refers to when (in which tax year) a given gain or loss is taxed. The rule is that a transaction is completed and taxed, in the year in which it is sold. It is sometimes desirable to take a loss in a given year while continuing to own the security. This can be accomplished by purchasing an identical number of the same securities 31 days before or 31 days after selling the securities in question. The gain or loss from the "old" securities is taken in the current tax year, but the same number of identical securities continue to be owned. Losses from security sales are not allowed if identical securities are purchased within 30 days of the sale. Another way of taking a loss, while continuing to effectively own a security, is to exchange the security sold for that of a different company having identical investment characteristics.

Securities sold at a discount which pay no periodic interest provide investors with the ability to defer payment of taxes on the income from these securities until the security matures. This feature is especially valuable for owners of Series E bonds because of their relatively long maturity feature.

Interest payments from municipal bonds are tax free to the recipient. This feature is very valuable to persons in the high income tax brackets or corporations because their income is taxed at high rates. Yields on municipal bonds are lower than those of taxable bonds of equal grade because of the feature of nontaxability. The capital gain from buying a municipal at a discount is taxable income. Some states exempt Treasury bond interest from state income taxes. Certain Treasury bonds are redeemed at par to pay estate taxes. These securities may be very profitable investments for persons having large potential estate tax liabilities. Retirement plans which meet certain federal guidelines allow persons to deduct contributions to these plans from their taxable income. This ability is valuable for most persons.

Record keeping is an important part of investing. Records are necessary for reporting income for taxation and for determining how profitable investments have been.

PROBLEMS

1. Tom Jones is tired of paying income taxes on his investments. He states to a friend that he is going to sell all his corporate bonds and invest the money in municipals. Currently, municipals yield 6 percent and corporates yield 9 percent.
   a. Tom pays taxes at a marginal rate of 25 percent. Is this exchange to his advantage?
   b. At what income tax rate would Tom be indifferent to whether he owned the corporates or the municipals?

2. Ann Parsons is computing her security transactions for the current year. She sold the following securities during the year of 1974.

Company	*Number of Shares or Bonds*	*Purchase Price*	*Purchase Date*	*Sale Price*	*Sale Date*
Excell. . . .	$2,000 par	$2,000	3/15/70	$1,950	1/11/74
Ajax	100 shares	4,600	7/12/71	5,200	6/1/74
Quick. . . .	200 shares	2,010	4/15/74	1,800	7/3/74
Bilco	500 shares	6,400	4/15/74	7,020	10/14/74

a. Construct a form resembling Part I and II of Schedule D (Figure 13–1), and determine Ann's taxable income from these security transactions. (Taxable income appears on line 15b of Schedule D. No alternative computation is necessary.

b. If Ann's other income is $16,000, how much tax will she pay on these investments? (Ann is unmarried and uses Schedule X tax rates.)

3. Three months ago you purchased 200 shares of stock in the New Process Data Processing Company. The stock cost $20 per share and is now priced at $45. The investment community is divided on the outlook for NPDP; some brokers recommend selling the stock while others say hold for long-term capital gains. You are in the 30 percent marginal income tax bracket. Outline the most important considerations in your decision to hold for long-term gains or to sell now.

4. In the current tax year your income has been unusually low. However, you hold several hundred shares of stock that have appreciated 100 percent in value over what you paid for them just eight months ago. You are convinced that the price of this stock will go higher, but you would like to pay taxes on this gain in the current tax year. How can you do this and continue to own the securities in anticipation of a higher gain?

5. Construct a chart like the data recording portion of Figure 13–7. Consult Moody's, Standard & Poor's, or any other financial reporting service to obtain interest and dividend payment dates, declaration dates of dividends, and a one-year price history for a selected bond and common stock. Record this information on the form.

6. Select several of the suggested two-way exchanges from Figure 13–4 and determine whether they were in fact good exchanges.

7. A person may contribute up to $6,000 per year into a *qualified retirement program*. The person is in the 35 percent income tax bracket. How much is this person out of pocket because of this contribution; or stated another way, how much current spending power is lost through this contribution?

QUESTIONS

1. Why have the tax courts defined convertible bonds or preferred stock in a given company as "substantially identical securities" to the common stock of that company, while not defining straight (nonconvertible) bonds or preferred stock as substantially identical?
2. Why do most investors try to defer the payment of taxes on investments as long as possible?
3. What is meant by the term *marginal income tax rate?*
4. Why is long-term capital gain income more desirable than ordinary income?
5. What are *paper profits* and *paper losses?* Do they alter income tax liabilities?
6. What is a *wash sale?*
7. When is the interest on Series E savings bonds taxed? Do these securities offer investors any particular tax advantages?
8. Why are most municipal bonds owned by corporations, commercial banks, and wealthy individuals?
9. What special tax advantages do the Treasury bond issues known as *flower bonds* have?
10. If you and your wife owned 200 shares of stock that paid dividends of $1.50 per share per year, and neither of you owned any other securities, how much of this income would be taxable if, (*a*) The securities were owned jointly by you and your wife or (*b*) If the securities were held in your wife's name only?

SELECTED READINGS

Haft, Robert J. *Tax Sheltered Investments*. New York: Boardman, Clark Co., Ltd., 1973.

Investors' Tax Kit. New York: Data Digests. This publication is distributed by many brokerage houses.

J. K. Lasser's: Your Income Tax. New York: Simon & Schuster, published annually.

1974 United States Master Tax Guide. Chicago: Commerce Clearing House, published annually.

Your Federal Income Tax, 1974 Edition for Individuals. Washington, D.C.: Internal Revenue Service, published annually.

14

Timing of Investment Decisions

INTRODUCTION

This chapter outlines several methods of *timing* purchases and sales of investments, and several investment plans which make timing decisions automatically. Even though an investor can identify an appropriate investment (one which meets all pertinent risk and return criteria) to be successful, this investment must be purchased at an appropriate price. Timing of investment purchases is at least as difficult as determining which investments to purchase. An enormous amount of effort has been directed toward the creation of accurate predictors of security prices, but without complete success.

This book has consistently set forth the premise that practically any investment can be a "good" investment—if it can be purchased at a price low enough so that its profit potential outweighs its potential for loss. An additional premise—really an observation—deals with irrationality of security markets. There is a definite tendency for markets to become "too high" during periods of optimism and to sink to unreasonably low levels during times of pessimism. These characteristics are partially documented in Chapters 2, 6, and 10, where the price/earnings ratios of various stocks were examined during periods of optimism and pessimism. Since almost all securities are affected by market upturns and downturns, if market turning points could be predicted, one could profit handsomely through correct timing of investment purchases and sales. Buy when the market is relatively low, and sell when it is high. The problem of security selection would be minimized, although to maximize profits from correct timing decisions, securities of companies that react most rapidly and consistently to changes in security market prices should be purchased and sold. At any rate, the potential rewards for correct predictive devices are great enough so that there is a never-ending attempt on the part of the investment community to discover "the correct way" to predict security market price levels and turning points.

No one has yet discovered a completely reliable method of predicting security price movements. Nevertheless, all investors should be aware of at least some of the many attempts that have been made, and their strengths and weaknesses. The predictive devices that are examined in this chapter have been placed into four classifications, although there is some overlap between the four.

The first classification is called *economic analysis*. As the term implies, economic conditions are examined in an effort to determine how the market prices of securities have been and will be affected by changes in economic activity.

The second classification is *fundamental analysis*. In this type of analysis individual companies and industries are examined to determine the future prospects of individual companies and/or industries. Because fundamental analysis was examined in detail in Chapter 6, it receives only brief mention in this chapter.

The next type of analysis attempts to forecast security price changes on the basis of the supply and demand factors in the security markets. This technique is usually called *technical analysis*. The theoretical bases for this type of activity are presented later in some detail. At this point it is sufficient to say that technical analysis does not make use of economic data. Its predictions are of a much shorter-term nature than those obtained through either fundamental or economic analysis.

The final grouping classifies and examines several *formula investment plans*. These are special investment programs, the simplest of which are based upon the assumption that accurate forecasts of future economic events cannot be made. Formula plans make timing decisions for investors automatically, with little regard to economic, fundamental, or technical analysis. These plans are all long-term in nature.

With some modifications, most of the theories and plans are applicable to bond, preferred stock, and common stock investments. Emphasis is placed upon common stocks because it is here that most investor interest is centered. All persons desiring to make use of any of these methods are encouraged to read further in the sources listed at the end of the chapter.

ECONOMIC ANALYSIS

At one time or another, practically every economic event has been used to predict security market trends. Increases or decreases in business activity, changes in production of certain basic commodities, changes in employment, wholesale and retail price changes, changes in the money supply, and other economic events, are all followed closely by economic forecasters. In some cases it is difficult to identify any logical relationship—the statisticians refer to this as *causality*—between the markets themselves and whatever measure is being used as the basis for the forecast. But if the predictor actually foretells market movements accurately, professionals and amateurs alike will grasp this measure as being "the" indicator to watch and follow.

Investors are advised to rely upon a variety of economic and business indexes rather than on a single one. These should constantly be reinterpreted and reevaluated as predictive devices, for none of them will be accurate all of the time. Many investors have made the costly error of continuing to invest on the basis of some "pet" economic or business indicator, only to learn—too late—that it has become useless.

Indexes of Economic Activity

Over the long run, the price of a company's common stock is determined largely by company earnings—high earnings, high prices; low earnings, low prices. Company earnings are strongly influenced by the state of the economy. A booming economy means that most companies will do well because the economy causes increases in sales, cash flows, and earnings. A depressed economy means the opposite. The relationship betwen stock prices and the level of economic activity is therefore a logical one easily accepted by most persons.

Some types of companies are able to increase their earnings more rapidly than the average firm during periods of high economic activity, while others characteristically are more "recession proof." But as Figure 14–1 indicates, there is a reasonably close relationship between total business activity—as measured by an index of industrial production—and stock prices—as measured by the Standard & Poor's *Industrial Index*. However, the relationship between these two indexes is not reliable enough to allow accurate prediction of how changes in one index will affect the other. The industrial production index dipped in 1953, 1957, 1960, 1962, 1970, and 1974. But by the time industrial production had turned down, stock prices had already moved lower.

FIGURE 14–1
Industrial Production and Stock Market Prices

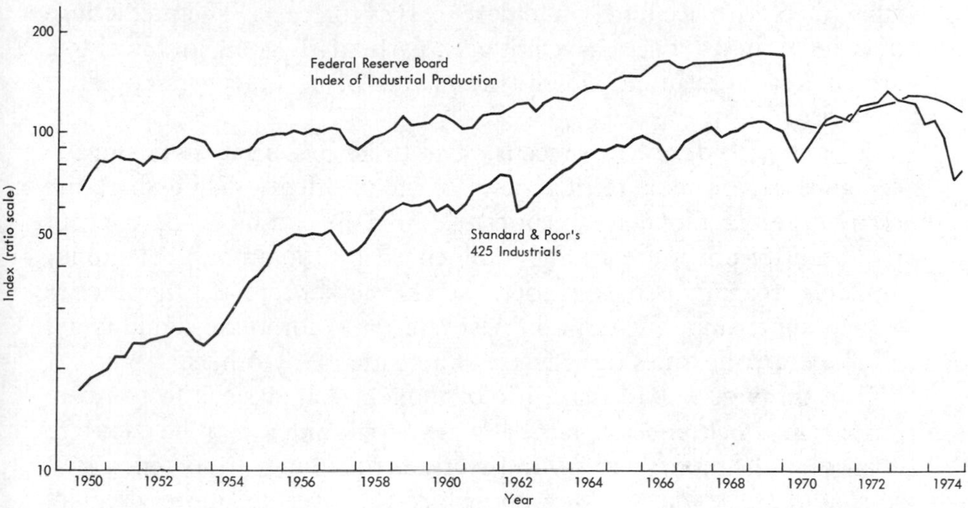

Source: Standard & Poor's, Inc. and Federal Reserve Board.

The explanation for this relationship is that knowledgeable investors foresee a reduction in business activity and sell stocks in anticipation of it. This drives down stock prices. When improved business conditions are anticipated, investors buy securities. The important point is that while there is a relationship between stock prices and business activity, it is the "wrong" relationship. Stock price changes usually *precede* changes in business activity;[1] this makes it impossible to use business activity to predict changes in stock prices.

The difficulty in making stock price predictions lies in finding an economic indicator which consistently *leads*, or even *coincides* with, changes in stock prices. There are literally hundreds of series of economic data which have been used at one time or another to predict turning points in stock prices. Some of these series have been accurate predictors—for short periods of time—but over the long run none of them have been consistently reliable. Investors are often asked to sub-

[1] The relationship between these two variables is nevertheless useful. Stock prices are used as a "leading indicator" of economic activity by the U.S. Department of Commerce in several of its statistical indexes.

The *Business Conditions Digest* (Washington, D.C.: U.S. Department of Commerce, Bureau of the Census) contains several hundred different series of data describing the economic activity of most sections of the U.S. and international economy. This is a good place to gather data for economic analysis.

scribe to market letters (sometimes at considerable cost) which promise to analyze economic conditions and through this method provide subscribers with accurate, up-to-date market forecasts. The predictions of some of these services have not been particularly good, and investors are advised to examine closely the claims of accuracy presented by these firms.

Monetary Indexes. In recent years there has been increasing acceptance of the monetarist's views of stock prices. While there are many different monetary theories, all hold in common the concept that security prices are strongly influenced by the amount of money available to purchase securities. Stock market credit, the money supply, short- and long-term interest rates, and corporate liquidity are all monetary measures in wide use. There are many others.

The simplest way to make use of monetary analysis is to compare changes in stock prices (practically any stock index may be used) to changes in the money supply. In theory, as the money supply increases, so should stock prices.[2] Most monetary theorists use more variables and more sophisticated techniques than were included in the above example. One stock market and business forecasting firm employs ten different measures of credit use and availability to construct what they call a "monetary thermometer."

> The ten underlying indicators making up the Thermometer fall in four main categories of policy, transactions, liquidity, banking liquidity, and combinations of each. The basic idea is that each of the ten indicators is potentially capable of obtaining 0, 1, 2 or 3 points (demerits) depending on the degree of deterioration in the particular series. The consensus reading can therefore lie between 0 and 30, but in practice has never been above +22. When the reading has moved up to +8 or higher, the Thermometer has consistently given major warning signals of impending trouble in the stock market and business.[3]

Figure 14–2 is a 55-year history of the Monetary Thermometer plotted against the *Dow Jones Industrial Index.* Whenever the Thermometer registered +8 or above, it indicated worsening stock market

[2] The Federal Reserve Board of Governors is the leading source of data for money supply analysis. The Federal Reserve Bank of St. Louis publishes monthly statistics on the money supply in a form especially relevant to persons desiring to use these data. A free copy of their publication, *Monetary Trends,* may be obtained by writing this bank. See also Beryl W. Sprinkel, *Money and Stock Prices* (Homewood, Ill.: Richard D. Irwin, 1964).

[3] *The Bank Credit Analyst,* 21, no. 12 (June 1970); 10.

FIGURE 14–2
The Monetary Thermometer

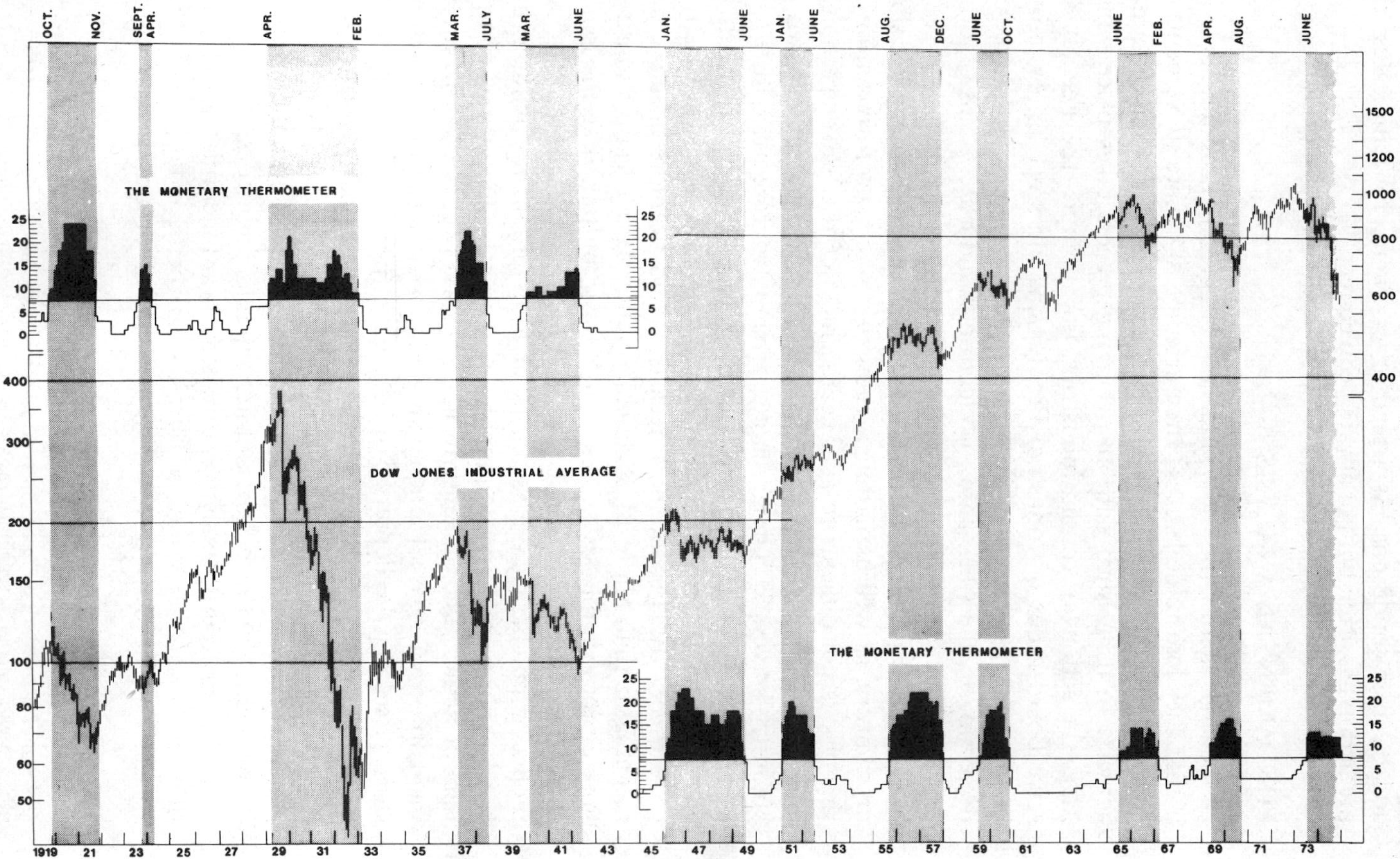

Source: "The Outlook for 1975," *The Bank Credit Analyst* (Supplementary Issue 1975), p. 33.

and business conditions. As a reading of Figure 14–2 indicates, the prediction has often but not always been correct.[4]

FUNDAMENTAL ANALYSIS

A charge against the use of indexes of aggregate economic activity is that they lose value because they attempt to equate movements in all stock prices (or at least all industrial companies) to total economic activity. In using such data an averaging process takes place which hides the actions of certain industries. For example, the Federal Reserve Board Index of Industrial Production, and stock prices, might be increasing *on average* while both production and stock prices were decreasing in the steel, auto, or electronics industry. Gains of other industries would outweigh the losses of these industries.

When it is possible, the investor should base investment decisions on industry, as well as national, economic forecasts. Information of this type is not difficult to get because most of the brokerage houses and several financial reporting services prepare what are known as "industry surveys."[5] These surveys attempt to forecast future economic conditions expected to prevail in specific industries and, by extension, the security prices and earnings of firms in these industries.

In theory these economic forecasts should be more accurate and meaningful than those of a general nature. If a certain industry—housing for example—is expected to increase output, it seems logical that an investor could participate in the expected sales growth and profits by purchasing the securities of firms producing building materials, or construction equipment, or some other important component of homes. The difficulty in making successful use of this investment strategy is that although a single industry is performing well, all stock prices may be depressed—in this case the reward in purchasing these securities may come from their doing "less poorly" than others. Nevertheless, the individual investor can often identify industries which will experience relatively rapid future growth and obtain profits from investing in the securities of firms in these industries.

The art of security analysis is directed toward identification of securities whose market values are lower than their fundamental values. In this type of analysis it is assumed that all securities have values

[4] See A. Hamilton Bolton, *Money and Investment Profits* (Homewood, Ill.: Dow Jones-Irwin, 1967) for a fuller explanation of the thermometer.

[5] Standard & Poor's *Industry Surveys* are probably more widely followed than any others. *Value Line* prepares similar surveys, as do many brokerage houses.

which are determined by their risk characteristics, future prospects of the company, expected yield, and other fairly easily measured things. Based upon these considerations all securities are assumed to have an intrinsic value. If securities can be purchased for less than this value (or sold short for more) future profits should result as the market recognizes that the security is priced differently from its intrinsic value and adjusts the price to this value.

TECHNICAL ANALYSIS OF MARKET DATA

The predictive devices examined earlier in this chapter attempted to link stock prices to fundamental economic events. Those now examined attempt to predict future price movements on the basis of events *internal* to the securities markets. All fall into the broad classification known as *technical analysis*.

The Odd-Lot Trading Index

The logic behind the use of odd-lot trading statistics as market predictors can be stated simply: (1) Small investors generally do the "wrong thing" at important turning points of the stock markets; (2) The action of the average small investor is revealed in the odd-lot statistics. It will be remembered that odd-lot purchases and sales are those of less than 100 shares. Such trades are widely believed to be those of the man in the street, the small-scale investor.

Figure 14–3 pictures what historical odd-lot data indicate the small investor does at various times in a stock market cycle. As prices rise, this person is cautious, a seller on balance. When prices near their peak, greed overcomes reason and securities are purchased aggressively. The small investor remains hopeful as prices decline, buying more shares than are sold. But as the bottom of the market approaches, fear sets in and large amounts of securities are sold. The small investor does the correct thing to generate profits *some of the time* by selling as prices increase and buying as they decrease. The errors are made at *turning points*.

Data on daily and weekly odd-lot sales and purchases are widely available in most newspapers having a financial section. The SEC publishes statistics of odd-lot trading monthly in its *Statistical Bulletin*. The most popular use of odd-lot information is through a ratio of selling to purchasing volume. This tells whether, and in what proportion, the small investor is a *net* seller or buyer.

FIGURE 14–3
Odd-Lot Investor Syndrome

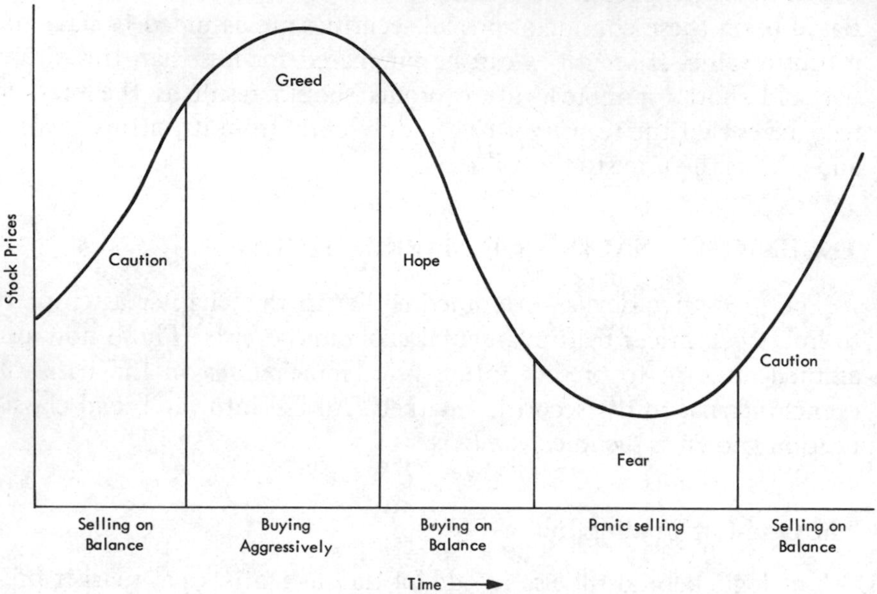

Some analysts relate total odd-lot to total round-lot purchases and sales in an attempt to measure whether the small buyer is *more or less active* than the round-lot purchaser.

Odd-lot data are usually used to verify that a turning point has occurred in the security markets, rather than as a leading indicator. For example, some persons believe that a declining market has not reached bottom until there is evidence of panic selling on the part of the odd-lotters. Since there are so many ways of using odd-lot data, we will make no attempt to evaluate carefully its usefulness as a predictor. The data have at times been misleading, particularly when markets have turned down. They have more accurately indicated when the market has bottomed out.[6]

Index of Short to Regular Sales

Investors make short sales when they expect prices to decline. Since these short sales will someday be covered by repurchased securities,

[6] See "Wrong Again? Small Investor Stays Bearish, So Analysts Foresee Market Upturn," *The Wall Street Journal*, June 17, 1970, p. 1, for a discussion of the use of odd-lot data.

they constitute a future demand for the stock.[7] Decreased short interest (a term used to indicate the amount of securities sold short) forecasts a lower future demand. These data are usually analyzed by constructing a ratio of the short interest outstanding on various dates to the average daily stock trading volume. An increasing ratio indicates that future demand for the stock is increasing. When these short sales are covered, the price of the stock should rise. A declining ratio indicates that short contracts are being covered and that the latent demand for the stock is being reduced.

A dramatic shift in short interest of a single firm may indicate that this corporation has impressed the investment community—favorably or unfavorably—with its future prospects. If short interest increases (or decreases) greatly, it is wise to try to find out why this has happened before purchasing (or selling) this stock.

The New York and American Stock Exchanges release short interest reports near the middle of each month. Figure 14–4 is a portion of a short interest report prepared for the month ended February 14, 1975. This report only lists securities having short positions of at least 20,000 shares and securities in which there was a short position change of at least 10,000 shares over the month.

Abbott Labs had outstanding 13,621,775 common shares on February 14, 1975. Of this number 18,056 were shorted. One month earlier only 7,873 shares were shorted. While this increase in shorted shares is unquestionably large, much of the increase may have been caused by the vastly increased volume of activity on the NYSE in late January and early February 1975. During this period the NYSE recorded four trading days in which volume exceeded 30 million shares.

Short interest data may be used to analyze the markets as a whole by constructing a ratio of total short interest to the daily average stock volume. NYSE data are usually used to make this calculation, although the AMEX provides similar information on the companies it lists. Those who follow this method of prediction expect a general market downturn soon after the ratio of short interest to average share volume declines to a predetermined figure. When this ratio rises to another predetermined level, a market upturn is expected. Different analysts use different ratios, of course, but the usual sell signal has been at a ratio of short interest to average daily trading volume of 0.75:1; the buy signal has come when the ratio reached 1.75:1.

[7] See Chapter 12 for a discussion of the mechanics of short selling. Not all short sales result in future purchases as some investors short securities they own. This is thought to be a small proportion of total short selling.

FIGURE 14–4
NYSE Short Interest Information

NEW YORK STOCK EXCHANGE

	Shares-Warants 2-14-75	1-15-75	Listed
Abbott Labs	18,056	7,873	13,621,775
†Amer Tel & Tel wts '75	690,012	1,084,262	31,312,621
ASA Ltd	61,547	74,977	4,800,000
Aetna Life Casualty	24,000	14,000	54,160,284
Air Products & Chem	33,498	26,847	13,375,309
Alcan Aluminum Ltd	215	37,908	34,712,069
Alco Standard Corp	18,000	34,707	10,014,960
Alison Mtg Inv Tr	25,800	30,900	2,339,417
Amax Inc	25,739	39,176	23,872,794
Amer Cyanamid Co	14,175	3,850	48,905,338
†Amer Home Products	152,232	148,969	166,348,739
Amer Hospital Supply	77,097	34,422	36,148,189
AMF Inc	3,795	22,950	19,638,277
†Amer Motors Corp	152,787	135,687	29,792,151
†Amer Telephone & Tel	103,484	142,787	560,940,626
Amfac Inc	100	34,881	10,944,290
AMP Inc	394,964	356,002	37,440,000
Apeco Corp	10,880	54,280	10,796,475
Arctic Enter Inc	20,000	20,000	3,050,396
ARA Services Inc	26,850	29,140	6,177,929
Armstrong Cork	12,095	24,620	25,930,860
Ashland Oil Inc	45,790	46,400	23,268,834
Atlantic Richfield	66,028	133,882	47,055,808
Atl Richf $2.80 cv pr	12,087	1,568	12,025,704
Auto Data Processing	25,290	19,004	6,434,059
Avon Products	255,949	254,848	57,991,239
Baker Oil Tools	29,565	20,050	10,699,051
Bandag Inc	19,400	32,948	12,634,215

Note: The dagger symbol in front of American Telephone and Telegraph warrants, American Home Products common stock, and others identifies securities which are believed to have short positions which are largely due to the fact that the company's stock can be exchanged for that of another company, or for a new issue. Short positions that arise through these conditions are not accorded the same meaning as those resulting from the usual reasons.

Source: *The Wall Street Journal*, February 24, 1975, p. 7.

On February 14, 1975, NYSE short interest was 25,121,419 shares, up 4,308,159 shares from the previous month. During early 1975 the daily NYSE stock volume averaged about 20 million shares per day. The ratio of short interest to average market volume was therefore about 1.25:1. At this time the ratio was almost completely neutral under the above formulation.

Odd-Lot Short Sales

As its name implies, this forecasting technique attempts to use data on these trades to indicate turning points in the markets. The interpretation of the action of small investors is the same as in the previous example. Under this theory, odd-lotters are not only wrong in that they sell securities at the bottom of a market downturn, but they are doubly wrong in that they short securities in great numbers at this critical time. The ratio used in this analysis is that of odd-lot short sales volume to that of total odd-lot market activity. The ratio usually averages about 2 percent, but at certain past stock market turnaround dates, it has risen to as high as 7 percent. The index appears to be a better predictor of upturns than downturns.

ADVANCE DECLINE INDEX

Many market analysts believe that the end of a *bull market* can be identified by a progressive weakening of security prices. While the stock prices of the larger and better known companies remain strong, and perhaps even rise, prices of securities of weaker firms decline. Eventually the market collapse spreads to practically all securities and a *bear market* begins. Because most stock market price indexes are made up of securities of larger, stronger, and better known companies, the indexes do not reveal the beginning price weaknesses that foretell of a major market downturn. The Dow Jones Industrial Average, because it is composed of a small number of blue chip securities, is particularly misleading in this respect.

The advance decline index is simply the number of securities that advanced compared to the number that declined in a given period of time. The most common way of arranging this information is by subtracting the number of gainers from losers at any given time. Most persons use a continuous sequence of weekly calculations. These computations can easily be made from data provided by the stock exchanges. Figure 14–5 is the Market Diary section taken from a *Wall Street Journal* published early in 1975. Over the six trading days listed there were on balance 598 more stocks which declined than advanced.

The absolute level of the index has no meaning because it depends entirely upon when the series of calculations was begun. What is

FIGURE 14–5
Market Diary Information

MARKET DIARY

	Thur	Wed	Tues	Mon	Fri	Thur
Issues traded	1,772	1,784	1,790	1,823	1,842	1,818
Advances	841	854	203	444	825	829
Declines	518	554	1,298	1,022	623	579
Unchanged	413	376	289	357	394	410
New highs, 1974-75	12	7	3	11	41	28
New lows, 1974-75 ..	2	0	4	0	0	1

Source: *The Wall Street Journal*, February 28, 1975, p. 29.

meaningful (in theory) is whether the net gains and losses move roughly in concert with the security averages. Logically, as security prices in general increase there should be a steady net increase in gains over losses, and vice versa. What users of the advance decline index look for is a situation where market measures—the Dow Jones Industrial Average for example—are increasing, while on balance more stock prices are declining than advancing.

This excess of declines over advances is interpreted to mean that a market downturn may have begun, but that the downturn is not yet revealed because the weakening of stock prices is currently limited to the shares of smaller, lesser known companies. Since these companies are usually not included in the security price indexes, these averages do not identify the market downturn until it is well underway.

Advance decline statistics are also used by some persons to identify the "bottom" of a bear market. Followers of the Dow Theory (discussed in the next section) believe that bear markets end with a major selloff of securities. Extraordinary increases in declines over advances are looked for by some analysts as the signal that a bear market has bottomed out and that the stage is set for a recovery in stock prices.

CHART PATTERNS AS PREDICTIVE DEVICES

There are dozens of different methods of using charts as predictors. Only the two most popular will be examined, leaving the interested reader to pursue the subject of charting in publications which present this topic in more detail than can be accomplished here.

Basing investment decisions on stock chart patterns is not new. Most of the present theories are modifications of the work of Charles Dow, the creator of the Dow Jones Stock Averages and the organizer of the Dow Jones financial news service. Other investors probably used methods similar to his, but because he wrote down his theories in editorials which appeared in *The Wall Street Journal* during the late 1800s he is usually identified as the father of stock charting.

The Dow Theory attempts to identify *trends* in stock prices and changes in these trends. The theory uses market statistics of stock averages and individual stocks. All data used in the analysis are internal to the market—the volume and price changes of securities. In their strictest form, none of the chart-based theories pay any attention whatsoever to the intrinsic value of a share or share price averages. Justification for this approach is that all the data that go into intrinsic value calculations—earnings, dividends, growth, and so on—are taken from historical accounting records which are meaningless so far as current decisions are concerned. The market looks ahead and discounts all future events.

> In brief, the going price as established by the market itself comprehends all the fundamental information which the statistical analyst can hope to learn (plus some which is perhaps secret from him, known to only a few insiders) and much else besides of equal or even greater importance.[8]

The theory further states that stock prices—individual companies and stock indexes—move in trends which continue until something happens which changes the supply and demand relationships which determine prices. *Major* or *primary* trends are the extensive market movements of long duration which are usually called bull or bear markets. *Secondary trends* are movements in the opposite direction of the primary trend. They have a shorter duration and amplitude than the primary trend but are larger and longer than minor trends. *Minor trends* closely resemble day-to-day fluctuations. Secondary and minor trends are superimposed on the major trend. When the Dow Jones averages are being analyzed, the transportation and industrial averages must "confirm" each other's actions by moving in the same direction at the same time. Without this confirmation no change can occur in a basic trend—so states the theory.

This basic theory has been modified by different analysts to make it more modern and/or reliable. Emphasis now seems placed upon the charting of individual stocks rather than averages, and several charting systems have extended the original Dow Theory goal of *identifying trends* to that of *predicting changes* in trends and *predicting future prices* of individual stocks and stock averages.

The purpose of this book is not to make chart analysts of our readers. In fact, our endorsement of charting is rather qualified because the chart patterns are difficult to interpret and sometimes give misleading information. Nevertheless, a significant proportion of the investment community follows the charts and reacts to signals of "trendline breakthroughs," "head and shoulders patterns," "support and resistance areas," and other formations (real or imagined) that are traced by the charts. Enough investors buy and sell on these signals that they help make predicted events happen. Therefore, whether or not one believes in the charts is immaterial. All investors should be

---

[8] Robert D. Edwards and John Magee, *Technical Analysis of Stock Trends*, 5th ed. (Springfield, Mass.: John Magee, 1966), p. 6.

familiar enough with their use to understand how they will affect the investment decisions of those who do. To illustrate this point, if the charts signaled the end of a bull market, and if enough investors believed the signal and began selling securities, they might well *cause* the end of the bull market.

Constructing a Bar Chart. Bar charts all resemble the graphs of the Dow Jones averages—the industrials, rails, and utilities—which are published daily in *The Wall Street Journal*. These stock indexes are, in fact, some of the earliest bar charts, the ones prepared by Charles Dow. Prices may be entered into a bar chart on a daily, weekly, monthly, hourly, or practically any other regular time period. Data usually plotted are the high, low, and closing price for the period as well as the volume of shares traded. These charts may record prices of stock averages, industry averages, groups of stocks, or individual companies. Price is usually plotted on the "Y" axis (the one that is vertical); time and volume are usually plotted on the horizontal "X" axis. A chart, Figure 14–6, has been prepared from the trading data for a single stock listed in Table 14–1.

TABLE 14–1
Hypothetical Trading Data

Date	*High*	*Low*	*Close*	*Daily Volume*
May 1.	$37	$36	$36 1/4	1,000
2.	36 7/8	36	36 1/4	1,200
3.	36 3/4	35 5/8	36	800
4.	36 1/4	35 3/8	35 1/2	1,500
5.	36 7/8	36	36 3/4	600

The vertical line at the top left of Figure 14–6 indicates that the stock of this company on May 1 was sold as high as $37 and as low as $36; it closed at $36¼. The closing price is indicated by the "tic" on the vertical line. The lower portion of the graph records the daily volume.

This chart cannot be used to predict any event because it covers only a short time period. After a stock has been plotted for a longer duration it may begin to trace patterns which are interpreted to mean certain things by the chart analysts. As can probably be imagined, the patterns traced by an individual company or a stock average may take many different shapes. Furthermore, the same data may generate different chart patterns, depending upon whether the chart is plotted

FIGURE 14–6
Bar Chart of Price and Volume Data

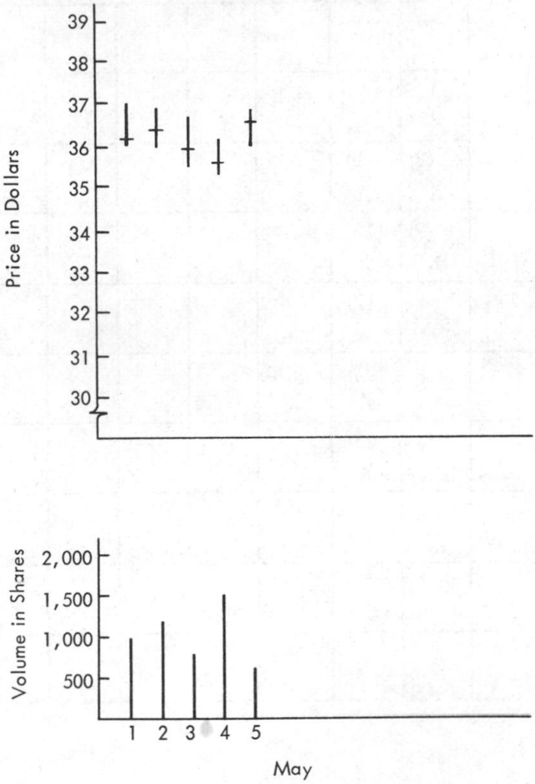

on a daily, weekly, monthly, or other time basis. Charts may be kept for a long period of time before they indicate anything of importance. Interpretation of some of the more common bar chart patterns can wait until the other leading method of constructing stock price charts has been examined.

Constructing a Point and Figure Chart. Point and figure charts are constructed from the same price data as the bar chart, but time and trading volume are not used. Stock price indexes may be plotted, but individual securities are more commonly analyzed this way. These charts are made on paper that is marked off into square blocks. The left-hand side of the paper contains a scale which indicates the closing prices of a single stock or stock index. Each square has a given dollar value which varies according to the market price of the stock or stock index. The squares are usually valued at $2 each for stocks trading at

FIGURE 14–7
Construction of a One-Point Point and Figure Chart

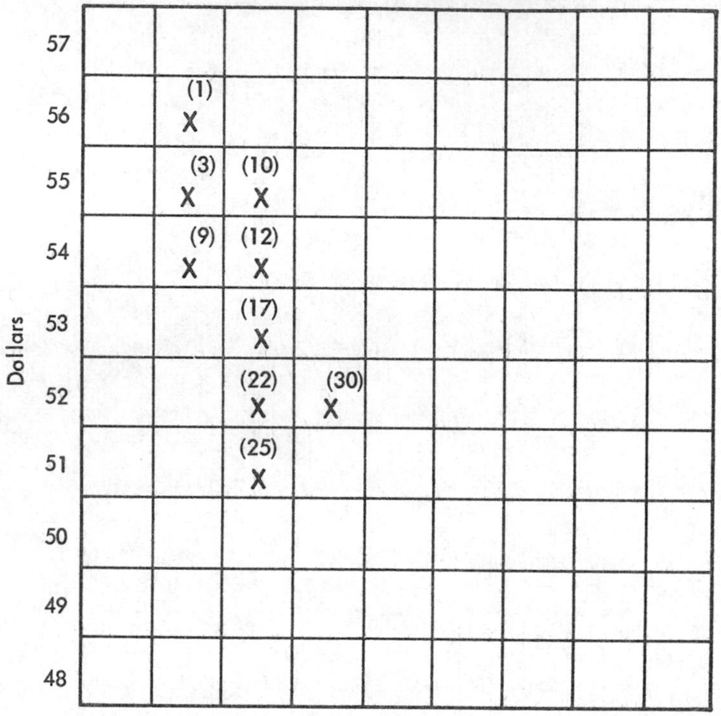

over \$100 and \$1 each for those trading below \$100 and above \$20. Units are valued at ½ or ¼ of a point for stocks having values of \$20 or less.

What the chart hopes to record is the supply and demand factors at work. To chart a stock under the point and figure method, an "X" (or any other symbol) is placed in a square on the chart to indicate that the stock has closed at a certain price. Fractional prices are usually ignored. No "X" is placed on the chart until the closing price has moved at least one complete unit (however this unit is defined) up or down. So long as a stock's price is moving in the same direction, all "X"'s will be in the same column. It is only when a stock "changes direction" that an entry is made in the next column.

Figure 14–7 has been constructed from the closing prices of a hypothetical stock listed in Table 14–2. Numbers in parentheses indicate the date on which each "X" was recorded. This has been done to make

TABLE 14–2
Hypothetical Closing Prices

Date	*Price*	*Date*	*Price*	*Date*	*Price*
May 1.	$56 1/2	10.	$55 1/4	19	$53 1/4
2.	56 1/4	11.	55	22	52 1/8
3.	55 1/2	12.	54 7/8	23	52 3/8
4.	55 3/4	15.	54 1/4	24	52 5/8
5.	55 7/8	16.	54 1/2	25	51 5/8
8.	55	17.	53 7/8	26	51 1/4
9.	54 7/8	18.	53 5/8	29	51 3/4
				30	52 1/2

it easier to follow the preparation of the chart; such dates would not normally be recorded.

Most chartists record the dates of major turning points or other events simply to give them an idea of when something took place. Time and volume data are not regularly recorded on the charts, nor are these measures used in the interpretation of chart patterns. These charts are as easy to prepare, and easier to maintain, than bar charts. If stock prices have fluctuated little or if all price movements are in the same direction, a month or more of trading activity may be recorded in very few X-axis spaces. Obviously, the value of the basic unit ($2, $1, $0.50, and so on) is critical because if it is "too small" the chart will record price reversals every few days. If the value is "too large," the chart will record practically no activity.

The chart was begun on May 1, so an "X" was placed in one of the squares next to $56. No record of the May 2 price was made because it was the same as May 1 since all fractions are ignored. On May 3, the price dropped to $55, and on the 9th it dropped to $54; these changes are recorded because they are a full dollar lower than the previous price. If the price had dropped from $56 to $54 in one day, an "X" would still have been placed in the $55 square. The other entries should be easy to follow by comparing the dates at which they occurred to the market prices.

Reading the Charts. The Dow theory, which underlies all chart analysis, attempts to identify stock market trends shortly *after* they occur. At this time the vast majority of investors will still be unaware that security markets in general, or the market for a particular security, have changed. The astute chart reader supposedly has time in which to benefit from the information revealed by the charts. Reading the charts consists of interpreting various patterns that are developed by the price changes of security price indexes or individual securities. There are many ways of preparing and interpreting charts, far too many to be covered in a book of this type. The following examples are provided to illustrate some of the more common patterns and types of charts. Interested readers are encouraged to further their abilities as chartists by pursuing some of the readings cited at the end of this chapter.

Figure 14–8 is a classic example of the "head and shoulders" pattern. This pattern is identified by rising stock prices—with high trading volume—which develops the beginning of the "left shoulder." Prices fall back and then rise to form the "head." They again retreat and begin their buildup which creates the right shoulder. The two "valleys" of the shoulders may be connected with a "neck line." Theory has it that when the neck line is "penetrated" after the right shoulder has been formed, the stock will decline in price and should be sold and/or

FIGURE 14–8
Bar Chart of Hughes Tool Company

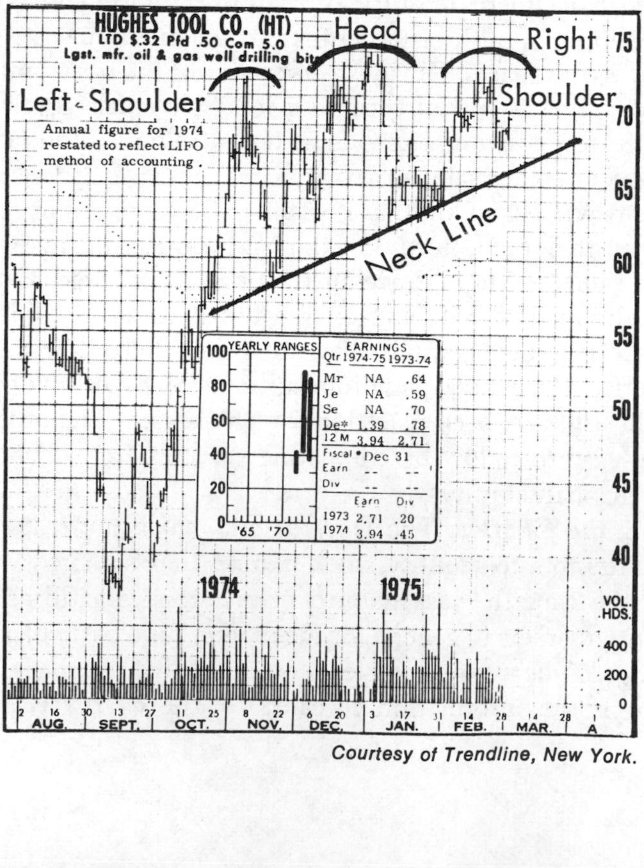

Courtesy of Trendline, New York.

FIGURE 14–9
Bar Chart of American Brands Incorporated

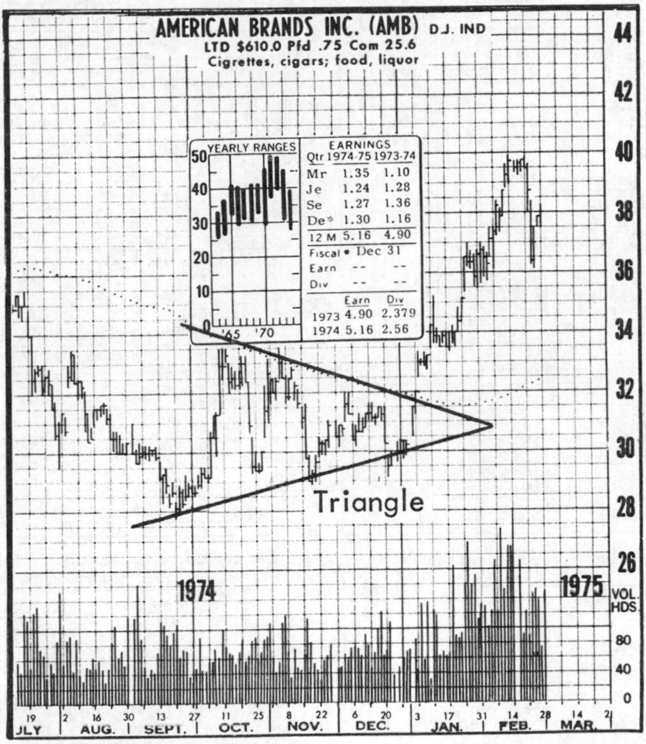

Courtesy of Trendline, New York.

shorted. If the neck line is not penetrated, the price is expected to continue rising.

Figure 14–9 pictures a triangle formation. These are relatively common since the triangle need not be symmetrical. Theory states that when prices break out of the triangle, they will continue in the direction of the breakout. This formation often appears at the end of a fairly large advance or decline. The dotted lines on Figures 14–8 and 14–9 are average prices of these stocks for the latest 30 weeks.

Figure 14–10 presents point and figure charts for four corporations: McCord, McCrory, McDonald's, and McDonnell Douglas. These charts are prepared and printed by a computer for a company which sells the completed charts by subscription to investors. The computer is programmed so that it enters price changes on the charts and creates *trendlines* which either slope upward or downward. The downward sloping line (the + marks) is called the *bearish resistance line.* This

FIGURE 14–10
Point and Figure Charts of Four Companies

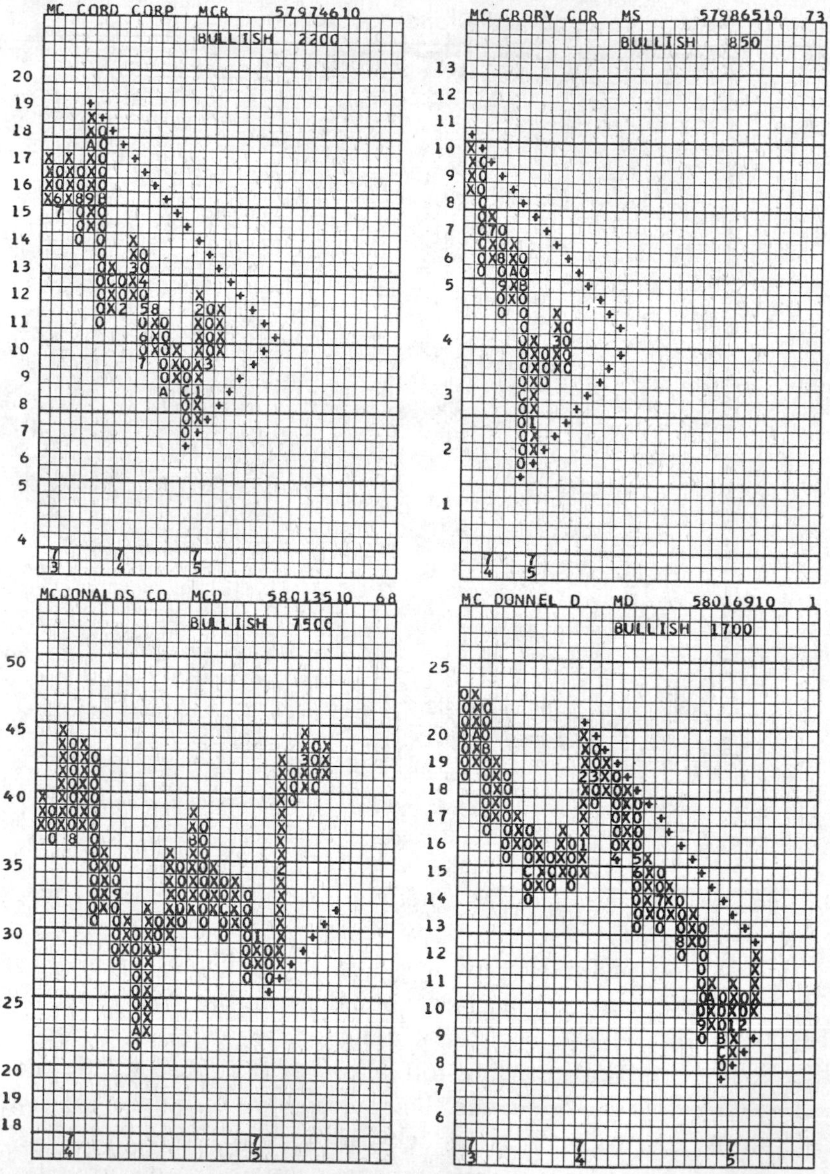

Note: The Chartcraft Company uses the following abbreviations. In the McCord Corporation example, MCR is the ticker symbol of the company's common stock. The eight digit number to the right of this symbol is a number used by the securities industry to identify the stock. Numbers to the right of this number (see McCrory Corporation) refer to the Standard & Poor's group index to which this stock is assigned, if it is assigned to such an index. It happens that the Chartcraft price prediction for all four securities is bullish, with a price objective of $22 for McCord and $8.50 for McCrory. Bearish predictions are also made along with price objective predictions. "X" marks refer to rising prices and "Os" indicate declining prices. Numbers and letters indicate months: 1 is January, 2 is February, A is October, B is November, and so on. Years are listed at the bottom of each graph and prices are listed on the left axis of the graph.

Source: *The Chartcraft Point and Figure Chart Book* (Larchmont, N.Y.: Chartcraft, Inc., April 1975), p. NYSE-104.

line indicates the price level at which the company preparing the charts expects that resistance to further price increases will be felt. The upward sloping line is called the *bullish support line*. This line indicates price levels at which the security is expected to find price support and reverse itself. Many charts contain both support and resistance lines.

One may also use these charts to identify certain patterns—double tops and bottoms, triangles, and others—which many persons believe will predict the direction of future price movements. There are many more of these chart patterns than can be identified or defined in the limited space devoted to this type of analysis. Identification of the patterns is at best an art since there are no universally accepted rules for determining either when a certain chart pattern has been begun or completed or exactly what the chart patterns indicate. Practitioners of this art claim their predictions are accurate a majority of the time. Interested readers are encouraged to study this topic on their own. Charts may be constructed and maintained by the individual, or already-constructed charts may be purchased from several companies.

FORMULA INVESTMENT PLANS

These investment strategies attempt to keep the investor from making poor *timing* decisions by setting down a formula which tells when to invest. The usual tendencies toward investor over-pessimism and over-optimism are controlled because investments are made according to a predetermined plan which was set with full awareness that prices are going to move down as well as up. These plans do not solve the problem of *selecting* the best security or securities. They have most appeal for investors who have little faith in economic analysis, fundamental analysis, or technical analysis.

Dollar Cost Averaging

Dollar cost averaging is a technique which allows an investor to realize profits so long as market prices fluctuate and so long as a constant dollar amount of investments can be periodically purchased. It is the simplest of formula plans.

A type of dollar cost averaging plan, which can be used as an illustration, is one in which an investor has $1,000 to invest in each of five periods. This money is to be invested in the stock of a single company, regardless of the current market price. To simplify the example

TABLE 14–3
Hypothetical Prices and Purchases of Stock Shares over a Five-Year Period

Period	Market Price	Number Purchased	Total Owned	Total Invested	Cumulative Value
1	$100	10.00	10.00	$1,000	$1,000.00
2	120	8.33	18.33	2,000	2,199.60
3	100	10.00	28.33	3,000	2,833.00
4	80	12.50	40.83	4,000	3,266.40
5	100	10.00	50.83	5,000	5,083.00

further, dividends and commission charges are ignored and it is presumed that fractional shares may be purchased. Table 14–3 presents a "no growth" situation in which the market price begins and ends at $100 per share while fluctuating an even amount above and below $100. One thousand dollars is invested each period at the current market price, and all investments are held until the fifth period is completed. Note that while the market price has fluctuated an equal amount above and below $100, the investor has realized a small profit of $83 over the period. Five thousand dollars were paid for securities worth $5,083. This profit resulted from the fact that when stock prices were "high" at $120, the investor could only buy 8.33 shares for $1,000; when prices were "low," 12.5 shares were purchased. At the average market price of $100, more low-priced than high-priced shares were acquired. Under these conditions dollar averaging will always result in a profit.

In fact, dollar averaging will fail to produce a profit only if share prices are constantly declining. Under these conditions the only way to profit is to sell short. If an investor had purchased $1,000 of stocks at the beginning of each year from 1950 through 1974, and if this investor realized the average investor experience of the Standard & Poor's industrial stock index, the portfolio would have increased in value as shown in Table 14–4.

Over the first five-year period $5,000 would have been invested; the market value of this portfolio would have been $6,418 and the annual return for this period would have been at a rate of about 13 percent per annum. Over the first ten-year period the investor would have done slightly better because market prices were increasing, but at a slower rate than before. Even though market averages dropped back drastically during 1974 (thereby lowering the market value of the entire

TABLE 14–4
Returns from Dollar Averaging of the Standard & Poor's Industrial Index (dividends and commission charges ignored)

Investment Period	*Total Invested*	*Value at End of Period*	*Approximate Annual Rate of Return*
1950–54	$ 5,000	$ 6,418	13 %
1950–59	10,000	19,255	14
1950–64	15,000	33,180	11
1950–69	20,000	46,286	8
1950–74	25,000	43,721	4.5

portfolio) this investment would have yielded about 4.5 percent over the 25 years of its existence.

This may not seem like a very large return, but remember that money doubles in about 16 years when compounded annually at 4.5 percent. Furthermore, to simplify the above calculations, neither dividends nor commissions were included. Dividend payouts have been higher than commission charges through this period so that the true rate of return would have been higher by at least two percentage points than the rates shown. If the dividends had been reinvested in additional shares, the returns would have been even higher.

The results from dollar averaging over any recent period of time are fair. But it should be remembered that for these plans to produce profits, several ingredients are necessary. First, the investor must be willing and able to purchase securities of an equal dollar amount when security prices are low as well as high. Dollar averaging, it should be remembered, is designed to *remove* the burden of making timing decisions. To be successful at this, investors must buy securities regularly. Second, security prices must be volatile, and they should be trending upward, or at least not be trending downward, over a period of time. Free markets produce volatile prices, so this characteristic can be expected to continue. As long as our nation's productivity continues to increase, stock prices should rise. Third, the investor must be prepared to purchase securities over a period of time long enough that purchases are made at both high and low prices. Ten years is probably a minimum amount of time for one of these plans to become effective, although if security prices are very volatile, a shorter time period might provide the required high and low prices. Purchases should be made often enough—semiannually, quarterly, or even monthly—so that price fluctuations are not missed because no purchases were made. Fourth, investors should not be under pressure—financial or psychological—to sell out quickly when prices are low. Most people advise liquidating a dollar cost averaging plan portfolio gradually so that all securities will not be sold at relatively low prices. Such a plan makes it impossible to sell out at relatively high prices either, but to attempt to do this would result in making timing decisions.

Is Dollar Averaging the Answer? The above conditions do not seem very difficult to attain, and success seems guaranteed. Investors constantly ask, "If dollar averaging is so good, why do professional investment managers not use it?" Many of them do! However, the professionals are equipped by their training to make decisions on timing. Most of them believe they can do better than the averages, and many of them do.

Dollar averaging does not solve the problem of which securities to purchase. Obviously, a dollar averaging plan which was made up of securities that rose in price will produce superior results to one which acquired securities which did not perform as well. Identifying the best possible securities—given certain risk and return characteristics—is the task of security analysis, however. At this point it will make the explanation of formula plans easier to follow if the reader assumes that the problem of selecting the best securities can be solved through the purchase of a diversified selection of stocks or bonds.

There are two ways of doing this. First, shares in a diversified mutual fund may be purchased. In fact, the investor may be able to reduce commissions by agreeing to purchase a certain amount of shares over a specified period. The dollar averaging program requires that this be done anyway. Second, diversification can be provided by purchasing securities in a few corporations that are themselves diversified. This has become increasingly easy to do as companies in entirely different fields have merged. Many of the larger manufacturing companies—GM, GE, Litton Industries, Textron, Genesco—are rather widely diversified in their operations.

Dollar cost averaging is used by millions of investors, many of whom do not recognize that they are using this technique. Buying securities under a monthly investment plan is really dollar averaging. Periodic contributions to a pension fund which invests its receipts in common stocks does essentially the same thing. Regular purchase of mutual fund shares may also be classified as a type of dollar averaging program.

Making the Basic Plan More (or Less) Profitable. Dollar cost averaging will do exactly what it is designed to do as long as the investor follows the rules. The temptation is often strong to "improve" the operation of the plan by making some personal decisions, which if correct will increase the return from the plan. For example, the investor may make no attempt to diversify security holdings. Investments might be made only in companies which are believed to have superior future prospects. If these securities can in fact be identified, the overall performance of the plan will be increased, perhaps greatly.

Purchases may be timed so that more money is invested when prices are "low" and less when they are "high." Attempting to purchase superior securities is not a very serious departure from the plan, but this practice is. The reason for using a plan in the first place is to make timing decisions automatic. By adopting such an approach the investor admits an inability to successfully predict what future security prices will be. By "tinkering" with the timing of the plan once it is adopted the plan's potential for long-run profit is reduced. It is obvious that if the investor's revised timing decisions are correct the profitability of the plan may be increased. But if the investor has the ability to make correct timing decisions, then the plan was not needed in the first place.

Individual securities can be sold out of the portfolio when their future prospects are poor or when they have become priced unrealistically high. This will usually not seriously affect the plan's purpose, but it does require that the investor be able to judge when prices of individual securities are relatively high or low. Not very many amateurs—and not all professionals—can consistently do this. There are many other ways that the basic dollar averaging plan can be altered, and in practice they are often changed to the point where they can no longer be called dollar averaging plans. They then belong to a group generally titled formula investing plans.

More Complex Formula Plans

Dollar averaging allows an investor to pursue an investment program unburdened by the need to make timing decisions. Other formula plans make timing decisions for the investor on the basis of predetermined rules (the formula) which attempt to cause the investor to buy stocks when prices are relatively low and sell them when they are relatively high. There are two general categories of these formula devices: *constant* and *variable ratio plans*. Many subclassifications exist but they all have two common characteristics: (1) the investment portfolio is divided into an aggressive and defensive portion, and (2) timing decisions are made automatically.

Constant Ratio Plans. These resemble dollar averaging in that once the plan has been started, the only decision that the investor makes is that of selecting the securities to be sold and those to be acquired. All decisions on timing are determined by the "formula." Under such a plan, an investor decides to place a certain proportion of an investment portfolio in aggressive and the remainder in defensive securities. If the requirement is that this ratio be maintained at 50–50, and it becomes greater or less than this due to changes in market prices, the portfolio is brought back into balance by selling the appropriate securities from the portion of the portfolio which is too large and replacing them with securities having the opposite investment characteristic. Security prices change daily, so the portfolio is almost never exactly in balance. To keep from constantly making adjustments, most investors allow the ratio to become out of balance by as much as 5 or 10 percent before making adjustments.

Aggressive investments are usually defined as common shares or senior securities convertible into common. Defensive investments are either straight debt or preferred stock of fairly high grade, savings accounts, or money-market mutual funds. Historically, when stock prices are high, interest rates are high and bond prices are therefore low. When stocks are low, interest rates are low and bond prices are high.

Such an inverse relationship between stock and bond prices guarantees profits because relatively high priced stocks are exchanged for relatively low priced bonds, which later rise in price and are exchanged for stocks which are then priced low. Unfortunately, the relationship has not held up very well in recent years. The market slump of 1973–74 has affected both bonds and stocks in that they sold both at low prices at the same time. This recent adverse bond/stock price relationship does not make the constant ratio plan unworkable, it just makes it less profitable because bond investments do not yield the anticipated profits. Under these conditions it is probably wise to invest the defensive portion of the portfolio in a savings account. Doing this protects one from a loss on the defensive portion of the portfolio, but it has the disadvantage of making it impossible to profit from increased bond prices (should this event occur). Many of the balanced mutual funds follow investment policies which are identical to fixed ratio formula plans.

Variable Ratio Plans. These are extensions of the constant ratio plan, extensions which allow the investor to follow a more aggressive investment policy while still being controlled by a predetermined set of decision rules which tell when to buy and sell. As the name implies, in the variable ratio plans, the aggressive-defensive ratio is altered as security market conditions change. When common stock prices rise, the investor *reduces* the proportion of the portfolio held in aggressive securities; at the same time *increasing* the defensive proportion. This is a significant departure from the fixed ratio plan. Under a fixed ratio plan the investor in effect says, "Regardless of what happens to the market, I want to have 50 percent (or 60 or 80 and so on) of my investments in aggressive securities and the remainder in defensive ones." An investor choosing a variable ratio plan might say this: "As stock prices rise, I want to own fewer and fewer aggressive securities; as stock prices become relatively low, I want to hold a high proportion of my investments in this form. By investing in this manner, I will amplify the profit potential of my portfolio." The logic of the statement is correct, but for this kind of plan to be successful several difficult conditions must be met. Before examining these conditions, let us organize and set in operation a simple variable ratio investment plan.

These are the decision rules.

1. The portfolio will be invested 50–50 in aggressive and defensive securities when the stock market is "normal."
2. As the market proceeds above normal, for every 10 percent increase, the basic ratio will be changed by a like percentage.
3. As stock prices decline, the ratio of defensive and aggressive securities will be substituted in the reverse of rule No. 2.

Table 14–5 lists the proportions of an investment portfolio that would be invested in aggressive and defensive securities under various

TABLE 14–5
Operation of a Hypothetical Variable Ratio Plan

Percent Market Is above or below Normal	DJIA	Percentage Invested in: Aggressive Securities	Percentage Invested in: Defensive Securities
+50	1,050	0	100
+40	980	10	90
+30	910	20	80
+20	840	30	70
+10	770	40	60
Normal level	700	50	50
−10	630	60	40
−20	560	70	30
−30	490	80	20
−40	420	90	10
−50	350	100	0

market conditions. When the stock market is 40 percent above normal (DJIA = 980) the portfolio would be only 10 percent aggressive and 90 percent defensive. When the market is 50 percent below its norm (DJIA = 350) the entire portfolio is invested aggressively.

On paper, this appears to be a practically infallible method of assuring one of high investment returns. It also appears to solve the problem of timing. Unfortunately, the recent history of the stock market is such that none of these variable ratio plans would have worked well without a great many changes in the rules—after the plan was in operation.

There is first of all the problem of arriving at a judgment of what is a "normal" level of stock prices. The plan should be started out with a ratio of aggressive to defensive investments which is determined by how far the market is above or below normal. Furthermore, since our stock markets have trended upward over the long run, even if a normal level could be determined for the *current* market, this figure would soon be too low. Analysts have solved this problem by using statistical techniques to determine the market trend line over a given period of time and then projecting this line into the future. Figure 14–11 is a graph of the Standard & Poor's industrial index from 1950 to 1974. Prices have been charted on a semi-logarithmic scale so that price increases that take place at a constant rate of increase are pictured as a straight line.

Assume that we started a variable ratio plan in early 1956 and that

FIGURE 14–11
Standard & Poor's 425 Industrials

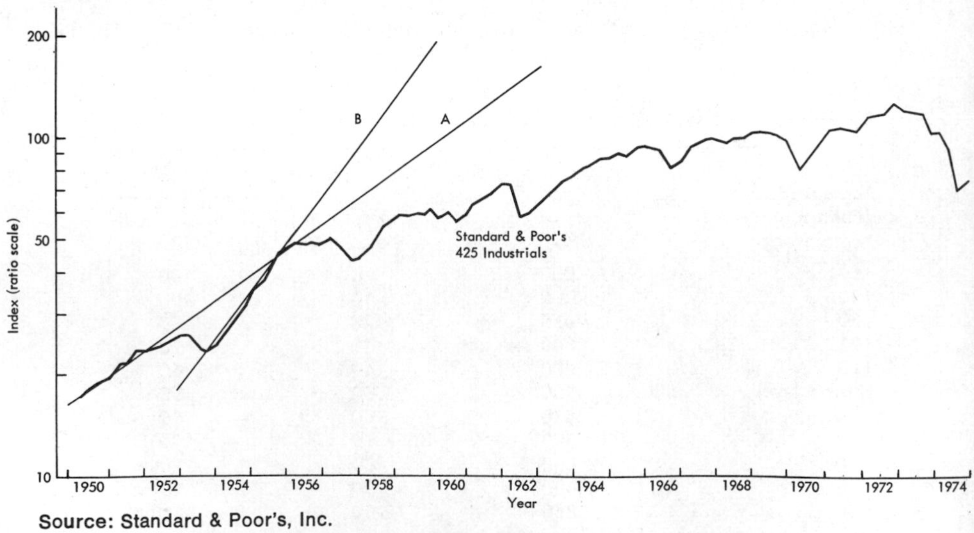

Source: Standard & Poor's, Inc.

we then attempted to choose a normal growth rate for stock prices—the basis of our plan. The easiest way to do this is to draw a straight line through the historical prices that *preceded* 1956 and project this line into the future. If we chose the period of 1950 to early 1956 as the norm, the line would be sloped like line "A." If we thought the normal period were from late 1953 through early 1956, the line would have the slope of "B." If we chose "A" as the norm, we would have started out in early 1956 with a 50–50 portfolio. By the third quarter of 1957, the normal level of the market is projected to be 64. The level actually was 43. The actual level is about 21 points below the calculated norm, so the portfolio should be invested about 83 percent aggressively and 17 percent defensively.[10] If line "B" had been chosen to represent the norm, the portfolio would have started off with a slightly higher proportion of aggressive securities and would have been 100 percent in aggressive securities by the third quarter of 1957. If the plan were followed faithfully, the investor would not have purchased a defensive investment again, because the actual market value was always less than 50 percent of the projected normal price. If projection "A" had been used, some defensive investments would have been held throughout 1958, but from this point on, no defensive securities would have been in the portfolio. Investing 100 aggressively from 1956 on would have yielded good profits because the market continued to trend upward. However, the plan would have been completely inoperative because projected market levels were always more than 50 percent higher than actual. Investors would have missed the profits which would have come from changing the ratio of aggressive and defensive securities during market downturns of 1960, 1962, 1966, 1969–70, and 1973–74.

In order for formula plans to operate correctly, the stock market must rise and fall with some regularity and within predictable limits. Stock prices should be high when bonds are low and vice versa. We have not had these conditions in recent years, and as a consequence the variable ratio plans have not had very wide usage. It is possible to make

10

Projected level	64
Less actual level	43
Equals the difference	21

(Difference/Projected level) × 100 = Percent difference between the projected and actual market levels.

$$(21/64) \times 100 = 33\%$$

When the market is 33 percent below normal, the correct proportion (from Table 14–5) is about 83 percent aggressive and 17 percent defensive.

such a plan work by changing the decision rules and the "normal level" of prices to fit current market conditions. But these are the very decisions that the plan is supposed to make automatically. If it does not make these decisions, or if it makes them incorrectly, the plan has no value. Variable ratio plans were adopted by a large number of individuals and investments managers who finally discarded them because they were not able to make them work without constant revision of the decision rules. However, if future security markets become more "normal" in their price fluctuations, these plans will probably again become popular, perhaps even valuable, investment aids.

Dollar averaging is especially well adapted for use by persons accumulating investments since it requires regular purchases of new securities to make it operate. Formula plans are used mainly to manage an already existing portfolio, but they can easily be modified to accommodate new investment funds. Instead of selling existing securities to bring the formula into balance, new money can be used to accomplish the same purpose.

CONCLUSIONS

This chapter will possibly have disappointed readers who expected it to reveal easy ways to investment profits through correct timing decisions. The truth of the matter is that there are no easy ways to investment profits, and there is no 100 percent accurate method of predicting security market price changes. This chapter was written to make investors aware of the more commonly used methods of making investment timing decisions and to point up the difficulties and shortcomings of each.

In doing so we may have appeared more skeptical and pessimistic than we intended. It is true that none of the timing devices is 100 percent accurate. It is equally true that formula plans are not always profitable and that dollar averaging does not always produce maximum profits. But few things in this world are perfect.

All the plans and predictive devices examined have at one time or another produced good results. Since the operation of most of them requires some skill of interpretation on the part of the user, it is not surprising that they have been more profitable for some investors than for others. These devices should be looked upon as tools which may be used to make better investment decisions. The secret to their successful use is not difficult to learn: Never rely completely upon any single predictive device. Rather, use several of the indicators which have proved reliable to you, checking the forecast of one against the others. Constantly reexamine and reevaluate investment plans and forecasting devices to determine whether they are performing as planned and whether they continue to be useful. Used carefully, these tools can provide better investment decisions.

SUMMARY

This chapter outlined several methods of *timing* investment purchases and sales. *When* investments are purchased and sold is important because markets for most investments—particularly equity securities—fluctuate more than they logically should. At one time prices are abnormally and unrealistically high; at another they are equally unrealistically low. If a person were able to always buy when prices were "low" and sell when they were "high," profitable investments could be made most of the time no matter which individual securities were purchased. Conversely, another investor might purchase the very "best" investments—on the basis of intrinsic value calculations—and lose money because the investments were purchased at abnormally high prices. Successful timing of investment purchases and sales minimizes the problem of individual security selection. Methods of timing investment decisions were presented in these four classifications: (1) economic analysis, (2) fundamental analysis, (3) technical analysis, and (4) formula investment plans.

Timing decisions based upon *economic analysis* use economic events to predict security price movements. Over the years, practically every economic event has been used as a predictor of security prices. This type of analysis has logical appeal because investment prices are related to company profits, which in turn are related to general economic conditions. The difficult part of this type of analysis is that of finding an economic indicator which reliably predicts changes. Industrial production has been used as such a predictor but with little success. Changes in industrial production usually *lag* changes in security prices. In recent years various indexes of the supply of money, credit, and other monetary variables have come into wide use as predictors. The theory underlying the use of these variables is that security prices are related more to the supply of credit than to other things.

Fundamental analysis makes use of economic data related to individual companies, industries, or security markets. These topics were covered in detail in Chapter 6, and received but brief treatment in this chapter.

Technical analysis encompasses a large number of theories which attempt to predict future security price changes on the basis of events *internal* to the security markets. These theories are complex and sometimes not completely logical, but large numbers of investors follow them. Stock charts record the history of prices of individual stocks or stock indexes. The patterns graphed by these prices are used, often along with other data, to predict future price movements.

Odd-lot statistics are used by many analysts to indicate turning points of stock markets. The theory is that the odd-lotter—the small investor—is usually *wrong* at major market turning points. If it can be determined that most small investors are selling, then the "smart investor" should be buying, and vice versa. An index of odd-lot trading is often used to measure whether the small investor is actively buying or selling. Data on short sales are also used to predict market turning points. The advance decline index attempts to identify major turning points in stock markets.

Formula investment plans are plans for making investment timing decisions automatically. The simplest of these is *dollar averaging*, a plan under which an investor periodically purchases a specified dollar amount of a given security or securities. If the market prices of these securities move up and down, as they are expected to do, the plan will result in profits. Ratio and other formula plans attempt to improve on dollar averaging by holding larger or smaller amounts of "aggressive" and "defensive" securities, depending upon whether security prices are relatively high or low. Such plans do increase profits, if they are successful, but to be successful it is necessary that investors be able to make accurate predictions of future security prices.

No timing devices have been 100 percent accurate, nor could one reasonably expect them to be. However, they are useful tools. Investors should have a basic understanding of their use.

PROBLEMS

1. Look through a recent copy of the *Business Conditions Digest* and pick out five economic indexes which you believe would most accurately predict future stock prices. Defend your choices on logical grounds.
2. Prepare a point and figure chart or a bar chart for a given security over a yearly period. What does this chart indicate to you? (We suggest

using weekly data on this exercise since a great number of plots must otherwise be made. *Barron's* presents weekly stock prices, or end-of-week prices can be obtained from any newspaper having a financial section.)

3. Design a dollar cost averaging program which operates over a five-year period with purchases at six-month intervals. Choose a security and obtain historical security price data which indicate how well the plan would have done if it had been followed over the past five years.
4. From data contained in *The Wall Street Journal* or other sources construct a ratio of total short interest to daily average stock volume. Interpret the meaning of the ratio.

QUESTIONS

1. "Any investment can be a good investment." Under what conditions is this statement true?
2. What is *technical analysis?*
3. What is the logic of using data on odd-lot trading to predict market turning points?
4. Explain how an increase in short interest of a security might indicate future increases in the price of this security.
5. What is *dollar cost averaging?* Explain how such a program operates. What arc its strong and weak points?
6. All formula plans are supposed to remove the burden of making investment timing decisions and forecasting from the investor. To what extent do they do this?
7. How do variable ratio plans differ from constant ratio plans?
8. Define *aggressive* and *defensive* investments.
9. Would the Federal Reserve Index of Industrial Production or a forecast of expected new car sales be a better indicator of the price of Ford Motor Company stock over the next six months?
10. How does *technical analysis* differ from *fundamental analysis?*

SELECTED READINGS

Bishop, George W., Jr. *Charles H. Dow and the Dow Theory*. New York: Appleton-Century-Crofts, 1960.

Bolton, A. Hamilton. *Money and Investment Profits*. Homewood, Ill.: Dow Jones-Irwin, 1967.

Cirino, Robert J. "Odd-Lot Short Sales: Are They Still a Reliable Barometer," *The Institutional Investor*, February 1975.

Cohen, A. W. *Technical Indicator Analysis by Point and Figure Technique*. Larchmont, N.Y.: Chartcraft, Inc., 1970.

Cohen, Jerome B.; Zinbarg, Edward D.; and Zeikel, Arthur. *Investment Analysis and Portfolio Management*, rev. ed. Homewood, Ill.: Richard D. Irwin, 1973.

Edwards, Robert D., and Magee, John. *Technical Analysis of Stock Trends*, 5th ed. Springfield, Mass.: John Magee, 1966.

Granville, Joseph E. *A Strategy of Daily Stock Market Timing for Maximum Profit*. Englewood Cliffs, N.J.: Prentice-Hall, 1960.

———. *Granville's New Key to Stock Market Profits*. Englewood Cliffs, N.J.: Prentice-Hall, 1963.

Kerrigan, Thomas J. "Behavior of the Short Interest Ratio," *Financial Analysts Journal*, November–December 1974.

Lerro, Anthony J., and Swayne, Charles B., Jr. *Selection of Securities: Technical Analysis of Stock Market Prices*. Aigencourt, Ont.: General Learning Corp., 1974.

Levy, Robert A. "Conceptual Foundations of Technical Analysis," *Financial Analysts Journal*, July–August 1966.

Schultz, John W. *The Intelligent Chartist*. New York: WRSM Financial Service Corporation, 1962.

Sprinkel, Beryl W. *Money and Markets: A Monetarist View*. Homewood, Ill.: Dow Jones-Irwin, 1971.

Tomlinson, Lucile. *Practical Formulas for Successful Investing*. New York: Wilfred Funk, 1953.

15
Managing Your Investments

INTRODUCTION

Managing investments is a difficult and often frustrating job, but one that cannot be delegated entirely to others. To this point the purpose of this book has been to provide the basic information necessary to select various types of investments. This chapter outlines a procedure for constructing and maintaining a personal investment program. Before taking up this topic, however, we shall briefly summarize the preceding chapters of the book, and thereby emphasize the main points that we were attempting to make. All are important to the development of a sound investment program.

Chapter 1 was concerned with basic definitions of investing and speculating, risk and return, and the concept of wealth. Chapter 2 carried these concepts further. From the viewpoint of an individual seeking to increase or conserve wealth through investments, the most important concepts were those of risk and return. All investments have some sort of risk attached to them. High-grade debt securities have little financial risk, but they usually make the investor liable to loss of purchasing power due to inflation. Market prices of these issues are controlled by changes in the market rates of interest, and price changes due to this source may be large. Equity investments have substantial amounts of financial risk, but because the returns from these investments can increase in value, they usually allow the investor some long-run protection against loss of purchasing power. Declining security prices during an inflationary period will in the short-run cause a great decline in purchasing power. Lack of marketability may affect both debt and equity investments; all high-grade investments—debt or equity—are marketable.

Chapters 3 and 4 examined the securities markets, sources of investor information, the broker-customer relationship, and the regulation of various aspects of investing. These chapters should have great value for the beginning investor because they describe the environment in which investments are made. Chapter 5 explained the use and meaning of financial statements. Chapter 6 was devoted to the general topic of investment analysis.

Chapters 7 through 11 described the risk, return, and other investment characteristics of the more usual forms of investments. Chapter 12 did the same thing for less common, but still important, types of investments. Of specific importance when planning an investment program, or in managing an existing one, are the risk and return characteristics of the many different types of investments. An investment program's success will usually depend upon the skill with which the risk and return characteristics of various different investments are merged. A correctly designed portfolio will perform closely to expectations while a poorly designed one probably will not.

Chapter 13 on investment taxation, and Chapter 14 on investment timing, dealt with two specific problems of investing. Taxes are important, even to small-scale investors, because you can only spend what remains after taxes are paid. Minimizing taxes—by legal means, of course—should be an important goal of every investor. Timing of security purchases and sales is also important. An investor who did everything else wrong—but who managed to time the purchase and sale of investments so that they were sold when markets were relatively high and purchased when they were relatively low—would probably do well regardless of the type of investment choices that were made. Unfortunately, there is no known way of consistently buying at lows and selling at highs, even though there are many ways of forecasting markets.

Constructing a successful investment program consists of balancing the bad or negative characteristics of investments—purchasing power risk, financial risk, or interest rate risk, for example—against the positive points—yield, growth, marketability, tax status, and so on—in such a way that the "best" mixture of risk and return is obtained. But what is best? A given mix of risk and return may be 100 percent suitable for investor A and completely unsuitable for investor B. Another type of investment program might be highly desirable for A at one time and be totally inappropriate at another. Designing an investment program is much like designing a house. The homeowner decides what the house must provide in terms of number of rooms required, room sizes, home location, and so on. The architect then plans a home around these basic needs and attempts to fit the cost of the house into the owner's budget. For persons of limited financial means, the compromise is usually in the direction of fewer or smaller rooms because the budget is less flexible than the home builder's desires. The compromise in designing an investment program is usually in deciding which risks to accept, and which to attempt to avoid, given certain goals of the program. Sometimes the program's goals must be scaled downward if the amount of principal is too small to provide a needed dollar amount of return. More on this topic later.

A further analogy between homes and investment programs is that the requirements of both change as persons move through their life cycles. When the children are still living at home, more bedrooms and recreation area is necessary. At a later time a smaller home is more appropriate because this space is not required. Investment programs must be tailored to fit changing lifestyles. When a person's earnings—and taxes—are high, returns in the form of capital gains will probably be preferred. Upon retirement, regular cash dividends and interest become more desirable.

DESIGNING AN INVESTMENT PROGRAM

As F. Scott Fitzgerald once said to Ernest Hemingway, "You see, Ernest, the very rich are different from you and me." And so they are, especially in how they administer their investments. Wealthy persons usually have available excellent legal, tax, and investment advice because (1) they can afford to pay for it, and (2) their accounts are of such size that the commissions generated provide a handsome income to investment advisors. Small-scale investors can obtain the same services and advice, of course, but at a price. As a result, most small investors must rely more on their own devices than their wealthy counterparts do. This chapter is not written for the Rockefellers, Du Ponts, Mellons, or others having vast wealth and much investment counsel, but rather to persons who must invest largely on their own.

Before beginning the actual design of an investment program some very basic questions must be answered. The first deals with the financial ability to invest.

A Total Financial Plan

An investment program cannot and should not be separated from the other financial dealings of the family.[1] It should be an integrated part of an overall financial plan which covers the complete life cycle of the family. While it is always uncomfortable to think of such matters, the plan should anticipate death and make arrangements for the settling and passing of the estate. Insurance needs should be satisfied. This is a difficult plan to devise because of the many uncertainties of the future. Questions such as the following must be answered: What will future earnings be? Will we have additional children? Are large unexpected expenses likely? These questions require careful analysis and decisions.

At this point many persons are tempted to throw up their hands in dismay and give up, citing the uncertainty of the future as making it impossible to plan effectively. However, even a plan which eventually proves to be inaccurate may have current value. It forces persons to think about the future in a way that they probably have never before done, and it indicates some of the basic constraints on their investment program.

Determining Net Worth. A first step toward a financial plan is to make up a current statement of family (or personal) net worth. This is accomplished by adding up the value of all the things you own and subtracting all debt. The remainder is net worth. This is intended as a rough-and-ready calculation. Do not try to include everything. Table 15–1 illustrates how this calculation might be made. Naturally, different families will have different types of assets and liabilities, but this general format can be used with minor changes.

This calculation often reveals that the person has more net worth than was imagined, and it allows one to see where cash might be obtained if it is necessary. By comparing current income to certain of the asset categories persons can tell whether they are "living within their means," at least in an average sense.

The Cash Reserve. A widely accepted rule of thumb is that a person's home may cost up to two or two-and-a-half times the family's

[1] This chapter is directed toward *family* financial planning for the following two reasons. First of all, most people will be married before they are 23 years old. Marriage and attendant responsibilities seem distant to the college sophomore or junior, but they will arrive, perhaps sooner than anticipated. Next, the single person is not really omitted from the discussion. In most cases the only difference between this person's financial plan and that of a family is that the single person has more money to invest and may be willing and able to take on more risk. We believe that single persons can benefit from financial planning as much as anyone.

TABLE 15–1
Simplified Statement of Net Worth

Assets		
Cash	$ 1,000	
Investments	2,000	
Savings deposits	3,000	
Cash value of life insurance	200	
Home and furnishings	17,000	
Automobile	2,000	
Other assets	6,000	
Total assets		$31,200
Liabilities		
Consumer debt*	$ 200	
Home Mortgage loan	11,000	
Total liabilities		11,200
Net Worth		$20,000

* Unpaid bills, credit card debt, department store credit, and so on. This amount should be the *average* of this type of debt.

yearly take home pay. Fifteen thousand dollars of after-tax income would "support" a house valued at between $30,000 and $37,500. Naturally, one would expect a family of nine to spend substantially more of their income on housing, while the family of two or three would spend less.

Many financial counselors advise having six months of after-tax income in a *liquidity reserve*, in anticipation of unexpected expenses. This money is usually held in a savings account or money-market fund—to earn interest—rather than in cash. However, it is doubtful that all persons need to hold this proportion of their earnings in a ready cash reserve. Many people now have unemployment insurance, insurance to continue salary in case of sickness or disability, medical and dental insurance, auto and home insurance, and life insurance. The well-insured family can probably get along with a rainy day reserve of three months' salary. An uninsured or underinsured family might need a larger cash reserve, as would one which had an erratic salary pattern. Single persons also need a cash reserve, but it is usually small.

Life Insurance as an Investment. The question of how life insurance relates to an investment program is of such importance to a large number of persons that we wish to answer it as best we can. First of all, *pure insurance* is not an investment, was never an investment, and cannot be an investment. Pure insurance simply allows a policyholder to obtain financial compensation if some statistically predictable event occurs, for example, the cash benefit received upon death. There is no compensation unless the event occurs, and there cannot be a profit to the beneficiary.[2] Many life insurance policies have savings features which cause them to become investments by virtue of the fact that the *insured* can obtain some benefit from the policy. Insurance policies are of three general types.

Term life insurance is pure insurance. This type of policy compensates the beneficiary only if the insured event—death of the policyholder—occurs. This type of insurance provides the maximum amount of coverage per dollar of premium because the policy includes no element of saving or investment. Term policies may be purchased which are automatically renewable at the option of the insured. Unless it is definitely known that insurance will not be needed after a certain time—when all children have graduated from high school for example—renewable term insurance should be purchased even though its premium is slightly higher than nonrenewable. Term insurance is practically a necessity for young married couples. It is often the only way that an estate of sufficient size can be built to provide financial support for the family in the event of death of the breadwinner. Premiums increase with the age of the insured to the point where term insurance is seldom purchased by people over 50. By that time, however, few need this kind of protection.

Straight life, ordinary life, and *whole life* insurance policies contain elements of saving. Part of the premium goes for term insurance, and another part accumulates as reserves. Premiums for these policies are "level" in that they remain constant over the life of the policy. Many of these policies prepay premiums so that the policyholder stops making premium payments at a fixed time—often age 65—but remains insured until death. The element of saving is small; it is merely the amount of premiums accumulated in excess of the protection part of the contract. This savings amount is known as cash surrender value and may be borrowed from the insurance company by the policyholder.

Endowment insurance resembles the above types except that in this policy the element of saving is even larger. Most of these policies are written so that the insured receives the face value of the policy after paying premiums for a specific time period. If the insured dies before this time the face value of the policy goes to the beneficiaries. Because the element of saving is such a large part of this policy, $1 of premium

---

[2] It might be argued that when old uncle Gottbucks dies and his nephew Frivolous becomes the beneficiary of his life insurance policy, that the nephew shows a profit on the transaction. It is true that he has more cash, but this is to compensate him for the premature death of his uncle. In theory there is no profit to him.

will buy less protection in this form than in either straight life or term insurance.

Before embarking on an investment program, an individual should make certain that family insurance coverage is adequate. This usually means that in the event of the death of the head of the household, insurance will support the spouse and family until the children are either out of school or until they are old enough so that the remaining parent can go to work. Term insurance provides this sort of protection best, but many people purchase policies having a saving feature because they feel that they will then be *forced* to save something. Savings accumulate at a slower rate in insurance policies than in bank savings accounts or in practically any other savings investment. For this reason most people are well advised to purchase term insurance to cover insurance needs and to place savings in the appropriate financial institution.

The Cash Budget. Assuming that insurance coverage and cash reserve are adequate, it is now time to attempt to answer the question of how much money can be invested. A cash budget is most useful in arriving at this amount.

The cash budget somewhat resembles the net worth calculation except that net worth is a value that exists *at a certain point in time,* while the cash budget lists income and expenses received and paid *over a period of time.* Begin this computation by estimating after-tax cash income from all sources for the coming year. From this amount deduct all anticipated cash expenses.[3] The difference between the two is the amount that is *surplus;* it is not necessarily the amount that should be invested (see Table 15–2).

Revenues, expenses, and surplus will become less predictable the further into the future the cash budget is projected. And yet, on a year to year basis the budget will probably be fairly accurate because budget figures are periodically reviewed as better information becomes available. Stated another way: In 1976, the 1980 projection is probably way off, but by 1979—due to constant revision of data—the anticipated 1980 revenues and expenses may be right on target. Preparing a budget such as this has definite advantages, whether or not there is any surplus. It allows one to see which are major expenses. Living expenses can be subdivided into such classifications as food, clothing, and so on,

[3] The emphasis is on cash although persons receive a part of their compensation in retirement benefits, stock options, profit sharing plans, housing, use of an automobile, or other service. These all have value and may indirectly affect investment decisions, but at this point our concern is only with cash revenues and expenses.

TABLE 15–2
Family Cash Budget

	1976	1977	1978
Revenue (after taxes)			
Take home pay	$12,000	$13,200	$14,520
Interest and dividends	250	300	350
Other income	300	300	300
Total income	$12,550	$13,800	$15,170
Expenses			
Ordinary living expenses	$ 6,000	$ 6,600	$ 5,600
Home mortgage and taxes	1,600	1,600	1,600
Insurance premiums	400	400	400
Retirement contribution (paid separately)	600	660	720
Large capital outlays			
Sailboat	1,000	-0-	-0-
Refurnish bedroom	-0-	1,500	-0-
College expense of child	-0-	-0-	2,000
Total expenses	$ 9,600	$10,760	$10,320
Revenue less expenses equals surplus	$ 2,950	$ 3,040	$ 4,850

which more precisely identify where the revenue is going. Separate unlisted classifications—entertainment for example—can be set up. Perhaps more importantly, it allows the family to ready itself for large capital outlays like sailboats and college expenses. Whether or not the budget is very accurate, it forces one to think in terms of future expenses and revenues, a distinct advantage in itself.

The cash budget and the net worth statement can and should be projected into retirement years. If this date is far into the future the figures will probably not be very realistic, but they will indicate in a general way what normal expenses are anticipated upon retirement and, from that, what revenues are necessary to cover them. The face value of insurance policies, and retirement income from Social Security and other plans, become important when these retirement calculations are made. If retirement is just too far away to plan toward, direct the plan toward specific events which will cause large financial outlays. A family having three children under five can project some rather heavy expenses beginning in 12 years and continuing on for perhaps nine more—if the children are expected to attend college.

Setting Investment Program Goals

Goals refer to what the investment program is supposed to do for the investor. A statement of these goals should be prepared at the time an investment program is begun. The statement should be in writing and should be specific enough that it is possible to determine whether the investment plan is actually accomplishing its goal or goals. Such a procedure may seem somewhat rigid and formal, but by proceeding in this fashion the investor is forced to do several things that might not ordinarily be done.

First of all, preparation of a goal statement causes in-depth thought about what the investment program seeks to do. When the investor attempts to balance program goals against whatever restrictions the program has, a more realistic view develops of what can be expected from the program. Preparation of goals usually cannot—and certainly should not—be done without reference to a total family financial plan. It is important that the investment program be integrated into this plan, and this is one way to guarantee that this is done.

Writing down the goal statement is desirable because it allows the investor to periodically review the investment program to see how well it is doing. But measuring the performance of a given program is impossible if the goal is not stated in terms which allow measurement. For example, a goal statement of "maximum long-term capital gains" may initially seem very specific and clear, but how could one tell whether maximum capital gains had in fact been attained? The goal is not related to a performance standard which provides the basis for appraising attainment of the goal. A more specific way of stating the goal would be in terms of capital gains appreciation relative to one of the common stock indexes. For example, one might revise the "maximum" statement to that of "obtaining long-term capital gains at least 10 percent greater than the increases of the Dow Jones Industrial Average over a ten-year period." A simple statement might define the goal as, "at least $2,000 (or 7 percent) per year in interest and dividends." These statements are precise enough to provide the basis for determining whether the goal was attained or how far below or above it the investment program performed.

Constraints on Investment Policy. It is unusual when the goals of an investment program can be stated in a single sentence, because most programs have goals which are constrained by factors unique to the investor. For instance, to attain the above-stated goal of capital gains performance at least 10 percent better than the Dow Jones Industrial Average, an investor would almost certainly have to invest in a limited number of common stocks that promised to perform exceptionally well over the next ten years. Shares chosen to implement this investment program may very well increase in value by the required amount over the ten-year period, but during this period they may decrease in value at some time by as much as 30 percent.[4] This action should be expected since this is the way common stock prices fluctuate. The question is, can the investor accept this type of price fluctuation? Are there any restrictions on his or her actions as an investor?

There are some constraints on practically every investment program which, if realistically considered, usually act to make the initial goal statement less aggressive. Constraints, as the word is used here, refer to conditions which keep the investor from maximizing the primary goal of an investment program—whatever that may be.

Constraints may take many forms. In the example of a goal of capital gains 10 percent greater than the Dow Jones industrials, the investor who set this objective may have done so because this amount of capital appreciation was *needed* to provide a given sum of money for retirement which was to take place in ten years. In other words, the goal of the investment program was integrated perfectly with this person's long-run financial plan and was in this sense "correct." However, to realize this goal the entire portfolio should probably be invested in fairly risky common stocks. Possible constraints to this investment program might be the following:

1. To provide liquidity, securities should always be marketable at no less than 80 percent of their purchase price. Obviously, securities which can be expected to decline in value by as much as 30 percent could not be used in an investment program so constrained.

2. Cash income (dividend income in this case) must be a minimum dollar amount per year. This may or may not be an important restriction depending upon the relationship of the minimum income necessary to the total securities purchased. However, if the minimum dollar amount is high relative to the amount of principal, the investor may be forced to purchase only very high-grade, dividend-paying stocks. These securities will probably not perform better than the Dow Jones Industrial Average.

The list of constraints could be extended almost indefinitely. The important point is that nearly every investment program contains limitations or restrictions. An investment program should be constructed so that these constraints are honored, because if they are not, the program is simply not going to do what the investor wants it to do. Constraints usually cause investors to act less aggressively than they

---

[4] During 1968 the low of the DJIA was 18 percent below the high. In 1969 it was 22 percent below. During 1974 the low was more than 50 percent below the high.

It should be remembered that many of the individual stocks that make up this average showed *greater* changes—60 percent or more—in market price. Higher grade stocks will usually experience less market price fluctuation than those of lower grade.

might prefer and may be seen as "standing in the way of profits." This is often true, because constraints almost always force the investor to revise the original investment program so that it is more prudent. Since risk and return are directly related, as risk declines so does the expected return from the investment portfolio.

One of the most common mistakes in investment management is to try to obtain "too much" return from a given amount of principal. This often happens when people are planning for retirement. They first decide how much income they need to live, then they decide how to get it. For example, next year Mr. X is retiring. He will receive a pension and Social Security of $4,000 per year, and he calculates his minimum yearly expenses at $7,000. Obviously he needs an additional $3,000 of income from somewhere. Suppose he has $20,000 for investment. The most direct solution to this financial problem is to invest the $20,000 so that it returns 15 percent ($3,000) per year.

If Mr. X decides on this course of action he will probably be disappointed. A 15 percent per annum return on investment is extremely difficult to obtain; it is impossible to obtain without accepting a rather great risk of loss of principal. Mr. X should realize that this goal is probably unattainable if he sets any constraints whatever on his investment program, and that he had better look to reducing his living expenses.[5] This is an undesirable solution perhaps, but in the long run probably the wisest one.

Most investment programs that are carefully and realistically planned contain several constraints. These should be listed in writing along with the goal or goals of the investment program. If possible, priorities should be assigned to each limitation. If liquidity is more important than protection of purchasing power, this fact should be noted. A way of approaching the problem of measuring the importance of various restrictions is to list them all and assign to each a measure of its importance. Table 15–3 is not an exhaustive list, but it identifies some of the more common constraints on investment programs. This list is no more than a formalization of what an investor should be considering when designing an investment program. Certain of these restrictions will possibly be relaxed as time passes, while others may become more important. This list should be revised periodically as the performance of the portfolio is appraised.

[5] Actually, there are several possible ways that Mr. X might make ends meet. He could purchase an annuity that would pay a certain amount per year until death. The return from this annuity would be constant and would be at a fairly high rate. He might also use part of the principal each year to make up the difference between what he can earn with the required amount of safety and what he needs.

TABLE 15–3
Listing of Investment Program Constraints

Need for	*High*	*Medium*	*Low*
Liquidity	X		
Constant income		X	
Constant purchasing power			X
Constant market prices			X
Tax exemption	X		

Psychological Constraints. Most constraints are set in an attempt to make an investment program more responsive to the needs of the investor, and most of them result from logical, dollar-and-cents analysis of the present and future financial situation of the family. It is difficult to bring the psychological attitudes of the investor or investors into this analytical decision-making process because numbers cannot be assigned to attitudes, but somehow it must be done. All investments contain a certain amount of risk, and one purpose of the investment program is to identify the types and degrees of risk that must be accepted by the investor in order for certain investment returns to be realized. The risk-return relationship is derived on the basis of what would be the most profitable course of action under given circumstances; it does not necessarily attempt to deal with the *preferences* of the parties involved. As an example of this type of logic, historical evidence indicates that an investor who purchased common stocks and held them for a period of time would have earned between 9 and 10 percent per annum after taking into consideration losses and costs of buying and selling the securities.[6] Savings deposits would have yielded something less than half this rate. Based upon these historical data, investors should forgo the safety of savings deposits for the profit of common shares whenever they have a choice of investment media.

The argument is logical because purchasing common stocks would enable the investor to make more profit. But from a purely psychological viewpoint, investment in common stocks may be very undesirable. Stock prices will fluctuate on a daily basis, while savings deposits will not. Fluctuating prices make some persons so nervous that they simply cannot endure the price uncertainty of investing in equity securities, even though they realize that in the long run this is probably the most

[6] Laurence Fisher and James H. Lorie, "Rates of Return on Investments in Common Stock, the Year by Year Record, 1926–1965," *Journal of Business*, July 1968, pp. 291–316 and ———, "Some Studies of Variability of Returns on Investments in Common Stocks," *Journal of Business*, April 1970, pp. 99–134.

profitable course of action. Others continue to invest in equities because it is "logical" in dollar-and-cents terms for them to do so, but they too might be better served by investments having more constant market prices. If an investor is the type of person who must check the stock quotes before breakfast, and if the stomach muscles tighten and the heart pounds every time stocks are off a point, caution may be in order. Such a person may not be psychologically equipped to invest in common stocks, or any other investment which has great market price fluctuations, even though the investor's financial situation is such that these investments should logically be purchased.

If this characteristic exists, it should be honored as a strong constraint in the investment program. Forcing one's self or one's partner into an investment program that is logical, but which causes undue anxiety or frustration is foolish. An investment program should be personally satisfying as well as profitable. Furthermore, the anxious, nervous person is the one most likely to panic and sell out at just the wrong time. The psychology of investing probably gets too little attention as a limitation on investment strategy because most people pride themselves on their ability to make "logical" and "businesslike" decisions. However, there can be no more logical or businesslike decision than that of recognizing and honoring any psychological constraints that affect one's desire or ability to invest in certain securities.

Tenure of Ownership. Psychological constraints are an overriding consideration which often restrict investment programs to less risky investments. Tenure of ownership is a consideration that may affect an investment program in two different ways. If tenure of ownership is weak—meaning there is a strong possibility that all or a portion of a security portfolio will have to be sold quickly—it limits an investment program to liquid securities. If tenure of ownership is strong—meaning there is little possibility that securities will have to be sold quickly—an investment program can be made up of less liquid securities having a wide range of price fluctuations. Such investors can "wait it out"; they will not be forced to sell securities at the wrong time.

Weak tenure of ownership may be caused by several things. If an investor has much personal debt, repayment of this debt may cause liquidation of a portion of the investment portfolio. This sort of expense can usually but not always be anticipated in the cash budget. Personal debts may come due at unexpected times and in unexpected amounts. When securities have been purchased on margin, tenure of ownership may become exceptionally weak during market downturns. Securities may have to be sold to meet margin requirements—just when security prices are low. Persons having fluctuating or uncertain incomes usually have weak tenure of ownership unless they have a large cash reserve.

Estate planning often identifies conditions of weak tenure of ownership. Death of even a modestly wealthy person causes formidable taxes to be levied against the person's estate. Unless plans have been laid carefully beforehand to have these taxes paid from a cash reserve or from insurance, securities may have to be sold unexpectedly. There is an element of probability in measuring strength or weakness of tenure of ownership from this cause. It is unlikely that a young person will soon die. Tenure of ownership of such individuals is therefore stronger than it would be for individuals of advanced age, all other considerations remaining the same.

Estate Planning

Estate planning is personal financial planning carried to the ultimate point of making arrangements for the complete settlement and passing on of the estate of the person or persons involved. Most people can plan their own investment programs, at least in general terms, but estate planning, because of its legal, tax, and liquidity problems, is the domain of the expert.[7] The purpose of including this topic in this book is *not* to tell how to plan for the settlement of an estate; this topic is far too complex for a book of this type. It is rather to indicate the need for such planning and to show some of the benefits to be derived from it.

Having no plan for disposition of an estate is for all practical purposes a type of estate planning. A person who dies *intestate* is a person who has left no valid will. In such circumstances the person's estate will be passed on in a legal procedure set down by the state in which the person resides. If the estate is small or held in joint tenancy by husband and wife, it may pass to the remaining party quickly, and with a minimum of cost. But even in this situation, the property may pass through the courts—a time-consuming and sometimes costly procedure. If the wife and husband die at the same time and there is no will, the property will pass to the legal heirs in accordance with state legal procedures. In either event, the law of the state "plans" for the

[7] Several books are listed at the end of this chapter for those who wish to read about this subject in more detail. Most banks which have active trust departments prepare literature written to the layperson which explains the purpose of estate planning and how one can begin a plan.

disposition of the estate, even though the owner of the estate had no written or otherwise stated plan. How property is held—in joint tenancy, as tenants in common, singly, or in some other form—helps determine how rapidly an estate can be settled.

Those people who wish to speed up the process of estate settlement, and make certain that their property is disposed of according to their wishes must either make a *will*, place property in a *trust*, or *give it away* before death. Under a will property is controlled by the owner until death, when the terms of the will take effect. Under a trust arrangement another person, the *trustee*, is granted control over the property. The trustee must manage the property in accordance with the wishes of the person who created the trust and in accordance with the state laws which control the actions of trustees.

There are more types of trusts than can be comfortably surveyed in a book of this limited size and scope. The device is so flexible that it can be used to control the disposition of property over many years (not indefinitely) and through several different users of the property. It is particularly useful when one wishes to grant the proceeds from an estate to a person, persons, or an institution without allowing control over the estate itself to pass into their hands. The most common example of this is when property is left in trust for a minor child. A trustee manages the property and holds title to it but pays out income from the property to the child. Often when the child becomes of legal age, the principal of the trust passes to the child's control.

People increasingly choose to give away part of their estate prior to death. Gifts can often be used to reduce federal and state estate taxes, and they allow givers to see what is done with their gifts.[8] Gifts also allow recipients to obtain a portion of an estate—which they are probably going to receive someday—earlier, when the gift is more meaningful or useful. Gifts of a limited amount are completely tax free to the persons receiving them. All gifts are taxed at rates lower than estate tax rates.

One of the greatest advantages of estate planning for individuals of substantial means is that it enables them to plan for the minimizing of federal and state estate taxes. Individuals can often lower their income taxes by making gifts of property to nonprofit institutions such as museums, colleges and universities, and even trusts. If these gifts are

[8] A person who had given a northwestern college money to build a fieldhouse requested that his name—which was chiseled in stone on the front of the building—be removed and the building be renamed. He had become dissatisfied with the uses to which the building had been put.

to be made anyway upon death, there is often a substantial tax advantage to making them early, while the person still has taxable income.

CONSTRUCTING AND ADMINISTERING AN INVESTMENT PORTFOLIO

At some point, a person will begin accumulating a portfolio of investments. Hopefully this is after enough financial planning has taken place to insure that the investor has a good idea of what the investment program should accomplish. After the investment program is begun, it should be administered so that the goals of the program, as well as the individual investments, come under the investor's regular scrutiny.

Constructing the Portfolio

Constructing any portfolio involves purchasing securities which have investment characteristics consistent with the goals of the investment program. Through the use of tools described earlier—mainly the net worth calculation and the cash budget—the investor will be able to develop investment program guidelines. At the same time one will also develop a reasonably good idea of the total amount of funds which can be devoted to investments, both now and in the future.

The Cash Reserve. It is now time to make some investments. Investing for liquidity is not difficult. The primary consideration is how rapidly can the investments be turned into cash without loss of principal; a secondary consideration is yield. For the small-scale investor, savings accounts at commercial banks or other financial institutions meet these requirements almost perfectly, as do some liquidity funds. U.S. savings bonds do about as well, except that they are not as quickly turned into cash. For the large-scale investor, Treasury bills provide a good liquidity reserve and usually the highest short-term yields available. Long-term government, corporate, or municipal bonds are unsuitable for use as a liquidity reserve. They are safe as far as financial risk is concerned, and they are marketable, but their market prices fluctuate greatly with changes in the market rates of interest. Turning these securities into cash quickly can result in large capital losses.

Defensive Investments. Ideal defensive investments are difficult to list because there are several things that an investor might wish to defend against. For example, one could seek to defend against loss of principal, loss of purchasing power, or loss of current income, or all three, in the defensive section of a portfolio. Unfortunately, securities which provide maximum protection of principal, and which promise to pay constant interest or dividends for the foreseeable future, are those securities which provide least protection against loss of purchasing power because of inflation. There is always an element of conflict in the defensive portion of an investment portfolio as long as there is inflation.

The investor usually resolves this conflict by redefining "defensive" to mean defense against financial risk. When this is done, the obvious choice of investments for the defensive portion of the investment portfolio is securities of high grade. These would ordinarily be government bonds, corporates, and/or municipals of A grade or better, or possibly high-grade mortgages. These investments are secure so far as principal and interest income are concerned. Prices of high-grade long-term bonds fluctuate because of changes in interest rates. But these securities are purchased because they provide constant interest income; they will probably be held for a long period of time. Staggering maturities so that some bonds mature every year or so guarantees the investor the ability to redeem some of these securities at par, thereby allowing a certain amount of cash to be obtained with no loss of principal. Buying the bonds of companies in several different industries—utilities, industrials, communications, and so on—provides additional diversification in this part of the portfolio. The same diversification, and probably more, could be obtained through purchase of shares of a mutual fund which invests in bonds exclusively.

Investors often attempt to protect themselves against loss of purchasing power in the defensive portion of their portfolio by purchasing securities which they hope will increase in price over the long run. High-grade convertible bonds and convertible preferred stocks can provide an element of price appreciation which may overcome losses from price inflation. The investor can also follow a policy of purchasing lower grade bonds at discounts and holding them to maturity. In the spring of 1975 many highly rated bonds having coupons of 9 to 11 percent were selling at fairly large discounts. The current yield and potential price appreciation made these securities good hedges against moderate rates of inflation. Shares of conservatively managed "balanced" or "income" mutual funds may be acquired. Perhaps the investor can acquire mortgages that allow participation in price inflation by paying a percent of gross rentals in addition to interest. These kinds of investments may provide defense against loss of purchasing power due to inflation, but this protection is purchased at a price. Investors must not delude themselves into believing that this last-mentioned group of investments is "just as safe" as the first group. They are not. Compromise is always involved in attempts to obtain protection against financial and purchasing power risk with the same securities.

Aggressive Investments. These may be defined as investments which have rather high potential for loss or gain. They are usually characterized by great market price fluctuation and a yield which may vary from year to year. Common stocks are the most obvious of these investments, but any investment having the above characteristics would qualify as "aggressive." For example, low-grade bonds, "risky" mortgages, mutual fund shares in performance funds, warrants and rights, low-grade preferred stock, and certain convertible securities are all aggressive investments.

It is apparent that the thing these investments are aggressive about is financial and market risk. The investments are usually of such low grade that interest rate risk or purchasing power risk is not much of a factor in determining their price. If the financial situation of the company improves, the prices of these investments will climb. This is most clearly seen when a company having bonds rated at B or Ccc, or a company having preferred stock that has passed dividends becomes more financially able. Grades of these fixed income securities increase, and so do their prices. A buoyant market, with the majority of investors in an optimistic mood, may cause an even more rapid increase in prices.

As an example of such securities, in the spring of 1975 several issues of McCrory Corporation bonds were selling at about 40 ($400 per bond having a par value of $1,000). The current yield on these issues was near 20 percent. The bonds were not in default but the interest coverage ratio was low. These were certainly speculative securities; only time will tell whether they were good speculations.

Diversification is the most important single thing to emphasize when constructing the aggressive portion of an investment portfolio. Over the long run, average returns can consistently be obtained from risky investments only if enough different securities are held so that returns are average. How many securities are enough to do this? There is no hard and fast rule, but the absolute number of different securities increases as the risk factor increases because risky securities imply widely fluctuating returns. To get "average" experience from these securities a large number of them must be held. Less risky securities, because returns are more constant, provide an average experience with less diversification.

Shares in a single mutual fund might provide adequate diversity of risk, if the investments of the fund are truly diversified. Industry funds, real estate funds, and other funds which stress concentration of investments will not normally meet the requirements for diversification. Shares of funds having broader investment policies might.

Directly held common stocks are usually diversified by purchasing securities of companies in several industries. It is not necessary to buy securities in all or most industries simply to obtain diversification. Adequate diversification is obtained when investments are made in enough different companies that economic downturns in one or two industries will not affect all securities. A general downturn will affect them all, unfortunately, but some less than others. Too many different securities can be purchased in the attainment of diversification; do not purchase so many securities that they cannot be conveniently managed. As a rule of thumb, from 9 to 15 carefully chosen stocks are believed adequate to provide sufficient diversification for most investors. Diversification does not allow the investor to sit back and wait for profits; the portfolio still requires regular attention.

There is a school of thought which advocates purchases of just a few securities which are carefully chosen for excellent future performance. "Put your eggs in one basket and watch that basket" is the way one writer describes this strategy. We have no quarrel with this policy, but we do wish to correctly identify it as being *speculation* rather than *investment*. Concentration of investments has no place in the average investment portfolio because it introduces more risks than are usually acceptable. If the basket drops, *all* the eggs may break.

Security Analysis and Portfolio Construction

Security analysis may be defined as the art (it is not a science) of examining individual securities, industries, and securities markets and assigning them probable future values. The professional security analyst is a person knowledgeable in accounting, finance, economics, and money and banking. In addition, this person may also be trained in specific areas—geology, engineering, or chemistry, for example—if the analysis of companies using these types of technology is the primary assignment of the analyst. Most professional analysts are not brokers. They work in the research departments of large brokerage houses, investment companies, financial institutions, or financial news services, and the sole products of their efforts are research reports and recommendations on the future prospects for various companies.

Analysts make use of both fundamental and technical analysis in their work, but most of their effort is of a fundamental nature. This usually means that the researcher thoroughly examines the history of the companies under study and is completely familiar with the way company earnings change with changes in various economic conditions. The analyst usually follows the management of the company carefully and attempts to measure this important variable. Many analysts attend company annual meetings and often visit with the top management of companies in which they have an interest. Good researchers often know nearly as much about a given company as do many members of the company's board of directors.

The point of this is that few "average" investors have the background, or the time, to perform their own security analysis. And yet it should be done. An investor who decides to purchase shares of a company in a certain industry (for purposes of diversification let us say) should not buy those of just any company. Instead the security that promises to best satisfy the risk-return criteria of the investment program should be sought. Many investors prefer to make these decisions on their own, and there is much information available to aid them in their selection.[9] To make these choices intelligently, the investor does not need to be a security analyst. But one should be able to read the analysts' reports with understanding and with discrimination. One of the goals of this book is to provide enough background information so that the average investor is prepared to make such decisions.

Most investors do not have to make investment decisions completely on their own, however. They will be purchasing security investments through a broker, and this broker should be willing and able to help with the selection of securities. It is important to specify what the securities are supposed to do within the totality of the investment program. This can be done by providing the broker with an outline of the entire investment program. The broker should not ordinarily be concerned with setting the goals of the program—this is the individual's responsibility.

Investors can delegate complete management of their investment portfolios to others. This service is not free. It usually varies in price

---

[9] Chapter 4 lists these sources of information and how to use them.

with the size of the portfolio and the amount of attention it requires, but for larger portfolios it is relatively inexpensive. The same service can be purchased by smaller investors, although the cost may be higher in relation to the value of the portfolio. A large number of banks and other financial institutions as well as firms and individuals offer financial management advice for a fee. In all but exceptional circumstances (a minor child, a senile person, and so on) the investor should have control over the setting and review of investment program goals. Without some such direction and control it is impossible to tell whether the investment program is "on target" and still responsive to the investor's financial situation.

Managing an Investment Portfolio

The job is not completed when an investment program has been set and investments purchased. Investors must periodically review their programs to see (1) if the stated goals of the program are still the most desirable ones, and (2) if presently held investments are the best ones to realize these goals. At a minimum the investor should review an investment program once a year, ideally more often.

First, one should consult with other affected persons and answer this question: Are the goals of this program as currently stated still desirable? Conditions may have changed over time, causing investment goals to be altered. Investors commonly go through three clearly identified phases in their investment programs, phases which coincide roughly with their age and earning power.

The average under-40 investor has many family responsibilities. Life insurance premiums use a large amount of money that might otherwise go for security investments. Buying and furnishing a house is expensive, as are children. The need for liquidity is likely to be great. It is often said that young people are most able to take large investment risks because they have so much time to make up their losses. "Buy risky common stocks and wait for them to rise." This simply is not true! The beginning investor usually has little money to invest, and this money may well be needed for emergencies. Furthermore, such persons may have limited time to spend managing investments. Young people are often *willing* to take great risks in their investment programs; such is the optimistic nature of youth. Cash budget/net worth calculations should help to temper this optimism by providing a realistic appraisal of the kinds and amounts of risk that can be accepted.

From roughly age 40 to retirement the investor is usually more settled in a job, business, or profession. The children have either flown the nest or their departure is imminent. The house may well be paid for and all other foreseeable financial obligations covered. This person's cash budget may show large amounts available for investment. When these conditions prevail, and if the investor is willing to accept rather high risk, investment program goals will likely become much more aggressive, to build up resources for retirement. By this time the person may be more "savvy" about investments, and may have a broker or financial advisor whose past recommendations have proved sound and profitable. This investor may seek very rapid portfolio growth through high-risk investments. Performance mutual funds, warrants, convertible securities, and other risky investments may make up the bulk of this person's portfolio. Income property or part ownership in small businesses may be acquired. After all, such a person can afford to take investment risks. Since current income is probably high, it may be desirable to seek to lower income taxes by investing in municipal bonds, to the extent defensive securities are used. If the original investment goals are changed to reflect this desire for higher returns and a more aggressive policy, the change should be recorded and kept with other investment information.

The third phase in an investment program occurs when retirement becomes imminent. At this point—hopefully before—the investor should begin some sort of estate planning. Investment program goals will probably shift back to a more conservative policy, and constant income from the portfolio will usually be important. It may become desirable to sell investments which require managerial effort—for example, rental properties, small businesses, and so on. But this differs with the individual. Some people do not want to retire completely, and proprietary investments may provide a desirable outlet for such a person's energy and time. Others do not want to be bothered about anything that smacks of business. They want to be completely retired. Retirement age investment plans are often stated contingently: As long as Mr. X lives, the program is of one type. In the event of death or disability of Mr. X, the program changes to another. Regardless of what the personal preferences are, the goals of these programs should be stated just as specifically and as formally as before.

Reviewing Individual Investments. It is unlikely that the goals of an intelligently conceived investment program will be changed very often. The annual, semiannual, or quarterly review of the investment portfolio will normally concern itself with the question of whether the goals of the investment program are being realized. Is the defensive section of the portfolio really defensive? Are aggressive investments doing what they are were acquired to do? Is the cash reserve producing as much return as possible under the circumstances?

This type of analysis must at one stage or another examine individual investments. Such examination usually requires that the performance of each stock, bond, savings account, or other investment be compared to similar investments having like grade and risk characteristics. The important question is always, "Can I replace any currently held investments with others that will make the total investment portfolio more efficient?" Efficiency in portfolio construction occurs when the goals of a program are met and return from the portfolio is maximized, given certain constraints.

Theoretically, this search for maximum portfolio yield is a continuing one which consists of comparing the historical and expected future yields of all investments one against another after classifying them by their most important risk characteristics. In practice, complete comparison is impossible because of the large number of different investments involved. There has recently been a great deal of research on the construction of efficient portfolios, with computers used to make the many comparisons. But most of this work cannot yet be practically applied to the individual investor's problems of portfolio planning and evaluation.[10]

The individual investor can simplify the problem of investment program maintenance by identifying the poorest investments in the portfolio and replacing them with better ones. This does not maximize the efficiency of the portfolio, but it acts to constantly improve efficiency, and this may be the best that can be hoped for under the circumstances. Under this approach, the worst investments are periodically exchanged for others which better meet the requirements of the portfolio.

There are two things to look for when seeking the "worst" investments—risk characteristics and returns. As an example, assume a portfolio which requires that $10,000 be invested in grade A or better corporate bonds. Several of the bonds have dropped in grade to Baa or lower. Although there will probably be a capital loss on the transaction, these bonds should be sold and replaced with securities of the

---

[10] See William F. Sharpe, *Portfolio Theory and Capital Markets* (New York: McGraw-Hill, 1970) or Keith V. Smith, *Portfolio Management: Theoretical and Empirical Studies of Portfolio Decision-Making* (New York: Holt, Rinehart and Winston, 1971) for a detailed discussion of the theory of portfolio construction.

required grade. If this is not done, the effect is to alter the risk characteristics of the portfolio.

Another example might be of a corporation whose stock had been purchased because of its anticipated growth in market price. Over the years the growth has taken place, and in every respect the shares have met the investment characteristics of the portfolio. It has recently become apparent that the rapid growth of the company has ended, management is now expected to concentrate upon paying large dividends (which had not been paid when the company was growing) and increasing earnings per share. These shares may continue to be excellent investments, especially from the yield standpoint, but their investment characteristics have changed. The shares may be held, but they should be reevaluated on the basis of their new investment characteristics. If there is no place in the portfolio for securities of their type, they too should be sold.

An easier type of replacement decision occurs when an investment has a poor performance record. Risk characteristics have remained constant as anticipated, but earnings have been lower than expected. The natural tendency is to continue to hold these securities in the hope that they will eventually justify their expectations and thereby prove that the investor's choice was correct. People generally do not like to admit that they have made a mistake, but these securities should be sold—and the losses taken—just as rapidly as securities whose investment characteristics have changed. Some investors overcome the psychological barrier to selling securities at a loss by requiring that the two, three, or four, worst performing securities be sold each time their portfolio is examined. By making this procedure a regular part of the management of the portfolio, it becomes less difficult to take losses.

Brokers and other financial advisors are helpful in identifying "poor performers" and securities to replace them. They have more time to examine investment data, and they may have better sources of information than the average investor. Figure 15–1 is an example of securities of several different types recommended by Merrill Lynch. Each group is made up of securities which promise to provide the investor with different types of risks and returns. Many brokerage houses provide similar information. Obtaining investment advice is no problem; evaluating the worth of this advice is.

Advice from Bernard Baruch. This book has been written to answer the questions of *who, what, why, when,* and *how,* as they relate to personal investments. It is our hope that these topics have been covered well enough so that the reader can construct and intelligently manage an investment program. We further hope that the reader's curiosity has been whetted to the point where additional reading will be done in areas of interest. The Selected Readings at the end of each chapter identify books and other publications which we have found interesting and informative.

It seems entirely fitting to close this book by paraphrasing and expanding upon several rules of investing that were given by Bernard M. Baruch, a man who was a far more successful investor and speculator than your authors ever hope to be. Mr. Baruch was a self-made man, a person of rather modest origin who made a large fortune in the securities markets. He was a financier, businessman, diplomat, and presidential advisor. His advice is worth repeating and following.[11]

1. *Speculation.* Normally, this type of investing should be done by professionals or persons who can devote their full time and energy to it.
2. *Tips.* Be cautious of free "inside information" of all types; it is usually worth exactly what it costs.
3. *Obtaining information.* Before investing, examine the company as thoroughly as possible. Seek information on management, competition, and earnings possibilities.
4. *Timing of purchases and sales.* It is nearly impossible to buy at the bottom and sell at the top, so don't waste a lot of effort attempting to do so.
5. *Taking losses.* If you have made an error and purchased the wrong investment, take your loss as quickly as possible. No one is right all the time.
6. *Diversification.* Don't buy so many securities that you cannot watch them all carefully. Invest only in areas you know best, even at a sacrifice of diversification.
7. *Portfolio examination.* Periodically examine all investments to see that they are living up to your expectations. If they are not, sell them.
8. *Taxes.* Examine your income tax position so that you know when it is advantageous to take profits and losses.
9. *Cash reserve.* Don't invest all your funds. Keep some cash in reserve for safety and to take advantage of unforeseen opportunities.

---

[11] From Baruch, *My Own Story*, p. 254.

FIGURE 15–1
Recommended Security Selections

MARKET

April 16, 1975

Investment Characteristics	Stock	Price 4/15/75	Price Range 1975	Est. 1975 EPS* Primary/ Fully Diluted	Current Fiscal P/E*	Yield %
	INVESTMENT GRADE					
G	Northwestern Natl. Life Ins. (j)	17	17¼-10⅛	$3.40-3.45/—	5/—	3.2
	GOOD QUALITY					
D	CPC International Ⓢ	42	42¼-32⅝	4.50/—	9/—	4.8
C-G	Diamond Shamrock Ⓢ	37	39⅜-21¾	6.05-6.15/—	6/—	3.8
G	General Signal	36	37 -23⅞	3.10/—	12/—	2.1
C-G	Great Western Financial Ⓢ	16	17⅜-14⅛	2.25-2.30/—	7/—	2.8
G	Hawaiian Electric Ⓢ	20	20⅞-16½	2.90/—	7/—	8.4
G	Public Service of New Mexico	16	16⅞-11⅜	2.50-2.65/—	6/—	7.5
C	Republic Steel Ⓢ	35	35⅞-22⅞	7.50-8.00/—	5/—	8.6e
C-G	United Aircraft Ⓢ	45	45⅞-31¼	—/5.50	—/8	4.4
	SPECULATIVE					
C-G	Blue Bell (b) Ⓢ	24	24½-12½	3.50/—	7/—	3.3
C-G	Fluor Corp. (b) Ⓢ	31	31½-15	3.00/—	10/—	1.3
G	General Automotive Parts (j) Ⓢ	20	20 -13	2.00-2.10/—	10/—	3.0
C-G	Northwest Airlines	17	19¾-11⅝	2.15/—	8/—	2.6
C-G	U A L Inc. Ⓢ	20	23 -13⅝	2.25/—	9/—	3.6e

A Research Report is available on each selection. See reverse side for explanation of footnotes.

SELECTIONS

FIGURE 15–1 (*continued*)

Merrill Lynch Pierce Fenner & Smith Inc.

Securities Research Division

MARKET SELECTIONS

We believe that Market Selections is an effective investment guide for intermediate-term investors.

The Market Selections include issues that our Securities Research Division considers to be the most attractive purchases for the intermediate term—i.e., for periods of up to one year. The stocks on the list may change frequently; in effect, the list is new each time it is issued. Deletion of a stock from the list, however, does not necessarily imply a sell recommendation. It simply means that other **buy-rated** issues are regarded as relatively more attractive for new purchases.

Investment Grade stocks are issues of companies that have strong balance sheets, sound capital structures, demonstrated earnings ability, and long dividend records. **Good Quality** stocks are of somewhat lower quality than Investment Grade, and prices of these issues may move over a wider range. **Speculative** stocks are of lower investment quality than the issues in the two above groups. Prices for these stocks fluctuate over a fairly broad range for a number of reasons, such as the unstable or cyclical character of a company's business or a large amount of debt, preferred stock, or both, which precede the common. **High Risk** stocks include securities of those companies which, we believe, possess an unusually high potential for price appreciation and, of course, entail considerable price risk. In addition to the reasons mentioned under the Speculative category, the price action of high risk stocks may be affected by a brief corporate history, new or untested management, participation in a new industry, and heavy dependence on one product. In addition, such issues may be unseasoned, may command a high price-earnings ratio, or may have a thin float.

Merrill Lynch, Pierce, Fenner & Smith, Inc.

FOOTNOTES:

*Accounting procedures require that companies with outstanding convertible securities, warrants, and stock options report their earnings per share on two bases. Primary earnings reflect the conversion of certain convertible securities, warrants, and options to common-stock equivalents. Fully diluted earnings reflect the conversion of all convertible securities, warrants, and options to common-stock equivalents. For certain cases, we have estimated earnings on both bases, and the column Current Fiscal P-E indicates the P-E as follows: Primary/Fully Diluted, and is based on estimated 1975 earnings, except where noted.

b–Estimated earnings are fiscal 1975.

e–Including extra.

j–This security is traded Over-the-Counter. Solicitation of orders may be prohibited in certain states. Merrill Lynch usually makes a market in this issue.

INVESTMENT CHARACTERISTICS:

C–Cyclical
D–Defensive
G–Growth

NOTE: It is the policy of Merrill Lynch, Pierce, Fenner & Smith Incorporated to disclose the Corporation's interest, as well as that of its elected officers and employee benefit program, in any security that is the subject of any printed material prepared by our Research Division. While the Corporation does not invest its capital in equity securities, it frequently maintains an inventory of those issues in which it functions as a market maker. Our full-disclosure policy is intended to permit our customers to judge for themselves the possibility of and possible extent of any bias in favor of companies discussed. At the time that this report was prepared, our total interests were as indicated: Ⓢ–Small–Less than $200,000; Ⓜ–Moderate–$200,000-to-$500,000; Ⓛ–Large–More than $500,000.

For more information on these securities, please contact your account executive.

The information set forth herein was obtained from sources which we believe reliable, but we do not guarantee its accuracy. Neither the information, nor any opinion expressed, constitutes a solicitation by us of the purchase or sale of any securities or commodities

Source: Merrill Lynch, Pierce, Fenner & Smith, Inc., New York.

SUMMARY

Persons owning investments must manage them, at least to the extent of setting investment program goals. Designing an investment program is much like designing a house. In both cases, the end product should satisfy the needs of the owner in an efficient manner. The most important limitations on home building are usually the amount of money available, preferred location, style, and number of persons in the family. While these limitations—or constraints—are fixed at one point in time, they change as the life cycle of the family changes. Limitations on investment programs are often more subtle. The amount available for investment is of obvious importance. Need for insurance protection is also important. Program goals may change several times during an investor's life. Other constraints deal with the ability and willingness of a person to accept risk and the need for certain levels of investment return.

An investment program is but one part of a *total financial plan* which should encompass all present and future financial aspects of an individual's or a family's existence. A good way to begin the formulation of this plan is by taking stock of how many assets the individual or family owns. This computation is the same as that for measuring the net worth of a business,

$$\text{Assets less liabilities} = \text{Net worth.}$$

To determine how much money can be invested it is necessary to construct a *cash budget*. This budget closely resembles a business income statement.

$$\text{Total income less total expenses} = \text{Surplus.}$$

It is this surplus amount that may be invested after setting aside funds for a cash reserve and for insurance. Projecting net worth statements and cash budgets into the future provides an indication of future uses for and sources of cash. These schedules provide the basic data for constructing investment program goals.

Goals are statements of what a given investment program is supposed to do for an investor. Goals should be presented in writing and in a form specific enough to allow measurement of attainment. Constraints almost always act to reduce the potential profitability of a given investment program because they usually reduce the investor's ability to accept risk. Stating goals and constraints in writing makes it easier to identify possible areas of conflict between them.

One of the more important, and less obvious, constraints is the psychological one. Some people are ill-suited to investments which have high financial risk, even though their financial position and the goals of their investment program indicate that they should be able to accept such risks. Investments should not cause anxiety and frustration; if they do, they should be replaced with ones that are more suitable.

Estate planning is financial planning carried to the point of arranging for the passing on of the estate of the person or persons involved. Legal advice is usually needed for this type of financial planning because trusts and wills are involved.

In managing an investment program, once it is constructed and set in operation, it is necessary to constantly review the plan to see if it is doing what it was designed to do. Individual securities must be purchased to allow realization of program goals. Understanding the characteristics of various investments is necessary to an intelligent choice of individual securities. Brokers and other investment counsel are helpful sources of information on which securities to purchase, but the investor should remain responsible for the overall management of the program. At the very least the program's goals should be set by the investor.

PROBLEMS

1. *a.* Construct a personal net worth statement.
   b. Construct a personal cash budget for a period of either several months or several quarters.
   c. Identify amounts for a "rainy day" and insurance.
   d. How much do you have available to invest?
2. Construct an investment program for you or your family.
   a. State the goals of the program in specific terms.
   b. State any investment program constraints that would act to alter the above goals.
   c. How would you expect this program to be changed in five years? Ten years?

QUESTIONS

1. Why is it desirable to state investment program goals and constraints in writing?

2. Of what value is a *net worth statement?* How is such a statement prepared?
3. What is a family cash budget? How is it prepared?
4. What contribution should a broker make to the setting of a person's investment goals?
5. How does life insurance relate to the setting of investment goals?
6. "Building an investment program is much like building a house." What are the similarities and dissimilarities of these two tasks?
7. What are *psychological constraints,* and how do they affect investment program goals?
8. What is *estate planning?*
9. What are *aggressive investments? Defensive investments?*
10. What is a *security analyst?* How can this person's services help the investor?

SELECTED READINGS

Bowe, William J. *Estate Planning and Taxation,* 3d ed. Homewood, Ill.: Richard D. Irwin, 1972.

Brosterman, Robert. *The Complete Estate Planning Guide,* rev. ed. New York: Mentor Books, 1970.

Dacey, Norman F. *How to Avoid Probate.* New York: Crown Publishers, 1965.

Dixon, Lawrence W. *Wills, Death and Taxes.* Totowa, N.J.: Littlefield, Adams, 1968.

Engle, Lewis. *How to Buy Stocks.* New York: Bantam Books, 1972.

Fisher, Lawrence, and Lorie, James H. "Rates of Return on Investments in Common Stocks." *Journal of Business.* July 1968, pp. 291–316.

Graham, Benjamin. *The Intelligent Investor,* rev. 4th ed. New York: Harper & Row, 1973.

The Life Insurance Fact Book. New York: Institute of Life Insurance, published annually.

West, David A. *The Investor in a Changing Economy.* Englewood Cliffs, N.J.: Prentice-Hall, 1968.

West, David A., and Wood, Glen. *Personal Financial Management.* Boston: Houghton Mifflin, 1972.

Glossary of Investment Terms

Most terms have been entered in alphabetical sequence except those under the general headings of Bonds, Investment Companies, Preferred Stock, Risk, Savings Accounts, and Yield. Terms pertaining exclusively to these headings have been entered there as an aid to locating them.

The definitions in this glossary are as brief as it was possible to make them. Most terms are defined in greater detail and explained in the context of the investment environment in the chapters. Look to the index for a listing of pages containing references to each term.

Advisory Service. An organization offering information for sale to investors. This information may be financial data only, or it may consist mainly of buy and sell recommendations.

After Market. The market which develops after a security issue has been sold. Trading in an after market occurs on exchanges and over-the-counter. Also called secondary market.

Agency Securities. Securities sold by federal agencies such as the Federal Home Loan Bank, The Federal National Mortgage Association, and so on.

American Depository Receipt. A negotiable security evidencing ownership in a block of foreign securities held in an American financial institution.

Amortization. The payment of a debt through scheduled installments.

Arbitrage. The act of buying securities in one market and immediately selling them, or equivalent securities, in a different market.

Asked Price. In security trading, the price at which a seller offers to sell securities.

Assets. An accounting term which refers to something that is owned.

Authorized Stock. The number of shares of stock that are authorized in the company's charter. Seldom are all authorized shares outstanding.

Balance Sheet. An accounting statement which shows the amount of a company's assets, liabilities, and capital as of a given date.

Bar Chart. A type of graph commonly used in the securities industry to show the high, low, and closing prices of securities over a given time period, usually one day. Technical analysts often use such charts.

Bear Market. A declining market. A bull market is a rising market.

Best Efforts. An arrangement in which an investment banking firm agrees to sell an issue using its best effort. Any unsold securities will be returned to the issuer. See underwriting.

Bid Price. The price currently offered for a security.

Blue Sky Laws. A general term which refers to all state laws which regulate the sale of investment securities.

Boiler Room Operation. High pressure selling of stocks by telephone. Stocks sold are often of dubious value.

Bonds

Assessment Bonds. Bonds issued by municipalities which are to be repaid through assessments made against property, usually that which has benefited from the improvements financed by the bond issue.

Collateral Trust Bonds. A debt issue secured by collateral such as other securities which are deposited with a trustee.

Convertible Bond. A debt security which is convertible at the option of the owner into a certain number of shares of common stock, usually of the company which issued the bond.

Coupon Bonds. Bonds which have interest coupons physically attached to the bond. As interest payments come due, coupons are presented to the issuer for redemption.

Debenture Bond. A debt security which has no specific collateral pledged as security.

Estate Tax Bonds. Certain issues of long-term Treasury bonds which may be redeemed at their par value for payment of federal estate taxes.

Full Faith and Credit Bonds. A type of municipal debt security which has no specific collateral. The issuer promises to use its "full faith and credit," to obtain funds to pay interest and redeem this security.

Guaranteed Bond. A debt security whose payment of interest and principal is guaranteed by another company.

Indenture. The agreement between the bond issuer and the owners of the bond which sets forth conditions of repayment and other legal obligations of the company.

Joint Bond. A debt security which is issued and guaranteed by two or more companies.

Mortgage Bond. A debt security which has a mortgage on a piece of real property as its collateral.

Municipal Bond. The name given to debt securities which are issued by states, local governments, or other nonfederal taxing agencies.

Revenue Bonds. Municipal bonds whose interest payments and the repayment of principal are to come from income generated by the facility which was financed through the issuance of these bonds. Common examples are bonds used to finance toll roads, sewers, bridges, transit systems, and so on.

Savings Bonds. Debt securities sold by the U.S. Treasury to individual investors. These are fully registered securities, usually sold in small amounts.

Serial Bond. A debt security issue which matures in relatively small amounts at periodic prestated intervals.

Book Value. Accounting term which in general means the value of an asset as it is listed on the company's balance sheet. A stock's book value is determined by deducting all liabilities from a company's assets and dividing this amount by the number of common shares outstanding.

Broker. An agent who handles buy and sell orders for securities or commodities for a commission charge. This person is often referred to as a registered representative, customers' representative, or account executive.

Bull Market. A rising market. A bear market is a declining market.

Call Option. A contract which gives its owner the right to buy a certain number of shares of stock, at a specific price, within a specified time period.

Call Premium. Compensation paid when a security is called.

Call Protection. A clause specifying the amount of time during which a company cannot call a security.

Callable. A term which indicates that an issuer may repurchase, or call back, a bond or preferred stock which it has issued before the indicated maturity date.

Capital Gain. The profit obtained from selling a capital asset. Short-term capital gains result from the sale of assets held less than six months. Long-term capital gains result from assets held six months or longer.

Capital Gain Dividends. Dividends paid by investment companies from the long-term capital gains they have realized from the sale of portfolio securities.

Capitalization. Total amount of securities (bonds, preferred and common stock) issued by a corporation plus its retained earnings.

Capital Stock. Preferred and common shares which represent the ownership of a business.

Cash Flow. The amount of money available for reinvestment by a company over a given period of time. Cash flow is retained earnings plus noncash expenses such as amortization, depreciation, and depletion charges occurring during a given period of time.

Central Market. The proposed integration of major U.S. securities markets—for example the NYSE, AMEX, regional exchanges, and the OTC into an electronically linked central marketplace. This would involve a common tape for reporting quotes and trades.

Chartered Financial Analyst (CFA). Designation given to someone who has met rigid criteria establishing knowledge and experience in the field of security analysis.

Chicago Board Options Exchange (CBOE). An auction market located in Chicago on which call options of selected securities are sold. Such contracts are also sold on the AMEX and OTC.

Commission. The amount paid to a broker or other agent to buy or sell securities.

Commission Broker. A member of the New York Stock Exchange whose function is to execute orders to buy and sell securities for the firm's customers.

Commodities. Items having useful value. Active trading occurs mainly in foodstuffs and metals. See futures market.

Commodity Trading. The buying and selling of contracts which provide for future delivery of certain numbers of units of commodities at a certain time in the future.

Common Stock. Securities which represent the primary ownership interest of a corporation.

The owners of these securities vote for the directors of the company.

Common Stock Dividends. The amounts paid to the owners of common shares. Dividends are usually in cash, but they may be in stock, merchandise, or practically any other thing.

Common Trust Funds. An arrangement to combine and invest funds which have been placed in trust for a bank to manage.

Competitive Bidding. A procedure in which investment bankers submit written bids to purchase new securities. This arrangement is used mainly for municipals and public utility issues.

Consolidated Accounting Statements. Accounting statements which record the combined financial condition of a corporation and its subsidiaries.

Constant Ratio Plans. A formula investment plan under which an investor purchases and sells securities so that the investment portfolio contains a constant ratio of two or more types of securities.

Corporation Charter. The federal or state authority under which a company does business.

Cumulative Voting. A type of voting for directors of a corporation which enables minority shareholders to elect one or more directors.

Dealer. Anyone who makes a market in a security by offering to buy or sell that security for his or her own account.

Deflation. An economic condition in which the purchasing power of the dollar increases.

Depreciation. A noncash accounting charge against earnings used to spread the cost of an asset over its useful life. Depletion and amortization are related terms.

Dilution. A term which refers to the actual or potential reduction in earnings per share, asset coverage, and so on, that has occurred or may occur because of the issuance of new shares of stock or stock options.

Discount. The amount that a bond or preferred stock sells below its par value.

Diversification. The act of purchasing securities having different risk characteristics.

Dividend. The amount paid to owners of common and preferred stock. It is usually paid in cash but may be paid in securities, in products, or practically any other thing.

Dollar Cost Averaging. A type of formula investment plan under which an investor purchases an equal dollar amount of the same security periodically.

Dow Jones Averages. Measures of the average prices for groups of stocks—industrials, transportation, utilities, and a composite group.

Dow Theory. A stock market theory which attempts to identify stock price trends shortly after they occur. Market price movements are divided into major or primary trends, secondary trends, and minor trends.

Dual Listing. The practice of listing a security on more than one stock exchange.

Earnings per Share. The amount of earnings obtained by a company over a given period of time for each share of common stock outstanding.

Economic Analysis. The examination of fundamental economic conditions (industrial production, gross national product increase, and so on) to determine the direction of stock prices.

Equipment Trust Certificate. A debt security issued to purchase equipment, usually railroad rolling stock. The certificate is usually secured by a first lien on the piece of equipment which it was issued to purchase.

Equity Security. The common and preferred stock which evidences ownership of a corporation.

Ex-Dividend. A term which means "without dividend." A person buying stock which is selling ex-dividend will not receive the most recently declared dividend. Later dividends will be received if the stock continues to be held.

Ex-Rights. A term meaning "without rights." A person buying a security which is ex-rights does not receive the rights.

Flat Quote. A bond price quote which includes both interest and principal. (Bonds are often sold on the basis of a market price plus accrued interest).

Floor Broker. A member of the New York Stock Exchange who executes orders to buy or sell securities. These individuals assist commission brokers by helping handle their orders during periods of heavy trading activity.

Formula Investment Plan. An investment technique which makes timing of investment decisions automatically.

Fundamental Analysis. A type of security analysis which emphasizes the study of accounting information, management, market position, and other "basic" data to determine the value that a security should have. Also referred to as basic analysis.

Futures Market. The market for trading contracts to deliver foodstuffs and metals. Often called commodity futures market.

Government Bonds. The title usually used to identify debt securities issued by the federal government. Often called "governments."

Grading Securities. The activity of assigning a relative ranking to securities based on their exposure to a particular risk.

Holding Company. A corporation which owns controlling interest in at least one but usually several other companies.

Housing Condominiums. An arrangement in which housing units are sold with an accompanying agreement for someone to manage the units and support facilities. They are considered to be security offerings.

Income Statement. An accounting statement which shows total revenues, costs, and profits of a firm realized over a certain period of time.

Inflation. An economic condition in which the purchasing power of the dollar decreases.

Insider. Someone who is closely connected with a publicly held corporation. Usually this means company officers, directors, and owners of 10 percent or more of the common stock, although the definition has been broadened in recent court actions.

Interest. The amount paid for the use of debt capital. The "rent" on money.

Intrinsic Value. The value that a security "should have" based upon the company's assets, earning power, dividends, future prospects, and its management.

Investing. The committing of money for the purchase of securities based on careful analysis of risks and rewards anticipated over a period of one year or more.

Investment Banking. The business of assisting organizations in raising funds, usually by helping to sell new security issues.

Investment Clubs. Groups of individuals who invest small sums that have been contributed by each member. A major purpose of the organization is to educate the membership about investing.

Investment Companies

Accumulation Plans. An arrangement under which a purchaser of mutual fund shares agrees to acquire more shares over a given period of time. There are two types of these plans, voluntary and contractual.

Automatic Dividend Reinvestment Plan. An agreement

between a mutual fund shareholder and the fund, whereby dividends are automatically used to purchase additional shares of stock in the fund.

Balanced Funds. A mutual fund which has an investment policy of balancing its portfolio, usually between bonds and common stocks.

Bond and Preferred Stock Funds. Mutual funds whose investment policy is to invest in bonds and preferred stock.

Capital Gains Funds. Investment companies which have the investment policy of seeking profits primarily through capital gains.

Closed-End Investment Company. An investment company which has a fixed number of shares of stock outstanding. These shares are traded like other shares of common stock and are not redeemed by the investment company.

Common Stock Funds. Investment companies whose investment policy is to seek profits by investing in common stocks.

Dual Purpose Funds. Closed-end investment companies which sell income shares and capital shares. Owners of income shares receive all the income that the company obtains through dividend and interest payments. Owners of capital shares receive the profit that the company obtains from capital gains.

Funding Companies. The name given to a new type of financial company which offers investors a package of mutual fund shares and life insurance.

Hedge Fund. A type of mutual fund which has an investment policy which seeks profits through purchase of risky investments, often using borrowed funds to increase profit potential.

Income Funds. A type of investment company which has as its main investment goal the obtaining of liberal current income for shareholders of the fund.

Investment Company. A generic term which includes mutual funds, closed-end funds, and the several other types of companies engaged in the business of investing the money of their shareholders in securities of other organizations.

Money-Market Funds. Investment companies which invest in short-term, high yield, high grade, debt securities. These mutual funds offer investors the promise of high dividends and are seen as an alternative to savings accounts.

Mutual Fund. The popular name given to open-end investment companies.

No-load Mutual Funds. A type

of mutual fund which does not charge sales commissions. These funds may be readily identified in the lists of mutual fund quotations presented in the press because bid and asked prices are identical.

Open End Investment Company. An investment company which can increase its size through regular sale of additional stock.

Regulated Investment Company. An investment company which has met the terms of the Investment Company Act of 1940 and has chosen to be regulated under this act.

Withdrawal Accounts. A type of mutual fund account which pays a certain amount of money periodically to the owner of the account. Most commonly used by retired persons as a source of income.

Legal Investments. A list of investments which may be purchased by insurance companies, banks, and other financial institutions which are regulated by state and federal governments. They are often called "Legal List Securities" and are invariably of the highest quality.

Leverage. In finance, a term used to indicate a condition whereby earnings per share of common stock is either increased or decreased because of the use of senior securities in the capital structure of the company. A non-leveraged company would have only common stock in its capital structure.

Liabilities. An accounting term which refers to the amounts that a company owes to others.

Limit Order. An order to buy or sell a security at a stated price or better.

Liquidating Value. The value of a company if it ceased operations, sold its assets, and paid off all creditors.

Liquidity. The ability to convert assets into cash with little money loss in relation to the original purchase price.

Listing. A procedure which involves meeting certain requirements for having a security traded on a stock exchange.

Margin. Involves the use of borrowed funds in security transactions. It is the down payment or owner's equity.

Marketability. The ability to buy or sell a security quickly without driving the price up or down.

Market Averages. Measures of price levels for groups of securities.

Market Letter. A brief publication issued by brokerage firms and investment advisory services to provide investors with recommendations to buy or sell securities and other investment information.

Market Order. An order to buy or sell securities at the most advantageous price obtainable at the moment.

Market Value. The price at which a security can be sold.

Merger. A form of consolidation under which two or more firms create a third company which is made up of the liabilities, assets, and capital of the original companies.

Monthly Investment Plan. A plan under which investors may purchase stock in small periodic amounts.

Moody's Investors Service. A company which provides information for investors. It assembles financial data, assigns ratings to securities, and offers buy and sell recommendations.

NASDAQ. Automated system developed by the NASD for reporting OTC trading information. System uses a central computer to tie dealers around the country together for instantaneous price quotes.

National Association of Securities Dealers (NASD). A self-regulatory body of broker dealer firms organized to develop, promote, and enforce standard procedures and ethical practices in the securities industry.

National Quotation Bureau. A company which publishes daily quotations on over-the-counter securities.

Negotiable. The property of a security which allows it to be sold to another investor.

Negotiated Sale. A procedure in which an investment banker and an organization seeking funds establish terms of a security issue which the investment banker will sell. See competitive bidding.

Net Asset Value. A term commonly used to define the value of shares in investment companies. To determine net asset value, the market values of all outstanding securities are totaled. From this amount, all liabilities are deducted. Dividing the remaining amount by the number of outstanding shares provides net asset value per share.

Net Worth. An accounting term which defines net worth as assets minus liabilities. The net worth is the capital of the business.

New Issue. Securities being offered by an organization for the first time.

Notes. Debt securities which are of shorter maturity than bonds.

Odd Lot. An amount of stock less than the standard trading unit of 100 or 10 units. A round lot of stock is usually 100 shares.

Odd-Lot Dealer. A member of the New York Stock Exchange who executes orders to buy or sell less than 100 shares.

Offering Price. The price at which a person is willing to sell securities. Often referred to as the asked price.

Opportunity Cost. The rate of return from the best alternative investment. Stated another way, it is the highest rate of return that will not be earned if funds are invested in a specific investment. If one purchased bonds, and the next best investment were a savings account which yielded 5 percent, the opportunity cost of investing in the bonds would be the 5 percent foregone by not investing in the savings account.

Over-the-Counter Market. Involves the buying or selling of securities without the use of stock exchange facilities. A vast communication network ties together security dealers in hundreds of cities for their OTC trading activities.

Paper Profits and Losses. These are profits or losses which an investor has had because of fluctuating market prices in his or her investments but which have not yet been realized by actually selling the securities.

Par Value. The dollar amount assigned to each share of stock by the corporate charter. This value has practically nothing to do with the market value of common shares; preferred shares may eventually be redeemed on the basis of their par value. In the case of bonds, par value is the amount the company pays upon maturity to redeem the security.

Point and Figure Charts. A charting device used by technical analysts which records security price changes only.

Portfolio. Securities which are held by an individual, trust, or institution.

Preemptive Right. The right enjoyed under common law by all shareholders to maintain their proportional share in the ownership of the company.

Preferred Stock

Convertible Preferred Stock. Preferred stock which is convertible at the option of the owner into a certain number of shares of common stock, usually of the same company.

Cumulative Preferred Stock. A preferred stock which has the feature of having passed dividends accumulate. These dividends must be paid in full before common stockholders can be paid any dividends.

Participating Preferred Stock. A

type of preferred stock which may receive higher than regular dividends if the company's earnings are high enough to warrant additional payment.

Preferred Stock. An equity security whose dividends must be paid before any dividend may be paid on the company's common stock. Preferred shareholders usually receive preferential treatment over common shareholders in case the company is liquidated. Preferred dividends are usually paid at a specified rate.

Premium. The amount that a bond or a preferred stock sells above its par value. Also the amount by which the market value of a convertible security exceeds its conversion value.

Primary Market. The original sale of securities.

Private Placement. An arrangement in which an organization's securities are sold to a small number of investors as opposed to a public offering.

Prospectus. A document issued to prospective purchasers of new securities. It describes the purpose and terms of the issue and the business and management of the issuer.

Proxy. A legal document which gives one person the power to act for another. A proxy is also the name given to the person who acts for another. In investments the most common use of the proxy is when a company's management asks shareholders for their proxies to vote at the annual meeting.

Proxy Statement. Required information which is sent to stockholders along with a request for their voting proxy.

Public Offering. An arrangement in which securities are offered for sale to the investing public. This requires filing a registration statement with a regulatory body, whereas a private placement avoids this requirement.

Put Option. A contract which gives its owner the right to sell a certain number of shares of stock, at a specific price, within a specified time period.

Ratio Analysis. A method of analyzing the performance and financial position of a company through ratios of balance sheet and income statement data.

Real Estate Investment Trusts (REITs). Companies formed to invest in real estate. These companies usually use high financial leverage to increase shareholder profits. "Mortgage trusts" are so named because they invest mainly in mortgages. "Equity trusts" are those which specialize in the purchase and management of real property.

Record Date. The date at which one must be registered as a shareholder on the books of a corporation to receive dividends or rights, or to vote on company matters.

Red Herring. A preliminary prospectus. Prepared when information about a proposed security offering is filed with the Securities and Exchange Commission.

Regional Stock Exchanges. A name used for all the stock exchanges except the New York and American Stock Exchanges.

Registered Security. Any security which is registered in the name of the owner by the issuing company. These securities can be transferred only if they are endorsed by the registered owner. The opposite type is a "bearer" security: ownership is not registered and the bearer is presumed to be the owner.

Registered Trader. A member of the NYSE who trades for his or her account. This member does not deal with the public.

Registration. A procedure required by various security acts for publicly held corporations, stock exchanges, and security firms which causes them to file data with regulatory bodies.

Regulation A. The Securities and Exchange Commission regulation that exempts corporations from a full registration procedure in the case of a public offering of securities. The maximum amount that can be raised under this exemption is $500,000.

Regulation Q. The Federal Reserve Board regulation which sets the maximum rates member banks may pay on savings deposits.

Regulation T. The Federal Reserve Board regulation which sets the maximum amount of credit which may be granted by brokers and dealers for the purpose of purchasing securities.

Regulation U. The Federal Reserve Board regulation which sets the maximum amount of credit which may be granted by a bank to customers for the purpose of purchasing securities.

Relative Strength Ratio. A measure obtained by dividing an industry stock price index by the market stock price index. The ratio indicates relative price performance.

Reorganization. A procedure under which the courts create a successor corporation from a bankrupt corporation.

Retained Earnings. The amount of capital that has been reinvested in the company.

Right. An option to purchase a specified number of shares of a new issue of securities at a designated price. This option is usually of short duration.

Rights Offering. An offering of new securities which is made to existing stockholders. The number of new securities which may be purchased is usually proportional to the number of old securities that were held on the date of record of the rights offering.

Risk

Financial Risk. The uncertainty of future returns from a security because of changes in the financial capacity of the organization that issued the security. Sometimes called business risk.

Interest Rate Risk. The uncertainty of future returns or security prices due to changes in market rates of interest.

Market Risk. The uncertainty of future prices because of changes in investor attitudes.

Political Risk. Uncertainty of future returns from a security because of political developments such as revolution, currency devaluation, nationalization of facilities, and so on.

Purchasing Power Risk. The uncertainty of the purchasing power of future returns due to changes in the price level.

Social Risk. Uncertainty of future returns from a security because of shifts in public attitudes. This may involve changing consumption patterns, pollution, population control, and so on.

Round Lot. A unit of trading securities on exchanges. In most cases, it involves 100 shares or one $1,000 par value bond.

Savings Accounts

Bonus Accounts. Savings accounts paying a higher than normal rate of interest.

Insured Deposits. Deposits in banks and other financial institutions which are insured by the FDIC, FSLIC, or any other federal-sponsored or state-sponsored insuring agency. If the institution fails, deposits are insured against loss.

Multiple Maturity Time Deposits. A type of savings deposit which has limited withdrawal privileges and pays a higher than normal rate of interest.

Mutual Savings Bank. A financial institution which accepts deposits from savers and reinvests most of these deposits in mortgages. These institutions differ from commercial banks mainly in the fact that they cannot offer checking accounts to depositors and that they make relatively few personal and business loans.

Notice Account. A type of savings account which requires the depositor to give notice of intent to withdraw funds. These accounts usually receive a premium rate of interest.

Saving and Loan Company. A financial institution which sells saving shares to investors, paying interest or dividends on each saving share.

Time Certificates of Deposit. Also called Certificate of Deposit, or abbreviated CD. A time deposit which is evidenced by a certificate rather than a passbook or any other device. These accounts are not redeemable until the certificate matures. Certificates may be negotiable.

Time Deposits—Open Account. A type of savings account into which a depositor may place funds at any time. A written request is necessary to withdraw money from this type of account.

Secondary Market. The trading of securities after they have been originally sold in the primary market. This includes both stock exchange and OTC transactions.

Securities Act of 1933. Its main provision requires issuers of securities to disclose relevant information about the organization and its offering to the investing public.

Securities and Exchange Commission (SEC). The federal agency which administers various federal acts and regulates the securities industry.

Securities Exchange Act of 1934. Its main provision regulates activities for trading securities in secondary markets.

Securities Investor Protection Corporation (SIPC). A nonprofit company organized to insure investors against loss of up to $50,000 per account when their brokerage firm fails.

Security. A certificate evidencing ownership or debt.

Selling Group. A group of brokerage firms who assist underwriters of an issue by helping to sell it.

Short Sale. A way that investors may profit from declining security prices. In expectation of lower prices, securities are borrowed and sold, and the loan is to be later repaid by reimbursing the lender with the same number of securities as were borrowed.

Sinking Fund. Required payments made by a company to retire a bond or preferred stock issue gradually before maturity, or to provide money to retire the issue at maturity.

Specialist. A member of a stock exchange who is responsible for maintaining a fair and orderly market in one or more securities. Specialists sometimes act as dealers by buying and selling for their own accounts. At other times they act as agents or brokers' brokers.

Speculation. The act of investing so as to assume relatively high short-term financial and other risks in the hope of better than average gains.

Standard & Poor's Corporation (S&P). An organization which publishes financial data on organizations which have issued securities. It also rates securities and offers advisory services.

Stock Dividend. A dividend which is paid in securities rather than in cash. A dividend is usually in additional shares of the issuing company, but it may be in shares of another company.

Stock Split. Increasing the number of outstanding shares of a corporation by granting existing shareholders more shares of the company in proportion to their original holdings. A person owning 10 shares of stock which were split 3 for 1 would own 30 shares after the split.

Stockholders' Equity. An accounting term which refers to the amount of capital that has been invested in a firm by the equity shareholders.

Stop Order. An order to buy or sell a security after the price reaches a certain stated level.

Straddle. The action of combining a put and a call option on the same security.

Subchapter S Corporation. A domestic corporation which has only one class of stock and no more than 10 shareholders. If all shareholders agree, the corporation's income may be taxed as income of the individual shareholders rather than as income of the corporation.

Subordinated Debentures. A debt security whose legal claim for payment of interest and repayment of principal is subordinated to that of another security.

Tax Avoidance. Managing of financial matters so as to lower taxes as much as is legally possible.

Tax Evasion. Not paying taxes owed. This is illegal.

Tax Exempt Bond. Debt securities of states, cities, and other public authorities, the interest of which is exempt from federal income tax.

Tax Free Dividend Income. Dividend income which is partially or wholly free from federal income taxes.

Technical Analysis. The analyzing of supply and demand factors in security markets to determine the direction of security prices.

Third Market. Over-the-counter trading of listed securities. Involves large orders.

Trading Posts. Locations on the floor of an exchange where stocks are bought and sold.

Transfer Agent. The person or firm who accounts for the changes of ownership in a company's shares and makes certain that shares redeemed and issued are genuine.

Treasury Bills. Debt securities having maturities of one year or less. These securities are sold at a discount by the U.S. Treasury.

Treasury Stock. Stock issued by a company and then later reacquired and held by the company. No dividends are paid to treasury stock nor may it be voted.

Trend Bucker. A company whose sales and earnings do not decline when the general economy recedes.

Trustee. Someone who holds the security for a bond issue and who carries out other duties specified by the indenture. Also someone who undertakes administrative obligations under a trust agreement.

Turnaround. A situation in which a company's declining sales and/or earnings are reversed.

Unbundling. The name applied to the separation of charges by brokerage firms. Investors would pay directly for research and other services and pay lower commission fees under this concept.

Underwriting. An arrangement in which an investment banker buys securities from an issuing organization in the hope of later selling them to investors.

Variable Ratio Plans. A formula investment plan under which an investor changes the ratio of certain types of securities in a portfolio depending upon whether the stock market is relatively high or relatively low.

Warrant. An option to purchase a certain number of securities at a certain price over a period of time which is usually longer than that allowed for exercise of rights.

Wash Sale. The sale and repurchase of substantially identical securities within a 30-day period. Losses from such transactions are not legal deductions from income when reporting federal income taxes.

Yield

Coupon Yield. The yield in percentage terms that is stated on the face of a bond. It can be determined by dividing the annual interest payment in dollars by the par value of the security and converting this figure into percentage terms.

Current Yield. The yield of a security determined by dividing its annual interest or dividend payment by the current market price and converting this figure into percentage terms.

Yield. Dividends or interest paid on a security expressed as a percentage of either the current price, the purchase price, or the par value of the security.

Yield to Maturity. A yield calculation which takes into account the relationship between the security's maturity value, time to maturity, current price, and coupon yield. This calculation allocates bond premium or discount over the life of the security and is the most accurate type of yield calculation.

Index

Index

This book has been set in 11 point Electra, leaded 2 points, and 10 point Electra, leaded 3 points. Part numbers and titles are 24 point (small) Helvetica italic. Chapter numbers are 48 point Helvetica and chapter titles are 18 point Helvetica. The size of the type page is 27 × 46 picas.